Moral Pressure for Responsible Globalization

International Studies in Religion and Society

Series edited by

Lori G. Beaman (*University of Ottawa*)
Peter Beyer (*University of Ottawa*)

Advisory Board

Afe Adogame (*University of Edinburgh*)
Elizabeth Coleman (*Monash University*)
Lene Kühle (*Aarhus University*)
Mary Jo Neitz (*University of Missouri*)
Linda Woodhead (*University of Lancaster*)

VOLUME 30

The titles published in this series are listed at *brill.com/isrs*

Moral Pressure for Responsible Globalization

Religious Diplomacy in the Age of the Anthropocene

By

Sherrie M. Steiner

BRILL

LEIDEN | BOSTON

Cover illustration: Furnished by shutterstock.com, image by Elena Schweitzer.

Library of Congress Cataloging-in-Publication Data

Names: Steiner, Sherrie M., author.
Title: Moral pressure for responsible globalization : religious diplomacy in
  the age of the Anthropocene / by Sherrie M. Steiner.
Description: Boston : Brill, 2018. | Series: International studies in
  religion and society, ISSN 1573-4293 ; VOLUME 30 | Includes
  bibliographical references and index.
Identifiers: LCCN 2018001817 (print) | LCCN 2018002582 (ebook) | ISBN
  9789004365018 (e-book) | ISBN 9789004363748 (hardback : alk. paper)
Subjects: LCSH: Globalization--Religious aspects. | Globalization--Moral and
  ethical aspects.
Classification: LCC BL65.G55 (ebook) | LCC BL65.G55 S74 2018 (print) | DDC
  201/.7--dc23
LC record available at https://lccn.loc.gov/2018001817

Typeface for the Latin, Greek, and Cyrillic scripts: "Brill". See and download: brill.com/brill-typeface.

ISSN 1573-4293
ISBN 978-90-04-36374-8 (hardback)
ISBN 978-90-04-36501-8 (e-book)

This book is dedicated to
Archbishop Mar Gregorios Yohanna Ibrahim
Syriac Orthodox Church
The People's Patriarch
Aleppo, Syria
(1948–)

⁂

Contents

Foreword XI
Acknowledgments XIII
List of Illustrations XIV
List of Abbreviations and Acronyms XV

1 **Introduction: Religious Engagement for More Responsible Governance** 1
  Beyond Sustainable Development as Oxymoron 1
  The Evolution of Religious Shadow Summitry 2
  Theoretical Account of the F8/F7/F20 Initiative 4
  Theoretical Development—Why Religion? Why Now? 5
  In Matters of Religion, Religion Matters 10

2 **G-plus System Diplomacy** 12
  The Origins and Evolution of the G-plus System 12
  The Rules of Governing without Government 15
  Broadening the Dialogue 16
  Engagement Group Recognition 18
  Monitoring of the G-plus System 20

3 **Governance in the Age of the Anthropocene** 24
  Primarily Human-Induced Global Environmental Changes 24
  Environmental Implications for Governance 26
  'Transition Science' Emerges to Inform Governance 28
  Governance for a Common Future 31
  Implications for G8/G7 and G20 Financial Deliberations 32
  Patterned Vulnerabilities and Anti-globalization Protests 35
  Governance without Government 38
  The Costs of Globalized Irresponsibility 41
  Conclusion 46

4 **The Return of Religion to Transnational Relations** 47
  Transnational Religious Resurgence 47
  The Crisis of Secularization 56
  Can Secularization be Taken Too Far? 64

Reimagining the Secular with 'Cosmopolitan Solutions'   67
    Religious Diplomacy   68
    Cosmopiety   69
Conclusion   74

5   The F8/F7/F20 Initiative   75
Origins and Evolution   75
    The F8   76
    The F7   76
    The F20   77
    The Merge   77
Patterning after the G-plus System   79
Distinguishing Factors   81
Invitees and Organizational Representation   82
Phases of Development   93
Conclusion   95

6   Illuminating the Unseen   96
Summary Overview   96
Annual Initiatives   100
    2005 United Kingdom—Civil Society Ecumenical Origins   100
    2006 Russia—An Interfaith State Affair   102
    2007 Germany—Consolidating the Vision   105
    2008 Japan—Decentering Anthropocentrism   108
    2009 Italy—A Natural Disaster   113
    2010 Canada—Engagement and Governance   117
    2011 France—Respecting the 'Other'   123
    2012 United States—Special Delivery   126
    2013 United Kingdom—All a Twitter   129
    2014 Australia—New Beginnings   134
    2015 Istanbul—Consolidation   137
    2016 China—Entering a New Phase of Dialogue   142
    2017 Germany—Officially Engaged   147
Conclusion   150

7   Organizing Details, External Relations, and Documentation   152
Organizing the Summits   152
    Leadership Rotation   155
    The Organizing Committees   156
    Financing   158

Religious Ritual   161
Special Events and Excursions   163
Aborted Events   166
External Relations   168
Heads of State   168
Government Advisors   170
Foreign Ministers   171
Sherpas   171
Members of Parliament   172
Mayors   174
Special Advisors   174
Civil Society   175
Academia   177
Business   178
Media   181
Conclusion   185

8   **Reform, Assessment, and Impact**   186
Reform   186
Accountability   188
Enduring Informality   194
Reflexive Engagement   197
Assessment   208
Information Technology   209
Influence of International Relations   212
Institutional Differentiation   214
Competing Assessments   222
Redundant   223
Replacement   224
Rejection   226
Reinforcement   227
Impact   228
G-plus System   228
Gender   236
Domestic Relations   243
Conclusion   246

9   **The Golden Thread**   247
A New Millennium   247
Global Ethic—Global Norm   249

The MDG Focal Point   252
F8/F7/F20 MDG Dialogue   254
Transition Dynamics   261
F20 SDG Dialogue   265
Non-human Agency   270
Conclusion   273

10   Collaboration for a Responsible Future   275
Religious Diplomacy in the Age of the Anthropocene   275
Tikkun Olam   280
Changing Times   282
SDG Implementation Challenges   283
Governance Forecasts   286
What an F20 Might Offer   287
Further Research   292

Appendix A: Theoretical Orientation, Methodology, Documentation
& Data   295
Methodology   297
Documentation   300
Data   301
Appendix B: Institutional Affiliations Reference List   303
References   309
Index   351

Foreword

Dr. Sherrie Steiner's *tour de force, Moral Pressure for Responsible Globalization: Religious Diplomacy in the Age of the Anthropocene*, is, in the first instance, an exercise in disciplined scholarship, addressing significant issues in the areas of the sociology of religion and international political complexity. But it is more than that.

The perennial cry of the realtor is *"location, location, location."* The privilege for one charged with offering a foreword to such a book as Dr. Steiner's is to set *"context, context, context."* In fact, for a book such as this, context is of the essence. Dr. Steiner's scholarship and narrative constitute an integrative whole of an extraordinary initiative, still in its generative stages, yet already possessed of tangible achievement and immense potential.

Solomon, King of Israel, is famously attributed with the observation that, "there is nothing new under the sun."

It would appear that His Late Hebraic Majesty may have been too sweeping in his generalizations; at least in this instance.

At the dawn of this already deeply troubled century, and in the wake of United Nations Secretary General Kofi Anan's Millennium Forum, the oft muted voices of the world's religions were raised in a new way. Former Canadian Foreign Minister, the Hon. Dr. Lloyd Axworthy, had ignited the imagination of leaders secular and religious with his vision of "Human Security": essentially the view that the interests of the world's peoples must ever trump the interests of the nation states system. The world's religious communities form the largest planetary civil society network extant. The time had surely come for that network to exercise its considerable "soft power" in the mission of Tikkun Olam: the Hebrew for the "Mending of the World." This religious soft power was to be neither diffident to political and economic power on the one hand, nor dogmatically and doctrinally hostile on the other. Rather, a new and collaborative posture was proposed: a posture committed to the healing of the entire created order.

The story and concomitant analysis of the responsive engagement of a hitherto informal network of global religious leaders, some of high rank and profile, most of more modest office and stature, is the warp and woof of Dr. Steiner's present oeuvre. She documents, discerns and dissects the G8 and subsequent G20 Interfaith Summits (now increasingly designated the F8 and F20 Summits) as phenomena in their own right, and in the context of the global cauldron of the twenty-first century.

The result is a gift to those of us who have and are participating in this nascent global effort; to the academy; and to that increasing number of global citizens of all faiths who, like the Hebrew prophet Habakkuk, be charged through religious conviction to "record the vision, write it on tablets, that the one who reads may run" (Habakkuk 2).

She records and analyses critically yet faithfully an international process which answers the heart wrenching and hopeful vision of theologian Hans Küng: "unity among the churches; peace among religions; community among the nations" (Spero contra spem, 1990).

In short, in *Moral Pressure for Responsible Globalization*, Dr. Steiner has harkened to the words of the prophet Isaiah, "And now, go, write it before them in a tablet and inscribe it in book, that it may be for the time to come, as a witness for ever" (Isaiah 30: 8).

The Rev. Prof. Dr. James Taylor Christie
Secretary General, G8 World Religious Leaders' Summit
Winnipeg, Canada, 2010

Acknowledgments

I would like to personally acknowledge several colleagues for their valuable comments in reviewing various drafts of this manuscript: Brian Adams, James Christie, Peter Hajnal, Katherine Marshall, Yoshinobu Miyake, Georgia Wralstad Ulmschneider, and Marco Ventura. Their insights proved immensely helpful for improving the manuscript. I would also like to express my appreciation to the staff at Brill and their peer reviewers for their interest, encouragement, support, and help in this project.

Special thanks go to my friend T. Eric Evans, who nurtured me through the final days of major manuscript revision, and to my daughter, Tamara Aeschliman, and grandson, Elijah, for their patience in putting up with the long hours spent completing this book.

This work was partially funded by a summer research grant from the Purdue Research Foundation. My university provided more than financial support, however. I would like to express my gratitude to Ludwika Goodson and members of the IPFW Faculty Writing Circle who encouraged me to continue with this writing project during a time involving some difficult transitions.

List of Illustrations

Figures

2.1   The solar system of G20 engagement groups   18

6.1   Millennium Development Kids alter ego network by groups   131

6.2   Anglican Twitter network by groups for Twitter campaign 2013   132

7.1   The delegation model phase—summit length & representation (2005–2013)   153

9.1   Generating political will for MDG/SDG fulfillment through informal dialogue   264

Tables

5.1   RNGO faith tradition representation at F8/F7/F20 summits (2005–2017)   86

5.2   Constituencies in excess of a million participating in F8 Canada Summit (2010)   90

5.3   Participant perspectives at the F8 2011 France Summit   91

6.1   F8/F7/F20 Initiative engagement with the G-plus System, 2005–2017   97

6.2   F8 and F20 secretaries-general (2005–2017)   98

8.1   F8 process compliance with the complex standard (2005–2010)   193

List of Abbreviations and Acronyms

B20	G20's business engagement partner
C20	G20's civil society engagement partner
ECOSOC	Economic and Social Council of the United Nations
HIPC	Heavily Indebted Poor Country Initiative
ICLRS	International Center for Law and Religion Studies
INGO	International non-governmental organization
ICC	International Continuance Committee
IMF	International Monetary Fund
ISIS	Islamic State of Iraq and Syria
L20	G20's labor engagement partner
LDS	Latter-day Saints
MDG	Millennium Development Goals
OECD	Organization for Economic Cooperation and Development
RfP	Religions for Peace
RNGO	Religious non-governmental organization
SDG	Sustainable Development Goals
UNAOC	United Nations Alliance of Civilizations
UNESCO	United Nations Educational, Scientific and Cultural Organization
UNICEF	United Nations Children's Emergency Fund
URI	United Religions Initiative
W20	G20's women engagement partner
WCRP	World Conference on Religion and Peace
WEA	World Evangelical Alliance
WFDD	World Faiths Development Dialogue
WWF	World Wildlife Fund

CHAPTER 1

Introduction: Religious Engagement for More Responsible Governance

This book details the historic evolution and development of a process where leaders of diverse faith traditions engage in serious and consistent credible conversation with the political leaders of the world. The process is distinctive and historically unprecedented.[1] The engagement process described in the pages that follow has evolved over time, convened under a variety of names, and developed from within different social contexts north and south of the equator. Religious summitry, referred to here as the F8/F7/F20 Initiative, has shadowed the G-plus System since 2005. This chapter outlines the theoretical framework used to explain the historical significance of this case study. Social science theories of secularization, international relations and globalization are critiqued as being too narrow for understanding the evolution of societal-environmental relations in the Age of the Anthropocene. Peter Beyer's theory of religious institutionalization in the context of globalization is situated in human ecology theory to advance a primarily human-induced, but non-human, causal explanation for the return of religion to the public sphere.

Beyond Sustainable Development as Oxymoron

For the first time in history, humans are changing the biosphere in ways that threaten our common future. Although the process of globalization has been variously described, both positively and negatively, as an economic process that is proceeding somewhat 'out of control,'[2] others consider it to be a political process.[3] Can the global economy be made compatible with the pursuit of sustainable development? Can our planet's common future be secured with

---

1 Karen Armstrong, *The Great Transformation: The Beginning of Our Religious Traditions* (Toronto, Canada: Vintage Canada, 2010); Hans Küng, *Global Responsibility* (New York, New York: Crossroad, 1991).

2 Jan-Erik Lane, *Globalization: The Juggernaut of the 21st Century* (New York, New York: Ashgate Publishing, 2008).

3 Peter Newell, *Globalization and the Environment: Capitalism, Ecology and Power* (Cambridge, UK: Polity Press, 2012), 2–3.

the economic and political institutions we currently have at our disposal? What forms of governance are probable, and can collective engagement evoke new possibilities? Can the wealth which globalization generates for the few be steered towards more equitable and sustainable forms of development for many, or is the very idea of sustainable development an oxymoron?

The Evolution of Religious Shadow Summitry

Since 2005, an alliance of religious, development and human rights representatives, moved by these conditions, have convened shadow summits to meetings of the Group of Eight (G8), the Group of Seven (G7) and the Group of 20 (G20) to strengthen exchanges between their networks and the G-plus System to address a broad range of issues that threaten the global network of interconnected societies. There are other world summits attended by a diverse array of leaders such as the Assisi meetings, the Congress of World Religions, the Doha International Center for Interfaith Dialogue process, the Inter-religious dialogue in Kosovo, Kazakhstan's model of religious dialogue, the meetings of the Parliament of the World's Religions, the work of Religions for Peace (RfP), and the World Humanitarian Summit. The alliance detailed in this case study is distinctive in its consistent evolving engagement with the G-plus System for more than a decade. Over time, participants have collectively developed recommendations covering the thematic scope of the G-plus System agendas. Initiative meetings have been variously referred to as The G8 World Religions Summit, The G20 Interfaith Summits, The Interfaith Leaders Summits, The Summit of World Religious Leaders, The Religious Leaders Summit, and The World Summit of Religious Leaders. In recent years, the G20 Interfaith Executive Committee has started exploring adoption of a nomenclature system consistent with the emergence of other engagement groups in the 'Solar System' of the G20.[4] Hereafter, I will refer to the alliance of representatives as the F8/F7/F20 Initiative where "F" refers to the faith factor and the number (8, 7 or 20—following the historical order when the G8 became the G7) refers to the political group in the G-plus System that the religious summit 'shadowed' in any given year.[5] Early summits (2005–2013) shadowed the G8, one interfaith

---

4   Nancy Alexander and Heike Loeschmann, "The Solar System of G20: Engagement Groups," *G20 Fundamentals* 4 (2016), https://www.boell.de/en/2016/12/08/solar-system-g20 -engagement-groups.

5   G20 Interfaith Executive committee members decided to adopt a nomenclature similar to other engagement groups according to an email from James Christie, May 27, 2016.

youth summit shadowed the G7 (2014–15), and recent summits (2014–2017) have shadowed the G20. "Initiative" refers to how annual summits only convene through the supportive apparatus of national hosts from within the rotating host country each year. Although the network of representatives incorporates development, academic and human rights organizations, the majority of participants represent religious non-governmental organizations (RNGOs) that are transnational in scope. The F8/F7/F20 Initiative is diverse and inclusive with regular participation by representatives from Bahá'í, Buddhist, Christian (Anglican/Episcopal, Catholic, Latter-day Saints (LDS), Orthodox, Protestant/Reformed), Hindu, Indigenous (Native American, Aboriginal, Islander), Jewish, Muslim (Shiite, Sunni), and Shinto traditions.[6]

Development of dialogue between governments, international financial organizations and religious leaders is more difficult to achieve than one might expect. In 1998, James D. Wolfensohn, then president of the World Bank, launched a series of high-level meetings centered on religious and development dialogue around topics like the Millennium Development Goals; unexpectedly, the World Bank's Executive Directors, who represented 184 countries at the time, raised many objections to building a structured dialogue with world religions because religion was seen as politically divisive, patriarchal, dangerous to progress and modernization, and a low priority as an outmoded social institution increasingly relegated to the private sphere.[7] In recent years, government officials, particularly in development circles, have begun to recognize religious concerns for how they affect multiple dimensions of society including, but not limited to, the economy, gender, environment, politics, peacemaking, human rights, disaster relief, development, and, of course, terrorism.[8] Although faith organizations are well positioned to help combat corruption, encourage integrity and promote public ethics in public policy because of their interest in, and support of, value-based behaviors and their extensive presence and reach into

---

6   Sherrie Steiner, "Religious Soft Power as Accountability Mechanism for Power in World Politics: The Interfaith Leaders' Summit(s)," *Sage Open* (2011).

7   Katherine Marshall, *Global Institutions of Religion: Ancient Movers, Modern Shakers* (2013), 191–192.

8   See, for example, Patrice Brodeur, "From the Margins to the Centers of Power: The Increasing Relevance of the Global Interfaith Movement," *Cross Currents* (*New Rochelle, N.Y.*) 55, no. 1 (2005); J. Casanova, *Public Religions in the Modern World,* (Chicago, IL: Chicago University Press, 1994); Anna Halafoff, "The Multifaith Movement," in *Global Risks and Cosmopolitan Solutions* (New York: Springer, 2013); G. Clarke and M. Jennings, *Development, Civil Society, and Faith-Based Organizations* (London, UK: Palgrave Macmillan, 2008).

local communities,[9] most policymaking continues to marginalize religious insights. The emergence of the F8/F7/F20 Initiative is historically significant for making consistent, persistent and evolving contributions oriented toward addressing that governance lacuna. Katherine Marshall, speaking from more than four decades of experience working at the World Bank with a focus on international development, describes the "F20 series," in particular, as "among the boldest interfaith efforts today in its explicit focus on the most global of global agendas, and in its more implicit goal of influencing the world's most powerful leaders."[10]

In the pages that follow, we examine how this religious (re)assertion in the "public sphere" reflects coterminous and changing relations among systems as new connections are being formed between religious and political networks under conditions of globalization. Several questions will be addressed: How is the Initiative shaped by the local host context? How does the Initiative handle the inevitable tensions that arise in relation to situations that privilege one or a very few religions over others? How does the Initiative process tensions when religious rights, human rights and women's rights diverge? To what extent is the F8/F7/F20 Initiative emerging in a postmodern form that is coterminous with civil society, or is it (re)asserting itself into the public sphere as a distinct societal system (representing religion *as religion*)? Does the F8/F7/F20 Initiative seek a determinative role in the functioning of the state, or are the new connections being formed dissolving expressions that differentiate religion as a distinct social institution?

Theoretical Account of the F8/F7/F20 Initiative

The theoretical explanation is developed in the book as follows. After introducing the Initiative in this chapter, I describe the evolution of the G-plus System in Chapter 2. In Chapter 3, I outline the changing material conditions that constitute the context within which governance occurs throughout the world. The social threats posed by environmental changes set the stage for why religion's return to transnational relations merits serious consideration. Religion is not a master variable in the field of international relations, but is considered by various theories to be a variable that acquires and loses salience at particular

---

9   Katherine Marshall, "Ancient and Contemporary Wisdom and Practice on Governance as Religious Leaders Engage in International Development," *Journal of Global Ethics* 4, no. 3 (2008).

10   "Shadowing the China G20 Summit: An Interreligious Gathering," *Huntington Post*, September 5, 2016.

historical moments.[11] Evidence from impact science in relation to population and resource pressures are provided as justification for *why* religion should be considered as a category for diplomatic analysis at this moment in history. Chapter 4 describes changing sociocultural conditions that are occurring in tandem with these environmental changes. I identify a worldview shift in the public role of religion. I survey a variety of ways the interface between religion and politics is being reconsidered that interested readers might want to further explore. In particular, the term *cosmopiety* is introduced to refer to a new historically emergent cosmopolitan governance stream in transnational relations. This chapter helps readers appreciate the significance of the F8/F7/F20 Initiative as a historic development making real and potentially important contributions to global governance. Chapter 5 details evolution of the F8/F7/F20 Initiative from 2005 through 2017. Although the process has waxed and waned over time, the F8/F7/F20 Initiative is far stronger in 2017 than when it first began in 2005 and 2006. Chapter 6 details the annual progression of each summit from 2005 through 2017. Chapter 7 presents organizing details, describes F8/F7/F20 external relations and lists documentation samples of scholarly evaluations, compilations of texts, official faith-based publications and media accounts of the summit process. Chapter 8 describes internal processes of F8/F7/F20 reform and offers a scholarly assessment of the F8/F7/F20 Initiative. Chapter 9 details the broad historical process at the macro level as driven by the non-human agency of environmental change. I describe the historical emergence of two parallel processes that the Initiative seeks to bridge: The Global Ethic emerged as a global norm among and between religions of the world. The MDGs emerged as a global governance response to human population and resource pressures at the turn of the millennium. I describe how the MDGS, and later the SDGs, have operated as a central theme and organizing principle for governance engagement throughout the F8/F7/F20 Initiative whose leaders collaborate in accordance with the common ground established by the Global Ethic. Chapter 10 provides a summary assessment of the F8/F7/F20 Initiative with attention to the ongoing process in the future and suggestions for future research.

Theoretical Development—Why Religion? Why Now?

The findings of this case study resonate with a stream of social-scientific observations over the past two decades that have variously described the 'return of religion' to public life in the context of globalization. Sociologists of religion

---

11   Rudolph and Piscatori, *Transnational Religion and Fading States.*

have increasingly come to recognize that secularization, even in Western Europe, may be a self-limiting process.[12] Some scholars talk about 'desecularization'[13] or the advent of a 'post-secular age,'[14] identifying emergent patterns of individualistic and unofficial expressions of spirituality;[15] other scholars talk about 'religious resurgence'[16] or even the 'revenge of God.'[17]

While social scientists tend to agree that religion is a factor that is becoming more influential in the public sphere, descriptions and observations seldom develop into theoretical explanations. Whether the focus is on changing official conceptions of religion, the understanding of how religion is becoming more integral to public policy, or on changing patterns of religious regulation in different states, any theoretical development of religion in the context of globalization must move beyond description toward offering an explanation for why and how these changes are occurring.[18]

---

12 Zachary R. Calo, "Higher Law Secularism: Religious Symbols, Contested Secularisms, and the Limits of the Establishment Clause," *Chicago-Kent Law Review* 87, no. 3 (2012); "Law in the Secular Age," *European Political Science* 13, no. 3 (2014); Peter Edge, "Law, State and Religion in the New Europe: Debates and Dilemmas," *Journal of Church and State* 55, no. 3 (2013); Bruce Ledewitz, *Church, State, and the Crisis in American Secularism.* Bloomington, Indiana: Indiana University Press, 2011; David Voas and Mark Chaves, "Is the United States a Counterexample to the Secularization Thesis?," *American Journal of Sociology* 121, no. 5 (2016); Thomas G. Walsh, "Religion, Peace and the Postsecular Public Sphere," *International Journal on World Peace* 29, no. 2 (2012).

13 Peter L. Berger, *The Desecularization of the World: Resurgent Religion and World Politics* (Grand Rapids, MI: Eerdmans, 1999); Julia Berger, "Religious Nongovernmental Organisations," *Voluntas: International Journal of Voluntary and Nonprofit Organisations* 14, no. 1 (2003).

14 Jürgen Habermas, "Religion in the Public Sphere," *European Journal of Philosophy* 14, no. 1 (2006).

15 Meredith McGuire, *Religion: The Social Context*, 5th ed. (Long Grove, Illinois: Waveland Press, 2002); Jeremy Carrette and Richard King, *Selling Spirituality: The Silent Takeover of Religion* (New York: Routledge, 2005).

16 S. Thomas, *The Global Resurgence of Religion and the Transformation of International Relations: The Struggle for the Soul of the Twenty-First Century.* (Basingstoke, UK: Palgrave Macmillan, 2005); S.M. Thomas, "A Globalized God: Religion's Growing Influence in International Politics," *Foreign Affairs* 89, no. 6 (2010); David Zeidan, *The Resurgence of Religion* (Netherlands: Brill, 2000).

17 Gilles Kepel, *The Revenge of God: The Resurgence of Islam, Christianity, and Judaism in the Modern World* (Cambridge, UK: Polity Press, 1994).

18 Lee Freese and Jane Sell, "Constructing Axiomatic Theories in Sociology," in *Theoretical Methods in Sociology: Seven Essays*, ed. Lee Freese (Pittsburgh, PA: University of Pittsburgh Press, 1980).

Peter Beyer has theorized how the religious landscape has been significantly shaped by globalization processes in a post-Westphalian circumstance to explain the rise of consumeristic versions of religious expression in tandem with religious change as transnational institutional *differentiation* (rather than fusion, dissolution or disappearance) of the religious from other institutional systems.[19] The case study presented in the following chapters will further develop this theory in two ways. Firstly, whereas Peter Beyer focused attention on the economic shaping of the differentiated sphere of religion with the rise of globalization, I highlight how the differentiated sphere of religion is also being shaped by the *transnational political sphere* in the form of the post-Westphalian G-plus System. As the nation-state system moved from the "statist" period into an era characterized by 'governance without government' and 'globalized irresponsibility,' these processes have shaped the way in which institutional differentiation has transformed the religious landscape.

Historically, however, the relationship between religion and governance has often been marked by violence. Empirical evidence consistently indicates that hostilities against religious minorities continue to be widespread.[20] Some of the participants in the F8/F7/F20 Initiative have themselves risked, if not lost, their lives as a consequence of their public engagement.[21] Collective religious rights are in need of direct international protection, and yet, "unlike many other human rights, there is as yet no focused United Nations (UN) Convention directly addressing the subject of freedom of religion or belief."[22] Given the history of violent conflict, the inadequacy of governance protection, and

---

19   Peter Beyer, *Religion in the Context of Globalization* (New York: Routledge, 2013).

20   Pew Research Center, "Trends in Global Restrictions on Religion," (2016), http://www
.pewforum.org/2016/06/23/trends-in-global-restrictions-on-religion/.

21   For example, Archbishop Ibrahim was a plenary speaker in the 2011 F8 Summit. He, along
with Archbishop Yazigi, were later kidnapped because of their peacemaking work on
April 22, 2013 along the road between Aleppo and the Turkish border. When the Syrian
Orthodox Patriarch Mar Ignatius Zakka I passed away on March 21, 2014, Christians in
Syria and the wider Middle East unanimously nominated the captive Archbishop Mar
Gregorios Yohanna Ibrahim by electronic polls as "The People's Patriarch." There has yet
to be confirmation of life or death since his abduction. See Wolfgang Danspeckgruber,
Huffington Post (2014). Published electronically April 21 http://www.huffingtonpost.com/
wolfgang-danspeckgruber/archbishop-mar-gregorios-yohanna-ibrahim-and-archbishop
-boulos-yazigi-_b_5186945.html.

22   Malcolm Evans, "Introductory Overview," ed. Malcolm Evans and Kay Carter, *Article 18:
An Orphaned Right* (Washington, D.C.: All Party Parliamentary Group on International
Religious Freedom or Belief, 2013), https://freedomdeclared.org/media/Article-18-An
-Orphaned-Right.pdf.

the high levels of hostility against religious minorities, why has the F8/F7/F20 Initiative emerged *now*? As international relations scholars Susanne Hoeber Rudolph and James Piscatori point out in *Transnational Religion and Fading States,* religion is *not* a master variable in international relations theory, but is a variable that acquires and loses salience at particular historical moments.[23] It is not enough to say that religion has become politically engaged in a manner that mirrors the G-plus System via processes of institutional differentiation in a context of globalization. Given the risk of high cost (and arguably low actual political benefit) of participation in the F8/F7/F20 Initiative, social theory must move beyond the *why* to address the question of: why *now*? In other words, religion will *not* be presented as a master variable in international relations. Which leads me to my second point of theory: primarily human-induced, but non-human, agency.

For the first time in history, more than seven and a half billion human beings are dependent upon, and transforming, the earth's biosphere.[24] The International Union of Geological Sciences, the professional organization in charge of defining Earth's time scale, has stated that humans are impacting earth systems in such a profound way that we have moved from the Holocene Epoch to the Age of the Anthropocene.[25] In the chapters that follow, I will argue that historically unprecedented population and resource pressures are inducing environmental changes that challenge, weaken and sometimes undermine states. Global governance must operate in a context of global-scale primarily human-induced environmental and human system threats that create both vulnerabilities and opportunities for cascading social-ecological change and transformation.[26] Many religious heritages retain connections to cultural roots from a time when religion was the foundation of the social system; religion

---

23   Susanne Hoeber Rudolph and James Piscatori, *Transnational Religion and Fading States* (Boulder, Colorado: Westview Press, 1997).

24   See www.worldometers.info/world-population.

25   Joseph Stromberg, "What Is the Anthropocene and Are We in It?," *Smithsonian Magazine* (2013), http://www.smithsonianmag.com/science-nature/what-is-the-anthropocene-and-are-we-in-it-164801414/.

26   Seth D. Baum and Itsuki C. Handoh, "Analysis: Integrating the Planetary Boundaries and Global Catastrophic Risk Paradigms," *Ecological Economics* 107 (2014). Måns Nilsson and Åsa Persson, "Analysis: Reprint of 'Can Earth System Interactions Be Governed? Governance Functions for Linking Climate Change Mitigation with Land Use, Freshwater and Biodiversity Protection,'" *Ecological Economics* 81, September (2012); Carl Folke et al., "Reconnecting to the Biosphere," *AMBIO: A Journal of the Human Environment* 40, no. 7 (2011); Jonathan Foley, "Boundaries for a Healthy Planet," *Scientific American* 302, no. 4 (2010).

has been shown to resurge when governments fail, or undermine traditional lifestyles.[27] For better or worse, once a state enters a legitimation crisis, religion becomes one of the only remaining legitimate structures for governance.[28]

The position presented in the following chapters considers the social scientific formulation of the relationship between secularization, international relations and globalization as too narrowly conceived. I argue that the core development with regard to the emergence of the F8/F7/F20 Initiative, specifically, and religious resurgence more generally, is the co-evolution of societal and environmental relations in the Age of the Anthropocene.[29] In particular, the primarily human-induced, but non-human, agency of environmental change[30] is offered as the causal explanation for the return of religion to public life. The term *cosmopiety* is introduced as an ideal type in the Weberian tradition to refer to a new historically emergent cosmopolitan governance stream in transnational relations. Discussion of secularization theories, international relations, and globalization should be understood in the context of evolving societal-environmental relations set within the complex, nonlinear, multidisciplinary systems theory of human ecology.[31] For further details on theoretical framework, method and data, see Appendix A.

---

27   M. Juergensmeyer, *The New Cold War?* (Berkeley: University of California, 1993); S.M. Thomas, "Taking Religious and Cultural Pluralism Seriously: The Global Resurgence of Religion and the Transformation of International Society," *Millennium* 29, no. 3 (2000); E. Sahliyeh, *Religious Resurgence and Politics in the Contemporary World* (New York: State University of New York Press, 1990); Jonathan Fox, "Religion and State Failure: An Examination of the Extent and Magnitude of Religious Conflict from 1950 to 1996," *International Political Science Review/Revue Internationale de Science Politique* 25, no. 1 (2010).

28   Fox, "Religion and State Failure: An Examination of the Extent and Magnitude of Religious Conflict from 1950 to 1996."; Juergensmeyer, *The New Cold War*; Jürgen Habermas, *Legitimation Crisis*, trans. Thomas McCarthy (Beacon Press, 1975); Jürgen Habermas, Joseph Ratzinger, and Florian Schuller, *The Dialectics of Secularization: On Reason and Religion* (Freiberg, Germany: Herder Verlag, 2005); Habermas, "Religion in the Public Sphere."

29   Dietz, Thomas, "Drivers of Human Stress on the Environment in the Twenty-First Century," *Annual Review of Environment and Resources,* 42 (2017):189–213.

30   Chris Pearson, "Beyond 'Resistance': Rethinking Nonhuman Agency for a 'More-Than-Human' World," *European Review of History: Revue Européenne d'Histoire* 22, no. 5 (2015); Gabriele Duerbeck, Caroline Schaumann, and Heather Sullivan, "Human and Non-Human Agencies in the Anthropocene," *Ecozon@2015,* no. 1 (2015).

31   Lee Freese, "Evolution and Sociogenesis: Parts I & II," in *Advances in Group Processes*, ed. E.J. Lawler and B. Markovsky (Greenwich, CT: JAI Press, 1988); *Environmental Connections* (Greenwich, Connecticut: JAI Press, 1997); *Evolutionary Connections* (Greenwich, Connecticut: JAI Press, 1997).

In Matters of Religion, Religion Matters

One of the lessons of secularization has been that religious monopolies and the practice of preferential treatment toward one religion at the expense of another is incompatible with democratic governance; empirical evidence suggests that political practices of religious favoritism may be a distinguishing factor influencing violent outcomes for religious minorities.[32] To the extent that the F8/F7/F20 Initiative emphasizes human rights, humanitarian assistance and sustainable development, the 'return of religion' to the public sphere may be regarded as an extension of civil society. But the Initiative also addresses freedom of religion or belief for the religious sector. This more controversial aspect of the Initiative provides evidentiary support for Peter Beyer's claim that modern religion is differentiated religion—maintaining its semantic and sociostructural identity even as it reasserts in the public domain of globalizing structures.[33] In addition to partnering for humanitarian assistance, the F8/F7/F20 Initiative consistently speaks to governance lacunas associated with the religious sector. Analysis of the empirical gap between religious freedom aspiration and practice is so large that the 2013 All Party Parliamentary Group on International Religious Freedom or Belief report refers to Article 18 as an 'orphaned right.' In his foreword to the report, Lord Singh of Wimbledon, member of the UK Parliament in the House of Lords, has written that

> we in Western Europe need to learn to approach questions of religion and belief with humility, recognizing that, globally speaking, secularism is a minority view, and that Western ways of operating will not necessarily be applicable in other parts of the world ... we must never fall into the danger of "cultural colonialism," whereby we assume that our culture is superior to other world cultures. We must never allow ourselves to believe that religion is somehow backward; it can be a positive force for good. Equally the bigotry and intolerance that sometimes attaches itself to religion will not just go away if we ignore it. We have a responsibility to expose and combat intolerant attitudes that attach themselves to and distort underlying ethical teachings.[34]

---

32   Brian Grim and Roger Finke, *The Price of Freedom Denied: Religious Persecution and Conflict in the Twenty-First Century* (Cambridge, MA: Cambridge University Press, 2010).

33   Beyer, *Religion in the Context of Globalization*, 5.

34   Lord Singh Wimbledon, "Introduction," *Article 18: An Orphaned Right* (2013), https:// freedomdeclared.org/media/Article-18-An-Orphaned-Right.pdf.

The time has come, says Tony Blair (former Prime Minister of Great Britain and Northern Ireland), to "put away the delusions ... that a debate about politics can be seriously conducted in the 21st century without discussing religion. We must discuss and debate it, and not just as social science, foreign affairs, or even psychology, but as religion."[35] Regardless of whether the return of religion to the public sphere is discerned to be good, bad or somewhere in-between, the point is this: *religion matters*. The chapters that follow document, detail and assess the F8/F7/F20 Initiative's ability to convince members of the G-plus System that religion should also matter *to them*.

---

35   Tony Blair, "Protecting Religious Freedom Should Be a Priority for All Democracies," *The Review of Faith and International Affairs* 10, no. 3 (2012): 7.

CHAPTER 2

G-plus System Diplomacy

This chapter describes the origins and evolution of the G-plus System, and explains why various interest groups have sought out ways to engage with the G7/G8 and the G20 to influence their dialogue process. Evolution of G7, G8 and G20 meetings are rooted in the advent of globalization. Major market democracies began to dialogue with one another as the progression of globalization intensified economic interdependencies. Governance gaps resulted in patterned inequities that interest groups slowly organized around. Attempts to engage in dialogue with the G-plus System have proceeded unevenly with some engagement groups achieving official recognition more easily than others. Efforts by religious leaders to engage with the G-plus System have gone largely unrecognized. Over time, engagement groups and think tanks have shifted their attention away from inputs toward outputs as various G-plus System research centers and civil society organizations have begun to monitor G-plus System performance.

The Origins and Evolution of the G-plus System

The first meeting of what would eventually become a continuing series of annual meetings of subgroups forming the G-plus System began more as an informal retreat in reaction to the rigidity of the existing bureaucratic international institutions of governance.[1] The heads of state for France, West Germany, Italy, Japan, the United Kingdom and the United States gathered at the Château de Rambouillet near Paris, November 15–17, 1975, to become better acquainted. The leaders of what were then considered the strongest 'core' economies recognized a need to dialogue about the increasing transnational problems. Although they convened as a group, they were in agreement that participants were not officially responsible for the resolution of problems that lay beyond the political jurisdiction of their respective national borders.

Over time, the G6 expanded and diversified into a G-plus System. A variety of informal transnational governing bodies have emerged to engage in

---

1   Bob Reinalda and Bertjan Verbeek, *Autonomous Policy Making by International Organizations* (London: Taylor and Francis, 1998), 205.

dialogue and diplomacy to address complex situations. On May 7–8, 1976, seven heads of state or government of the major industrial democracies began to meet annually to address major economic and political issues facing their domestic societies and the international community as a whole. Representatives from Canada, France, the United States, United Kingdom, Germany, Japan and Italy met at No. 10 Downing Street in London. The European Community first participated in 1977 when the group met at the former official residence of the Federal Chancellor in Bonn on July 16–17. This Group of Seven, or G7, met regularly thereafter with various levels of broader post-summit dialogue that included the USSR (and later Russia) and developing countries. By 1997, Russia was participating in all except financial and certain economic discussions, and on May 15–17, 1998, the Group of Eight was formed at the Birmingham Summit. France, the United States, the United Kingdom, Germany, Japan, Italy, Canada, and Russia continued to meet as the G8 until Russia's actions in Ukraine on March 2, 2014 sparked suspension of their participation in what would now be ongoing G7 meetings.[2]

When the 1997–99 global financial crisis occurred, the informal political process broadened. Finance ministers and central bank governors from 19 countries and the European Union began to meet informally with representatives of the International Monetary Fund and the World Bank. The Group of Twenty (G20) forum of finance ministers and central bank governors was formally created at the September 25, 1999 meeting of the G7 Finance Ministers. Heads of state from this informal network began meeting in 2008 at the invitation of US President George W. Bush in response to the US financial crisis. The G20 was formed as a deliberative (rather than decisional) body that was focused on policy formation to promote the creation of consensus on international issues that would avoid the traditional north-south divide and stabilize the global economy. In addition to the G7 members, the G20 was expanded to include Argentina, Australia, Brazil, China, India, Mexico, Russia, Saudi Arabia, South Africa, South Korea, Turkey and two unfilled positions reserved for Asian countries. The G7 and the G20 continue to meet to address international issues of global concern.[3] Other transnational bodies have also emerged over time (e.g., the European Union, the Council of Europe, UNICEF) to respond to growing concerns.

---

2   Peter I. Hajnal, *The G7/G8 System: Evolution, Role and Documentation* (Brookfield, Vermont: Ashgate Publishing Company, 1999).

3   John Kirton, "What Is the G20?," *G20 Information Centre* (1999), http://www.g20.utoronto.ca/g20whatisit.html.

Despite the ongoing series of summitry, the G-plus System has remained decidedly informal. None of the manifestations—G6, G7, G8 or G20—exist as international institutions. There is no fixed summit structure or enduring administrative or bureaucratic support structure. Even websites produced by national hosts to document the process are frequently dismantled once the summit process has been handed over to the next host. The various G-plus System meetings have no charter, rules, headquarters, permanent secretariats, buildings or pension plans.[4] But neither is the process an unfocused, *ad hoc* intermittent exchange of information.

Statements are frequently issued following G-plus System summits. The effectiveness of the dialogue has been heavily critiqued since conformity to collaborative statements is unenforceable rendering the process effectively toothless. Lack of process control, however, does not mean the process is lacking in authority or influence.[5] Dr. John Kirton (Co-Founder and Director, G8 Research Group; Founder and Co-Director, G20 Research Group, Munk School of Global Affairs, University of Toronto, Canada) suggests that the lack of solid institutional structure may be a contributing factor to the G-20's accomplishments; the informality of the process motivates international cooperation and facilitates human agency in a complex network influenced by repeated crisis and high uncertainty.[6] Cesare Merlini, Chairman of the Board of Trustees of the Istituto Affari Internazionali and Nonresident Senior Fellow of the Brookings Institution, has made similar suggestions in his description of the dynamics associated with the semi-personal and quasi-institutional structure of the G-plus System.[7] British diplomat Nicholas Bayne has observed that the contradictory institution/anti-institution approach of the G-plus System may be "the secret of its survival."[8] Peter Hajnal, also from the Munk School of Global Affairs, has certainly noted the importance of informality in his analysis of the ongoing G-plus System.[9]

---

4   Hajnal, *The G7/G8 System: Evolution, Role and Documentation*; Peter I. Hajnal, "The G20," in *Evolution, Interrelationships, Documentation* (Burlington, VT: Ashgate, 2014); John J. Kirton, "G20 Governance for a Globalized World," (Burlington, VT: Ashgate, 2013).

5   For example, see Kirton, "G20 Governance for a Globalized World," 1–51.

6   Ibid.

7   Cesare Merlini, "The G-7 and the Need for Reform," *The International Spectator* 29, no. 2 (1994).

8   Nicholas Bayne, "The G7 Summit and the Reform of Global Institutions," 30, no. 4 (1995).

9   Hajnal, "The G20."; Hajnal, *The G7/G8 System: Evolution, Role and Documentation*.

The Rules of Governing without Government

Since the end of the Cold War, Raymond Cohen has referred to diplomacy as the 'engine room' of international relations where the action happens.[10] Scholar-diplomat Smith Simpson contends that much of the rationale attending to the world's affairs can be credited to the daily activities of diplomats and consular officers around the world.[11] As the G-plus System has expanded, diplomacy has somewhat declined in importance, but it nevertheless remains a key factor influencing transnational policy-making.[12] The resolution of transnational social problems in an increasingly interdependent world requires dialogue where the explicit construction, representation, negotiation, and manipulation of identities are "necessarily ambiguous."[13]

Ambiguous conversations about commitments to resolving global problems should not obfuscate a defining feature of the post-Westphalian context: it is a nation-state system. When diplomats gather for dialogue in informal transnational governing bodies such as the G7 and the G20, one must understand whom they represent. Representatives gather within a normative framework that would negatively sanction any diplomat presuming to claim transnational, yet alone global, political jurisdiction. As Paul Sharp has pointed out,

> Diplomats and the diplomatic system continue to derive their authority from the claim that they represent sovereign states in their relations with one another and not from some wider notion of international community, of which states are but one expression. Failures of diplomacy in places as different as Maastricht, Mostar, and Mogadishu involved over-ambitious attempts at international management for which no consensus existed in the great powers expected to supply the resources.[14]

To the extent that transnational and global social problems are addressed within the Westphalian nation-state system, collective responses must be

---

10 Raymond Cohen, "Putting Diplomatic Studies on the Map," *Diplomatic Studies Programme Newsletter* 1998.

11 Smith Simpson, "Of Diplomats and Their Chroniclers," *Virginia Quarterly Review* 71, no. 4 (1995): 758.

12 Paul Sharp, "For Diplomacy: Representation & the Study of International Relations," *International Studies Review* 1, no. 1 (1999):33–57.

13 Ibid., 33.

14 "Who Needs Diplomats? The Problem of Diplomatic Representation," *International Journal: Canada's Journal of Global Policy Analysis* 52, no. 4 (1997): 609.

negotiated through collaborative engagement in the absence of a global government; dialogue becomes a critical means by which collective responses are
negotiated for development and implementation of more responsible policies
(e.g., the Sustainable Development Goals). The dialogue process necessarily
avoids, or negatively sanctions, extraterritorial jurisdictional behavior by any
individual nation-state. For this reason, individual nation-states are appropriately reluctant to accept responsibility for addressing social problems that
span or emanate from beyond their national borders.

But appropriate reluctance can become problematic irresponsibility. For
example, many local governments have encountered resistance from national
laws when they have adopted sustainable management practices in relation
to the global commons.[15] If the nation-state system and other transnational
organizations (e.g., the European Union, the Council of Europe, UNICEF) are
not pressured into acting more responsibly in a timely manner, scholars point
out that the unintended consequence may eventually culminate in the tragedy
of the global commons.[16]

Broadening the Dialogue

There are patterned gaps in global governance. The unintended consequences
of these patterned transnational governance gaps have attracted civic responses from a variety of special interest groups over time. Attempts to gain the attention of G-plus System leaders have taken many forms over the years from
direct action protests to letter writing campaigns directed at the spouses of
participating diplomats. One enduring strategy for bringing diverse experts
together to discuss issues relevant to the G-plus System agenda has been the

---

15   Jonathan Rosenbloom, "Local Governments and Global Commons," *Brigham Young Uni-
      versity Law Review* 2014, no. 6 (2015).
16   Juan Carlos Castilla, "Tragedia De Los Recursos De Uso Comun Y Etica Ambiental In-
      dividual Responsible Frente Al Calentamiento Global," *Tragedy of the Common Pool Re-
      sources and Environmental Ethics Individually Liable to Global Warming* 21, no. 1 (2015);
      Aidan Hollis and Peter Maybarduk, "Antibiotic Resistance Is a Tragedy of the Commons
      That Necessitates Global Cooperation," *The Journal Of Law, Medicine and Ethics: A Journal
      Of The American Society Of Law, Medicine and Ethics* 43, Suppl. 3 (2015); Frederick A.B.
      Meyerson, "Population, Development and Global Warming: Averting the Tragedy of the
      Climate Commons," 1998; Ghulam Mujaddid, "Second Tragedy of Global Commons: Stra-
      tegic Competition and Conflict over Humanity's Common Assets," *Strategic Studies* 32,
      no. 4/1 (2013); Eduardo Araral, "Ostrom, Hardin and the Commons: A Critical Apprecia-
      tion and a Revisionist View," *Environmental Science and Policy* 36 (2014).

convening of shadow summits in tandem with G-plus System gatherings. Shadow summits may, or may not, be officially recognized by the G-plus System. Duplicate protest summits—or just protests—are sometimes convened, if the shadow summit is considered too compromised to effectively address the issues.[17] The degree to which civil society operates in reciprocity with government remains unclear,[18] and analysts question whether civil society expansion reflects a strengthening of democracy, or a response to the increasingly precarious position of sovereign states.[19] In the past few years, civil society has started contracting. Scholars have begun to explore the meaning, potential and limits of global civil society.[20] Shadow summitry can be expensive and less productive than more focused strategies such as developing G20 communiques and targeted policy briefs. For example, over 180 civil society groups formed InterAction in the United States to develop annual briefs that are delivered to the G7 and G20.

Several engagement groups have coalesced to engage with political leaders at their summits. The first engagement partners formed in relation to the G20 as business (B20) and labor (L20) who provided consultation focused on key financial, economic, trade, and development issues. As G20 topics broadened to address a wider array of issues from terrorism to climate change, the number of engagement partners was formalized to include civil society (C20), academia/think tanks (T20), youth (Y20), and, most recently, women (W20).[21] Under the German Presidency in 2017, an association of research academies formed a science (S20) engagement group.[22] The most influential groups are the Business 20 (B20) alliance of leading G20 trade associations which represent more than 6.8 million businesses, and the Labor 20 (L20) which is convened by the International Trade Union Confederation and the Trade Union Advisory Committee to the OECD.[23] Some groups have developed advisory groups to the G20 (e.g., the International Chamber of Commerce formed a G20

17   Julia Damphouse, "Storming the Stage: An Interview with Emily Laquer," (2017), https://jacobinmag.com/2017/06/g20-summit-protests-eu-globalization-neoliberalism.

18   Hajnal, "The G20."

19   Jeffrey Haynes, "Transnational Religious Actors and International Politics," *Third World Quarterly* 22, no. 2 (2001).

20   Evan Berry, "Religion and Sustainability in Global Civil Society," *Worldviews: Global Religions, Culture and Ecology* 18, no. 3 (2014).

21   Sharan Burrow et al., "G20 2014: Perspectives from Business, Civil Society, Labour, Think Tanks and Youth," *G20 Monitor* 9, March (2014); Hajnal, "The G20."; Tristram Sainsbury, "G20 Outreach to Society in 2015," *G20 Monitor* 18, October (2015).

22   Alexander and Loeschmann, "The Solar System of G20: Engagement Groups."

23   Ibid.

CEO Advisory Group) as a way of leveraging direct links with governments in each of the G20 economies.

Engagement Group Recognition

Over time, the G-plus System has slowly come to acknowledge the importance of engaging in broader policy consultation with civil and private sector networks as part of their deliberations. Several groups have obtained varying degrees of recognition by the G-plus System, more generally, and as official engagement partners for dialogue by G20 hosts, specifically. By 2017, the Heinrich Böll Institute was referring to engagement groups as the 'Solar System' of the G20 (See Figure 2.1). National hosts determine which engagement groups will be recognized during their year of hosting the summit, so there is variation year-to-year regarding which groups are invited by the G-plus System to

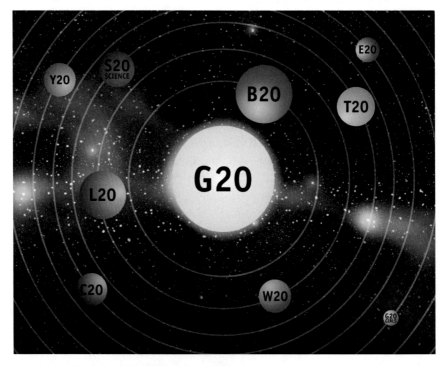

FIGURE 2.1   *The solar system of G20 engagement groups*
SOURCE: NANCY ALEXANDER AND HEIKE LOESCHMANN, "THE SOLAR
SYSTEM OF G20: ENGAGEMENT GROUPS," *G20 FUNDAMENTALS* 4 (2016),
USED WITH PERMISSION OF THE HEINRICH BÖLL FOUNDATION NORTH
AMERICA, LICENSED UNDER CC-BY-NC-ND 4.0.

actively provide input into the process. In 2017, Germany officially recognized Women (W20), Business (B20), Think Tanks (T20), Civil Society (C20), Science (S20), Labour (L20), and Youth (Y20) as engagement groups. Officially recognized groups are invited to participate in multiple meetings to provide ideas and recommendations for discussion and negotiation.

Informal engagement groups are interest groups seeking engagement that go unrecognized in any given year by the G20 (or even by other documenters of the process). For example, the Heinrich Böll Stiftung Foundation (a non-profit political foundation affiliated with the German Green Party and the documenter of engagement groups in the USA) identified only one informal engagement group in the 2017 Germany G20 'Solar System' that is displayed in Figure 2.1—the Girls (G20) engagement group. By way of contrast, China formally recognized only the B20 and C20 as engagement groups just the year before, despite informal national dialogue occurring with several of the groups on the side.[24] Although the L20 went unrecognized in China in 2016, they were officially recognized by Turkey in 2015 along with the B20, C20, T20, W20 and Y20.[25]

Some religious groups have participated in the official engagement process, but they have done so as part of other engagement groups—either civil society (e.g., Tear Fund and World Vision in C20 Australia in 2014)[26] or think tanks (e.g., F20 participation in T20 Germany in 2017). The G7 leaders have recently begun to recognize some of the concerns expressed by religious leaders, but even after the 2016 China F20 Summit, keynote speaker Katherine Marshall (Senior Fellow, Berkley Center for Religion, Peace and World Affairs, Georgetown University, US) noted in her post-summit reflections that "world leaders meeting in Hangzhou, China may be unaware that a few days earlier a shadow group of religious scholars met in Beijing."[27] Key leaders in the Initiative process are aware that their work has low visibility. Yet, they continue.

Obtaining recognition involves a fluid process that may take decades, if it ever happens at all. Consider, for example, the case of the C20. Civil society draws together a diverse network of organizations concerned across a range of issues affecting vulnerable communities including development, trade, climate financing, and food security.[28] Peter Hajnal documents how the C20

---

24   See http://www.g20chn.org/English/Engagement/, accessed June 28, 2017.
25   See http://g20.org.tr/engagement-groups/, accessed June 28, 2017.
26   J.A. Scholte, "Introduction," in *Building Global Democracy? Civil Society and Accountable Global Governance*, ed. J.A. Scholte (Cambridge: MA: Cambridge University Press, 2011).
27   Marshall, "Shadowing the China G20 Summit: An Interreligious Gathering."
28   Hajnal, "The G20."

has developed through five stages of relationship with the G-plus System: Phase I (1975–80) marked the early years of 'mutual ignorance' or 'mutual non-recognition.' Phase II (1981–94) involved one-sided recognition where civil society acknowledged the G7 but civil society organizations had not yet reached the G7's consciousness. Phase III (1995–97) represented the stage of mutual recognition starting with the 1995 Halifax G7 Summit. Phase IV (1998–2001) marked development of well-established, systematic contact between G8 and civil society. Phase V (2002 to the present) marked the phase of regularized mutual interaction.[29] Hajnal documented a linear progression of increasing recognition, but his book was published before civil society began to recently shrink. This could change.

Official recognition, when it occurs, triggers a year-long process of information exchange between the engagement group and the G-plus System. The leaders of nations and governments use Sherpas to dialogue with the official engagement partners to develop institutional arrangements that facilitate more effective responsible transnational policies in ways that are appropriate to the governance norms of the Westphalian nation-state system.[30]

Monitoring of the G-plus System

According to scholar of diplomacy Kai Monheim, process matters in global negotiations much more than analysts have cared to acknowledge.[31] Multilateral negotiations on worldwide challenges have grown in importance with rising global interdependence, and effective negotiation of the process is itself invoked as an explanatory factor.[32] It is not enough that talks be inclusive and transparent, they must be perceived as such, and diplomatic skill is important to the social construction of trust and respect. Presidencies where negotiations have been successful, says Monheim, have paid attention to transparency and inclusivity, have included large and non-mainstream countries, and have ensured that all delegates feel respected.[33]

---

29   Ibid.

30   Sherpas are the senior civil servants at the level of deputy minister or equivalent whose task it is to navigate the G-plus System for the heads of state and senior delegations.

31   Kai Monheim, *How Effective Negotiation Management Promotes Multilateral Cooperation: The Power of Process in Climate, Trade, and Biosafety Negotiations*, Routledge Research in Global Environmental Governance (London: Routledge, 2015).

32   Ibid.

33   Ibid.

Several academic institutes and engagement groups monitor the G-plus System in some manner. Canada has at least three monitoring groups: the Centre for Global Studies at the University of Victoria, the Centre for International Governance Innovation in Waterloo, and the Munk School of Global Affairs at the University of Toronto. In particular, the Munk School of Global Affairs has a G7 Research Group, a G8 Research Group and a G20 Research Group; they also host a series of documents at the G8 Information Centre including compliance reports and articles on evolving partnerships with groups such as the G20, B20, BRICS and the United Nations. The Lowy Institute for International Policy is an Australian think tank that follows the G-plus System. They also have a G20 Studies Centre and they quarterly publish the *G20 Monitor* that brings together policy contributions from wide cross-sections of society interested in feeding into the G20 process. They also publish a *Global Diplomacy Index* which maps and ranks the diplomatic networks of all G20 and OECD nations. Top rated think tanks such as The Brookings Institution, Chatham House, and The Heinrich Böll Foundation critically comment on G-plus System activities.

Engagement groups tend to follow which, if any, of their recommendations have been included by leaders in their official final communiqués. The Heinrich Böll Foundation uses policy brief inclusion as one measure for determining engagement group influence within the engagement group 'Solar System.'[34] Engagement groups that tend to be more critical of the G-plus System, such as the L20 and C20, tend to focus on G-plus System performance and follow-through on promises they have made over time. The L20 (Labour) publishes annual policy tracking reports where they critically assess the effectiveness of G20 policies as pertains to issues of employment.[35] In the United States, InterAction drafts policy briefs and advocates to influence the annual G7 and G20 summits including attention to G7 and G20 accountability. Some civil society organizations track G-plus System progress on more targeted issues. Transparency International, for example, tackles financial corruption and advocates for the G20 to show global leadership to establish a cleaner, more opaque and rigorous financial system. ActionAid has long called for reform of the economic development aid system to hold donors to account.

Ella Kokotsis, Director of External Relations of the G8 and G20 Research Group for The Munk School of Global Affairs, has argued that a landmark shift from inputs to outcomes occurred when the Canadian G8 chair issued *The Muskoka Accountability Report* in 2010. Analysts for the Canadian G8 compared

---

34   Alexander and Loeschmann, "The Solar System of G20: Engagement Groups."

35   Visit the International Trade Union Confederation website at https://www.ituc-csi.org and search for L20 Policy Tracking for reports.

their rhetoric against reality by tracking specific deliverables against commitments across a wide set of G8 issue areas.[36] Since that time, G7/8 performance has reportedly risen across all six dimensions of governance being measured. State reports variously attend to issues of failed diplomacy (e.g., climate change) and broken promises (e.g., payment of 0.7% of GDP to implement the MDGS) as well as to notable signature achievements (e.g., the 2010 Muskoka Initiative on Maternal, Newborn, and Child Health), strong performance on diplomatic dynamics (e.g., the 2013 G8 Lough Erne Summit that addressed trade, tax, transparency and terrorism), and effective crisis intervention and management (e.g., the G20 finance intervention in 2008).[37]

The Muskoka Accountability Report was the first demonstration of a collective effort within the G-plus System to create a mechanism of enforcement to hold themselves accountable to back their words with action.[38] Since that time, comprehensive state issued accountability and transparency reports have been intermittent but steady. For example, *The 2013 Lough Erne Accountability Report* was issued under the UK Presidency of G8 2013. Increasingly, accountability reports focus on issue areas rather than on overall governance. For example, the G7 Germany 2015 issued the *G7 Elmau Progress Report* on Biodiversity, and the G7 Japan 2016 issued the *Ise-Shima Progress Report: G7 Accountability on Development and Development-Related Commitments.*

The G20 has also begun to monitor their activities. For example, the Russians and Chinese both focused on development. The G20 Russian Presidency released the *Saint Petersburg Accountability Report on G20 Development Commitments* in 2013. The G20 China 2016 released the *Hangzhou Comprehensive Accountability Report on G20 Development Commitments.* The Turkish Presidency focused on corruption with the release of *Accountability Report: G20 Anti-Corruption Working Group* in 2015.

The self-monitoring by states does not often agree with the type of independent assessments that are provided by think tanks such as the G8 Research Group's annual *Compliance Reports* that score states in accordance with what is (or is not) fulfilled across summits, and ONE's annual *DATA Report* that

---

36   Ella Kokotsis, "The Muskoka Accountability Report: Assessing the Written Record," *International Organisations Research Journal* 5, no. 5 (2010).

37   For more information on accountability of the G7/8 and G20, see Part IV of Marina Larionova and John Kirton, *The G8-G20 Relationship in Global Governance* (Burlington, VT: Ashgate, 2016).

38   Andrew Schrumm, "Muskoka Accountability Report: G8 Rhetoric Versus Reality," *Centre for International Governance Innovation* (2010), https://www.cigionline.org/articles/muskoka-accountability-report-g8-rhetoric-versus-reality.

zeros in on G8 commitments to Africa. Nevertheless, issuance of accountability reports does represent the first step toward recognition within the G-plus System that they are accountable for their actions and answerable to stakeholders for the decisions that they make.[39] The degree to which political leaders recognize the value of engaging with stakeholders that are concerned with religion or belief and human rights for their insights into governance crises is another matter entirely.

---

39   Ibid.

CHAPTER 3

Governance in the Age of the Anthropocene

This chapter considers material changes in social and primarily human-induced environmental conditions as an explanation for why religion has become salient in transnational relations at this historic moment. Religion is not presented as a master variable in international relations. Rather, the case study is situated in a broader context of primarily human-induced environmental changes, globalization and transnational governance to provide an account for the real and potential contributions the F8/F7/F20 process makes to global governance. This chapter describes how we have left the "statist" period and entered an era characterized by 'governance without government' and 'globalized irresponsibility.' Administrating globalization leaves democratic deficits that have drawn sharp criticism from segments of society potentially putting the legitimacy of the system at-risk. As we 'make things work,' are we adequately engaged with the kind of world we are making? Multi-faith dialogue is one means of addressing this question during uncertain times of social change.

Primarily Human-Induced Global Environmental Changes

This is a unique historic moment in relation to societal-environmental relations. Human population and consumption growth are exerting unprecedented pressures on ecosystems and, for the first time in history, primarily human-induced environmental changes are observable throughout the biosphere.[1]

---

1 J. Rockström et al., "Planetary Boundaries: Exploring the Safe Operating Space for Humanity," *Ecology and Society* 14, no. 2 (2009); Johan Rockström, "A Safe Operating Space for Humanity," *Nature* 461, no. 7263 (2009); Stephen Mosley, *The Environment in World History*, 1st ed, *Themes in World History* (Milton Park: Routledge, 2010). Robert Costanza, "Ecosystem Health and Ecological Engineering," *Ecological Engineering* 45 (2012); Della Dennis, "Idealism to Realism: Applying Ecological Science to Society's Environmental Problems: The Sustainable Biosphere Initiative Project Office Creates Implementation Plan," 1992; Jane Lubchenco et al., "The Sustainable Biosphere Initiative: An Ecological Research Agenda: A Report from the Ecological Society of America." *Ecology* 72, no. 2 (1991): 371–412; Charles W. Fowler, "Maximizing Biodiversity, Information and Sustainability," *Biodiversity and Conservation* 17, no. 4 (2008); Clive L. Spash and Iulie Aslaksen, "Research Paper: Re-Establishing an Ecological Discourse in the Policy Debate over How to Value Ecosystems and Biodiversity," *Journal of*

© KONINKLIJKE BRILL NV, LEIDEN, 2018 | DOI 10.1163/9789004365018_004

Scientific data indicate that the environmental and social changes, from floods and severe storms to droughts and wildfires, are having greater effects now than in the 20th century.[2] During the latter part of that century, scientists began to explore the possibility that there might be limits to socioeconomic growth in relation to the second law of thermodynamics of physics.[3] By the turn of the century, scientists began to consider the possibility that the optimum carrying capacity might not be equated with maximum population density and that the impact of per capita consumption should be taken into consideration.[4] Some analysts consider the trajectory of primarily human-induced changes as potentially undermining the necessary conditions for human existence if current patterns remain unchecked.[5] World Wildlife Fund, one of the world's largest and most experienced independent conservation organizations, releases a bi-annual science-based analysis of planetary health and the human impact of human activity upon it. After analysis of social-environmental interactions in 2012, the scientific conclusion was that the global community may already be exceeding the carrying capacity by as much as 50%.[6] The 2014 report details a 50% decline in biodiversity between 1970 and 2010 even as humanity continues to make unsustainable demands on nature.[7] Reports emphasize how taking more from ecosystems and natural processes than can be replenished jeopardizes our common future. Even the oceans are now impacted. An estimated 60% of the world's population lives within 100 kilometers of coasts with nearly 3 billion people reliant on fish as a major source of protein. Marine vertebrate populations declined 49% between 1970 and 2012 primarily due to

---

    Environmental Management 159 (2015); Clem Tisdell, "Global Warming and the Future of Pacific Island Countries," *International Journal of Social Economics* 35, no. 12 (2008).

2   Richard H. Moss and Meredith A. Lane, "Decision-Making, Transitions, and Resilient Futures: The Newly Established National Research Council Board on Environmental Change and Society Explores Insights and Research Frontiers for Understanding Coupled Human-Environment Systems," *Issues in Science and Technology*, no. 4 (2012).

3   Kenneth D. Bailey, "System Entropy Analysis," *Kybernetes* 26, no. 6/7 (1997); William R. Catton, *Overshoot*. (Urbana, Illinois: University of Illinois Press, 1980); Nicholas Georgescu-Roegen, *The Entropy Law and the Economic Process* (Cambridge, MA: Harvard University Press, 1971); *Energy and Economic Myths* (New York, New York: Pergamon, 1976).

4   Gary W. Barrett and Eugene P. Odumuch, "The Twenty-First Century: The World at Carrying Capacity," *BioScience* 50, no. 4 (2000).

5   Freese, *Environmental Connections; Evolutionary Connections.*

6   WWF, Living Planet Report 2012: Biodiversity, Biocapacity and Better Choices, (Gland, Switzerland: World Wildlife Fund International, 2012).

7   Living Planet Report 2014: Species and Spaces, People and Places, (World Wildlife Fund International, 2014), https://www.worldwildlife.org/pages/living-planet-report-2014.

overfishing.[8] Temperature rise is undermining coral reef habitat; plastic pollution has become problematic with more than 5 trillion plastic pieces weighing over 250,000 tons in the sea. The number of oxygen-depleted dead zones in the ocean is growing from continued nutrient run-off, threatening the economic benefits of oceans that have been estimated to be worth at least $2.5 trillion per year. Only 3.4 per cent of the ocean is protected, and increasing marine protected area (MPA) coverage to 30 per cent of marine and coastal areas could generate between US$490 billion and US$920 billion from industries such as fishing and tourism. The employment structure would also improve through the creation of 150,000–180,000 full-time jobs in MPA management by 2050.[9] The relationship between society and the environment need not be win-lose when we already understand ways in which actions can be undertaken that generate win-win outcomes.

Environmental Implications for Governance

Deterioration of the modern international system may have already begun as industrialism approaches limits to further expansion due to environmental degradation and reorganization.[10] As globalization increasingly induces global environmental changes, global threats to humanity and the environment create governance challenges as decreasing ecosystem capacities are expected to support increasing, high consuming human populations.[11] The globalization

8   Living Blue Planet Report: Species Habitats and Human Well-Being, (Gland, Switzerland: World Wildlife Fund International, 2015).

9   Ibid.

10   Catton, *Overshoot*; Álvaro Fernández-Llamazares et al., "Rapid Ecosystem Change Challenges the Adaptive Capacity of Local Environmental Knowledge," *Global Environmental Change Part A: Human and Policy Dimensions* 31 (2015); Helena Kahiluoto et al., "Taking Planetary Nutrient Boundaries Seriously: Can We Feed the People?," *Global Food Security* 3 (2014); Rockström et al., "Planetary Boundaries: Exploring the Safe Operating Space for Humanity."; Miriam L. Diamond et al., "Review: Exploring the Planetary Boundary for Chemical Pollution," *Environment International* 78 (2015); Rockström, "A Safe Operating Space for Humanity."; Foley, "Boundaries for a Healthy Planet."; Will Steffen, Johan Rockström, and Robert Costanza, "How Defining Planetary Boundaries Can Transform Our Approach to Growth," *Solutions: For a Sustainable and Desirable Future* 2, no. 3 (2011).

11   Koko Warner, "Environmental Change and Migration: Methodological Considerations from Ground-Breaking Global Survey," *Population and Environment* 33, no. 1 (2011); Frank Biermann, "Planetary Boundaries and Earth System Governance: Exploring the Links," *Ecological Economics* 81 (2012); Baum and Handoh, "Analysis: Integrating the Planetary

of chemical production in relation to agricultural and industrial production is causing harm and creating hazards in core as well as peripheral countries.[12] Whether the emphasis is on global environmental threats created by environmental footprints that transgress planetary boundaries,[13] or the global catastrophic risks that threaten civilization,[14] what becomes clear is globalization may be transgressing global environmental tipping points which threaten human progress. Environmental changes associated with drought and food insecurity are expected to contribute to unprecedented rates of migration to Europe and create problems associated with environmental refugees that are expected to impact policy decisions.[15] Global governance is now operating in a context of global-scale environmental and human system threats that create both vulnerabilities and opportunities for cascading social-ecological changes and transformation.[16]

Some limited human adaptability may be possible through reorganization in the context of environmental constraints,[17] but it would be fallacious

---

Boundaries and Global Catastrophic Risk Paradigms."; K. Fang, R. Heijungs, and G.R. De Snoo, "Understanding the Complementary Linkages between Environmental Footprints and Planetary Boundaries in a Footprint-Boundary Environmental Sustainability Assessment Framework," *Ecological Economics* 114 (2015).

12 Tomás Sheoin, "Controlling Chemical Hazards: Global Governance, National Regulation?," *Social Justice* 41, no. 1/2 (2015).

13 Fang, Heijungs, and De Snoo, "Understanding the Complementary Linkages between Environmental Footprints and Planetary Boundaries in a Footprint-Boundary Environmental Sustainability Assessment Framework."

14 Seth D. Baum, "The Far Future Argument for Confronting Catastrophic Threats to Humanity: Practical Significance and Alternatives," *Futures* 72 (2015).

15 Allan M. Findlay, "Migrant Destinations in an Era of Environmental Change," *Global Environmental Change Part A: Human and Policy Dimensions* 21 (2011).

16 Baum and Handoh, "Analysis: Integrating the Planetary Boundaries and Global Catastrophic Risk Paradigms." Nilsson and Persson, "Analysis: Reprint of 'Can Earth System Interactions Be Governed? Governance Functions for Linking Climate Change Mitigation with Land Use, Freshwater and Biodiversity Protection.'"; Folke et al., "Reconnecting to the Biosphere."; Foley, "Boundaries for a Healthy Planet."

17 Miguel A. Gual and Richard B. Norgaard, "Bridging Ecological and Social Systems Coevolution: A Review and Proposal," *Ecological Economics* 69 (2010); A.I. Gaziulusoy, C.A. Boyle, and R. McDowall, "A Conceptual Systemic Framework Proposal for Sustainable Technology Development: Incorporating Future Studies within a Co-Evolutionary Approach," *Civil Engineering and Environmental Systems* 25, no. 4 (2008); Jeroen C.J.M. van den Bergh, *Evolutionary Economics and Environmental Policy: Survival of the Greenest.* (Cheltenham, UK: Edward Elgar Publishing, 2007).

to take for granted that humans will make choices to adaptively reorganize.[18] Several civilizations have disappeared over the course of history rather than adapt when the environment became irreversibly disorganized (e.g., Aztecs, The Mayan Civilization, Rapa Nui Civilization on Easter Island, Indus Valley Civilization, etc.).[19] The process of adaptive reorganization of human systems is problematic for several reasons including, but not limited to, the social construction of denial,[20] leadership timidity in bureaucratic organizations,[21] and the 'iron chains' of rationalized societies.[22]

'Transition Science' Emerges to Inform Governance

Governance in changing ecological contexts involves reduction of system stress, understanding and responding to risks and vulnerabilities, triggering and navigating transformation of economic activity, and development of a diversity of options.[23] Information shapes the ability to develop a common

---

18   P.R. Ehrlich and A.H. Ehrlich, "Can a Collapse of Global Civilization Be Avoided?," *Proceedings of the Royal Society B: Biological Sciences* 280, no. 1754 (2013).

19   Clive Ponting, "The Burden of the Past," *Global Dialogue* 4, no. 1 (2002); *A New Green History of the World: The Environment and the Collapse of Great Civilizations* (New York, New York: Penguin Books, 2007); J.C. Flores, "A Phase-Transition Model for the Rise and Collapse of Ancient Civilizations: A Pre-Ceramic Andean Case Study," *Physica A: Statistical Mechanics and its Applications* 440 (2015); Sherrie Steiner-Aeschliman, "Transitional Adaptation: A Neoweberian Theory of Ecologically-Based Social Change," ed. Lee Freese (JAP Press, 1999); Jared Diamond, *Collapse: How Societies Choose to Fail or Succeed* (Viking, 2004); Joseph A. Tainter, *The Collapse of Complex Societies* (Cambridge: Cambridge University Press, 1990).

20   Peter J. Jacques, "A General Theory of Climate Denial," *Global Environmental Politics* 12, no. 2 (2012); Kari Marie Norgaard, *Living in Denial: Climate Change, Emotions and Everyday Life* (MIT Press, 2011).

21   John M. Jermier, "Complex Systems Threaten to Bring us Down," *Organization and Environment* 17, no. 1 (2004); Sendil K. Ethiraj and Daniel Levinthal, "Bounded Rationality and the Search for Organizational Architecture: An Evolutionary Perspective on the Design of Organizations and Their Evolvability," *Administrative Science Quarterly* 49, no. 3 (2004).

22   Richard M. Weiss, "Weber on Bureaucracy: Management Consultant or Political Theorist?," *Academy of Management Review* 8, no. 2 (1983); Robert D. Miewald, "The Greatly Exaggerated Death of Bureaucracy," *California Management Review* 13, no. 2 (1970).

23   Nilsson and Persson, "Analysis: Reprint of 'Can Earth System Interactions Be Governed? Governance Functions for Linking Climate Change Mitigation with Land Use, Freshwater and Biodiversity Protection.'"

future by influencing culture, politics and responses to climate change.[24] But the process of changing biophysical conditions and the changing conditions of human society is not a simple, causal relationship.[25] Rather, the process of changing human-environmental connections is complex, nonlinear, and multidimensional.[26] 'Transition science' is an emergent field of knowledge that explores, among other things, how unprecedented rates of rapid ecosystem changes challenge the adaptive capacities of strategies that rely primarily upon local environmental knowledge.[27] It is becoming increasingly clear that, if existing systems are to be sustained, new knowledge must be generated that incorporates how earth systems are changing.

'Transition science' has begun to develop in behavioral economics, risk communication, governance, decision science, and environmental science to provide new data and information to inform the process and develop strategies, warning systems and coping strategies for decision makers.[28] For example, in the United States, The National Research Council now has a Board on Environmental Change and Society and the University of Maryland has a Global Change Research Institute. The integration of social science research with climate and environmental research provides insights into the potential effectiveness of different approaches to increase resilience or reduce human contributions to drivers of change.[29] Governance in this new historic context is a multi-level problem involving coherent interaction between (at least) four earth sub-systems: climate change, freshwater use, land use and biodiversity.[30]

---

24 Deserai Crow and Maxwell Boykoff, *Culture, Politics and Climate Change: How Information Shapes Our Common Future* (New York, New York: Routledge/Earthscan, 2014).

25 Armand L. Mauss, "Beyond the Illusion of Social Problems Theory," in *Perspectives on Social Problems*, ed. R.L. Henshel and A.M. Henshel (JAI Press, 1989).

26 Freese, *Environmental Connections*; *Evolutionary Connections*; Richard B. Norgaard and John A. Dixon, "Pluralistic Project Design," *Policy Sciences* 19, no. 3 (1986); David LePoire, "Interpreting 'Big History' as Complex Adaptive System Dynamics with Nested Logistic Transitions in Energy Flow and Organization," *Emergence: Complexity and Organization* 17, no. 1 (2015).

27 Fernández-Llamazares et al., "Rapid Ecosystem Change Challenges the Adaptive Capacity of Local Environmental Knowledge."

28 Moss and Lane, "Decision-Making, Transitions, and Resilient Futures: The Newly Established National Research Council Board on Environmental Change and Society Explores Insights and Research Frontiers for Understanding Coupled Human-Environment Systems."

29 Ibid.

30 Nilsson and Persson, "Analysis: Reprint of 'Can Earth System Interactions Be Governed? Governance Functions for Linking Climate Change Mitigation with Land Use, Freshwater and Biodiversity Protection.'"

Scientists are beginning to operationalize a set of global scale planetary boundary measures into less-aggregated national and sub-national scales to provide frameworks that align socio-economic and ethical decision-making processes with biophysical changes for more robust sustainability decision-making.[31] The knowledge base for informing the process remains a work in progress.

The year 2015 marked a troubled, but pivotal, year of hope for the global community in terms of restoring degraded landscapes, reaching global agreement on sustainability goals, spurring companies to cut emissions, and inspiring urban leaders to take actions to cut emissions. The groundwork was established for the Paris agreement, and China prioritized green financing for their G20 Presidency.[32] The transition from Millennium Development Goals to Sustainable Development Goals reflected the shift in governance focus from a human-centered prioritization of development to societal development in collaboration with the biosphere.[33] The global community is now taking more of a planetary boundaries approach which aims to define a safe operating space for humanity as a precondition for sustainable development. But governance of earth systems within a larger framework of identified planetary boundaries also creates challenging political conflicts.[34] For example, estimates indicate that operating within planetary nutrient boundaries limits the food supply more than population growth does.[35] Steffen and Stafford Smith suggest that it may be in the best interest of wealthy nations to redistribute resources to facilitate more equitable international development if planetary boundaries are going to be respected.[36]

31   Tiina Häyhä et al., "From Planetary Boundaries to National Fair Shares of the Global Safe Operating Space—How Can the Scales Be Bridged?," *Global Environmental Change* (2016).

32   James A. Harmon and Andrew Steer, "Letter from the Chairman & President," *Pivotal Year: WRI 2015 Annual Report* (2016), http://www.wri.org/annualreport/2015/welcome/letter-from-the-chairman-president/.

33   Folke et al., "Reconnecting to the Biosphere."

34   Biermann, "Planetary Boundaries and Earth System Governance: Exploring the Links."; Steffen, Rockström, and Costanza, "How Defining Planetary Boundaries Can Transform Our Approach to Growth."; Will Steffen and Mark Stafford Smith, "Planetary Boundaries, Equity and Global Sustainability: Why Wealthy Countries Could Benefit from More Equity," *Current Opinion in Environmental Sustainability* 5 (2013).

35   Kahiluoto et al., "Taking Planetary Nutrient Boundaries Seriously: Can We Feed the People?"

36   Steffen and Stafford Smith, "Planetary Boundaries, Equity and Global Sustainability: Why Wealthy Countries Could Benefit from More Equity."

Governance for a Common Future

The United Nations has come to recognize that everyone is implicated and we are all in this together—we share a common future.[37] The concept of sustainability was first introduced in 1987 with release of the *Brundtland Report*.[38] Since then, several different indices and indicators have been created in association with development of a Worldwide Sustainable Society Index, the results of which are contributing to increasing concerns about the well-being of future generations.[39]

Many cities and governments are taking action to try to anticipate, mitigate and adapt to the consequences of environmental changes for both abrupt and gradual shifts where the consequences are experienced over time.[40] For example, analysts largely attribute the differences in death tolls from the 2010 earthquake between Chile and Haiti to the consistent willingness (and capability) of the Chilean government to heed the advice provided by its natural and social scientists and engineers.[41] Decision-making informed by the best 'transition science' has to offer will nevertheless encounter limitations. Understanding sustainability is a complex process of multidimensional interactions.[42] Decisions and policies have to be made in a context of uncertainties. The nature of complex, multidimensional systemic changes is that there will always be more than one possible result of a decision. Uncontrollable and uncertain forces affect the feasibility of implementing decisions and some possibilities will likely involve catastrophic loss or other undesirable outcomes.[43]

---

37   Erling Holden, Kristin Linnerud, and David Banister, "Sustainable Development: Our Common Future Revisited," *Global Environmental Change* 26 (2014); World Commission on Environment and Development, *Our Common Future*, Oxford Paperbacks (New York: Oxford University Press., 1987); Joseph Dewey, "Our Common Future," (Salem Press, 2015).

38   Gro Harlem Brundtland, "Report of the World Commission on Environment and Development: Our Common Future (Brundtland Report)," (Oslo, Norway: United Nations, 1987).

39   Isabel Gallego-Álvarez, Mª Galindo-Villardón, and Miguel Rodríguez-Rosa, "Analysis of the Sustainable Society Index Worldwide: A Study from the Biplot Perspective," *Social Indicators Research* 120, no. 1 (2015).

40   Yuliya Voytenko et al., "Urban Living Labs for Sustainability and Low Carbon Cities in Europe: Towards a Research Agenda," *Journal of Cleaner Production* 123, June (2016).

41   Moss and Lane, "Decision-Making, Transitions, and Resilient Futures: The Newly Established National Research Council Board on Environmental Change and Society Explores Insights and Research Frontiers for Understanding Coupled Human-Environment Systems."

42   Liu Jianguo et al., "Multiple Telecouplings and Their Complex Interrelationships," *Ecology and Society* 20, no. 3 (2015).

43   Moss and Lane, "Decision-Making, Transitions, and Resilient Futures: The Newly Established National Research Council Board on Environmental Change and Society

Implications for G8/G7 and G20 Financial Deliberations

Consideration of environmental limitations have enormous implications for how the economy is structured.[44] At the international level, agreement has been reached that if nations are going to build a common future together, all three dimensions—environmental, economic and social—must be considered together as an interrelated system. The normative idealizations underpinning the systemic operation of trade and development must adapt to changing circumstances or they will degrade environments and constrict opportunities for economic and social advancement.[45] Bank governance occurs in a context of systemic risk that needs to be better understood, if not reformed, in the interest of securing and maintaining global financial stability.[46] The changing distribution of risks poses a threat to the legitimacy of business firms, as well. In the past, businesses derived their legitimacy from operating in compliance with the legal rules of democratic nation-states, but now they increasingly operate under conditions of the growing interconnectedness of the global economy.[47] For this reason, the legitimacy of business firms is increasingly tied to effective governance of the global commons.

There has been considerable growth in management studies on corporate sustainability practices,[48] but intensifying environmental degradation has implications for asset impairment that have yet to be fully recognized or defined.[49] Humanity has already exceeded four of the nine planetary boundaries,[50] each

---

Explores Insights and Research Frontiers for Understanding Coupled Human-Environment Systems."

44 Herman E. Daly, *Steady-State Economics* (San Francisco: W.H. Freeman, 1977).

45 Mark Langan, "A Moral Economy Approach to Africa-EU Ties: The Case of the European Investment Bank," *Review of International Studies* 40 (2014).

46 Luci Ellis, Andy Haldane, and Fariborz Moshirian, "Systemic Risk, Governance and Global Financial Stability," *Journal of Banking and Finance* 45 (2014).

47 Anselm Schneider and Andreas Scherer, "Corporate Governance in a Risk Society," *Journal of Business Ethics* 126, no. 2 (2015).

48 Gail Whiteman, Brian Walker, and Paolo Perego, "Planetary Boundaries: Ecological Foundations for Corporate Sustainability," *Journal of Management Studies* 50, no. 2 (2013).

49 Martina K. Linnenluecke and Andrew Griffiths, "Firms and Sustainability: Mapping the Intellectual Origins and Structure of the Corporate Sustainability Field," *Global Environmental Change* 23, February (2013).

50 The nine planetary boundaries that define maximum values for human-driven environmental changes are climate change, biodiversity loss, stratospheric ozone depletion, ocean acidification, changes in biogeochemical flows, land-system changes, freshwater use, atmospheric aerosol loadings and chemical pollution. The four which have already exceeded the safe levels are climate change, biodiversity loss, land-system change and

of which has direct implications and flow-on effects for business activities over different time frames.[51] For example, with regards to climate, regulatory changes have begun to limit carbon-intensive production and clean technology is rapidly expanding, but financial risks also result from increased physical damages due to more frequent weather extremes. Risk is also introduced in association with changing technological landscapes as more environmentally friendly technologies come to replace obsolete technologies.[52] Assets become impaired when fossil fuel deposits become 'unburnable,' technologies become 'obsolete,' or investments become 'stranded.'[53] Analysts have just begun to assess the investment consequences of impaired assets but the process is hampered by the indicators which firms use that are not yet attuned to planetary boundaries.[54] Firms that depend upon ecosystem services such as flood protection or natural resource inputs (e.g., agriculture, fisheries, forestry and tourism) cannot function if ecosystems are severely degraded.[55] Firms are also drivers of global environmental changes (e.g., due to farming, large-scale deforestation, burning of fossil fuels, etc.), including production of novel substances through the chemical industry that are released at local to regional scales, which in aggregate threaten ecosystem and human viability.[56] Whether asset impairment stems from the inability to adapt to changing environmental conditions or from the need to mitigate human inducement of environmental change, financial governance will be required to make changes in regulatory requirements (or their interpretations), and make changes in the application of existing laws and legislation.[57] Although the overall situation continues to worsen in response to current patterns of globalization, analysts hope to build

---

changes in biogeochemical flows. The planetary boundaries for chemicals is still in the process of being identified. See Linn M. Persson et al., "Confronting Unknown Planetary Boundary Threats from Chemical Pollution," *Environmental Science and Technology* 47, no. 22 (2013). Rockström et al., "Planetary Boundaries: Exploring the Safe Operating Space for Humanity."; Rockström, "A Safe Operating Space for Humanity."

51   Martina K. Linnenluecke et al., "Planetary Boundaries: Implications for Asset Impairment," *Accounting & Finance* 55, no. 4 (2015).

52   "Divestment from Fossil Fuel Companies: Confluence between Policy and Strategic Viewpoints," *Australian Journal of Management* 40, no. 3 (2015).

53   Linnenluecke et al., "Planetary Boundaries: Implications for Asset Impairment."

54   Ibid.

55   Ibid.

56   Diamond et al., "Review: Exploring the Planetary Boundary for Chemical Pollution."

57   B. Caldecott and J. McDaniels, "Stranded Generation Assets: Implications for European Capacity Mechanisms, Energy Markets and Climate Policy," (2014); Linnenluecke et al., "Planetary Boundaries: Implications for Asset Impairment."

on the one past governance success story: the reversal of stratospheric ozone depletion after implementation of the Montreal Protocol.[58] But progress is slow, and in the absence of adequate governance responses, intensified competition for increasingly scarce resources is contributing to the 'securitization' of issues that were previously regarded as 'technical.'[59]

International economic organizations that govern trade, production and finance (e.g., World Trade Organization, International Monetary Fund, World Bank, etc.) are critical to the possibilities of effective environmental governance, even if they are not typically thought of as environmental regimes. International economic organizations have substantive environmental profiles in terms of the authority they exercise over resource access, use and environmental impact.[60] Similarly, there are environmental and social dimensions to the financial decisions made by the G-plus System.[61] Shortly after passage of the SDGs, the United Nations Environment Programme launched the Environment and Trade Hub, an initiative established to assist countries to use sustainable trade as a vehicle for achieving the 2030 Agenda for Sustainable Development, including the SDGs and the Financing for Development Action Agenda. Efforts are underway to implement an inclusive green economy in countries across all continents and incorporate sustainability into national trade policies and trade agreements that are negotiated at bilateral, regional and international levels.[62] The Hub provides capacity building services, targeted stakeholder training, identification and dissemination of best practices and the identification of sector or region specific sustainable production and trade opportunities to enhance the capacity of countries to realize a shift of trade practices to more sustainable pathways and contribute to global value chains. But the former UN Deputy Secretary-General Jan Eliasson made it clear that implementation of the SDGs is dependent upon development of a

---

58   Linnenluecke et al., "Planetary Boundaries: Implications for Asset Impairment."; Rock-
        ström, "A Safe Operating Space for Humanity."

59   John Ravenhill, "Resource Insecurity and International Institutions in the Asia-Pacific Re-
        gion," *Pacific Review* 26, no. 1 (2013); Jon Barnett, "Security and Climate Change," *Global En-
        vironmental Change* 13 (2003); Hans Günter Brauch, "Conceptualising the Environmental
        Dimension of Human Security in the Un," *International Social Science Journal* 59, no. 193
        (2008).

60   Newell, *Globalization and the Environment: Capitalism, Ecology and Power.*

61   Kirton, "G20 Governance for a Globalized World."; Hajnal, "The G20." Laura A. McKin-
        ney, "Foreign Direct Investment, Development, and Overshoot," *Social Science Research*
        47 (2014).

62   UNEP, "UNEP Launches Environment and Trade Hub to Support Countries in Sustainable
        Development Goals Implementation," *News Release,* 2015.

comprehensive development financing framework that includes financing from public, private, domestic and international sources. Illicit financial flows and international trade, and debt sustainability and relief impact international financial stability. "It is clear," said Eliasson, "that today's financing and investment patterns will not deliver sustainable development—even though current global savings are actually sufficient to finance sustainable development needs."[63]

Commitments to sustainability continue to generate tensions within the business community,[64] raising ethical as well as practical considerations that need to be addressed as part of the development of meaningful public policies and business strategies.[65] Sustainability raises ethical questions related to social justice (both within and between generations) along dimensions of gender, race and ethnicity. Ethical issues associated with humanistic solidarity, a concern for the world's poor, and respect for the ecological limits to global development also factor into sustainability commitments.[66]

Patterned Vulnerabilities and Anti-globalization Protests

No matter how you define it, globalization is a strong force with technological, ideological, institutional, and political as well as economic dimensions.[67]

---

63   UN, "Deputy Secretary-General Says Achieving Sustainable Development Goals Requires 'Coherent and Holistic' Financial, Non-Financial Implementation Means," 2015.

64   Joseph DesJardins, "Is It Time to Jump Off the Sustainability Bandwagon?" *Business Ethics Quarterly* 26, no. 1 (2016); John Gerring, "Global Justice as an Empirical Question," *PS: Political Science & Politics* 40, no. 1 (2007).

65   Göran Svensson, Greg Wood, and Michael Callaghan, "A Corporate Model of Sustainable Business Practices: An Ethical Perspective," *Journal of World Business* 45 (2010); Jack McCann and Matthew Sweet, "The Perceptions of Ethical and Sustainable Leadership," *Journal of Business Ethics* 121, no. 3 (2014); Denis G. Arnold, Kenneth E. Goodpaster, and Gary R. Weaver, "Past Trends and Future Directions in Business Ethics and Corporate Responsibility Scholarship," *Business Ethics Quarterly* 25, no. 4 (2015); Jr. Benton, Raymond, "Business, Ethics, and the Environment: Imagining a Sustainable Future," *Business Ethics Quarterly* 18, no. 4 (2008). Abul Hassan, "Islamic Ethical Responsibilities for Business and Sustainable Development," *Humanomics* 32, no. 1 (2016).

66   Oluf Langhelle, "Sustainable Development: Exploring the Ethics of 'Our Common Future,'" *International Political Science Review* 20, no. 2 (1999): 129–149; Judith Treas and Daisy Carreon, "Diversity and Our Common Future: Race, Ethnicity, and the Older American," *Generations* 34, no. 3 (2010).

67   Anthony Giddens, *Runaway World: How Globalization is Reshaping Our Lives* (New York: Routledge, 2003). Ulrich Beck, *What Is Globalization?* (Malden, MA: Polity Press, 2000).

Many benefits of globalization have been identified such as how it often lowers infant mortality rates in low and middle income countries, particularly in democratic contexts that provide access to nutrition.[68] When globalization leads to greater prosperity in developing contexts, child labor goes down, 'spicy hybrid cultures' emerge, literacy rates rise, and if proper environmental regulations are employed, pollution does not necessarily increase.[69] But globalization also negatively impacts particular groups in patterned ways.[70] In addition to the negative environmental externalities that more commonly accompany globalization,[71] Indigenous peoples are going extinct, the health gap is widening, people are being dispossessed from their lands, cultures are dying, languages are disappearing, and poor women and children are disproportionately affected by environmental degradation.[72] Although globalization proponents thought that transnational expansion of the economy would reduce the severity of internal ethnic conflicts, fatalities have remained high; empirical findings indicate that (1) economic globalization and cultural globalization significantly increase fatalities from ethnic conflicts, (2) sociotechnical aspects of globalization increase deaths from ethnic conflict but decrease deaths from non-ethnic conflict, and (3) regime corruption increases fatalities from non-ethnic conflict.[73] Whether the benefits of globalization outweigh the costs is a matter not easily settled.

Zygmunt Bauman describes how globalization 'liquifies modernity' by annulling the temporal-spatial distance that used to preserve local communities. Individuals at the top of the stratification structure are increasingly freed from their obligations to the perpetuation of daily communal life as they become

---

68   Anna Welander, Carl Hampus Lyttkens, and Therese Nilsson, "Globalization, Democracy, and Child Health in Developing Countries," *Social Science & Medicine* 136–137, July (2015).
69   Jagdish N. Bhagwati, *In Defense of Globalization* (New York: Oxford University Press, 2004).
70   Julian Kunnie, *The Cost of Globalization: Dangers to the Earth and Its People* (Jefferson, North Carolina: McFarland & Company, 2015).
71   David Ehrenfeld, "Globalisation: Effects on Biodiversity, Environment and Society," *Conservation & Society* 1, no. 1 (2003); Claus Emmeche, "Bioinvasion, Globalization, and the Contingency of Cultural and Biological Diversity: Some Ecosemiotic Observations," *Sign Systems Studies* 29, no. 1 (2001).
72   Kunnie, *The Cost of Globalization: Dangers to the Earth and Its People*; Salikoko S. Mufwene, "Language Birth and Death," *Annual Review of Anthropology* 33, no. 1 (2004); Muhammad Tariq Khan et al., "Languages in Danger of Death—and Their Relation with Globalization, Business and Economy," *International Journal of Information, Business & Management* 7, no. 2 (2015).
73   Susan Olzak, "Does Globalization Breed Ethnic Discontent?" *Journal of Conflict Resolution* 55, no. 1 (2011).

freed up to travel, physically as well as virtually, anywhere they please; individuals at the bottom of the stratification structure find their local spaces shrinking and their social power to generate local meaning weakening.[74] As the 'throw away' culture expands, the human bonds associated with local communities wilt and 'decompose'. The increasing mobility of capital means that the rich no longer need the poor, a factor which contributes to a corporate shedding of responsibility for the consequences of corporate social behavior.[75] Bauman describes development of collective impotence among more vulnerable communities as traditional public spaces disappear and people have nowhere to elevate their private concerns into public issues.[76] Giddens has a different take on it, however. Globalization, he says, liberates people from tradition so that, rather than disappear, traditional involvement becomes a choice rather than fate or obligation.[77] But Giddens agrees that globalization pulls power upward and away from local communities and nations while also pushing downward, creating new pressures for local autonomy. In response to these new pressures, local identities either intensify, diversify into new nationalisms, or die.[78] The new identities that form are often unstable, reflexive and ever changing.

The political ramifications of globalization have increased over time. Globalization has been described by some groups as a form of neocolonialism.[79] Anti-globalization protests oriented toward civil disobedience first began to emerge in conjunction with the 1999 World Trade Organization meetings in Seattle and soon spread to other parts of the world.[80] Participating groups included anti-racist groups, feminist groups, environmentalist groups, gay and lesbian groups, students, peasants, labor unions, and political parties.[81] Protestors engaged in civil disobedience, mass demonstrations, consumer activism, electronic activism, teach-ins, and direct action tactics.[82] Activists have

---

74   Zygmunt Bauman, *Globalization: The Human Consequences* (New York: Columbia University Press, 1998); *Liquid Modernity* (Cambridge: Polity Press, 2000).

75   Bauman, *Globalization: The Human Consequences*.

76   Ibid.

77   Giddens, *Runaway World: How Globalization is Reshaping Our Lives*.

78   Ibid.

79   M. Habib, "Globalization and Literature,"*Language in India* 15, no. 9 (2015): 14–21.

80   Selin Bengi Gumrukcu, "The Rise of a Social Movement: The Emergence of Anti-Globalization Movements in Turkey," *Turkish Studies* 11, no. 2 (2010).

81   Ibid.

82   Ibid.

continued to reject consumerism and advocate for a holistic globalization that delivers social justice to people across all nations and across generations.[83]

The anti-globalization movement has persistently targeted international financial organizations such as the G8/G7 and the G20, but also the Organization for Economic Cooperation and Development, the International Monetary Fund, the World Bank and the World Trade Organization.[84] One of the first widely publicized deaths of a protester occurred when the G8 met in Italy in 1999 when Carlo Giuliani, a history student from Genoa, was shot by police as he hoisted a fire extinguisher to throw through a broken window. After that, the civil-disobedience anti-globalization movement advocating for social reform began to attract activists advocating violent agendas or no-agendas at all.[85] A more professional, formally organized civil society stream has emerged over time.

Governance without Government

Governance has changed in response to how national economies have integrated during the last quarter of the 20th century through foreign investment, technological change, international trade, and immigration.[86] As countries promoted the increased flow of goods and services across borders, there has not been any simultaneous integration of political regimes; new horizontal regulatory regimes emerged inclusive of international organizations, firms, NGOs and other civil society organizations to address a broad range of substantive issues such as human rights, health and healthcare, housing, poverty, security and counter-terrorism.[87] Power has been slowly shifting away from the nation-state's ability to hold multinational corporations accountable to serve the interests of citizens within their respective borders. As such, we have left the 'statist' period where countries have been the strongest arbiters of power and entered an era of globalization characterized by 'governance without government.' States are increasingly contracting services and engaging in public-private partnerships signaling a move away from the traditional role

---

83   Jeffrey M. Ayres, "Framing Collective Action," *Journal of World-Systems Research* 10, no. 1 (2004).

84   Ibid.

85   Rod Nordland et al., "First Blood," *Newsweek* 138, no. 5 (2001).

86   Patricia Kennett, *Governance, Globalization and Public Policy* (Cheltenham, UK: Edward Elgar Publishing, 2008).

87   Ibid.

nations have played as the central source of the 'authoritative allocation of values.'[88]

Governance patterns have become characterized by an unstructured complexity composed of a diverse array of players.[89] As globalization has progressed, the ability of national governments to create public policies that influence the economy and society has become weaker in tandem with the growing importance of networks, partnerships and international markets where power is negotiated in multiple parallel spaces.[90] States have become 'hollowed out,' no longer as capable of steering as they have done in the past.[91] Governance power has become dispersed across new sites of action, augmented by new structures and technologies.[92] Governance power has expanded upwards to the supranational level of the G-plus System, outwards to include private firms and markets, and downwards through agencies and quasi-autonomous INGOs.[93] As governance has become more inclusive, the boundaries between public and private parties have become blurred. Societies become increasingly steered by less direct means as self-organizing networks come to dominate public policy.[94] If governments attempt to impose control over policy in these networks, the networks have enough resiliency that they are often able to evade government control.[95]

At the transnational level, interaction based on institutional authority has increasingly given way to governance via network influence as a way of respecting the legitimate national interests of those affected by decisions, programs

---

88   B. Guy Peters and John Pierre, "Governance without Government? Rethinking Public Administration," 1998.

89   Bob Jessop, "Hollowing out the 'Nation-State' and Multilevel Governance," in *A Handbook of Comparative Social Policy* (Cheltenham: Edward Elgar Publishing, 2004).

90   Peters and Pierre, "Governance without Government? Rethinking Public Administration."; R. Mayntz, "Common Goods and Governance," in *Common Goods: Reinventing European and International Governance* (Lanham, MD: Rowman & Littlefield, 2002); Arne Heise, "Governance without Government," *International Journal of Political Economy* 41, no. 2 (2012).

91   R.A.W. Rhodes, "The New Governance: Governing without Government," *Political Studies* 44, no. 4 (1996); H. Bekke, W. Kickert, and J. Kooiman, "Public Management and Governance," in *Public Policy and Administrative Sciences in the Netherlands*, ed. W. Kickert and F.A. van Vught (London: Harvester-Wheatsheaf, 1995).

92   Nikolas Rose and Peter Miller, "Political Power Beyond the State: Problematics of Government," *The British Journal of Sociology* 43, no. 2 (1992).

93   Kennett, *Governance, Globalization and Public Policy*.

94   Rhodes, "The New Governance: Governing without Government."

95   Peters and Pierre, "Governance without Government? Rethinking Public Administration."

and interventions.[96] Transnational governance occurs without a supranational government via informal patterns and practices that have domestic impact at the national level. Transnational governance generally seeks to maintain the stability of the international financial system and avoid the negative consequences of uncooperative distribution games.[97] An asymmetrical regulatory pattern emerges where supranational regulation in the context of a single market limits the national capacity to act even as nation-states maintain an illusion of self-determination.[98] Accountability for these decisions shifts from vertical to new forms of horizontal dialogue with complex combinations of public and private agencies involved in partnerships and joined-up service delivery.[99] A growing body of global regulatory governance mechanisms have emerged that Kingsbury and Stewart describe as a spontaneously evolving, untidy regulatory mass without center or hierarchy that is largely administrative in character, reaching decisions by reference to sources such as staff employment contracts, staff rules and regulations, and internal orders.[100] While this curb on the exercise of public power promotes more orderly patterns of globalization, the highly fragmented, horizontally organized regimes function with considerable autonomy, outstripping any global governance ability to control and legitimate regulatory decisions.[101] Administrating globalization so that it unfolds with a measure of decency and order leaves huge democratic deficits that have drawn sharp criticism from concerned INGOs, citizens, and media who question the nature and direction of globalization itself.[102] To the extent that the hegemonic nation-states are characterized by democratic norms, there may arise *expectations* among people in regions throughout the world

---

96   Ulrich Beck, A. Giddens, and S. Lasch, *Reflexive Modernization: Politics, Tradition and Aesthetics in the Modern Social Order* (Stanford, CA: Stanford University Press, 1994).

97   Heise, "Governance without Government."

98   Otto Holman, "Trans-National Governance without Supra-National Government: The Case of the European Employment Strategy," *Perspectives on European Politics & Society* 7, no. 1 (2006).

99   M. Considine, "The End of the Line? Accountable Governance in the Age of Networks, Partnerships, and Joined-up Services," *Governance* 15 (2002).

100   B. Kingsbury and R.B. Stewart, "Legitimacy and Accountability in Global Regulatory Governance: The Emerging Global Administrative Law and the Design and Operation of Administrative Tribunals of International Organizations," in *International Administrative Tribunals in a Changing World*, ed. S. Flogaitis (Esperia, Italy: 2008).

101   Ibid; L.M. Wallach, "Accountable Governance in the Era of Globalization: The WTO, Nafta, and International Harmonization of Standards.," *University of Kansas Law Review* 50 (2002).

102   Newell, *Globalization and the Environment: Capitalism, Ecology and Power.*

that global governance be characterized by democratic norms in its various manifestations (e.g., transparency, participation, reasoned decision-making, accountability, etc.). Although democratic norms have continued to expand, the pace is slow, the process is mostly internal, the manifestations are diverse, and the democratic deficits in governance remain large.[103] How the recent rise in nationalism in the United States and Europe during the latter part of 2016 will affect this trend is uncertain.

The Costs of Globalized Irresponsibility

The process of globalization has been described as an out-of-control juggernaut that is proceeding forward at a pace that eludes governance.[104] Some view this as a positive development. When analysts consider the evidence regarding globalization's impact with the commonly used KOF indices that measure economic, social and political dimensions, allowing globalization to proceed unfettered seems to be improving the overall socioeconomic conditions for the majority of people worldwide, despite widening socioeconomic gaps within countries.[105] But the KOF indices that are used to come to these conclusions do not take into account environmental conditions and changes. Empirical environmental conditions suggest that this is an oversight that matters. With the singular exception of ozone depletion, none of the key environmental indicators or trends show signs of significant improvement or reversal despite nearly four decades of intense institutional activity aimed at containing an array of environmental threats.[106] The scale of population growth and economic development continues to outpace environmental gains from new technologies and policies despite calls that were issued at the turn of the century to redirect globalization so that it resolves, rather than aggravates, the serious imbalances

---

103   Janet E. Lord, David Suozzi, and Allyn L. Taylor, "Lessons from the Experience of U.N. Convention on the Rights of Persons with Disabilities: Addressing the Democratic Deficit in Global Health Governance," *Journal of Law, Medicine & Ethics* 38, no. 3 (2010); John Glenn, "Global Governance and the Democratic Deficit: Stifling the Voice of the South," 2008; C.U. Schierup, A. Ålund, and B. Likić-Brborić, "Migration, Precarization and the Democratic Deficit in Global Governance," *International Migration* 53, no. 3 (2015).

104   Lane, *Globalization: The Juggernaut of the 21st Century*. R. Alan Hedley, *Running out of Control: Dilemmas of Globalization* (Bloomfield, CN: Kumarian Press, 2002); Uri Dadush and William Shaw, *Juggernaut: How Emerging Markets Are Reshaping Globalization* (Washington D.C.: Carnegie Endowment for International Peace).

105   Niklas Potrafke, "The Evidence on Globalisation," *World Economy* 38, no. 3 (2015).

106   Newell, *Globalization and the Environment: Capitalism, Ecology and Power*.

that divide the world.[107] Popular accounts in the anti-globalization move-ment construct an image of a world out of control where volatile capital and transnational corporations move rapidly so as to elude government control.[108] Regardless of whether globalization is, or is not, controllable, the pattern of societal-environmental relations associated with globalization represents a new form of "organized irresponsibility."[109]

Humans have been exposed to threats throughout human history, but globalization exposes people to an accumulated array of risks (e.g., envi-ronmental, terrorist, military, financial, biomedical, etc.) that are primarily human-induced.[110] Risk-as-anticipation embraces the future as an extended present that presupposes human decisions. In risk society, people come to question the confidence placed in large-scale planning, and social expecta-tions emerge for less speculative and more responsible and accountable policy making.[111] When pressured to be more accountable to the public, policymakers frequently justify the trade-offs using a probability calculus followed by the implementation of mitigation strategies. But the global market also creates manufactured uncertainties that are incalculable, uncontrollable and not pri-vately insurable.[112] Manufactured uncertainties are also dependent upon hu-man decisions, but they are created by society itself, immanent to society, and collectively imposed (e.g., climate change, fisheries collapse, acid rain, finan-cial collapse). Because manufactured uncertainties are not limited to one geo-graphical location and the consequences associated with some of the induced changes may already be a foregone conclusion (e.g., biodiversity loss, climate change), the foundations of modern society have become shaken putting the perceived legitimacy of the global order at-risk.[113]

Administrating globalization so that it unfolds relatively undirected but with a measure of decency and order has drawn sharp criticism from con-cerned INGOs, citizens and media who question the nature and direction of globalization itself. Since representatives from hegemonic nation-states con-sistently claim to uphold democratic norms, there is an expectation among people throughout the world that global governance also be characterized

---

107   UNEP, *Global Environmental Outlook 2000* (London, UK: Earthscan, 1999).

108   Neil Thomas, "Global Capitalism, the Anti-Globalization Movement and the Third World," *Capital & Class*, no. 92 (2007).

109   Ulrich Beck, "The Cosmopolitan Society and Its Enemies," *Theory, Culture & Society* 19, no. 1–2 (2002).

110   "World Risk Society and Manufactured Uncertainties," *Iris* 1, no. 2 (2009).

111   Ibid.

112   Ibid.

113   Beck, "World Risk Society and Manufactured Uncertainties."

by democratic norms. Although this global regime absorbs some democratic norms (i.e., transparency, participation, reasoned decision-making, accountability, etc.) and democratic norms continue to expand, because the pace is slow, the process is mostly internal, setbacks occur, and the accountability gaps in governance remain large, the future stability of the international system may be increasingly at-risk.

Civil society has emerged to address accountability gaps in global governance, but the ad hoc aspects of the anti-globalization movement, in particular, have also been somewhat destabilizing. The contestation of INGOs and activists in the anti-globalization movement represent the "voices of the weak and powerless" to exercise a form of accountability that is *claimed from below* rather than *conferred from above*.[114] Willetts refers to civil society NGO activism as the "conscience of the world" as they use "shaming" tactics to affect the reputation of organizations through media exposure and government lobbying. They command the allegiances of large constituencies to influence public opinion.[115] As civil society activism has increased over time (until recently), the security costs associated with hosting G8, G7 and G20 Summits has become substantial causing some constituencies to question whether the meetings are worth the expense.[116] In 2007, Germany spent so much on security that some journalists began to wonder if the protests themselves had become the whole point of the summit.[117] Canada spent the most on security concerns when they hosted both the G8 and the G20 meetings in 2010.[118] Despite the spending of an unprecedented sum for G8 and G20 Summit security, over-turned burning cars and citizen face-offs with police in riot gear still dominated Summit coverage on the Canadian nightly news during the meetings.[119] In the end, more than

---

114 Newell, *Globalization and the Environment: Capitalism, Ecology and Power.*

115 P. Willetts, *The Conscience of the World: The Influence of Non-Governmental Organizations in the UN System* (London, England: Hurst & Co., 1996).

116 John Kirton, Jenilee Guebert, and Shamir Tanna, "G8 and G20 Summit Costs," (2010), http://www.g8.utoronto.ca/evaluations/factsheet/factsheet_costs.pdf; Patrick McGuire, "Brisbane, Australia's 2014 G20 Security Costs Were $500M Less Than Toronto's," (2014), http://www.vice.com/en_ca/read/brisbane-australias-2014-g20-security-costs-were-six-times-lower-than-torontos-647; Henry McDonald, "Treasury to Foot Most of 50 Million Pound G8 Summit Security Bill," (2013), https://www.theguardian.com/world/2013/jun/03/treasury-g8-summit-security-bill.

117 Kirton, Guebert, and Tanna, "G8 and G20 Summit Costs."

118 Ibid.

119 Adrian Morrow, "Toronto Police Were Overwhelmed at G20, Review Reveals," *The Globe and Mail* (2011), http://www.theglobeandmail.com/news/toronto/toronto-police-were-overwhelmed-at-g20-review-reveals/article2073215/.

1000 people were arrested, 39 citizens and 97 police were injured, and millions of dollars in damage occurred from a break-away group from a peaceful labor march.[120]

The conditions associated with the stability of democratic governance have been a leading concern for political scientists. As long as citizens perceive the overall quality of the social order with its associated institutions and norms to be legitimate, people voluntarily comply with the political order even at great cost. However, should the social order's legitimacy become questioned, compliance ceases to be voluntary and political upheaval can put the entire governing system at-risk.[121] Should this happen, the social order would face a legitimation crisis. Understandably, scholars have begun to question the degree to which some of the more vulnerable countries in the global network may be already facing a legitimation crisis (e.g., Greece, Afghanistan).[122] But concerns are becoming more widespread than that. Some scholars have begun to question whether the European Union,[123] if not the entire nation-state system,[124] might be entering a crisis of legitimation. The Syrian refugee crisis is the largest wave of human migration in recent history and the impact on Western Europe continues to unfold. Immigration concerns significantly influenced the United Kingdom's 2016 BREXIT vote to leave the European Union, and the decision is significantly influencing international finance.[125] Marshall wonders whether we may have already entered into a legitimation crisis given the impact of environmental changes.[126]

For Anthony Giddens, current conditions are characterized by a 'paradox of democracy.' Conditions are requiring more democratic involvement even as conditions are also creating increasing disillusionment with modern

---

120   Ibid. David Rider and Susan Delacourt, "Pressure Builds on Ottawa for Compensation," *The Star* (2010), https://www.thestar.com/news/gta/2010/06/29/pressure_builds_on_ottawa_ for_compensation.html.

121   Habermas, *Legitimation Crisis.*

122   W.R. Polk, "Legitimation Crisis in Afghanistan," *Nation* 290, no. 15 (2010); Peter Bratsis, "Legitimation Crisis and the Greek Explosion," (2010).

123   Hauke Brunkhorst, "The Legitimation Crisis of the European Union," *Constellations: An International Journal of Critical and Democratic Theory* 13, no. 2 (2006).

124   R. Lhotta et al., "The Democratic Nation State: Erosion, or Transformation, of Legitimacy: Is There a Legitimation Crisis of the Nation-State?," *European Review* 13, no. 1 (2005).

125   Tim Adams, "Statement by IIF President and CEO Tim Adams on the U.K. Referendum," (2016), https://www.iif.com/press/statement-iif-president-and-ceo-tim-adams-uk -referendum.

126   Brent Marshall and Warren Goldstein, "Managing the Environmental Legitimation Crisis," *Organization & Environment* 19, no. 2 (2006).

democratic processes.[127] Giddens' answer to the situation is increased democratization of democracy through constitutional reforms, stronger civic culture, and greater political transparency.[128] Without greater democratic engagement by broader sectors of society, however, what we are left with is governance as technique. Governance as technique is incapable of offering a vision for human life. Langdon Winner reflects on the limitations of technique as a guiding principle. "As we 'make things work,'" he asks,

> What kind of world are we making? This suggests that we pay attention not only to the making of physical instruments and processes, although that certainly remains important, but also to the production of psychological, social, and political conditions as part of any significant technical change. Are we going to design and build circumstances that enlarge possibilities for growth in human freedom, sociability, intelligence, creativity, and self-government? Or are we headed in an altogether different direction?[129]

Robert Keohane reminds us that common values are lacking in what is a highly interdependent and violence-prone international system. Global society is inevitably partial rather than universal. "A universal global society remains a dream," says Keohane, "and one that may be receding from view rather than becoming closer."[130] The very conditions in which we find ourselves undermine traditional ethics.[131] But this may be a necessary part of the process. Traditional ethics have been dangerously human-centered to the neglect of the environment. To the extent that the human-centeredness of traditional ethics have helped to perpetuate unsustainable approaches to the environment, their transformation may be necessary to the development of a common future. And so, "now we shiver in the nakedness of a nihilism in which near-omnipotence is paired with ... knowing least for what ends to use it," says Hans Jonas.[132] It is not enough to deconstruct unsustainable ethics. The global

---

127   Giddens, *Runaway World: How Globalization is Reshaping Our Lives.*

128   Ibid.

129   Langdon Winner, *The Whale and the Reactor: A Search for Limits in an Age of High Technology* (Chicago, IL: The University of Chicago Press, 1986).

130   R.O. Keohane, "Global Governance and Democratic Accountability," in *Taming Globalization: Frontiers of Governance*, ed. D. Held and M. Koenig-Archibugi (Cambridge, UK: Polity Press, 2003).

131   Richard J. Bernstein, "Rethinking Responsibility," *Social Research* 61, no. 4 (1994).

132   Hans Jonas, *The Imperative of Responsibility: In Search of an Ethics for the Technological Age* (Chicago: University of Chicago Press, 1984).

environmental changes of this unique historic moment, asserts Jonas, requires us to also transform our ethics to replace the principle of hope with the principle of responsibility.[133] Ethics for a sustainable common future do not just appear *ex nihilo;* they must be socially constructed through humanitarian action as well as words.

Conclusion

This chapter has described historically distinctive changes in the material conditions that 'set the stage' for why stakeholders concerned with religion or belief and human rights have returned to politics. Primarily human-induced global environmental changes present governance challenges that require more than the deconstruction of human-centered ethics and the development of sustainable governance techniques. Administrating globalization leaves democratic deficits that have drawn sharp criticism from segments of society that could potentially put the legitimacy of the system at-risk. As we 'make things work,' are we adequately engaged with the kind of world we are making? Social change for a sustainable common future also involves the transformation of ethical social systems which do not appear *ex nihilo* but must be socially constructed through humanitarian action and insight. The global interfaith movement has a potentially valuable contribution to make to this historic moment of uncertainty and social change. The material changes discussed in this chapter reflect a co-evolution of societal and environmental relations that are theoretically relevant to a foundational reconsideration of the role stakeholders concerned with religion or belief and human rights might play in transnational relations. How the religious sector has interfaced with the political sector in the past is abruptly distinctive from how stakeholders concerned with religion or belief and human rights might potentially interface with political leaders in the future. The precipitating factor setting the stage for understanding the importance of the F8/F7/F20 Initiative has been the unintended consequences of globalization, population pressures, resource pressures and primarily human-induced global environmental changes. This chapter has detailed some of these changes and their impacts on global financial institutions engaged in global governance that create conditions requiring a new set of ethical behaviors if we are to build together a common future.

---

133   Ibid.

CHAPTER 4

The Return of Religion to Transnational Relations

This chapter describes the return of public religion and the influence of religious soft power on transnational relations. The secularization crisis is explored with attention to concerns regarding inappropriate religious influences on political deliberations. But can secularization be taken too far? The chapter concludes with a discussion of ways the secular is being reimagined. The term *cosmopiety* is introduced to refer to the governance role of religion in transnational relations where religious actors are participating in providing cosmopolitan solutions to global social problems. *Cosmopiety* goes beyond contributions that are coterminous with civil society in that many of the cultural resources are firmly rooted in networks within the differentiated institution of the religious sector.

Transnational Religious Resurgence

It is now widely recognized that religion has returned to transnational relations since the end of the Cold War and the advent of globalization.[1] To some extent, the religious resurgence is related to trends in human migration, urbanization

---

1   Thomas Banchoff, ed., *Religious Pluralism, Globalization, and World Politics* (New York, New York: Oxford University Press, 2008); Jonathan Fox and Shmuel Sandler, *Bringing Religion into International Relations*, 1st ed, Culture and Religion in International Relations (New York: Palgrave Macmillan, 2004); J. Fox, "Integrating Religion into International Relations Theory," in *Routledge Handbook of Religion and Politics*, ed. Jeffrey Haynes (New York, New York: Routledge, 2009); Jeffrey Haynes, "Religion and International Relations in the 21st Century: Conflict or Co-Operation?," *Third World Quarterly* 27, no. 3 (2006); J. Snyder, *Religion in International Relations Theory* (New York, New York: Columbia University Press, 2011); F. Petito and P. Hatzopoulos, *Religion in International Relations: The Return from Exile* (New York, New York: Palgrave MacMillan, 2003); Jeffrey Haynes, "Religion and Foreign Policy Making in the USA, India and Iran: Towards a Research Agenda," *Third World Quarterly* 29, no. 1 (2008); "Religion and Foreign Policy," in *Routledge Handbook of Religion and Politics*, ed. Jeffrey Haynes (New York, New York: Routledge, 2009); *Religion in Global Politics* (London, England: Longman, 1998); *Religion in Third World Politics* (Buckingham, England: Open University Press, 1993); "Transnational Religious Actors and International Order," *Perspectives: Central European Review of International Affairs* 17, no. 2 (2009); Haynes, "Transnational Religious Actors and International Politics."

and demographic shifts in population growth from the developed countries of the North to the developing countries of the so-called South.[2] In Europe, the Syrian refugee crisis represents the largest wave of human migration in recent history and its impact on Western Europe continues to unfold.[3] Germany has recently undergone enough of a Muslim demographic revolution that German society can no longer be presumed to be neutral toward immigrants, homogeneous and well integrated.[4] Immigration concerns significantly influenced the United Kingdom's June 23, 2015 BREXIT vote to leave the European Union, and this decision, in tandem with other populist movements, is expected to influence international finance.[5] Following the BREXIT vote in England and Wales, hate crimes and incidents in Britain rose 37% from the same timeframe the previous year with 3,219 incidents reported to police from June 16–30, 2016.[6] Jo Cox, the British MP who was killed on June 16th in 2016, was an avid supporter of religious diversity and a tireless campaigner for Syrian refugees.[7] After assessing the rise of nationalism in countries like Finland, France and Hungary, the European Central Bank issued a warning in their mid-year report about weak profitability expectations for the European Union and increasing uncertainty associated with the implementation of orthodox economic reforms.[8]

Globalization increases interconnectedness and interdependence not just between economies, states, and cultures, but also among and between religious communities.[9] Religious influences are not always supportive of globalization; anti-globalization local resistance is significant as local forces join with political leaders to adopt statutes and regulations that restrict foreign religious

2   Thomas, "A Globalized God: Religion's Growing Influence in International Politics."

3   Fabrice Balanche, "The Worst of the Syrian Refugee Crisis is Coming for Europe," *Business Insider* (2016).

4   Soeren Kern, "Germany's Muslim Demographic Revolution," (2015), http://www.gatestone institute.org/6423/germany-muslim-demographic.

5   Lalita Clozel, "U.S. Banking Regulators Concerned About BREXIT: Report," *American Banker* 181, no. 76 (2016); Peter Grier, "The Year of Disruption," *The Christian Science Monitor*, December 24, 2016.

6   Jon Kelly, "In Numbers: Has Britain Really Become More Racist?," *BBC News Magazine*, August 10, 2016.

7   Rosi Scammell, "Britain Sees an Increase in Anti-Muslim Attacks," *Religion News Service* (2016), http://national.deseretnews.com/article/20804/britain-sees-an-increase-in-anti-muslim -attacks.html.

8   Becky Bradford, "Is Populism a Threat to Europe's Economies?," *BBC News*, May 26, 2016.

9   Akira Iriye, *Global Interdependence: The World after 1945* (Cambridge, MA: Harvard University Press, 2014).

rivals that they see as undermining their culture.[10] Dubbed 'the year of disruption,' the latter part of 2016 saw a wave of protectionist nationalism spread throughout Western Europe and the United States.[11] The United States elected Donald Trump as the national chief executive; he ran on a platform advocating for religious freedom that won him the support of more than 80% of white evangelical voters, but the type of federal level religious exemption measures being considered has the ACLU concerned that discrimination against minorities will increase as a consequence.[12]

But a noteworthy qualitative shift is also occurring. For the first time in history, a multi-faith movement has emerged that has been growing exponentially and developing a new emerging democratic network that is attentive to a diverse array of social issues and global environmental problems.[13] In addition, the number and visibility of faith-based organizations (FBOS) that derive inspiration and guidance for their activities from the teachings and principles of particular religious traditions has dramatically increased in recent decades.[14] Several explanations are offered for the growth in FBOS such as a religious response to the historic challenges of traditional religious identities and the postmodern breaking apart of modern culture.[15] One of the unintended consequences of structural adjustment programs that required government devolution for many social supports has been an increase in funding of FBOS-as-NGOS

---

10   Katherine Marshall, *Global Institutions of Religion: Ancient Movers, Modern Shakers* (New York, New York: Routledge, 2013).

11   Grier, "The Year of Disruption."

12   Eugene Scott, "ACLU Expecting More Religious Freedom Bills in 2017 Than Ever," *CNNPolitics*, December 16 2016.

13   Christy Lohr, "Building the Interfaith Youth Movement: Beyond Dialogue to Action," *Reviews in Religion & Theology* 14, no. 4 (2007); Brodeur, "From the Margins to the Centers of Power: The Increasing Relevance of the Global Interfaith Movement."; Halafoff, "The Multifaith Movement."; Anna Halafoff, "Netpeace and the Cosmopolitan Condition: Multifaith Movements and the Politics of Understanding," *Political Theology* 11, no. 5 (2010); Nathan R. Kollar, "The Interfaith Movement in a Liminal Age: The Institutionalization of a Movement," *Journal of Ecumenical Studies* 51, no. 1 (2016); G. Yukich, "Encounters at the Religious Edge: Variation in Religious Expression across Interfaith Advocacy and Social Movement Settings," *Journal for the Scientific Study of Religion* 53, no. 4; Grace Yukich and Ruth Braunstein, "Encounters at the Religious Edge: Variation in Religious Expression across Interfaith Advocacy and Social Movement Settings," *Journal for the Scientific Study of Religion* 53, no. 4 (2014); Kusumita P. Pedersen, "The Interfaith Movement: An Incomplete Assessment," *Journal of Ecumenical Studies* 41, no. 1 (2004).

14   Clarke and Jennings, *Development, Civil Society, and Faith-Based Organizations.*

15   Kollar, "The Interfaith Movement in a Liminal Age: The Institutionalization of a Movement."

(RNGOs as NGOs) and the development of public-private partnerships.[16] Some of the largest development organizations are now faith-based (e.g., Tear Fund, Islamic Relief, Aga Khan Foundation, Christian Aid, Caritas, Catholic Relief Services).[17] But religious engagement is not confined to development; religion has become observable as active participants in social issues related to human rights, education, health, law, infrastructure, social services, defense, religious freedom, peacemaking, environmentalism, humanitarian aid, and gender.[18] As the international state system has given way to globalization, Casanova describes a process of "religious deprivatisation" where religion has once again become an influential player in the international arena.[19] For example, groups of congregations became publicly engaged to leverage congregational infrastructures for maximum impact on disease and poverty as the 2015 MDG deadline approached.[20]

Despite the significant increase in faith-based efforts to address social problems, most of the scholarly (and media) attention has been given to how religion has become highly visible in the troubling form of Islamic extremism, and the Islamophobic backlash, that is impacting the international order.[21] And for good reasons. This resurgence of religious influence was unexpected and disconcerting because the prevailing expectation was that the Western trend would be religious privatization due to secularization.[22] That said, by the turn of the century, some scholars had already begun to question the inevitability of the secularization process.[23]

Religion is only one of a diverse array of interest groups that have recently become influential in international relations.[24] RNGOs, along with other forms

---

16   G. Clarke, "Faith Matters," *Journal of International Development* 18, no. 6 (2006): 836; Marie Juul Petersen, "International Religious NGOs at the United Nations: A Study of a Group of Religious Organizations," *The Journal of Humanitarian Assistance* (2010).

17   Ben Jones and Marie Juul Petersen, "Instrumental, Narrow, Normative? Reviewing Recent Work on Religion and Development," *Third World Quarterly* 32, no. 7 (2011).

18   Petersen, "International Religious NGOs at the United Nations: A Study of a Group of Religious Organizations."

19   Casanova, *Public Religions in the Modern World.*

20   Andreas Hipple, "The Center for Interfaith Action and the MDGs: Leveraging Congregational Infrastructures for Maximum Impact on Disease and Poverty," *Cross Currents* 60, no. 3 (2010).

21   Haynes, "Religion and Foreign Policy."

22   Steve Bruce, *Secularization: In Defence of an Unfashionable Theory* (Oxford, UK: Oxford University Press, 2011); B. Wilson, *Religion in Secular Society* (London, UK: C.A. Watts, 1966).

23   Rodney Stark, "Secularization, R.I.P.," *Sociology of Religion* 60, no. 3 (1999).

24   Berry, "Religion and Sustainability in Global Civil Society."

of civil society actors, exercise what Lloyd Axworthy and J.S. Nye, Jr. have de-scribed as soft power in the transnational arena. As power has diffused away from the state, the "hard power" of coercion has given way to include the "soft power" influence of persuasion.[25] Foreign policy continues to use traditional forms of coercion, but the influence of diplomacy in relation to a diverse array of interest groups marks a noticeable change, particularly in the post September 11th period. According to Nye, soft power refers to the ability to get what you want through attraction, rather than coercion or payment, through the use of culture, values and foreign policies.[26] In contrast to the command pow-er that accompanies possession of resources and the ability to reach desired outcomes, soft power refers to the ability to shape what others want through attraction, co-optation, the framing of the agenda, persuasion, cultural attrac-tiveness and the mastery of institutions and information technologies to dis-seminate persuasive information.[27]

The division between hard and soft power is not always clear. Whereas US military forces can be clearly considered hard power, the Canadian military has a long tradition of being requested to use their military to intervene in humanitarian roles.[28] The effectiveness of soft power also remains unclear, because it sometimes reinforces, and sometimes interferes with, hard power as an independent social force. By and large, a soft power approach to inter-national relations has been identified as more compatible with the necessi-ties of responsible living in an interdependent world[29]—with the exception of religious soft power.[30]

The cultural dimension of soft power becomes particularly salient when it is applied to religion.[31] When globalization brings with it culture, what Nye re-ferred to as "attraction" in the West may be experienced as "the insidious threat of seduction" by Islamic cultures that reject Western lifestyle choices, clothing

25   Lloyd Axworthy, *Navigating a New World* (Toronto, Canada: Vintage Canada, 2003); Joseph S. Nye, *Soft Power: The Means to Success in World Politics* (New York, New York: Public Af-fairs, 2004).

26   Nye, *Soft Power: The Means to Success in World Politics.*

27   Brooke A. Smith-Windsor, "Hard Power, Soft Power Reconsidered," *Canadian Military Journal*, Autumn (2000).

28   Ibid.

29   Joseph M. Dondelinger, "Cultural Contradictions of Soft Power and Islam," *Journal of In-terdisciplinary Studies* 20 (2008).

30   Haynes, "Religion and International Relations in the 21st Century: Conflict or Co-Operation?"

31   "Religion and Foreign Policy."

preferences, and access to pornography.[32] Soft power attraction, according to Nye, is produced by the resource assets of cultural attractiveness, political values, and the moral authority of legitimate foreign policies.[33] Robert Seiple, the first US Ambassador-at-Large for International Religious Freedom, has referred to freedom of religion as America's single greatest soft power for its central influence on important strategic issues including conflict mitigation, post-conflict stabilization operations, immigration and integration, women's rights, and engagement of multilateral institutions and international law.[34]

But if values are viewed as hypocritical, soft power will detract rather than attract.[35] People of faith believe in something greater than the government. They have the capacity to organize, "and therefore the capacity to rebel against the state;" religious dynamics occur in a complex context shaped by global trends, regional geo-politics, national narratives, ethnic majority-minority relations, gender and family dynamics, and educational development policies.[36] Religion often pays limited respect to state boundaries, exercising transnational influence via diaspora networks, religious organizations and spiritual communities.[37]

In transnational relations, the reentry of religion into international relations initially reignited the "clash of civilizations" controversy between Islam and the West. At the time, religious jihadism versus conservative US evangelicalism under the Bush administration carried with it an underlying assumption that religious soft power's influence primarily resided in fueling the abuse of power in world politics or serving as a reminder that culture has international consequences.[38] As time has progressed, although this may significantly change under the influence of President Donald Trump's administration, it has become clearer that Islam and the West may be compatible in some dimensions (e.g., science, technology), but incompatible in others (e.g., culture of eroticism). For radical Islam, in particular, fanaticism becomes fueled by its

---

32   Dondelinger, "Cultural Contradictions of Soft Power and Islam."

33   Nye, *Soft Power: The Means to Success in World Politics.*

34   Liora Danan, "A Public Diplomacy Approach to International Religious Freedom," *The Review of Faith and International Affairs* 10, no. 3 (2012): 59.

35   Dondelinger, "Cultural Contradictions of Soft Power and Islam," 40.

36   Chris Seiple, "Building Religious Freedom: A Theory of Change," *The Review of Faith and International Affairs* 10, no. 3 (2012): 97.

37   Jeffrey Haynes, *Religious Transnational Actors and Soft Power* (Surrey, England: Ashgate Publishers, 2012); Robert Wuthnow and Stephen Offutt, "Transnational Religious Connections," *Sociology of Religion* 69, no. 2 (2008).

38   Dondelinger, "Cultural Contradictions of Soft Power and Islam."

encounter with Western cultural soft power.[39] In reaction, radical Islam creates an anti-Western soft power and uses technology to recruit new members. For this reason, religious soft power has been characterized as either *denying* or *reinforcing* the legitimacy of the world system by either *repudiating* or *affirming* the foundational norms, values and institutions on which it is based.[40]

Dualistic characterizations of religious soft power are inherently problematic. Scholarly discussion of religious soft power differs from the way in which the concept has been understood in relation to government diplomacy or NGOs. Soft power was initially understood as a contribution to governance where diplomatic negotiations were now influencing outcomes in addition to coercion.[41] In soft power diplomacy, attention gets paid to how the stability of democratic legitimacy allows for the "peaceful 'play' of power—the adherence by the 'outs' to decisions made by the 'ins' and the recognition by the 'ins' of the rights of the 'outs'."[42] Soft power uses knowledge to shape the debate through evolving norms. When it comes to religion, however, the characterizations become decidedly dualistic with inadequate attention paid to the diverse ways in which a wide array of possible outcomes are negotiated (or negotiable) through the influence of religious diplomacy.[43] Scholarship on the relationship between religion, nationalism and violence has been critiqued for subsuming religion into nationalism rather than treating the relationship between them as variable so that scholars can explore under what conditions religious-nationalist mobilization does, or does not, lead to violence.[44] In development circles, for example, religious voices have made contributions to public discourse, although less than one might expect, by bringing attention to corruption, accountability and responsibility in ways that are resulting in new forms of partnership, dialogue and alliances, but this activity has been given

39   Ibid.

40   Banchoff, ed., *Religious Pluralism, Globalization, and World Politics*; Richard Falk, *Religion and Humane Global Governance* (New York, New York: Palgrave, 2001); Petito and Hatzopoulos, *Religion in International Relations: The Return from Exile*; Haynes, "Religion and International Relations in the 21st Century: Conflict or Co-Operation?"

41   Nye, *Soft Power: The Means to Success in World Politics*; Axworthy, *Navigating a New World*.

42   S.M. Lipset, "Some Social Requisites of Democracy: Economic Development and Political Legitimacy," *Political Science Review* 53 (1959): 71.

43   Robert Hefner, *Civil Islam: Muslims and Democratization in Indonesia* (Princeton, NJ: Princeton University Press, 2000); Berna Turam, "The Politics of Engagement between Islam and the Secular State: Ambivalences of 'Civil Society,'" *British Journal of Sociology* 55, no. 2 (2004).

44   Philip S. Gorski and Gülay Türkmen-Dervişoğlu, "Religion, Nationalism, and Violence: An Integrated Approach," *Annual Reviews* 39 (2013).

little scholarly (or media) attention.[45] Consider the following three concrete examples:

- *World Faiths Development Dialogue:* In 1998, the President of the World Bank, James Wolfensohn, and the Archbishop of Canterbury, Lord George Carey, formed WFDD as a not-for-profit organization focused on the intersection of religion and global development to build cultural bridges between major world religions and secular international development organizations. Based in Washington, DC, WFDD has formal relationships with Georgetown University's Berkley Center for Peace, Religion, and World Affairs and the World Bank. WFDD supports dialogue and conferences, collects case studies on faith-based organizations, fosters communities of practice, and promotes mutual understanding on religion and development with specific insights into poverty and equity challenges. A series of reports, case studies, policy briefs, event summaries, and scholarly books are hosted by Georgetown University's Berkley Center for Peace, Religion, and World Affairs.[46]
- *The International Partnership on Religion and Sustainable Development/ PaRD*: The Federal Ministry for Economic Cooperation and Development hosted an international conference February 17–18, 2016 in Berlin called "Partners for Change: Religions and the 2030 Agenda for Sustainable Development." PaRD was subsequently formed as a partnership between development organizations and registered non-profit religious organizations or initiatives whose mission and activities in the field of development and/or humanitarian assistance are explicitly inspired by religion and a peaceful and impartial approach. Participants dialogue to improve their own work through mutual exchange and cooperation in knowledge sharing and learning exchange, networking, capacity-building, policy advice, monitoring, reviewing and joint learning. Membership is open to bilateral donors and multilateral development agencies as well as intergovernmental

---

45   Marshall, "Ancient and Contemporary Wisdom and Practice on Governance as Religious Leaders Engage in International Development." Although technological approaches to corruption reduction are relatively effective in Asian countries where Confucianism is being affected by Western culture and interfaith dialogue for norm evolution takes longer, E-governance is less effective in Arab and Muslim countries where the religious factor is more prominent. See Chon-Kyun Kim, "Anti-Corruption Initiatives and E-Government: A Cross-National Study," *Public Organization Review* 14, no. 3 (2014).

46   For more information, see https://berkleycenter.georgetown.edu/wfdd/publications.

programs active in the field of religion and development or humanitarian assistance.[47]

- *T20 Inclusion of Religious Policy Briefs to G20 Germany 2017*: Representatives from the Think20 (T20) reached out to some religious leaders including three who were heavily involved in executing the 2017 F20 Summit—Cole Durham, Ulrich Nitschke, and Katherine Marshall. They contributed to two briefs on famine[48] and refugee resettlement.[49] Out of the 74 policy briefs produced at the Berlin T20 Summit,[50] theirs were the only briefs that incorporated religious perspectives. Both policy briefs were included in the final document that was sent to the G20 Sherpas.[51]

The governance role of religion in world affairs challenges dualistic characterizations of religion, and is a role that has been neglected and under-researched.[52] Scholars have recently begun to critically revisit the relationship between religion, democracy, and political discourse to 'remedy the problematic neglect of religion in extant scholarship.'[53]

---

47 Ulrich Nitschke and Bennet Gabriel, "The International Partnership on Religion and Sustainable Development/PaRD: A Global and Inclusive Partnership to Harness the Positive Impact of Religion in Development and Humanitarian Assistance," *Ecumenical Review* 68, no. 4 (2016).

48 Mohammed Abu-Nimer et al., "Engaging Religious Actors in Addressing the Famine Emergency in South Sudan, Nigeria, Somalia, and Yemen," *T20 Policy Vision* (2017), http://www.g20-insights.org/policy_briefs/engaging-religious-actors-addressing-famine-emergency-south-sudan-nigeria-somalia-yemen/.

49 Robert Vitillo et al., "G20 Policy Makers Should Support Wider Religious Roles in Refugee Resettlement," *T20 Policy Brief* (2017), http://www.g20-insights.org/policy_briefs/g20-policy-makers-support-wider-religious-roles-refugee-resettlement/.

50 There were 15 briefs on Digitalization, 8 on Climate Policy and Finance, 13 on The 2030 Agenda, 8 on Global Inequality and Social Cohesion, 6 on Forced Migration, 5 on Financial Resilience, 5 on Trade and Investment, 5 on Toward Ending Hunger and Sustainable Agriculture, 3 on International Cooperation in Tax Matters, 1 on Resilience and Inclusive Growth, 3 on Circular Economy, and 2 on G20 and Africa. See http://www.g20-insights.org/policy_briefs/.

51 Dirk Messner and Dennis Snower, "20 Solution Proposals for the G20 from the T20 Engagement Group," (Bonn, Germany 2017).

52 Halafoff, "The Multifaith Movement."; Douglas Johnston, ed. *Faith-Based Diplomacy: Trumping Real Politik* (New York, NY: Oxford University Press, 2003); Douglas Johnston and Cynthia Sampson, eds., *Religion, the Missing Dimension of Statecraft* (New York, New York: Oxford University Press, 1994).

53 Timothy Samuel Shah, Monica Duffy Toft, and Alfred Stepan, *Rethinking Religion and World Affairs* (Oxford: Oxford University Press, 2011).

The Crisis of Secularization

The mere suggestion that religion is becoming more, rather than less, publicly influential conjures up images of partisan religious influence on political decision-making and public policy development. Although scholars are
increasingly acknowledging that public religion is 'here to stay,' the democratic
principle of the institutional separation of church and state found in several
countries has tended to delimit religious public engagement so as to discour-
age the governmental establishment of religion and to ensure religious liberty.[54] The conventional liberal understanding is that religious discourse, by
itself, is inappropriate in the public sphere because it employs restrictive comprehensive doctrines that are not equally accessible to all citizens.[55] Scholars
such as John Rawls have emphasized that *legitimate* political regimes demand
the use of public reason as a source of justification open to all.[56] According to
conventional liberal logic, the use of religious reasons for political decision-
making *undermines* political legitimacy by replacing the use of public reason
with reasons based on restrictive comprehensive doctrines of truth that are
not reasonably accessible to all citizens. According to John Rawls, the "zeal to
embody the whole truth in politics is incompatible with an idea of public reasons that belongs with democratic citizenship."[57] According to Rawls, it is the
'duty of civility' for citizens of faith to engage in the public forum 'as if they
were legislators' by presenting 'proper political reasons'—and not reasons giv-
en solely by comprehensive doctrines in the wider public political domain.[58]
According to the liberal model, it is the responsibility of citizens with a social
conscience to translate their concerns into secular language if they seek to influence public policy.

   Jürgen Habermas is also attentive to how religious actors engage in public
dialogue although he approaches the issue differently. Habermas agrees that
fundamentalist communicative action, for example, works *against* the democratic process, contributing to political polarization around a master cleavage

---

54   C.J. Eberle, *Religious Conviction in Liberal Politics* (Cambridge, MA: Cambridge Universi-
      ty Press, 2002); Rajeev Bhargava, *Secularism and Its Critics* (Oxford, England: Oxford Univer-
      sity Press, 2005); O.P. Shabani, "The Role of Religion in Democratic Politics: Tolerance and
      the Boundary of Public Reason," *Religious Education* 106 (2011).

55   Christopher Nadon, *Absolutism and the Separation of Church and State in Locke's Letter
      Concerning Toleration* (Cambridge, MA: Gale, 2007).

56   John Rawls, "The Idea of the Public Reasons Revisited," *University Chicago Law Review* 64
      (1997).

57   Ibid.

58   Ibid, p. 769, 784.

of some kind.[59] But for Habermas, the key indicator for religion as governance is *reflexivity*. Legitimate and constructive faith-based dialogue in the public sphere, he says, must have "the epistemic ability to consider one's own faith reflexively from the outside and relate it to secular views."[60] But reflexivity is a socio-historical process and not meant to be reduced to a cognitive, individual-istic process that leaves out social influences and treats the social construction of identities as subjective individual processes.[61] Individualistic approaches uncritically assume a teleology of self-mastery and misleadingly imply person-al sovereignty and political emancipation in a way that "celebrates a form of middle-class individualism" masking how underlying assumptions derive from structural privilege.[62]

According to Ulrich Beck and Anthony Giddens, reflexivity is a structurally embedded process that varies and is influenced by organizational dynamics, and the power hierarchies within them. Micro identities are shaped within the structural constraints of differing social contexts.[63] Reflexivity emerges out of social contexts where exclusivist national or religious identities give way to transnational recognitions that nation-states and/or religious communities are interdependent and entangled with one another.[64] Inner globalization

---

59   Habermas, "Religion in the Public Sphere," 8.

60   Ibid, 9–10.

61   Ulrich Beck, "Reply and Critiques," in *Reflexive Modernization: Politics, Tradition and Aes-thetics in the Modern Social Order*, ed. Ulrich Beck, Anthony Giddens, and S. Lash (Stan-ford, CA: Stanford University Press, 1994), 177; Ulrich Beck, W. Bonss, and C. Lau, "The Theory of Reflexive Modernization: Problematic, Hypotheses and Research Programme," *Theory, Culture & Society* 20, no. 2 (2003): 3; D. Farrugia, "Addressing the Problem of Reflex-ivity in Theories of Reflexive Modernisation: Subjectivity and Structural Contradiction," *Journal of Sociology* 51, no. 4 (2015); K.S. Chang and M.Y. Song, "The Stranded Individual-izer under Compressed Modernity: South Korean Women in Individualization without Individualism," *British Journal of Sociology* 61, no. 3 (2010); K.J. Arrow, "Methodological Individualism and Social Knowledge," *American Economic Review* 84 (1994); C. Cramer, "Homo Economicus Goes to War: Methodological Individualism, Rational Choice and the Political Economy of War," *World Development* 30 (2002).

62   Farrugia, "Addressing the Problem of Reflexivity in Theories of Reflexive Modernisation: Subjectivity and Structural Contradiction," 2; P. Sweetman, "Twenty-First-Century Dis-Ease? Habitual Reflexivity or the Reflexive Habitus," *Sociological Review* 51, no. 4 (2003); S. Threadgold and P. Nilan, "Reflexivity of Contemporary Youth, Risk, and Cultural Capi-tal," *Current Sociology* 57, no. 1 (2009).

63   Ulrich Beck and Edgar Grande, "Varieties of Second Modernity: The Cosmopolitan Turn in Social and Political Theory and Research," *British Journal of Sociology* 61, no. 3 (2010): 258.

64   S. Randeria, "Beyond Sociology and Sociocultural Anthropology," *Soziale Welt* 50 (1999).

results from the lived experience of 'glocal' boundary crossing as involved actors socially construct collective identities as historically imagined communities regarding what is practicably possible within the constraints of structurally embedded decision-making.[65] Technological innovation and globalization are 'flattening' global culture such that previously marginalized groups are increasingly able to influence the social construction of identities. Rayner and McNutt describe how networks operate around, and within, institutional structures via processes that must maintain credibility as they negotiate their own legitimacy at "reflexivity interfaces."[66] According to Feindt, whether and how the plurality of diverse perspectives are taken into account and become effective "are at the heart of the quest for reflexive governance."[67]

From this perspective, the rise of religious engagement as a new sort of identity politics poses a challenge.[68] Religious language is difficult to reconcile with the logic of economic progress, individualism and bureaucratic rationalisation.[69] People of faith, says Tony Blair, need to know that "their faith and their reason are aligned;" if democracy is going to take root in the world, people of faith become important partners in the political process for developing an open attitude of mind that is committed to defending the equal right for others to practice what they believe in.[70] Until recently, Western European faith-based organizations have downplayed their identities despite being at the forefront of service delivery and social movements in development in order to distance themselves from the worst excesses of their faith, access secular funding, partner with other groups, and keep a diverse staff team together. This may

---

65   Ulrich Beck and Elisabeth Beck-Gernsheim, *Individualization: Institutionalized Individualism and its Social and Political Consequences* (London, England, 2002), 37.

66   J. Rayner and K. McNutt, "Valuing Metaphor: A Constructivist Account of Reflexive Governance in Policy Networks," in *5th Annual Conference on Interpretive Policy Analysis* (Grenoble, France 2010).

67   P.H. Feindt, "Reflexive Governance and Multilevel Decision Making in Agricultural Policy: Conceptual Reflections and Empirical Evidence," in *Reflexive Governance for Global Public Goods*, ed. E. Bronsseau, T. Dedeurwaerdere, and B. Siebenhuener (Cambridge, MA: The MIT Press, 2012).

68   M. Castells, *The Power of Identity* (Cambridge, MA: Blackwell, 1997); Casanova, *Public Religions in the Modern World.*

69   Jones and Petersen, "Instrumental, Narrow, Normative? Reviewing Recent Work on Religion and Development."

70   Blair, "Protecting Religious Freedom Should Be a Priority for All Democracies," 8.

be changing as the shift away from classical political economy frameworks allows space for religion within more heterodox approaches.[71]

The creation of any 'religious space' for public religion is problematic according to strict separationists, while for many religious groups, the public space is still too narrow. According to Ulrich Beck, public religion today develops primarily in interaction and negotiation with the "world religions,"[72] such that the only 'legitimate' public expression of religion is in the form of an individualized religiosity that is itself an expression of secularized culture.[73] When Annette Wilke tested Beck's theory, she critiqued Beck's binary model of juxtaposing reflexive cosmopolitanism against fundamentalism as an overly simplistic model that does not fit the data and has "little impact on the heated debates about religion in public discourse."[74] Her findings point to the importance of recognizing cultural differences within nations and religions with specific attention to minority Muslim populations. She concluded that

> [b]oth secularization and individualization theories, as well as the recent theories of desecularization or the demise of the secularization thesis for Western Europe need cautious critical revision. The subject of critique includes a latent eurocentrism and the crucial fact that it is not only a question of empirical data whether religion, secularity, or "de-secularization" is perceived, but also one of the concept of religion and scholars' predispositions.[75]

Because the German paradigm was designed to explain a specific religious, historical and socio-cultural context, Wilke concluded that theories such as Beck's are not easily transportable to other regions and religions, and that "much knowledge and cultural sensitivity is needed to evaluate data where other cultures are concerned."[76]

Attention needs to be paid to the social dynamics associated with religious organizations at the meso-level of analysis, something Ulrich Beck did not do.

---

71   EA Brett, *Reconstructing Development Theory: International Inequality, Institutional Reform and Social Emancipation* (Basingstoke: Palgrave MacMillan, 2009).

72   Ulrich Beck, "A God of One's Own," in *Religion's Capacity for Peace and Potential for Violence* (Thousand Oaks, CA: Sage, 2010), 273.

73   Annette Wilke, "Individualisation of Religion," *International Social Science Journal* 64, no. 213–214 (2013).

74   Ibid., 271, 74.

75   Ibid., 275.

76   Ibid., 276.

Beck rooted risk society theory in two, and only two, levels of analysis: from that of the whole and from the standpoint of individuals.[77] When Beck theorized about religion, he theorized about the macro-micro relationship of declining religious monopolies and increasing individualized religiosity with inattention to meso-level religious organizational dynamics.[78] Although Beck recognized immigration as an influential factor affecting risk society,[79] his meso-level 'blind spot' is consistent with a similar black box in immigration research, more generally, which has been critiqued for assuming that the host society is itself neutral, homogeneous and well integrated.[80] This is often not the case, however. Immigration analyst Thomas Faist contends that attention to the meso-level is crucial to immigration research.[81]

Times have changed since Beck originally formulated his sociology of religion. The Syrian refugee crisis is the largest wave of human migration in recent history and the impact on Western Europe continues to unfold.[82] Germany has recently undergone enough of a Muslim demographic revolution that German society can no longer be presumed to be neutral toward immigrants, homogeneous and well integrated.[83] Beck's model that individuals are autonomous subjects ignores gender and class differences, is inattentive to discrimination against religious minorities, and ignores the social realm more generally.[84] Jamrozik and Nocella critique the individualization of social problems for protecting, rather than reforming, existing exploitative capitalist structures.[85]

77   Beck and Beck-Gernsheim, *Individualization: Institutionalized Individualism and Its Social and Political Consequences*, 4.

78   Beck, "A God of One's Own."

79   Ulrich Beck, "Critical Theory of World Risk Society: A Cosmopolitan Vision," *Constellations* 16, no. 1 (2009).

80   Christian Joppke and Eve Morawska, *Toward Assimilation and Citizenship: Immigrants in Liberal Nation States* (Palgrave MacMillan: New York, NY, 2003).

81   Thomas Faist, "The Crucial Meso-Level," in *Selected Studies in International Migration and Immigrant Incorporation*, ed. Marco Martinello and Jan Rath (Amsterdam: Amsterdam University Press, 2009).

82   Balanche, "The Worst of the Syrian Refugee Crisis Is Coming for Europe."

83   Kern, "Germany's Muslim Demographic Revolution."

84   P. Taylor-Gooby, *Reframing Social Citizenship* (Oxford, England: Oxford University Press, 2009); C. Mackenzie, "Autonomy: Individualistic or Social Rational?," in *Risk, Welfare and Work*, ed. G. Marston, J. Moss, and J. Quiggin (Melbourne, Australia: Melbourne University Press, 2010); Jens O. Zinn, "Risk, Social Inclusion and the Life Course—Review of Developments in Policy and Research," *Social Policy & Society* 12, no. 2 (2013).

85   A. Jamrozik, *Social Policy in the Post-Welfare State: Australian Society in the 21st Century* (Frenchs Forest, NSW: Longman, 2005).

Although the 'institutional individualism' in Beck's work is now being debated in youth research,[86] the impact on his sociology of religion has not yet been fully explored. One need not adopt a rational choice market theory approach to the sociology of religion to pay attention to the meso-level. Beck's theoretical black box neglects important social integration issues associated with diverse populations as well as ignores the private sector's role in responding to the new social realities as "governance from below."[87] By paying attention to the meso-level of religious, human rights, and development organizations, we can refine our understanding of different forms of agency exercised on behalf of collectives, as well as individuals, and we can improve our understanding of how religion or belief operates in contemporary risk society.

Our understanding does need to be improved. Take the case of the increasing number of Muslim religious organizations involved in development. Muslim organizations are less dependent on public funds, are more explicit about their faith identity, and are more homogeneously staffed with younger personnel than organizations in the Judeo-Christian tradition.[88] Muslim organizations cultivate stronger and more youthful religious identities that press against the restrictive social space allotted in the public square for religion. Several well-meaning moderate Islamic organizations have gotten caught up in the global war on terror regime.[89] For example, in the immediate years following September 11th in the United States, more than a dozen Islamic organizations were closed after being either accused of financing or supporting terrorist networks even though only one accusation resulted in an actual conviction. In some contexts, the US government has closely scrutinized charities without any findings of wrongdoing, causing

---

86   D. Woodman, "Class, Individualization and Tracing Processes of Inequality in a Changing World: A Reply to Steven Roberts," *Journal of Youth Studies* 13, no. 6 (2010); "The Mysterious Case of the Pervasive Choice Biography: Ulrich Beck, Structure/Agency and the Middling State of Theory in the Sociology of Youth.," *Journal of Youth Studies* 12, no. 3 (2009); Zinn, "Risk, Social Inclusion and the Life Course—Review of Developments in Policy and Research."; S. Roberts, "Misrepresenting Choice Biographies? A Reply to Woodman," *Journal of Youth Studies* 13, no. 1 (2010).

87   Jean Grugel and Nicola Piper, *Critical Perspectives on Global Governance: Rights and Regulations in Governing Regimes* (New York, New York: Routledge, 2007).

88   Rick James, What Is Distinctive About FBOS? How European FBOS Define and Operationalise Their Faith, (INTRAC, 2009). 3.

89   Jones and Petersen, "Instrumental, Narrow, Normative? Reviewing Recent Work on Religion and Development," 1293.

serious harm to the charity's reputation and opening the door to public backlash.[90]

Lorenzo Zucca argues that the crisis in the secular state associated with Europe's failure to manage religious diversity has itself contributed to the emergence of less-than-reasonable forms of religious fundamentalism.[91] For Zucca, the emergence of fundamentalisms, both religious and secular, is not the disease. Rather, fundamentalisms are the reflection of failed secular politics.[92] As attitudes toward public religion shift, however, Western donors are beginning to intensify their co-operation with 'moderate' Islamic NGOs as "potential bridge-builders in their attempts to reach out to the Muslim world;" in the 1960s and 1970s, Western donors similarly invested in Judeo-Christian development agencies as bridge-builders in the fight against Communism during the Cold War.[93] Whether this trend will continue given the recent rise in nationalistic fervor is unclear.

Michael Walzer has made a similar argument in a recent study of three states created after World War II: India, Israel, and Algeria. Each state was birthed by a secular political liberation movement and then challenged approximately 25 years later by a militant fundamentalist religious movement that has remained in power. His recommendation is for the left to undertake a project of critical engagement with cultural and religious traditions to help prevent the type of toxic polarizations that breed extremism. By recognizing the power that faith exercises in people's everyday lives and working with, and through, them, Walzer suggests that more inclusive and progressive societies can be developed.[94]

In the meantime, secularization appears to be in crisis.[95] Scholars have begun to question the neat divide between politics and religion that makes any

---

90   K. Guinane, "Muslim Charities and the War on Terror," (2006), http://foreffectivegov.org/files/pdfs/muslim_charities.pdf; J.B. Alterman and K. Von Hippel, eds., *Understanding Islamic Charities* (Washington, DC: Center for Strategic and International Studies, 2007).

91   Lorenzo Zucca, "A Secular Europe: Law and Religion in the European Constitutional Landscape," (Oxford, UK: Oxford University Press, 2012).

92   Ibid.

93   Jones and Petersen, "Instrumental, Narrow, Normative? Reviewing Recent Work on Religion and Development," 1293.

94   Michael Walzer, *The Paradox of Liberation: Secular Revolutions and Religious Counterrevolutions* (New Haven, CN: Yale University Press, 2015).

95   Calo, "Higher Law Secularism: Religious Symbols, Contested Secularisms, and the Limits of the Establishment Clause."; "Law in the Secular Age."; Ledewitz, *Church, State, and the Crisis in American Secularism*; Elizabeth S. Hurd, *The Politics of Secularism in International Relations*, ed. Thomas Christiensen, G. John Ikenberry, and Marc Trachtenberg, Princeton

form of interaction between the two illegitimate or dangerous.[96] The secular/religious binary is critiqued as a dualistic factor influencing jurisprudence and fueling culture wars by creating sharp and irresolute cleavages.[97] Neither secularism nor religion are monolithic structures. Charles Taylor has identified a diverse array of secularisms that have historically emerged in different social contexts,[98] and religious landscapes are ever changing and always difficult to define.[99] For some, secularism refers to the development of spheres of society that exist apart from religion, possessing jurisdictional autonomy from religious organizational control but not having any ground of its own; rather than being oppositional to religion, the secular finds its meaning in relation to a plural array of religious traditions.[100] For others, secularism refers to the intellectual rebellion against Western political theology in association with the historical development of the modern state following the Wars of Religion; secularism as revolt against religious traditions explicitly minimizes any public and political religious influences.[101] To the extent that this latter version "strains the metaphysics out of politics,"[102] law comes to "possess its own logic unrelated to any supervening moral system, while religion is relegated to the private sphere."[103] As immigration increases cultural heterogeneity and

Studies in International History and Politics (Princeton, New Jersey: Princeton University Press, 2007).

96   Charles Taylor, *A Secular Age* (Cambridge, MA: Harvard University Press, 2007); Snyder, *Religion in International Relations Theory*; Judith Butler et al., *The Power of Religion in the Public Sphere* (New York, NY: Columbia University Press, 2011); Thomas Banchoff and Robert Wuthnow, eds., *Religion and the Global Politics of Human Rights* (New York, New York: Oxford University Press, 2011). Jocelyne Cesari, "Religion and Politics: What Does God Have to Do with It?," *Religions* 6, no. 4 (2015); Karen Murphy, *State Security Regimes and the Right to Freedom of Religion and Belief: Changes in Europe Since 2001* (Hoboken: Taylor and Francis, 2013); Ledewitz, *Church, State, and the Crisis in American Secularism.*

97   Zucca, "A Secular Europe: Law and Religion in the European Constitutional Landscape."; Calo, "Higher Law Secularism: Religious Symbols, Contested Secularisms, and the Limits of the Establishment Clause."

98   Charles Taylor, "Modes of Secularism," in *Secularism and Its Critics*, ed. Rajeev Bhargava (Oxford, England: Oxford University Press, 2005); Taylor, *A Secular Age.*

99   McGuire, *Religion: The Social Context.*

100   Graeme Smith, *A Short History of Secularism* (London, UK: I.B. Tauris, 2007).

101   Iain T. Benson, "That False Struggle between Believers and Non-Believers," *Oasis* 12, Dec. (2010).

102   William E. Connolly, *Why I Am Not a Secularist* (Minneapolis, MN: University of Minnesota Press, 2007).

103   Calo, "Higher Law Secularism: Religious Symbols, Contested Secularisms, and the Limits of the Establishment Clause," 3.

shared cultural self-understandings continue to deteriorate, the issue becomes whether there exists some necessary point of contact between liberal separationism and religions for the ongoing social construction of cultural character as societies change.[104]

Can Secularization be Taken Too Far?

Scholars since Max Weber have recognized that too much privatization of religion through the process of rationalization may eventually become problematic. When rationalization is taken too far, a dual crisis of management and meaning emerges: (1) the public crisis occurs when there is inadequate political will and ethical direction to publicly manage pressing social problems, even as (2) a private crisis occurs as people of faith seek to provide ethical direction about the pressing social problems but they are relegated to the private sector.[105] Max Weber considered the dual crisis of management and meaning a threat to the future of Western civilization. He was concerned that overly rationalized broad social contexts would result in bureaucratic governments incapable of generating the necessary political will to resolve social problems.[106] Too much rationalization would create a public management crisis as 'vacated answers' become replaced by "questions that continue to be asked" in relation to pressing social problems.[107] Given mounting evidence of accumulating environmental degradation and global environmental changes, such public management crises can be expected to substantially increase, raising numerous questions in relation to emergency response systems, the relationship between law and morality in exigent circumstances, and norm evolution for adaptive social reorganization.[108]

---

104   Ibid.

105   Max Weber, *Economy and Society*, vol. 1 (Los Angeles, CA: Regents of the University of California, 1978), 223.; Guenther Roth and Wolfgang Schluchter, *Max Weber's Vision of History* (Berkeley, CA: University of California Press, 1979), 40, 43, 53.

106   Roth and Schluchter, *Max Weber's Vision of History*.

107   The impact of rationalization is distinguishable from the disenchanting effects that accompany transformation of an authentic religious tradition into its self-alienated form. See H. Blumenberg, *Saekularisierung und Selbstbehauptung.* (Frankfurt, Germany: Suhrkamp, 1974).

108   Steiner-Aeschliman, "Transitional Adaptation: A Neoweberian Theory of Ecologically-Based Social Change."; Demetris Tillyris, "'Learning How Not to Be Good': Machiavelli and the Standard Dirty Hands Thesis,"*Ethical Theory & Moral Practice* 18, no. 1 (2015).

The liberal understanding of a strict separation has been critiqued as more restrictive than what the principle of separation of church and state demands.[109] Even John Locke can be interpreted as advocating a minimalist, not an absolutist, approach to separation.[110] While citizens should provide *public justification* for their claims, argues Christopher Eberle, they should not be required to *exercise restraint* in offering faith-based reasoning.[111] Nicholas Wolterstorff contends that the liberal understanding unfairly impairs the "ethics of democratic citizenship" by essentially excluding religious reasoning from the public sphere—a principle that a growing number of scholars consider to be incompatible with the freedom of religion.[112] As Shabani explains,

> Many religious citizens cannot separate or recast their religious convictions from their political ideals as easily as the 'principle of secular justification' demands. This would mean that citizens of faith cannot be expected to justify their political claims independently of their religious convictions.[113]

Wolterstorff suggests *impartiality*, rather than separation, as sufficient to meet the neutrality requirement for political engagement, thereby permitting a more inclusive and diverse setting for reasoned argument. There would continue to be restrictions pertinent to the ethics of citizenship, but such restrictions would relate to the specific positions taken and the manners with which one conducts oneself.

In some contexts, religion can make distinctive contributions that strengthen political legitimacy in the public square. In his more recent work, Jürgen Habermas describes how religion communicates *meaning* in ways philosophy and science cannot. To repress it, or attempt to replace it, would do more

109 J. Waldron, "Religious Contribution and Public Deliberation," *San Diego Law Review* 30 (1993).

110 Nadon, *Absolutism and the Separation of Church and State in Locke's Letter Concerning Toleration.*

111 Eberle, *Religious Conviction in Liberal Politics*, p. 10.

112 R. Audi and N. Wolterstorff, *Religion in the Public Square: The Place of Religious Convictions in Political Debate* (Lanham, MD: Rowman & Littlefield, 1997); Veit Bader, "Religious Pluralism: Secularism or Priority for Democracy?," *Political Theory* 27 (1999); K. Greenawalt, *Private Consciences and Public Reasons* (New York, New York: Oxford University Press, 1995); B.C. Parekh, *Rethinking Multiculturalism: Cultural Diversity and Political Theory* (Cambridge, MA: Harvard University Press, 2000).

113 Shabani, "The Role of Religion in Democratic Politics: Tolerance and the Boundary of Public Reason," p. 336.

than unfairly exclude religion; it would deprive "secular society from important resources of meaning."[114] Habermas seeks to validate a particular type of
religious reasoning in the public sphere—one that is reflexive as well as communicative. While Habermas would agree with the liberal position that fundamentalist expressions of religious reasoning undermine political legitimacy,
he believes that the liberal requirement that citizens translate their faith-based
reasoning into public/secular reasons puts an 'undue cognitive burden' that
de facto restricts and separates religious reasoning—including the beneficial
type—from the public sphere.[115] In place of this barrier, Habermas propos-
es an "institutional translation proviso" that would allow a particular type of
faith-based reasoning into the public sphere—one that has "the epistemic
ability to consider one's own faith reflexively from the outside and to relate it
to secular views."[116] According to Shabani,

> The difference between Habermas and Rawls is *when* proper political
> reasons (public reason) should be demanded from citizens and officials.
> For Rawls it is earlier in the public sphere and for Habermas it is later at
> the formal institutional level.[117]

Habermas' defense of the legitimacy of faith-based public debate replaces the
one-way liberal model dialogue with an informal and deinstitutionalized two-
way public conversation between sacred and secular. "Habermas wants to alter
the asymmetrical burden of reason-giving", says Shabani, where the secular
citizen shares in the responsibility to "recognize the continued existence of
religious communities in diverse liberal democracies", and hence to also recognize "the conflict between secular and sacred as among 'reasonably expected
disagreement.'"[118]

Religious pluralism is a policy approach that can be traced as far back as
539 B.C. As recorded by the Cyrus Cylinder, the Persian king Cyrus the Great
restored religious traditions after taking control of Babylon. The Persian king
permitted those who had been deported to return to their settlements in and
around Babylonia.

---

114   Jürgen Habermas, *Future of Human Nature* (London, UK: Polity Press, 2003), p. 109.
115   Habermas, "Religion in the Public Sphere," p. 8.
116   Ibid, p. 9–10.
117   Shabani, "The Role of Religion in Democratic Politics: Tolerance and the Boundary of
       Public Reason," p. 337.
118   Habermas, "Religion in the Public Sphere," p. 15.

A modern version of pluralism found in the United States, according to Roger Finke, is provided by the legal framework of the separation of church and state. The political act of *religious deregulation* aimed to protect the free expression of religious minorities in the religious market and introduced a new era of religious diversity.[119] Religious liberty means more than tolerance; democracy dismantles the monopolization of religion in support of free expression and *equal rights*.[120] More than 90% of people in the world adhere to one of the top ten major religions, and every major religion exists as a subculture elsewhere in the world where they are often victims of discrimination and hate crimes. Thus, the separation of church and state may have been intended more as a removal of religious monopolization than of religion, per se. For this reason, Finke suggests that diverse religious inclusion, rather than exclusion, might be the future mark of democracy.[121]

Reimagining the Secular with 'Cosmopolitan Solutions'

A variety of new models of nation-state politics are emerging that create space for religious voices in the public sphere such as associational democracy,[122] consocial politics,[123] higher law secularism,[124] and multi-faith dialogue.[125] The scholarly interest in opposition and clash has left a diverse array of state-Islam

---

119   Roger Finke, "Religious Deregulation: Origins and Consequences," *Journal of Church and State* 32, no. 3 (1990).

120   Ibid, p. 609.

121   Ibid.

122   Robert Putnam, *Making Democracy Work: Civic Traditions in Modern Italy* (Princeton, NJ: Princeton University Press, 1994); Veit Bader, "Sciences, Politics, and Associative Democracy: Democratizing Science and Expertizing Democracy," *Innovation: The European Journal of Social Sciences* 27, no. 4 (2014); Pierpaolo Donati, "Social Capital and Associative Democracy: A Relational Perspective," *Journal for the Theory of Social Behaviour* 44, no. 1 (2014).

123   Audi and Wolterstorff, *Religion in the Public Square: The Place of Religious Convictions in Political Debate*.

124   Zachary Calo focuses specifically on legal discourse to develop a pluralistic post-secular higher law jurisprudence. See Calo, "Higher Law Secularism: Religious Symbols, Contested Secularisms, and the Limits of the Establishment Clause."; "Law in the Secular Age."

125   Brodeur, "From the Margins to the Centers of Power: The Increasing Relevance of the Global Interfaith Movement."; Halafoff, "The Multifaith Movement."; "Netpeace and the Cosmopolitan Condition: Multifaith Movements and the Politics of Understanding."

interactions understudied with regard to civil society.[126] New particularistic theologies of public engagement and discourse ethics are emerging in other religions, as well.[127] An emerging theme across different approaches is that the interface between religion and politics is a negotiated nexus where several possible outcomes can, and do, occur in relation to the various influences of an array of diverse and competing interpretations.

Religious Diplomacy

As a wider array of particular religious traditions become publicly engaged, pragmatic approaches that advance a compromise between achievement of a neutral state and the state opening public space to multiple particularistic religious expressions are reimagining the secular. Casanova has argued that the re-entry of religion into the political sphere can be understood within a Habermasian framework as forcing modern nation-states to confront inequalities and environmental destruction and reflexively reconsider their normative foundations. By pushing back against secularization pressures for marginalization, public religion can be understood as 'on the side of human enlightenment' helping modernity save itself through practical rationalization of the traditional lifeworld.[128]

Within a global framework, reimagining the secular occurs in the context of a political nation-state system, economic and cultural globalization, global communication systems, governance without government and global environmental changes.[129] In transnational relations, public religion operates within

---

126   Turam, "The Politics of Engagement between Islam and the Secular State: Ambivalences of 'Civil Society.'"; Hefner, *Civil Islam: Muslims and Democratization in Indonesia*.

127   For example, see Bhikshuni Lozang Trinlae, "rospects for a Buddhist Practical Theology,"*International Journal of Practical Theology* 18, no. 1 (2014); Anning Hu, "Gifts of Money and Gifts of Time: Folk Religion and Civic Involvement in a Chinese Society," *Review of Religious Research* 56, no. 2 (2014). Stephen Winter, "Engaging with Globalization: A Matter of Life or Death?," *Political Theology* 3, no. 1 (2001); Hefner, *Civil Islam: Muslims and Democratization in Indonesia*; Seyla Benhabib, "Beyond Interventionism and Indifference: Culture, Deliberation and Pluralism," *Philosophy and Social Criticism* 31 (2005).

128   Casanova, *Public Religions in the Modern World*, 234; Halaffoff, "Netpeace and the Cosmopolitan Condition: Multifaith Movements and the Politics of Understanding."

129   Bauman, *Globalization: The Human Consequences*; *Liquid Modernity*; Ulrich Beck, "The Cosmopolitan Society and Its Enemies," *Theory, Culture & Society* 19, no. 1–2 (2002); Beck, "A God of One's Own."; Ulrich Beck, "Incalculable Futures: World Risk Society and Its Social and Political Implications," *Ulrich Beck: Pioneer in Cosmopolitan Sociology & Risk Society* (2014); Ulrich Beck and Natan Sznaider, "A Literature on Cosmopolitanism: An Overview," *British Journal of Sociology* 57, no. 1 (2006); Mayntz, "Common Goods and Governance."

highly interdependent, interconnected and rapidly changing networks. Because risks and manufactured uncertainties cross borders while governments defend them, the need for collaborative governance for combating existing threats and minimizing risks has greatly increased.

Cosmopiety

Cosmopolitan political theory has emerged to provide a de-centered nation-state perspective capable of identifying how the nation-state system exacerbates, mitigates and adapts to global changes.[130] The crisis of secularism de-absolutizes the secular ideals that once marginalized and critiqued religion resulting in 'a disenchantment of the disenchanters.'[131] In this regard, cosmopolitan mindsets are radically reflexive, attentive to the interdependence of all life with an emphasis upon equal rights alongside respect for diversity. The perspective that emerges out of interdependent and interconnected social experiences is "inclusive and deliberative, collaborative and multilateral, [and] concentrated at local and global, as opposed to national, levels."[132]

Cosmopolitan political theory may be useful for addressing a void in transnational theories of religion. Although the concept of soft power has usefully described the governance role of secular INGOs in transnational relations, when it has been applied to religion, the concept has been influenced by Western dualistic conceptions of the religious-political nexus, categorizing religious soft power into only two streams—as either endorsing or opposing globalization—and rendered less useful.[133] Dualistic approaches to religious-political relations obscure the governance role of religion, a factor which may

---

130 Beck, "The Cosmopolitan Society and Its Enemies."; Ulrich Beck and Ciaran Cronin, "The European Crisis in the Context of Cosmopolitization," *New Literary History*, no. 4 (2012); Ulrich Beck, "The Reality of Cosmopolitanism," *Ulrich Beck: Pioneer in Cosmopolitan Sociology & Risk Society* (2014); Ulrich Beck and Patrick Camiller, "The Truth of Others: A Cosmopolitan Approach," *Common Knowledge*, no. 3 (2004); Ulrich Beck, "We Do Not Live in an Age of Cosmopolitanism but in an Age of Cosmopolitization: The 'Global Other' Is in Our Midst," in *Ulrich Beck: Pioneer in Cosmopolitan Sociology and Risk Society*, ed. Ulrich Beck (New York, New York: Springer, 2014); Beck, "World Risk Society and Manufactured Uncertainties."

131 Jean-Paul Willaime, "Religion in Ultramodernity," in *Theorising Religion: Classical and Contemporary Debates*, ed. James A. Beckford and John Wallis (Aldershot: Ashgate, 2006).

132 Halafoff, "The Multifaith Movement," 20.

133 Haynes, "Transnational Religious Actors and International Politics."; "Religion and International Relations in the 21st Century: Conflict or Co-Operation?"; Jeffrey Haynes, *Religion and Development: Conflict or Cooperation?* (Basingstoke, England: Palgrave Macmillan, 2007); Haynes, "Religion and Foreign Policy."

be contributing to why it is under researched.[134] But religious organizations are not just pro- or anti-globalization, and this is a difference that matters since, by and large, a soft power approach to international relations has been identified as more compatible with the necessities of responsible living in an interdependent world.

The term *cosmopiety* may be useful as a way of distinguishing a third stream of religious soft power in transnational relations that is both cosmopolitan and engaged in governance. Cosmopiety refers to the social space where the practice of religious diplomacy occurs. People of faith or belief are exposed to the same processes that, according to Ulrich Beck, shape the development of cosmopolitan mindsets. People of faith or belief are shaped by exposure to others where they develop a shared morality within an inclusive community composed of diverse people from different places.[135] Where *cosmopiety* diverges from Beck, however, is in his presumption that religious commitments are subject to eventual individualization and privatization.[136] *Cosmopiety* maintains commitments to meso-level subcultures of religion or belief, but exposure to other religions and recognition that identities are interlinked permeates the walls of separation enough to develop a shared community that disempowers the bonds of religious favoritism and blurs the boundaries of difference.

The term *cosmopiety* was first introduced at the F20 2015 Turkey Summit by Paul Morris in a presentation drawing upon a monograph currently in progress that looks at the global rise of cosmopolitan pieties and religiosities. As he reflected upon the immensity of tasks associated with implementation of the SDGs, he proposed an agenda for what he termed 'Cosmopolitan Pietists.' Against the backdrop of cosmopolitan politics, he suggested that *cosmopiety* recognizes that the politics of human rights are not limited to the nation-state, but are extended beyond *all* political borders to include values and the validity of others' values.[137] Although religious diversity is not new, most religious traditions practice a prejudicial pluralism where they rarely acknowledge other traditions as equal. Rather than revive an uncritical model of prejudicial pluralism, Paul Morris encouraged attendees to develop a critical theory of religious equality and reflect upon how they might partner with secular

---

134   Halafoff, "The Multifaith Movement."; Johnston and Sampson, eds., *Religion, the Missing Dimension of Statecraft*; Johnston, ed. *Faith-Based Diplomacy: Trumping Real Politik*.

135   Beck, "The Cosmopolitan Society and Its Enemies."

136   "A God of One's Own."

137   Paul Morris, *Cosmopiety* (New Zealand: Palgrave, 2017). For an edited short summary of his 2015 presentation on the topic, see Sherrie Steiner, "G20 Interfaith Summit Summary Report" (2015), 22–23.

cosmopolitans to implement the SDGs. He then presented an account of religious equality from the Jewish tradition. The Talmud defines a city as a community of obligation. A 10% tithe is used in this tradition to open the community
to the needs of vulnerable people within its walls as a balance to responsibility
for one's intimate community. This entails that the needs of the vulnerable
are on equal footing to all other legal privileges as a matter of justice. He then
extended the modern application to develop a rabbinical-based *cosmopiety* in
support of faith-based commitment to SDG fulfillment. He identified five links
between faith-based organizations and development organizations that position them to make a significant impact on SDG fulfillment if their constituencies were sufficiently mobilized: (1) Religious communities offer strong models
of sustainable communities, (2) Charity and support is widely advocated as a
religious duty rather than as tax relief, (3) Religions offer cogent alternatives
to liberal capitalism, (4) Religions appreciate teachings on contingency with
recognition that life is dynamic and fragile (resiliency), and (5) Religions are
depositories of values and give adherence to orienting narratives of position,
place and purpose that are absent from contemporary social thought.[138]

Diana Eck takes a similar critical approach to religious equality when she
distinguishes pluralism from exclusivism and inclusivism. Her use of the term
pluralism is not to be confused with plurality which refers to the conditions
of diversity. Pluralism is a broader term that incorporates the *social response*
to the conditions of diversity in a positive and active way.[139] Eck has studied
the religious landscape in the United States through the Pluralism Project at
Harvard University. She lays out three prevalent responses to religious diversity
in the United States.[140] Most dualistic approaches to public religion focus on
either the position that "my way is the only way" of exclusivism or the approach
that considers there are grains of truth in other ways, but ultimately under-
stands that "my way is the better way" of inclusivism. Diana Eck's third option
is the pluralist response which seeks to find new ways of positively engaging
with diversity, exploring differences whilst seeking common understanding.
On the website for Harvard University's Pluralism Project, Eck describes the
four principles of pluralism as: (1) Pluralism is not diversity alone, but the energetic engagement with diversity; (2) Pluralism is not tolerance, but the active seeking of understanding across lines of difference; (3) Pluralism is not
relativism, but the encounter of commitments; and (4) Pluralism is based on

---

138   Steiner, "G20 Interfaith Summit Summary Report," (2015), 22–23; Morris, *Cosmopiety*.
139   Diana Eck, *Encountering God: A Spiritual Journey from Bozeman to Banaras* (Boston: Bea-
       con Press, 2003).
140   "What Is Pluralism?," (2006), http://pluralism.org/what-is-pluralism/.

dialogue.[141] The scope conditions of Diana Eck's work, however, is national rather than transnational, and Eck does not explore the governance role of religion in transnational relations.

Cosmopiety is *not* syncretism. *Cosmopiety* does *not* fuse, combine or amalgamate different religions. Neither is *cosmopiety* reducible to civil society. *Cosmopiety* develops within the institutionally differentiated religious sector where religious organizations maintain distinctive religious identities. The interlinked identities that form through encounters of individualizing comparisons continue to respect diversity of beliefs and particularlistic commitments. Just as the calming of nationalistic fervor that accompanies development of the cosmopolitan mindset does not eliminate national identity and affiliation, so does the calming of religious fervor that accompanies development of the *cosmopietal* mindset not eliminate religious identity and organizational commitments. What *cosmopiety* achieves is the ability to imagine, understand and relate to the other.

David Inglis and Roland Robertson were some of the first scholars to discuss development of cosmopolitan ways of understanding one's place in the world within religious traditions.[142] They describe the evolution of ecumenical sensibilities in association with the historic development of colonialism. In the context of risk society, Willaime suggests that religions may be strengthening democracies by contributing to political will and emphasizing the importance of accepting political responsibility.[143]

Halafoff describes how the multi-faith movement and multi-actor peace-building networks embody cosmopolitan responses for countering global risks.[144] According to Beck, research into the pluralization of borders is the most basic indicator of reflexive modernization. When people are reflexive, borders that demarcate categories, such as national/international and society/nature "are no longer predetermined—they can be chosen (and interpreted) ... redrawn and legitimated anew."[145] In keeping with Beck's methodological cosmopolitanism,[146] Halafoff focused on looser social forms where the boundary-transcending effects of globalization were expressed within

---

141   Ibid.

142   David Inglis and Roland Robertson, "The Ecumenical Analytic: 'Globalization', Reflexivity and the Revolution in Greek Historiography," *European Journal of Social Theory* 8, no. 2 (2005).

143   Willaime, "Religion in Ultramodernity," 22.

144   Halafoff, "The Multifaith Movement."; "Netpeace and the Cosmopolitan Condition: Multifaith Movements and the Politics of Understanding."

145   Beck, "The Cosmopolitan Society and Its Enemies," 19.

146   Ibid.

multi-local interfaith networks to provide empirical evidence in support of her claims.[147] In contrast to the oversights from more dualistic approaches, Halafoff documents how a diverse grouping of religious actors within the multi-faith and peacebuilding movements have been acting in accordance with cosmopolitan principles to constructively critique and partner with state actors to advise on policies that address the underlying causes of terrorism and build more inclusive societies. Instead of viewing global tensions as a clash of civilizations[148] or as a battle between civil society and the state,[149] Halafoff provides evidence in support of her claim that the multi-faith movement and multi-actor peacebuilding networks are cosmopolitan actors in clash with anti-cosmopolitans seeking to impose their will and policies upon others. In a similar vein, Dondelinger points out that radical Islamism and Arab Salafist traditionalisms are not just hostile to Western popular culture, they are also putative globalization movements in direct conflict with the "rich texture and diversity of the Muslim world's many local, regional, and national cultures ... they are forms of cultural imperialism in their own right."[150] There are not just multiple modernities, says Dondelinger; there are multiple global-izations competing for the hearts and minds of Muslims.[151] Tapping into anti-globalization sentiment, Dondelinger critiques the homogenizing tendencies of globalist radical Islamism as an oppressive force that eliminates Muslim cul-tural diversity and replaces it with an inauthentic culture.[152] If the real issue is the unsustainable cultural homogenization that accompanies globalization, and not religion, per se, then certain streams of religious engagement can be understood as joining with other cosmopolitan actors who, rather than reject modernity, "seek to create a public sphere through dialogical means in which all actors, be they religious or non-religious, have a role to play in governance and in refining policies. In this way, they extend and refine modern principles of democracy to be more truly inclusive and participatory."[153] Mara Leichtman has also applied cosmopolitanism to her study of contemporary Islam and the

---

147 Halafoff, "The Multifaith Movement."
148 Samuel P. Huntington, *The Clash of Civilizations and the Remaking of the World Order* (London: Simon & Schuster, 2003).
149 Mary Kaldor, "New & Old Wars: Organized Violence in an Global Era," (Cambridge: Polity, 1999).
150 Joseph Dondelinger, "Cultural Contradictions of Soft Power and Islam," 58.
151 Ibid., 57.
152 Ibid., 58.
153 Halafoff, "The Multifaith Movement," 31.

transformation of religious authority in Senegal.[154] In the pages that follow, the F8/F7/F20 process will be discussed as an example of *cosmopiety* in transnational relations.

Conclusion

Whereas the previous chapter identified material changes in social and environmental conditions to explain why religion has become salient in transnational relations at this historic moment, this chapter has surveyed a variety of explanations for how religion is operative in the public realm that interested readers might want to further explore. The purpose of this chapter was not to provide a convincing case of any particular detailed examination or justification of how religious organizations should engage the public sphere. Rather, the point was to describe how a worldview shift is underway that opens the door for examining, understanding and appreciating the significance of new emerging and distinctive cosmopolitan approaches for how RNGOS engage in the public sphere. The term *cosmopiety* was introduced to describe this emergent historically distinctive governance role of religion where religious diplomacy can be practiced in transnational relations. *Cosmopiety* was distinguished from syncretism and civil society. The concept had an expanded application beyond peacebuilding to incorporate broader concerns (e.g., development, human rights, religious freedom, etc.). In the remainder of the book, the F8/F7/F20 Initiative will be considered as an historical example of *cosmopiety* making real and potentially important contributions to global governance. It is to that which we now turn.

---

154   Mara A. Leichtman, "Shi'i Islamic Cosmopolitanism and the Transformation of Religious Authority in Senegal," *Contemporary Islam* 8, no. 3 (2014).

CHAPTER 5

The F8/F7/F20 Initiative

This chapter details the origins and evolution of the F8/F7/F20 Initiative from 2005 through 2017. The participants and invitees are described in terms of faith tradition and political representation. Evolution of the Initiative is detailed from its ecumenical origins in 2005 (F8), the youth interfaith event in 2014–15 (F7), and spontaneous F20 emergence in 2014 (F20), through the merge in 2015, into the era of consolidated co-production of engagement with the G-plus System. The chapter also describes changes in the agenda over time.

Origins and Evolution

The F8/F7/F20 Initiative emerged in association with the *Make Poverty History* civil society campaign[1] which had a significant policy impact on the 2005 G8 Summit. Since 2009, the World Bank, the International Monetary Fund, and other multilateral, bilateral and commercial creditors had been working through the Heavily Indebted Poor Country (HIPC) Initiative to ensure that the poorest countries in the world were not unduly hampered by unmanageable debt. The structured program required the privatization of basic services and adoption of economic liberalization policies as a condition for obtaining debt relief.[2] By 2005, a civil society movement had emerged to pressure HIPC to offer debt relief without preconditions. *The London Forum on G8* was part of an assemblage of over 540 organizations that mobilized 225,000 people to pressure the G8 to commit to more equitable terms of trade for developing

---

1 The concept of civil society as used in this book denotes not-for-profit groups of citizens engaging in collective action around particular public issues of concern. Another way of describing civil society is as a political space where associations seek, from outside political parties, to shape societal rules through collective action. For theoretical development of this concept, see J.A. Scholte, "Global Governance, Accountability and Civil Society," in *Building Global Democracy? Civil Society and Accountable Global Governance*, ed. J.A. Scholte (Cambridge, UK: Cambridge University Press, 2011).

2 The HIPC program has continued to work for developing country debt relief. By the end of 2015, 36 participating nations—30 of which are in Africa- had $99 million in debt relief which reduced the overall debt stocks by 97%. For more information, see http://www.worldbank.org/en/topic/debt/brief/hipc.

countries, cancel debts of the poorest countries, and improve international aid.[3] The involvement of religious leaders brought a more conservative tone, if not some measure of credibility, to a movement marked by anti-globalization protesters and civil unrest. *Make Poverty History* claims to have had significant impact on public policy. The 2005 G8 made between $15 and $20 billion of new commitments toward poverty alleviation and agreed to drop $1 billion per year of debt for 18 of the most highly indebted poor countries. All UK political parties agreed to maintain the aid target of spending 0.7% of national income on development aid.[4] The benefits of civic engagement were immediately apparent to participating religious leaders. The F8/F7/F20 Initiative has remained engaged with the G-plus System ever since, although the conversation with political leaders has been largely one-sided.

The F8

The F8 portion of the Initiative traces its origins to the *London Forum on G8* when the Archbishop of Canterbury instigated the organization of an ecumenical religious leaders' summit on June 29, 2005 at Lambeth Palace to coincide with the UK G8.[5] The first multi-faith *World Summit of Religious Leaders* was hosted the following year by the Moscow Patriarchate of the Russian Orthodox Church the following year in Moscow, Russia on July 3–5, 2006. In September of 2008, an International Continuance Committee was formed consisting of religious representatives from previous hosts, the upcoming host, and the immediate host(s) thereafter. F8 engagement with Sherpas began as a Canadian initiative in 2008 and continued thereafter. The F8 process was continuous over the 9-year span from 2005 to 2013 through a complete cycle of G8 meetings: United Kingdom (2005), Russia (2006), Germany (2007), Japan (2008), Italy (2009), Canada (2010), France (2011), United States (2012), and the United Kingdom (2013).

The F7

The F7 portion of the Initiative traces its history to Interfaith youth who convened a 2014 pre-conference on July 13–18, 2014 in Kaub, Germany that was attended by 19 youth from 19 countries with faith representation from Muslim, Jewish, Bahá'í, and Christian faith traditions to focus on three overarching

---

3   Nicolas Sireau, *Make Poverty History: Political Communication in Action* (New York, New York: Palgrave Macmillan, 2009).

4   Make Poverty History, "Policy Impact," http://www.makepovertyhistory.com.au/mdg -highlights-and-achievements/.

5   Charles Reed, "Project Proposal—2013 G8 Religious Leaders' Initiative," (London, UK: International Continuance Committee, 2013).

issues: peace, justice and education. The policy and advocacy team drafted a statement in preparation for the 2015 MDG deadline that was circulated for feedback from civil society networks in each participant's home country. Youth continued to make plans for a summit scheduled to convene May 23–30, 2015 that planned to bring delegates from many countries to talk about local projects and the transition from the MDGs to the SDGs. The event was unexpectedly canceled by the German hosts. After incorporating feedback, the Interfaith Youth posted their F7 statement online as an Open Letter to the G7.

The F20

In October of 2014, Christie presented on the F8 history at the *21st International Law and Religion Symposium* convened by the Center for Law and Religion Studies, founded by Dr. Cole Durham, Jr. within the Faculty of Law at Brigham Young University. Dr. Frederick Axelgard, lawyer and former diplomat with an extensive career in public policy and international business centered in Washington DC, heard the presentation and invited Christie to present at the first iteration of the F20 Summit in Australia the following month. In Australia, the Church of Jesus Christ of Latter-day Saints (LDS) is very active in interfaith engagement. The Australian LDS was able to provide volunteers and advice for appropriate religious engagement in support of the first F20 multi-faith event.[6] Dr. Brian J. Adams, Director of the Centre for Interfaith and Cultural Dialogue of Griffith University, did some community consultation with faith groups and, together with some local colleagues, innovated the idea of having a G20 Interfaith shadow summit. On November 16–17, 2014, Griffith University's Center for Interfaith & Cultural Dialogue, independent of any directives or funding from the LDS church and Salt Lake City,[7] hosted a three-day conference in relation to the G20 Australian Summit with international dialogue centered on economic development, religious freedom and social cohesion.

The Merge

After the 2014 F20 Summit, Adams asked Christie to join the review team and continue with future planning. Christie suggested, and existing members of the F20 process agreed, that additional members from the F8 steering committee join the planning team—Rev. Yoshinobu Miyake (Superior General, Konko Church of Izuo, Japan), and Rev. Dr. Karen Hamilton (General Secretary, Canadian Council of Churches, Canada). The F8 leadership brought a history of international engagement experience to the F20 leadership's vision

---

6   Cole Durham, Email, March 15, 2017.
7   Brian Adams, Email, March 15, 2017.

of engagement with the G20 process. In response to the changing world, the F8 and F20 steering committees evolved into the F8/F7/F20 Initiative.[8] As of the middle of 2017, none of the F7 Interfaith Youth Leadership are members of the F20 Executive Committee although some of the youth leaders maintain informal relationships with committee members.

Christie describes the transition—from the F8 process, connection to the F20, and evolution into the F8/F7/F20 Initiative—as an organic process that could not have happened without the support structure of the Church of Jesus Christ of Latter-day Saints (LDS).[9] Brigham Young University (BYU) is the largest religiously affiliated university in the United States. It ranks among the largest of private universities with an enrolment exceeding 30,000 students. BYU established the International Center for Law and Religion Studies (ICLRS) on January 1, 2000 to "institutionalize ongoing academic work on law and religion and religious freedom in settings around the world."[10] The Center's operations are funded primarily from contributions made by individual private donors and foundations. The LDS Church is a major world religion that indigenously emerged in the United States as a persecuted minority.[11] Durham, in his organizational role as a law professor, has close ties to friends working in the Office of Legal Counsel for the LDS Church through whom he has learned about global religious freedom problems and the role religion can play in various world settings. Given their strong interest in law and religion issues, the ICLRS has "played a prominent role in a number of primarily academic initiatives around the world, including support for the G20 Interfaith Summits in 2014, 2015 and 2016."[12] The ICLRS hosted the conference that became the bridge between the F8, the F7, and the F20. Several LDS academics and religious leaders have drawn upon their distinctive identity during their involvement in the F20 process to make connections with other religious leaders that have high, as well as low, tensions with the globalization process. When organizing international summits, local LDS volunteers and personnel often assist with logistics together with volunteers from many faith communities with whom they interact in a practical setting of attending and running an international conference. That said, LDS support for the process should not be overstated. Financing for the conferences is diverse and minimally reliant upon LDS resources (see the

---

8   Interview by Sherrie Steiner, November 17, 2015.
9   James Christie, Email, June 21 2016.
10   Durham.
11   Alex Beam, *American Crucifixion: The Murder of Joseph Smith and the Fate of the Mormon Church* (New York, New York: Public Affairs/Perseus Books Group, 2014).
12   Durham.

section on finances in Chapter 6).[13] Conference content is independent and autonomous from any LDS directives.

The first jointly organized Summit occurred on November 16–18, 2015. About 130 leaders from 37 countries met for the G20 Interfaith Summit in Istanbul, Turkey for dialogue about religious freedom, human rights, law, social cohesion, interfaith cooperation, finance and economic development. Rather than focus on high-profile religious leaders, the F20 process now targeted influential opinion leaders and political advisors primarily from three sectors of society—policy making (e.g., political advisors), the judiciary (e.g., legal scholars), and civil society (e.g., development organizations, medicine, business, and faith leaders).

In 2016, the F8/F7/F20 Initiative expanded to include two regional pre-conferences in addition to the F20 Summit. A Pacific Regional Pre-Conference was convened at Pacific Theological College in Suva, Fiji May 2–4. A South Asia Regional Pre-Conference was convened at Hotel Apollo Dimora in Trivandrum in Kerala, India July 25–26. The Pacific Regional Pre-Conference issued a Conference Statement that made specific recommendations for G20 consideration.[14] An F20 Summit convened along the theme of *Dialogue among Civilizations and Community of Common Destiny for All Mankind* and met at the China Palace Hotel in Beijing, China on August 31st-September 2nd. On June 15–17, 2017, more than a hundred experts and leaders on economy, law, politics, religion, development and humanitarian aid from 30 nations gathered for the fourth consecutive F20 Summit at Potsdam, Germany along the theme of *Religion, Sustainable Development, and the Refugee Crisis.*

Patterning after the G-plus System

There are several questions that will be addressed in the following pages: Does the F8/F7/F20 Initiative seek a determinative role in the functioning of the state? Are participating world religions seeking to 'turn back the clock' from what the West has learned about the dangers of religious monopolies and the practice of favoritism in church/state relations? Is there any evidence in the history of the F8/F7/F20 Initiative of intent to form a common world platform of merged religious resources for purposes of global governance?

---

13   Ibid.

14   F20-China, "Conference Statement: G20 Interfaith Summit Pacific Regional Preconference," (2016), http://www.g20interfaith.org/sites/default/files/Conference%20Statement%20%28Website%29.pdf.

Evidence presented in the pages that follow consistently indicates that the Initiative is seeking to advise, but not exercise a determinative role in, the functioning of the state. Summit content does not lend support to formation of religious monopolies. If anything, summit content challenges the practice of favoritism in church-state relations. The organizational structure of the Initiative mirrors the G-plus System's approach to the transnational situation of 'governance without government'[15] in a post-Westphalian context. The Initiative is a relatively informal process whose leaders have resisted formal organization. Steering committee members are mindful of working within the national and institutional biases that characterize transnational governance processes to strengthen collaborative problem-solving approaches to transnational social and environmental problems. Nicholas Bayne, who was simultaneously involved in the G8 and the F8, has observed how this model of summitry is both institutional and anti-institutional—an approach he considered as crucial to the survival of the G-plus System's processes.[16] For the F8/F7/F20 Initiative, the informal leadership structure minimizes bureaucratic encumbrances and facilitates development of a deeper understanding of how religion or belief factors into transnational and domestic governance issues. The F8/F7/F20 Initiative has no charter, rules, headquarters, permanent secretariat, building or pension plan. The F8/F7/F20 Initiative is not an international institution. In the absence of any fixed summit structure or enduring administrative/bureaucratic support structure, each year the process must scramble to find a local organization capable of hosting the event. The semi-personal nature of the process keeps it fluid, but neither is the process an unfocused, *ad hoc* intermittent exchange of information. The process develops cultural capital for religious diplomacy.

The F8/F7/F20 Initiative uses a serial summit structure to guide dialogue across consistent integrative themes. The use of a leadership rotation model in tandem with the absence of a fixed summit support structure creates a situation whereby each summit is significantly shaped by the national context and the religious organizations in the nation that hosts the event. The F8/F7/F20 Initiative provides a forum for the sharing of best practices to develop international action that tends to be reflective of, and grounded in, a full respect for religious beliefs and domestic policy. The F8/F7/F20 Initiative has no collective information effort such as a public relations department, an

---

15   We have left the 'statist' period where countries are the strongest arbiters of power and entered an era of globalization where governance occurs transnationally in the absence of a global government. See Mayntz, "Common Goods and Governance."

16   Bayne, "The G7 Summit and the Reform of Global Institutions."

information service or a singular, all-encompassing web site. National hosts frequently publicize the annual summit and disseminate briefing materials, but communication materials are temporarily associated with the rotating summit event and websites are frequently dismantled or not maintained once the national responsibility for hosting meetings has been transferred. This is not to imply that the F8/F7/F20 Initiative is analogous to the G-plus System except to say that the informality of the process, and the problems that stem from that, should not be considered reasons for dismissal. If anything, commitment to informality becomes even more important when assessing religious transnational engagement in governance given the long history of violent religious and political relations.

Distinguishing Factors

There are four distinguishing factors that identify the F8/F7/F20 Initiative from other interfaith groups. First, the F8/F7/F20 shadows the G-plus System. The Initiative seeks to become one of the engagement partners providing input into the governance process.

Second, the Initiative is a "stand-alone" process that does not depend on a parent international organization for its existence. This distinguishes the Initiative from RNGOS such as Religions for Peace (RfP) and the Universal Peace Federation (UPF). RfP and UPF develop formally organized interfaith peacemaking councils that have Special Consultative Status with the United Nations Economic and Social Council.[17] The Initiative is not developing an infrastructure.

Third, the 'faith factor' has been salient at several of the summit gatherings in various ways (e.g., prayer, worship, cultural events, leadership commentary, etc.). Although some summits have been run more like a business meeting, such an approach is more the exception rather than the rule. Religious leaders consistently broaden the scope of governance discussion beyond a delimited scope that would constrict conversation to the functional significance of religion or belief's contribution to development, peacemaking, immigration, employment, etc. Religious leaders involved in the Initiative consistently critique governance approaches that instrumentalize religion as narrowing the discussion in ways that significantly undermine what religion can contribute

---

17   William F. Vendley, "The Power of Inter-Religious Cooperation to Transform Conflict," *Cross Currents*, Spring (2005); Walsh, "Religion, Peace and the Postsecular Public Sphere."

to governance.[18] The F8/F7/F20 Initiative takes a broad-based approach to dialogue that includes an emphasis on religious freedom that goes beyond the sacred/secular dualism to facilitate a demystification of polarizing processes catalyzed by religious insensitivities.

Fourth, the F8/F7/F20 Initiative is thematically oriented toward dialogue focused on progressive implementation of UN goals. Initially, F8 dialogue was primarily structured around application of moral pressure for G8 countries to create the financial conditions that would enable successful implementation of the MDGs. As such, F8 dialogue was more oriented toward global governance than global development, per se. According to Brian Adams, an important and significant differentiating factor as the Initiative evolved into F20 dialogue has been a shift in emphasis away from global governance toward increasing emphasis upon global development. F20 dialogue is now structured around a broader framework surrounding fulfillment of the Sustainable Development Goals. Over time, the F8/F7/F20 Initiative has evolved to address a broader array of ways in which the faith factor connects to global governance in tandem with G-plus System issue expansion.[19]

Invitees and Organizational Representation

The meetings have taken on various forms that reflect the organizational capacity of the national host and their understanding of the local relationship between religion and politics. In some instances, local hosts managed financial and organizational pressures and boosted participation by dovetailing summits with other local events (e.g., the EKD's Kirchentag in Germany 2007, a broader Chinese Academy of Social Sciences forum in China 2016). In other instances, individual participants managed financial pressures by dovetailing their involvement with participation in other transnational meetings, particularly in European contexts (e.g., Sub-Saharan African participants for United Kingdom 2005, International Ecumenical Peace Convocation participants for France 2011). Working within fiscal organizational constraints, the governance

---

18   Jones and Petersen, "Instrumental, Narrow, Normative? Reviewing Recent Work on Religion and Development."

19   Hajnal, *The G7/G8 System: Evolution, Role and Documentation*; "The G20."; Kirton, "G20 Governance for a Globalized World."; John J. Kirton and Ella Kokotsis, *The Global Governance of Climate Change: G7, G20, and UN Leadership*, Global Environmental Governance (Surrey, England: Routledge, 2015).

focus of the F8/F7/F20 Initiative has become increasingly evident over time both in terms of religious diversity and country delegations.

Participation in the F8/F7/F20 Initiative can be understood within the broader context of civil society's governance role in representing those who do not otherwise have a say in the making or enforcing of rules created by global governing institutions. Civil society responds to the democratic deficit of the G-plus System by challenging corporate and government irresponsibility through local participation and partnership with other governance actors.[20] INGOs have proliferated in recent years growing from approximately 37,000 in 2000 to what is now referred to as 'global civil society.' Strengthening global governance through civil society INGOs is a complex process with well-intentioned actors often working at cross-purposes. While intergovernmental networks tend to favor "delegation" models, INGOs tend to favor "participation" models.

The F8/F7/F20 process has been variously influenced by both delegation models (for G8/G20 member and non-member nations) and participation models (representing the religious landscape) depending upon the local context. The F8 Initiative initially convened delegations from the G8 countries which are Canada, France, Germany, Italy, Japan, Russia, the United Kingdom and the United States (Russia has since been excluded by the G7). Beginning in 2010 with Canada, each delegation was asked to choose delegates that would inclusively represent the religious landscape in their country.[21] Efforts were made to involve top tier religious leader engagement from G8 contexts, but consistent top level engagement proved difficult to maintain over time. For example, Archbishop Rowan only attended the F8 meetings in 2005. After that, he identified people to represent him. The Bishop of London was sent to Moscow in 2006, accompanied by the Archbishop on Ecumenical Affairs. In 2007 with Germany, Charles Reed (the UK Foreign Policy Advisor) and Bishop of Guildford attended, but only staff officers attended in France in 2011. When the United Kingdom hosted the meetings in 2005, they involved UK religious leaders but also UK heads of faith-based development organizations such as Tear Fund and Jewish Relief. When they hosted the Initiative in 2013, they heavily emphasized the participation model by augmenting the collaborative

---

20   Kennett, *Governance, Globalization and Public Policy*.

21   Karen Hamilton, "To Boldly Go: Innovations Originating through the F8 Canadian Inter-faith Leaders Summit Which Strengthen Human Destiny and Community," Unpublished paper (2016); James Christie, "In Sundry Places: The Domestic Impact of the F8/F20 International Interfaith Summit Process," in *Dialogue among Civilizations and Human Destiny Community CASS Forum* (Beijing, China 2016).

statement with a Twitter Campaign of civil society political engagement. In 2012, the United States also focused on practical impact prioritizing RNGO development organizations (e.g., Bread for the World) over religious leader representation. By way of contrast, the Russian Summit in 2006 was more of a state affair, emphasizing high level religious leader engagement and church representation. President Vladimir Putin opened the meetings, the Catholic Church sent five cardinals, and the General Secretary of the World Council of Churches attended. In 2010, Canada incorporated public engagement a year in advance of the meetings, and invited participants from all over the world. In 2007, Germany only invited participants from the G8 states and from Africa.

The F20 Initiative invites delegations from all G20 countries,[22] and participation from G20 member states averages around 70%. The meetings have focused less on religious leader representation (although the diverse religious landscape is certainly represented), and more on academicians and political advisors with particular attention paid to the interface of law and religion. For example, at the 2014 Summit in Australia, speakers participated from Griffith University, International Islamic University of Malaysia, The Ma'din Academy, Brigham Young University, University of Adelaide, Monash University, University of Melbourne, University of Winnipeg, University of Pennsylvania, ICLRS, Berkley Center for Religion, Peace and World Affairs, University of Oslo, Nalsar University of Law, Charles Sturt University, Universidad de Montevideo, and University of Notre Dame. In terms of political advisors, speakers included the Embassy of the Arab Republic of Egypt for Canberra, the State Minister for Aboriginal and Torres Strait Islander and Multicultural Affairs, a Member of Parliament at the Turkish Grand National Assembly, Members of Parliament for Ikaroa Rawhiti and Mangere in New Zealand, the Ambassador and former General Director of the Emirates Institute of Diplomacy for the United Arab Emirates, the Chair and the Former Executive Director of the US Commission on International Religious Freedom, the Samoa Law Reform Commission, the United Arab Emirates' Minister of Culture, Youth and Community Development, the Australian Minister of Public Enterprises, and the Australian Human Rights Commissioner. European participation was even greater for the Turkey meetings in 2015, and even though a much smaller Summit was convened in China in 2016,[23] the F20 process expanded to include two pre-conference Summits in South Asia and the Pacific.

---

22 The G20 consists of the G8 countries plus Argentina, Australia, Brazil, China, India, Indonesia, Mexico, Saudi Arabia, South Africa, the Republic of Korea and Turkey, and the European Union.

23 Steiner, "G20 Interfaith Summit," (2016).

In years where development issues have been prioritized on the agenda, additional efforts have been made to include participation from vulnerable regions, such as sub-Saharan Africa and small island countries that are not members of either the G8 or G20 (e.g., United Kingdom 2005, Canada 2010, France 2011, Australia 2014, Turkey 2015, pre-conference Summits in South Asia and the Pacific 2016). G8 membership is certainly exclusive, but even G20 membership is not universal. The G20 is estimated to represent 66% of the world's population, 88% of the world's gross domestic product, and 60% of the world's poor.[24] The parties that are excluded are capable smaller countries (e.g., Norway, Switzerland, Chile, Singapore and New Zealand) and the poorest developing countries. There is no formal criteria for G20 membership except that member countries be able to contribute to global economic and financial stability, reflect regional balance and remain small enough as a governance network to 'facilitate frank and open discussion.'[25] To address the lack of representation for the most vulnerable people in the G-plus System, the F8/F7/F20 Initiative has consistently and persistently sought to include delegations, where possible, from the most vulnerable regions of the world and provide an avenue for conveying their interests to government and other civil society organizations who collaboratively share responsibility for the collective human future.[26] The inclusiveness of the F8/F7/F20 Initiative offers the G-plus System a politically impartial point of contact for governance that respects freedom of religion. F8/F7/F20 participants have frequently developed consensus statements that document agreement on the morality (derived from diverse origins) of the recommended actions. On several occasions (e.g., most notably Turkey in 2016), interfaith dialogue at the face-to-face meetings made use of the meetings to also explore differences between different faith traditions to identify diverse interpretations of public morality and integrity on an array of topics such as the role of women in the family, gender violence, environmental ethics and anthropocentrism in world religions.

Although the 2005 meetings were ecumenical, the meetings became increasingly representative of religious diversity over time. Table 5.1 shows the increasing religious diversity among Initiative participants between 2005 and 2017. The religious representation model complements the G8/G20 faith

---

24   Paul Martin, "The G20: From Global Crisis Responder to Global Steering Committee," in *The Oxford Handbook of Modern Diplomacy*, ed. A.F. Cooper and Jorge Heine, and Ramesh Thakur (Oxford, UK: Oxford University Press, 2013).

25   Hajnal, "The G20," 20.

26   Brodeur, "From the Margins to the Centers of Power: The Increasing Relevance of the Global Interfaith Movement."

delegation model, which was used from 2005–2013, to reasonably ensure inclusive and diverse representation by people of faith and academicians who are well-versed in the faith-based reasoning of particular traditions from the majority of the world's religions; one can conclude that the reasons provided on their communiqués are equally accessible to all citizens despite diverse origins in an array of faith traditions. In this manner, the F8/F7/F20 Initiative strategy affirms democratic principles to overcome objections against their employ of restrictive comprehensive doctrines that are often used to keep their concerns marginalized from public discourse.

Many of the invitees blend religious beliefs and activism to fulfill explicit public missions. Berger defines RNGOs as "formal organizations whose identity and mission are self-consciously derived from the teachings of one or more religious or spiritual traditions and which operate on a non-profit, independent, voluntary basis to promote and realize collectively articulated ideas about the public good at the national or international level."[27] Although RNGOs are subject to the same laws as secular civil society, RNGOs *differ* from INGOs in that they claim a moral authority focused on *ends* rather than

TABLE 5.1   *RNGO faith tradition representation at F8/F7/F20 summits (2005–2017)*

2005	2006	2007	2008	2009	2010–2017
Catholic	Buddhist	Buddhist	Buddhist	Buddhist	Baha'i
Protestant	Catholic	Catholic	Catholic	Catholic	Buddhist
	Hindu	Hindu	Hindu	Hindu	Catholic
	Jewish	Indigenous	Indigenous	Indigenous	Hindu
	Muslim	Jewish	Jewish	Jewish	Indigenous
	Protestant	Muslim	Muslim	Muslim	Jewish
	Shinto	Protestant	Protestant	Protestant	Muslim
		Shinto	Shinto	Shinto	Protestant
			RfP[a]	RfP	Shinto
					Sikh
					RfP

[a] RfP = Religions for Peace, a sort of 'United Nations' for religion consisting of inter-religious bodies in more than 70 countries, led by 60 senior religious leaders from around the world representing all major religious traditions.

27   Berger, "Religious Nongovernmental Organisations," 15.

means that is unavailable to secular non-profits.[28] The sacred writings and traditions of RNGOs (that are unavailable to secular INGOs) provide content-independent, non-coercive criteria that strengthen the ability of RNGOs to function as external epistemic actors in global politics. Unlike most INGOs, even the largest of RNGOs are connected to faith networks deeply rooted in local communities, representing some of the best-organized civil institutions in the world.[29] The sacred nature of RNGOs employs duty-oriented language that emphasizes obligation, a concern for justice, and a belief in reconciliation and the transformative capacities of people and society.[30]

To measure the potential participation size of RNGO civic engagement, a total of 68 semi-structured short interviews using open-ended questions were conducted of participants of the Canadian Summit in 2010 shortly after the event (between August and October). Data was collected using a combination of phone conversations and email correspondence. Approximately 24 organizations were contacted to determine the size of the constituency they might potentially mobilize for purposes of advocacy. Responses to the question "How many people do you represent?" given by RNGO representatives revealed the difficulties in defining an organization's constituency. A representative from the Canadian Council of Imams was unable to answer the question claiming that "representation at all Summits was never based on number, but faith ... No one can claim that they were representing all adherents of their faith," adding that "we are a Canadian Organization." The distinction between "participation" and "representation" was equally challenging for a Japanese representative who mentioned difficulties between Eastern and Western understandings of religion, language barriers and differences in organizational networks between Shinto Shrines, Konko Churches, and Shugendo and Bahá'í community Congregations. The pivotal issue in discerning the size of the constituency was self-identification rather than an independent measure. In the case of the International Anglican Communion, respondents expressed ambivalence as to whether or not the entire international network should be included; since the Church of England does bring issues to the attention of the entire Anglican Communion on *rare* occasions, I included the entire network as a potential resource for advocacy, but it merits mentioning that the Anglicans did not mobilize their entire network for the 2013 Twitter Campaign.

---

28 T. Heferen, "Finding Faith in Development," *Anthropological Quarterly* 80, no. 3 (2007): 888.

29 Berger, "Religious Nongovernmental Organisations," 16.

30 Falk, *Religion and Humane Global Governance.*

In accordance with Berger's work,[31] four significant dimensions of RNGOs were explored: (1) religious orientation and pervasiveness, (2) organizational representation, geographic range, structure and financing, (3) strategic process, and (4) orientation, geographic range and beneficiaries of service.[32] Any attempt to identify the size of RNGO constituencies is fraught with measurement issues. Some of the RNGOs do not keep records of their networks and some of the RNGO participants did not respond to my queries (e.g., Finland, France, India, Italy and delegates attending from South America). Even so, participants at the 2010 Summit reported a constituency that altogether added up to more than 800 million, but this sum should be cautiously interpreted. Some of the RNGO constituencies overlap. That said, religious people are more likely to be influenced and politicized if they hear consistent messages of moral concern from multiple RNGOs that they respect, so an overlapping constituency, while numerically problematic, is nevertheless meaningful.

Delegations from Canada, Germany, England, the United States and Japan brought sufficient multi-faith representation to the 2010 Summit to justify their claim of pervasive national representation. In the case of Saudi Arabia, pervasive national representation is a reflection of how church and state are socially organized in that context. The delegation represented the Ministry of Islamic Affairs in Saudi Arabia—a government agency that licenses and supervises all of the mosques in the kingdom; there are about 15,000 mosques, each with a membership of 400–800 worshipers.

In some cases, delegations claimed regional representation by their RNGOs. The Anglican Communion represented a significant portion of the United Kingdom. The Russian Orthodox Church, a hierarchically organized monolithic RNGO, claimed to represent 73% of the Russian population in 14 nations. The Pacific Conference of Churches and World Vision Africa also claimed pervasive regional representations; as para-church organizations, they are much more loosely organized than either the Russian or Saudi Arabian delegations, but their constituencies are more politicized from the effects of rising ocean waters, extreme poverty and illness.

The Anglican Communion, the World Evangelical Alliance (WEA) and the Salvation Army had significant transnational representation. The WEA is more loosely organized and more politicized than the Anglicans; The WEA explicitly uses their network of 420 million to advocate on issues relating to poverty, anti-human trafficking, religious freedom, peace and reconciliation, and nuclear weapons. The Salvation Army is a hierarchically organized monolithic RNGO that is more oriented toward social services among at-risk populations

---

31   Berger, "Religious Nongovernmental Organisations."
32   Ibid., 9.

than advocacy, but the 2010 chairman of the International Doctrine Council indicated a willingness to advocate their constituency of 1,400,000 people. That said, leadership frequently changes in the Salvation Army, and the General's support is critical to mobilization of this network. Several of the RNGOs indicated that they had posted the 2010 consensus statement to their websites and held press releases about the event in their home country. For example, the leadership of the Anglican Communion works with a constituency spanning 140 nations, the Salvation Army network spans 121 nations, and the World Evangelical Alliance spans 128 nations; the network of RfP has affiliated interreligious bodies in 70 countries that is networked at the national, regional and global level throughout an untold number of countries. These organizations understand many of the issues associated with global governance because they, like the G8 leaders, have a constituency experiencing tensions related to transnational issues of poverty, the environment, and shared security. Although some world religions have more monolithic organizational structures than others, even loosely organized religious networks such as the World Evangelical Fellowship provide a network of potential relationships, decentralized organizations and religious communities which contribute to a subcultural emphasis upon moral achievement and religious experience in an international context.

RNGOs such as the International Economic Development arm of the Catholic Church, Tear Fund, Mennonite Central Committee, and the Salvation Army are heavily involved in poverty alleviation, child health and welfare and other issues associated with global governance. World Vision International—a frequent participant in the summits—operates in nearly 100 countries with an estimated 80 per cent of its funding coming from private sources. In 2015, their organization responded to 128 humanitarian emergencies around the world, sponsored 4.1 million children, and disbursed more than $771 million in microloans to over 1.1 million people in 32 countries. World Vision International also impacted more than 1.6 million jobs and improved the lives of nearly 3.9 million children who experienced increased family income during the same timeframe. They involve 50,000 staff and volunteers who engage 10 million financial supporters to impact an estimated 100 million people in World Vision supported communities.[33] The Salvation Army, Catholic Social Services and the Jewish Federation are well known for their involvement in social services, and mosques are known in many regions of the world as the place where suffering people can find assistance.

---

33   Rich Stearns, "2015 Annual Report," (2016), https://www.worldvision.org/wp-content/uploads/2015-annual-report-brochure-F3.pdf.

TABLE 5.2   *Constituencies in excess of a million participating in F8 Canada Summit (2010)*

Organization	Constituency	Location
Anglican Communion	78,000,000	International (140 countries)
Canadian Council of Churches	22,000,000	National (Canada)
Catholic Church in Germany	25,000,000	National (Germany)
Churches of the Reformation in Germany	24,000,000	National (Germany)
Evangelical Lutheran Church of America	4,540,000	Regional (Americas)
US Jewish Council of Public Affairs	2,500,000	National (USA)
Ministry of Islamic Affairs: Saudi Arabia	6,000,000	National (Saudi Arabia)
National Council of Churches USA	50,000,000	National (USA)
Pacific Conference of Churches	5,600,000	Regional (14 island countries)
Russian Orthodox	164,000,000	Regional (14 countries)
The Salvation Army	1,650,000	International (121 countries)
Turkish Muslims in Germany	3,000,000	National (Germany)
World Evangelical Alliance	420,000,000	International (128 countries)
World Vision Africa	8,000,000	Regional (25 countries)

Participants in the 2010 Canada Summit who represented constituencies of more than a million are listed in Table 5.2. Religious leaders represent the oldest and most fundamental of social institutions outside of the human family and they remain key actors with significant mobilization potential in community life, particularly in times when the political economy fails.[34]

However, the existence of significant mobilization potential does not necessarily mean that this network is easily politicized toward civic engagement. Attendees at the French Summit in 2011 were surveyed about their attitudes toward the F8 process and civic engagement (see Table 5.3).[35] Respondents

---

34   Marshall, *Global Institutions of Religion: Ancient Movers, Modern Shakers*, 191.

35   The response rate was 33% (n = 9). Survey items were recorded on a Likert type scale with values ranging from 1–5 (1 = Unimportant to 5 = Very Important).

TABLE 5.3 *Participant perspectives at the F8 2011 France Summit*

Item	Mean	SD	N
1. That faith involvement in public issues preserve and respect the integrity of a secular state	4.11	.78	9
2. That people from the most vulnerable regions of the world be represented at the World Religions Summits	4.44	.53	9
3. That religious leaders intervene in public debate on important social issues to challenge the State on moral issues	4.78	.49	9
4. For delegates to involve their religious constituencies after the Summit to lobby their government about statement issues	4.11	.78	9
5. For delegations to have higher level representation at the Summits (e.g., the Pope or the Dalai Lama)	3.62	.74	8
6. For development of a website for ongoing use	3.44	1.33	9
7. For religious organization to help meet the needs of the most vulnerable people in the world (e.g., social services)	4.40	.97	10
8. That religious and political leaders collaborate together to meet the needs of the most vulnerable people in the world	4.78	.44	9

Note: descriptive statistics of items range from 1.00 to 5.00.

considered *collaboration* with political leaders to meet the needs of the most vulnerable people in the world (item 8) and offering words of *challenge* to the State (item 3) as the most important issues (M = 4.78). These were also the items of strongest agreement among respondents (SD for challenging the state = .49 and SD for political collaboration = .44). The second most important item of strong agreement was for a willingness to be frank with politicians; respondents felt that it was important to be involved in public issues without undue concern about preserving the integrity of the secular state (item 1, M = 4.11). The second most important issue, also displaying strong agreement (SD = .53) related to the democratic deficit in global governance; respondents thought it very important that people from the most vulnerable regions of the world be represented at the summits (M = 4.44). This priority was evident in how they described themselves to the G8 in the collaborative statement as "[t]ogether with colleagues from Africa, a continent which should be included in the G8 and the G20 meetings".[36] Delegates often spoke of the G8 leaders' *de facto* responsibility to represent more than their own interests; they spoke of a shared responsibility to "care for the rest of the world and make sure that the world doesn't become a jungle." Of least importance was getting higher level religious representation at the summits (M = 3.62) and developing an F8 website for ongoing use (M = 3.44). Respondents felt it was more important for them to actually meet the needs of the most vulnerable people in the world (M = 4.40) than it was for them to lobby their constituencies to lobby governmental officials (M = 4.11) after the summit. This indicates that the 2011 delegates had more of a service orientation (where they are open to dialogue with G8 leaders) than a political orientation toward civic engagement, per se. The high standard deviations associated with the organizational questions, however, indicate that this was a topic of wide disagreement among attendees (e.g., SD for the website question = 1.33). Furthermore, the leadership rotation model employed by the F8/F7/F20 Initiative cautions against generalizing these observed 2011 perspectives across the entire Initiative from 2005–2016. Although similar responses were obtained from questionnaires distributed at the 2012 US Initiative, if one considers the entire cycle of summits, there is no single way of furthering the process. National hosts heavily shape the process in ways that reflect national organizational capacities and the local understanding of how faith and politics relate. The topics under discussion are differently emphasized depending upon the host country and current events. This creates evident tension within the group (which is further explored in Chapter 8).

A variety of tensions are observable in summit dynamics. Tension is evident between development practitioners and educators concerned with leadership development. Tension is evident between anthropocentric themes prioritizing humanitarian aid and Indigenous traditions concerned about the environment. Some of these differences are evident in how summit mottoes change as each country takes turns hosting the Initiative. For example, the British emphasized *Action on Poverty Needed Now*—United Kingdom 2005 and *Striking at Causes of Poverty*—United Kingdom when they hosted the Initiative a second time in 2013. The Canadians emphasized the importance of developing religious diplomacy with *A Time for Inspired Leadership and Action*—Canada 2010.

---

36   F8-France, "Statement of the Bordeaux Religious Leaders Summit," (2011), http://www
          .g8.utoronto.ca/interfaith/.

After the Russian summit, the Germans emphasized democratic inclusivity with *Just Participation*—Germany 2007. The Japanese were more attuned to the environment and the threat of warfare with *Living with the Earth*—Kyoto-Osaka and *Shared Security*—Sapporo in Japan 2008. Turkey and China were more concerned with developing dialogue between East meeting West with *Religion, Harmony and Sustainable Development*—Turkey 2015, and *Dialogue among Civilizations and Human Destiny Community*—China 2016. Tensions were even evident in conversations around symbols such as logos. For example, the logo for the 2010 Summit featured a square background border conveying, in the words of the Secretary-General of the 2010 Canadian Summit and the General Secretary of the Canadian Council of Churches, a background of grounding overlaid with a fluid shape symbolizing an embrace of complexity which deliberately has neither beginning nor end.[37] This was far too abstract for some of the more pragmatically inclined delegates from the United States who, at that point, began to question their involvement in the ongoing process. I will describe internal divisions further in the section on reform in Chapter 8.

Phases of Development

If we consider the Initiative as a distinctive informal engagement group that is not coterminous with civil society or think tanks, we see a slightly different timeline than the one proposed by Peter Hajnal in his study of civil society engagement with the G20. Hajnal identifies five phases in the evolution of civil society relations with the G-plus System—Phase I (1975–80) Mutual Ignorance, Phase II (1981–94) One-Sided Recognition, Phase III (1995–97) Mutual Recognition, Phase IV (1998–2001) Regular Contact, and Phase V (2002 to the present) Regularized Relationship.[38] If we consider the historic evolution of the Initiative, we see that the years for direct engagement by the F8/F7/F20 Initiative with the G-plus System has followed a similar, albeit delayed, pattern:

· Phase 1 (1975–2004): Notwithstanding James D. Wolfensohn's 1998 efforts to connect the World Bank to religious leaders, these are the years of 'mutual ignorance' where G-plus leaders did not recognize religious leaders as

---

37   Karen Hamilton, *Logo*, ed. Sherrie Steiner (email, 2016); James Christie, Email, July 20, 2016. The logo can be viewed at F8-Canada, "A Time for Inspired Leadership and Action," (2010), http://www.g8.utoronto.ca/interfaith/.

38   Hajnal, "The G20," 86.

potential interlocutors and religious leaders, by-and-large, did not yet realize the power and importance of the G-plus System.

- Phase II (2005–2015): These are the years of one-sided recognition during which religious leaders have acknowledged the G-plus System but the importance of the F8/F7/F20 Initiative still had not reached the collective recognition of the G-plus System's leaders. F8 leaders engaged with G8 finance ministers, ministers of foreign relations, Sherpas and national leaders. In 2012, the F8 communication strategy expanded to address the G20 meeting in Mexico in addition to the G8 meeting in the US. Religious leaders began to see this group of powerful states as important partners for dialogue and their communiqué was recognized in documentation of outside communications addressed to the G20.[39] In 2013, the F8 process was redesigned to utilize e-governance methods for statement development (e.g., Open Letter, Twitter Campaign). In 2014, F20 summit meetings autonomously emerged in Australia and F7 attention shifted to shadow the G20. The F8 and F7 statements are hosted on the University of Toronto's G8 Information Centre web site (www.g7.utoronto.ca) which serves as a permanent, focused, and comprehensive record of G7/G8 activities and documents, from the founding of the G7 forum in 1975 onwards.
- Phase III (2016 to the present): This phase notes the beginning of mutual recognition beginning with the G7 acknowledgment of the importance of cross-religious, interfaith dialogue, and freedom of religion or belief in the *Joint Communiqué* from the G7 Foreign Ministers' meeting on April 10–11, 2016 in Hiroshima, Japan.[40] In 2017, the T20 Engagement Group invited F20 Executive Committee participation in development of policy briefs; both briefs were included in their submission to the G20.[41]

At this point in the process, the Initiative has successfully recommended to the G20 that they consult with religious leaders on issues pertaining to famine relief and hunger resettlement. The Initiative has yet to progress through Hajnal's last two phases (IV and V) where systematic contact becomes bidirectional and regularized.

---

39   Ibid., 178.

40   G7 Foreign Ministers, *Joint Communique*, (2016), http://www.mofa.go.jp/mofaj/files/000147440.pdf.

41   Messner and Snower, "20 Solution Proposals for the G20 from the T20 Engagement Group."

Conclusion

This chapter outlined the F8/F7/F20 Initiative at the macro level and identified four distinguishing factors relevant to the case study illustration of *cosmopiety*: (1) The Initiative is organizationally patterned after the G-plus Summit process in a manner that retains existing religious forms that are compatible with a post-Westphalian nation-state system; (2) The Initiative represents a dialogue process not a formal organization; (3) Distinctive religious identities are preserved and diplomacy is cultivated from the standpoint of engaging religion *as religion*; and (4) The Initiative is oriented toward religious governance, shadowing the G-plus System summits with an agenda consistently oriented around implementation of the MDGs and SDGs. The description in this chapter focused on evolution of the overall summit process. In order to fully appreciate the depth and breadth of Initiative dialogue, additional attention at a lower-level of analysis identifies a more detailed description of each summit. It is to that which we now turn.

CHAPTER 6

Illuminating the Unseen

This chapter provides a brief history of F8/F7/F20 Initiative meetings convened beginning in 2005. Distinctive characteristics associated with each context are identified. Different meetings are compared to demonstrate how the Initiative is influenced by the way in which the host country regulates religion into public policy. Some aspects and elements of the Initiative appear to be coterminous with civil society, but the institutionalized form of religion remains salient, thus differentiating the Initiative from secular society.

Summary Overview

A list of annual F8/F7/F20 Initiative engagement activities with the G-plus System is provided in Table 6.1. The record begins with the ecumenical origins in 2005 and the multi-faith origins in 2006. The record continues through to the most recent summit that was convened in 2017. The G-plus System presidency that is being shadowed is identified for each year along with the venue and dates for summit meetings. The first time the Initiative directed their communiqué to the G20 was in 2010, but that was because Canada was system president for both summits that year. The G20 had already been meeting for two years by that point and they convened another meeting in November of 2010 in South Korea, but the Initiative did not address any of those three meetings because the shadow process was primarily focused on the G8 at the time. In 2011, France also assumed the Presidency of both summits, so the Initiative's communiqué was again addressed to both the G8 and the G20. The next year was different. The Initiative shadowed the G8 in the USA, but had an emissary deliver the common statement to the G20 meetings that were convened under the Presidency of Mexico where their communiqué was received and documented. In the case of London in 2013, the Initiative turned to internet activism in lieu of a physical summit; April 5 was the date for publication of the Open Letter on the internet that was directed at the G8. The Initiative did not communicate with the G20 Summit under the Russian Presidency in 2013. The Initiative shifted to shadowing the G20 in 2014; their communiqué was not sent to the G8 that year. In the transition year between the end of the MDGs and the SDGs, a youth delegation published an Open Letter communiqué directed to what was now the G7. That same year, the Initiative

TABLE 6.1   *F8/F7/F20 Initiative engagement with the G-plus System, 2005–2017*

G8/G7/G20 system presidency	Venue	Date
G8-United Kingdom	London, United Kingdom	29 June 2005
G8-Russia	Moscow, Russia	3–5 July 2006
G8-Germany	Cologne, Germany	6 June 2007
G8-Japan	Kyoto/Osaka, Japan	27–29 June 2008
G8-Japan	Sapporo, Japan	2–3 July 2008
G8-Italy	Rome, Italy	16–17 June 2009
G8 & G20-Canada	Winnipeg, Canada	21–23 June 2010
G8 & G20-France	Bordeaux, France	23–24 May 2011
G8-United States/ G20-Mexico	Washington, D.C.	17 May 2012
G8-United Kingdom	London, United Kingdom	5 April 2013
G20-Australia	Gold Coast, Australia	16–18 November 2014
G7-Germany/ G20-Turkey	Istanbul, Turkey	16–18 November 2015
G20-China	Beijing, China	30 August–1 Sept. 2016
G20-Germany	Potsdam, Germany	15–17 June 2017

shadowed the G20 in Turkey. The Initiative has continued to shadow the G20 ever since.

The Secretaries-General for each year of the Initiative, and their respective positions, are listed in Table 6.2. Religious infrastructures vary from state to state. The history of church-state relations is reflected in the type of leadership exhibited in the list of Secretaries-General. On several occasions, religious leaders innovated or partnered with other organizations (e.g., academic institutions, RNGOS, etc.) when the religious infrastructure was not capable of hosting a summit. For example, the Archbishop of Canterbury is the senior bishop and principal leader of the Church of England and the symbolic head of the worldwide Anglican Communion. Although the majority of funding for the Church of England today comes from parishioners, the legacy of government funding is still evident in the national funding that continues to assist dioceses with the least resources.[1] When it came time for the United Kingdom

---

1   For more information, see https://www.churchofengland.org/about/leadership-and -governance/church-commissioners.

TABLE 6.2   *F8 and F20 secretaries-general (2005–2017)*

Country	Year	Secretaries-General	Position
UK	2005	Archbishop Rowan Williams	104th Archbishop of Canterbury,Church of England
Russia	2006	Patriarch Alexey II of Moscow	15th Patriarch of Moscow,Russian Orthodox Church
Germany	2007	Bishop Dr. Wolfgang Huber	Chairperson, Council of the Evangelical Church in Germany
Japan	2008	Rev. Yoshinobu Miyake	Superior General, Konko Church of Izuo, Japan
Japan	2008	Rev. Nichiko Niwano	President of Rissho Kossei-kai International Buddhist Congregation, President, World Conference of Religions for Peace Japan
Italy	2009	Bishop H.E. Msgr. Vincenzo Paglia	Bishop of Terni-Narni-Amelia and Chairman, Commission for Ecumenism and Dialogue of the Italian Bishops Conference
Canada	2010	Rev. Dr. James Christie	Professor of Whole World Ecumenism and Dialogue Theology, Director of the Ridd Institute for Religion and Global Policy, University of Winnipeg,
France	2011	Metropolitan Emmanuel Adamakis	Metropolitan, Greek Orthodox Metropolis of France
USA	2012	Rev. Bud Heckman	Executive Director, Religions for Peace USA
UK	2013	Dr. Charles Reed	*Foreign* Policy *Advisor* at Archbishops' Council of the Church of England
Australia	2014	Dr Brian J. Adams[a] Dr. W. Cole Durham, Jr.[a]	Director, Centre for Interfaith & Cultural Dialogue, Griffith University, Australia Director, International Center for Law and Religion Studies, Italy
Turkey	2015	Dr. Recep Şentürk	Director, Alliance of Civilizations Institute, Faith Sultan Mehmet University, Turkey

Country	Year	Secretaries-General	Position
China	2016	Dr. Zhuo Xinping	President, Society of Chinese Religious Studies; Director, Institute of World Religions, Chinese Academy of Social Sciences
Germany	2017	Kathy Ehrensperger, Co-Secretaries-General	Research Professor, Universität Potsdam, Germany
Germany	2017	Patrick Schnabel, Co-Secretaries-General	Evangelische Kirche Berlin-Brandenburg-Schlesische Oberlausitz, Kirchlicher Entwicklungsdienst, Germany

a   Brian Adams and Cole Durham continued to serve as Secretaries General the following years, assisting Secretaries-Generals from the host country.

to host the Initiative a second time, leadership for the Archbishop position was in transition, so the Foreign Policy Advisor at the Archbishops' Council of the Church of England facilitated the process in a manner that did not require authorization of funds for hosting a summit. That year, all communications were done via internet and no face-to-face summit was convened. Very different church-state dynamics were observable in Russia when it was their turn to host the Summit in 2006. The Patriarch of Moscow is the Primate of the Russian Orthodox Church which has close ties to the government. The history of persecution under communist rule complicated a relationship where throughout Patriarch Aleksey's reign, significant finances were invested in a massive program of costly restoration and reopening of devastated churches and monasteries. The government provided much of the financial support for hosting the Summit that year and the religious leaders' communiqué reflected the history of state persecution. On more than one occasion, no single religion had a strong enough infrastructure to finance a summit, so Secretaries-General came from national representatives with the international interfaith organization RfP (e.g., Sapporo in Japan, USA). More recently, Secretaries-General have come from academicians where a university offers infrastructural support (e.g., Canada, Australia, Turkey, China). Most recently, the German summit in 2017 was co-hosted by Secretaries-General from academics (Potsdam University) and the national religious infrastructure (Evangelical Church in Germany which encompasses the vast majority of Protestants in the country).

Annual Initiatives

The F8/F7/F20 Initiative is an ongoing process. This book was completed immediately following the 2017 Germany F20 Summit. Thirteen years have passed since the first ecumenical gathering in London—twelve if we mark the history from the Initiative's multi- faith beginnings. In this section, highlights from each year are presented and summarized.

2005 United Kingdom—Civil Society Ecumenical Origins
In 2005, the initial F8 process emerged from the civil society *Make Poverty History* campaign that pressed for transformative change on poverty through international debt cancellation.[2] In the weeks leading up to the Gleneagles Summit in Perthshire, Scotland, tens of thousands of people from around the world mobilized in and around Edinburgh, Scotland. People participated in alternative summits, conferences, workshops, marches, and protests to debate economic and environmental responsibilities associated with G8 policies.[3] Faith communities were asked to be part of that platform. It seemed sensible for religious leaders to organize a complementary event to explore from a faith perspective what transformative change might look like in practice. In retrospect, organizers of the 2005 F8 Initiative have noted that it would have been difficult to create enough momentum for a religious summit had it not been for the activism of the secular INGOs. The first F8 meetings focused primarily on development issues in keeping with half of the G8 agenda. The United Kingdom, as G8 host, had decided to focus on global climate change and the

---

2 For a full discussion of this movement, see Sireau, *Make Poverty History: Political Communication in Action*.

3 This represented a significant increase in civil society protests from 2004. The impetus behind the increase in civil society protests was due, in part, to a campaign launched at the 2005 World Social Forum in Brazil. A worldwide alliance of existing coalitions, civil society INGOs, trade unions, faith groups, individuals and campaigners including Action Aid, Amnesty International, CIVICUS, Oxfam, Red Cross, UNICEF, World Vision, and World Wildlife Fund had met earlier that year. Three alternative civil society summits were hosted between 3–5 July: G8 Alternatives Summit, Corporate Dream, Global Nightmare and Global Warming 8 Conference. Although no arrests or injuries were reported at protests of the Royal Navy's Faslane Base and the Dungavel Detention Centre, protests on opening day of the G8 Summit resulted in the use of force, mass arrests and dozens of police injuries. More than 10,000 police officers from 50 forces were accessed for crowd control of civil society engagement with the G8 process. See Hanae Baruchel and Steve Dasilva, "Global Civil Society Action at the 2005 G8 Gleneagles Summit," (2005).

lack of economic development in Africa.[4] The F8 roundtable, organized only a couple of months in advance, had a fairly open attendance list, ecumenically speaking. They drew first and foremost upon church leaders from the United Kingdom. There was a US delegation, representatives from the Russian Orthodox Church, and a few representatives from Sub-Saharan Africa who were already in Europe for other meetings. A bilateral ecumenical relationship between leaders significantly contributed to organization of the initial event.[5] Archbishop Rowan Williams and Rev. Jim Wallis had a series of conversations that developed into a transatlantic relationship engaging churches around the MDGs. Wallis organized a US delegation for the ecumenical meetings.[6] Whether or not this one-day event in 2005 marks the first 'Summit' is somewhat disputed given that, at this point, the process was not multi-religious. This gathering, however, established the initial model of convening a roundtable dialogue, developing a statement addressing responsibility for global injustices directed to the G8 leaders, and hosting a press conference at the end of the meeting. At the 2005 United Kingdom F8 Summit, participants:[7]

- Asked the G8 to provide political leadership for the eradication of extreme poverty
- Asked the G8 to provide the resources needed to eradicate extreme poverty
- Ask the G8 to expand debt cancellation to include all multilateral creditors and more impoverished and heavily indebted nations without attaching conditions that reinforce existing patterns of inequality or undermine pro-poor policies of local governments
- Called for the G8 to reform the structural inequities and power imbalances in trade rules that tilt trade relations to benefit rich nations at the expense of impoverished nations so that people in developing countries can earn a sustainable income and the private sector can generate jobs and wealth for the common good
- Acknowledged the importance of public-private partnerships for building and sustaining education and health infrastructures in developing countries

---

4 Nicholas Bayne, *Staying Together: The G8 Summit Confronts the 21st Century* (United Kingdom: Ashgate, 2005).

5 Christie, "In Sundry Places: The Domestic Impact of the F8/F20 International Interfaith Summit Process."

6 Pauline J. Chang, "Ecumenical Forum: Poverty is the New Slavery and Silent Tsunami," (2005) *Christian Post,* http://www.christianpost.com/news/ecumenical-forum-poverty-is-the-new-slavery-and-silent-tsunami-3703/.

7 F8-United Kingdom, "Action on Poverty Needed Now," (2005), http://www.g8.utoronto.ca/interfaith/.

· Called for the G8 to reform their subsidies to prevent the dumping of produce on world markets and strengthen special and differential treatment for poor countries to protect vulnerable producers and support new industries

· Expressed a commitment for faith-based organizations to do their part to end extreme poverty in collaboration with other grassroots organizations

At the conclusion of the 2005 Gleneagles G8 Summit, civil society assessment of G8 outcomes were mixed. *Make Poverty History* identified significant advances for development goals. Several of the prominent civil society debt cancellation campaigners were not as optimistic. For example, Jubilee South, expressed disappointment with the debt cancellation agreement claiming that it did not go far enough. From their perspective, the conditions "attached to debt cancellation would only exacerbate poverty rather than end it."[8]

2006 Russia—An Interfaith State Affair

The Interreligious Council of Russia, a representative body comprising representatives of Russian Orthodox, Islamic, Buddhist and Jewish communities of Russia, hosted with state support a high level multi-faith Summit the following year in Moscow. Organizers of the Russian Summit indicated that the interreligious communities were not active enough to speak as a driving force in Russian society, so the state helped organized this F8 event. In contrast to the UK context where the summit emerged out of a civil society movement, the F8 Summit in Russia was a process entirely separate from the Russian Civil G8 consultative process.[9]

---

8 Baruchel and Dasilva, "Global Civil Society Action at the 2005 G8 Gleneagles Summit."

9 Russia disrupted the civil society momentum associated with the G8 process from 2005 even as they strongly supported the faith-based process. Although Russian representatives participated in civil society meetings hosted by the think tank Chatham House leading up to their event and Russia created a Civil G8 Advisory Council of Russian and international experts, the Russian Duma also passed new legislation on 21 December 2005 that went into effect in April of 2006 that curtails the freedom of activity within Russia of NGOs with links to international or foreign NGOs. Russia's Civil G8 Advisory Council aimed to bring the G8 agenda closer to the public and for the first time, two civil society pre-summit consultations were held where all nine Sherpas engaged in direct dialogue with NGOs. Many of the INGOs from the World Social Forum were excluded from this process, so they convened an alternative summit called "The Other Russia" where they challenged antidemocratic governmental processes and advocated for an increased rule of law affirming civil rights in Russia. Russian officials criticized western diplomats that attended this alternative summit, but the meetings were permitted to be openly convened as a functioning opposition. See Peter I. Hajnal,

The Russian 2006 Summit was a multi-faith state affair that was hosted by the Interreligious Council of Russia. The Summit was initiated by the head of Moscow Patriarchate's External Church Relations Department, Metropolitan Kirill, and convened by the Russian Orthodox Patriarchate of Moscow, the Patriarch Alexey II of Moscow. Only Russian communities were involved in the planning because, at this point, there was no team of international organizers. The Summit was rooted primarily in religious church traditions and planned a year in advance. Although the G8 remained the focus of who received the statement, the Russians invited representatives from all continents including Africa and Asia. The opening of the Summit was attended by the President of the Russian Federation, Vladimir Vladimirovich Putin. More than 200 leaders of religions from 49 countries met from July 3 to 5, including the Catholic Cardinal responsible for relations with the Orthodox Church at the Vatican; Chairman of the World Jewish Congress; the National Council of Churches, United States; the Chief Rabbi of Israel; leadership from the World Council of Churches; Syria's highest ranking Mufti; an Iranian Ayatollah; and Muslim, Buddhist, Catholic, and Orthodox Christian officials from China. The Catholic delegation included all relevant ecumenical dialogue partners except the Pope; this would be the Catholic Church's greatest show of support within the first round of religious summitry. Pope Benedict XVI addressed the gathering from St. Peter's Square in the Vatican, and Kofi Annan, UN Secretary General, sent greetings.

In some ways, hosting the Summit was a "coming out party" for Russia, politically and religiously. Russian relations were warming with the United States and NATO.[10] Working together to organize the F8 Summit raised Russia's international profile and strengthened the relationships for interreligious communities in relation to the Russian state.[11] The Russian approach to summitry set the precedent for investing significant financial resources in face-to-face dialogue over several days and making linkages with heads of state. The Russians also established the precedent of closing the Summit with an invitation for a host in the following year. In this case, Patriarch Alexey II of Moscow

---

"The 2006 St. Petersburg Summit and Civil Society," (2006), http://www.g8.utoronto.ca/scholar/hajnal_061202.html.

10   NATO, "Relations with Russia," (2016), http://www.nato.int/cps/en/natolive/topics_50090.htm; Office of the Historian, "United States Relations with Russia: After the Cold War," (2001–2009), http://2001-2009.state.gov/r/pa/ho/pubs/fs/85962.htm.

11   Sherrie Steiner, "Reflexive Governance Dynamics Operative within Round One of the World Religious Leaders' Dialogue with the G8 (2005–2013)," *Sage Open* 3, no. 4 (2013).

invited Bishop Dr. Wolfgang Huber, Chairperson of the Council of the Evangelical Church in Germany, to host the 2007 Summit.

The Russian version of the F8 process was heavily shaped by the history of religious repression in that context. Strong emphasis was placed on religious freedom. Religious leaders expressed repeated resistance to instrumentalism, whether in the form of political manipulation, religious manipulation, or the economic commodification of human beings. Although the religious leaders were in agreement that the time had come to develop a more systemic partnership between religious leaders and the United Nations, the collaborative statement they developed was only tangentially related to the 2006 G8 agenda. The Russian political Summit focused on energy security, education, and health/infectious diseases. The F8 communiqué made no mention at all as to how faith traditions might help the G8 fulfill MDG commitments. The F8 communiqué was not clearly directed toward the G8 leaders, at all. Rather, the statement was diffusely directed toward heads of states, more generally, to internal religious communities, and "to all people of good will." Given the understandable sensitivities to getting too close to government, the 2006 Russian F8 Summit participants:[12]

· Affirmed the importance of dialogue and partnership between civilizations for democratic, participatory decision-making processes in national and international relations
· Affirmed the importance of protecting religious freedom, human rights, and religious minorities
· Condemned terrorism and all forms of extremism
· Called for responsible engagement with civil society
· Called for the integration of sustainable ethics into the educational system, the practice of business, and the stewardship of natural resources

At the conclusion of the 2006 St. Petersburg G8 political Summit, civil society organizations were generally critical of the process. For example, Debt AIDS Trade Africa wanted better follow-through on promises to make trade work for Africa. Oxfam felt the meetings downplayed the fight against poverty. Greenpeace rejected the G8's claims on energy security, and Friends of the Earth criticized the G8 energy plan as fueling, rather than stemming, climate change.[13]

---

12   F8-Russia, "World Summit of Religious Leaders," (2006), http://www.g8.utoronto.ca/interfaith/.
13   Hajnal, "The 2006 St. Petersburg Summit and Civil Society."

2007 Germany—Consolidating the Vision

The German F8 Summit was also convened with state support. The 2007 F8 refocused the summitry process on civil society engagement and global governance on behalf of the world's poor along the theme of "Just Participation." The F8 leaders pressed the G8 to incorporate Africa's participation in the G8 process. German cultural commitments to democratic governance affected the planning and procedure of the way the religious hosts convened the F8 Summit. The process was more transparent and solicited more international input than what had occurred in Russia. An international committee helped draft the statement which was circulated in advance of the Summit along with the international invitations. For the first time, achievement of the MDGs was heavily emphasized in the statement that was ultimately delivered to the G8. Another first was involvement of African participation in the Summit process under the leadership of Archbishop Desmond Tutu (Archbishop of Cape Town, Anglican Church of Southern Africa, South Africa).[14] Summit organizers wanted to increase the participation of global religious leaders so, to facilitate their participation, the F8 Summit 'piggy backed' on a biannual event, the "Deutscher Evangelischer Kirchentag." The Kirchentag began in 1949 and is attended by as many as 2,000 religious leaders over a period of four days with as many as 500,000 local attendees in a single day. The F8 Summit was held in a hotel at the entrance of the exhibition grounds hosting the Kirchentag. The religious leader's Summit collaborated with Kirchentag to host a conference on "The Power of Dignity" the day before the F8 Summit. Fifty nine participants came primarily, but not exclusively, from G8 countries representing diverse Bahá'í, Christian (Anglican/Episcopal, Catholic, LDS, Orthodox, Protestant/ Reformed), Hindu, Indigenous (Native American, Aboriginal, Islander), Jewish, Muslim (Shiite, Sunni), Shinto and other religious traditions and communities. The Summit itself was a two-day event held in English that culminated in a statement delivered to media and political leaders using the Kirchentag press office.

For the first time, religious leaders at the F8 meetings expressed an international commitment to ongoing religious summitry with consistency and persistency. During the meetings, Christopher Hill proposed that the MDGs become the 'golden thread' for the ongoing process to provide consistency of content for dialoguing with state parties. Christie emphasized in response that persistence of presence throughout an entire G8 cycle was equally important

---

14   Christie, "In Sundry Places: The Domestic Impact of the F8/F20 International Interfaith
       Summit Process."

to maintain.[15] From this point on, the F8 process used the watchword "consistency of message and persistency of presence" using the MDGs as what Christie referred to as a 'Rosetta stone.' When it was clear, at the end of the German F8, that this process was worth replicating, the invitation to continue came from Miyake. Upon his return to Japan, Miyake immediately reached out to the World Council of RfP Japan, and then to religious leaders across all of Japan, to raise sponsorship money and begin preparations for hosting a meeting in June of the following year.

In contrast to the Russian process, the German F8 collective communiqué was tailored to the German G8 Presidency's agenda. German organizers circulated a draft statement to religious participants during the month ahead of the Summit to solicit multi-religious and international feedback before fine-tuning the communiqué at the face-to-face meetings.[16] The Ecumenical Advocacy Alliance delivered a letter to the heads of G8 countries with over 570 signatories of religious leaders and people of faith (most of which were active in the response to HIV and AIDS) urging G8 leaders to take critical steps in fulfilling the promises they made at prior summits to respond to the HIV/AIDS epidemic.[17] Religious leaders welcomed German steps taken to encourage better integration of Southern economies into the system of democratic global governance, but expressed concerned that their motto of "Growth and Responsibility" was putting too much emphasis on expanding market-driven mechanisms at the expense of sufficient support for clear and coherent poverty eradication programs focused on human development. Germany's Presidency marked the half-way point for the MDG process. Religious leaders were dismayed at the slow and uneven progress made on the collective responsibility that had been accepted in 2000. The religious leader communiqué spoke to the G8 with recognition that they operate within a broader network of other transnational institutions influencing the governance process. Although not all of the G8 German agenda was addressed (e.g., little religious leader attention was given to financial market transparency, intellectual property, and energy efficiency), rethinking economic development to strengthen Africa's position in international relations for poverty eradication was clearly and directly

---

15   James Christie, "How Well Does the G8 Deliver: Compliance with G8 Commitments," (Tokyo, Japan 2008).

16   For example, a delegate representing the Federation of Protestant Churches of Italy provided feedback on the importance of taking remittances to international migrants into consideration when discussing development.

17   Sara Speicher, "Tutu, Religious Leaders Call on G8 Leaders to Keep Promises on Aids," news release, May 23, 2007.

addressed (as was climate change, peace and security). The 2007 German F8 Summit participants:[18]

- Asked the G8 to develop binding frameworks and effective mechanisms within the "Guidelines of the Organisation for Economic Co-operation and Development (OECD) for Multinational Enterprises" for monitoring private corporation social and ecological accountability
- Proposed creation of a permanent forum involving the G8 and Africa for strengthening Africa's governance position in international relations given Africa's weak position with the World Bank and the IMF
- Asked for increased G8 support for the African Union to strengthen security structures capable of resolving endemic conflicts
- Reminded the G8 of their 2005 development promises for poverty eradication and expressed disappointment in the limited delivery on those commitments
- Requested that any international climate agreement incorporate development friendly mechanisms by which developed countries could fund clean development activities in less developed countries

Civil society was very active in relation to the German G8 meetings. Civil society protests succeeded in blocking the G8 meeting entrance for three days. G8 leaders had to be flown in by helicopter to participate in the Heiligendamm meetings.[19]

Religious leaders were less confrontational than civil society organizations. Religious leaders preferred to use a delegation model to shadow the G8 Summits from 2005–2013, interacting with individual Sherpas before and after the event. This process was not limited to national hosts. For example, after the Germany meetings, the director of the G8 Research Group at the Munk Centre took the F8 Germany statement to the Canadian G8 office to communicate the on-going work of Canadian faith groups, and Canadian delegates sought meetings with their G8 Sherpas.

---

18   F8-Germany, "Just Participation: A Call from Cologne," (2007), http://www.g8.utoronto
      .ca/interfaith/.
19   Joanna Dafoe and Miranda Lin, "The Choreography of Resistance: Civil Society Action
      at the 2007 G8 Summit," (2007), http://www.g8.utoronto.ca/evaluations/csed/index
      .html. Rob Augman, "G8-Summit Protests in Germany: Against Globalisation and Its
      Non-Emancipatory Responses,"*Libcom.org* (2007), https://libcom.org/library/g8-summit
      -protests-germany-against-globalisation-its-non-emancipatory-responses-rob-augm.

At the conclusion of the 2007 Heiligendamm Summit in Germany, initial news headlines reported that in response to public pressure, G8 leaders had committed to a $60 billion aid package for Africa. Closer analysis of the package by NGOs such as Oxfam pointed out that the G8 had fallen short of the 2005 pledges in disbursement by 10 billion; Moreover, of the $60 billion currently committed, half was pledged by the US to span over a 5 year timeframe. Most of the funds were earmarked for humanitarian aid rather than development.[20] In a post-summit reflection on the G8 outcomes, one of the religious leader participants from the Canadian delegation described the G8 outcomes as dismal, with failure to act on climate change as frightening, the promises made to finance HIV/AIDS at Glen Eagles largely unfulfilled, and the failure to cancel debt as immoral.[21]

2008 Japan—Decentering Anthropocentrism
Two Summits took place back-to-back in Japan indicating a certain fragmentation and rivalry within the local context. As promised at the F8 Germany in 2007, Miyake worked with the Indigenous Japanese churches. He partnered with the President of the Japanese Buddhist Federation and leaders in the mainstream Buddhist, Shinto and Christian traditions to raise $400,000 to host a June 27–29 International Summit in Kyoto and Osaka, Japan.[22] Many professors and religious, political, diplomatic, and business leaders came from the G8 states, Middle Eastern and African states.[23] Approximately 200 participants gathered, 47 of whom were from 39 countries. The international network of RfP had not been very involved in the German context. In Japan, they have a strong representation, so despite having conveyed an initial disinterest in the Summit process to Miyake when the idea was vetted at a World Council of RfP board meeting in July of 2007, RfP Japan ultimately decided to collaborate with the Japanese Association of Religious Organizations to host a fully international Summit in Sapporo on July 2–3, 2008. Over 300 delegates, including

---

20 Anup Shah, "G8 Summit 2007," *Global Issues* (2007), http://www.globalissues.org/article/719/g8-summit-2007.

21 Karen Hamilton, "A Few Comments from Karen's Participation in the G8 Religious Leaders' Conference June 5–7, 2007—Koln, Germany," (Toronto, Canada: Canadian Council of Churches, 2007).

22 Alliance of Religions and Conservation, "Religious Leaders Remind G8 Summit that the Eco Crisis is a Crisis of the Heart," *News Release* (2008). Published electronically July 1, http://www.arcworld.org/news.asp?pageID=242.

23 Michael Shackleton, "Religious Leaders Call for Global Partnership: Members of the Host Committee," *The Japan Times*, July 3 2008. Meeting proceedings in Japanese can be found at http://www.relnet.co.jp/g8/info03.htm

100 religious leaders from 23 countries, assembled under the leadership of Rev. Nichiko Niwano serving as Secretary General.[24] In addition to serving as President of Rissho Kossei-kai International Buddhist Congregation, he was also President of WCRP Japan at the time. The RfP sponsored summit drew religious delegates from the G8 countries, as well as participants from Africa, Asia and the Pacific, Europe, Latin America and the Caribbean, the Middle East and global religious bodies and ecumenical organizations (e.g., the Pontifical Council for Inter-Religious Dialogue, the World Council of Churches and the World Alliance of Reformed Churches). Participants at both Summits represented an array of traditions including Christianity, Islam, Judaism, Jinja Honcho, Buddhism, Hinduism, Zoastrianism, and Indigenous Japanese traditions. The F8 Kyoto-Osaka Summit convened under a Summit theme of "Living with the Earth." Academics moderated sub-committee work in accordance with three topics: Living with Nature, Living with Ethnic Diversity, and Reckoning with Africa's Poverty. The F8 Sapporo Summit convened under a Summit theme of "Shared Security." The dialogue in Sapporo occurred in accordance with four sub-themes: Environment and climate change, the MDGs, nuclear disarmament, and violent conflicts and terrorism. An internal power struggle within F8 summitry was now apparent, and the UK delegation began to raise questions encouraging reflection about the overall F8 process.[25] Statements from both summits were delivered to the Japanese Prime Minister in advance of the G8 meetings.[26] Each statement was characterized by a noteworthy and distinctive theme: the importance of environmental priorities.

Japan is the only F8 context where the summitry process came close to de-centering anthropocentrism.[27] For the Kyoto-Osaka meetings, the environment

---

24   Jennifer Gold, "Religious Leaders in Peace Call to G8 Leaders," *Christian Today* (2008), http://www.christiantoday.com/article/religious.leaders.in.peace.call.to.g8.leaders/20131.htm.

25   Charles Reed, "The G8: Our Spiritual and Moral Responsibilities: Does the G8 Matter?," in *World Religious Leaders Summit for Peace on the Occasion of the G8 Hokkaido Toyako Summit* (Sapporo, Japan 2008).

26   Yoshinobu Miyake and an African Catholic priest brought the Kyoto-Osaka statement to the Prime Minister's Official Residence in Tokyo on June 30th, 2008, just as the UN Secretary General came to visit the Prime Minister. They handed the declaration to the Deputy Cabinet Minister.

27   Anthropocentrism refers to a worldview that places humans as the most significant species on the planet with a moral status higher than other life forms. Anthropocentrism is increasingly critiqued for contributing to unsustainable ways of life. For example, see Christian Breyer, Sirkka Heinonen, and Juho Ruotsalainen, "New Consciousness: A Societal and Energetic Vision for Rebalancing Humankind within the Limits of Planet

was the central theme through which other concerns were addressed. Sub-committee discussions were convened in centuries-old Sumiyoshi Grand Shrine, Nempo Temple and Konko Church to highlight the practical relevance of Indigenous traditions for maintaining sustainable social organization through disruptive histories. In Sapporo, the environment was discussed as a subtheme under the overarching theme of shared security. Both Summits emphasized the importance of sustainability. Japan's ongoing involvement in religious summitry is the singular consistent voice in the F8 process for prioritizing environmental concerns in and of themselves. This aspect of their role in the F8/F7/F20 Initiative will become even more important beginning in 2015, to be discussed later, when the UN commitment to the MDGs gives way to a new focus on sustainability with the SDGs. The Sapporo and Kyoto-Osaka statements have both been incorporated into the history of the F8/F7/F20 process.

Both F8 Summits were somewhat reflective of the Japan Presidency's G8 focus on the world economy, environment and climate change, development and Africa and political issues.[28] Although the Kyoto-Osaka Summit's three working groups—living with nature, ethnic and religious diversity, Africa reckoning with poverty—reflected the Japan Presidency's agenda, the only concrete 'ask' from the Kyoto-Osaka Summit to the G8 political leaders was for establishment of a Scholarship Foundation for student exchange between Africa and the G8 to address the history of neo-colonialism through education.[29] By way of contrast, the Sapporo statement made a series of recommendations to the G8 under the peacemaking theme of "Shared Security." The Sapporo statement issued calls to action in relation to the destruction of the environment and climate change, the MDGs, nuclear disarmament, terrorism and violent conflict. Participants in the 2008 Sapporo Summit asked the G8 to:[30]

· Redirect national defense and military funds to establish an Earth Fund for environmental protection and MDG promise fulfillment

---

Earth," *Technological Forecasting & Social Change* (2016); Kusumita P. Pedersen, "Religious Ethics and the Environment," *Journal of Religious Ethics* 43, no. 3 (2015); Charles S. Brown, "Anthropocentrism and Ecocentrism: The Quest for a New Worldview," *Midwest Quarterly* 36 (1995).

28   Ministry of Foreign Affairs, "Summary of the Hokkaido Toyako Summit," (2008), http://www.mofa.go.jp/policy/economy/summit/2008/news/summary.html.

29   F8-Japan/Kyoto-Osaka, "A Proposal from People of Religion," (2008), http://www.g8.utoronto.ca/interfaith/.

30   F8-Japan/Sapporo, "Call from Sapporo-World Religious Leaders Summit for Peace," (2008), http://www.g8.utoronto.ca/interfaith/.

- Establish a binding climate change framework
- Expand other 'green' policies (e.g., expand energy efficiency and conservation efforts to reduce carbon emissions, increase carbon dioxide sequestration efforts, implement the Kobe 3R Action Plan of Reduce, Reuse, Recycle, etc.)
- Pursue rigorous implementation of nuclear reduction and nonproliferation policies leading to the goal of total nuclear disarmament; implement UN Security Council Resolution 1540 to control the transfer of nuclear materials
- Strengthen its commitments to utilize non-violent means including standards of international law, and acknowledgment of the importance of multi-religious partnerships and peace education to thwart terrorism and resolve disputes

The Kyoto-Osaka Summit seemed aware of the Japanese Science Academy's recommendations to the G8, and the Sapporo Summit made several references to UN resolutions and articles, but both Summits appeared otherwise disengaged from the broader G8 process. Neither the Kyoto-Osaka Summit nor the Sapporo Summit reflected any significant depth of engagement with civil society activism in Japan. Religious leaders were focused more on developing long-term sustainability and stability. Civil society was focused on the urgency of meeting immediate humanitarian concerns as part of the political ramifications of the food crisis.[31] World food prices had dramatically increased in 2007 and during the first two quarters of 2008, causing political and economic instability, and social unrest (including food riots) in poor and developed countries. Civil society organizations delivered an anti-poverty petition with over a million signatories to the Japanese Prime Minister at a June civil society leader meeting.[32] Although the Sapporo statement recognized the importance of the food crisis as one of several social issues to be addressed, neither of the F8 Summit statements reflected the pressing urgency expressed in civil society activism. Japanese Indigenous religions were heavily involved in the Kyoto-Osaka meetings, but the Kyoto-Osaka collaborative statement showed no awareness

---

31   For example, see Susan Jean Taylor, "The 2008 Food Summit: A Political Response to the Food Price Crisis in Gauteng Province, South Africa," *Development Southern Africa* 30, no. 6 (2013); Neha Kumar and Agnes R. Quisumbing, "Gendered Impacts of the 2007–2008 Food Price Crisis: Evidence Using Panel Data from Rural Ethiopia," *Food Policy* 38, February (2013).

32   Peter I. Hajnal, "Civil Society and the 2008 G8 Hokkaido Summit," (2008), http://www .g8.utoronto.ca/evaluations/2008hokkaido/2008-hajnal.html.

of the Indigenous People's Summit convened in Sapporo, Hokkaido ahead of the G8 Summit nor did the Kyoto-Osaka statement reflect any of the concerns adopted by Indigenous peoples in the *Nibutani Declaration* (e.g., implementation of the UN Declaration on the Rights of Indigenous Peoples).[33]

At the conclusion of the G8 Hokkaido Toyako Summit, outcomes reflected few of the concerns expressed in the F8 Summit communiqués. The G8 did not mention redirecting defense spending toward development, establishing an Earth Fund or an African Scholarship Foundation or a binding climate change framework; the G8 did not even agree to stimulate renewables such as wind, solar, geothermal and hydro (although they did agree to boost second-generation biofuels).[34] From a G8 leadership perspective, however, many of the religious leader concerns and calls to action were addressed. On behalf of the UK Prime Minister, a letter was sent to Religions for Peace International on August 6, 2008 thanking religious leaders for their valuable contribution and offering an itemized list of G8 advances that were made in the key areas of climate change, development and counter terrorism.[35] Civil society organizations were not pleased with those advances. In a post-summit press release, the Global Campaign against Poverty described the G8 as "out of touch" with the main issues related to ending poverty. Oxfam expressed similar disappointment in G8 progress on development issues.[36] Several civil society organizations expressed concern over whether or not continued investment in G8 Summit dialogue represented a strategic choice for their organization. Factors contributing to a diminishment in civil society engagement in G8 advocacy included increasing budgetary constraints for NGOs, diminishing G8 relevance for addressing global issues, diminishing access to the remote and secluded G8 meeting sites, and the pattern of limited G8 follow-through on promises made through the summit process.[37] *African Monitor*, for example, did not think that the recent G8 Summit held in Japan was acting with sufficient urgency to circumvent the current crises:

> Year in and year out, the G8 conducts its business as usual, regurgitating the same commitments with very little progress. Yet, the crises that the

---

33   Indigenous People's Summit, "Nibutani Declaration," (2008), http://www.tebtebba.org/index.php/content/100-nibutani-declaration-of-2008.

34   John Kirton, "Hokkaido Analysis: Assessment of the 2008 G8's Climate Change Performance," (2008), http://www.g8.utoronto.ca/evaluations/2008hokkaido/2008-kirton-climate.html.

35   Neil Day, Letter, August 6 2008.

36   Hajnal, "Civil Society and the 2008 G8 Hokkaido Summit."

37   Ibid.

world faces are even more pronounced today, and deteriorate with every year that passes ... There has been an increasing impatience with the lack of accountability shown by both African and G8 governments. It is time for African and international civil society organizations to come together and regroup.[38]

Meanwhile, as the global economic and financial crisis continued into late 2008, the Group of Twenty (G20) met on November 15–16 for the first time in Washington, DC, then again on April 2–3, 2009 in London. Religious leaders consulted with the Italian Prime Minister's G8 Sherpa, Ambassador Massolo, to clarify the evolving process. The Sherpa confirmed that the Italian G8 Summit would significantly differ from past G8 summits. In terms of the division of labor between the G20 and the G8, at that point the G20 was going to focus mainly on financial regulation and economic emergency, leaving the G8 to focus more on long-term issues dealing with structural problems associated with financial and economic globalization. The G8 would continue to take a more informal approach to developing like-minded approaches for effective implementation. The G20 would take a more formalized representative approach that broadens contributions for inclusion in the public-policy decision-making process.[39]

2009 Italy—A Natural Disaster

Shortly after the second meeting of the G20 concluded their deliberations on April 3, an earthquake struck Italy on April 9, 2009 just as it was preparing to host the G8. The Italian Summit was overshadowed by the aftermath effects of the earthquake which struck the architecturally rich city of L'Aquila, killing and injuring more than 300 people and destroying several churches. Religious communities of the world expressed their solidarity with the Italian people, praying for the victims and sending financial support. This international flow of support was well received by the Italian people and the trust-building capacity of multi-religious collaboration for humanitarian response[40] became

---

38   African Monitor, "The Time to Act Is Now! African Monitor's Response to the G8 Summit 2008," (*African Monitor*, 2008).

39   Antonio Tricarico, "Minutes of Consultation Meeting with Italian Prime Minister's G8 Sherpa, Ambassador Massolo," (Rome, Italy: CRBM, 2009).

40   The earthquake undermined trust in seven seismologists and geologists, however, who had met shortly before the quake struck and decided not to issue a safety warning despite weeks of frequent small tremors. Seven prominent Italian experts were initially convicted of manslaughter and sentenced to six years in prison for failing to give warning. The conviction was eventually overturned upon appeal for all except one, but the process

very apparent in the aftermath of the natural disaster, but the situation did not exactly build confidence that the G8 was the most effective means for maintaining international financial stability.[41]

Bishop Paglia of Terni-Narni-Amelia served as Secretary-General for the F8 Summit in Italy. The 2009 Summit was organized as a top-down state affair by the Episcopal Conference of the Italian Bishops of the Catholic Church and the Department of Foreign Affairs. The Italian F8 hosts decided to hold their Summit by standing with the victims of the earthquake. Religious delegations involving 120 participants brought some financial assistance for earthquake victims, Summit participants visited the earthquake site, and the Japanese made a presentation on behalf of all religious leaders to the Italians to assist their suffering people. Religious leaders were convened to provide the spiritual support drawn from diverse faith traditions that is required to deal with all social issues. After spending most of the first day in the earthquake areas, the Italian Foreign Ministry hosted an official reception at the Villa Madama in Rome where the Prime Minister usually hosts state guests. The event had top-tier representation from Italy's Ministry of Foreign Affairs and the Pontifical Council for Inter-religious Dialogue from the Vatican. The second day was spent discussing peacebuilding from an interfaith perspective in the main room used for hosting foreign delegations. Discussion was convened in accordance with the same theme used by RfP the year before in Sapporo: "Shared Security." Every delegation was given an opportunity to speak to issues of particular concern (e.g., the Japanese were particularly concerned about nuclear disarmament, William Vendley emphasized the importance of drawing upon shared values among different religions to prevent conflict, etc.).

The Italian F8 Summit was organized last minute and invitations were issued to participants with relatively short notice. It was a top-tier event, but the Summit almost didn't occur at all. Organizers invested in the ongoing process realized that if F8 meetings were going to continue, the process needed to be stabilized with some measure of committee support. Organizers had already been discussing possible ways to go about it without making the process too

---

has raised many questions associated with responsible risk analysis under conditions of uncertainty. See Edwin Cartlidge, "Updated: Appeals Court Overturns Manslaughter Convictions of Six," *Sciencemag.org* (2014), http://www.sciencemag.org/news/2014/11/updated-appeals-court-overturns-manslaughter-convictions-six-earthquake-scientists; Elisabetta Povoledo, "Italian Appeals Court Overturns Guilty Verdicts in Earthquake Trial," (2014).

41   Peter I. Hajnal, "Civil Society at the 2009 G8 Summit in L'Aquila," (2009), http://www .g8.utoronto.ca/evaluations/2009laquila/2009-hajnal.html.

formal. The conceptual structure of an international committee had been delineated at an earlier 2008 meeting in New York that convened in the offices of the late Robert Edgar who was at the time the General Secretary of the National Council of Churches of Christ. On June 15th, 2009 the first meeting was convened of an International Continuance Committee (ICC). It was envisioned that the ICC would help organize ongoing summits and provide a place for the discussion of broad and deep interfaith issues and their global impact as they relate to ongoing religious summitry.

The Italian F8 host laid out five priorities that were in keeping with the 2009 G8 Summit agenda: the global economic crisis, climate change, terrorism and nuclear proliferation, development in Africa, and regional security. Several of the items emphasized by the religious leaders were mirrored in the outcome of these meetings. The 2009 Italy F8 Summit participants emphasized the following key points:[42]

- They called for a new financial pact that would acknowledge the need for moral principles, address the causes of financial crisis, include all stakeholders (especially the poor), partner with civil society, and create sustainable financing for development
- They agreed to partner with the G8 to fulfill MDG promises according to schedule
- They asked for coordinated efforts between conventional disarmament and nuclear disarmament efforts to avoid provocation of a new arms race
- They called for the development of uniform standards for protection of the growing number of undocumented immigrants
- They called for the establishment of mechanisms for dialogue between religious communities, political leaders, international organisations and civil society structures

Twelve days later, on June 29, Pope Benedict XVI gave a lengthy encyclical, *Caritas in Veritate* [Charity and Truth], directed to all people of good will where he commented on human development, economic development, civil society, the environment, co-operation and technology.[43] In the days leading up to the G8 Summit, the Municipality of Rome collaborated with the Italian Prime

---

42   F8-Italy, "IV Summit of Religious Leaders on the Occasion of the G8," (2009), http://www
      .g8.utoronto.ca/interfaith/.

43   Pope Benedict XVI, "Caritas in Veritate," *Third Encyclical Letter* (2009), Published electronically http://w2.vatican.va/content/benedict-xvi/en/encyclicals/documents/hf_ben
      -xvi_enc_20090629_caritas-in-veritate.html.

Minister's office, the Italian Foreign Ministry and the Italian Coalition against Poverty to sponsor a *Roma Civil G8* on May 4–5, 2009. Civil society dialogue was convened with all nine Sherpas in the presence of over 200 attendees.[44] NGO leaders directly conveyed their issues of concern about the world economy, development finance and labor, common goods including health and education, food sovereignty and agriculture, global governance, climate change and environment, and expectations for accountability.[45] An alternative G8 Summit (nicknamed *GSott8*) convened in Sardinia July 3–5, to condemn wastefulness and exploitation and demand drastic changes in lifestyle to phase out the oil economy.[46] Additional gatherings included a poor people's summit, a farmers' union meeting, trade unions, a Global Health Forum, a delegation from academies of science, and the G8 Parliamentarians group. *Global Call to Action Against Poverty Italy* delivered a petition with 1.5 million signatories to Prime Minister Berlusconi asking him to deliver on health, water and education issues. There were some street demonstrations in Rome on July 7 and some military clashes with the police at a US military base, but demonstrations were much more peaceful than when Italy hosted the previous G8 Summit in 2001.[47]

At the completion of the G8 Summit, political leaders agreed to reform financial regulations so as to strengthen business ethics with common standards to be brought to the next G20 Summit in Pittsburgh. G8 leaders did not agree to include all stakeholders in financial reform, but they did agree to repair the financial system in ways that would ensure a level playing field and sustainable growth. For the first time, the G8 decided to monitor their own progress on development efforts to strengthen the effectiveness of their actions and improve the quality of service delivery. The G8 committed to mobilize $20 billion (US) over three years through the L'Aquila Food Security Initiative to address the food crisis. The United States agreed to convene a conference in spring 2010 to secure vulnerable nuclear material around the world, and consider revision of the Non Proliferation Treaty. Some of the religious leaders' concerns such as development of uniform standards for immigrant protection and direct dialogue with religious leaders remained unaddressed by the G8.[48]

Civil society organizations had a mixed response to the outcomes of the L'Aquila Summit. Most major NGOs (e.g., ONE, Oxfam, Save the Children UK)

---

44   Hajnal, "Civil Society at the 2009 G8 Summit in L'Aquila."
45   Ibid.
46   Ibid.
47   Ibid.
48   Berlusconi, "Chair's Summary."

welcomed the $20 billion (US) Food Security Initiative and advances made on maternal, newborn and child health, but fulfilment of MDG aid promises and climate change undertakings were widely regarded as insufficient.[49] The year 2009 represented a time of significant G-plus System growth with continued expansion of various types of interest groups seeking engagement in accordance with their areas of specialized concern.

Meanwhile, regularized G20 meetings solidified with the third meeting of the G20 in Pittsburgh in September where the G20 would declare itself to be the 'premier forum for international economic cooperation.'[50] Bread for the World and the Alliance to End Hunger partnered with other faith organizations to bring more than 25 national religious leaders representing the Christian, Muslim and Jewish faiths to discuss development work and humanitarian relief at a Summit on September 22–23. They pressed the G20 to make food security and poverty alleviation the most important indicator of economic recovery.[51] This network of leaders would continue to advocate for development and humanitarian concerns as part of the emerging civil society C20 process.

2010 Canada—Engagement and Governance

In 2010, Canada hosted both the G8 and G20 meetings. Canadian religious leaders had been preparing for civic engagement with this process for almost two years, collaborating with 47 faith-based church, parachurch and secular organizations (e.g., Academics Stand Up against Poverty, the Canadian Council for International Cooperation, The Mosaic Institute, and the University of Winnipeg) to join in an F8 interfaith partnership with a consensus model of decision-making.[52] The Canadian Council of Churches provided the organizational support for national hosting, but given that their financial resources are among the most limited of the world's regional Councils of Churches, and that they have a limited population despite being a large country, their religious leaders took a cooperative and collaborative approach to summit organizing.[53] The Canadian Interfaith Partnership intentionally built collaborations

---

49 Hajnal, "Civil Society at the 2009 G8 Summit in L'Aquila."

50 "The G20," 24.

51 Shawnda Hines, "Faith Leaders to Press for Action During G-20 Summit in Pittsburgh," *Agriculture Week*, October 8 2009.

52 Hamilton, "To Boldly Go: Innovations Originating through the F8 Canadian Interfaith Leaders Summit Which Strengthen Human Destiny and Community."

53 Christie, "In Sundry Places: The Domestic Impact of the F8/F20 International Interfaith Summit Process."

with secular organizations to build trust in a national context where there had been a "tendency for secular organizations to view faith-based ones with suspicion and lack of understanding and for faith-based groups to be disinclined to engage with secular organizations."[54] Their democratic process was modeled upon the German Summit, but further expanded to mobilize widespread grassroots support for the process at the initiative of Axworthy, Christie, and Hamilton. A Canadian Interfaith Partnership, hereafter referred to as the Partnership, was formed to organize the Summit which drew upon the resources of the Canadian Council of Churches (the broadest ecumenical network in Canada which represents 22 churches of Anglican, Eastern and Oriental Orthodox, Protestant, Evangelical, and Roman Catholic traditions), the Aboriginal community, the Hindu community, the Sikh community, the Bahá'í community, the Canadian Council of Imams, and various development organizations (e.g., Tear Fund, Christian Aid, Micah Challenge, Kairos, etc.).

As with past summits, the main task of the Partnership was to draft a statement for religious leaders to develop and deliver to political contacts associated with the G8 (and increasingly the G20), but the Canadians expanded the process in several ways. Firstly, a draft statement was widely circulated and publicly posted almost two years in advance of the actual meetings with requests for national and transnational feedback; more than fifty pages of feedback from nearly twenty organizations was incorporated into the process.[55] Secondly, the Partnership worked with the G8 Research Group based at the University of Toronto, one of the leading G8/G20 research bodies in the world, to integrate G8 commitment compliance data into the summit process. Kirton spoke at five regional gatherings for the dual purpose of providing education on the MDGs and enhancing regional interfaith relationships. As an academic body, the University of Toronto's G-plus research groups have included faith-based participants in the Partnership in writing and research on G-plus System accountability.[56] Thirdly, the Summit statement was communicated to political leaders involved in the G8 and the G20 processes, engaging with the offices

---

54   Hamilton, "To Boldly Go: Innovations Originating through the F8 Canadian Interfaith Leaders Summit Which Strengthen Human Destiny and Community"; Christie, "In Sundry Places: The Domestic Impact of the F8/F20 International Interfaith Summit Process."

55   Interfaith Partnership, Faith Community Responses, Policy Responses, Previous Statements, (2010). The International Continuance Committee wanted to ensure that global leaders would have an opportunity to work on the draft statement at the summit itself rather than have their comments confined to an addendum.

56   Hamilton, "To Boldly Go: Innovations Originating through the F8 Canadian Interfaith Leaders Summit Which Strengthen Human Destiny and Community."

prior to the political summits for the first time.[57] The Chair of the Partnership had been in conversation with the Canadian G8 Sherpa since the 2007 F8 Summit in Germany. As a result of this dialogue, the draft 2010 F8 statement was released nine months before the Canadian Summit so that the Sherpas, the national political leadership, the media and faith communities could seriously engage with, and provide feedback to, the draft.[58] Fourthly, an extensive series of interfaith dialogue dinners were convened before and after the Summit with Members of Parliament to discuss ethical issues related to the G8 and G20 process. A Parliamentary Petition was added to the post-summit MP dinner process which was then taken forward through the federal Speaker's Office to be addressed by the house. The MP dinner dialogues directly impacted an estimated 30,000 people. Conservative estimates related to documented media coverage in the weeks immediately surrounding the Summit event indicate that coverage of the process reached a faith based audience exceeding 800,000 and a general audience exceeding 1.5 million people for a total reach of approximately 2.5 million people. At the close of the conference, the collaborative statement was delivered to Prime Minister Harper by Member of Parliament Steven Fletcher (Minister of State for Democratic Reform), and delivered to the Canadian G8 Office shortly thereafter by Hamilton.

Canada was the first summit since 2005 to include significant youth participation. The Partnership involved Tony Blair Faiths Act Fellows in the planning process preceding the Summit. A hundred youth from a variety of faith traditions met in a parallel Summit during the international religious leader's Summit and in follow-up efforts after that Summit.[59] Thirteen of the youth delegates participated in the discussion and consensus building of the collaborative statement where they encouraged and challenged delegates to build increased grassroots support for the content in their home contexts.[60] Youth involved in this process would continue to build upon this experience to organize the F7 Interfaith Youth Summit convened in Germany in 2014. A children's component, the Millennium Development Kids, was also initiated in tandem with the Canadian process which focused on civil society education for fulfillment of the MDGs (and later, the SDGs).

Canada was the first to host an F8 summit without state financial support. Although the United Church of Canada has preaching points coast to coast

57   Ibid.
58   Martin Affolderbach, Email, July 15, 2010.
59   Hamilton, "To Boldly Go: Innovations Originating through the F8 Canadian Interfaith Leaders Summit which Strengthen Human Destiny and Community."
60   Ibid.

and is national in scope, it receives no special treatment from the government other than that shared by other religious non- profits—tax exempt status. Summit organizers obtained a government grant to host the MP dinners, but no government funds were used for the Summit itself. The 2010 F8 Summit was made possible through the generous financial support of the ecumenical and interfaith religious infrastructure in Canada and the support of the University of Winnipeg. The 2010 Summit brought together 80 senior religious delegates from faith traditions from more than 20 countries of all regions of the world and more than nine religious traditions and 47 different denominations, 13 youth delegates, and numerous observers including an official observer from the G8/G20 Research Group.

The gathering took place June 21–23, 2010 on the campus of the University of Winnipeg, Canada at the invitation of Axworthy.[61] Pre-conference events included a human rights and religious freedom seminar, an interfaith bus tour, and the lighting of a sacred fire. Keynote addresses included, but were not limited to, presentations by Axworthy on human security and the responsibility to protect, Justice Murray Sinclair on the Truth and Reconciliation Commission process in Canada, Roméo Dallaire who called for statesmanship to take precedence over political expediency, Andre Karamaga who addressed extreme poverty, Jim Wallis who spoke about faith-based activism, Francois Pihaate on the socioeconomic impacts of climate change on the Pacific Islands, Miyake who provided a Shinto perspective on environmental ethics, John Siebert on nuclear disarmament as peacemaking, and John McArthur who spoke about current advances being made toward fulfillment of the MDGs.[62] Language translation was provided in French, German and Japanese throughout the process to facilitate dialogue. At the conclusion of the proceedings, leadership for the following summit was passed to Metropolitan Emmanuel Adamakis who was serving as the Metropolitan for the Greek Orthodox Metropolis of France. The 2010 Canada F8 Summit participants emphasized the following key points:[63]

· Invest 0.7% of Gross National Income to fulfill MDGs, cancel the debt and halt capital flight from poor countries, combat corruption, support small businesses, educate girl children and ensure basic needs

---

61   Christie, "In Sundry Places: The Domestic Impact of the F8/F20 International Interfaith Summit Process."

62   Peter Hajnal, "The World Religions Summit 2010—Interfaith Leaders in the G8 Nations: Notes of an Observer," (2010), http://www.g8.utoronto.ca/evaluations/2010muskoka/hajnal-faith.html.

63   F8-Canada, "A Time for Inspired Leadership and Action."

- Develop concrete plans to ensure that global average temperatures do not exceed a 2°C increase from pre-industrial levels and address poverty reduction and environmental stewardship together in developing countries
- Halt the arms race, invest in peace, stop ethnic cleansing, disarm nuclear weapons, and establish effective dialogue mechanisms between international organizations and faith communities

Despite the media coverage surrounding the Winnipeg Summit that reached more than 2.5 million people, the serenity of the F8 Summit in Winnipeg occurred somewhat removed from the political process occurring on the East Coast where civil society activism contributed to expensive security costs.[64] But serene meetings removed from the political process should not be interpreted as political disengagement by the religious leaders. Several F8 participating organizations were also involved in the civil society activities that were occurring in Toronto.[65] *Save the Children,* for example, issued its own "Call for Action for the G8 and G20 Leaders" to fulfill their promises specific to the Maternal and Child Health MDGS.[66] KAIROS participated in the G8/G20 People's Summit held in Toronto in addition to the F8 Summit. KAIROS also organized a Climate Justice Tour of Canada involving some of the religious leaders who were in Canada for the F8 Summit.[67]

For the first time in the history of the G8 and G20 meetings, the two political summits were convened back-to-back near one another. The G8 met in Huntsville just north of Toronto June 25–26, and the G20 met in Toronto on June 26–27. Despite the spending of an unprecedented sum for G8/G20 Summit security, over-turned burning cars and citizen face-offs with police in riot gear still dominated Summit coverage on their nightly news during the Summits.[68] In the end, more than 1000 people were arrested, 39 citizens and 97 police were injured, and millions of dollars in damage occurred from a break-away group from a peaceful labor march.[69] Although the F8 Summit heavily emphasized civil society engagement, a missing sense of urgency contributed to a growing internal division within the civil society network and frustrated several faith leaders from RNGOs that were heavily involved in direct practical response to the humanitarian crisis.

---

64   Kirton, Guebert, and Tanna, "G8 and G20 Summit Costs."
65   Abdi Aidid et al., "Report on Civil Society and the 2010 G8 Muskoka Summit," (2010).
66   Ibid., 41.
67   Ibid.
68   Morrow, "Toronto Police Were Overwhelmed at G20, Review Reveals."
69   Ibid. Rider and Delacourt, "Pressure Builds on Ottawa for Compensation."

The legitimacy of the G8/G20 system was increasingly being called into question by civil society. Religious leaders were now engaging the G8/G20 system on both fronts, although these were the early stages for engagement with the G20 process. (An independent, persistent religious leader G20 engagement process would not emerge until 2014.) The G8 was finally beginning to hold itself publicly accountable and admit to commitment shortfalls.[70] Canada spent more on hosting the two meetings ($1.2 billion for staging two summits including security costs) than it committed to its premier initiative, the *G8 Muskoka Initiative: Maternal, Newborn and Under-Five Child Health* ($1.1 billion).[71] As for the G8 overall, Canada failed to motivate much political will among colleagues; a total of $5 billion ($1.1 billion of which came from Canada) in new money was pledged at the Summit for the next five years to implement the new initiative—an initiative that was closely related to MDG goals 4 and 5 and partly related to goals 1 and 6.[72] Although the G8 leaders slightly opened the process to consult with leaders from vulnerable regions during the Summit, the self-assessment diplomatically refused to name and shame G8 countries that had fallen behind in keeping their commitments; the group decided to focus future accountability reports on specific sectors and avoid comprehensive assessment.[73]

As for the G20, now that recovery from the 2008 global economic crisis was underway, they focused on reforming the financial sector as promised in Pittsburgh. They developed a regulatory framework for effective oversight and supervision of financial institutions that addressed systemic issues. They implemented a transparent, peer-reviewed international assessment in co-operation with the IMF, the World Bank and the Financial Stability Board that could be differentiated and tailored to national circumstances.[74] Developed countries committed themselves to reducing their government

---

70   For several years, NGOs such as the DATA group and the G8 Research Centre had been is-
      suing G8 compliance reports assessing the degree to which the G8 was following through
      on promises made at the summits. In 2009, the G8 promised to begin holding itself ac-
      countable and at Muskoka, the G8 released the *Muskoka Accountability Report* where
      data and narrative evidence was used to analyze 56 development-related commitments
      for compliance. See G8 Canada, "Muskoka Accountability Report," (2010), http://www
      .g8.utoronto.ca/summit/2010muskoka/accountability/.

71   Peter Hajnal, "Head to Head: Summits in Canada in June 2010: The Muskoka G8 Meets the
      Toronto G20," *Academic Council on the United Nations System* 83, Summer (2010).

72   Ibid.

73   Ibid.

74   Ibid.

debt-to-GDP ratios and they launched the G20 Financial Inclusion Experts Group.[75]

Faith-based organizations expressed dissatisfaction with the outcomes of the G8 and G20 Summits.[76] For example, the advocacy director for Tear Fund said that the G8 had yet to issue a plan of action to deliver on the MDGS, most of which could be financed by a nominal Financial Transaction Tax on global business transactions. He called for country-by-country monitoring by civil society. KAIROS denounced Canada's aggressive policing, and World Vision assessed G8 commitments as woefully inadequate to meet existing needs.[77]

2011 France—Respecting the 'Other'

The religious landscape in France is predominantly Roman Catholic. Although the Catholic Church affirms the importance of interreligious dialogue and dialogue between religion and politics for purposes of the common good,[78] the form of dialogue is usually bilateral between the Catholic Church and other faith traditions.[79] The process of obtaining official Roman Catholic Church sponsorship for a summit would be too lengthy and complex to maintain summit continuity within the existing timeframe. As with Canada, the G8/G20 political leaders would both be meeting in France in 2011: the G8 on May 26–27, 2011 in Deauville and the G20 on November 3–4, 2011 in Cannes. If the F8/F7/F20 summit process was going to continue, it would have to be organized by leaders of religious minorities in a context where the national inter-religious infrastructure was too weak to support a process comparable to that which had just occurred in Canada.

His Eminence Metropolitan Emmanuel Adamakis served as Secretary-General for the 2011 F8 Summit. He worked with leaders from the Greek Orthodox and Bahá'í community traditions to form a 2011 Inter-Faith Partnership that hosted, under the patronage of the Council of the Christian Churches in France, a two-day Summit on May 23–24, 2011 at the Hotel Pullman in Bordeaux, France. Invitations were issued on short notice in large part because there was a shortage of funds available for sponsoring delegation

---

75 Hajnal, "The G20," 25.

76 Aidid et al., "Report on Civil Society and the 2010 G8 Muskoka Summit."

77 Ibid.

78 For commentary on Pope Francis' attitude, for example, see Paola Bernardini, *Contending Modernities*, March 6, 2014, https://blogs.nd.edu/contendingmodernities/2014/03/06/dialogue-between-the-catholic-church-and-the-modern-world/.

79 Bradford Hinze, *Practices of Dialogue in the Roman Catholic Church* (New York, New York: The Continuum Publishing Group, 2006), 192–195.

transportation costs. Thirty eight religious leaders, many from Europe, representing all G8 delegations and most regions of the world convened to develop
a collaborative statement of concerns for conveyance to government leaders.
Representatives came from a variety of faith traditions including Buddhism,
the Bahá'í faith, Islam, the Jewish tradition, Protestantism, Catholicism, the
Russian Orthodox Church, the Anglican Communion, the Greek Orthodox
Church, the Armenian Church, the Konko tradition, and the All Africa Conference of Churches. This was the first summit for the majority of participants,
but a third of the participants had been present at the Canadian Summit and a
tenth of the attendees had attended four or more summits since 2005. Keynote
addresses included "Justice in Economic Reform" by Rabbi Richard Marker,
"Urgent Action for the Achievement of the Millennium Development Goals"
by Hamilton, and "The Power of Multi-Religious Cooperation for Peace" by
Vendley.

There were five moderated working sessions. Session 1 focused on Reforming
Global Governance and was moderated by Bishop Marc Camille Michel Stenger
following comments given by Andre Karamaga and Hegumen Philaret Bulekov. Session 2 focused on The Macro Economic Situation and was moderated
by Dr. Sayyid M. Syeed following comments given by Rev. Rüdiger Noll. Session 3 focused on Climate Change moderated by Rev. Dr. John Chryssavgis
following comments given by Canon Guy Wilkinson and Miyake. Session 4
focused on Development and was moderated by Bhai Sahib Bhai Mohinder
Singh Ji following comments made by Ms. Doris Peschke (General Secretary,
Churches Commission for Migrants in Europe) and Dr. Jan de Volder (Editor,
Tertio magazine, Community of Sant'Egidio, Belgium). Session 5 focused on
Investing in Peace and was moderated by Dr. Mohammad Sammak following
comments given by Mar Gregorios Yohanna Ibrahim and Martin Affolderbach.

Religious minority rights and the problems that flow from state favoritism toward religious majorities, particularly in relation to growing tensions
within Syria, were extensively discussed during the two days of dialogue. This
agenda was in-keeping with aspects of the French G8 agenda which focused on
international peace and security, development in Africa and accountability as
well as the French G20 focus on reform of the international monetary system,
corruption and economic development.[80] The 2011 France F8 Summit participants emphasized the following key points:[81]

---

80   Religious leaders did not specifically address the Euro zone crisis stemming from Greece's
     financial problems that came to unexpectedly dominate the French G20 agenda. See
     Hajnal, "The G20," 25–26.
81   F8-Canada, "A Time for Inspired Leadership and Action."

- Expanded dialogue & partnership between religious communities and the G8/G20 system
- Integration of the G8/G20 more fully into the UN System, increasing representation for vulnerable countries
- Greater transparency and accountability to ensure G8/G20 promise keeping
- Development of a just and binding climate change agreement
- Increased development budgets to reach the promised 0.7% of GDP assistance, attainment of universal access for HIV/AIDS treatment, and implementation of prior commitments
- Increased financial support for non-military instruments, including dialogue, for peacemaking

Immediately following the Summit, the collaborative statement of concerns was delivered to the governments participating in the upcoming 37th G8 Deauville Summit and the G20 Cannes Summit through the French Secretary-General of the G8 and G20.[82] Hamilton and Vendley called upon the G8 and G20 countries via the French Secretary-General to foster an expanded partnership with the religious communities.[83] In particular, Hamilton spoke to the importance of developing a deeper understanding of how Islam and democracy are not incompatible, and how improved dialogue can help identify implications for nations with a religious majority undergoing changes in contexts where religious minorities are experiencing persecution.

President Sarkozy claims to have spent a tenth of what Canada spent hosting the Summits in Deauville and Cannes, but they also turned the meeting venues into veritable fortresses to contain civil society protests. Civil society still managed to issue press statements, protest, convene public awareness events and workshops, collaborate with other civil society organizations, and participate in formal consultations and special events.[84] Civil society's "big push" to address growing inequities and finance for MDG fulfillment to meet 2015 targets was beginning to gain momentum.[85] The day before the Summit,

82   Anna Keller, "World Religious Leaders Urge G8 and G20 Governments to Invest in Peace," (2011), http://www.cimer.org.au/documents/WorldReligiousLeadersUrgeGovernments .pdf.

83   Kate Bruce-Lockhart et al., "Report on Civil Society and the 2011 G8 Deauville Summit," (2011).

84   Bruce-Lockhart et al., "Report on Civil Society and the 2011 G8 Deauville Summit."

85   Gorik Ooms et al., "Financing the Millennium Development Goals for Health and Beyond: Sustaining the 'Big Push,'" *Globalization & Health* 6 (2010); Jan Vandemoortele, "The MDG Conundrum: Meeting the Targets without Missing the Point," *Development Policy Review* 27, no. 4 (2009).

Oxfam called on G8 leaders to take an active stance on unfulfilled past promises before committing to something new. On May 26, World Vision wrote an Open Letter to the spouses of G8 leaders, encouraging them to draw attention to food security, hunger and poverty as they enjoyed the French cuisine served at summit events.[86]

When the political leaders met, they agreed to support democracy in the Arab Spring. They established the *Deauville Partnership* to further development and agreed to host a global immunization summit. They produced a *Cannes Action Plan for Growth and Jobs* targeted toward stimulating the global economy, promising to be fully transparent in meeting their pledges.

Faith based civil society organizations praised leaders for improving financial transparency and affirming aspirations for freedom of religion in the Arab world.[87] Even so, most still considered G8 and G20 meeting outcomes to be too slow, vague and inadequate to fulfill MDG commitments by the impending 2015 deadline when existing commitments were currently set to expire.[88]

2012 United States—Special Delivery

The separation of church and state in the United States meant that whichever religious representative hosted the Summit would need to do so without state financial support. The National Council of Churches in the United States had not been involved in past summits. Pragmatic American culture offered little motivation for faith-based NGOs and other parachurch organizations to invest funds in a costly summit with the MDG 2015 deadline fast approaching. Galvanizing religious support for meetings proved difficult. Neither transportation nor housing costs were covered for delegates. The G8 political leaders made a last minute venue change on March 5, 2012 from Chicago to Camp David. This caught many civil society groups by surprise and impacted what little faith-based organizational efforts had managed to get underway.[89] Internal tensions within the International Continuance Committee disrupted the communication flow about available resources and summit expectations between past Secretaries-General and the US Summit hosts. In the end, a Joint Religious Leadership Coordination for the Summits (JRLCS) was formed consisting primarily of RfP US and the Berkley Center at Georgetown University. A short summit would convene to develop a common statement of concerns to be shared with G8 and G20 leaders.

---

86   Bruce-Lockhart et al., "Report on Civil Society and the 2011 G8 Deauville Summit."
87   Hamilton, "The G8 Speaks but is There Action to Follow?"
88   Bruce-Lockhart et al., "Report on Civil Society and the 2011 G8 Deauville Summit."
89   Tejas Parasher et al., "Media Analysis of the G8 and the 2012 Camp David Summit," (2012), http://www.g8.utoronto.ca/evaluations/csed/.

Rev. Bud Heckman served as Secretary-General for the 2012 F8 US Summit. He provided leadership to the JRLCS which hosted a one-day Summit in Washington DC in the Berkley Center's office on May 17. International invitations were sent out last minute (less than one week ahead of time) which resulted in a greatly reduced international representation. US hosts gave international delegates such short notice that several who wanted to come, simply couldn't. Japanese delegates came despite such short notice, but the one-day event was over before they had recovered from jet lag. Japan and Canada were the only international G8 delegations present. The process was run more like a business meeting than prior summits due, in part, to the shortness of the event (9 am to 5 pm) and unexpected problems that prevented the opening speaker from attending. When the opening speaker didn't show, organizers began the Summit by having participants work on the draft statement.

Presentations were made by Father Thomas J. Reese who briefed delegates on the US political context, Max Finberg who spoke about the domestic collaborative process between religion and politics that operates through 13 faith-based advisory centers, Sarah Hildebrandt who spoke about the Millennium Kids' work promoting MDG promise fulfillment in Canada, and Marshall, who spoke about the Berkley Center's work that focuses on religion and global development with attention to gender and the environment. Twenty three representatives from faith based organizations representing Muslim, Catholic, Protestant, Episcopal, Shinto, Jewish, Jain, Russian Orthodox, and Quaker traditions participated in a closed meeting for the day at the Berkley Center. A Fellow for the JRLCS compiled a six page briefing document for participants providing information on the G8 and G20 2012 agenda. The 2012 F8 Summit took place in advance of the 38th G8 Summit at Camp David May 18–19, and the G20 Summit in Los Cabos, Mexico June 16–17. Issues for discussion at the Berkley Center meeting included the Deauville Partnership (regarding governance reforms in light of the Arab Spring), global health, food security, and an array of economic concerns. Participants were interviewed during the day and a professional video was created that recapped the summit process. A press release was issued that resulted in minimal media reports. The DC hosts networked with their counterparts in Mexico, and Rabbi Elías Szczytnicki delivered the joint statement via a religious leader delegation to the Sherpas working on the G20. The 2012 Religious Leaders' Statement for the G8 and G20 Summits has been documented as one of seven other outside communications addressed to the G20 that year from NGOs and coalitions, business groups and individuals.[90] Despite the late organization of the Summit process, the US F8 Summit managed to extend the long history of religious and interreligious organizations

---

90   Hajnal, "The G20," 178.

using the occasion of global summits to articulate shared moral concerns and articulate policy recommendations. In the absence of a UK delegation, Miyake offered to pass leadership on to the United Kingdom for hosting the process in 2013, then he offered prayers to close Summit proceedings. The 2012 US F8 Summit participants emphasized the following key points:[91]

- Regulate, reform and stabilize the economy to be just as well as sustainable, paying particular attention to the marginalized, the poor, women and children
- Publish self-accountability reports and fulfill past commitments with particular attention to meeting the 2015 MDG deadline
- Attend to basic needs in ways that support local farmers, encourage plant-based nutrition, and provide all peoples with access to clean water and nutritious food

As for the G8 and G20 process, they continued with further signs of evolution and change. For the first time since joining the G8 in 1997, Russia did not attend the G8 Summit. The last minute venue change to Camp David prevented civil society from the type of direct G8 engagement characteristic of past summits; there were very few US on-site protests and civil society activities in 2012.[92] Information about the process was dependent upon communication from government representatives and official press releases, and G8 interaction with civil society groups was rarely discussed.[93]

Civil society inclusion was emphasized by the Mexican president of the 2012 G20 Summit in Los Cabos, however. In the months leading up to the Summit, the Mexican Sherpa, Lourdes Aranda, met continually with representatives of business, labor, think tanks, and civil society and publicly posted information about the dialogue process on their website at g20mexico.org where the parallel language associated with official engagement partners began to crystallize (e.g., B20, L20, etc.).[94] Considerable resources were devoted to hosting side events (e.g., Young Entrepreneurs Summit, Youth20, Rethinking20, Girls20, Trade20), ensuring full access to the media centre, providing daily briefings, and providing a cultural pavilion for NGO exhibitions to ensure comprehensive

---

91   F8-United States, "Religious Leaders' Statement for the G8 and G20 Summits," (2012), http://www.g8.utoronto.ca/interfaith/.

92   Parasher et al., "Media Analysis of the G8 and the 2012 Camp David Summit."

93   Ibid., 8.

94   Tristen Naylor, "Civil Society Inclusion at Los Cabos 2012," (2012), http://www.g20.utoronto.ca/analysis/120626-naylor.html.

representation of global stakeholders.[95] Civil society influence on the process itself, however, was somewhat marginally inclusive. Accreditation for civil society NGOs was provided last and only three days prior to the Summit, they were denied access to the B20 meetings, and the rooms designated for their activities was physically located a significant distance from the convention centre and the media rooms. When civil society organizations hosted their own press conference, the Mexican Foreign Ministry shut-down the press conference midstream, stopping a reporter in the middle of a question to the assembled panel of activists.[96] Although civil society organizations were invited to participate in the Mexican Presidency's preparatory process, no mention was made of civil society and their concerns in the *Los Cabos Communiqué*.

The 2012 F8 Summit marked completion of one full round of engagement with the evolving G8/G20 system. The US host, Bud Heckman, coauthored an article with Canadian leader Hamilton that was published in *G8*. The preparatory Summit publication was distributed to participants at both G8 and G20 2012 Summits. In their article, Hamilton and Heckman used the imagery of an 'open spiral' to describe the 2012 F8 Summit: the process was 'complete' and 'finished,' but 'continuing' and 'ongoing; was 'not just a closing of the eight-year cycle,' but also 'part of the open spiral, continuing to build on the parallel faith leaders' summits that have gone before'; as 'building collaboration and unity for common witness on shared moral concerns (soft advocacy),' but also 'working in specific ways to influence the policy agenda (hard advocacy)'; and 'as both an end and a new beginning'.[97] Now that civil society's participation in global governance was beginning to be recognized by the G20 in a somewhat limited, subordinate, and marginalized way,[98] the F8 International Continuance Committee would begin to discuss how the F8 process, too, might appropriately evolve.[99]

2013 United Kingdom—All a Twitter

Not all F8 Initiatives have involved face-to-face meetings. The Anglican Church was positioned for hosting the F8 summit on the occasion of the G8, but they were unable to conduct advanced planning because of a leadership turnover

---

95   Ibid.

96   Ibid., 3.

97   Karen Hamilton, "The Open Spiral: The Ongoing Commitments of Faith Leaders," in *G8 the Camp David Summit: The Road to Recovery*, ed. John Kirton and Madeline Koch (Toronto, Canada: Newsdesk Media Group, 2012).

98   Naylor, "Civil Society Inclusion at Los Cabos 2012."

99   Steiner, "Reflexive Governance Dynamics Operative within Round One of the World Religious Leaders' Dialogue with the G8 (2005–2013)."

with the Archbishop of Canterbury. Once the new Archbishop Justin Welby took office, little time remained for hosting face-to-face meetings. Extensive ICC conversations had already been exploring a variety of possible formats. Defenders of summits lasting 2 or more days considered longer summits to be worth the expense if only for practical reasons. The time gap in combination with the physical challenge of people coming from half way around the world necessitated opportunities for rest. Advocates for change were a bit more critical. UK representatives questioned how the summit seemed to have developed a life of its own since 2005, expanding without checks and balances "as part of the interfaith industry." The opportunity to explore alternative formats was opened-up once delegates began "to question what we want to achieve and if this is the best way of operating." In 2013, Charles Reed led the Initiative for reworking the model, "despite the success of previous encounters." Organizers did not want financial and organizational pressures to impede the ability of hosts to offer religious leaders "the opportunity to make a recognisable and credible impact on public and political debates ahead of the G8 Summit ... with attention squarely focused on desirable outputs rather than on process."[100] The United Kingdom decided to sponsor a social media campaign. They used electronic communication to develop an international statement that would be released to the media which they published as an open letter and directed to the G8 leadership.

Religious leaders also launched a #1000DaysToGo Twitter Campaign on April 5, 2012 as part of the civil society 'MDG push' which was now in full swing. This date marked 1000 days to go before arrival of the deadline agreed upon by the international community for MDG goal completion. As each person used Twitter, they formed networks as they followed, replied, retweeted and mentioned one another. Participants used the hashtag #1000daystogo.

Twitter campaigns can be analyzed to reveal information about the degree to which participants are publicly engaged. The #1000DaysToGo Twitter Campaign network was visualized and analyzed using the software package NodeXL.[101] The tweeting behavior of socially isolated tweeters typically displays a star-shaped ego-network pattern. When people are socially connected, however, the tweeting behavior displays a different pattern that reflects how users direct their tweets to other groups and develop followers. Socially connected Twitter

---

100   Ibid.

101   NodeXL is a free and open add-in for Excel 2007/2010/2013. NodeXL is a project from the Social Media Research Foundation, a not-for-profit organization dedicated to creating open tools, open data, and open scholarship related to social media. NodeXL is commonly used by Pew Research Center to analyze Twitter social media networks.

users display what is referred to as an alter-ego network pattern that breaks down into identifiable groups. The more socially engaged a Twitter campaign becomes, the more it displays alter-ego networks of multiple groupings. Social media network data for the #1000DaysToGo Twitter Campaign was collected from Twitter, analyzed and visualized for two Twitter Campaign participants in the #1000DaysToGo Initiative: the Millennium Development Kids (from the Canadian delegation) and the Anglicans (representing the UK hosts). Millennium Development Kids is a non-profit formed as part of the Canadian F8 process to mobilize civil society for purposes of fulfilling MDG commitments. Visualization of their network indicates that they are socially networked with six identifiable groups (see Figure 6.1). Millennium Development Kids is represented by the square on the left. Some of the groups with which they engage include government representatives (red), civil society (blue), faith-based groups (light green), and family members (dark green). There is some indication of a star-shaped ego network (purple), but the lines emanating outward toward other groups on the right indicate that the dominant pattern is one of social engagement. The Archbishop of Canterbury's network (@lambeth-palace) is visualized in Figure 6.1. In this figure, the size of each circle has been adjusted to reflect the size of each tweeter's following. The Archbishop's

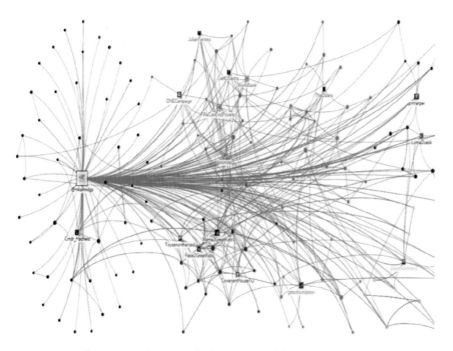

FIGURE 6.1 *Millennium Development Kids alter ego network by groups*

star-shaped ego network (purple) includes a diverse array of connections including media (BBCNews), high-level political leadership (BarakObama), and RNGOs (ChristianAid). At the time of this analysis in 2013, the Archbishop's social network organizes into five groupings of largely faith-based tweeters that range from a more general faith-based (blue) and individual (dark green) orientation to denominationally specific identifications (red). Unlike predominantly star-shaped social network patterns that indicate the self-referential behavior of socially isolated individuals, analysis of the 2013 F8 #1000DaysToGo Twitter Campaign indicate an outwardly focused pattern of social engagement with a variety of groups in different sectors of society including governance, media, and civil society (faith-based and secular). The social media campaign provided the first visual display of the type of civic engagement networks involved in the religious summitry process (see Figure 6.2), and connected the F8 process with a new generation of social media users who utilize modern technologies.

Using email, the ICC also developed a collaborative statement. They solicited and incorporated interfaith feedback on the draft over a period of several months before obtaining signatories. On April 5, 2013, 80 religious leaders collectively wrote to G8 leaders, "urging them to keep promises on foreign aid and invest in sustainable development.[102] The statement was sent to the *Financial Times*, and posted on various religious and news websites. The UK Initiative

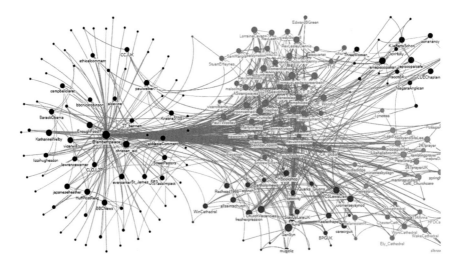

FIGURE 6.2 *Anglican Twitter network by groups for Twitter campaign 2013*

---

102   Hajnal, "The G20," 99.

allowed the F8 process to continue despite financial constraints and organizational fragility during a time of transition and reorganization. Unlike recent
years where religious leaders had directed their concerns to the G20 as well
as the G8, the UK Initiative focused only on the G8 in relation to the United
Kingdom's Presidency's agenda of tax, trade and transparency. The 2013 UK F8
participants emphasized the following key points:[103]

- Although new goals are being discussed by the G8, meeting existing MDG
  commitments remains morally imperative
- The G8 agenda referencing tax, trade and transparency presents an opportunity for the G8 to make policies that strike at the underlying causes of
  poverty with fair tax practices, fair trade & tax transparency
- Leaders specifically asked G8 leaders to spend 0.7% of Gross National Product on aid, launch a G8 Convention on Tax Transparency, and press for
  greater financial transparency from developing countries

Communications with G20 leaders was less direct that year. Hamilton published
again in the *G8* publication that was distributed at both G8 and G20 Summits.
In 2013, she spoke about the UK Initiative and the history of the process dating
back to 2005, emphasizing the importance of fulfilling MDG promises made
to the global community in 2000.[104] Some RNGOs participated in civil society
engagement with the G20 which met in St. Petersburg, Russia in 2013.[105] The F8
Initiative did not direct a communication to the G20 in 2013 because, in part,
relations with Russia were showing signs of increasing strain. Their religious
leader representative to the ICC had gone silent after failing to show at the
2012 meetings that were convened in the United States. In the absence of a
national host, religious leaders chose not to address the 2013 G20 leaders meeting in Russia where civil society organizations were struggling to find a way to
legitimately engage with the process even as political leaders struggled to enter
a new phase of productivity, accountability and effectiveness.[106]

---

103   F8-United Kingdom, "UK Can Lead G8 in Striking at Causes of Poverty, Say Religious
       Leaders," (2013), http://www.archbishopofcanterbury.org/articles.php/5045/archbishop
       -joins-call-on-g8-to-strike-at-causes-of-poverty.
104   Karen Hamilton, "After 13 Years, the Millennium Development Goals Are Still Pertinent,"
       in *G8 the UK Summit Lough Erne: Helping Global Trade to Take Off*, ed. John Kirton, Mad-
       eline Koch, and Nicholas Bayne (London, UK: Newsdesk Media, 2013).
105   Burrow et al., "G20 2014: Perspectives from Business, Civil Society, Labour, Think Tanks
       and Youth," 17–18.
106   Mike Callaghan et al., "Challenges Facing the G20 in 2013."

2014 Australia—New Beginnings

The ICC's decision to not further the F8 process in the absence of a national host made the ongoing process particularly vulnerable in 2014 when it was Russia's turn to host the G8. The ICC had not expanded their membership to incorporate G20 representation even though they had been directing statements toward their leadership representatives since 2010. Russia's actions in Ukraine began early in the year, further complicating matters.[107] On March 24, Prime Minister David Cameron, President Barack Obama and other world leaders suspended Russia from the elite group of leading economies on the basis of President Putin's breach of international law. The G8 officially became the G7.[108] Political leaders agreed to meet without Russia until such a time as their head of state indicated a willingness to engage in 'meaningful discussion.' The previously scheduled G8 Sochi Summit was cancelled, and the G7 met in Brussels on June 4–5. The F8 Russian Summit was also cancelled. "While a 2014 interfaith leaders' summit in Russia would have been an important opportunity to strengthen global faith relationships and to make a strong statement about future directions for the faith leaders and the G7/8 in pursuit of sustainable living and equity for all people," wrote Hamilton, "the interfaith leaders' summit process has gained such strength and momentum that its continuity, consistency and persistency will carry its statements and priorities into 2015 and beyond."[109]

Interfaith youth connected to the F8 2010 Canadian Summit convened a 2014 pre-conference on July 13–18, 2014 in Kaub, Germany that was attended by 19 youth from 19 countries with faith representation from Muslim, Jewish, Bahá'í, and Christian faith traditions to focus on three overarching issues: peace, justice and education. The policy and advocacy team drafted a F7 statement directed to the G7 in preparation of the 2015 MDG deadline. The draft statement was circulated for feedback from civil society networks in each participant's home country. Youth continued to make plans for a summit scheduled to convene May 23–30, 2015 that planned to bring delegates from many countries to talk about local projects and the transition from the MDGs to the SDGs.

---

107   Uri Friedman, "Russia's Slow-Motion Invasion of Ukraine," *The Atlantic*, August 29 2014.

108   Tamara Cohen, "G8 Becomes the G7 as Leaders Kick Russia Out: It's Not a Big Problem, Says Putin's Foreign Minister," *Daily Mail* (2014), http://www.dailymail.co.uk/news/article-2588490/G8-G7-leaders-kick-Russia-Its-not-big-problem-says-Putins-foreign -minister.html.

109   Karen Hamilton, "Keeping the Faith: Still Focused on Goals," in *G7 the Brussels Summit: Strengthening the Global Network*, ed. John Kirton and Madeline Koch (London, UK: Newsdesk Media, 2014).

As Hamilton wrote about the importance of "keeping the faith" and "staying focused on goals" despite the disruption that interrupted the planned F8 interfaith leaders' Summit for 2014,[110] an independent F20 process was emerging halfway around the globe. Later that year, Christie was asked to present on the F8 history at the 21st International Law and Religion Symposium convened by the Center for Law and Religion Studies, founded by Durham. When Dr. Frederick Axelgard—lawyer and former diplomat with an extensive career in public policy and international business centered in Washington DC— heard the presentation, he invited Christie to present at the first iteration of an F20 Summit that had been independently planned to convene in Australia the following month.

On November 16–18, 2014, immediately following the political G20 Summit, Brian Adams and Durham served as Secretaries-General to convene a three-day Summit in relation to the G20 Australian Summit. From the beginning, the F20 was convened to enable subjects such as religious freedom to become part of G20 political discourse. The Summit was co-sponsored by the State of Queensland, the United Arab Emirates Ministry of Culture, Youth and Community Development, and the International Centre of Law and Religion Studies at Brigham Young University.

More than 100 academic, faith and government leaders convened at the Crowne Plaza Surfers Paradise Hotel to engage in international dialogue centered on economic development, religious freedom and social cohesion. The Summit was built on a strong international base. Significant emphasis was placed on the relationship between the freedom of religion and free enterprise, profiling evidence in support of a positive relationship between economic growth and religious freedom. Many positive relations were developed between scholars, lawyers, political leaders, and faith and interfaith leaders from a variety of traditions including Anglican, Bahá'í , Buddhist, LDS, Muslim, Jewish, Catholic, Protestant, and Orthodox traditions. Presentations were videotaped, archived, and made available for public access.[111] Keynote addresses included, but were not limited to, presentations on religious freedom by Commissioner Tim Wilson from the Australian Human Rights Commission and Dr. Katrina Lantos Swett; presentations that identified connections between religious freedom, religion and the economy by Dr. Brian Grim and Dr. Ram Cnaan; presentations that explored relations between law, religion and economic issues by Dr. Augusto Zimmerman from Murdoch University,

---

110   Ibid.

111   Presentations   can   be   viewed   at   http://www.g20interfaith.org/content/archive
          -presentations.

Dr. Paul Babie from University of Adelaide, Dr. Neil Foster from University of Newcastle, and Dr. Nigel Zimmermann from University of Notre Dame; and presentations on religious rights and economic development by Dr. Carmen Asiain Pereira, Dr. Juan Navarro Floria (Pontificia Universidad Católica Buenos Aires, Argentina), Dr. Faizan Mustafa (Vice Chancellor of Nalsar University of Law, India), and Durham. Parallel Sessions were convened on "Interfaith Dialogue and Social Cohesion," "International Perspectives on Humanitarian Aid, Economic Development and Religious Charities," "Youth Perspectives on Religious Freedom and Human Rights," "International Perspectives on Interfaith Relations and Religious Freedom," and "Dialogue and Diapraxis." In keeping with G20 culture, the F20 Summit dedicated a session to a Parliamentary Panel where four Australian Members of Parliament engaged with participants on religion and the economy. Several media outlets discussed the Summit including *Daijiworld, Gulf Today,* and *The Australian. ABC Australia* ran several podcasts from interviews conducted during the event that ran through November and December.[112] Although the F20 convened the day following the end of the G20, the 2014 Australian F20 Summit nevertheless published a communiqué intended to become part of G20 culture that emphasized the following key points:[113]

- Careful regulation of the global financial systems should be done with attention to the shared humanity and equality of all people with transparency and affirmation of religious diversity
- Employment outcomes should provide job security, reasonable working conditions, fair wages, and equal access for the young, the old, women and minorities
- Natural resources should be ethically and sustainably developed; development should protect both climate and societies
- Development should focus on the root causes of global hunger and poverty
- Women should be supported in leadership roles to act as change agents for promoting sustainable civil societies

Although the G20 did not receive this statement prior to their deliberations, they did hear from faith leaders afterwards. For example, on June 13, 2014, Miyake visited the Japanese Parliament and directly handed over a letter addressed to the G20 Leaders to Hon. Katsunobu Kato, the Deputy Chief Cabinet

---

112   See http://www.g20interfaith.org/content/media-coverage.

113   F20-Australia, "Statement from the G20 Interfaith Summit 2014," (2014), http://www
      .g20interfaith.org/sites/default/files/2014-interfaith-summit/Consensus-Statement.pdf.

Minister of the Japanese Government, along with an oral explanation about the ongoing activities of the F8/F7/F20 Initiative. His visit was part of ongoing ICC internal communication encouraging civic engagement with the G-plus System.[114]

For the first time, civil society was officially recognized by the G20 as an engagement partner. The coordinator for the C20 engagement group was Reverend Tim Costello, CEO of World Vision Australia which is an RNGO. Whereas B20 engagement helps the G20 restore the confidence of investors and consumers in the wake of the global financial crisis, the C20 was engaged by the G20 to reinvigorate community engagement as a way of restoring confidence *in* governments, business, and institutions by encouraging policymakers to listen more intently to the voices of the excluded.[115] A collaborative policy development process utilizing an open web platform was used for dialogue during the months leading up to the Melbourne Summit. The C20 submitted four, detailed policies into the G20 system for Sherpa consideration, but getting C20 policies actually onto the G20 formal agenda remained a challenge.[116] G20 leaders engaged in dialogue with the C20 were motivated by an increasing recognition that growth is not an automatic job-creator, and policies must be attentively guided to address the 'youth bulge,' the needs of women, minorities and the elderly.[117] The advantage for religious involvement with the C20 was having direct access to the governance process, but the drawback of this strategy was that faith-based input became more narrowly confined to development and sustainability concerns.

2015 Istanbul—Consolidation

The MDG deadline arrived. After speeches from Pope Francis and the Nobel Laureate Malala Yousafzai, on September 25, 2015, a new set of Sustainable Development Goals was adopted by 193 countries at the start of a three-day UN Summit on sustainable development.[118] The SDGs expanded the eight MDGs to an agenda consisting of 17 goals designed to end poverty and hunger by 2030. Pope Francis became the first Pope to address the UN assembly. He made a

---

114 Yoshinobu Miyake, Email, June 14 2014.

115 Burrow et al., "G20 2014: Perspectives from Business, Civil Society, Labour, Think Tanks and Youth."

116 Ibid., 20.

117 Ibid.

118 Sam Jones and Carla Kweifio-Okai, "World Leaders Agree Sustainable Development Goals—as It Happened," *The Guardian* (2015), https://www.theguardian.com/global -development/live/2015/sep/25/un-sustainable-development-summit-2015-goals-sdgs -united-nations-general-assembly-70th-session-new-york-live.

forceful speech to the UN warning against selfishness. He asserted that nature, as well as humanity, had rights. "Any harm done to the environment," he said, "is harm done to humanity. The ecological crisis, and the large-scale destruction of biodiversity, can threaten the very existence of the human species."[119]

The F8/F7/F20 Initiative continued to evolve and strengthen in 2015. After the 2014 Australian F20 Summit, Adams had asked Christie to join the review team and continue with future planning. Christie suggested, and existing members of the independent F20 process agreed, that additional members from the F8 steering committee join the planning team—Miyake and Hamilton. The F8 leadership brought a history of international engagement experience to the F20 leadership's vision of engagement with the G20 process. In response to the changing world, the steering committees evolved into the current F8/F7/F20 Initiative.[120] Christie describes the transition from the F8 process to connection with the F20 process and the subsequent evolution into the F8/F7/F20 Initiative as an organic, grace-filled process (from a Christian religious perspective) that could not have happened without the support of the Church of Jesus Christ of Latter-day Saints.[121] Brigham Young University's ICLRS hosted the conference that became the bridge between the two processes that resulted in the F8/F7/F20 Initiative in its current form.

More than 300 participants including 140 speakers and session chairs met on November 16–18, 2015 for the F20 Summit in Istanbul, Turkey. Participants represented all continents and more than 40 individual countries. The highest representation was from Turkey itself, followed by strong delegations from North America, Europe, Central Asia, China, India, the Pacific, South America, and Africa. Plenary and breakout sessions were organized around themes inspired by the United Nations' new SDGs.

Dynamics at the 2015 Summit were significantly influenced by international events immediately preceding the Summit. Three days prior, just as many international speakers were catching airplanes to attend the Summit, terrorist attacks at six locations in and just outside of Paris on November 13, 2015 resulted in 128 deaths and hundreds of wounded in France.[122] When the Summit convened on November 16, 2015, almost every speaker opened their talks with some form of reflection on the Paris bombings. In some cases, speakers set aside their prepared comments entirely to address international terrorism

---

119   Ibid.

120   Adams.

121   Christie.

122   Steve Almasy, Pierre Meilham, and Jim Bittermann, "Paris Massacre: At Least 128 Die in Attacks," CNN (2015), http://www.cnn.com/2015/11/13/world/paris-shooting/.

from an interfaith perspective. Dynamics quickly shifted to include panelist commentary on the Ankara blasts in October where more than 90 were killed by blasts from suicide bombings in the Turkish capital.[123] Eventually participants paid attention to international terrorism in many other parts of the world that often go unacknowledged in international circles.[124] Significant and unplanned dialogue occurred throughout the conference exploring concrete ways participants could exercise leadership to reduce and interrupt the culture of terrorism and terrorist behavior. Delegates discussed how they might draw upon their networks and resources to provide alternatives to the 'lost generation' from the youth bulge to better integrate them into the global economy. Diverse pathways for democratic engagement were presented by Islamic scholars. For example, Professor Emre öktem from Galatasaray University explained and critiqued the religious logic behind the Daish (ISIL) destruction of pre-monotheistic religious heritage in Iraq and Syria. He then offered a counter-religious logic rooted in Islamic tradition. In recent years, Daish has intentionally destroyed pre-monotheistic remnants of ancient civilizations under the pretext that this heritage was idolatrous, not Islamic, and against the spirit of prayer. Their sect teaches that if they encounter objects that have been used for idolatry, they must be destroyed. There is a double standard, he said, in that many of these artifacts have been smuggled through Turkey and sold on the black market to fund their operations. Their behavior illustrates the inherent conflict between their rigid religious ideology and the intransigent realities of life. After critiquing the selling of archaeology under a façade of Islamic legality as hypocritical, öktem presented an alternative Islamic perspective regarding the destruction of archeological heritage. He identified seven chapters in the Qur'an where the text invites Muslims to contemplate and learn from the ruins of ancient civilizations. His main point was that destruction of this heritage prevents devotees from doing their Islamic duty to contemplate what these civilizations did to result in their destruction. At the Summit, alternative interpretations, such as the one presented by Emre öktem, were shared as cultural resources to offer religiously motivated individuals an alternative

---

123   Constanza Letsch and Nadia Khomami, "Turkey Terror Attack: Mourning after Scores Killed in Ankara Blasts," *The Guardian* (2015), https://www.theguardian.com/world/2015/oct/10/turkey-suicide-bomb-killed-in-ankara.

124   Even media professionals acknowledge this oversight. See, for example, Jonathan Kealing, "This Weekend's Terrorist Attacks Are Just a Handful among Hundreds. Most of Them You Don't Hear About," *Public Radio International* (2016), http://www.pri.org/stories/2016-03-22/paris-there-have-been-hundreds-terrorist-attacks-many-have-gone-unnoticed.

to what is currently being distributed by ISIL and disinformation campaigns against Islam.[125]

The 2016 G20 Interfaith Summit in Istanbul Turkey was organized by Adams, Durham, and Recep Şentürk who served as Secretaries-General to convene the *G20 Interfaith Summit: Religion, Harmony, and Sustainable Development* summit at the Barceló Eresin Topkapi Hotel in Istanbul, Turkey. More than 150 scholars, political, religious and interfaith leaders from around the world convened for dialogue as a contribution to the G20 economic forum. The event facilitated academic, faith, interfaith, economic, media, professional and political contributions from around the world to highlight a missing element in the G20 discussions. This was done in the belief that "to engender harmony and contribute to the achievement of the SDGs, there must be broad civil society discussion and action from grassroots to policymaking levels."[126] The 2015 F20 Turkey Summit convened a special panel on the impact of women of faith on sustainable development, a topic that was highlighted by Turkey's G20 Presidency which created the Women 20 (W20) engagement group.[127] Additional priorities of Turkey's G20 Presidency that were addressed at the F20 Summit include development in low-income countries, climate change, and immigration issues.[128]

Speakers included, but were not limited to, Brian Adams, Carmen Pereira, Pieter Coertzen, Cole Durham, Sharon Eubank, Marie-Claire Foblets, Brian Grim, Karen Hamilton, Peter Howard, Mark Hill QC, Tahir Mahmood, Shan Manocha, Katherine Marshall, Knox Thames, Javier Martinez-Torron from Complutense University, Faizan Mustafa, Peter Petkoff, David Saperstein, Recep Şentürk, and Katrina Swett. Attention was paid to Islamic Finance and the integration of Muslim insights into the international financial economy and sustainable development. Special NGO, youth, religious minority and women panels addressed important issues of difference that influence outcomes in relation to religion and economic development. Panelists discussed the complexities associated with religious heritage protection and how appropriate emotion management of public environments can positively contribute to dialogue among civilizations.

---

125   Islamic Culture and Relations Organization, "German Evangelical Church Leaders Meet Iranian Religious Scholars," (2015).

126   Karen Hamilton and Brian Adams, "Inspiring Leadership and Action for Development," G20 Turkey: The Antalya Summit, edited by Kirton, John and Madeline Koch, 194–195. London, UK: Newsdesk Media, 2015.

127   Ibid.

128   Ibid.

Media coverage in 2015 was somewhat of a missed opportunity. There were no media packets or public briefings. The few media representatives that did attend scrambled for space. Because organizers of the Summit did not provide adequate support for media engagement, post event media coverage was significantly less than it might have otherwise been. For example, Rachel Kohn, producer from ABC Radio National, interviewed several participants for international podcasts, but in the absence of any dedicated interview space, finding quiet venues for appropriate professional program development proved challenging.

The F20 Summit did not issue a statement in 2015, but youth connected to the process had been organizing to develop an interfaith youth statement since 2012 to present their concerns to the G-plus System. The interfaith youth Summit was supposed to have convened on May 23–30, 2015, but was abruptly canceled by the German hosts in January—but not before a preliminary interfaith and international statement had already been drafted at a pre-forum youth Summit convened on July 13–18, 2014 in Kaub, Germany with support from the Evangelical Church of Germany. The F7 youth statement was developed by 19 youth from 19 countries with faith representation from Muslim, Jewish, Bahá'í, and Christian faith traditions. When it became clear that the statement was not going to be finished with feedback at a 2015 Summit, youth created an online petition to solicit civil society support and publish their concerns as an open letter directed to the G7. The statement was subsequently endorsed by 103 people.[129] The Interfaith Youth Pre-Conference issued a Conference Statement that explored an oft-neglected determinant of the political process, the interfaith perspective. The 2015 German F7 Youth Summit participants made the following recommendations on the occasion of the G7 2015 Summit in Germany:[130]

· That the G7 fully commit to SDG implementation and achievement
· That the G7 implement human rights to food, health and social security
· That the G7 ensure transition to efficient and sufficient economic systems that address structural causes of inequality and discrimination and that accord with ecological boundaries
· That the G7 curtail human trafficking, the arms trade and land grabbing to promote peace and commit to peaceful ways of conflict resolution
· That the G7 commit to ensuring quality education for all

---

129   F7-Germany, "Interreligious Youth Forum on Sustainable Development," (2015), ekd.de/ekd_de/ds_doc/IYF_Shared_Statement_Release_01_06_2015.pdf.
130   Ibid.

Civil society engagement under the Turkish G20 Presidency was taken seriously with formation of a 14 member C20 Turkey Steering Committee that sought out the views of a broad range of institutions and countries. Although the C20 steering committee was NGO based, there was little to no RNGO representation on it. Consequently, the 2015 C20 approach to civil society engagement was decidedly more secular than what had occurred in Australia the year before.[131]

Given the history of F8 engagement with the G-plus System, the G8 and G7/G20 Research Group from the University of Toronto solicited commentary on the 2015 process from Hamilton for publication in *G7*. In reference to the 2015 G7 agenda, Hamilton said that "the G7 must work towards establishing peace and security, and ensuring that people can live a self-determined life. Freedom and human rights, democracy and the rule of law, peace and security, prosperity, and sustainable development are core principles agreed to by the G7."[132] Now that the MDGs were coming to a kind of completion in 2015, "with success achieved on some specific goals and failure on others", she noted, "the transition to the post-2015 SDGs marks an opportunity both to develop strategies, goals and objectives, and to deepen commitment to actions that will make a substantive difference in the lives of vulnerable peoples." But the process won't be easy, she acknowledged. "The SDGs' focus on creating peaceful and inclusive societies may be even more difficult to measure than the goals and objectives of the MDGs. Regardless, and in the context of the many detailed goals and objectives of the SDGs, the imperatives continue."[133]

2016 China—Entering a New Phase of Dialogue

The year 2016 marked entry into a new phase of F8/F7/F20 dialogue with the G-plus System. Since 2005, the dialogue had been characterized by a one-sided recognition during which religious leaders acknowledged the G-plus System but the importance of the F8/F7/F20 Initiative had not yet reached the collective recognition of the G-plus System's leaders. Over time, religious leaders committed increasing amounts of resources toward engagement with this group of powerful states as important partners for dialogue. Although the G8, the G7 and the G20 Research Centres at the University of Toronto attentively documented F8/F7 engagement with the G-plus System throughout Phase II, and

---

131   Sainsbury, "G20 Outreach to Society in 2015."

132   Karen Hamilton, "The Global Agenda from an Interfaith Perspective," in *G7 Germany: The Schloss Elmau Summit*, ed. John Kirton and Madeline Koch (London, UK: Newsdesk Media, 2015).

133   Ibid.

evidence showed that communiqués such as the 2012 F8 United States' Summit statement was making it into historical records of external communications received by the G20,[134] mutual recognition did not begin from within the G-plus System until early 2016. Following a G7 meeting of Foreign Ministers on April 10–11, 2016 in Hiroshima, Japan, the G7 Foreign Ministers issued the *Joint Communiqué* wherein they acknowledged the importance of cross-religious, interfaith dialogue, and freedom of religion or belief.[135] Release of this document marks the beginning of Phase III and the beginning of mutual recognition between the G-plus System and religious leaders.

In 2016, the F8/F7/F20 Initiative expanded to include regional pre-conference engagement in association with the G20 Interfaith Summit process. Two-regional pre-conferences were convened in 2016. Forty participants (Members of Parliament, academics, faith and interfaith leaders, development and peacebuilding specialists) convened at Pacific Theological College in Suva, Fiji May 2–4 at a Pacific Regional Pre-Conference, and 29 participants (Members of Parliament, academics, faith and interfaith leaders, legal experts, intercultural and terrorism experts) convened at Hotel Apollo Dimora in Trivandrum in Kerala, India July 25–26 at a South Asia Regional Pre-Conference. The Pacific Regional Pre-Conference issued an F20 Summit Statement that made the following recommendations for G20 consideration:[136]

· To address SDG4, Quality Education, that emphasis be made on holistic lifelong learning, that Pacific curricula be localized and assessed with attention to Indigenous approaches, that practical solutions be developed to build school infrastructure, and that educational outcomes be equitable for all
· To address SDG8, Decent Work & Economic Growth, faith communities commit to prophetically oppose unsustainable exploitation of natural resources, educate themselves about sustainable alternatives, and communicate details of best practices to appropriate UN and other agencies
· To address SDG 13, Climate Action, faith communities commit to model sustainable living and lobby policy makers for climate change action, and ask the G20 to establish a UN Framework to protect threatened people and nations in low lying atolls

---

134   Hajnal, "The G20," 178.
135   Ministers, *Joint Communique,* (2016).
136   F20-China, "Conference Statement: G20 Interfaith Summit Pacific Regional Preconference."

· To address SDG16, Peace, Justice and Strong Institutions, faith communities commit to the coordinated and collaborative pursuit of peace and
justice, attentive to gender justice and purposeful collaboration with
governments

With regards to F20 2016, Adams, Durham, and Zhuo Xinping served as Secretaries-General to convene the *Dialogue among Civilizations and Community
of Common Destiny for All Mankind* which met at the China Palace Hotel in
Beijing, China on August 31-September 2, 2016. Although the organizing process began a year in advance with the Secretaries-General meeting in Beijing
on multiple occasions to coordinate the process, bureaucratic constraints
delayed the ability to finalize arrangements for the event. The F20 2016 convened some 70 speakers, about 20 of whom attended from outside of China,
to discuss four topics: "Religion and Dialogue among Civilizations," "Religion
and Human Destiny Community," "G20 Interfaith Study," and "Internet Religion and Global Governance." The Summit was smaller than the meetings held
in Turkey and Australia and was convened as part of a broader Chinese Academy of Social Sciences' Forum convened August 30-September 1 in association
with the Society of Chinese Religious Studies and the Institute of World Religions. National scholars from across China engaged in two days of dialogue
with more than 20 international scholars from an array of countries including
Australia, Canada, Japan, New Zealand, Spain and the United States. Unlike the
2015 F20 meetings where the Sustainable Development Goals provided significant scaffolding for interfaith dialogue centered on SDG goal implementation,
the 2016 F20 meetings focused more on movement toward development of a
harmonious common destiny through common values that outrank divides
linked to culture or religion. Topics emphasized in Istanbul such as religious
freedom, migration, radicalism, human rights, and the perils of instrumentalizing religion were deemed less important for dialogue than a revisiting of
Samuel Huntington's 1993 'clash of civilizations' thesis.[137] Religious violence
was largely discussed in relation to discussions about developing appropriate
governance mechanisms for the Internet in relation to religion.[138]

For the first time, reflection on the F20 process itself became a thematic
topic for dialogue. Chinese scholars focused on governance developments
under discussion within the nation-state of China in relation to religion. For
example, Liu Peifeng spoke about evolving government norms and laws for

---

137   Huntington, *The Clash of Civilizations and the Remaking of the World Order.*
138   Marshall, "Shadowing the China G20 Summit: An Interreligious Gathering."

regulating the relationship between religion and charitable organizations;[139] presenters variously emphasized the wall of separation and secularization. Fang Wen spoke about the dangers of reification and the importance of developing cultural self-consciousness when engaging in social categorization.[140] International scholars, who were more familiar with the F8/F7/F20 process, tended to focus more on transnational governance contributions. For example, Elizabeta Kitanović spoke about how the interfaith forum emphasizes diversity and highlights human and religious minority rights violations; provides religious leaders with a means to caution G20 leaders against instrumentalizing religion for political purposes; allows religious leaders a means for bringing ethical perspectives into sustainable development to help address corruption; and provides opportunities to develop better knowledge across religions to reduce social hostilities and create the positive climate that is necessary for governments and businesses to do their work properly.[141] Marco Ventura identified how interfaith forums contribute to G20 governance as a component of civilization; they are indispensable to human welfare, enhancing human agency by providing purpose and energy for the formation and implementation of policies. He spoke about how religion has been empirically shown to impact global economic and financial structures, contribute to reform of the financial sector and the development of green finance, and facilitate consensus on anti-corruption measures. He identified real and potential ways in which interfaith dialogue facilitates innovation, strengthens solidarity to facilitate interconnectedness, and influences social integration to strengthen inclusion. He also addressed substantial challenges religion poses for G20 member states and G20 partner international organizations to engage with, and listen to, interfaith forums. Perhaps the biggest challenge, he said, was the challenge these possibilities and opportunities present to many religion or belief groups themselves to bridge traditional doctrines enough to share their strategies and engage with, and listen to, other communities of religion or belief.[142] Desmond

---

139   Liu Peifeng, "A Reflection on the Rationality and Paradox of Religion and Charity," in *Dialogue among Civilizations and Human Destiny Community CASS Forum* (Beijing, China2016).

140   Fang Wen, "Cultural Self-Consciousness: Transcending the Escape-Proof Net of Social Categorization," Ibid.

141   Elizabeta Kitanović, "The Impact of the G20 Interfaith Summit on the G20," Ibid.

142   Marco Ventura, "Religion as a Resource in G20 Contributions to an Innovative, Invigorated, Interconnected and Inclusive World Economy," in *Dialogue among Civilizations and Human Destiny Community CASS Forum* (Beijing, China 2016).

Cahill spoke about the real and potential role religious leaders play in protecting vulnerable groups in the current Asian context.[143]

Finally, Paul Morris addressed the role of religion in civilizational dialogue in an opening plenary address. He spoke about how human beings have organized themselves in a myriad of ways over the course of human history, and how the 353 year-old Westphalian nation-state system inadequately reflects the multiple dimensions associated with the history of governance diversity. The Westphalian agreement settled European wars enough to allow shipping and trade to proceed, but the treaties also established the principle that the sovereign state would determine the established religion operative within its borders in accordance with a minimal degree of minority recognition. As Europeans states conquered the known world, they exported this European nation-state model; part of this heritage has been a particular attitude toward religion. But every majority religion exists as a minority religion somewhere else. Migration patterns and the increasing interconnected interdependencies of a globalizing network of nations have contributed to increasing tensions within, and between, states that often involve genuine religious differences. When political leaders assert common values, he said, they draw upon current majority communities to the exclusion of minorities. This can lead to a misreading of situations. It is an approach that consigns religion to be considered only as a threat, to the exclusion of religion's possibilities for positive engagement. Paul Morris provided empirical examples where religion has positively contributed to the construction of community, and where nation-states have turned to religious communities for assistance in developing cultural continuity to ensure order during times of failed states, weak states, and social change. Those who only consider established religion within civilization dialogue offer little to nothing for religious minorities. Modern states need to explore a variety of ways for managing their religious minorities, and reflect upon how their minorities are supported or suppressed. This cannot be understood, he said, by looking at the states; one needs to listen to the actual religious minorities themselves. When state regulation of religion is deemed as excessive, a clash of sovereignties occurs. The history of religions has repeatedly involved challenges to state sovereignty. This alone may be reason enough for religions and politics to avoid developing toxic relationships so that religion and culture might be incorporated into the dialogue within, and between, civilizations. Religious traditions have long histories full of insights, not just

---

143   Desmond Cahill, "The Role of Religious Leaders in the Protection of Vulnerable Groups in the Context of 21st Century Asia," in *Dialogue among Civilizations and Human Destiny Community CASS Forum* (Beijing, China 2016).

for understanding the other, but also for the possibilities of extending equal religious rights to others. Working together with religious communities within, and between, nation-states develops a deeper understanding of religious diversity and produces fruitful dialogue about sovereignty, and the autonomy of religion and difference.[144]

2017 Germany—Officially Engaged

On June 15–17, 2017, more than a hundred experts and leaders on economy, law, politics, religion, development and humanitarian aid from 30 nations gathered in Potsdam, Germany for the fourth consecutive F20 summit to convene *Religion, Sustainable Development, and the Refugee Crisis* which met at Potsdam University. Participants stayed at a series of nearby hotels and traveled to the conference using local transportation. Durham and Adams continued to assist Secretaries-General from the host countries. Two chairs teamed up as Co-Secretaries-General to organize the event: Kathy Ehrensperger, Research Professor from Universität Potsdam and Patrick Schnabel from the Evangelische Kirche Berlin-Brandenburg-Schlesische Oberlausitz, Kirchlicher Entwicklungsdienst. As with past summits, a diverse array of religious traditions or beliefs were represented including, but not limited to, Baháʼí, Jewish, humanitarian, Konko, and various Christian traditions. Participants from a variety of interfaith (e.g., the King Abdullah bin Abdulaziz International Centre for Interreligious and Intercultural Dialogue—KAICIID, Coexister, RfP Europe), human rights (e.g., Office of UNHCR, Human Rights Department for the German Commission of Justice and Peace) organizations contributed to the dialogue. Faith representatives from the majority of G20 nations were represented. Ulrich Nitschke discussed how they are engaging civil society and non-governmental organizations such as religious and value-driven organizations, secular NGOs, community initiatives, foundations, academic institutions and other relevant development organizations to help implement the Sustainable Development Goals.

Plenary sessions developed in accordance with three themes: sustainable development, religious freedom or belief, and the economic sector. The relationship between religion and sustainable development paid particular attention to religious contributions to alleviating the refugee and famine crises. The plenary on religious freedom or belief explored the contributions faith based organizations make in contexts of weak or failed states, and the challenges associated with religious contribution to SDG fulfillment given the deep privatization of religion, the confessional nature of religious communities, and

---

144 Paul Morris, "What Is the Role of Religion in Civilizational Dialogue?"

the barriers of denominationalism. The plenary on religion and the economic sector focused on developing religious literacy for organizations to improve the quality of conversation because religion is important to the economy. Several parallel sessions focused on the relationship between religion and special interest groups important to the successful implementation of the SDGs. Delegates from Africa including Mussie Hailu Gebrestadik and Nicta Lubaale contributed perspectives focused on *Developing Partnerships with Africa*. Two concurrent sessions were focused on the interfaith youth movement: *Youth Interfaith Engagement* and *A Common Word among the Youth: Interfaith Development Goals*. A parallel session on *Women, Faith, and Human Rights* was also convened for the second time in the history of the Interfaith Summits.

A few parallel sessions addressed recent political developments. Delegates discussed the US withdrawal from the Paris Agreement in a session on *Faith, Sustainable Development and the Environment*. Delegates struggled with the need for new communication strategies in a session on *Religion, Media, and Development in the Post-Truth World*. Delegates discussed in a session on *Shrinking Space of Civil Society* how security concerns are increasingly misused to limit the freedom of religious minorities and what might be done to strengthen and defend human rights.

Several advances were made in relation to the shadowing of the G20. Prior to the Interfaith Summit, representatives from the Think20 (T20), an official engagement group during Germany's G20 Presidency that brings together research institutes and think tanks from the G20 countries to develop policy recommendations within thematic Task Forces, reached out to some religious leaders including three who were heavily involved in executing the 2017 F20 Summit: Cole Durham, Ulrich Nitschke and Katherine Marshall. They contributed to two briefs on famine[145] and refugee resettlement.[146] Both briefs were included in the final document that was sent to the G20 Sherpas.[147] German

---

145   Abu-Nimer, Mohammed, Cole Durham, Manoj Kurian, Katherine Marshall, Ulrich Nitschke, Rabbi Awraham Soetendorp, Arnhild Spence, *Engaging Religious Actors in Addressing the Famine Emergency in South Sudan, Nigeria, Somalia, and Yemen*, see http://www.g20-insights.org/policy_briefs/engaging-religious-actors-addressing-famine -emergency-south-sudan-nigeria-somalia-yemen/

146   Vitillo, Msgr. Robert, Rabbi Awraham Soetendorp, Alberto Quatrucci, Azza Karam, Attalah Fitzgibbon, Ulrich Nitschke, and Katherine Marshall. *G20 Policy Makers Should Support Wider Religious Roles in Refugee Resettlement*, see http://www.g20-insights.org/ policy_briefs/g20-policy-makers-support-wider-religious-roles-refugee-resettlement/

147   *20 Solution Proposals for the G20 from the T20 Engagement Group*, see http://www .t20germany.org/2017/05/30/20-solutions-g20/

F20 Summit participants in the T20 policy brief process emphasized the following key points:

· G20 policy makers should support wider religious roles in refugee resettlement
· Religious actors should be part of policy discussions on issues like criteria for resettlement, engagement with host communities to assure welcome, a sharp focus on the protection of unaccompanied or separated children, special measures to counter risky transit like the humanitarian corridor proposal, and post arrival reintegration in including education and trauma healing
· The G20 should engage religious actors in addressing the famine emergency in South Sudan, Nigeria, Somalia, and Yemen
· The G20 should link their support for action on famine relief to UN resolutions; a request for quarterly reporting on progress of engagement of religious institutions and leaders could help chart the future course of engagement and ensure rigor in following up on Summit commitments
· Success requires that the G20 fully engage religious leaders at senior levels in highlighting the ethical issues at stake in the famine emergency, specific engagement of religious leaders in efforts to negotiate access to areas acutely affected by famine, and cooperative (track two) peacemaking efforts with religious communities in famine affected areas

In anticipation of the 2018 G20 meetings, the Interfaith Summit Organizing Committee invited several delegates from Argentina to participate in the Potsdam meetings including the Government of Argentina's Director of Religious Freedom and Diversity from the Ministry of Foreign Affairs and Worship, the Director of Global Affairs from the National Senate, and the President of the Argentine Council for Religious Liberty. Interfaith Summit participants in the T20 think tank process reported having an impact on other think tank participants. T20 participants had been unaware of the complexity of religious organizations and interfaith participants were able to deconstruct simplistic associations of religion with violence and patriarchy. Out of the 74 policy briefs produced at the Berlin T20 Summit,[148] the briefs they work on were the only ones that incorporated religious perspectives; both policy briefs were included

---

148   There were 15 briefs on Digitalization, 8 on Climate Policy and Finance, 13 on The 2030 Agenda, 8 on Global Inequality and Social Cohesion, 6 on Forced Migration, 5 on Financial Resilience, 5 on Trade and Investment, 5 on Toward Ending Hunger and Sustainable Agriculture, 3 on International Cooperation in Tax Matters, 1 on Resilience and Inclusive

in the final document that was sent to the G20 Sherpas. As a result, the 2017 F20 Potsdam Summit marked a notable shift in strategy away from collaborative statements toward policy recommendations aimed at practical application. Members of the F20 Summit Organizing Committee advised session chairs to facilitate discussion to identify points for dialogue with the G20 to be included in the *G20 Interfaith Summit 2017 Summary Report*.[149] The G20 Interfaith Summit Executive Committee will use this information for planning purposes as they prepare for 2018 in Argentina. It is too soon to assess the impact of the policy briefs on the G20. I am completing this manuscript for the publisher prior to the G20 meetings in Hamburg scheduled for July 7–8.

Conclusion

This chapter has detailed evolution of the F8/F7/F20 Initiative from 2005 through 2017. Although the process has waxed and waned over time, the F8/F7/F20 Initiative is far stronger and more engaged with the G-plus System in 2017 than when it first began in 2005/2006 and 2014. The process is multi-faith and participative, emphasizing engagement with civil society, local communities, humanitarian relief and business. The process is consistently and persistently engaged with the G-plus System, communicating concerns on a wide variety of issues that affirm human dignity, environmental sustainability, and international security. Over time, the process has shifted from high-level religious leader participation toward engaging academia, lawmakers, and opinion makers and advisers to political leaders. Since the G-plus System first began, F8/F7/F20-G8/G7/G20 relations have moved through three phases of relations. Phase 1 (1975–2004) were the years of 'mutual ignorance' where G-plus leaders did not recognize religious leaders as potential interlocutors and religious leaders, by-and-large, did not yet realize the power and importance of the G-plus System. Phase II (2005–2015) were the years of one-sided recognition during which religious leaders acknowledged the G-plus System but the importance of the F8/F7/F20 Initiative still had not reached the collective recognition of G-plus System leaders. Phase III (2016 to the present) notes the beginning of mutual recognition beginning with the G7 acknowledgment of the importance of cross-religious, interfaith dialogue, and freedom of religion or belief in the *Joint Communiqué* from the G7 Foreign Ministers' meeting on April 10–11,

---

Growth, 3 on Circular Economy, and 2 on G20 and Africa. See http://www.g20-insights .org/policy_briefs/.

149   *Summary Reports* for the annual summits are posted at https://www.g20interfaith.org/.

2016 in Hiroshima, and ending with an invitation for engagement by a recognized engagement group—the T20. This chapter has documented the annual progression of this process as one way of 'illuminating the unseen.' We now turn attention to organizing details, external relations and various types of documentation associated with the F8/F7/F20 Initiative.

CHAPTER 7

Organizing Details, External Relations, and Documentation

The governance role of the F8/F7/F20 process in transnational relations is highlighted in this chapter. I detail variation and consistency in how the F8/F7/F20 process has been internally organized and externally engaged with the broader society. Internal organization includes discussion of steps that have been taken over time to provide organizational stability and continuity to a process that has remained an informal network. Variation in religious rituals, special events and excursions are highlighted to demonstrate how summits differ from one another depending upon the national context of the host. Organizational failure is also explored in relation to events that were planned and then aborted. In the section on external relations, I detail ways in which the F8/F7/F20 process has engaged with political leadership at different levels of government from city officials to heads of state. F8/F7/F20 engagement with other sectors of society are discussed including civil society, academia, business and the media.

Organizing the Summits

Initial F8 meetings were informally organized using a leadership rotation model. The informality has been maintained over time, allowing the international process to proceed within a nation-state framework. The Summits varied depending upon which national religious leaders hosted the event in any given context. Some leaders had more organizational infrastructural support than others. From 2005 through 2013, national hosts used a delegation model to shadow the G8 summit process (hence the name F8 and the national location of Initiative leadership provided during that time frame). Summits averaged two days in length. The Canadian meetings (2010) were the longest, although more time was spent on summitry in Japan (2008) because two meetings were convened. That same year, the international financial crisis created lasting strains on the budgets of faith-based organizations, many of which preferred to direct dwindling funds toward the humanitarian crisis rather than international gatherings. Internal pressures to reform the F8/F7/F20 process eventuated in shorter summits after Canada's hosting in 2010 (see Figure 7.1).

© KONINKLIJKE BRILL NV, LEIDEN, 2018 | DOI 10.1163/9789004365018_008

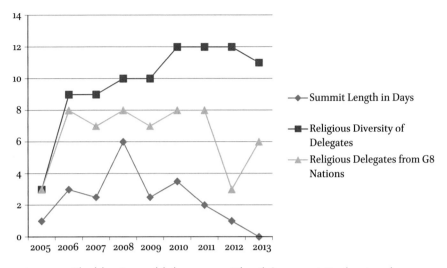

FIGURE 7.1   *The delegation model phase—summit length & representation (2005–2013)*

More pragmatically oriented Secretaries-General began to organize the process with diminishing enthusiasm. International invitations were issued on short notice which impacted international participation. The US Summit was the low point after which reform replaced face-to-face meetings with e-governance. This allowed delegates to remain involved without incurring financial pressures to redirect funds away from the humanitarian crisis.

Once it became clear that the G-plus System was expanding, the religious leaders began directing their communiqués throughout the broader G-plus System network. F8 summit communiqués were delivered to the G8 *and* the G20 in Canada 2010, France 2011, and the US 2012. The UK leadership wanted to reform the F8 Initiative in 2013; no face-to-face meetings were held that year. The communiqué was developed with ICC feedback by email, and directed only to the G8 leadership via an Open Letter.

The next two years (2014 and 2015) were transition years for the Initiative. In 2014, the G8 became the G7. Russia did not host the intended F8 Summit, but a Pre-Conference Youth Summit was convened in Germany in preparation for the G7 2015 Summit. Senior religious leaders decided not to convene an F7 summit without Russia's participation. The F7 Youth Pre-Conference developed a statement intended for delivery to the G7 the following year in accordance with arrival of the MDG deadline in 2015.[1] Senior religious leadership shifted attention from the G7 to the G20 process. A separate F20 process

---

1   F7-Germany, "Interreligious Youth Forum on Sustainable Development."

had emerged in Australia where the G20 was meeting. A new hosting pattern was established to convene summits to follow the G20 leadership rotation. The 2014 F20 Summit was co-hosted by a national-international team of Secretaries-General. This would become a new pattern for hosting international summits. Adams served as national Secretary-General. Durham served as international Secretary-General. Christie participated in the 2014 Australian Summit, presenting on the history of the F8 process. The F20 Summit developed a communiqué that was directed to the G20 leadership. In 2015, the MDGs were replaced by the SDGs. In early 2015, the 2015 F7 Youth Summit was unexpectedly canceled.[2] The F7 youth solicited civic feedback on their draft statement and posted the communiqué directed to the G7 on the internet.[3] This was the last F7 communiqué to emerge out of a summit process following the G8 and G7 leadership rotation.

Since 2015, the Initiative has been shadowing the G20 Summits. With more than twenty nations involved, it has no longer been feasible to use a delegation model. That said, international involvement remains significant. The 2015 F20 Summit was co-hosted by a team of three Secretaries-General. Adams now served as an international Secretary-General along with Durham. Şentürk served as a national Secretary-General. The team organized the F20 Summit in Istanbul, Turkey.

In 2016, the F8/F7/F20 Initiative was now hosting summits in locations set by the G20 meetings. The meeting process expanded to include two presummit conferences hosted by the international team of Secretaries-General, Adams and Durham. The 2016 China Summit was convened by Dr. Zhuo Xinping serving as national Secretary-General and Adams and Durham serving as International Secretaries-General. The Initiative continued to follow the G20 in 2017 when the G20 met in Germany; no pre-summit conferences were hosted by the F20 that year.

The informality of the leadership rotation model used for the initial F8 Summit process assured some measure of continuity but also contributed to division and confusion during the leadership transition from Germany in 2007 to Japan in 2008. In that year, summit organizing responsibilities were passed on to multiple hosts. Miyake was asked, and accepted, the hosting role at the Germany Summit in 2007. Given the strong organizational presence and capacity of RfP in Japan, German hosts later asked Niwano to host the Summit. However, by then, Miyake had already set a process fully in-motion. The ensuing confusion and competition threatened to disrupt the ongoing continuity

---

2 Interreligious Youth Forum, "Canceled:Interreligious Youth Forum," http://www.iyf2015.de/.

3 F7-Germany, "Interreligious Youth Forum on Sustainable Development."

of the process, so when a summit was organized last-minute by Paglia the following year in Italy, the International Continuance Committee (comprised of past, present, and future F8 Secretaries-General) was inaugurated.[4] Some members of the ICC have merged into the G20 Interfaith Summit Executive Committee now that the process has evolved to shadowing the F20 process. To assist with this larger shadow summit model, an international-national team of Secretaries-General are now organizing F20 summits and occasional regional pre-conferences for ongoing engagement with the G-plus System.

Leadership Rotation

The chief organizing person for the national summit host was referred to as the summit's Secretary-General. A list of summit Secretaries-General for the F8/F7/F20 Initiative from 2005 through 2016 was provided in the last chapter (Table 6.2). Secretaries-General accept the responsibility for organizing the summit venue, raising the finances to cover associated costs, sponsoring a limited number of international participants (flight, hotel, food for a portion of delegations), issuing invitations, arranging the interface with the G-plus System (communiqué delivery, Sherpa interaction, etc.), connecting with local media, and developing any special events and/or excursions for participants.

In some cases, additional positions were acknowledged to assist the Secretary-General with hosting the summit process. For example, Miyake served as Secretary-General for the F8 Kyoto-Osaka Summit, Most Venerable Juntoku Deguchi served as Summit President and four people served as Honorary Summit Presidents: R.H. Baron George L. Carey, H.E. Francis Cardinal Arinze, H.R.H. Prince Samdech Norodom Sirivudh and the Most Venerable Yukei Matsunaga.[5] The F8 Sapporo Summit also had an Organizing Committee with the Rev. Keishi Miyamoto serving as Chairman and Vendley serving as Member.[6] The US Summit in 2012 had a facilitating local host, Katherine Marshall, who provided hospitality and organized arrangements at the facility where the Summit took place.

The F8/F7/F20 Initiative struggles to maintain a balance between informality and formalization. When the F8/F7/F20 Initiative makes the international process more formally organized, it creates tension with the political leadership, who operate within the nation-state system with which they engage.

---

4   James Christie and Karen Hamilton, Email exchange, August 2009.

5   Shackleton, "Religious Leaders Call for Global Partnership: Members of the Host Committee."

6   Keishi Miyamoto and William Vendley, "Welcome: World Religious Leaders Summit for Peace—on the Occasion of the G8 Hokkaido Toyako Summit," (Sapporo, Japan 2008).

Relations between the Initiative and the G-plus System operate in a context of governance without government. To be effective, the leadership structure of the F8/F7/F20 Initiative must maintain enough structural informality as to be compatible with the transnational governance realities. Too much informality, however, undermines the stability of the ongoing process.

The Organizing Committees

The conceptual structure of the first organizing committee—the International Continuance Committee (ICC) for the F8—was delineated at a 2008 meeting in New York. A small group convened in the offices of the late Robert Edgar who was at the time the General Secretary of the National Council of Churches of Christ. It was envisioned that the ICC would help organize ongoing summits. The ICC would also provide a place for the discussion of broad and deep interfaith issues and their global impact as they relate to ongoing religious summitry. In August of 2009, the Canadians circulated a concept paper for discussion in support of developing an ICC that would deepen interfaith conversation and strengthen the ongoing continuity of the process.[7] In September of 2009, the ICC was formed consisting of religious representatives from all of those who had hosted, the upcoming host, and the immediate host(s) thereafter.

The purpose of the ICC was to help organize ongoing summits and provide a place for the discussion of interfaith issues and their global impact as they pertain to the ongoing summit process. The first ICC meeting was convened on June 15, 2009 where the leadership rotation model was endorsed and clarified with domestic impacts in mind. At the 2009 Italy Summit, religious leaders clarified that the leadership rotation model used by the summit process meant that national variation would affect possible hosts as well. In some countries, the chair of a national interfaith body would have enough infrastructure to host a summit. In other countries, the host might be a senior religious leader or the representative of the major religion of the country in question.

A very different process unfolded when a summit was hosted by a religious leader than when it was convened with the support of religious infrastructures. The strength of using a leadership rotation model is that it ensures national ownership of the process by the local religious culture in ways that are compatible with the nation-state system. The weakness of using a leadership rotation model is that it depends upon people in the G-plus System countries taking up the idea in further years. Following the large Canadian 2010 Summit, ICC members encouraged Hamilton to contact Metropolitan Emmanuel to offer

---

7   Christie and Hamilton.

assistance for organizing a summit in France.[8] The different character and size of the religious conferences mirror the different kind of readiness and means in the different countries. The ICC became an important resource for ensuring continuity.

It was initially envisioned that the ICC would appoint one of its representatives to house within their home organization appropriate files and resources (e.g., all the statements since 2005, budget templates, invitation lists, strategic plans for hosting etc.).[9] The committee would make organizations hosting summits in the future aware that these resources are available to them as helpful or necessary. In looking to the future, it was suggested that the members of the ICC meet in person once a year. Making this a reality, however, would prove to be a financially insurmountable challenge. Even so, the ICC met on a number of occasions and discussed questions such as what constitutes a faith group; conversations have continued within the committee by email. Canadian representatives have maintained files via the Canadian Council of Churches in Toronto on all summits attended and they have made these resources available (and offered support) to the hosts of the 2008, 2009, 2011, and 2012 Summits to assist them as needed.[10] The ICC also served as a vehicle for discussion of Initiative reform in 2013, circulating the UK Open Letter which proposed launching a social media campaign in lieu of face-to-face meetings.

The G20 Interfaith Summits have developed a G20 Interfaith Summit International Organizing Committee that has its own Executive Committee. The G20 Interfaith Summit Executive Committee members are Adams, Christie, Durham, Kitanović, Marshall, and Petkoff. Additional Association Members who consult with the Executive Committee about the ongoing F20 meetings have included Pereira, Coertzen, Ferrari, Foblets, Hamilton, Khasru, Kirton, Mahmood, Miyake, Mustafa, Petkoff, Şentürk, and Zheng.

The G20 Interfaith Summit also has a Summit Secretariat that provides administrative support for conference details from Griffith University in Australia and Brigham Young University in the United States. The Secretariat consists of Ricky Lashand, Blythe Shupe, Donlu Thayer and Deborah Wright. I have served as Special Rapporteur from 2014–2017.

Some overlap exists between the F8/F7 and F20 organizing committees. Christie, Hamilton, Kirton, Miyake and Marshall have been heavily involved in both processes.

---

8   Affolderbach.

9   Christie and Hamilton.

10   Hamilton, "To Boldly Go: Innovations Originating through the F8 Canadian Interfaith Leaders Summit Which Strengthen Human Destiny and Community."

Financing

The summits have been variously financed over the years depending upon the national context. Summit hosts have generally covered transportation and housing costs for portions of the F8 delegations from G8 countries. The costs often exceed the organizational capacity of national religious infrastructures, so religious organizations have frequently partnered with government to ensure adequate participation and representation. For religious delegates coming from national contexts with strong separationist policies, government financing of the summits was thought by some critics to compromise the integrity of the process. The ICC disagreed with this position contending that this was an ongoing process of international participation where delegates could variously choose to 'speak truth to power' through collaborative teamwork. Consistency and continuity of the process was seen to outweigh any compromises stemming from government sponsorship.

National contexts that involved government sponsorship were generally countries with comparatively homogenous religious landscapes. For example, the F8 Italy Summit was sponsored by Italy's Ministry of Foreign Affairs and the Episcopal Conference. Italy is predominantly Roman Catholic and was not offering, at that time, to sponsor a summit of diverse interreligious representation for engagement with the network of political leaders. The Episcopal Conference is comprised of religious minorities in Italy and could not finance a summit of this stature. The head of each delegation received full coverage for both accommodation and flights by the Italian Ministry of Foreign Affairs (MFA). The MFA only covered accommodation for the second member from each delegation. The third delegation member was personally responsible for both accommodation and flight. Despite being organized on short notice, the event had significant international participation, in part, because the Italian Ministry of Foreign Affairs and the Episcopal Conference paid for some transportation costs for participants from locations such as Asia and the Middle East. The MFA covered all transportation costs for any excursions planned for during the meetings.

The religious landscape of Germany has historically been homogenous enough to have developed a strong Protestant organizational structure (although the religious landscape is rapidly becoming more diverse). The Evangelical Church of Germany (EKD) was interested in hosting the 2007 F8 Summit when Germany hosted the G8 and they were financially capable of carrying the costs at that point in time. The EKD financial situation changed by the time it was their turn to host the G7 Summit in 2015. Plans would be cancelled despite having already financed a pre-summit with the youth in preparation the year before. The United Kingdom is also comparatively religiously homogenous and the Archbishop of Canterbury hosted the London Forum at Lambeth Palace in 2005.

Japan may have been the most expensive F8 year because two meetings were convened. The F8 Kyoto-Osaka Summit was sponsored by Japan's Ministry of Environment, the Osaka Promotion Committee for the G8 Finance Ministry Meeting, the Kyoto Committee for the 2008 G8 Foreign Ministers Meeting, the Kyoto Chamber of Commerce and Industry, the Japan Committee of UNICEF, the National Federation of UNESCO Associations of Japan, the UN Association of Kansai, and the Kyoto Convention Bureau. The Japanese Ministry of the Environment also helped sponsor the F8 Sapporo Summit which was organized by the RfP Japan, and the Japanese Association of Religious Organizations. Additional sponsorship was obtained from the Japan Religious Committee of the World Federalist Movement.

Canadian organizers funded the F8 Summit through private sector donations. Hamilton and Christie raised close to $300,000 to cover traditional costs such as delegate transportation ($80,000), accommodation ($17,000), food ($42,000), administration and conference coordination ($50,000), and French/German/Japanese language translation ($6,000). They also solicited funds to host an interfaith media communications forum ($1000). They raised funds to develop a website that was used for civic engagement, solicitation of statement feedback, and document preservation ($15,000).[11] A full-color handout of event sponsors was distributed at the Summit. Sponsors included, but were not limited to, Ecclesiastical Insurance, The Salvation Army, World Vision, Modern Earth Web Design, United Church Women, and the Hindu Federation of Canada. The Partnership obtained a government grant ($77,959) from the Multiculturalism Program of the Department of Citizenship and Immigration Canada to host interfaith dialogue and religious education dinners with Members of Parliament to discuss spiritual and ethical aspects of the three 2010 G8 agenda issues of poverty, care for the earth and peace and security.[12]

Academic sponsorship has greatly increased since the F8/F7/F20 Initiative began shadowing the G20 process. With organizational support from the Centre for Interfaith and Cultural Dialogue at Griffith University, the 2014 F20 Summit in Australia was financed by the Queensland Government, United Arab Emirates Ministry of Culture, Youth and Community Development, and the International Centre of Law and Religion Studies at Brigham Young University with additional sponsorship from IBAQ, Seekers Hub Global, Ma'din

---

11   Canadian Council of Churches, "2010 Religious Leaders Summit High Level Financial Budget," (2009).

12   Jason Kenney, August 6, 2010.

Academy, Adelaide University, Queensland Churches Together, Queensland Jewish Interfaith, the Australian Bahá'í Community, and Queensland Intercultural Society.

The 2015 F20 Summit in Turkey was sponsored primarily by academic organizations with some ecumenical faith-based sponsorship. The conference sponsors were African Consortium for Law and Religion Studies, Amity University, Brunel University London, Canadian Council of Churches, Consejo Argentino para la Libertad Religiosa, Consorcio Latinaamericano de Libertad Religiosa, Dersaadet Kültür Platformu, Fatih Sultan Mehmet Vakıf Üniversitesi, Griffith University, ICLRS, International Consortium for Law and Religion Studies, Madin Academy, Max Planck Institute for Social Anthropology, Medeniyetler İttifakı Enstitüsü, Nalsar Hyderabad, Oslo Coalition on Freedom of Religion or Belief, Oxford Journal of Law and Religion, RfP (Middle East/North Africa Council), Royal Academy of Jurisprudence and Legislation (Section on Law and Religion and Canon Law), The Economic Policy Research Foundation of Turkey, The International Religious Liberty Association, The Universidad Complutense Departamento de Derecho Eclesiástico del Estado, Universitas Studiorum Insubriae, and University of Oxford.

The 2016 F20 process expanded to include two pre-conferences. The Centre for Interfaith and Cultural Dialogue at Griffith University and the International Centre of Law and Religion Studies at Brigham Young University helped sponsor both pre-conferences and the Summit in Beijing. In addition, Pacific Theological College, the United Nations Educational, Scientific and Cultural Organization, and Victoria University of Wellington supported the Pacific Regional Pre-Conference. Ma'din Academy, the Government of Kerala, and the Institute for Policy, Advocacy and Governance supported the South Asia Regional Pre-Conference. The Summit in Beijing had the additional support of the Institute of World Religions at the Chinese Academy of Social Sciences and the Government of China.

By 2017, the ICLRS was raising over half of total conference costs, primarily from individual donors. The ICLRS solicits funds from a diverse array of collaborating institutions and religious traditions. Collaborating institutions have included the following: African Consortium for Law and Religion Studies; Alliance of Civilizations Institute at Fatih Sultan Mehmet Vakif University, Turkey; Amity Institute of Advanced Legal Studies in New Delhi, India; Brunel Law and Religion Research Group, UK; Canadian Council of Churches, Canada; Insubria University's Center on Religion, Law and Economy in the Mediterranean Area of Como, Italy; Centre for Interfaith and Cultural Dialogue at Griffith University in Australia; Center for Research and Training in Interfaith Relations, Morocco; Consejo Argentino para la Libertad Religiosa, Argentina;

Consorcio Latinoamericano de Libertad Religiosa; Department of Law and Religion at Complutense University, Spain; Institute for Policy, Advocacy, and Governance in Bangladesh; International Consortium for Law and Religion Studies in Milan; International Religious Liberty Association; Ma'din Academy in India; Max Planck Institute for Social Anthropology in Halle, Germany; National Academy of Legal Studies and Research in the University of Law, Hyderabad, India; Oslo Coalition on Freedom of Religion or Belief, Norwegian Centre for Human Rights, Norway; Oxford Society of Law and Religion, UK; Regents College, Oxford University, United Kingdom; Royal Academy of Jurisprudence and Legislation, Section on Law and Religion and Canon Law, Spain; Sant' Edigio Community, Italy; and World Faiths Development Dialogue, Georgetown University, United States.[13]

Religious Ritual

The incorporation of religious ritual into the summit process has, at times, been a point of contention among more pragmatically oriented participants. According to Hamilton,

> The use of words and language can be a very delicate one in any interfaith relationship, particularly the words and language used to refer to what so many traditions call 'God'. It can be easy to arrive at common terminology for the addressing of world hunger and climate change issues but harder to determine how faith traditions, in their diversity and yet working together, will refer to the foundation and centre of their faith. At the 2007 F8 Summit, it was determined that all the faith traditions gathered could use the term Divine Imperative. It was not the first choice for all faiths but one that they could live with in the deep spirit of relationship ... the term 'Divine Imperative' is gaining global acceptance.[14]

Most, but not all, of the summit meetings began and ended with prayers that emphasized common ethics (e.g., prayers of peace), offering of thanks (e.g., common reading of interfaith prayers for the religions of the world) and requests for sacred blessings on the political engagement efforts around areas of shared concern. In addition to the structured prayers embedded in the opening and closing of meetings, and the distribution of handouts that identify the golden rule across the world's religions in thirteen sacred texts, the following

---

13   Durham.

14   Hamilton, "To Boldly Go: Innovations Originating through the F8 Canadian Interfaith Leaders Summit Which Strengthen Human Destiny and Community."

religious rituals were variously incorporated into the summit process over time:

- The F8 Kyoto-Osaka Japan Summit convened the meetings to intentionally incorporate a 'religious flavour' by convening working group sessions in shrines and temples (e.g, the oldest Buddhist temple in Japan—Shitennoji Temple) as a complement to the plenary sessions that were hosted in an academic setting at Osaka University. The three days of meetings were interspersed with various performances such as Bugaku "Ranryo-o" and "Gar yo-kai." This traditional music and dance is of 6th Century origin. When delegates refined their collaborative statement, delegates were intentional that the document have a 'religious flavour not a political one.' Summit meetings were closed with a ringing of a bell of thanksgiving for Mother Earth.
- The 2009 Italy Summit convened an official moment of public prayer and witness in the main square of L'Aquila to recognize the earthquake victims and hand over a good will token of financial assistance from religious participants for humanitarian aid to local victims.
- The 2010 Canada Summit hosted a sacred fire for the duration of the event since the Summit was physically held on the treaty land of the Indigenous, First Nations Anishnaabe peoples.[15] The First Nations spiritual event involved the lighting of a sacred fire, guarded by Anishnaabe fire-keepers from Circle of Turtle Lodge, to open and close Summit ceremonies next to a teepee in the university's quadrangle. The fire remained visible to participants for the duration of the Summit. Anishnaabe songs, accompanied by drumming and the casting of tobacco pouches, carried prayers into the fire. Additional spiritual and cultural events in Canada included performances of Japanese traditional dance, Zane Zalis' holocaust oratorio *I Believe,* and *Strike,* a play by Danny Schur dramatizing a Winnipeg strike that was a milestone on securing human rights and fair employment in Canada. The *I Believe* oratorio was written by a Ukrainian Catholic Christian.
- The 2015 Turkey Summit organized a Mosque visitation (providing participants with appropriate clothing to indicate respect) and facilitated participant observation of a Whirling Dervish service at the Fatih Sultan Mehmet Vakif Üniversitesi in Istanbul to conclude the Summit on November 18.

Additional tensions surrounding the incorporation of religious ritual centered on pragmatic pressures for increased response to the humanitarian crisis.

---

15   Ibid.

Participants from RNGOs expressed concerns that religious ritual would divert attention away from civic engagement, practical application and public policy relevance. The US 2012 Summit, for example, was a one-day session that was convened somewhat like a business meeting with scant attention to the cultivation of mutual understanding through interfaith dialogue and relationship. By way of comparison, at the closing of the first G20 shadow Summit in Australia, Adams, in his closing statement at the end of the Summit, proposed that a measure of the event's success be the degree to which the summit process generated respect, increased mutual understanding and formation of new multi-faith relationships.

Special Events and Excursions
National hosts often convened special events reflective of their national culture and local context. Some of the specific special events and excursions include:

- Regional Pre-Conferences (China 2016): The Secretaries-General organized two regional pre-conferences in association with the 2016 G20 Interfaith Summit. Forty participants (Members of Parliament, academics, faith and interfaith leaders, development and peacebuilding specialists) convened at Pacific Theological College in Suva, Fiji May 2–4 at a Pacific Regional Pre-Conference, and 29 participants (Members of Parliament, academics, faith and interfaith leaders, legal experts, intercultural and terrorism experts) convened at Hotel Apollo Dimora in Trivandrum in Kerala, India July 25–26 at a South Asia Regional Pre-Conference.
- A Dignity Pre-Conference (Germany 2007): On June 5, 2007 in Cologne, Germany, a special one-day optional pre-conference was held on the theme "The Power of Dignity." The Kirchentag Secretary, with Evangelische Kirche in Deutschland (EKD) sponsorship, organized a one-day conference open to participation by religious leaders on human rights themes.
- Human Rights and Religious Freedom Pre-Conference (Canada 2010): An optional pre-conference seminar entitled "Facing the Challenge of Poverty, the Environment and Peace and Security" was convened on June 21 by the late Dr. Redwan Moqbel, a leader of the Canadian Bahá'í community, on the theme of religious freedom and human rights. Four international human rights experts from four different faith backgrounds addressed the relationship between religious freedom and challenges associated with eliminating extreme poverty, achieving peace and security and confronting the environmental crisis. Speakers looked at current concerns about the relationship between religious freedom and freedom of expression, women's rights, minority rights, environmental rights, and other rights in light of efforts to impose barriers to religious freedom based on claims about

public order, secularization and the defamation of religion. The event was convened at the insistence of the honourable Dr. Lloyd Axworthy, president of the University of Winnipeg and titular host of the 2010 Summit. Axworthy was Canada's foreign minister from 1996–1999 and is the only foreign minister of Canada who convened roundtables on religious issues to broaden the topic of human rights.

· Media Communications Pre-Conference (Canada 2010): An optional pre-conference seminar was convened on June 21 for interfaith participants and media professionals on engaging media for purposes of interfaith advocacy on G8 issues. Described as an interfaith journalists professional development day, religion communicators and journalists covered a variety of topics addressing how religion is covered in the context of religious marginalization, media upheaval, social media and blogging. Media accreditation was processed for an array of media representatives including, but not limited to, Radio Canada, Canadian Broadcasting Corporation, Salt and Light Television (French and English) and Golden West Radio.

· A Poverty Excursion (Japan 2008): The F8 Kyoto Japan Summit took religious leaders to the "Airin" area (Nishinari Ward) which has the largest concentration of homelessness and joblessness in Japan. In the spirit of transparency and compassion, religious leaders were brought to the Airin Labor's Public Employment Security Office and they visited the Roman Catholic Charity's outreach program to vulnerable populations.

· Humanitarian Outreach (Italy 2009): The first half of the day, June 16, 2009 in Italy was spent meeting with people in the areas affected by the L'Aquila earthquake. Participants presented financial contributions from their faith traditions to assist the local community in rebuilding.

· Climate Justice Tour (Canada 2010): Under the leadership of KAIROS, participants were taken on a Canada wide tour to bring forward the voices of those most affected by climate change. Speakers included Naty Atz Sunc from Guatemala, Isaiah Kipyegon Toroitich from Kenya, Francois Pihaatae from Tahiti, and Fred Sangris from Yellowknife to address the impact of climate change in their communities and dialogue about how Canadians can work toward solutions.[16]

· Millennium Kids (Canada 2010): On the occasion of hosting the 2010 Summit in Canada, a national affiliate of the Millennium Kids movement (www .millenniumkids.ca), an RNGO with leadership from Canadian children born in the year 2000, was formed to educate civil society about fulfilling promises made in relation to the MDGs (and now the SDGs). Millennium

---

16   Aidid et al., "Report on Civil Society and the 2010 G8 Muskoka Summit."

Kids was founded by Australian twelve-year-olds in 1996 following a visit to the United Nations where they learned about environmental issues and the MDGs. Millennium Kids has additional connections with organizations in South Africa, Indonesia, China and Malaysia. In Canada, events were held in schools, mosques and temples to develop moral pressure for keeping promises made to fulfill the MDGs/SDGs. The Canadians have developed a downloadable song on YouTube and a Millennium Development Goals game for grassroots education and engagement.[17]

- Interfaith Bus Tour (Canada 2010): The 2010 Canadian Summit organized an Interfaith Bus Tour of houses of worship in Winnipeg for participants to visit different religious traditions in the vicinity during the day on June 20. The bus tour was sponsored by the Manitoba Interfaith Council and the Manitoba Interfaith and Immigration Council and Beaver Bus Lines.
- French INGO Caravan (France 2011): A caravan was organized by NGOs including ONE, CIDSE, and Catholic Committee Against Hunger and Development to travel through France informing the public on global financial alternatives to address hunger, climate change, support for democratic struggles in the Arab region, critiques of austerity policies and income inequality, and questions about the legitimacy of the G8. The caravan finished with a rally and street party on the weekend of May 21 in L'Havre.[18]
- Youth Delegation (Canada 2010): On June 22, a youth delegation, chaired by Hilary Keatchie, and comprised of 13 Tony Blaire Faith Act Fellows, facilitated a dinner with over 100 young adults from various local faith traditions to dialogue about the issues addressed in the draft statement. On June 23, Hilary Keatchie chaired a panel during which the Youth Delegation addressed summit participants.
- Hospitality (United States 2012): On May 16, Katherine Marshall hosted a personal dinner reception in her home for participants to engage in informal, relaxed and extended conversation with one another.
- Dinner Out (Turkey 2015): On November 18, the 2015 Summit provided dinner at a local restaurant for participants to experience local cuisine to conclude the conference. Participants traveled together on a bus and ate at a local restaurant between visiting a local mosque and observing a Whirling Dervish worship service. This cultural event occurred at the close of the conference.

---

17   Hamilton, "To Boldly Go: Innovations Originating through the F8 Canadian Interfaith Leaders Summit Which Strengthen Human Destiny and Community."

18   Bruce-Lockhart et al., "Report on Civil Society and the 2011 G8 Deauville Summit."

- Parliamentary Panel (Australia 2014/Istanbul 2015): In keeping with G20 culture, the F20 meetings dedicate part of the summit program for engagement with Members of Parliament from the host country. In 2014, four Australian Members of Parliament interacted with participants for a session on November 17, 2014. A Parliamentary Panel made comments during the luncheon in 2015.

Aborted Events

Three summits have been aborted that were either hoped for, partially planned or publicly announced and then dropped. All three events occurred in relation to the transition years when the G8 became the G7, the MDGs transitioned to the SDGs, and civic engagement shifted from the G8 and G7 to the G20. The three aborted events were:

- 2014 Russia F8 Summit: Although past organizers spoke about intentions to host this event during interviews conducted in 2012, plans were always qualified pending government approval. As the time drew closer, political tensions accompanying Russia's 'invasion/incursion/aggression/staycation' in Ukraine made the event untenable.[19] In 2012, the Russian delegation had communicated to the US Secretary-General that they would be attending the US Summit, but the delegates never arrived. ICC attempts to communicate with the Russian representative went unanswered from that point on. Russian delegates did not sign the Open Letter generated by the UK F8 process in 2013. In 2014, the G8 became the G7.[20] At that point, hosting an F8 Summit became politically untenable for the Russian religious infrastructure. Even if they had managed to organize some type of gathering, it is unclear whether or not other international delegates would have participated.
- 2015 Germany F7 Summit: In anticipation of the arrival of the MDG deadline, Martin Affolderbach began working with young leadership to plan an interfaith youth event two years in advance of Germany's planned hosting of the G7 meetings. An F8 Interreligious Youth Forum was to be organized by the Protestant Youth Federation of Germany. The first planning meeting was convened in June, 2012. Hilary Keachie was brought from Canada to begin organizing the process in January of 2013 for an interreligious youth summit to be held in Stuttgart in 2015. Youth were going to emphasize

---

19   Friedman, "Russia's Slow-Motion Invasion of Ukraine."

20   Cohen, "G8 Becomes the G7 as Leaders Kick Russia Out: It's Not a Big Problem, Says Putin's Foreign Minister."

accountability for ways in which the G7 fell short of achieving their MDG commitments. Hamilton wrote about the plans in the *G8* publication that was distributed to G8 and G20 leaders in 2014.[21] A pre-forum Youth Summit was convened on July 13–18, 2014 in Kaub, Germany that was attended by 19 youth from 19 countries with faith representation from Muslim, Jewish, Bahá'í, and Christian faith traditions to focus on three overarching issues: peace, justice and education. The policy and advocacy team drafted a statement in preparation of the 2015 MDG deadline that would be circulated for feedback from civil society networks in each participant's home country. During the planning stages, Affolderbach retired and his replacement was less supportive of the youth summit process. Youth continued to meet, developing an interfaith planning team with RNGO representation. Summit dates were selected for May 23–30, 2015 to bring delegates from many countries to talk about local projects and the transition from the MDGs to the SDGs. In January of 2015, the entire process was unexpectedly cancelled[22] without discussion citing financial constraints.[23] Youth delegates created an online petition that obtained 103 supporters in hopes of reviving the process and to publish the pre-conference statement.[24]

- 2016 Japan F7 Summit: During 2014, the ICC had been communicating among themselves encouraging ongoing civic engagement with the G-plus System. In Japan, Miyake hand delivered on June 13, 2014 a letter of concerns directed at the G20 leaders to the Deputy Chief Cabinet Minister of the Japanese Government, along with an oral explanation of the F8/F7 process. On that occasion, he also publicly announced intention to host an F7 Summit when Japan was next scheduled to host the G7 in 2016.[25] By 2016, however, the F8/F7/F20 Initiative, along with other civil society organizations, had shifted the summits away from the G7 to shadow the G20.

Although the cancellation of these three events disrupted an already fragile process, nevertheless summit communiqués have been continuously published, and usually directly delivered, to the G-plus System even during the transition years.

---

21   Hamilton, "Keeping the Faith: Still Focused on Goals."
22   F7-Germany, "Interreligious Youth Forum on Sustainable Development." Also see their Facebook page at https://www.facebook.com/IYF2015?fref=ts.
23   Hilary Keachie, April 1 2015.
24   F7-Germany, "Interreligious Youth Forum on Sustainable Development."
25   Miyake, Email, June 14, 2014.

External Relations

The F8/F7/F20 exercise of soft power diplomacy has occurred in the transnational context of governance without government. Previously marginalized groups are increasingly able to influence international relations due to the "flattening" of global culture through technological innovation and globalization. As risk society theorists have noted, institutional authority has increasingly given way to governance via network influence as a way of respecting the legitimate interests of those affected by decisions, programs, and interventions.[26] As the global community has left the "statist" period where countries are the strongest arbiters of power and entered a new era of globalization,[27] new forms of complex combinations of public and private agencies involved in partnerships and joined-up service delivery, such as represented by the F8/F7/F20 Initiative, now characterize emergence of a shift in governance accountability from vertical to horizontal dialogue.[28] Although a governance role for religion remains under-researched,[29] some scholars have begun to identify a diplomatic role for religion in international relations.[30]

One way of gauging the diplomatic role of the F8/F7/F20 system is to assess levels of engagement with different levels of political officials. In some cases (e.g., France 2011), the F8 Secretary-General delivered the religious statement to officials at the highest levels that are connected to the G-plus System. In other contexts (e.g., Japan 2008, Italy 2009, Canada 2010), political representatives came to the religious leaders to receive the collaborative statement. This next section details levels of diplomatic engagement with various government officials.

Heads of State

At some summits, the heads of state were involved in the religious leader meetings. In 2006, President Vladimir Putin opened the Summit and met with the religious leaders. In his end-of-summit press conference, Putin also stated that "our discussions took into account recommendations made by two very

---

26   Beck, Giddens, and Lasch, *Reflexive Modernization: Politics, Tradition and Aesthetics in the Modern Social Order.*

27   Mayntz, "Common Goods and Governance."

28   Considine, "The End of the Line? Accountable Governance in the Age of Networks, Partnerships, and Joined-up Services."

29   Halafoff, "The Multifaith Movement"; Johnston, ed. *Faith-Based Diplomacy: Trumping Real Politik.*

30   For example, Johnston, ed. *Faith-Based Diplomacy: Trumping Real Politik.*

important forums that took place in Moscow at the beginning of July—the World Summit of Religious Leaders and the International Forum of Non-Governmental Organizations/the Civil G8 2006."[31] Exactly how, if at all, religious leaders' concerns impacted G8 deliberations was not stipulated, however.

At other summits, F8 Secretaries-General met with heads of state to deliver the summit communiqué. For example, both statements were delivered to the Japanese Prime Minister in advance of the G8 meetings, each one characterized by a noteworthy and distinctive theme: the importance of environmental priorities.

On August 6, 2008, one of the F8 ICC members, William Vendley, received a letter from the UK Prime Minister's G8 Team Assistant. The letter clearly identified how G8 outcomes reflected many of the concerns and calls to action addressed in the Sapporo Statement. The letter also stated that religious leaders made a valuable contribution to the G8 discussions:

> [T]he G8 made a number of advances in the key areas of climate change, development and on counter terrorism. On climate change we agreed on the adoption of a long-term goal of a reduction of at least 50% in global greenhouse gas emissions by 2050, as part of an agreement under the United Nations Framework Convention on climate change. We also launched the Climate Investment Funds, with G8 pledges approaching $6 billion—this was a key priority for the United Kingdom. On Development, our commitment to deliver $60 billion over 5 years for infectious diseases, along with 100 million bed-nets to combat malaria will make a huge impact on the well-being of people in developing nations. The G8 is also contributing over $10 billion collectively to help tackle the global food crises. On international security, the G8 sent a strong message condemning acts of terrorism and on the need to counter this global threat. I am glad that you have made common cause in tackling these shared agendas, and hope that we can take this forward into the Italian Presidency of the G8 in 2009. Your work and multi-religious cooperation for peace is greatly admired.[32]

That same year, F8 religious leaders from the Canadian delegation were asked by conveners of a one-day governance conference to present a civil society perspective on July 1, 2008 about how well the G8 actually delivers on its

---

31   Hajnal, "The 2006 St. Petersburg Summit and Civil Society."
32   Day, Letter, August 6 2008.

promises.[33] Referencing data from the G8 Research Group, religious leaders reported mixed results citing a current 2008 overall track record of 47% for the G8 keeping of its own commitments.[34] The United Nations University, the Centre for International Governance Innovation and the G8 Research Group collaborated to bring the concerns of developing countries and development institutions into the Japanese-led preparatory process for the 2008 Summit.[35]

At each summit, religious leaders made efforts to contact the head of state for the national host. Although some delegations continued to deliver communiqués to their heads of state during years when they were not hosting a summit, most delegates only reached out to their heads of state once every eight years when it was their turn to host again. One of the goals in reforming the F8 process in 2013 was to develop a new model of collaboration where religious leaders could use the results of collaborative initiatives for ongoing advocacy with their respective governments in advance, *and between,* political summits.[36] For example, although Canadian delegates sought meetings with their G8 Sherpa after the 2008 meetings in Germany, Sherpa engagement during years when it was not their turn to host was sporadic. The Canadian delegation changed their advocacy efforts in response to the 2013 reform efforts, and they began reaching out to their prime minister every year even when they were not national hosts.[37] The Japanese delegation was already in continuous contact with their head of state.

Government Advisors

Various government advisors have been involved throughout the process over time. Usually, government advisors are recipients of religious leader advocacy and dialogue, but sometimes, they participate in the program. For example, the F8 Kyoto-Osaka statement was handed by Miyake to the Honorable Mr. Matsushige Ono, Deputy Chief Cabinet Secretary for the Japanese Government on June 30, 2008. The Chief Cabinet Secretary holds multiple daily news conferences and is the most often quoted politician by Japanese media outlets. The Deputy Chief Cabinet Secretary also presides over the Cabinet

---

33   Christie, "How Well Does the G8 Deliver: Compliance with G8 Commitments."

34   Karen Hamilton, "For Just Such a Time as This: Reflections on the Statement 'Translating Shared Concerns into Action,'" (Sapporo, Japan 2008).

35   United Nations University, "Global Development Challenges, Desired G8 Responses: A G8-Developing Country Dialogue for the Hokkaido Summit," (Tokyo, Japan 2008). See also CIGI, July 1, 2008, http://library.utoronto.ca/g7/conferences/2008/program-unu .html.

36   Reed, "Project Proposal—2013 G8 Religious Leaders' Initiative."

37   Karen Hamilton, Email, June 6, 2013.

Secretariat—the staff at the Prime Minister's office. Since the late 1990s, the position of the Chief Cabinet Secretary was expanded so that the holder of that title now presides over "key advisory panels, administrative organizations and high-ranking officials, including the Deputy Chief Cabinet Secretary for Crisis Management, the National Security Secretariat, the Cabinet Intelligence and Research Office, and the Cabinet Affairs Office."[38] The F8 Sapporo statement was delivered to Japanese Prime Minister Yasuo Fakuda for conveyance to the G8 Summit.

Foreign Ministers

Foreign Ministers have been involved on several occasions in summit sponsorship and communiqué delivery to the G-plus System. For example, in 2008, the Vice Foreign Minister for Japan, Mr. Yashuhide Nakayama, welcomed the delegates to the F8 Kyoto-Osaka Summit on behalf of the Prime Minister. The Foreign Ministry, along with the Ministry of Environment, was involved in sponsorship of the events. In 2009, the Italian Ministry of Foreign Affairs helped sponsor the Summit. The Italian Foreign Minister met with delegates on the afternoon of June 16, 2009. The G7 Foreign Ministers have been the first in the G-plus System to acknowledge the ongoing concerns expressed by the F8/F7/F20 Initiative. In the *Joint Communiqué* from the G7 Foreign Ministers' meeting on April 10–11, 2016 in Hiroshima, the Ministers acknowledged the importance of cross-religious, interfaith dialogue, and freedom of religion or belief to transnational governance.[39] The G7 Foreign Ministers continued to acknowledge, in their 2017 *Joint Communiqué*, the importance of engaging with religious leaders as one, among a wide array, of civil society representatives.[40]

Sherpas

Sherpas are key senior officials who provide a central coordinating point to support leaders in their work for the Summit. The term Sherpa is derived from Nepalese ethnic porters who guide people climbing in the Himalayas. The term has been adapted to refer to the personal representative of a head of state or government at an international summit. All of the G8, G7, and G20 participating states have representative Sherpas. Although Sherpas can be quite

---

38   Reiji Yoshida, "Chief Cabinet Secretary Is Much More Than Top Government," *Japan Times* (2015), https://www.japantimes.co.jp/news/2015/05/18/reference/chief-cabinet-secretary-much-top-government-spokesman/.

39   Ministers, *Joint Communiqué*, (2016).

40   Ministers, *Joint Communiqué*, (2017).

influential, they generally lack any authority to independently make final decisions about any given agreement.[41]

The Canadian delegation first reached out to their Canadian G8 Sherpa—Mr. Len Edwards, Associate Deputy Minister—in relation to the F8 Summit in Germany, 2007.[42] By early 2008, the Canadian G8 office had already taken the voice of religious leaders seriously and contacted them on two occasions for further dialogue.[43] Other F8/F7/F20 former Secretaries-General made contact with Sherpas as well (except for the Japanese who often had higher level, direct access to their political leaders).

As the F8/F7/F20 process has shifted from shadowing the G8 and G7 to shadowing the G20, Sherpa contact has become increasingly important. To make the final summit more efficient and effective, Sherpas host multiple conferences in advance of the G20 Leaders' Summit. There are multiple Sherpa conferences where agenda topics and other matters are developed and possible agreements laid out.[44] The host nation will often produce a communiqué following Sherpa meetings leading up to the summit to convey the current state of negotiations.

The C20 (Civil Society G20 engagement partner) has begun to consistently engage with the G20 Sherpa process.[45] Scholarly analysis of effective engagement with the G-plus System recommends continuous engagement with Sherpas, involvement in their meetings, and consistent dialogue in relation to their agendas.[46] But F8/F7/F20 Initiative engagement with Sherpas has been intermittent. The Initiative has yet to develop a thorough, consistent, regularized and systematic Sherpa engagement process.

Members of Parliament

By far, the Canadian Summit engaged most thoroughly with Members of Parliament. At the conclusion of the 2010 Summit, delegates presented the collaborative statement to Member of Parliament Steven Fletcher, Minister of State for Democratic Reform; He promised to pass it on to Prime Minister Harper.[47] The

41   Heather Smith, "What Is a Sherpa?" *G20 Watch* (2014).
42   Christopher Shapardanov, Email, 2007.
43   Brenda Suderman, "Economics and the Pulpit," *Winnipeg Free Press*, February 3 2008.
44   Smith, "What Is a Sherpa?"
45   Mike Callaghan et al., "Challenges Facing the G20 in 2013," *G20 Monitor* 1, Dec. (2012); Burrow et al., "G20 2014: Perspectives from Business, Civil Society, Labour, Think Tanks and Youth."
46   Hajnal, "The G20," 79–118.
47   See https://parliamentofreligions.org/content/religious-leaders-call-action-2010-world-religions-summit.

following week, Hamilton additionally delivered the statement to the Canadian G8 office who promptly responded to summit organizers confirming receipt of the document and interest in the content. But this was only the beginning. Canadian F8 Participants engaged in dialogue with Members of Parliament through a series of MP dinners that were convened to facilitate extensive and thorough spiritual and ethical dialogue on issues related to the G8 Summit in the months preceding, and immediately following, the F8 Canada 2010 Summit. Prior to the Summit, thirty-four Bahá'í Local Spiritual Assemblies, working with at-risk youth as part of an interfaith mentoring service learning project, coordinated the interfaith hosting of dinner dialogues with the following MPs: Ed Fast, Jim Abbott, Don Davies, Sukh Daliwal, Assistant to Joyce Murray, Gary Lunn, Keith Martin, Denise Savoie, Kelly Block, Brad Trost, Guy Lauzon, Terence Young, Paul Dewar, David McGuinty, John Rafferty, Bruce Hyer, Harold Albrecht, Peter Braid, Stephen Woodworth and Michael Chong.[48] Some MPs declined to meet with interfaith leaders for dialogue. A small delegation of interfaith leaders planned follow-up visits to MPs who did not attend an interfaith dinner to present them with information on faith commitments to MDG fulfillment. Initiative participants wanted to ensure that the MPs knew that the Canadian Government was being made aware that participating diverse faith traditions share common beliefs about concrete actions that need to be taken on the issues. Post-Summit MP dinners added a Parliamentary Petition to the process which was then taken forward through the Federal Speaker's Office to be spoken to by MPs in the house. Of those who participated, Don Davies, Sukh Daliwal, Keith Martin, Gary Lunn, Denise Savoie, David McGuinty, and Peter Braid reported to have found the exchange with the interfaith community to be very useful; they expressed interest in participating in ongoing events to be convened in the future. The dinner dialogues directly impacted an estimated 30,000 people.

The 2014 Australian and 2015 Turkey F20 Summits incorporated Parliamentarian Panels (with host and international participation) into the program. For example, at the 2015 Turkey F20 Summit, Pereira spoke about her experience of defending religious freedom and serving in parliament in Uruguay. She challenged the aura of mistrust that tends to surround politicians. She spoke about political engagement as one of the highest forms of charity. It allows a person to contribute to the well-being of the common good. Katrina Lantos Swett (Commissioner, United States Commission for International Freedom, US) also spoke about parliamentarians who are working to fight for fundamental human

---

48   Office of Governmental Relations, "G8 Religious Leaders' Summit—MP Dinners Interim Report," (Ottawa, Canada 2010).

rights. The Summits also involved Members of Parliament from the host country (e.g., Turkey involved Vecdet Öz, Founding General Chairman of the Justice
Party, and Fatih Gürsul, Advisor to the Republican People Party Leader).

Mayors

One of the summit traditions was some type of welcome by the local mayor.
Sometimes it took the form of a welcome speech (e.g., Japan 2008). At other
times, the mayor would host an actual reception (e.g., the Mayor of Cologne in
Germany 2007) or deliver a written message of welcome that was given to all
participants (e.g., Mayor Sam Katz in Canada 2010). Generally, mayoral involvement was limited to hospitality functions.

Special Advisors

A shift in strategy occurred when the Initiative changed from convening in
tandem with the G8/G7 to shadowing the G20. Initiative participants began to
pay greater attention to lower-level positions in key advisory roles. Organizers
began to focus on cultural opinion leaders. For example, Knox Thames was
asked to give a keynote address at the 2015 Turkey Summit. He addressed what
can, and should, be done from his perspective as Special Advisor for Religious
Minorities for the US State Department. He talked about the challenging task
associated with bringing parliamentarians together who are engaged in both
religion and politics. He illustrated his points with reference to a 2014 meeting
in Oslo and a 2015 meeting in New York that produced several action letters
that were sent to prime ministers. Not much came from that. He spoke about
efforts to identify new ways to create international connections for parliamentarians around religious freedom.

Nazila Ghanea was another special advisor invited to speak at the 2015 Turkey Summit. Ghanea serves on the OSCE Advisory Panel of Experts on Freedom of Religion or Belief in the United Kingdom. She participated in a panel
on women, faith and sustainable development. She spoke about how, in terms
of peacebuilding and security, Security Council Resolution 1325 (S/RES/1325)
on women, peace and security recognizes a qualitative benefit that women
bring to peace negotiations and peacebuilding. She asked whether or not there
might be a qualitative benefit women bring to faith and sustainable development. She talked about the importance of conducting research that isolates
out the gender factor to develop empirical evidence as a first step toward
obtaining legal protection for vulnerable women of faith.

Additional advisors participating in the 2015 Turkey Summit included:
Cüneyt Orman—Advisor to the Central Bank of the Republic of Turkey—who

discussed the relationship between religiosity and state welfare spending; Dmitry Kabak—Member of the Panel of the OSCE/ODIHR Advisory Council on Freedom of Religion or Belief for Kyrgyzstan—spoke about religious freedom issues in the Kyrgyzstan context; and Roman Podoprigora explained how, in Kazakhstan, the President and the Cabinet of Ministries has established special advisory bodies to address issues of sustainable development in the system of public administration.

Civil Society

From the beginning, the F8 Initiative has emphasized civil society engagement. Most of the London Forum participants were from RNGOs engaged in development work. UK participants would continue to emphasize RNGOs until recently when UK delegates began to shift their attention to linkages between religion and the business community. The United States has consistently emphasized a pragmatic approach that prioritizes RNGO representation on the participant list. By way of contrast, RNGOs were not emphasized on the participant list in Russia, Italy, Japan, or France where the focus was more on worshiping faith traditions.

Canada developed the most elaborate engagement with civil society. Planning activities began two years in advance of their national F8 Summit. In early 2008, Kirton spoke across Canada on a cross-country tour co-sponsored by the Canadian Council of Churches and the University of Winnipeg's Faculty of Theology.[49] As a political scientist, Kirton referred to the religious network hosting the 2010 F8 Canada meetings to be the most organized and internationally connected network available to Canadians interested in influencing policy and priorities for G8 summits. In Canada, the faith-based network is more organized and internationally engaged than environmental, peace and development NGOs.[50] Canadian hosts developed a website that was used to foster dialogue from participating faith traditions on a draft collaborative statement during the year preceding the Summit. Comments were compiled in a document and systematically reviewed in preparation for the Summit. Faith traditions and youth were engaged to host MP dinners (see above). Twenty-five at-risk youth from different faiths, including Christianity, Jewish, Muslim and Hindu, were mentored through the religious education dinner dialogue process to foster civic responsibility and strengthen communities. Several domestic faith groups (e.g., Canadian Churches Forum for Global Ministries)

---

49   Suderman, "Economics and the Pulpit."
50   Ibid.

wrote summit organizers following the Summit indicating that the process impacted, and "will continue to shape" their work.[51]

After the 2010 Summit, the newly formed Canadian Interfaith Partnership collaborated with *Beyond 2015*, a civil society campaign for adoption of new development goals to replace the MDGs after the 2015 deadline. The campaign—which ended March 31, 2016 after the UN successfully adopted a new set of SDGs—was comprised of a network of 1,581 organisations from 142 countries. Of these, 69% were southern civil society organizations and 31% were northern civil society organizations; civil society organizations came from 44 countries in Africa, 38 countries in Europe, 26 countries in Asia, 25 countries in Latin America, 7 countries in the Pacific, and 2 countries in North America. As a result of the Canadian Interfaith Partnership's collaborative partnership with *Beyond 2015*, Hamilton was invited to address the United Nations High Panel on the MDGs as it determined what and how the MDGs should be built upon. Hamilton was the only faith leader among civil society participants that was invited to address the High Panel.[52] The 21 members of the High Panel were placed at roundtables with the 30 representatives of global civil society to discuss specific questions. Hamilton's contributions addressed the question of how inequality can be addressed to promote inclusive development.[53]

The Canadian leadership has continued to promote ongoing domestic civic engagement. The Canadian Council of Churches sponsored a national Justice Tour 2015 where leaders traveled across the country to stimulate and focus dialogue on issues of climate justice and poverty eradication.[54] During the first half of May, they visited four cities to develop a church leaders' pastoral statement to encourage Canadians to connect with elected officials to call for increased action. Despite recently tightened budgets, faith groups drew upon their spiritual capital to exercise some moral authority for the common good.

51   Jonathan Schmidt, June 30, 2010.

52   Hamilton, "To Boldly Go: Innovations Originating through the F8 Canadian Interfaith Leaders Summit which Strengthen Human Destiny and Community."

53   Karen Hamilton, "UN High Panel on the Millennium Development Goals" *Canadian Council of Churches* (2012). Published electronically December 6 https://www.council ofchurches.ca/whats-new/un-high-panel-on-the-millennium-development-goals/

54   Dennis Gruending, "Justice Tour 2015: Churches Focus on Climate Change and Ending Poverty," (2015), http://rabble.ca/print/blogs/bloggers/dennis-gruending/2015/05/justice-tour-2015-churches-focuses-on-climate-change-and-end.

William Vendley, a member of the ICC,[55] participated in a transnational 2015 faith-leader consultation on the moral dimensions of sustainable development and climate change held at the Vatican on April 28, 2015 in Rome. In his role as Secretary-General, he led an RfP group of senior religious leaders to collaborate with the Pontifical Academies of Sciences, the United Nations Sustainable Development Solutions Network, and Columbia University's Earth Institute. They dialogued with senior Vatican officials, some heads of states, the Secretary-General of the United Nations, and leading thinkers in science, economics and business. The dialogue focused on the moral and religious dimensions of climate change and sustainable development with particular attention to the impact on the world's poor.[56] The conference, *Protect the Earth, Dignify Humanity: The Moral Dimensions of Climate Change and Sustainable Development*, was convened five months prior to the UN adoption of a post-2015 sustainable development agenda. Eight months later, 196 countries met for the December talks in Paris that produced the universal climate change agreement.

Academia

The F8/F7/F20 Initiative has related to academia in a variety of ways over time. The F8/F7/F20 process has been the subject of academic analysis by the G8 Research Group and the G8/G20 Research Group at the Munk School of Global Affairs at University of Toronto.[57] On multiple occasions, academic institutions have provided the venue for summit meetings or offered other forms of organizational support. The University of Winnipeg provided the venue for F8 Canada in 2010, and Pacific Theological College provided the venue for

---

55   Vendley's participation in the ICC has been intermittent. His somewhat reluctant engagement is part of an ongoing legacy of the tensions associated with the double summit year of 2008.

56   William F. Vendley, "Vatican City: United Call for Moral Awakening on Climate Change," *Religions for Peace Global Newsletter* (2015).

57   Hajnal, "The 2006 St. Petersburg Summit and Civil Society"; "Civil Society and the 2008 G8 Hokkaido Summit"; "Civil Society at the 2009 G8 Summit in L'Aquila"; Peter I. Hajnal and Jenilee M. Guebert, "A Civil Society," in *G8 the Italian Summit 2009: From La Maddalena to L'Aquila*, ed. John Kirton (Toronto, Canada: Newsdesk Communications Ltd, 2009); Hajnal, "The G20"; *The G7/G8 System: Evolution, Role and Documentation*; "Head to Head: Summits in Canada in June 2010: The Muskoka G8 Meets the Toronto G20"; "The World Religions Summit 2010—Interfaith Leaders in the G8 Nations: Notes of an Observer"; John Kirton, "Leveling the Playing Field," in *G8 the UK Summit Lough Erne: Helping Global Trade to Take Off*, ed. John Kirton, Madeline Koch, and Nicholas Bayne (London, UK: Newsdesk Media, 2013).

the F20 Regional Pre-Conference in Suva, Fiji in 2016. University faculty have invested significant amounts of time in the Initiative. Griffith University's Adams and Durham have both expended enormous energy organizing the F20 Summits (2014–2017). Since the shift to shadowing the G20 process, academic institutions have played important roles by providing venues for meetings and opportunities to dovetail summits to existing events.

In 2010, a representative from the G8 Research Group at the University of Toronto collaborated with the Initiative in 2010 to convene five regional gatherings across Canada. Meetings were convened to educate civil society on the MDGs, and the G-plus System. The Canadian Interfaith Partnership convened activities directed toward holding Canada accountable for past commitments to ensure MDG fulfillment.[58] Between 2010 and 2016, the G8 Research Group invited the F8 Secretaries-General to make annual contributions to the *G8/G7* publication.

In the early years of the F8 Initiative, summit speakers and participants were predominantly represented by religious practitioners of either church-based or RNGO-based networks involved in development or interfaith activities. With the shift to shadowing F20 Summits, the process has become increasingly professionalized. The percentage of academics among the participants has been slowly increasing over time.

Business

The F8/F7/F20 Initiative has been slow to engage with the business community, but that is beginning to change with the F20. The early F8 process focused on NGO civil society and political engagement with the G-plus System. In recent years, the process has begun to engage with business communities. Brian Grim—President of the Religious Freedom and Business Foundation— has been a keynote speaker at the 2014 Australian and 2015 Turkey Summits. At Istanbul, Edmund Newell spoke about his congregation's past involvement in the *Make Poverty History Campaign* when the F8 was initially born. He said that, in retrospect, if he had to do it all over again, he would have strategized about how business can work *for*, rather than against, the poor as a strategic approach.[59]

The F20 Summit presentations have increasingly highlighted connections between religion and economics. Panels and keynote addresses repeatedly focus on the relationship between religion, business and economic development

58   Hamilton, "To Boldly Go: Innovations Originating through the F8 Canadian Interfaith Leaders Summit Which Strengthen Human Destiny and Community."

59   Steiner, "G20 Interfaith Summit Summary Report," (2015), 35.

in various regions of the world. For example, the 2015 Turkey F20 Summit thematically addressed several ways in which business is impacted by religion including:

· How socioeconomic development relates to human rights and religious freedom (empirical data was often provided from countries to support claims)
· How religious freedom, human rights and interfaith dialogue can be concretely integrated into development issues through several of the Sustainable Development Goals (e.g., Goal 1: No Poverty; Goal 2: Zero Hunger; Goal 4: Quality Education; Goal 5: Gender Equity; Goal 8: Decent Work & Economic Growth; Goal 15: Life on Land; Goal 16: Peace, Justice and Strong Institutions; etc.)
· How the existence of interfaith groups can reduce social hostilities and enable governments and businesses to engage religious traditions without showing religious favoritism of one tradition over another[60]

Diverse perspectives are often considered. For example, in 2015, Brian Grim presented research explaining how religious freedom contributes to sustainable development. He was at the United Nations for the launch of the SDGs, and he met with Facebook Founder/Director, Bono from U2, and CEOs from a variety of companies to discuss how business can be a constructive part of the process, rather than enemies of the process. He reported how the UN Secretary-General emphasized *Goal 16: Ensuring Peace,* and the way faith and business can contribute to it. Later, at the 2016 Para-Olympics, the Religious Freedom and Business Foundation together with the UN presented global and interfaith peace awards to salute CEO commitments to advancing interfaith understanding and peace worldwide. The awards have become an annual event.

A very different perspective toward business was offered at the same Summit by Mohamad Hammour who is Chair of Guidance Financial Group in France. Hammour described how the narrative of modern economics becomes anti-religious. "Something to consider from finance," he said, "is that commercial trade and exchange is rooted in metaphysics. Commercial exchange involves intrinsic values. Exchanging shadows for shadows, whether money or derivatives, in the absence of intrinsic values, results in merchants of shadows building houses of cards. We should not be surprised if we observe chronic tendencies for these houses of cards to collapse."[61]

---

60   Ibid.
61   Ibid., 15.

An F20 2015 panel on Islamic Finance and Theories of Development focused on the history of Islamic financial institutions and ways Islamic finance contributes to sustainable economic development. Moderated by Mehmet Bulut who is President of Istanbul Sabahattin Zaim University in Turkey, presenters were Needet Şensoy (Chairman, Audit Committee, International Islamic Liquidity Management Corporation, Turkey), Cüneyt Orman (Advisor, Central Bank of the Republic of Turkey, Turkey), Asad Zaman (Vice Chancellor, Pakistan Institute of Development Economics, Quaid-i-Azam University, Pakistan), and Murat Çizakça (Emeritus and Adjunct Professor of Islamic Finance, Luxembourg School of Finance, University of Luxembourg, Luxembourg).[62]

In an F20 2015 panel on spiritual capital and economic development in China, Lin Li from the Chinese Academy of Social Sciences addressed what Islam contributes to China's economy. There are currently an estimated 13 million Chinese Muslims comprising ten officially recognized ethnic groups in the country. There is an Islamic Economic Community in China that contributes to the development of regional transnational economic relationships that are mutually beneficial to participating countries. In 2015 alone, China created 163 investment projects in collaboration with the Muslim international community.

In the same panel, Nanlai Cao from Renmin University spoke about the Chinese Christian diaspora network created by the immigration of Chinese merchants to France from Wenzhou, a coastal city popularly referred to by residents as 'China's Jerusalem.' China is home to one of the largest Protestant populations in the world (estimated at 40 million). China's Christian transnationalism has contributed to the international expansion of Chinese commerce. The ethnic trading community provided a transnational bridge for commerce. Participation in Christian congregations also embedded people in the community. In this way, he showed how Christianity played an important role in migrants' adaptation to dramatic socioeconomic changes brought about by transnational living circumstances. He described the migrant church as a large civil society structure where the family, market and state intersect. The migrant traders operate small businesses such as garment factories and restaurants. They trade in light industrial products across Europe. The diaspora actively expand their business networks thereby planting an indigenous model of Chinese life throughout Europe. Chinese merchants celebrate doing business as a celebration of authentic faith reconciling the conservative spiritual tradition of the Chinese house church movement with the utopian dreams of capitalist success. The Christian merchants emphasize an entrepreneurial

---

62   Ibid., 37–42.

logic of being resourceful and capable church members, particularly in the face of state pressures, whether in China or in France. They utilize an informal finance mechanism for both business and church development that operates significantly outside of the state sanctioned economic framework using house churches and transnational immigrant networks.[63]

Although more attention has been given recently to how religion and business can work for, rather than against, the poor, the F8/F7/F20 Initiative has not lost its prophetic edge to become a blind endorser of globalization. One of the opening keynote addresses given by Marshall at the 2015 Turkey F20 Summit emphasized the critical nature of the problems facing the world. Marshall emphasized how the problems present groups with a rare opportunity for coming together with a variety of foci from the Sustainable Development Goals, the Paris COP 21 meetings, and the F20 meetings, to the countless meetings on refugee issues and negotiations on Syria, Iraq, Philippines, and Columbia. "Part of the challenge," she said, "is understanding how all of these come together, to disentangle the threads, establish links and discern what can and should be done." She discussed the governance crisis affecting international development. She identified four important trends as particularly relevant to the Istanbul discussions in relation to business: 1) the need for new approaches to fragile states, 2) the enormous challenges associated with inequity, 3) divergent models of development, and 4) how human rights and religious freedom relate to the challenges of socioeconomic development.[64]

Media

The F8/F7/F20 Initiative has engaged with the media in a variety of ways depending upon the local context over time. In countries where government sponsorship was involved, professional media coverage was sometimes sought (e.g., Japan 2008). In countries that heavily emphasize civic engagement, media professionals were mentored about reporting on the Initiative in a manner that greatly increased diverse coverage of the process (e.g., Canada 2010). The media has also been used as a tool for e-governance (e.g., United Kingdom 2013, Youth Pre-Conference process 2014–15).

Media professionals have been involved in several of the summits. In 2008, the F8 Kyoto-Osaka meeting organizers involved the Japan Broadcasting Corporation in covering the event. After the summit, a professional information video about the summit and the delivery of the statement to Japanese government officials was distributed. A press conference was convened at the end of

---

63   Ibid., 71–74.
64   Ibid., 11–12.

the event and a full page newspaper article was published describing the event in *The Japan Times,* Japan's largest English-language newspaper.

The F20 shadow summits have involved media representatives such as Rachael Kohn, producer and broadcaster for the American Broadcasting Corporation Radio National (ABC Radio National) since 1992. Kohn made presentations at the 2014 Australia and 2015 Turkey F20 Summits and interviewed several of the participants for follow-up podcast coverage of the summit process on ABC's *The Spirit of Things.* Rachel Kohn has produced award winning features for *Encounter* as well as two-part television documentaries on ABC TV; she is a popular speaker on religion and spirituality in Australia.

The Canadians not only involved media, they made efforts to track and measure how extensive the media coverage was across Canada in faith-based communities and secular contexts. To cultivate relationships with media professionals in 2010, the Canadian Summit hosted an interfaith media forum where presentations were made about the responsibility people of faith have to engage with the media on ethical issues related to the common good. Presenters discussed which media outlets were most important, how to develop talking points, media contacts, and appropriate content for print, radio or television. Information Resource Kits were developed and distributed for participants to use prior to, during and as part of the post-summit follow-up process that contained information on common religious ethics, the statement, and information on the MDGs.[65] The summit website hosted live streaming of the event and many of the summit meetings were open to the general public. Keynote speeches were recorded and archived for public access on the www .faithchallengeg8.com website for several years following the summit. A press conference was hosted immediately following closing ceremonies. Some of the requests for interviews were so numerous that delegates could not accommodate the volume.[66] Organizers kept a record of media coverage immediately surrounding the June Summit. Several faith-based magazines, websites and blogs reported on the event including the *Anglican Journal* (circulation 170,000), the *Bahá'í World News Service* (online publication), *Christian News*, *Canadian Jewish Congress* (online publication), *Canadian Mennonite* (circ. 15,000), *Catholic Courier* (circ. 111,000), *Catholic News Service* (circ. 30,000), *Christian Week* (circ. 20,000), *Ecumenical Press* (online publication), *Episcopal Life* (circ. 220,000), *Indian Country Today* (online publication), *IQRA—Muslim* (online publication), *Jewish Independent* (online publication), *Council for a*

---

65   Hamilton, "To Boldly Go: Innovations Originating through the F8 Canadian Interfaith Leaders Summit Which Strengthen Human Destiny and Community."
66   Ibid.

Parliament of the World's Religions (online publication), *Presbyterian Church US* (online publication), *The Canadian Jewish News* (circ. 35,000), *The Catholic Register* (circ. 30,000), the *United Church Observer* (circ. 60,000) and the *Winnipeg Jewish Review* (circ. 122,000). Radio and podcast coverage included *CBC Radio* (English and French), *CJOB, Church Matters,* and *Voice of Russia.* Secular media coverage included articles in the *Amherst Daily News* (circ. 2,600), *Daily Herald* (circ. 2,100), *Edmonton Metro* (circ. 40,000), *G8 Information Centre* (online publication), *Moosejaw Times Herald* (circ. 8,300), *Rabble. ca* (online publication with monthly viewers of 100,000), *South Asian News* (online publication), *The Huntsville Forester* (online publication), *Toronto Star* (circ. 284,000), *Truro Daily News* (circ. 5,400), and the *Winnipeg Free Press* (circ. 162,000). Television coverage was provided by *CTV* on June 21, 2010 (1,000,000 viewers). Conservative estimates drawn from this information indicate that coverage of the Canadian Summit reached a faith-based audience exceeding 800,000 and a general audience exceeding 1.5 million people for a total exposure of approximately 2.5 million people.

In 2013, the United Kingdom's approach combined the Open Letter technique with e-governance. The Youth Pre-Conference also did this, but with less intentionality, purpose and direction. The Open Letter is a popular format that utilizes the letter format for media distribution via the internet, newspapers, magazines and books to direct the personal concerns, often critical, of an individual or group to individuals or groups for social and political commentary. The process is public and intended for wide circulation. The Open Letter technique can be an effective tool for social change. For example, during the second wave of the women's movement in France, Gaullist feminist Françoise Parturier wrote Open Letters from 1968–1974 to intellectually intervene and politically engage an audience as a way of shattering conventions and contributing to social change.[67] In her case, the medium used was a magazine; she was a regular columnist with *Le Figaro* from 1956–1975. Although research appears scant on use of the Open Letter technique, initial research indicates that computer mediated Open Letters (posting them on the internet) are high in personalization (private impact) and low in exclusivity (public impact), and they represent an epistolary genre that bridges the gap between mass and personal communication.[68]

---

67   Imogen Long, "Writing Gaullist Feminism: Francoise Parturier's Open Letters 1968–1974," *Modern & Contemporary France* 19, no. 3 (2011).

68   Irina Chesnokova, "The Addressee Types of the Internet Open Letters," *Procedia—Social and Behavioral Sciences* 206 (2015).

E-governance refers to the use of electronic information and communication technologies to exchange information, communicate transactions, and deliver government services. The approach integrates various stand-alone systems and services between government-to-customer (G2C), government-to-business (G2B), and government-to-government (G2G); e-governance also cultivates interaction within the entire government network. E-governance is considered a convenient, efficient and transparent approach to connecting with citizens. Although e-governance is usually used to cut costs and more efficiently manage service delivery, e-governance is increasingly seen as a way to strengthen democratic engagement for social and economic development through what has been termed 'e-democracy'.[69] E-governance is considered a valuable tool for expanding government-citizen communication to bring citizens as a group closer to political officials, particularly in developing contexts affected by financial pressures and corruption; the 'written record' of interactions increases both transparency and accountability.[70] Government to citizen use of e-governance for service delivery has been shown to have a problematic impact on citizens' security or privacy concerns,[71] but citizens have also been shown to push back and proactively flip the service delivery model to alter how government solves public problems.[72] Although e-governance is still under-researched, early case studies indicate that technological systems can be useful ways for citizens and governments to collaboratively innovate solutions that address barriers and design comprehensive strategies for addressing social problems.[73]

Citizen use of the internet for purposes of civic engagement is increasingly referred to as Web 2.0. Civic acts are accomplished or advanced through the use of online tools such as blogging, chatting, editing, texting, Facebook

---

69   Kelvin Joseph Bwalya and Stephen Mutula, *Digital Solutions for Contemporary Democracy and Government* (Hershey, PA: ICI Global, 2015).

70   Ibid.

71   Jyoti Kharade, "G2C E-Governance Project Implementation at Local Level in a Pune Division Context," *BVIMSR Journal of Management Research* 8, no. 1 (2016).

72   Dennis Linders, Calvin Zhou-Peng Liao, and Cheng-Ming Wang, "Proactive E-Governance: Flipping the Service Delivery Model from Pull to Push in Taiwan," *Government Information Quarterly* 8, no. 4 (2015).

73   Albert Meijer, "E-Governance Innovation: Barriers and Strategies," *Government Information Quarterly* 32, April (2015): 198–206; Carlos Nunes Silva, *Citizen E-Participation in Urban Governance: Crowdsourcing and Collaborative Creativity*, Advances in Electronic Government, Digital Divide, and Regional Development (Hershey, PA: Information Science Reference, 2013).

or tweeting to engage citizens in deliberation and action on public issues.[74] When the United Kingdom innovated the F8 summit process in 2013 to combine publication of an Open Letter with the social media #1000daystogo Twitter Campaign, they adopted Web 2.0 as a new strategy for civic engagement. Although the F20 process records events using the hashtag #G20Interfaith and they have a handle @F20News, the Web 2.0 strategy used in 2013 was not repeated from 2014–2017.

Conclusion

This chapter provided empirical support for the claim that use of a leadership rotation model by the F8/F7/F20 Initiative resulted in summit diversity that varied in accordance with different national contexts between 2005 and 2017. National differences created internal tensions that threatened process continuity. Steps taken to strengthen the organizational process with formation of the ICC initially only made matters worse, but eventually the ICC provided enough organizational stability for continuity and growth over time. Variation in religious rituals, special events, excursions and engagement with external relations were highlighted to demonstrate various ways in which the process has been differently conducted over time depending upon the national context of the host. Aborted events were also detailed in relation to events that were planned and then canceled.

---

74   Laura W. Black, "Blog, Chat, Edit, Text, or Tweet? Using Online Tools to Advance Adult Civic Engagement," *New Directions for Adult and Continuing Education*, no. 135 (2012).

CHAPTER 8

Reform, Assessment, and Impact

This chapter highlights cosmopolitan aspects of the F8/F7/F20 process, and focuses on reform, assessment and impact. The first section considers the variety of pressures for internal reform of the Initiative. The entire cycle of F8 summits is discussed through the lens of scholarship on reflexive governance. In the second section, the F8/F7/F20 process is assessed for how it has been shaped by changes in information technology, by changes in international relations, and by changing norms of religious public engagement.

Reform

Proposals to reform, improve, replace or abolish the F8 process arose from the beginning. As early as 2006, religious leaders were questioning the authenticity of a 'top-down' summit process that was not significantly influenced by civil society RNGOs. Reform proposals have ranged widely in scope and kind. Some have addressed the composition of the Initiative through increasing (Canada 2010), reducing (US 2012) or changing (UK 2013) participation. Canada was the first to adopt a delegation model that reflected the religious landscape of national hosts; this was adjusted when the shadowing process shifted from the G8 to the G20. Other reform proposals have suggested institutional changes including whether and how to establish an International Continuance Committee (ICC).[1] Once established, reform proposals explored the degree of organizational authority and type of leadership structure it might offer the ongoing process. When shadow summitry shifted from the G8 to the G20, the committee shifted from a 'crisis committee' to being more of an 'advisory committee.' Expanding or contracting the agenda has been much discussed, as has been the degree of practical application[2] and pragmatic relevance of the summit model.[3] RNGO-based summits (UK, US) were more supportive of developing specific public policy recommendations than gathering top-tier religious

---

1 Christie and Hamilton, Email exchange, August 2009.
2 Steiner, "Reflexive Governance Dynamics Operative within Round One of the World Religious Leaders' Dialogue with the G8 (2005–2013)," 9.
3 Reed, "Project Proposal—2013 G8 Religious Leaders' Initiative"; Christie, "In Sundry Places: The Domestic Impact of the F8/F20 International Interfaith Summit Process."

© KONINKLIJKE BRILL NV, LEIDEN, 2018 | DOI 10.1163/9789004365018_009

leaders (Russia) or galvanizing widespread civic engagement with high-level moral statements (Canada).[4] The Initiative's evolving relationship with civil society organizations (e.g., Christian Aid, Tear Fund), academic think tanks (e.g., the G8/G7 and G20 Research Groups), academia (e.g., the Centre for Interfaith & Cultural Dialogue at Griffith University in Australia and the ICLRS in Italy), business (e.g., The Religious Freedom and Business Foundation), development (e.g., Berkley Center for Religion, Peace, and World Affairs) and youth (e.g., Faiths Act Fellows with the Tony Blair Faith Foundation) have also influenced reform efforts.

Although shadow summitry would not shift from the G8 to the G20 until 2014, religious leaders were asking "Does the G8 Matter?" as early as 2008.[5] Charles Reed from the UK delegation noted that the F8 summits had become part of a larger civil society process applying pressure to the G8 to lead the world in a different direction, but he challenged religious leaders to consider whether or not this approach might be "exaggerating the power of the G8, almost to the point of caricature" as if the G8 "could make poverty history, if it so chose, more or less as a matter of political will."[6] He critiqued this overly agentic focus of attention on the G8 as misplaced, but then went on to identify ways in which attention to the G8 is "entirely merited, and this relates to the issue of governance."[7] He further clarified his statement:

> We have come to realise that the new global political economy is not operating totally anarchically; it is actually being governed, however unsatisfactory that process may be from various normative points of view. To many people, the G8 now represents prospectively the effective centre of global governance. The G8 has now expanded from its traditional fire side chats to embrace meetings of foreign, finance, trade, justice, environment, home, employment, energy and education ministers as well as *ad hoc* meetings, task forces and working groups to address pressing issues. These meetings are backed-up by associated meetings of officials, thereby adding to a growing sense that a system of rule may be emerging in and around the annual summits of leaders. Seen from this perspective, the G8 is more than a mere symbol of power, but less than an actually powerful institution that routinely takes and carries into practice

---

4 Steiner, "Reflexive Governance Dynamics Operative within Round One of the World Religious Leaders' Dialogue with the G8 (2005–2013)."

5 Reed, "The G8: Our Spiritual and Moral Responsibilities: Does the G8 Matter?"

6 Ibid.

7 Ibid.

major decisions of global significance. What it does best is play an overarching role in relation to other, more formal institutions of global governance, seeking to coordinate, legitimise, prioritise and steer the actions of the leading states in relation both to each other and to the global institutions.[8]

This self-awareness of the power of informal governance has significantly shaped how the F8/F7/F20 Initiative continues to self-organize.

Accountability[9]

Participation in the civil society accountability movement has resulted in pressure for RNGOs to be increasingly transparent and accountable themselves. Religious leader delegates have occasionally raised questions about a summit process that seemed to have taken on a life of its own, proceeding without checks and balances. At one point, the UK member of the International Continuance Committee, Rt. Rev. Nicholas Baines who currently serves as the Bishop of Leeds, said, "I can see how the host nation might benefit from this experience; but do these summits really have a global impact, or is this just religious tourism for the elite?" His committee colleagues considered the question brutal, but honest, and worthy of ongoing consideration.[10] In response to increasing pressures for civil society accountability, several of the participating RNGOs (e.g, Tear Fund, World Vision) have begun to issue and publish self-accountability reports.[11] Several of the larger participating RNGOs have become members of the International NGO Accountability Charter (e.g., Islamic Relief, Tear Fund, World Vision International).[12]

Strengthening the accountability of organizations is a complex, difficult process with well-intentioned actors often working at cross-purposes. Koppel has identified five dimensions of accountability: transparency, liability,

---

8   Ibid.

9   Portions of this section were previously published in Steiner, "Religious Soft Power as Accountability Mechanism for Power in World Politics: The Interfaith Leaders' Summit(s)."

10   Christie, "In Sundry Places: The Domestic Impact of the F8/F20 International Interfaith Summit Process."

11   Bryony Norman, "Monitoring and Accountability Practices for Remotely Managed Projects Implemented in Volatile Operating Environments," (2012), *Tearfund.* Published online at http://betterevaluation.org/sites/default/files/remote_monitoring_and_accountability _practice_web_2.pdf; Elie Gasagara, "Accountability," *World Vision International Accountability Report 2014* (2014), http://www.wvi.org/accountability/publication/2014 -accountability-report.

12   See http://www.ingoaccountabilitycharter.org/charter-members/.

controllability, responsibility, and responsiveness. He explains the difficult process in terms of how conflicting expectations born of different conceptions of accountability can undermine a global organization's effectiveness.[13] Competing models of accountability can destabilize even-handed assessments of INGO contributions with intergovernmental networks favoring "delegation" models, and INGOs favoring "participation" models.[14] As noted earlier, the F8/F7/F20 process has been influenced by both models, often leaning more toward one or the other depending upon the 'bent' of the national host. When shadowing shifted from the G8/G7 to the G20, the practicality concerns of ensuring comprehensive delegations shifted the emphasis more toward participation models. According to Steffek and Ferretti, although there are potential trade-offs between delegation and participation approaches, civil society organizations tend to be torn between their deliberative and watchdog functions.[15] This ongoing tension has been evident within the Initiative.

Disclosure of information has become a heavily relied upon tool used to strengthen accountability, so much so, that Gupta considers transparency to be a moral and political imperative in global governance.[16] The F8/F7/F20 process is not formally organized as a non-profit organization, so official reports and financial records are not filed; the process works as a collaborative effort of other organizations such as the Canadian Council of Churches which has kept records of the G8 shadow summit process since 2007. Hamilton provided open access to this author into all of their records associated with the Initiative, including financial, upon request in December 2014.

Buchanan and Keohane have noted how the "soft power" of INGOs operates in a transnational civil society channel of accountability as broad accountability mechanisms under terms of broad transparency where reliable information gets used to assess some of the most fundamental goals of the institution in the pursuit of global justice.[17] Broad accountability offers provision for the contestation of the terms of accountability, whereas narrow accountability does not provide for the revision of existing standards. This is important for

---

13   J. Koppell, "Pathologies of Accountability: ICANN and the Challenge of 'Multiple Accountabilities Disorder'" *Administration Review* 65 (2005).

14   R.W. Grant and R. Keohane, "Accountability and Abuses of Power in World Politics," *American Political Science Review* 99 (2005).

15   J. Steffek and P.M. Ferretti, "Accountability or 'Good Decisions'? The Competing Goals of Civil Society Participation in International Governance," *Global Society* 23 (2009).

16   A. Gupta, "Transparency under Scrutiny: Information Disclosure in Global Environmental Governance," *Global Environmental Politics* 8 (2008).

17   A. Buchanan and R. Keohane, "The Legitimacy of Global Governance Institutions," *Ethics and International Affairs* 20 (2006).

understanding F8 engagement with the G-plus System where the accountability process has continued to evolve and innovate over time. Broad transparency is critical for the operation of broad accountability. Reliable information must be highly accessible by civil society to function as accountability mechanisms. If deliberation occurs behind closed doors, INGOs cannot do their work. For this reason, civil society accessibility to, and engagement with, the G-plus System becomes very important. Buchanan and Keohane discuss how, in the absence of global government, the soft power of INGOs influences the functioning of global governing institutions with regard to the people whose interests they believe the governing institutions should represent. In the absence of democracy, legitimacy becomes highly dependent on the activities of these institutionally organized INGOs that function as external epistemic actors in the transnational civil society channel of accountability.[18] From this perspective, the legitimacy of global governing institutions can only be assessed in relationship with the informed ongoing contestation of INGOs. INGOs often tackle the most difficult accountability challenges, representing the "voices of the weak and powerless." Willetts refers to them as the "conscience of the world,"[19] exercising a form of accountability that Newell describes as *claimed from below* rather than *conferred from above.*[20] In keeping with this approach, civil society assessments of G-plus System outcomes were included in year-by-year descriptions of the F8/F7/F20 process in Chapter 4.

But who (or what) holds civil society organizations accountable? Although INGOs face their own problems of internal accountability,[21] their effectiveness often rests on their claim to moral authority and their use of "shaming" tactics to affect the reputation of organizations through media exposure.[22] Because INGOs are more single minded and agile than states, they have an advantage over states in media struggles. They can lobby governments. To the extent that they command the allegiances of large constituencies, they are able to influence public opinion. Their activities augment statist politics with civic life politics, playing on the fact that governments and corporations are vulnerable to public opinion. INGOs can use knowledge as a form of power to shape the

---

18   Ibid.

19   Willetts, *The Conscience of the World: The Influence of Non-Governmental Organizations in the UN System.*

20   Peter Newell, "Civil Society, Corporate Accountability and the Politics of Climate Change," *Global Environmental Politics* 8 (2008).

21   T. Risse, "Transnational Governance and Legitimacy," in *Fifth Pan-European Conference on International Relations* (The Hague, Netherlands 2004).

22   Keohane, "Global Governance and Democratic Accountability."

nature and terms of the debate through evolving norms and ideas that can serve to either strengthen, or undermine, the legitimacy of the global system.[23] But the ad hoc aspects of INGO activism can be destabilizing. Which INGOs should be taken seriously and why?

In response to this question, Buchanan and Keohane developed a complex standard useful for the broader horizontal network of leaders who must identify valuable INGO accountability partners engaged in holding political leaders accountable even when the leaders themselves do not recognize a corresponding obligation.[24] The complex standard, were it to be widely accepted by governing institutions, would provide a principled proposal to bring order to the messy process that currently characterizes the assessment of global governance. It was their hope that the complex standard would help guide reform efforts in an evolving historic context. Their ideal "external epistemic actor"—composed of individuals and groups outside the institution in question—would appeal to a normative concept of justice that is separate from the standard used to assess the legitimacy of the global governing institution. That is, the external epistemic actor would have content-independent, non-coercive reasons for their choice to comply (or not comply) with the institution they assessed. The external epistemic actor would gain knowledge about the institution, use their own norms to interpret and asses that knowledge, and exchange it with others in ways intended to influence institutional behavior. "The complex standard almost makes it clear," say Buchanan and Keohane, "that whether the institution is legitimate does not depend solely upon its own characteristics, but also upon the epistemic-deliberative relationships between the institution and epistemic actors outside it."[25] The complex standard is their proffered solution to the governance issues that arise from situations where people want to hold governing bodies accountable for redress but the governing bodies do not recognize a corresponding obligation. Their proposal was not initially rooted in any specific historical illustration, but was offered as a temporary, fluid guide with the suggestion that, "were such a standard widely accepted, it could bolster public support for valuable global governance institutions that either satisfy the standard or at least make credible efforts to do so."[26]

---

23   T. Risse, "Transnational Actors and World Politics," in *Handbook of International Relations*, ed. W. Carlsnaes, T. Risse, and B. Simmons (London, England: Sage, 2002).

24   Buchanan and Keohane, "The Legitimacy of Global Governance Institutions."

25   Ibid., 411.

26   Ibid., 406.

Although Buchanan and Keohane had human rights organizations more in mind when they considered its specific INGO application,[27] Steiner applied the standard to the F8 process in 2011 in order to *systematically* address the value of the F8 process for global governance since the value cannot be logically determined by lack of mutual response by one party in relation to the other in the G-plus System context. Steiner drew on Buchanan and Keohane's proposal for a complex standard and analyzed the extent to which the F8 process met the six criteria they proposed.[28] For data, Steiner conducted content analysis of summit communiqués, pre-summit responses to the 2010 draft, press releases, and website information from 2005 to 2010. Data was additionally collected from UN MDG documents, the sacred texts and traditions of the diverse religious traditions involved in the initiative, and the participants at the 2010 Canadian Summit. Steiner's assessment of the F8 process from origins through the 2010 expression in Canada estimated a remarkable degree of compliance with the Complex Standard (see Table 8.1). The first two standards showed weakest compliance and the last four standards showed strongest compliance. Steiner concluded that one of the greatest strengths of the Initiative's network—and the strength of their service to the leadership of the G-plus System as dialogue partners—is their shared understanding of the moral vulnerabilities that stem from the accountability gaps of global 'governance without government.' Senior religious leaders have heightened moral sensibilities on behalf of the most vulnerable people in the global community. But their strengths are related to their greatest areas of weakness. The other-worldly idealism associated with sacred vocations may not be sufficiently distinguished from this-worldly judgements of what is realistically possible for governments to achieve. Religious leaders live in tension between the ideal and the real, between what exists in 'the now' and what is envisioned as possible in the 'not yet,' whereas the legitimacy of political leaders is often outcome dependent on services rendered. Thus, politicians tend to be more interested in making decisions that are probable rather than possible. The dialogue that emerges between those concerned primarily with moral will and those concerned primarily with political will is a conversation that—if it does not collapse into posturing, dismissal, or condemnation—has the potential to push the language of probability toward

---

27 A. Buchanan and R. Keohane, "The Legitimacy of Global Governance," in *Human Rights, Legitimacy, and the Use of Force*, ed. A. Buchanan (Oxford, UK: Oxford University Press, 2010).

28 Steiner, "Religious Soft Power as Accountability Mechanism for Power in World Politics: The Interfaith Leaders' Summit(s)."

TABLE 8.1   *F8 process compliance with the complex standard (2005–2010)*

Complex standard desiderata	Estimated level of compliance
1. The standard must provide a reasonable public basis for coordinated support of the institutions in question on the basis of moral reasons that are widely accessible in spite of the persistence of significant moral disagreement about the requirements of justice.	PARTIAL COMPLIANCE
2. The standards must not confuse legitimacy with justice but nonetheless must not allow that extremely unjust institutions are legitimate.	PARTIAL COMPLIANCE
3. The standard must take the ongoing consent of democratic states as a presumptive necessary, but not sufficient, condition; given the limitation of formal democracies, consent is incorporated when institutions satisfy the criteria of minimal moral acceptability, comparative benefit, and institutional integrity.	COMPLIANCE
4. The standard should be consonant with democratic values but must not make authorization by a global democracy a necessary condition.	COMPLIANCE
5. The standard must reflect the dynamic character of global governance institutions, able to respond to changing institutional goals, means and conditions over time.	COMPLIANCE
6. The standard must be able to provide broad accountability in the context of the accountability gap through a functioning transnational civil society channel of accountability—addressing the problem of bureaucratic discretion and the tendency of democratic states to disregard the legitimate interest of foreigners.	COMPLIANCE

objective possibility.[29] Together, decisions can be made that dare to address the question raised by Langdon Winner: "As we make things work, what kind of world are we making?"[30]

The Complex Standard has been used a few times to assess civil society accountability processes. Buchanan and Keohane applied the Complex Standard themselves to human rights organizations.[31] A few years later, the Complex Standard was used to assess climate change geoengineering ventures.[32] Campbell, Kumar and Slagle engaged with Buchanan and Keohane's Complex Standard for its usefulness in discerning the basis upon which civil society organizations confer legitimacy on global governance institutions, but the proposed Complex Standard has not been broadly applied in political science.[33] For this reason, Steiner has not updated with a more recent Complex Standard assessment of the F8 process.

Enduring Informality

The F8/F7/F20 Initiative has remained an informal process despite the problems informality has, at times, created. A tradition had been established since the 2006 Russian Summit of handing over leadership to the next host to close the meetings. At the close of the Germany 2007 Summit in June, Miyake was present. He accepted the invitation to host the 2008 Japan Summit as part of the German closing ceremonies. Shortly thereafter, Hamilton proposed that an International Continuance Committee be formed and that it adopt a leadership model in which the Summit is chaired by a country where the G8 was meeting and then had as Vice-Chairs, the leadership of the previous host and the religious leadership of the country where the G8 will be the following year. The proposal was not immediately adopted.[34] Religions for Peace (RfP) had not attended the Germany Summit as their organization is not strong in that context. Japan, however, is a context where RfP has such a strong and influential presence, that in August, RfP Japan began organizing a summit based on an 'in principle' agreement associated with their organizational history. By then,

---

29   Ibid.

30   Winner, *The Whale and the Reactor: A Search for Limits in an Age of High Technology.*

31   Buchanan and Keohane, "The Legitimacy of Global Governance."

32   Andrew L. Strauss and William C.G. Burns, *Climate Change Geoengineering: Philosophical Perspectives, Legal Issues, and Governance Frameworks* (Cambridge: Cambridge University Press, 2013).

33   Joel R. Campbell, Leena Thacker Kumar, and Steve Slagle, "Bargaining Sovereignty: State Power and Networked Governance in a Globalizing World," *International Social Science Review* 85, no. 3/4 (2010).

34   Karen Hamilton, Email, June 15, 2017.

however, Miyake had already set key organizational processes in motion.[35] Follow-up international efforts among religious leaders to create a singular summit using informal mechanisms were unsuccessful now that two separate national summits were already in motion. Process continuity was even more difficult to determine for Italy the following year since two summits had been convened in Japan. The Japan experience raised several questions associated with the ongoing informal process: How authoritative is the summit closing ceremony hand-off (Germany to Japan)? What happens if there is no ceremonial hand-off at all (Japan to Italy)? In Italy, the leadership network would organize an International Continuance Committee, but even then, the process would remain decidedly informal. More questions would continue to emerge. What happens if a ceremonial hand-off occurs to a religious leader with weak national infrastructural supports (e.g., Canada to France)? What happens if the only national delegates present are unable to host the next year's event (e.g., France to the US)? What happens if the hand-off is accepted by a host who refuses to host a summit at all (e.g., United States to United Kingdom)?

At a deeper level, why have religious leaders remained so committed to maintaining such an informal, and therefore fragile, process? What value attracts sustained religious leader engagement to a process that 'rejectionists' have called into question as a 'necessary fiction'?[36] Is dialogue an outmoded 'fireside chat' model of governance or is it a form of religious leader engagement appropriate to transnational relations and G-plus System engagement?

As noted earlier, F8/F7/F20 shadow summitry mimics G-plus System summitry in organizational form. Although scholars have offered diverse explanations for why the G-plus System operates as it does, there is widespread agreement that G-plus System summitry is decidedly informal. Kelly Grant has pointed out that the informality allows leaders to sit down together in person to develop innovative responses to financial crisis.[37] David Shorr and Thomas Wright have described the 'institutionalized informality' as an intentional strategy whereby the lack of a solid institutional structure keeps the focus on the discussions of the decision makers.[38] The informality of the process has been repeatedly analyzed as crucial for the development of shared expectations,

---

35   Yoshinobu Miyake, "2008 G8 Religious Leaders Summit: Memorandum of Intent," (2008).
36   Steiner, "Reflexive Governance Dynamics Operative within Round One of the World Religious Leaders' Dialogue with the G8 (2005–2013)."
37   Kelly Grant, "Paul Martin," Globe and Mail, May 31, 2010.
38   David Shorr and Thomas Wright, "The G20 and Global Governance: An Exchange," Survival: Global Politics and Strategy 52, no. 2 (2010); Guoxing Wang, "Financial Crisis: Its Impacts on International Economic System and Geopolitics," Global Review 3 (2009).

the generation of positive pressure and leadership momentum and the development of domestic and international compliance. Bruce Jones, Carlos Pascual, and Stephen John Stedman have described the process as a form of institutionalized dialogue.[39] For Kirton, informality allows the G-plus System to operate as the hub of a global network where the "agency, visions, calculations, and choices of individual leaders, alone and together," influence a system of global governance.[40] Paul Masson and John Pattison describe how international financial cooperation around the G20, in particular, suffers from a free-rider problem.[41] Kirton clarifies that while informality makes it difficult to "transform international consensus into domestic law, which renders the group toothless," it also generates consensus and facilitates human agency to influence a network of nation-states operating in a complex system of high uncertainty.[42] Although the F8/F7/F20 Initiative is not analogous to the G-plus System in either substance or function, the informality that characterizes its organization, and the problems that stem from that, should not be considered reason enough for dismissal. If anything, commitment to informality becomes even more important when assessing religious transnational engagement in governance given the long history of violent religious and political relations. The informality of the F8/F7/F20 process may be one of the secrets to its ongoing survival and is certainly important for effective engagement with a nation-state network engaged in transnational 'governance without government.'

An enduring intention of the F8/F7/F20 process has been to create moral pressure to induce G-plus System leaders to embrace a stronger sense of cross-border responsibility for the resolution of particular transnational social problems. Informality is essential to the process of generating political will for addressing transnational social problems. Data was presented in Chapter 4 indicating religious leaders' strong agreement that '*collaboration* with political leaders to meet the needs of the most vulnerable people in the world' and 'offering words of *challenge* to the State' were important issues they wanted addressed at the summits. During interviews, religious leaders expressed concern about the democratic deficit in global governance and often spoke of the

---

39   Bruce Jones, Carlos Pascual, and Stephen John Stedman, *Power and Responsibility: Building International Order in an Era of Transnational Threats* (Washington, D.C.: Brookings Institution, 2009).

40   Kirton, "G20 Governance for a Globalized World."

41   Paul R. Masson and John C. Pattison, "Financial Regulatory Reform: Using Models of Cooperation to Evaluate Current Prospects for International Agreement." *The Journal of Economic Asymmetries* 6, no. 3 (2009): 119–136.

42   Kirton, "G20 Governance for a Globalized World," 7.

G8 leaders' *de facto* responsibility to represent more than their own interests and "to care for the rest of the world and make sure that the world doesn't become a jungle."[43]

From a transnational perspective, diplomacy, to be effective, must remain attentive to recognizing nation-state dynamics associated with 'governance without government.'[44] Data on religious leaders' perspectives indicate strong agreement that they 'respect the integrity of the state' in their efforts to motivate political leaders to accept responsibility for transnational social problems.[45] This mindful attention to the importance of borders, and how they politically demarcate limits of responsibility, even as dialogue explicitly embraces an agenda of increasing cross-border responsible engagement is a form of reflexive engagement that, according to Ulrich Beck, lies at the heart of issues associated with global governance.[46] In particular, for Beck, the pluralisation of borders is the most basic indicator of reflexive modernization. When people are reflexive, borders that demarcate categories such as national/international and society/nature "are no longer pre-determinate—they can be chosen (and interpreted)...redrawn and legitimated anew."[47]

Reflexive Engagement[48]

For Beck, reflexivity is indicated where there is an increase in "plausible ways of drawing new borders and a growing tendency to question existing borders in all different fields (e.g., climate crisis, biopolitics, genetically modified food, terrorist threats)."[49] Since the F8/F7/F20 process pressures G8/G7 and G20 leaders to demarcate new borders of moral responsibility for global issues, analysis of their reflexivity becomes important for a well-developed understanding of the overall process. Elsewhere, Steiner has analyzed reflexivity in the F8 external religious leaders' summit communiqués (2005–2012) to G8 political leaders

---

43   Sherrie Steiner, "Faith-Based Accountability Mechanism Typology: The 2011 Interfaith Summit as Soft Power in Global Governance," *Sage Open* April-June (2012).

44   Rhodes, "The New Governance: Governing without Government"; Peters and Pierre, "Governance without Government? Rethinking Public Administration"; Heise, "Governance without Government"; Mayntz, "Common Goods and Governance."

45   Steiner, "Faith-Based Accountability Mechanism Typology: The 2011 Interfaith Summit as Soft Power in Global Governance."

46   Beck, "The Cosmopolitan Society and Its Enemies."

47   Ibid., 19.

48   A version of this section of the book was previously published in Steiner, "Reflexive Governance Dynamics Operative within Round One of the World Religious Leaders' Dialogue with the G8 (2005–2013)."

49   Ibid.

as a form of social (re)construction of cosmopolitan responsibility by world religious leaders.[50] Internal pressures for reform of F8 shadow summit engagement with the G8 can also be analyzed through the lens of transnational governance dynamics involving first order and second order reflexivity.

First and Second Order Reflexivity

According to Beck, reflexivity is a process that *includes* the *otherness of the other* by *accepting* a logic of *inclusive oppositions* and *excluding a logic* of *exclusive oppositions* that reifies differences into dualisms used to form a master cleavage along various dimensions such as religion, nature, citizenship, nationality, etc.[51] Reflexivity is understood as a requirement of surviving the modern world that emerges out of social experience; strategies of self-limitation are adopted through the "recognition of the legitimate interests of others and their inclusion in the calculation of one's own interests" given a realistic experience of global risks and material interdependencies.[52]

Reflexive *governance* has been said to 'loop learning,' according to single-loop and double-loop learning, as a way of giving citizens an active role in the decision-making process and moving the governance process forward in a post-national model of democracy.[53] Single-loop learning is primarily reactionary, reflecting upon a first-order response to the unintended consequences of actions. First-order reflexivity, characterized predominantly by single-loop learning, takes a straightforward, problem-solving approach to governance according to specialised purpose, worldview and skill. Single-loop learning employs instrumental rationality to study aspects of modernity such as technology impact, scientific knowledge production, legitimacy and the effectiveness of democracy.[54] 'Double-loop learning' adds an additional second-order reflection on the governing decisions that led to the initial actions that created the unintended consequences that require governance.[55] Second-order reflexivity, characterized predominantly by double-loop learning, leaves the

---

50   Sherrie Steiner, "Reflexivity in External Religious Leaders' Summit Communication Sequences (2005–2012) to G8 Political Leaders: The Social (Re)Construction of Cosmopolitan Responsibility by World Religious Leaders," *Sage Open* (2013).

51   Beck, "The Cosmopolitan Society and Its Enemies," 18–19.

52   Beck and Grande, "Varieties of Second Modernity: The Cosmopolitan Turn in Social and Political Theory and Research," 437.

53   Ibid.

54   Jan-Peter Voss, Dierk Bauknecht, and Rene Kemp, *Reflexive Governance for Sustainable Development* (Cheltenham, UK: Edward Elgar, 2006).

55   C. Argyris and D. Schön, *Organizational Learning: A Theory of Action Perspective* (Reading, PA: Addison-Wesley, 1978).

isolation of instrumental specialisation. Discourse is widened across cognitive and institutional boundaries, undermining the modernist problem-solving approach.[56] Second-order reflexivity is forced to expand and amalgamate, rather than specialize and narrow, in order to get an adequate grasp of the problems that require governance. Second-order reflexivity is more open, experimental and learning oriented when compared to first-order reflexivity. Second-order reflexivity considers not only the self-induced problems, but its very own working conditions and effects—actively exploring the uncertainties, ambivalences and control problems associated with the confrontation of multiple rationalities embedded in diverse worldviews. 'Double-loop learning' distinguishes conceptual/political learning from instrumental/technical learning and incorporates self-conscious learning practices that question the underlying goals and values of a strategy when necessary. Reflexive governance, shaped by the dynamic interplay between these two approaches, develops a new logic of action and decision-making that responds to shifting scales and multi-level decision-making. Reflexive governance involves conflict regulation as well as problem handling via rule altering politics as modernity reflects upon itself.[57] The interplay between first-order and second-order reflexivity is said to shape the ongoing process of reflexive governance, facilitate intentional reflection on the structures and systems that produce (and reproduce) unintended consequences, and encourage reflection on how best to improve the chances of achieving stipulated goals.[58] Modernist governance processes are dominated by first-order reflexivity processes. When second-order reflexivity becomes dominant, all but clearly unambiguous problem-solving processes cease in favour of integrative, unrestrained, open-ended "second order" governance processes such as goal definition, transdisciplinary research, foresight exercises, participatory decision-making, cooperative policy making, and modulation of ongoing developments, etc.[59] According to Beck, Bonss and Lau, second-order reflexivity de-traditionalizes the foundations of modernity enough to enable conversations over border conflicts to be transformed into conflicts over the drawing of boundaries.[60] When first-order reflexivity returns to dominance,

---

56   Voss, Bauknecht, and Kemp, *Reflexive Governance for Sustainable Development.*

57   Ibid.

58   A. Stirling, "Precaution, Foresight and Sustainability: Reflection and Reflexivity in the Governance of Science and Technology," in *Reflexive Governance for Sustainable Development*, ed. J.P. Voss, D. Bauknecht, and R. Kemp (Cheltenham, UK: Edward Elgar, 2006).

59   J.P. Voss and R. Kemp, "Sustainability and Reflexive Governance: Introduction," Ibid. (Edward Elgar Publishing).

60   Beck, Bonss, and Lau, "The Theory of Reflexive Modernization: Problematic, Hypotheses and Research Programme."

however, the focus shifts away from integrated knowledge production towards implementation and the maximization of control in recognition that
incomplete information and uncertainty remain.[61] As the different orders of
reflexivity interplay, the process of reflexive governance becomes variously
characterized by complex combinations of opening-up and closing-down, and
is therefore vulnerable to opportunistic behavior, power struggles and the dis-
proportionate domination of interaction processes by particular actors.[62]

Rhodes suggests that governance focused on second-order consideration of
beliefs, practices, traditions and dilemmas is more effective for a global context characterized by the decline of state power, the blurring of boundaries,
and increasing economic interdependence.[63] Without global polity, argue
Rayner & McNutt, reflexive governance is constrained to steer the process of
rule formation, adoption, enforcement and evaluation increasingly through
a type of network reflexivity that uses metaphors of openness, closed-ness,
cohesion and transparency in policy design.[64] If the process closes-down too
soon, the quality of problem definition and the learning about societal ends
is short circuited, effectively shutting out the insights that come from social
pluralism and distributed intelligence.[65] If the process reflects on foundational assumptions too long, the pressure to problem-solve and identify concrete
solutions can create insurmountable political tensions. As Mayntz puts it,
choosing effectiveness may come at the cost of democracy or even integrity;
choosing democratic process may come at the cost of reducing performance
levels.[66]

Trommel describes good governance as an art that engages, and works
within, the tensions of value-conflicts.[67] Rip describes these contradictory

---

61   J.P. Voss and R. Kemp, "Sustainability and Reflexive Governance: Introduction," in *Re-
      flexive Governance for Sustainable Development*, ed. J.P. Voss, D. Bauknecht, and R. Kemp
      (Cheltenham, UK: Edward Elgar Publishing, 2006).

62   Ibid.

63   R.A.W. Rhodes, *Understanding Governance: Policy Networks, Governance, Reflexivity and
      Accountability* (Philadelphia, PA: Open University Press, 1997); "Understanding Gover-
      nance: Ten Years On," *Organizational Studies* 28 (2007).

64   Rayner and McNutt, "Valuing Metaphor: A Constructivist Account of Reflexive Gover-
      nance in Policy Networks."

65   Voss and Kemp, "Sustainability and Reflexive Governance: Introduction."

66   R. Mayntz, "Modernization and the Logic of Interorganisational Networks," in *Societal
      Change between Market and Organisation*, ed. J. Child, M. Crozier, and R. Mayntz (Alder-
      shot, UK: Avebury, 1993).

67   W. Trommel, "Good Governance as Reflexive Governance: Towards Second-Order Evalua-
      tions of Public Performance," in *EGPA Conference* (Rotterdam, Netherlands 2008).

forces inherent within reflexive governance as the *efficacy paradox of complexity*.[68] The dynamics are paradoxical because the 'opening-up' and 'closing-down' processes that result from the tension are *both* necessary aspects of the governance process. Rather than choosing between *keeping up action capacity* or *opening problem handling for further contextualization*, reflexive governance is best understood, says Rip, as *both* that interplay and combine in a variety of ways depending upon the content and timing of what is variously opened-up or closed-down. Voss & Kemp identify four typologies describing how the interplay shapes reflexive governance: problem-solving with blinders (totally closed), erosion of strategic capabilities (totally open), sequential opening and closing (taking turns), and exploring experiments (phases of opening and closing utilized within a diverse portfolio strategy of experiments and alternate frameworks of problem definition, goals and options).[69]

Problem-solving with blinders is dominated by single-loop learning where the primary pursuit is a modernist problem-solving approach to a given problem within a given problem definition that cannot be called into question. Voss & Kemp refer to this as 'closed with blinders' because performance management within historically developed implementation cultures is characterized by lack of stakeholder involvement, blind spots for the public values underpinning the approach, and presumptuous expectations regarding the stability of the system.[70]

Voss & Kemp's second typology, 'erosion of strategic capabilities,' is a 'totally open' approach that emerges in polarized tension with the 'totally closed with blinders' model. The governance process is opened-up in all dimensions, involves diverse representation and participation of actors, identifies values and diversity of worldviews, encourages diverse definitions of the problems, and explores diverse options for response. When taken to an extreme, the capacity for collective action totally erodes due to uncertainty about problem dynamics, ambivalence about the sustainability of goals, and the diversity of options; this approach runs the risk of becoming practically irrelevant, producing pointless

---

68   A. Rip, "A Co-Evolutionary Approach to Reflexive Governance—and Its Ironies," in *Reflexive Governance for Sustainable Development*, ed. J.P. Voss, D. Bauknecht, and R. Kemp (Cheltenham, UK: Edward Elgar Publishing, 2006).

69   J.P. Voss and R. Kemp, "Reflexive Governance for Sustainable Development: Incorporating Feedback in Social Problem Solving," in *6th International Conference of the European Society for Ecological Economics* (Lisbon, Spain 2005).

70   Ibid; Trommel, "Good Governance as Reflexive Governance: Towards Second-Order Evaluations of Public Performance."

statements on a large number of issues.[71] Trommel describes this as a good governance normative ideal in search of utopia that risks political 'totalitarianism' by implying that a world without evil is even possible.[72] Trommel suggests that the 'good' of governance, if it is to avoid either irrelevance or political tyranny, needs to remain historically embodied and realistically immersed in institutional arrangements that grapple with imperfection, struggle with normative ambiguity, and recognize the limitations of what is practicably possible in given contexts. Trommel suggests vigilantly organizing a public spirit of trust in the implementation of an imperfect public project that embraces irony as a form of productive pragmatism that encourages modest realistic solutions, including identification of acceptable 'possible failures,' as a way of avoiding the unintended side-effect of cynicism and political intolerance.[73]

Voss & Kemp's third typology, sequential opening and closing, is a form of governance characterized by 'turn taking' where strategies of problem handling dominated by first order reflexivity, single-loop learning and prioritization of keeping up action capacity sequentially alternates with strategies dominated by second order reflexivity, double-loop learning and prioritization of opening-up problem handling for further contextualization. What makes this a distinguishable typology is that, unlike the first two typologies, this form of governance embraces the ongoing struggle delimited by tension between the diverse approaches, creates space for the expression of both styles, and trusts in the ongoing project as shaped by the sequential expressions. This typology, as an adaptive strategy that can be probed and further revised, is somewhat amenable to incremental pragmatic policy advances; but it also risks the formation of camps around the two approaches, making the typology vulnerable to power struggles that undermine the governance process.[74] Trommel suggests organizing public vigilance into the governance process as a way

---

71   Voss and Kemp, "Reflexive Governance for Sustainable Development—Incorporating Feedback in Social Problem Solving."

72   Trommel, "Good Governance as Reflexive Governance: Towards Second-Order Evaluations of Public Performance"; H. Achterhuis, *De Erfenis Van De Utopie* (*The Legacy of Utopia*) (Amsterdam, Netherlands: Ambo, 1998); M. Waltzer, *Spheres of Justice* (New York, New York: Basic Books, 1983); J. Gray, *Black Mass: Apocalyptic Religion and the Death of Utopia* (New York, New York: Farrar, Straux, Giroux, 2007).

73   Trommel, "Good Governance as Reflexive Governance: Towards Second-Order Evaluations of Public Performance."

74   Voss and Kemp, "Reflexive Governance for Sustainable Development—Incorporating Feedback in Social Problem Solving."

of planning for inevitable discontinuities so that change becomes accepted as normative.[75]

Voss & Kemp's final typology, exploring experiments, describes a governance process characterised by both: opening-up in one or more dimensions where diverse perspectives are explored *combined with* a set of closing-down strategies developed according to alternative selection criteria and priorities. Governance processes may open and close in various combinations along dimensions such as problem definitions, goals of action, solutions to be assumed, and the degree of inclusion of diverse people in the participatory governance process itself. Unlike the sequential opening and closing 'turn taking' model, this typology implements both processes simultaneously through a complex diverse portfolio of diverse experimental strategies that support learning. Rather than prioritize one consistent problem-handling framework, this governance model embraces a portfolio of strategy experiments, inducing variation that balances more or less risky approaches with the stability that comes with diversity. An exploring experiments approach to reflexive governance remains oriented toward solving specific problems while also remaining flexible enough to adapt to, and reflect upon, the problems at hand in a manner congruent with the context and the available resources at hand. Most importantly, this approach recognizes the dangers associated with closing-down too soon and retains the ability to re-open the discussion, as needed, when the results of closing-down are viewed as inadequate. The dilemma of reflexive governance is that the issues of *erosion of action capacities* and *erosion of problem handling for contextualization* cannot be resolved without losing out on either side. By embracing the 'efficacy paradox of complexity,' this approach recognizes, rather than attempts to resolve, the paradox and works with it to balance the two contradicting requirements to cultivate an adequate combination of opening-up and closing-down for specific governance situations. In a review of reflexivity research, Widmer, Schippers & West concluded that, to the extent that governance partners may be considered a team, team characteristics such as trust, psychological safety among group members, a shared vision, diversity, inspirational leadership, and cooperative management of conflict enhance reflexivity; research also indicates that team reflexivity is related to a team's output in terms of innovation, effectiveness, and creativity.[76]

75 Trommel, "Good Governance as Reflexive Governance: Towards Second-Order Evaluations of Public Performance."

76 P.S. Widmer, M.C. Schippers, and M.A. West, "Recent Developments in Reflexivity Research: A Review," *Psychology of Everyday Activity* 2, no. 2 (2009).

Reflexive Analysis of the F8 Summits

If we consider the International Continuance Committee as a team, and consider communiqué production, summit hosting, use of e-governance and the social media Twitter Campaign as team output, the F8 process can be reviewed using Voss & Kemp's typology of first and second order reflexivity.[77] Between 2005 and 2013, the F8 process shadowed a complete round of G8 summits. Reflexive governance dynamics for the F8 summit process are analyzed in this section, treating 2005–2013 as a single macro-level unit. Data analyzed in this section include summit presentations (2005–2012), summit statements (2005–2013), qualitative interviews and questionnaires (33% response rate) conducted on May 23–24, 2011 in France, qualitative interviews and questionnaires (45% response rate) conducted on May 17, 2012 in Washington, DC, and qualitative interviews of summit hosts from October 2012 to January 2013 (75% response rate).

As noted earlier, F8 summits began in 2005 with the UK ecumenical 1-day conference that emerged out of the *Make Poverty History* civil society campaign, and continued with a multi-faith process in Russia (2006), Germany (2007), Japan (2008), Italy (2009), Canada (2010), France (2011), and United States (2012). A complete round of G8 shadow summitry concluded with a UK (2013) Initiative comprised of an e-governance Open Letter and social media Twitter Campaign. The year-by-year process was detailed in Chapter 4. In this section, we consider how team dynamics developed over time as a reflexive process.

The harshest critics of the summit process came from US delegates, some of whom described the leadership as "fighting over who gets to control the legacy of a series of ineffectual meetings" (US interview). RfP has been a significant participant in the process. Their large international coalition of representatives from world religions has a strong presence in some, but not all, of the G8 countries. As leaders in the international multi-faith movement, their involvement has been significant but their weak presence in Germany, Canada and France presented problems for the summit rotation. As leadership emerged throughout the summit process, an inevitable power struggle resulted in two meetings in Japan, which is also where the ongoing value of investing in religious summitry was first publicly questioned by UK participants.[78] Some delegates felt that parallel events set a bad example, demonstrating a type of competition not admissible in this type of context (Russia interview). The costs of hosting

---

77   Voss and Kemp, "Reflexive Governance for Sustainable Development—Incorporating Feedback in Social Problem Solving."

78   Reed, "The G8: Our Spiritual and Moral Responsibilities: Does the G8 Matter?"

the political G8 and G20 summits were receiving increasing public scrutiny.[79] Financial pressures on religious hosts, particularly in light of the ongoing impact of the 2008 financial crisis, sharpened the division. US delegates failed to see any measurable effect of the F8 process on global policies, and the meetings failed to consistently attract from the top-tier hierarchy of world religions. When it was their turn to host, US hosts gave international delegates such short notice that several who wanted to come, simply couldn't. Japanese delegates came despite short notice, but the one-day event was over before they had recovered from jet lag. Defenders of summits lasting 2 or more days considered longer summits worth the expense if only for the practical reason of adjusting to the time gap in combination with the physical challenge of people coming from half way around the world. UK delegates questioned how the summit seemed to have developed a life of its own since 2005, expanding without checks and balances "as part of the interfaith industry," saying "I think we have to be careful about that. We need to question what we want to achieve and if this is the best way of operating" (UK interview). In 2013, the UK leadership led the Initiative for reworking the model, "despite the success of previous encounters," so that the financial pressure would not impede the ability of hosts to offer religious leaders "the opportunity to make a recognisable and credible impact on public and political debates ahead of the G8 Summit...with attention squarely focused on desirable outputs rather than on process."[80]

The leadership that hosted summits in Germany and Canada emphasized *process*. They prioritized galvanizing *civil society* to create summits that were highly collaborative, inclusive and transparent. The level of dialogue resulted in statements that challenged the misplaced priorities, western paternalism and implicit economic imperialism embedded in the political process, working together to overcome nationalism. Press releases were distributed to a wide variety of media personalities and outlets without concern about the risk of wider society interpretations (Canada interview).

In Russia and Italy, press releases were arranged through civil and church officials, with the summits funded and organized by the state establishment in a manner that showcased collaboration between religion and civil society. For the most extreme critics, this was enough to dismiss their portion of the process. More collegial participants, however, recognized that government co-sponsorship also meant that statement contents were conveyed to top levels of government strengthening religious linkages with heads of state. It also often meant provision of summit translation services and involvement (through

---

79   Kirton, Guebert, and Tanna, "G8 and G20 Summit Costs."
80   Reed, "Project Proposal—2013 G8 Religious Leaders' Initiative."

travel sponsorship) of representatives from poorer parts of the world (e.g., Ethiopia). Despite the significant investment Russia had made in the 2006 state affair, it was unclear whether the Russians would organize anything, yet alone revive the face-to-face summit process for 2014. In the end, Russia ceased participating in the Initiative. Even so, past Russian delegates defended summitry expenses as a worthwhile investment in interreligious peace and security. "When we know that thousands of conferences are being organized in the world every year, isn't the religious dimension just as important to humanity?" said a delegate from Russia.

If we consider the interpersonal dynamics in light of the *efficacy paradox of complexity* that gives rise to Voss & Kemp's four typologies of reflexive governance,[81] we can see how religious summitry is affected by reflexive governance during the period of 2005–2013. The leadership rotation model results in the culture and context of the national host significantly shaping the relative dominance of first or second order reflexivity, thus affecting the content and timing of the opening-up, or closing-down, of the reflexive governance process during the round of nine consecutive years. The 2005 Summit began with Voss & Kemp's problem-solving modernist approach to poverty reduction. Looking back on this time, UK hosts now recognize that the modernist 'blinders' were problematic:

> By its very nature this mode of politics tends very much to exaggerate the power of the G8, almost to the point of caricature, such that at the time of the Gleneagles Summit the watching global public was encouraged to believe that the G8 could make poverty history, if it so chose, more or less as a matter of political will. To say the least, such an argument hugely oversimplified the real politics involved in approaching, let alone realising, such an ambition.[82]

The next seven years of reflexive governance were characterized by Voss & Kemp's sequential opening and closing (taking turns). In 2006, the Russian Summit opened-up the process to involve multiple religions, religious representatives from all G8 nations, and extend dialogue over several days. Action capacity, however, was diminished. The statement made no reference to specific policies and was the only statement to not reference the MDGs.[83] The 2007

---

81   Voss and Kemp, "Reflexive Governance for Sustainable Development—Incorporating Feedback in Social Problem Solving."

82   Reed, "The G8: Our Spiritual and Moral Responsibilities: Does the G8 Matter?" 2–3.

83   F8-Russia, "World Summit of Religious Leaders."

German Summit emphasized process even more, internationalizing the planning process, circulating the statement draft for international contributions and utilizing a more transparent approach to media. Summit planners sought out international religious leaders to further contextualize dialogue so that the Summit included women and took the perspectives of religious leaders from marginalized parts of the world into account (German interview). The 2008 Japanese Summits were paradoxical, simultaneously opening problem handling to further contextualize governance to prioritize the environment and de-center anthropocentrism, while also reducing civil society involvement with state sponsored events that included dialogue with the head of state over very specific policy recommendations.[84] One of the Japanese hosts described the religious dialogue with political leaders in Japan as "unstoppable"[85] even as UK delegate Charles Reed began to publicly question the entire process.[86] The Initiative began to close-down again in 2009, with action capacity prioritized to the point of responding to earthquake victims face-to-face. The process opened-up again in 2010. Canadians emphasized process so much that, as the Canadian Summit was drawing to a close, a pragmatically oriented US delegate whispered into the ear of the US delegate that had invited him, "Tell me again, why did we come here?" (US interview). The Canadian statement most clearly questioned the underlying goals and values of the G8, emphasizing inclusive democratic process, and using phrases such as 'inspired leadership' to challenge political leaders and question their 'misplaced priorities.' Specific actions were recommended, encouraged and actually taken, but the approach encouraged thoughtful reflection upon rule altering politics in a manner that was lost on delegates who were impatient toward the opening-up of problem handling for further contextualization. After Canada, the process began to close-down with France in 2011, and then came close to shutting-down in 2012 with international participation at the lowest since the summits began in 2005 (see Figure 7.1). For the second time, the paradoxical aspects of the religious summit process surfaced. The US host, Rev. Bud Heckman, co-authored an article with Hamilton from Canada that was published in *G8*, a preparatory summit publication distributed at the G8/G20 Summits. Hamilton and Heckman used the imagery of an "open spiral" to describe the 2012 F8 Summit as "being complete" and "finished" but "continuing" and "ongoing";[87] as being "not just a

---

84   F8-Japan/Kyoto-Osaka, "A Proposal from People of Religion"; F8-Japan/Sapporo, "Call from Sapporo-World Religious Leaders Summit for Peace."

85   Yoshinobu Miyake, "Purpose," (2008), http://www.relnet.co.jp/g8/english/purpose1.htm.

86   Reed, "The G8: Our Spiritual and Moral Responsibilities: Does the G8 Matter?"

87   Hamilton, "The Open Spiral: The Ongoing Commitments of Faith Leaders," 220.

closing of the eight-year cycle," but also "part of the open spiral, continuing to build on the parallel faith leaders' summits that have gone before"; as "building collaboration and unity for common witness on shared moral concerns ('soft' advocacy), " but also "working in specific ways to influence the policy agenda ('hard' advocacy)"; "as both an end and a new beginning"; and "as a continued unveiling of the open spiral."[88] Voss & Kemp's diverse portfolio strategy of experiments and alternate frameworks was evident in 2013 when the United Kingdom decided several things:[89] they made changes to reduce financial pressures in response to a context of changing leadership and increasing fiscal constraint; they replaced face-to-face summitry with e-governance; and they introduced a social media Twitter Campaign. These changes were not entirely unexpected. Reed had raised concerns about face-to-face summitry in 2008, again in 2010, and once more in 2012 culminating in the "problem handling via rule altering politics" of replacing the summit with an Initiative in 2013.

Voss and Kemp's complex and nuanced understanding of the interplay between first and second order reflexivity provides a lens for interpreting how the ongoing governance process of the F8 has been shaped by the dynamic interplay of camps concerned with *keeping up action capacity* or *opening problem handling for further contextualization*. These governance dynamics have been observed elsewhere in secular transnational political processes; they can also be observed here as operative in religious soft power transnational governance dynamics. Rather than discontinue when sharp disagreement emerged within the leadership structure, the summit process evolved and innovated a new logic of action through self-conscious learning practices that questioned the underlying goals and values of a strategy when necessary. Religious leaders refused to choose between *keeping up action capacity* or *opening-up problem handling*, and instead embraced what Rip[90] refers to as the *efficacy paradox of complexity* so that the summit process could sequentially open and close, eventually embracing a complex portfolio of exploring experiments.

Assessment

In this section, the F8/F7/F20 process is assessed for how it has been shaped by technological changes, international relations and the secularization crisis.

---

88   Ibid., 221.

89   Voss and Kemp, "Reflexive Governance for Sustainable Development—Incorporating Feedback in Social Problem Solving."

90   Rip, "A Co-Evolutionary Approach to Reflexive Governance—and Its Ironies."

Technological changes have significantly shaped social relations with the advent of globalization, so the F8/F7/F20 Initiative is assessed for ways in which the process has been shaped by changes in information technology. Although the F8/F7/F20 religious leaders seek to influence global governance, in this section, the process is assessed for ways in which it has been shaped by changes in international relations. Finally, norms are changing for religious public engagement in association with the secularization crisis. One way this is expressed is through pressures for religion to be recognized as religion in the public square. The F8/F7/F20 Initiative is assessed for indications of this change in transnational relations.

Information Technology

The F8/F7/F20 Initiative is assessed for how it used information technology for civic engagement. The rapid growth of the internet over the past 20 years has changed how citizens express concerns on public issues with significant implications for civic engagement for social change.[91] Citizen use of the internet for purposes of civic engagement, increasingly referred to as Web 2.0, are accomplished or advanced through the use of online tools such as blogging, chatting, editing, texting, Facebook or tweeting to engage citizens in deliberation and action on public issues.[92] As of mid-year 2016, 95% of the global population now live in an area that is covered by a mobile-cellular network, 84% of the global population and 67% of the rural population live within mobile-broadband networks (3G or above), and 53% of the global population has access to LTE networks that enhance the quality of Internet use.[93] The Arab Spring brought international attention to how information technology plays a role in governance, particularly when the Egyptian government shut-down the Internet on January 29, 2011 in an attempt to control citizen's freedom of expression and assembly. Civil society actors have been increasingly using information technology to engage global political processes and forge new linkages between access to the Internet and human rights.[94] The UN's specialized agency for information technology, The International Telecommunication Union,

---

91   Lauren Movius, "The Influence of Global Civil Society on Internet Governance Negotiations," *Florida Communication Journal* 43, no. 2 (2015).

92   Black, "Blog, Chat, Edit, Text, or Tweet? Using Online Tools to Advance Adult Civic Engagement"; Silva, *Citizen E-Participation in Urban Governance: Crowdsourcing and Collaborative Creativity*.

93   Information Technology Union, "ICT Facts and Figures 2016," (2016), http://www.itu.int/en/ITU-D/Statistics/Documents/facts/ICTFactsFigures2016.pdf.

94   Movius, "The Influence of Global Civil Society on Internet Governance Negotiations."

has established a Telecommunication Development Bureau to facilitate using information telecommunication capacities for implementation of the 17 SDGs and their 169 targets.[95]

The F8/F7/F20 Initiative has made use of information technology in several ways, but their usage has been underutilized in comparison to what many other INGOs have been doing in recent years. All communiqués (2005–2016) are posted online in various locations (but not altogether). Video presentations for Canada (2010), Australia (2014) and Turkey (2015) are also posted online. At several points, the internet has been used to solicit feedback on the process. In 2013, the UK innovated the summit process to combine publication of an Open Letter with the social media #1000daystogo Twitter Campaign. Religious leaders were intentional about trying the technique of e-governance. The hashtag #G20Interfaith is used to record events associated with the F20 process and there is a handle @F20News that religious leader organizers have created to make official tweets, but little has been done using those platforms. The strategy of Web 2.0 remains underutilized in several ways. When the Twitter Campaign #1000daystogo was launched, a goal of 2 million tweets was specified but never measured. Without tracking the campaign to provide feedback related to outcomes, there was no information to motivate later hosts to continue using the Web 2.0 strategy. Not surprisingly, the Web 2.0 strategy used in 2013 has not (yet) been repeated. In addition, the #1000daystogo is a hashtag now associated with other events such as the Canada Winter Games in Red Deer, Alberta. Very few leaders tweet using the hashtag and Twitter handle specific to the F8/F7/F20 process. Neither does the process have a Facebook page. Finally, the F8/F7/F20 Initiative has not connected to the UN's specialized agency for information technology, The International Telecommunication Union, whose Telecommunication Development Bureau is using information technology to facilitate implementation of the SDGs.

There are limitations associated with civic engagement using information technology. The digital gap continues to affect more than half the world's population and is largest in fragile states where only one out of seven people use the internet; internet use is higher for men than women in all regions of the world and is highest in fragile states where the gender gap is currently at 31%; and, although 83 development countries achieved the affordability target by end of 2015, information technology remains unaffordable for the majority of

---

95   Smart Sustainable Development Model Advisory Board, "Report 2015: Smart Sustsain-able Development Model," (2015), http://www.itu.int/en/ITU-D/Initiatives/SSDM/Documents/SmartSustainableDevelopmentModel_Report2015.pdf.

the world's poor.[96] There are significant cultural barriers to e-governance innovation which Meijer's research suggests can be overcome using strategies focused on fixing problems and framing stories conducive to motivating people to connect technological opportunities to public value.[97] Although 'government to citizen' use of e-governance for service delivery has been shown to have a problematic impact on citizens' security or privacy concerns,[98] citizens have also been shown to push back and proactively flip the service delivery model to alter how government solves public problems.[99] Although e-governance is still under-researched, early case studies indicate that technological systems can be useful ways for citizens and governments to collaboratively innovate solutions that address barriers and design comprehensive strategies for addressing social problems.[100] Religious leaders have many stories that could be told in association with implementation of the SDGs. Given that public administration is being pressured to drive service delivery toward a more personalized, outcome-driven, participative, efficient and collaborative model, Web 2.0 technologies have immense potential for supporting civic engagement.[101] Moreover, stronger incorporation of social media into the summit program would provide an attractive venue for engaging youth who are more likely to utilize cyber participation.[102] There are significant limitations, however, to the effectiveness of Web 2.0 for F8/F7/F20 purposes. Globalization may be 'flattening' the world, but several countries are building thicker walls of censorship in response.[103] Moreover, any strategy should be mindful of the digital gap and the gender divide within it.

---

96   Union, "ICT Facts and Figures 2016."

97   Meijer, "E-Governance Innovation: Barriers and Strategies."

98   Kharade, "G2C E-Governance Project Implementation at Local Level in a Pune Division Context."

99   Linders, Liao, and Wang, "Proactive E-Governance: Flipping the Service Delivery Model from Pull to Push in Taiwan."

100 Meijer, "E-Governance Innovation: Barriers and Strategies"; Silva, *Citizen E-Participation in Urban Governance: Crowdsourcing and Collaborative Creativity.*

101 Manuel Pedro Rodríguez Bolívar et al., "The Influence of Political Factors in Policymakers' Perceptions on the Implementation of Web 2.0 Technologies for Citizen Participation and Knowledge Sharing in Public Sector Delivery," *Information Polity: The International Journal of Government & Democracy in the Information Age* 20, no. 2/3 (2015).

102 W. Lance Bennett, Chris Wells, and Deen Freelon, "Communicating Civic Engagement: Contrasting Models of Citizenship in the Youth Web Sphere," *Journal of Communication* 61, no. 5 (2011); Alan Steinberg, "Exploring Web 2.0 Political Engagement: Is New Technology Reducing the Biases of Political Participation?" *Electoral Studies* 39 (2015).

103 Rebecca MacKinnon, "Flatter World and Thicker Walls? Blogs, Censorship and Civic Discourse in China," *Public Choice* 134 (2008).

Influence of International Relations

Although the F8/F7/F20 Initiative seeks to influence international relations, the process is also clearly shaped by changing relations between different nation-states. In this section, I consider how the F8/F7/F20 Initiative has waxed, waned and evolved over the years in tandem with changes in international relations by treating the relationship between religion and nationalism as variable. Scholarship on the relationship between religion, nationalism and violence has been critiqued for subsuming religion into nationalism rather than treating the relationship between them as variable so that scholars can explore under what conditions religious-nationalist mobilization does, or does not, lead to conflict.[104] Four changes in international relations are discussed in relation to the F8/F7/F20 process: changing relations between Russia and Western Europe, the 2008 global financial crisis, the civil society campaign surrounding arrival of the 2015 MDG deadline, and acts of terrorism in late 2015.[105]

Evolving relations with Russia and Western European countries clearly affected the F8/F7/F20 Initiative. In 2006, Russia hosted a lavish F8 Summit with top-tier religious leader participation and representation. At the time, relations were warming with the United States and NATO.[106] Russian support would not be repeated in 2014 when it was their turn to host a second round of F8 meetings. Russia's 'invasion/incursion/aggression/staycation' in Ukraine had begun early in the year, further complicating matters.[107] On March 24, Prime Minister David Cameron, President Barack Obama and other world leaders suspended Russia from the elite group of leading economies on the basis of President Putin's breach of international law; the G8 officially became the G7.[108] Although political leaders agreed to meet without Russia until such a time as their head of state indicated a willingness to engage in 'meaningful discussion,' religious leaders decided against meeting without Russia. The previously scheduled G8 Sochi Summit was cancelled, and the G7 met in Brussels on June 4–5. The F8 meeting on the occasion of the G8 Russian Summit was also cancelled. By then, however, civil society attention had shifted away from the G8 toward the

---

104   Gorski and Türkmen-Dervişoğlu, "Religion, Nationalism, and Violence: An Integrated Approach."

105   At the time of finalizing this manuscript, it was too soon to assess the case of white evangelical support for President Trump and rising nationalism in the USA.

106   NATO, "Relations with Russia."

107   Friedman, "Russia's Slow-Motion Invasion of Ukraine."

108   Cohen, "G8 Becomes the G7 as Leaders Kick Russia Out: It's Not a Big Problem, Says Putin's Foreign Minister."

G20 in the wake of the 2008 global financial crisis and Initiative religious leaders decided to follow suit. The 2016 F7 Summit was subsequently canceled.

The 2008 global financial crisis affected the F8 process in several ways. Internal discontent among the religious leaders grew over failure of the summit process to concretely respond to immediate humanitarian crises. The MDG deadline was fast approaching, so leaders felt that the summit process must continue to maintain political pressure as part of the 'big push,' but the costs associated with face-to-face meetings became harder and harder to justify. Summits became shorter with fewer participants until, in 2013, a shift was finally made from summitry to e-governance. The 2015 Interfaith Youth Summit was unexpectedly canceled due to financial constraints.

The MDG 2015 deadline, and the civil society campaign to adopt a new set of goals to replace the MDGs, also shaped the F8/F7/F20 process. In 2014, the C20 became a recognized G20 engagement partner under the 2014 Australian G20 Presidency. As F8/F7 leader Hamilton wrote about the importance of "keeping the faith" and 'staying focused on goals' despite the disruption that interrupted the planned interfaith leaders' Summit for 2014 and the interfaith youth summit in 2015,[109] an independent F20 process was emerging halfway around the globe in Australia where a national faith leader was leading the C20 engagement process. The 2015 MDG/SDG transition provided motivation along with civil society momentum to continue the F8/F7/F20 process despite the legacy of the 2008 financial crisis, or perhaps even because of it. Given the immense needs associated with the ongoing humanitarian crisis, how could the Initiative not continue? In the critical transition year, despite the unexpected cancellation of their 2015 German Summit, the interfaith youth used the internet to post their communiqué to the G7 about the importance of fulfilling the MDGs and adopting a new set of goals. Just as the MDGs had provided a theme for summit discussion, the SDGs have been consistently discussed at F20 Summits once they were adopted by the UN.

Acts of terrorism have also influenced summit dynamics. Three days before the 2015 Turkey Summit, just as many international speakers were catching airplanes for travel, terrorist attacks at six locations in and just outside of Paris on November 13, 2015 resulted in 128 deaths and hundreds of wounded in France.[110] When the F20 Summit convened on November 16–18, 2015, almost every speaker opened their talks with some form of reflection on the Paris bombings. In some cases, speakers set aside their prepared comments entirely to address international terrorism from an interfaith perspective.

---

109   Hamilton, "Keeping the Faith: Still Focused on Goals."
110   Almasy, Meilham, and Bittermann, "Paris Massacre: At Least 128 Die in Attacks."

Dynamics quickly shifted to include panelist commentary on the Ankara blasts in October where more than 90 were killed by blasts from suicide bombings in the Turkish capital.[111] Eventually, participants paid attention to international terrorism in many other parts of the world that often go unacknowledged in international circles.[112] Significant and unplanned dialogue occurred throughout the conference. Participants explored concrete ways they could exercise leadership to reduce and interrupt the culture of terrorism and terrorist behavior. They considered how they might draw upon their networks and resources to provide alternatives to the 'lost generation' from the youth bulge to better integrate them into the global economy. Alternate pathways for inter-civilization engagement were presented by Islamic scholars who challenged ISIL's fundamentalist interpretations, exposed the hypocrisy of ISIL behavior, and presented alternative interpretations in support of intercultural dialogue that could be distributed through mosques as a cultural resource offered to religiously motivated individuals. Scholars offered an alternate interpretation to what was being distributed by ISIL and disinformation campaigns against Islam.[113]

Institutional Differentiation

Another question to be addressed when assessing the F8/F7/F20 Initiative is the degree to which, if at all, the new connections being formed are strengthening, or dissolving, the expressions that differentiate religion as a distinct social institution. A distinguishing factor of the F8/F7/F20 Initiative that sets it apart from competing transnational RNGOs, interfaith and humanitarian processes is how the culture is comfortable with explicit rejection of an instrumentalized approach to religion even as it promotes civic engagement for service delivery and activism in relation to the MDGs and SDGs. This apparent contradiction has been observed more broadly as characteristic of transnational INGOs. Mitchell and Schmitz observed a contradiction in transnational NGO behavior whereby INGOs are portrayed as 'principled' actors animated by global norms that appear to also act in instrumental ways that are seemingly inconsistent with their principled nature. Mitchell and Schmitz conducted in-depth research based on a diverse sample of 152 top organisational leaders that

---

111   Letsch and Khomami, "Turkey Terror Attack: Mourning after Scores Killed in Ankara Blasts."

112   Even media professionals acknowledge this oversight. See, for example, Kealing, "This Weekend's Terrorist Attacks Are Just a Handful among Hundreds. Most of Them You Don't Hear About."

113   Organization, "German Evangelical Church Leaders Meet Iranian Religious Scholars."

resulted in the introduction of a new heuristic of 'principled instrumentalism' to provide a new theoretical framework for understanding the seemingly contradictory behavior observed among transnational NGOs.[114] Although they acknowledge that the scope conditions may delimit the applicability of their model to organizations based primarily in the United States and may obscure important differences among various types of transnational NGOs, they suggest that their work 'opens the door' to more specific operationalizations that take transnational NGO heterogeneity into account.[115] In this section, the F8/F7/F20 Initiative is a case that contributes to a more heterogeneous understanding of how religion factors into concerns over instrumentalization in transnational relations.

Religious freedom and civic engagement is emphasized at the F8/F7/F20 summits in ways that goes beyond the sacred/secular dualism. As noted earlier, the F8/F7/F20 Initiative has been critiqued for giving too much attention to process, but Kai Monheim[116] presents an evidentiary case for how process matters in global negotiations much more than analysts have cared to acknowledge. Effective negotiation of the process is itself invoked as an explanatory factor in multilateral negotiations on worldwide challenges.[117] Diplomatic skill is important to the social construction of trust and respect, even when talks are inclusive and transparent. Successful presidencies of negotiations, says Monheim, pay attention to transparency and inclusivity, large and non-mainstream countries, and ensure that all delegates feel respected.[118] It is hard for delegates to feel respected if they feel they are being used, but pressures to be useful affects organizational cultures, as well. Zinn describes how increased dependency on state funding transforms the culture of charities,[119] and Murphy describes a 'marketisation' process that contradicts the charities' ethical ethos.[120] If the only point of contact between policy makers and religion is

---

114   George E. Mitchell and Hans Peter Schmitz, "Principled Instrumentalism: A Theory of Transnational NGO Behaviour," *Review of International Studies* 40 (2014).

115   Ibid., 503.

116   Monheim, *How Effective Negotiation Management Promotes Multilateral Cooperation: The Power of Process in Climate, Trade, and Biosafety Negotiations.*

117   Ibid.

118   Ibid.

119   Zinn, "Risk, Social Inclusion and the Life Course—Review of Developments in Policy and Research," 326.

120   J. Murphy, "Welfare Regimes and Risky Speculations," in *Risk, Welfare and Work*, ed. G. Marston, J. Moss, and J. Quiggin (Melbourne, Australia: Melbourne University Press, 2010).

instrumental in its approach, religious leaders will continue to feel not only marginalized, but disrespected and unduly constrained.[121]

A non-instrumentalized approach to religion contradicts European approaches to religion in the public square, particularly the German school. Ulrich Beck, for example, insisted that religious leaders embrace the use of public language with an instrumental emphasis upon peace (rather than truth) as the only approach compatible with the modern context that he referred to as risk society.[122] This may be true to the extent that risk society is unsustainably organized, but if the global community wants to successfully adapt to a sustainable common future, an instrumental approach to religion may be too narrow to support the successful negotiation of the contradictions of capitalism.[123] From this perspective, approaches emphasizing the usefulness of religion represent an improvement from anti-religious secularist biases that have long marginalized religion from the public sphere. To the extent that these approaches become dismissive of the meaning-making contributions of religious truth claims, however, they perpetuate the sacred/secular dualism that currently hampers governance structures. Dismissing deeply held beliefs communicates disrespect to religious leaders.[124] Instrumentalized religion delimits the scope of discussion to the useful contributions faith-based organizations make to immigration, employment, social cohesion, etc.[125] Usefulness is important, but if religious leaders feel disrespected, collaboration can quickly transform into repulsion. The public validation of resistance to religious instrumentalization may be an increasingly important component for development of collaborative religious-political relations in an increasingly flat world where the governmentality technique of 'regulating aversion' may be a self-limiting process.[126]

---

121   Jones and Petersen, "Instrumental, Narrow, Normative? Reviewing Recent Work on Religion and Development."

122   Beck, "A God of One's Own"; Ulrich Beck, "The Two Faces of Religion," *Ulrich Beck: Pioneer in Cosmopolitan Sociology & Risk Society* (2014); Habermas, Ratzinger, and Schuller, *The Dialectics of Secularization: On Reason and Religion.*

123   Jones and Petersen, "Instrumental, Narrow, Normative? Reviewing Recent Work on Religion and Development."

124   Ledewitz, *Church, State, and the Crisis in American Secularism;* Calo, "Higher Law Secularism: Religious Symbols, Contested Secularisms, and the Limits of the Establishment Clause"; "Law in the Secular Age"; Taylor, "Modes of Secularism."

125   Jones and Petersen, "Instrumental, Narrow, Normative? Reviewing Recent Work on Religion and Development."

126   Michael Foucault, "Governmentality," *Ideology and Consciousness* 6 (1979); Wendy Brown, *Regulating Aversion: Tolerance in the Age of Identity and Empire* (Princeton, NJ: Princeton

Toward the end of his life, Jürgen Habermas defended a new approach to public religious dialogue. As noted in Chapter 3, he defended how religion communicates *meaning* in ways philosophy and science cannot. He argued that to repress it, or attempt to replace it, would do more than unfairly exclude religion; it would deprive "secular society from important resources of meaning."[127] Habermas sought to validate a particular type of religious reasoning in the public sphere—one that was reflexive as well as communicative. While Habermas agreed with the liberal position that fundamentalist expressions of religious reasoning undermined political legitimacy, he believed that the liberal requirement that citizens translate their faith-based reasoning into public/secular reasons put an 'undue cognitive burden' that *de facto* restricts and separates religious reasoning—including the beneficial type—from the public sphere.[128] In place of this barrier, Habermas proposed an "institutional translation proviso" that would allow a particular type of faith-based reasoning into the public sphere—one that had "the epistemic ability to consider one's own faith reflexively from the outside and to relate it to secular views."[129] Habermas' defense of the legitimacy of faith-based public debate replaced the one-way liberal model dialogue with an informal and deinstitutionalized two-way public conversation between sacred and secular.

A consistent behavioral pattern has been evident among religious leaders involved in the F8/F7/F20 process: A declaration of resistance to religious instrumentalization commonly precedes dialogue about religious contributions to the common good. This occurs repeatedly as an apparent shared norm among participating transnational religious leaders. Sometimes, leaders add it quickly after beginning almost as if they had almost forgotten to mention it. But mentioning it is clearly important, even if it is not developed as a theme in his or her talk. First comes the disclaimer, then participants engage in discussion of religion's usefulness for collaborative engagement to 'mend the world.' For example, at the 2015 F20 Turkey Summit, a theme that was discussed throughout the Summit was how instrumentalized religion contributes to unsustainability. The exclusion of metaphysical reasoning from the public domain prevents advance of the moral character, legal reforms and

---

University Press, 2006); Ina Merdjanova, "Overhauling Interreligious Dialogue for Peace-building," *Occasional Papers on Religion in Eastern Europe* 36, no. 1.

127   Habermas, *Future of Human Nature.*, p. 109.

128   "Religion in the Public Sphere." p. 8.

129   Ibid., pp. 9–10.

enduring institutions necessary for adjusting socioeconomic development to be sustainable.[130] In her keynote address, Marshall discussed the importance of addressing concerns about the tendency to instrumentalize religion, whether in actuality or merely as a perception. Şentürk also spoke against the instrumentalization of religion in a keynote address; he identified a double standard that exists in sustainable development circles: The economy justifies everything, but it does not itself need justification whereas religion must justify its presence through contributions to sustainable development. But religion is also needed in the economy for its intrinsic value, said Şentürk, and yet economic reductionism keeps religion on the margins. *Sustainable* economic development involves values and nonmaterial sources of meaningfulness, but economic reductionism forces people to choose between values or economic development. This is a false dichotomy, he said. Religious metaphysical reasoning provides the humanistic values and develops the moral behavior constitutive of *sustainable* production and consumption. Only the combination of instrumental and metaphysical reasoning will enable the global community to overcome the challenges ahead.[131]

One way of understanding the behavioral pattern observed at the F8/F7/F20 Summits is to contextualize them as an expression of the cultural contradictions of capitalism: The pathway to religion becoming useful is the political validation of its right *not* to be (aka, religious freedom). Of course, there are several Marxist scholars who consider any notion of a collaborative future toward 'sustainable capitalism(s)' to be an oxymoron.[132] Karl Marx argued that capitalism was not indicative of "natural liberty" in the market-place but was rather a system that exploited human labor through the structure of economic relations.[133] But much of the 'it's impossible' dialogue occurred before the international community agreed to commit to the SDGs. Critics of the Marxist materialist analysis have long argued that Marxism does not adequately develop the role of culture, treating socialization and resocialization as a relatively unproblematic 'theoretical blackbox.' While several sub-streams have

---

130   Steiner, "G20 Interfaith Summit Summary Report," (2015), 2.

131   Ibid.

132   Joel Kovel, *The Enemy of Nature : The End of Capitalism or the End of the World?*, vol. 2nd ed. (London: Zed Books Ltd, 2007), Book; David Schweickart, "Is Sustainable Capitalism an Oxymoron?" *Perspectives on Global Development & Technology* 8, no. 2/3 (2009); James O'Connor, *The Second Contradiction of Capitalism* (Santa Cruz, CA: Guilford, 1991); *Is Capitalism Sustainable? Political Economy and the Politics of Ecology* (New York: The Guilford Press, 1994).

133   R.J. Holton, *The Transition from Feudalism to Capitalism* (London: MacMillan, 1985).

emerged in Marxist thought that emphasize social relations rather than ex-change relations[134] and which eclectically draw upon non-Marxist literature to augment this Marxist oversight,[135] the classic Marxist approach tends to view ideas and mentalities as reflex rationalizations of material systems; as such, they cannot pre-date (or post-date) the existence of a system in which they are embedded.[136] In the end, the nay-sayers may yet have the last word because implementation of the SDGs presents nations with numerous signifi-cant challenges,[137] not the least of which may entail development of collab-orative religious-political relations. But critics of the material embeddedness approach to class consciousness have argued that this perspective places the researcher in a privileged position and results in what has been referred to as 'the paradox of emancipation': What if the people, whose interests you know, do not want what you say they want? Class consciousness does not always co-incide with actors' material conditions.[138]

Ever since Daniel Bell first wrote about the cultural contradictions of capitalism,[139] scholars have explored ways in which people negotiate forces promoting values in conflict with one another. For example, O'Hara describes how a consumption ethic of sexual liberty and status emulation contradicts values of frugality, industry, justice, modesty and humility.[140] And Taylor talks about the cultural contradictions associated with motherhood as women vari-ously juggle work and family depending upon their social location based on race and class.[141] In relation to religious identities, Steiner-Aeschliman has ar-gued that the cultural contradictions of unsustainably organized capitalism

134   For example, R. Brenner, "Agrarian Class Structure and Economic Development in Pre-Industrial Europe," *Past and Present* 70 (1976); R. Hilton, *Bond Men Made Free, Medieval Peasant Movement and the English Rising of 1381* (London: New Left Books, 1973).

135   For example, P. Anderson, *Passages from Antiquity to Feudalism* (London: New Left Books, 1974).

136   M. Dobb, *Studies in the Development of Capitalism* (London: Routledge and Kegan Pauul, 1963); Holton, *The Transition from Feudalism to Capitalism*.

137   Mathilde Bouye, "6 Lessons on Sustainable Development from the High-Level Political Forum," (2016), http://www.wri.org/print/444310.

138   W. Doyle, *Origins of the French Revolution* (New York: Oxford University Press, 1980); Con-rad Russell, *The Crisis of Parliaments* (Oxford: Oxford University Press, 1971).

139   Daniel Bell, *The Cultural Contradictions of Capitalism* (New York, New York: Basic Books, 1996).

140   Phillip Anthony O'Hara, "Cultural Contradictions of Global Capitalism," *Journal of Eco-nomic Issues* 38, no. 2 (2004).

141   Tiffany Taylor, "Re-Examining Cultural Contradictions: Mothering Ideology and the Inter-sections of Class, Gender, and Race," *Sociology Compass* 5, no. 10 (2011).

induces contradictory forms of religious agitation that, unless successfully negotiated, produce disempowered selves trapped within an 'iron cage.'[142] Different religious subcultural streams differently negotiate the impact of capitalism in the West, variously combining an emphasis on the human capacity for exercising private judgement and the inherent goodness in humans.[143] Colin Campbell describes how religious culture was shaped over time to where all reference to thought eventually disappeared and an ethic of feeling emerged which emphasized the validity of feelings 'in and of themselves,' closely linking morality and emotion. By the mid-eighteenth century in England, says Colin, moderation in feeling had become a vice rather than a virtue, and individuals were now experiencing a moral obligation to express powerful emotions without constraint even if it went against convention. Sub-cultural streams evolved that embodied a moral determination to live with emotional freedom according to an 'inner-directed' quality, empowering the self from within and developing the potential to break free of Weber's iron cage.[144] Steiner-Aeschliman describes how this process variously evolved over time, influenced by rationalization, to develop an internal consistency with the capacity for self-control through therapeutic renewal. But unlike the hegemonic modernist ethic, this subcultural stream required mutual responsiveness to the needs, desires, and feelings of both self and other, combining imaginative passion and liberated emotion with moral earnestness and ethical sincerity.[145] In the West, streams of religious subcultures have diversely evolved in relation to the impact of industrialization processes to develop new means of self-mastery and forms of empowerment to permit selves to remaster the institutions they had created.[146]

Understanding how religious identities are socially constructed is particularly salient for understanding modern dynamics associated with religion in transnational relations.[147] As noted earlier, because globalization brings with

---

142 Sherrie Steiner-Aeschliman. *The Religious Construction of Intimacy for Emotional Renewal: The Parallel Protestant Ethic*, vol. 9, Research in the Social Scientific Study of Religion (Stamford, CN: JAI Press, 1998).

143 Ibid., 13.

144 C. Campbell, "The Romantic Ethic and the Spirit of Modern Consumerism," (New York: Basil Blackwell, 1987), 143–144.

145 Steiner-Aeschliman. *The Religious Construction of Intimacy for Emotional Renewal: The Parallel Protestant Ethic*, 13–14.

146 Ibid.

147 David S. Gutterman and Andrew R. Murphy, *Political Religion and Religious Politics: Navigating Identities in the United States*, Routledge Series on Identity Politics (New York, New York: Routledge, 2016); Cameron McAuliffe, "A Home Far Away? Religious Identity and Trans National Relations in the Iranian Diaspora," *Global Networks* 7, no. 3 (2007); Weng Hew Wai, "Beyond 'Chinese Diaspora' and 'Islamic Ummah': Various Transnational

it culture, what Nye referred to as "attraction" in the West may be interpreted as "the insidious threat of seduction" by Islamic cultures that reject Western lifestyle choices, clothing preferences, and access to pornography.[148] Soft power attraction, according to Nye, is produced by the resource assets of cultural attractiveness,[149] but if values are interpreted to be hypocritical, soft power will detract rather than attract.[150] Because people of faith believe in something greater than the government and they have the capacity to organize, "and therefore the capacity to rebel against the state," attention to how religious dynamics are socially constructed in complex contexts provides important insights that are relevant to regional geo-politics, national narratives, ethnic majority-minority relations, gender and family dynamics, and development policies.[151] Such influences were certainly apparent in the unexpected outcome of the 2016 US Presidential election. Culture has international consequences,[152] and it is becoming clearer that Islam and the West must negotiate multiple dimensions to develop new ways of living together, as well as deconstruct the processes that fuel the radicalization of Islam when it encounters the West, and vice versa.[153]

Religious actors are engaging in public discourse *as religion*. To put it within the framework of Peter Beyer's theory,[154] the F8/F7/F20 Initiative is evidence of the further institutional differentiation of the religious sector. Successful democratic negotiation of the religious-political nexus has a much greater chance of succeeding if conversation between religion and the state is two-way. Public religion has become a new form of identity politics.[155] Nuraan Davids explains this in relation to Muslim women whose bodies, she says, have become the site of symbolic confrontations between a re-essentialized understanding of religious and cultural differences and the forces of state power. When the state insists that individuals not be allowed to enter public discourse as religious beings, what emerges is a situation of either liberal democratic constraints on Muslim women or the exclusion of Islam, as represented by Muslim women,

Connections and Local Negotiations of Chinese Muslim Identities in Indonesia," *SOJOURN: Journal of Social Issues in Southeast Asia* 29, no. 3 (2014); Nuraan Davids, "Muslim Women and the Politics of Religious Identity in a (Post) Secular Society," *Studies in Philosophy & Education* 33, no. 3 (2014).

148 Dondelinger, "Cultural Contradictions of Soft Power and Islam."
149 Nye, *Soft Power: The Means to Success in World Politics*.
150 Dondelinger, "Cultural Contradictions of Soft Power and Islam," 40.
151 Seiple, "Building Religious Freedom: A Theory of Change," 97.
152 Dondelinger, "Cultural Contradictions of Soft Power and Islam."
153 Ibid.
154 Beyer, *Religion in the Context of Globalization*.
155 Castells, *The Power of Identity*.

from democratic citizenship. The politics of religious identity posed by Muslim women in the context of globalization presents an opportunity to explore and rearticulate a more inclusive form of democratic citizenship.[156]

Sarosh Arif and Linda Hyökki made similar arguments at the 2015 F20 Turkey Summit. Arif addressed the challenge to democratic inclusion posed by the presence of Muslim women. She discussed women's rights as a universal issue that is manifested differently in different social contexts. Rather than conflate women's rights with western feminism, Muslim women should define rights in a way that is better suited to their culture, religion and social context. This approach, said Arif, is consistent with the fundamental feminist tenant that women have the right to self-determination.[157] Linda Hyökki explained how the self-identification of women as Muslim through the wearing of headscarves, for example, is unproblematic for social relations when the diversity of women's hybrid identities is recognized and respected. Arguing for equal access to the social construction of hybrid-identities, she described a process of social exclusion that occurs when women are monolithically labeled only in terms of their religion. She said, "I would reject the label because otherwise it becomes too easy to exclude me as 'The Other.' If I am seen only as a Muslim, what gets disregarded is that I am also a fan of metal music, a lover of nature and my family stems from eastern Finlandia. All of this defines me, yet at the same time, I am a Muslim. These aspects of myself do not contradict the other aspects."[158] She described Islamophobia as a forced reduction of hybrid identities that fails to recognize other important aspects of people's cultural involvements that strengthen social integration. "Problems occur in social relations," she said, "when self-identification is unidirectional and one-sided." She described women's self-identification as an activist assertion of bi-directional hybrid identities and a quest for social recognition of the commonalities that we all share. "That is what brings us together, so let us be us."[159]

Competing Assessments

Ongoing summit diversity has contributed to development of competing assessments of the F8/F7/F20 process. The emergence and establishment of the F8/F7/F20 Initiative occurred over the course of a two-year period

---

156   Davids, "Muslim Women and the Politics of Religious Identity in a (Post) Secular Society."
157   Steiner, "G20 Interfaith Summit Summary Report," (2015), 4–5.
158   Ibid., 4.
159   Ibid.

during which two very different summits were convened: the 2005 Summit in the United Kingdom and the 2006 Summit in Russia. The contrast between the 2005 UK roundtable that emphasized civil society engagement on development issues with the high-level, expensive, three-day event in Russia shows how a leadership rotation model produced summits that strongly reflect the national particularities, involvement of communities, local contexts, and particular approaches to the organizing process, and the cultural events of the regional hosts. Once established, the Initiative has clearly taken on a life of its own, but just exactly what kind of life that is remains unclear. Four general schools of thought can be identified: redundant, replacement, rejection and reinforcement.

Redundant

The first general school of thought in the debate over the significance of the F8/F7/F20 Initiative is that the long-term summit process is too cumbersome and informal to justify the associated costs of a dedicated process that can be more effectively accomplished by the more than 300 religious NGOs that have been granted consultative status at the Economic and Social Council (ECOSOC) in the United Nations (UN).[160] According to this perspective, the UN provides an adequate diplomatic forum for faith based consultation. Article 71 of the UN Charter states that the UN would consult with NGOs to carry out its work through the Economic and Social Council (ECOSOC). NGOs can register with ECOSOC to obtain consultative status as general (large international NGOs), special (smaller groups with limited areas of concern) or rosters (for those with a technical focus). Although the UN is a formally secular organization, religion becomes visible in the UN within the constitutions of individual nation-states, within the consultative process of the UN (such as through the UN Alliance of Civilizations), in the work of The Holy See (Vatican), in groups of nation-states (e.g., the Organisation of Islamic Cooperation), and within the NGO network.[161] Analysts estimate that somewhere between 8 and 10% of the NGO network is faith-based.[162] RNGOs engage with the UN framework on concerns with peace building, environment, human rights, religious minority

160 "Reflexive Governance Dynamics Operative within Round One of the World Religious Leaders' Dialogue with the G8 (2005–2013)."

161 Jeremy Carrette and Hugh Miall, eds., *Religious NGOs and the United Nations in New York and Geneva* (Canterbury, United Kingdom: University of Kent, 2013).

162 Berger, "Religious Nongovernmental Organisations"; Carrette and Miall, eds., *Religious NGOs and the United Nations in New York and Geneva*; Petersen, "International Religious NGOs at the United Nations: A Study of a Group of Religious Organizations."

protection, gender, economic issues, international cooperation, development and health.[163] RNGOs relate to the UN process through a range of activities including lobbying, implementation of projects and monitoring sometimes either directing their work at religiously defined beneficiaries or taking a more universalistic approach in support of the common good.[164] While the F8/F7/F20 Initiative is considered to be largely redundant, it is valued in this perspective for how it has served to inspire existing interfaith networks such as Religions for Peace (RfP) and the Universal Peace Federation to meet the new need for interfaith dialogue and engagement with the G-plus System.

Replacement

According to this general school of thought, RfP and/or United Religions Initiative (URI) could (or should) replace the F8/F7/F20 Initiative.[165] Whether the work of the F8/F7/F20 Initiative is replaced by RfP or URI or some combination thereof, traditionalists who maintain a binary approach to the secular find this approach appealing.

RfP has been involved in the F8 process since 2008, and they have a strong presence in five of the G8 countries and many of the G20 regions. Some consider RfP to have the organizational capacity to continue picking up where the F8 process left off in 2013, engaging with the G7 as a formally recognized UN partner in a manner compatible with dominant European thought on how religion should engage in the public sphere (e.g., Ulrich Beck). After the 2014 crisis with the Soviet Union, the F8 ceased convening meetings in tandem with the G7 once their attention shifted to the G20. However, RfP recently partnered with the United Nations Alliance of Civilizations (UNAOC) to continue engagement with the G7 at the April, 2016 meetings in Hiroshima, Japan. They brought together high-level religious leaders from the Middle East to reaffirm the foundational

---

163   Carrette and Miall, eds., *Religious NGOs and the United Nations in New York and Geneva.*

164   Petersen, "International Religious NGOs at the United Nations: A Study of a Group of Religious Organizations."

165   The World Faiths Development Dialogue has opened dialogue and debate with international financial institutions such as the World Bank and the International Monetary Fund more narrowly targeted to development issues. See Marshall, "Ancient and Contemporary Wisdom and Practice on Governance as Religious Leaders Engage in International Development." The Council for a Parliament of the World Religions has been meeting since 1993, but analysis of the Parliament indicates that they have limited conceptions of globalization and have partial knowledge claims on how religion can resolve global problems. See Jon P. Bloch, "A Whisper toward Peace: A Theoretical Analysis of the Council for a Parliament of the World Religions," *Journal for the Scientific Study of Religion* 47, no. 4 (2008).

importance of developing pluralistic communities with full citizenship for all and developed an action plan to strengthen citizenship within their respective religious communities.[166]

RfP is the largest coalition of the world's religions committed to common action consisting of interreligious bodies. The International Secretariat headquarters is in New York and they have Regional Conferences in Europe, Asia, Middle East, Africa and the Americas with more than 90 affiliates at the national level, and several local units. RfP has consultative status with the United Nations Economic and Social Council (ECOSOC), with UNESCO and with UNICEF. The INGO builds inter-religious councils to help religious communities cooperate together in the work of transforming conflict. RfP utilizes public language, rather than religious language, for communicating across faith traditions.[167] The use of public language and the instrumental emphasis upon peace (rather than truth) is compatible with existing dualistic European theories of the role of religion in contemporary society.[168] Although RfP breaches the principle of national sovereignty by formally organizing as a transnational coalition, RfP has the needed universality, social network, consultative status, organizational infrastructure, hard legal status, and staff to maintain consistent, persistent and evolving engagement with the G-plus System on behalf of religious traditions.

United Religions Initiative (URI) is a grassroots interfaith peacemaking coalition that was established in 2000 and headquartered in San Francisco to promote interfaith cooperation to end religiously motivated violence. URI has more than 500 members who work through cooperation circles that are active in 22 of 30 conflict ridden regions.[169] URI is open to a wide range of Indigenous religious communities and new religious traditions. Like RfP, URI maintain a focus on youth and women. The United Religions Initiative at the United Nations provides an ongoing presence for their concerns for NGOs, Ambassadors and UN agency staff. URI focuses their cooperation circle action on economic development, health care, humanitarian aid, Indigenous people, labor, nuclear disarmament, religious freedom, service to the poor and spirituality. Although URI activities have been more directed to the UN System than the G-plus

---

166   Religions for Peace, "Mena Leaders Address Violent Extremism & Advance Citizenship Ahead of G7 Summit," (2016), http://religionsforpeaceaustralia.org.au/2016/05/17/mena-leaders-address-violent-extremism-advance-citizenship-ahead-of-g7-summit/.

167   Vendley, "The Power of Inter-Religious Cooperation to Transform Conflict."

168   Beck, "A God of One's Own"; "The Two Faces of Religion"; Habermas, Ratzinger, and Schuller, *The Dialectics of Secularization: On Reason and Religion.*

169   Marshall, *Global Institutions of Religion: Ancient Movers, Modern Shakers.*

System, their less formally organized grassroots orientation may be more compatible with the principle of national sovereignty operative in transnational governance than RfP.

Rejection

According to another school of thought, the F8/F7/F20 Initiative should be rejected as a process. Rejectionists outside the religious framework reject the F8/F7/F20 Initiative for a very different set of reasons than those given by religious leaders. Advocates of traditional governance models tend to reject civil society engagement, of which the F8/F7/F20 Initiative is a part, as an interfering distraction that drains energy and resources away from the G-plus System, making an already difficult task even more challenging. Religious leaders who have considered the F8/F7/F20 Initiative and come to reject it over time generally support civic engagement but either consider the costs to outweigh any tangible benefits, or they have found another venue better suited to their form of advocacy.

The F8/F7/F20 Initiative's use of the rotating host model puts undue financial pressure on local hosts to organize a fragile unorthodox process that is outside of anyone's official job description. But rejection runs deeper than cost/benefit analysis. Development NGOs, in particular, place heavy emphasis on pragmatic policy development that request procedural things from the governments. One US delegate explained that "in the American context, there is heavy emphasis to be focused on concrete things...there is not a strong taste for a joint worship service or a joint statement, although there is some value in that."[170] Several US NGOs chose not to attend the US Summit (2012) given their shrinking budgets and distaste for spending resources for writing "high-level moral statements." One of the people who had been involved in the G8 process for some time and did not attend the 2012 Summit referred to the process as a

> necessary fiction, meaning that it is important and valuable for religious leaders and communities to meet together and to try to hold political leaders accountable to the standards...but at the same time a fiction in the sense that the people that come together, the way in which they come together, the temporary character of it and the lack of continuity between the summits as not having any power to it.[171]

---

170   Steiner, "Reflexive Governance Dynamics Operative within Round One of the World Religious Leaders' Dialogue with the G8 (2005–2013)."

171   Ibid.

If the goal is to exercise influence through influential religious leadership, other global interfaith conferences command a "higher level" of religious leader representation than the F8/F7/F20 Initiative which reduces the credibility of any statements emanating from the summits. The breadth of support for the F8/F7/F20 process is questioned given that its roots were in a broader *Make Poverty History* civil society campaign that pressured political leaders on poverty issues:

> Faith communities were asked to be part of the campaign, and it seemed sensible to organize a complementary event involving church leaders to add to the details of what that transformative change might look like in practice. If the *Make Poverty History* campaign hadn't been taking place, it would have been much harder to have the awareness of the issues themselves.[172]

After the Canada (2010) meetings, several of the more pragmatically oriented RNGOs disengaged from the F8/F7/F20 Initiative to participate in the C20— the G20's Civil Society engagement partner. The C20 works continuously between meetings and develops policy briefs pertinent to the G20 meeting agenda. More development oriented hosts, such as the United Kingdom, the United States and Australia, continue to influence the F8/F7/F20 process toward "more of an NGO way than a church way," emphasizing the importance of involving faith-based development organizations for purposes of strengthening understanding by policy makers that "churches and faith communities are reliable and expert partners in development."[173]

Reinforcement

According to the reinforcement school of thought, the F8/F7/F20 Initiative has had considerable success in the past, but the model needs to be adapted to changing circumstances. The ability of leaders in religion or belief to shape public and political debate need to be improved. For example, the model of hosting large scale interfaith gatherings was said to put too much strain on national hosts, so a social media campaign was substituted for face-to-face meetings in 2013 as an alternate model. Retirements and leadership turnover within host organizations have weakened commitment to the process at critical junctures. To ensure ongoing support, proponents of the reinforcement perspective

---

172   Ibid.
173   Reed, "Project Proposal—2013 G8 Religious Leaders' Initiative."

suggest that meetings need to develop a clearer focus on desirable outputs as a complement to process, set priorities in relation to the agendas emerging from the G-plus System, and take the wider schedule of G-plus System events into consideration when developing plans. The diverse range of methods and topics that characterize summit meetings blurs the focus and interferes with constructive and concerted action. The "golden strand" running through the F8/F7/F20 Initiative that is considered worthy of reinforcement is the foci on fulfillment of the MDGs/SDGs. The MDG/SDG style Initiative offers national religious leader hosts the opportunity to inform this debate from their own starting point and is an area where considerable interfaith consensus already exists. The MDG/SDG consensus can be built upon with little risk of fragmentation. Early and advanced organization of summit activities reinforce advocacy with respective governments when done in advance of the political summit itself. To ensure that the process is worthwhile, this school of thoughts suggests that national hosts meet at least six months in advance, target particular agenda issues and prepare views/statements, do a public relations program a month or two ahead, and continue the media coverage while the G8/G20 leaders are meeting. From this perspective, the value of improving the process is to increase public pressure on policy makers as moral entrepreneurs to mobilize the necessary political will and resources to fulfill SDG goals. In the wake of the financial crisis of 2007–08, the Initiative's attention has shifted toward incentivizing G20 attention to religion by building on linkages between religious freedom and economic growth. In either case, this perspective finds significant flaws with the existing process but considers it valuable enough to warrant continuing support with attention to ways the process might be improved.

Impact

The F8/F7/F20 process has had intended and unintended impacts on religious and political national and transnational relations. The intended impact considered here involves discussion of how the F8/F7/F20 process has influenced the G-plus System. Two unintended impacts are also explored: on gender relations in religious transnational relations and on domestic interfaith relations in national contexts that hosted a summit.

G-plus System

Scholars have commonly assessed G-plus System outcome documents for references to civil society activities and concerns as an indicator of civil society impact since summit documents are the main vehicle used for communicating outcomes.[174] The F8/F7/F20 Initiative has been treated by scholars as part of civil society for some time now.[175] So one indicator of the F8/F7/F20 Initiative's impact is to assess the degree to which summit communiqué concerns resonate with civil society acknowledgements in G-plus System outcome documents. For example, Peter Hajnal reviewed the documents produced from the 2006 Russia Summit to see the degree to which civil society concerns impacted outcomes. He found no evidence of impact on the twin documents on energy security (*Global Energy Security* and the *St. Petersburg Plan of Action on Global Energy Security*), but he did find evidence of civil society impact in *Education for Innovative Societies in the 21st Century*, the *G8 Summit Declaration on Counter-Terrorism* and the *Report of the Nuclear Safety and Security Group*.[176] Of these, the following excerpts are consistent with the content of the collaborative religious leaders' communiqué:

> The document *Education for Innovative Societies in the 21st Century* promises: "Our governments will promote dialogue and synergies with business, higher education and labor to develop sound higher education and human resources policies" (para. 10), and states that the leaders "welcome active participation of the business community and non-governmental organizations in the development of continuous education that provides the competences and skills needed by our societies and economies" (para. 17). More vaguely, the statement undertakes that the G8 countries "will adhere to the...principles...[of] continued involvement of all relevant partners, including civil society...in the activities to tackle the HIV/AIDS pandemic and to reduce stigma and discrimination against people with this disease" (para. 17). The *G8 Summit Declaration on Counter-Terrorism* reaffirms the commitment to engage "in active dialogue with civil society to prevent terrorism" (para. 4).[177]

This type of outcome document matching could be continued for all G-plus System summit outcome documents through 2016 when, for the first time, the

---

174   Hajnal, "The 2006 St. Petersburg Summit and Civil Society"; "Civil Society and the 2008 G8 Hokkaido Summit"; "Civil Society at the 2009 G8 Summit in L'Aquila"; "The G20"; *The G7/G8 System: Evolution, Role and Documentation*; Kirton, "G20 Governance for a Globalized World."

175   See, for example, Hajnal, "Civil Society at the 2009 G8 Summit in L'Aquila."

176   "The 2006 St. Petersburg Summit and Civil Society."

177   Ibid., 5.

G7 Foreign Ministers made specific reference to religious concerns apart from civil society organizations:

> We emphasize the importance of promoting pluralism, moderation, tolerance, and gender equality, as well as cross-cultural, cross-religious, and interfaith dialogues, and promoting freedom of expression and freedom of religion or belief as useful tools to prevent and counter violent extremism and terrorism.[178]

In 2017, Foreign Ministers again identified religious leaders as an important civil society group that leaders should dialogue with as a way of preventing radicalization to violent extremism.[179]

However, the G-plus System is notoriously poor at translating prioritized values into specific promises, and even poorer at keeping those promises, once made, for numerous reasons including, but not limited to, high leadership turnover, weak political will for resolving transnational problems, and short-term record keeping. For this reason, a more challenging impact indicator has been assessment of the degree to which, if at all, priorities and promises emerging from the G-plus System are followed-up with concrete behaviors.

A civil society accountability network has emerged over time that has developed various indicators for measuring the degree to which the G7, the G8 and the G20 were keeping their promises. The F8/F7/F20 has participated in this broader civil society accountability process for some time, drawing upon measures produced by other NGO-centered think tanks and academic centers to exercise reputational accountability toward the G-plus System.[180] Civil society accountability reports usually focus on a specific topic. For example, since 2006, ONE has been issuing annual *DATA Reports* that monitor development promises to Africa emerging from the G-plus System.[181] ActionAid

---

178   Ministers, *Joint Communiqué*, (2016).

179   Ministers, *Joint Communiqué*, (2017).

180   Steiner, "Faith-Based Accountability Mechanism Typology: The 2011 Interfaith Summit as Soft Power in Global Governance"; "Religious Soft Power as Accountability Mechanism for Power in World Politics: The Interfaith Leaders' Summit(s)"; Sherrie Steiner, "Is Religious Soft Power of Consequence in the World Today?" in *Religious Diversity Today*, ed. Jen-Guy A. Goulet (Santa Barbara, CA: Praeger, 2016).

181   See, for example, Catherine Blampied et al., "The Data Report 2015: Putting the Poorest First," (*One*, 2015), https://www.one.org/us/policy/data-report-2015/.

issues reports specific to hunger.[182] New Rules for Global Finance focuses on economic reform, and Transparency International emphasizes public disclosure of activities.[183] World Health Organization reports are specific to health commitments.[184] Project Ploughshares is frequently referenced for the reports they produce on nuclear disarmament and compliance with the Nuclear Non-Proliferation Treaty.[185] The business sector has launched a 'performance dashboard' and the International Chamber of Commerce has devised a *G20 Business Scorecard* to assess the performance of G20 countries on trade and investment, green growth, transparency and anti-corruption, and financing for growth and development.[186] The G8 Research Group assessed the G8's compliance record on climate change from 1975–2011.[187] Many civil society organizations, including participants in the F8/F7F20 Initiative, have drawn upon these types of reports when determining their public response to the ongoing G-plus System process.

F8/F7/F20 leaders have maintained close relations with the G8/G7 and G20 Research Groups at the University of Toronto's Munk School of Global Affairs, a premier research institution studying the G8/G7 and G20 summit

---

182 Katie Campbell, "G8 Accountability Report a Big Step Forward for Transparency, but Underscores Unfinished Agenda on Global Hunger," *ActionAid* (2012), https://www.interaction.org/document/g8-accountability-report-big-step-forward-transparency-underscores-unfinished-agenda-global.

183 Hajnal, "The G20," 94.

184 World Health Organization, "G8 France 2011 New World New Ideas: Deauville Accountability Report," *G8 Commitments on Health and Food Security: State of Delivery and Results* (2011), http://www.who.int/pmnch/media/membernews/2011/20110518_accountability-report.pdf.

185 Cesar Jaramillo, Transparency and Accountability: NPT Reporting 2002–2012, (Waterloo, Ontario: Project Ploughshares, 2012).

186 Hajnal, "The G20," 164.

187 John Kirton, Jenilee Guebert, and Caroline Bracht, "Climate Change Accountability: The G8's Compliance Record from 1975–2011," (2011), www.g8.utoronto.ca/evaluations/climate-acc-111205.pdf. *G8 and G7* is distributed by mail to government officials, ministers, leaders, and diplomatic missions, with their personal names on the envelopes (in their professional positions). The Munk School also distributes *G8 and G7* to participants of the G8, G7 and G20 summits and the media center. At times, the annuals are hand-delivered to press clubs. *G8 and G7* are summit preparatory documents. It regularly features editors' introductions, articles from G8/G7 heads of state, and articles on each chosen summit theme, real-world conditions, global governance, and the G8/G7 process (including, but not limited to, compliance reports), and evolving partnerships with groups such as the G20, B8, BRICS, and the United Nations, depending on the dynamics at a given historical moment.

process. Since 2009, reports on the F8/F7/F20 process have been included in the G8/G7 Research Group's publication *G8* (and later, *G7*) which is a glossy 300 page document that is published and distributed at the G8/G7 and G20 Summits by Newsdesk Media.[188] On several occasions, F8/F7/F20 leaders have been asked to present public assessments of G-plus System's progress on the MDGs.[189] F8/F7/F20 leaders partnered with the G8 Research Group in 2010 to integrate G8 commitment compliance data into the summit process. Kirton spoke at five regional gatherings for the dual purpose of providing education on the MDGs and enhancing regional interfaith relationships. The G8 Research Group at the University of Toronto has released reports of G8 compliance with summit commitments since 1996. The annual compliance reports are prepared in collaboration with the International Organisations Research Institute, Higher School of Economics, and the National Research University (Moscow). The G20 Research Group at the University of Toronto has prepared, in collaboration with the International Organisations Research Institute, similar reports since the first 2008 G20 Summit in Washington, DC.[190]

In response to increasing civil society pressures, the G-plus System has engaged in limited self-assessment. In 2009, the G8 established an ad hoc working group that created an accountability tool to define a consistent and robust methodology to harmonize reporting and enhance transparency on implementation of commitments.[191] The following year, the G8 released its first, and only, comprehensive *2010 Muskoka Accountability Report*, after which reporting would be issue specific.[192] The Earth Institute and the Institute for Economics

---

188   See Steiner, "Is Religious Soft Power of Consequence in the World Today?"

189   Hamilton, "For Just Such a Time as This: Reflections on the Statement 'Translating Shared Concerns into Action.'"; Karen Hamilton, "Inspired Leadership: Civil Society's Contribution to G8 and G20 Summitry," in *G8/G20 the 2010 Canadian Summits: Recovery and New Beginnings*, ed. John Kirton and Madeline Koch (Toronto, Canada: Newsdesk Media, 2010); Hamilton, "The G8 Speaks but Is There Action to Follow?"; "UN High Panel on the Millennium Development Goals"; "The Open Spiral: The Ongoing Commitments of Faith Leaders"; "After 13 Years, the Millennium Development Goals Are Still Pertinent"; Karen Hamilton, "Faith in Sustainability: How Faith Communities Have Helped Move the Discussion around Sustainability Forward," *Open Canada.Org* (2013); Hamilton, "Keeping the Faith: Still Focused on Goals"; "The Global Agenda from an Interfaith Perspective"; Hamilton and Adams, "Inspiring Leadership and Action for Development"; Christie, "How Well Does the G8 Deliver: Compliance with G8 Commitments."

190   Hajnal, "The G20," 148.

191   G8, "G8 Accountability Tool," http://78.41.128.109/images//Holding_G8_Accountability _to_Account.pdf.

192   Hajnal, "Head to Head: Summits in Canada in June 2010: The Muskoka G8 Meets the Toronto G20s".

and Peace immediately issued an INGO assessment of the G8's comprehensive self-assessment.[193] As for the G20, it initiated the Mutual Assessment Process (MAP) "through commissioning a series of IMF reports with the World Bank and other IGOs also playing a role."[194] InterAction, a US based alliance of more than 180 member organizations working in every developing country, has published civil society assessments of the G20's self-assessment process.[195] InterAction members are faith-based and secular, large and small, with a focus on the world's most poor and vulnerable populations. Common commitments that define InterAction work include fostering economic and social development, provision of relief to those affected by disaster and war, assistance to refugees and internally displaced persons, the advancement of human rights, support for gender equity, protection of the environment, the addressing of population concerns, and agreement to press for more equitable, just and effective public policies. InterAction releases a score-card on G20 accountability in relation to these common commitments.[196] Improvement of the G20's self-assessment process also attracts ongoing analytic attention.[197] The G8 Research Group, the G7 Research Group, and the G20 Research Group have been among the first analyst groups to develop comprehensive performance measures for rating the G-plus System process. Peter Hajnal details the processes for how the G-plus System has been monitored and evaluated in his section on Civil Society in *The G20*.[198]

Political leaders have not been particularly pleased with the development of civil society assessment of the G-plus System, so another indicator often used for impact has been the degree to which the political leaders have been

---

193   Jeffrey D. Sachs and Steve Killelea, "Holding G8 Accountability to Account," Institute for Economics and Peace and the Earth Institute, Columbia University, 2011.

194   Hajnal, "The G20," 164.

195   John Ruthrauff and Sue Pleming, "Establishing G8 Accountability: Still a Work in Progress," (2013), https://www.interaction.org/document/establishing-g8-accountability-still-work-progress.

196   See, for example, http://www.g8.utoronto.ca/evaluations/2009laquila/2009performance090713.html.

197   Dirk Willem te Velde, "Accountability and Effectiveness of the G20's Role in Promoting Development," in *Workshop on an Accountability Mechanism for G20 Development Commitments* (Bali, Indonesia: Overseas Development Institute, 2012); Zhenbo Hou and Dirk Willem te Velde, "The Accountability of the G20's Development Agenda: Perspectives and Suggestions from Developing Countries of the Commonwealth and Francophonie," in *Commonwealth-Francophonie-G20 Development Working Group Meeting* (Washington, D.C. 2013).

198   Hajnal, "The G20," 148–170.

willing to engage with civil society. The G7, in its early years, and now the G20 have been slow to acknowledge civil society.[199] Some summit presidencies have provided more civil society access to the G-plus System than others. Just as civil society initiated contact with the G7, civil society initiated contact with the G20. Recently, the G20 has begun to officially recognize (with national variation) a variety of engagement partners.

There is a wide range of civil society organizations interacting with the G20 whose concerns include, but are not limited to, poverty, peace and disarmament, consumer affairs, development, environment and climate change, human rights, gender issues, health, education, financial regulations and others.[200] Scholte includes faith-based groups, labor unions, research institutes, think-tanks and academies of sciences under the broad umbrella of civil society,[201] but several of these groups have come to specialize and obtain autonomous recognition by the G20. In Peter Hajnal's discussion of civil society engagement with the G20, he considers four special groups as outside of the broad 'civil society' category: business, private philanthropies and foundations, celebrities and parliamentarians.[202] Hajnal has included contributions from the F8/F7/F20 under the broad umbrella of civil society.[203]

In this book, the F8/F7/F20 Initiative has been consistently treated as overlapping with, and yet distinctive from, civil society. Although this approach is a bit murky, civil society is itself a rather murky process, and without autonomous recognition, faith-based organizations can play leading roles within civil society one year (e.g., Australia 2014), and be excluded from the process in the next (e.g., Turkey 2015). The F8/F7/F20 process shares many concerns with secular INGOs, and often overlaps in how they engage with the G-plus System, but they also represent faith-based concerns that are not subsumable under secular and instrumentalized agendas. Marshall has identified several distinctive elements that apply to religious freedom that "deserve more focus than they have received" when subsumed under development concerns. She writes that "the stakes are often high—and as such, distinctive and nuanced consideration of these issues needs to be better incorporated into development analyses, dialogues, education, and policy development processes."[204]

---

199   Ibid., 104.

200   Ibid., 81.

201   Scholte, "Introduction."

202   Hajnal, "The G20," 79–118.

203   Ibid.

204   Katherine Marshall, "Religious Freedom in US International Development Assistance and Humanitarian Relief: Ideas, Practice and Issues," *Review of Faith & International Affairs* 11, no. 1 (2013).

The original intention behind engagement groups was to demonstrate that the G20 has links to broader segments of society rather than being a closed government forum. The first engagement partners to be recognized by the G-plus System were business (B20) which was first recognized by the South Korean Presidency in 2010 and labor (L20) which was first recognized by the French Presidency in 2011. Business and labor have provided consultation appropriate to the G20 focus on key financial, economic, trade, and development issues ever since. Civil society engagement has been slower. In 2012, Mexican President Calderón, host of the Los Cabos G20 Summit, appointed a Special Representative charged with engaging non-state actors before and during the Summit with particular emphasis on young people, academia, and the business community, but Peter Hajnal reports that the impression of several NGO participants and observers were that the events had minimal impact on the Summit outcome.[205] In 2013, the Russian Presidency at the 2013 G20 Summit involved a Think 20, Civil 20, and Youth 20 in addition to the B20 and L20. Despite the impressive agenda, reports Peter Hajnal, the process was accompanied by increased restrictive legislations that compromised the promising development of increased engagement.[206] The engagement process began to shift from consultation toward collaboration for policy improvement the next year when the Australian Presidency expanded engagement groups to five in 2014: B20, L20, T20 and now C20 (civil society) and Y20 (young people).[207] A collaborative policy development process utilizing an open web platform was used for dialogue during the months leading up to the Melbourne Summit. The C20 submitted four, detailed policies into the G20 system for Sherpa consideration, but getting C20 policies actually onto the G20 formal agenda nevertheless remained a challenge.[208] As the G20 focus broadened to address a wider array of topics from terrorism to climate change, the number of engagement partners was broadened again in 2015 under the Turkish Presidency to include women (W20). National hosts decide which of these engagement partners will be recognized in any given year, so there is fluctuation in the recognition process. In 2016, the China Presidency published on their website a meeting with the W20, but did not recognize on the official website, engagement

---

205   Hajnal, "The G20," 105–106.
206   Ibid., 107–108.
207   Burrow et al., "G20 2014: Perspectives from Business, Civil Society, Labour, Think Tanks and Youth."
208   Ibid., 20.

with other groups such as civil society and interfaith leaders who were permitted to convene meetings.[209]

When officially recognized, the G20 chair appoints a lead coordinator for the groups engaged within any given year. The appointed coordinator pulls together contributions from that segment of society in both G20 and non-G20 countries to identify policy priorities. National hosts determine which groups are recognized, consulted with and given access to officials and ministers throughout the year. Officially recognized engagement partners usually hold shadow summits of their own, in tandem with G20 meetings, where they put forward specific policy recommendations in relation to the G20's agenda. As of 2016, the F8/F7/F20 Initiative has yet to become an officially recognized engagement partner by any of the G20 presidencies, a factor which has limited the impact the F8/F7/F20 process might otherwise have upon the G-plus System. The F8/F7/F20 Initiative's weak focus on what Smith and Larimer refer to as 'the how and why of policymaking'[210] may be contributing to the G-plus System's delayed recognition given their pragmatic and immediate concerns with stabilizing the international economy. In the long run, however, the F8/F7/F20 process has demonstrated strong familiarity with what James and Jorgensen have identified as the 'analysis and evaluation'[211] stream of the policy process. Additional policy streams where the F8/F7/F20 exhibit strengths for G-plus System's considerations relate to the problem stream and the politics stream of the policy process.[212]

Gender

The F8/F7/F20 Initiative has provided an opportunity for women to exercise religious leadership as a contribution to transnational relations. The gender composition of high-level leadership within the F8/F7/F20 Initiative is reflective of a broader transnational cultural shift, though not without setbacks, plateauing and geographic variation, where opportunities to provide more female religious leadership has been slowly increasing over time as women rise

209   G20-China, "Equal Participation, Innovative Development: 2016 W20 Meeting Highlights 'She Power' to the World," (2016), http://www.g20.org/English/G20Priorities/Engagement/201606/t20160628_2345.html.

210   Kevin B. Smith and Christopher W. Larimer, The Public Policy Theory Primer (Boulder, Colorado: Westview Press, 2009).

211   Thomas E. James and Paul D. Jorgensen, "Policy Knowledge, Policy Formation, and Change: Revisiting a Foundational Question," Policy Studies Journal 37, no. 1 (2009).

212   For additional discussion of the streams of policy scholarship, see Matthew C. Nowlin, "Theories of the Policy Process: State of the Research and Emerging Trends," Ibid., 39, April (2011).

within the leadership circles of various faith traditions. In the case of the F8/ F7/F20 Initiative, two women in particular, have obtained heightened transnational profiles from their involvement in the process. Since 2010, Hamilton has been consistently asked by the University of Toronto's G-plus research groups to publish, and co-publish with rotating national hosts, articles on the F8/F7/ F20 process in the annual *G8* and *G7* publications that are annually distributed to participants at the G-plus summits.[213] Her leadership profile has risen over time to the point where she was the only faith leader asked to participate in the roundtable civil society consultation process between *Beyond 2015* (the network of 1,581 organizations from 142 countries) and the *United Nations High Panel on the Millennium Development Goals* during the transition phase when they were determining what, if anything, should follow the MDGs.[214] Marshall has also figured prominently in recent F20 summits. She has presented keynote addresses in Australia 2014, Turkey 2015, China 2016, and Germany 2017. Hamilton serves on the G20 Interfaith Summit International Organizing Committee and Marshall serves on the G20 Interfaith Executive Committee. Hamilton and Marshall have both called for greater attention to be paid to gender relations in ongoing summit agendas.

Hamilton became engaged with the F8/F7/F20 process in 2007 when members of the international planning team for the German Summit solicited her involvement. When she asked them why they approached her, they indicated that Canadians are good on process, they provide a bridge between Europeans and Americans, and they wanted her, as the only female Regional General Secretary in the National Council of Churches network, to provide a degree of gender balance to the planning committee.[215] Although she was not the Secretary General of the 2010 Canadian Summit, she played the second most prominent role that year in her national position as General Secretary of the Canadian Council of Churches. Hamilton has played a leading unofficial role within the ICC leadership structure. At several points in the ongoing F8/F7/F20 process, Hamilton's activities ensured leadership continuity between prior and upcoming summits. She has maintained files on the F8/F7/F20 process at the office of the Canadian Council of Churches in Toronto and forwarded relevant documents to Secretaries-General national hosts, as needed. Had she remained detached and uninvolved with the ongoing process apart from Canada's turn

---

213   Steiner, "Is Religious Soft Power of Consequence in the World Today?"

214   Hamilton, "To Boldly Go: Innovations Originating through the F8 Canadian Interfaith Leaders Summit Which Strengthen Human Destiny and Community."

215   Karen Hamilton, interview by Sherrie Steiner, October, 2012.

to play host, it is questionable whether the Italy 2009, France 2011, or US 2012 summits would have convened.

Katherine Marshall's involvement stems from her academic role as Professor of the Practice of Development, Conflict, and Religion at Georgetown University and her extensive career in the development field, including several leadership positions at the World Bank. She helped to create and now serves as the Executive Director of the World Faiths Development Dialogue at Georgetown University in Washington, DC. She has been involved in the summit process since 2008, and she helped host the F8 US Summit in 2012.

Although women are earning more educational degrees than men, they continue to be underrepresented at the top of institutional leadership hierarchies, particularly in patriarchal religious organizations, so how have these women come to exercise such prominent leadership roles? For example, recent US data indicate that although an estimated 10% of US religious organizations employ a female senior pastor, representation significantly lags behind other sectors where women's leadership is far higher (e.g., 24.5% of positional leaders in academia, and 51% of managerial and professional workers).[216] Even when women serve as senior pastors, their leadership is often largely confined to local or regional communities in ways that are not yet comparable to that of men.[217] Most major world religions continue to bar women from access to high-level positions within religious hierarchies, and the relationship between women and religion in Western civilization has tended to associate women with piety, relegating them to the private sphere (a practice being challenged in a variety of traditions) in ways that tend to work against their self-actualization in public service.[218] Scholars have suggested that this may change as more women rise within the leadership circles of various faith traditions, which may be the case here with the F8/F7/F20 Initiative.[219]

Key factors to take into consideration when seeking to understand gender relations in the F8/F7/F20 Initiative include the organizational structure of the

---

216   Amy B. Diehl and Leanne M. Dzubinski, "Making the Invisible Visible: A Cross-Sector Analysis of Gender-Based Leadership Barriers," *Human Resource Development Quarterly* 27, no. 2 (2016).

217   Adair Lummis and Paula Nesbitt, "Women Clergy Research and the Sociology of Religion," *Sociology of Religion* 61, no. 4 (2000).

218   Andrea Radasanu, "Introduction: The Pious Sex?" in *The Pious Sex: Essays on Women and Religion in the History of Political Thought*, ed. Andrea Radasanu (Lanham, MD: Lexington Books, 2010).

219   James Davison Hunter and Kimon Howland Sargeant, "Religion, Women and the Transformation of Public Culture," *Social Research* 60 (1993).

Initiative, the national leadership positions held by the women involved, the transnational context within which the Initiative operates, and the agenda addressed by the process. Mimicking the informal process of the G-plus System with which they engage, the F8/F7/F20 Initiative is committed to remaining an informal network of national representatives that operate in a post-Westphalian transnational context of 'governance without government.' Although this commitment to informality makes the process more fragile (e.g., the Initiative has no permanent secretariat and the ongoing process is constantly subject to the willingness of sponsors and national hosts), attentiveness to transnational dynamics is politically astute and may be, in the long run, one of the central factors contributing to the success of the long-term process. Unlike organizations such as Religions for Peace International or the United Religions Initiative, the F8/F7/F20 process is *not* building a transnational religious infrastructure. This means that, although women may be exercising power in the process, they are not being given official positions because the organization simply does not exist.

Research indicates that groups without any leadership at all often produce anarchic environments that favor the strong.[220] Although this process usually favours men, as women rise in leadership circles, this creates opportunities for changing gender patterns. In the case of the F8/F7/F20 Initiative, people such as Hamilton and Marshall have made their contributions to the F8/F7/F20 Initiative from the basis of their national positions that are separate from, rather than formally rising from within, the Initiative. Hamilton has entered from within the leadership ranks of Canadian faith traditions. Marshall's pathway has flowed from her achievements in transnational development work and her academic achievements in the US. Since the Initiative is not a formal organization and even the ICC remains a loose network of participants with varying levels of ongoing engagement, internal organizational dynamics have been significantly influenced by interpersonal relationships rather than internal bureaucratic positionality and hierarchy.

Recent research on gender-based leadership patterns in faith based small group NGOs[221] suggest that the influential roles of Hamilton and Marshall within the F8/F7/F20 Initiative may be related to the agenda addressed by the ongoing process, that of 'mending the world.' Research indicates that women,

---

220   Benjamin D. Zablocki, *Alienation and Charisma: A Study of Contemporary American Communes* (New York: Free Press, 1980).

221   John Levi Martin, Tod Van Gunten, and Benjamin D. Zablocki, "Charisma, Status, and Gender in Groups with and without Gurus," *Journal for the Scientific Study of Religion* 51, no. 1 (2012).

both female elected officials[222] and clergywomen,[223] tend to take more action on 'care issues' than men, although evidence is mixed on whether women are perceived to be doubly expert when they act on certain "gendered" social issues.[224] Research on the practice of world religions in contemporary Asia suggests that women in religion may exercise power in indirect and more dynamically fluid ways than do men.[225] Several empirical studies indicate that groups with patriarchal ideologies frequently offer women more day-to-day opportunities for women to exercise interpersonal power.[226] In particular, small religious networks composed of charismatic leaders are more likely to be "compatible with receptivity and decoupled from gender characteristics that tend to disadvantage women, leading charismatic women to have greater status than they would otherwise have."[227] Women are not just "less structurally advantaged than one might think given the official ideology, nor even that there are forms of countervailing power that are open to those who buy into an ideology of male dominance," write John Martin, Tod Van Gunten and Benjamin Zablocki, "[i]t is that women actually seem to have *more* interpersonal power in such groups than they do in other groups."[228] Females more frequently than males have been shown to use the transformational (as opposed to transactional) leadership style[229] that Max Weber described as a form of "emotional

222   Kathleen A. Bratton, "The Effect of Legislative Diversity on Agenda Setting: Evidence from Six State Legislatures," *American Politics Research* 30, no. 2; Michele Swers, "Research on Women in Legislatures: What Have We Learned and Where Are We Going?" *Women and Politics* 23, no. 1/2 (2002).

223   Laura R. Olson, Sue E.S. Crawford, and Melissa M. Deckman, *Women with a Mission: Religion, Gender, and the Politics of Women Clergy* (Tuscaloosa: University of Alabama Press, 2005).

224   Paul A. Djupe, "The Effects of Descriptive Associational Leadership on Civic Engagement: The Case of Clergy and Gender in Protestant Denominations," *Journal for the Scientific Study of Religion* 53, no. 3 (2014).

225   G. Lowes Dickinson and Susan Sered, "Prologue: Negotiating Women's Roles and Power in the Practice of World Religions in Contemporary Asia," *Religion* 37, no. 2 (2007).

226   Angela A. Aidala, "Social Change, Gender Roles, and New Religious Movements," *Sociology of Religion* 46, no. 3 (1985); Sylvia Fuller and John Levi Martin, "Women's Status in Eastern NRMs," *Review of Religious Research* 44, no. 4 (2003); Martin, Van Gunten, and Zablocki, "Charisma, Status, and Gender in Groups with and without Gurus."

227   Martin, Van Gunten, and Zablocki, "Charisma, Status, and Gender in Groups with and without Gurus," 20.

228   Ibid., 21.

229   James MacGregor Burns, *Leadership* (New York: Harper and Row, 1978); Vannessa Urch Druskat, "Gender and Leadership Style: Transformational and Transactional Leadership in the Roman Catholic Church," *Leadership Quarterly* 5, no. 2 (1994).

faith."[230] In small group contexts, if some of the exhibited behavior is particularly forceful, social space opens up for women to increase their status through the exercise of a different type of charisma that is connected with both dynamism and prosocial characteristics.[231]

When considered altogether, the informality of the F8/F7/F20 Initiative, the transnational context, the prominent national positions held by participating women, and the pro-social caring agenda of the Initiative may help to explain the observed gender relations at work in the leadership behavior of the F8/F7/F20 Initiative.

Gender has also been an important theme in the summit process, a topic which has been highlighted as noticeably absent in some of the European interreligious dialogue circles[232] and peacebuilding studies.[233] As early as 2008, Mary Robinson, former President of Ireland, pressed hard on issues of human rights and the responsibility of religious leaders to keep girls and women on the agenda of the F8 Summit in Kyoto-Osaka, Japan.[234] In her work, Marshall has identified a range of areas where religion and gender intersect, each illustrating some reasons for tensions, areas for common ground, and potential avenues for productive engagement including, but not limited to, female genital cutting, domestic violence, preference of families for male offspring, rape as a tool of war and conflict, sex trafficking, family planning, early marriage, and HIV/AIDS.[235] In 2015, the year the Turkish G20 Presidency officially recognized the W20 as an engagement partner, religion and gender equity was repeatedly mentioned at the F20 Summit as an issue to be prioritized for further dialogue.[236] Several presentations addressed the topic and a parallel session on Women, Faith and Sustainable Development was a 'standing room only' event. In his keynote address on November 17, Brian Grim spoke about how religious freedom aligns with SDG Goal 5: Gender Equity. He quoted research by Dr. Jo Anne Lyon, General Superintendent of the Wesleyan Church, whose empirical data indicated that religious freedom promotes empowerment for

230   Weber, *Economy and Society*, 1122.
231   Martin, Van Gunten, and Zablocki, "Charisma, Status, and Gender in Groups with and without Gurus," 38.
232   Merdjanova, "Overhauling Interreligious Dialogue for Peacebuilding."
233   Susan Hayward and Katherine Marshall, *Women, Religion and Peacebuilding* (Washington, D.C.: United States Institute of Peace Press, 2015).
234   Katherine Marshall, "A Religious G8," *The Washington Post* (2008), onfaith.washingtonpost.com/onfaith/Georgetown/2008/07/a_religious_g8.html.
235   "Development, Religion, and Women's Roles in Contemporary Societies," *Review of Faith & International Affairs* 8, no. 4 (2010).
236   Steiner, "G20 Interfaith Summit Summary Report," (2015), 3.

women along with political freedom, freedom of conscience and civil liberties. In 14% of countries worldwide, girls are discriminated against in education by government policies. He presented data showing that in contexts where there are high governmental restrictions on religious freedom, girls are twice as likely to be discriminated against in education compared to countries where restrictions on religious freedom are low.[237]

On November 18, 2015, Hamilton moderated a parallel session on Women, Faith and Sustainable Development. Nazila Ghanea raised several questions related to what the added value, or distinction, of the involvement of women of faith in sustainable development might be and, in turn, which rights might need to be protected to support this. Anita Soboleva (Associate Professor, Faculty of Law, Department of Theory and History of Law, National Research University Higher School of Economics, Russia) spoke about religious opposition to a law that protected women in Russia from domestic violence. SDG goals support development of protections for women. Since 1999, UN committee recommendations have consistently indicated that Russia needs to enact domestic violence laws. The Ministry of Interior estimates that 40% of violent crimes in Russia are committed within families and incidents of domestic violence continue to increase. In the absence of special legislation, these are considered private indictment cases leaving women on their own to move the case forward in the system. Dr. Soboleva said that they modeled their proposed law on special legislation that, after it was successfully implemented in Kazakhstan and Moldova, resulted in a 40% decrease in crime. Although the Russian State Duma is expected to create some mechanism of protection for women, the legislation itself had not yet been introduced to the State Duma, in part, because public opinion had become divided due to unanticipated strong resistance from Orthodox communities. Religious communities have denied the extent of the social problem, challenged the State's statistical data, and opposed development of new legislation claiming that adequate legal protections are already in place. Opposition considered the proposed law as 'demonizing' the family and inappropriately authorizing the state to intervene in private family matters. Without the law, victims of domestic violence must often continue living with their abusers because the legal system is not able to provide women with adequate protection.

Lena Larsen spoke about her engagement in a process that has identified a theological basis and methodology for promoting an argument in favor of gender equality before the law within the Islamic tradition. Treating sharia law as a social construction, she and her colleagues deconstructed the patriarchal

---

237   Ibid., 13–14.

interpretations that result in the mistreatment of women and children and impede sustainable development. They then reconstructed Islamic arguments for gender equality. She spoke about how these arguments are useful for garnering religious support for promoting gender equality in fulfillment of the SDGs.[238]

A pre-conference on Equality, Inclusiveness and Non-Discrimination was also convened on November 16, 2015 where participants discussed how Muslim women's distinctive social location differentiates their struggle for rights from that of western feminism. Panelists described how Islamophia is rooted in the social construction of "The Other" and the disregard of women's hybrid-identities, how woman's rights should be understood as a universal concept that is variously manifested in different contexts, and how Muslim women should define rights in a way suitable to their situation.[239]

The relationship between women's rights, the family and sustainable development has continued to elicit significant discussion among participants as evident in the most recent German Summit convened at Potsdam in 2017.[240]

Domestic Relations

The mere process of hosting a summit has a domestic impact, whether intended or unintended. The type of impact varies depending upon the national context. For Russia 2006, the process of hosting a large interreligious summit built a measure of much-needed trust between diverse faith traditions who worked together in a common project in a national context where the interreligious infrastructure is weak and fragile. It is unclear whether that trust has had any long-lasting effects. Russia did not host an F8 Summit when it was their turn again in 2014. The summit process deepened national religious divides among competing religious groups in the context of Japan 2008. Hosts of the 2009 Italian Summit spoke about how the process expanded their network of religious constituencies and connected several Italian politicians to faith traditions that they previously did not even know existed within their country.

Hosting the 2010 Summit in Canada initially resulted in formation of the Canadian Interfaith Partnership. Prior to this, Canada did not have a national interfaith body; some city-based multi-faith councils existed, but most interreligious networks were bilateral councils usually focused on Christian–Jewish dialogue. Two prior attempts to form a national multi-faith body such

---

238   Ibid., 75–77.
239   Ibid., 4–6.
240   Steiner, Sherrie, et. al., "G20 Interfaith Summit Summary Report," (2017).

as a Canadian Council of Religions, one in the 1980s and another at the turn of the millennium, had both failed.[241] The collaborative efforts of the 47 various expressions of Christian, Jewish, Hindu, Sikh, Muslim, Buddhist and Indigenous faith traditions to organize the 2010 Summit developed sufficient buy-in within Canadian faith communities to make this attempt at forming a national multi-faith body successful, even if it has continued to evolve.[242] Credibility came when the conservative government of Stephen Harper commissioned (and funded) the Canadian Interfaith Partnership to produce a study for the Government of Canada on the Summit's domestic impact in September of 2010.[243] The subsequent report indicated that the Summit had demonstrated a new type of interfaith dialogue and religious-secular dialogue that had facilitated significant media coverage and multi-faith political engagement across Canada. Faith traditions were convinced that relationships between and among faith traditions should continue to be strengthened, but they were also equally convinced that any type of structured formal multi-faith organization was premature.[244] The Canadian Interfaith Partnership became the Canadian Interfaith Conversation after Canada's Catholic Bishops pulled out of the national interfaith dialogue network they helped to establish in March, 2012.[245] The Canadian Catholic Bishops cited concerns over unrealistic expectations, unclear goals, affordability and lack of clarity around the ends and means of the network's ambitions, but they remain firmly committed to interfaith conversations and collaborations and they continue to participate as observers.[246] The Canadian Interfaith Conversation is now a national multi-religious dialogue between representatives of 39 faith communities and faith-based organizations who engage in ongoing faith-based advocacy in Canadian society for the common good. They continue to bring local and regional faith groups together with their Members of Parliament for the purposes of working together on fulfillment of the MDGs and, now, SDGs.[247] In 2013, the Canadian Interfaith

---

241   Christie, "In Sundry Places: The Domestic Impact of the F8/F20 International Interfaith Summit Process."

242   Ibid.

243   Ibid.

244   Ibid.

245   Deborah Gyapong, "Canadian Bishops Pull out of Interfaith Group," *Catholic Register* (2012), http://www.catholicregister.org/item/14064-canadian-bishops-pull-out-of-interfaith -group.

246   Ibid.

247   Hamilton, "To Boldly Go: Innovations Originating through the F8 Canadian Interfaith Leaders Summit Which Strengthen Human Destiny and Community."

Conversation successfully applied for the Doha International Award for Inter-faith Dialogue.[248] The $25,000 DICID award is being used to further their work in interfaith relations. The 2015–2018 term is being co-chaired by senior representatives of the Muslim and Evangelical Christian communities in Canada.[249] Although the Canadian Interfaith Conversation does not have a constitution or set of by-laws, they continue to operate under an agreed upon Charter Vision.[250] Three examples illustrate how the Canadian Interfaith Conversation has continued to have a domestic impact on issues of common concern. In 2011, the Canadian Interfaith Council issued the first national interfaith united call for climate justice asking the Government of Canada to take specific action against climate change at the UN conference in Durban.[251] Beginning in 2013, the Canadian Interfaith Conversation has played a role in convening bi-annual "Our Whole Society" Conferences that bring together religious, secular, humanist and agnostic constituencies to dialogue in a national roundtable.[252] Finally, when Canada's Truth and Reconciliation Commission released a list of 94 Calls to Action in June of 2015, Call to Action #48 asked Canadian church, faith and inter-faith groups to issue a statement by March 31, 2016 as to their implementation of the *United Nations Declaration of the Rights of Indigenous Peoples.* Shortly before the deadline, the Canadian Interfaith Conversation released a statement to Canadian society and faith communities indicating public support for reconciliation with Canada's Indigenous population and First Nations, support for the UN Declaration, and commitment to developing understanding of the Declaration as a framework for reconciliation within Canadian faith communities.[253] The Canadian Interfaith Conversation continues to evolve as they struggle to develop dialogue principles better

---

248   Canadian Interfaith Conversation, "Doha International Award," (2013), http://www
      .interfaithconversation.ca/documents-and-responses.

249   Hamilton, "To Boldly Go: Innovations Originating through the F8 Canadian Interfaith
      Leaders Summit Which Strengthen Human Destiny and Community."

250   Christie, "In Sundry Places: The Domestic Impact of the F8/F20 International Interfaith
      Summit Process." Canadian Interfaith Conversation, "Charter Vision," http://www.council
      ofchurches.ca/wp-content/uploads/2013/11/The-Canadian-Interfaith-Conversation
      -January-2013-Final.pdf.

251   Ali Symons, "Faith Leaders Call for Climate Justice," *Anglican Church of Canada News,*
      October 28 2011.

252   Christie, "In Sundry Places: The Domestic Impact of the F8/F20 International Interfaith
      Summit Process."

253   Kairos, "Churches' Response to Call to Action #48," http://www.kairoscanada.org/
      what-we-do/indigenous-rights/churches-response-call-action-48.

suited to facilitating action when controversies flare during times of cultural retrenchment.[254]

Conclusion

This chapter has described the F8/F7/F20 Initiative as a vulnerable process rendered even more fragile by moments of posturing, dismissal and condemnation. The group has been so divided at times that two summits were held, and yet, they have remained united enough to consistently include both statements in the accounts of their shared history. The diverse expression of various summits has contributed to competing assessments regarding its overall value. The religious summitry leadership, even at its highest points of tension and lowest points of process, demonstrates an approach committed to *including the otherness of the other* through the logic of *inclusive oppositions*. Religious leaders appear consistently shaped by contradictory forces whether it be the *efficacy paradox of complexity* inherent within reflexive governance dynamics, the *cultural contradictions of capitalism,* or pressures to *instrumentalize* religion. When the cycle looked as if it might come to an end, the process evolved and adapted to the new context creatively responsive to the historic moment of the "Big Push" for the MDGs and adoption of the SDGs. Despite the fragility and vulnerability of the process, the F8/F7/F20 Initiative has maintained an enduring informality whose collaborative partnership has, over time, continued to expand its commitment to help 'mend the world.'

---

254   In 2013, the Canadian Interfaith Conversation was unable to make a public statement without violating their current dialogue principles when Quebec attempted to introduce legislation that would restrict the public use of religious symbols. For a more complete discussion of this situation, see Christie, "In Sundry Places: The Domestic Impact of the F8/F20 International Interfaith Summit Process."

CHAPTER 9

The Golden Thread

In this chapter, we return to the governance role of the F8/F7/F20 Initiative as shaped by larger historical processes involving non-human agency. We consider how the turn of the millennium contributed to the evolution of a *global ethic* among (and between) world religions, a *global norm* among (and between) states and governments, and the F8/F7/F20 dialogue efforts to link them. We consider how the content of dialogue was initially centered on faith-based reasons for fulfilling the MDGs, but shifted to focus on the Sustainable Development Goals after the SDGs were adopted by the UN in 2015. Global governance relations with civil society are described in relation to the arrival, and passage, of MDG deadlines. Adoption of the SDGs is discussed as representative of a paradigm shift that may be changing how civil society relates with transnational governance institutions in the years ahead. The Initiative's future value in considered for its ability to bring together religious traditions in partnership with governing institutions to better orient the global economy toward the common good, not only as providers of citizen 'political will,' but as essential partners given the impact environmental changes will inevitably make upon state resources. Pressures to downsize the state have only just begun. In the days ahead, religious organizations would make much better partners than enemies as providers of essential services in contexts of weakened, if not failed, states. As we look to our common future, religious diplomacy will be needed more than ever.

A New Millennium

This is a chapter for taking a step back and assessing *cosmopiety,* as illustrated by the F8/F7/F20 case study, in light of longer term trends, historical backdrops, and future trajectories. We live in the Age of the Anthropocene. The very sociocultural developments that have supported human flourishing now threaten to undermine our very future. We are slowly beginning to understand that. The turn of the millennium in 2000 marked a moment of new beginnings in the global community's efforts to address extreme poverty.[1] In

---

1 Marshall, "Ancient and Contemporary Wisdom and Practice on Governance as Religious Leaders Engage in International Development," 220.

September of that year, world leaders adopted the MDGs that set time-bound targets for implementation of eight priority development objectives. The dawn of a new century also marked a broader collaborative moment between faith institutions and development organizations engaged in responding to social injustice. Prior to that time, relations between development institutions and faith-based organizations had been marked by isolation, separation, division, criticism and conflict.[2] Marshall describes how, for decades, faith institutions and development institutions had largely operated in separate spheres with little overlap—in subcultures that used different vocabularies and worked through different kinds of organizational networks. There were, of course, notable exceptions. The UN's International Labor Organization established a faith adviser in 1921 and bilateral aid programs have frequently worked with religious organizations, but this approach has been the exception to the rule. Most development officials have focused on state-centered leadership programs that use economic and technical approaches to individual project design. Development officials have largely operated unaware of, and disconnected from, the wide array of religious programs in education (e.g., Fe y Alegria in Latin America), water (e.g., INWRDAM), microcredit (e.g., Oikocredit, Opportunity International), health (e.g. IMA World Health), etc. As the millennium approached, this began to change, but the initial connection that was forged was tense and full of misunderstanding and conflict. Religious organizations were highly critical of the impact structural adjustment programs had on the poor.[3] The conflictual relationship detracted from development effectiveness and undermined the quality of development operations.

Efforts were made on both sides to transform demonstrations into dialogue. By 2000, common ground had been reached on several issues such as: the importance of putting people at the heart of development, recognizing the importance of spiritual life to development, affirming community-driven development, protecting the natural environment, promoting debt relief and cancellation, and improving mutual understanding and accountability.[4] Marshall identified six primary arguments in support of the new collaborative partnerships:

---

2   Ibid.

3   Ibid.

4   Deryke Belshaw, Robert Calderisi, and Chris Sugden, *Faith in Development: Partnership between the World Bank and the Churches of Africa* (Oxford, UK: Regnum Books, 2001).

1.   The large and varied development roles played by many faith institutions (especially in education, health and HIV/AIDS) called for cooperation and engagement.

2.   An historic lack of knowledge and interchange with the world's faith communities was an important lacuna ('blind spot') in development thinking that was contributing *inter alia* to flawed project design and suboptimal approaches to community, sectoral, national and transnational engagements. Continuing to ignore faith and religion was neither sensible nor viable for any development institution.

3.   Faith communities, religious leaders, and their relation to public institutions and many G8 governments were of strategic importance, notably in the areas of conflict, social cohesion and aspects of governance.

4.   Faith institutions have vast networks of mobilized and engaged followers who have an active interest in how international development relates to them, and who influence general support for development.

5.   Notwithstanding religious diversity, the ethical and practical engagement of faith informed broad perspectives on social responsibilities, equity and change might encourage faith leaders and communities to apply development values more critically to their own work and institutions.

6.   There were serious risks both of negative reaction and of missed development opportunities in curtailing current partnerships and work in this area.[5]

Although signing of the United Nation's MDGs by all national leaders created a strong consensus for the eradication of extreme poverty, it was the new collaborative partnerships between religious organizations, civil society and development organizations that would generate momentum for goal implementation in the years ahead.

Global Ethic—Global Norm

Agreement upon the MDGs marked emergence of a new global norm among nation-states. The MDGs represented one of the global community's most concerted responses to growth in rates of population, consumption, and environmental degradation resulting from globalization. Initially written by the UN

---

5   Marshall, "Ancient and Contemporary Wisdom and Practice on Governance as Religious Leaders Engage in International Development," 223.

Secretary-General in 2001, the UN membership embraced the MDGs as a useful development guide and incentive structure for a pro-poor policy.[6] The MDGs have been described as 'human development meets results based management' in that they identified 8 goals with 21 quantifiable targets and 60 indicators for fulfillment by 2015. The MDGs reflected six fundamental values: freedom, equality, solidarity, tolerance, respect for nature, and shared responsibility. Academic research on the MDGs has been largely polarized between 'rejectionists' who critique how development has been conceptualized or measured,[7] and 'technicians' who focus on MDG implementation.[8] Despite the division, scholars noted that the MDGs became accepted as a global norm identifying a minimally morally acceptable standard for national responses to the living conditions of the most vulnerable; the norm was also useful for mobilizing resources from donors to implement the goals.[9] Unlike prior development goals, the MDGs put the lives of people in poverty, rather than economic growth, at the center of the global development agenda for the new millennium.[10]

A global ethic also emerged among world religions around the same time.[11] Hans Küng and his colleagues identified core teachings common to the world's major religions that provided the foundation for a global ethic. The World Parliament of Religions endorsed the global ethic in 1993,[12] and the ethic has been incorporated into university ethics curricula by numerous universities and discussed by transnational economic institutions (e.g., the International Monetary Fund, World Economic Forum).[13] In 1996, an assembly of former heads

---

6   Andrew Sumner and Thomas Lawo, "The MDGs and Beyond: Pro-Poor Policy in a Changing World," in *EADI Policy Paper* (European Association of Development Research and Training Institute, 2010).

7   For example, see W. Easterly, "How the Millennium Development Goals are Unfair to Africa," *World Development* 37, no. 1 (2009).

8   F. Bourguignon et al., "The Millennium Development Goals at Midpoint: Where Do We Stand and Where Do We Need to Go?" in *European Report on Development* (2008).

9   Sumner and Lawo, "The MDGs and Beyond: Pro-Poor Policy in a Changing World."

10   Sakiko Fukudo-Parr, "Millennium Development Goals: Why They Matter," *Global Governance* 10 (2004).

11   Küng, *Global Responsibility*; Hans Küng, *Yes to a Global Ethic* (UK: UCS Press, 1996); "A Global Ethic for Global Politics and Economics," (Oxford, UK: Oxford University Press, 1997).

12   Parliament of the Worlds Religions, "Declaration toward a Global Ethic," (1993), https://parliamentofreligions.org/pwr_resources/_includes/FCKcontent/File/TowardsAGlobalEthic.pdf.

13   Marshall, "Ancient and Contemporary Wisdom and Practice on Governance as Religious Leaders Engage in International Development," 224.

of state, the InterAction Council, considered the Global Ethic. After affirming that sovereign states remain the primary vehicles of change, they encouraged religions to closely cooperate, collaborate and include women in the process to discuss concrete action plans to promote and disseminate a common code of ethics.[14] Taking into consideration the responses by the Parliament of the World Religions and Interaction Council, Hans Küng identified four ethical imperatives for the global community:

1. *Have respect for all of life.* The ancient precept—"You shall not kill"—evokes today the human responsibility for a culture of non-violence and respect for life; this is especially urgent in a time of children killing children.
2. *Deal honestly and fairly.* The very old commandment—"You shall not steal"—speaks today to our responsibility for a culture of solidarity and a just economic order; this is more important than ever in the age of globalization.
3. *Speak and act truthfully.* The ancient axiom—"You shall not lie"—today calls up our responsibility for a culture of tolerance and a life of truthfulness; it is particularly incumbent upon politicians and the media to attend to this axiom.
4. *Respect and love one another.* The age-old directive—"You shall not abuse sexuality, shall not commit sexual immorality"—today means we share a responsibility for promoting a culture of equal rights and partnership between men and women; this is even more important in an age which seems to be without taboos.[15]

Emergence of a global ethic has played an important role in the historic rise of a transnational multi-faith movement.[16] Emergence of collaborative agreement to collectively support and implement the MDGs has played an important role in the historic rise of a global normative agreement about what constitutes minimally morally acceptable behavior. The F8/F7/F20 Initiative would work to bring the global ethic and the global norm into consistent, persistent and evolving dialogue for purposes of governance.

---

14   Interaction Council, "In Search of Global Ethical Standards," (1996), http://interaction council.org/in-search-of-global-ethical-standards.
15   Hans Küng, "A Global Ethic: Development and Goals," *Interreligious Insight* (2003), http://www.interreligiousinsight.org/January2003/Jan03Kung.html.
16   Halafoff, "The Multifaith Movement."

The MDG Focal Point

Over the years, the MDGs became a focal point by which global governance became judged by people throughout the world.[17] Also known as a Schelling point, a focal point is a concept derived from game theory to refer to how people choose the most salient and notable solution to a problem because it is what "each person's expectation of what the other expects him to expect to be expected to do."[18] The MDGs established measurable goals that provided a concrete framework that was monitored for accountability for fifteen years. The MDG Monitor was created to be the central source of all information regarding progress on MDG goal implementation.[19] Available to the public, the Monitor was created through a partnership between the United Nations Development Programme, Relief Web of the UN Office for the Coordination of Humanitarian Affairs, the Statistics Division of the UN Department of Economic and Social Affairs, and the UN Children's Fund (UNICEF). The MDG Monitor was a continuously updated data set offered in multiple variations in other languages with country-level data and information available using Google Earth. Anyone could access the data to track progress, identify different country's achievements and challenges, and identify organizations to support who were working to implement the MDGs across the globe. The Eight Millennium Development Goals (MDGs) were:

> Goal 1: Eradicate extreme poverty and hunger.
> Goal 2: Achieve universal primary education.
> Goal 3: Promote gender equality and empower women.
> Goal 4: Reduce child mortality.
> Goal 5: Improve maternal health.
> Goal 6: Combat HIV/AIDS, malaria and other diseases.
> Goal 7: Ensure environmental sustainability.
> Goal 8: Develop a global partnership for development.

The MDGs established input goals for developed countries related to technology transfer, development aid and a commitment to open markets, and development output goals for the less developed countries. For example, as a way of implementing the first goal of eradicating extreme poverty, countries committed themselves to halve the proportion of people whose income is less than $1

---

17   Fukudo-Parr, "Millennium Development Goals: Why They Matter."

18   T.C. Schelling, *The Strategy of Conflict* (Cambridge, MA: Harvard University Press, 1960).

19   The public could view progress on each goal at http://www.mdgmonitor.org/.

a day between 1990 and 2015. The best known target in international aid to finance the programs that would be needed to accomplish this proposed to raise official development assistance (ODA) to 0.7% of donors' national income. The 0.7% target served as a reference for the 2005 political commitments at the G8 Gleneagles Summit and the UN World Summit. In 2005, the 15 countries that were members of the European Union as of 2004 agreed to reach the target by 2015.[20]

But promises made are not necessarily promises easily kept. The Nordic countries have been among the strongest supporters of the process. Sweden, Norway, Denmark, and Luxembourg kept their commitments to 0.7% financing since the MDGs were launched in 2000. The Netherlands met their commitments until 2013. Finland met the development goal once in 1991, but not since the MDGs were actually launched. The United Kingdom attained it from 2013 to 2015, but no other OECD countries met the target. The weighted average of members has never exceeded 0.4% of national income.[21] It has been difficult to implement the MDGs without sufficient financing.

Civil society organized grassroots support to increase political will to finance and implement the MDG goals. Grassroots civil society movements such as the *Make Poverty History* campaign, from which the initial 2005 ecumenical F8 Summit emerged, referenced the MDGs in their push for social justice. Pop culture icon Bono of U2 famously referred to the MDGs at the 2006 US National Prayer Breakfast as the "Beatitudes for a Globalized World."[22] Additional celebrities and campaigns that have appealed to the MDGs as a focal point for civic engagement include, but are not limited to, Leonardo DiCaprio, Susan Sarandon, Angelina Jolie, Brad Pitt, Nicole Kidman, BAND AID, Make Promises Happen, Global Call to Action Against Poverty, Live 8, Jubilee, the ONE Campaign, Stand Up against Poverty, and the Micah Challenge. Civic participation was encouraged to monitor progress on the eight goals and use the information to apply political pressure for governments to keep their commitments. As the MDG deadline of 2015 drew closer, popular appeals for governments to keep their promises became increasingly widespread and more intense. In 2009, as the global community passed the half-way mark to 2015, more than one hundred and sixteen million people were recorded as participating in the on-line civil society *Stand Up against Poverty Campaign*, setting a Guinness

---

20   OECD, "The 0.7% ODA/GNI Target: A History," *Development Assistance Committee Journal* 3, no. 4 (2002).

21   Ibid.

22   Paul David Hewson, "Transcript: Bono Remarks at the National Prayer Breakfast," *USA Today*, February 2 2006.

World Record.[23] The MDGs had come to define the minimally morally acceptable standard of behavior for global governance, and faith based organizations had become important participants in the civil society campaign.[24]

F8/F7/F20 MDG Dialogue

The F8/F7/F20 process has referenced the MDGs as an organizing theme throughout the process with the one exception of Russia in 2006. The ICC formalized the centrality of the MDG theme during their first meeting on June 15, 2009 when Christopher Hill proposed that the MDGs become the 'golden thread' for the ongoing process to provide consistency of content for dialoguing with state parties. Christie emphasized, in response, that persistence of presence throughout an entire G8 cycle would be equally important to maintain civic pressure for MDG implementation.[25]

Reference to the MDGs took many forms. Specialists were brought in to brief participants on MDG progress. For example, at the 2010 Canada Summit, John McArthur informed participants about how MDG financing was making a difference in the lives of real people:

> I have spent most of the past decade getting up out of bed every morning and going to bed most nights wondering what can be done to achieve the MDGs...I have never had the opportunity to discuss it with a group like this one. I am not qualified to talk about fundamentals of faith like you, but I do want to talk about...the faith in the possibility of the impossible...I was in a village in Western Tanzania recently and I was stunned by what I saw...I went to a clinic...People were lined up—mostly mothers with children and most of whom had fever....I spoke with mothers, asking 'What is the problem?" "My child has a fever and it is probably malaria, so I brought him to the clinic." I saw a farmer, trained as a clinic worker, pull out a strip test from his pocket. He tested the child in front of me and we watched, in a matter of minutes, the diagnosis that showed the child had malaria. The worker also had a cell phone in his pocket and

---

23   United Nations Non-Governmental Liaison Office, "Stand against Poverty 16–18 October," (2009), https://www.unngls.org/index.php/un-ngls_news_archives/2009/1912-stand -against-poverty-16-18-october.

24   Hipple, "The Center for Interfaith Action and the MDGs: Leveraging Congregational Infrastructures for Maximum Impact on Disease and Poverty."

25   Christie, "How Well Does the G8 Deliver: Compliance with G8 Commitments."

he had medicine in his cabinet.... Five years ago, there were no rapid di-
agnostic tests and no cell phone coverage in that community...Now this
community health worker was a farmer with grade 3 education, 2 wives,
6 children and 3 months of health worker training. This breakthrough
is...quietly occurring throughout the world because of the MDGs...There
is a lot being said today about the MDGs and many talk as if they will
be achieved, or not, based on the current trajectory. That is like asking
in 1750 if slavery will end. It is tough until you get a breakthrough via
coalitions, collaborations with people...who refuse to accept unethical
inattention to the worlds' poorest who die because they lack the simplest
tools that others have not seen fit to deliver.[26]

The F8/F7/F20 process also used the MDGs as the basis for dialogue with governance officials about accountability for promises made at the turn of the
century. For example, the 2010 Canadian F8 Summit communiqué that was
delivered to G8 and G20 officials and Members of Parliament elaborated on
three themes from the MDGs: poverty, environment and peace. In the body
of each section, the religious leaders identified a problem point in global governance, specifying *misplaced priorities* of wealthier countries, and *leadership
expectations* of wealthy *and* developing countries. The 2010 statement spoke of
"a shared responsibility to be and act for the change we want to see," affirming
their own commitment to call on their faith communities and members to
explicitly "monitor the compliance of our governments in meeting the Millennium Development Goals and, whenever possible, hold them publicly accountable for such compliance."[27] Consider what the Catholics had to say in
their response to the 2010 statement as it was being drafted:

Men and women of goodwill may suggest different ways to meet the
United Nations Millennium Development Goals for ending poverty, to
address climate change, or to build peace. Not only do we expect disagreement about how to proceed, we welcome it, since these practical
differences can lead to authentic dialogue that aims to find practical
solutions now. Christians want to be part of such a dialogue. But when
international conversations become paralyzed by posturing, or when the
interests of power are seen as more important than the basic needs of
our brothers and sisters, then we must speak out. The community of all

---

26 John W. McArthur, "To Boldly Go," in *World Religions Summit 2010* (Winnipeg, Canada
    2010).
27 F8-Canada, "A Time for Inspired Leadership and Action."

believers stands up with the victims of violence and war, with the poor and the broken, and with the whole of creation to remind world leaders of their obligations.[28]

The Canadian Yeshiva and Rabbinical School similarly emphasized that leaders are judged by how they treat the needy and downtrodden of the earth. In their response to the 2010 draft statement, they prayed that the leaders of 2010 would consciously strive "to take the broad view, to join the world below with the world above."[29]

The MDGs were referenced internally during discussions among religious leaders in relation to exploring how to address problems of political impasse where national leaders have yet to forge effective consensus. At the 2011 France F8 Summit, one delegate became quite agitated about global warming (relevant to MDG goals 7 and 8), saying:

> Where is the political will? Where is the political vision? That is a question asked by...Regional Ecumenical Organization's General Secretaries... There are 9 of us globally representing the different regions of the world. Several of us are here at the Summit. We meet and talk once a year. The one from the Pacific will just say, "If you ask me what's happening in my region, well, I tell you this many more islands have disappeared this year." [slow whistle] Yeah. And unfortunately, he says it quite matter-of-factly because he is so used to it. But one should *never* be used to that. *Never.* And what are we doing? Nothing. *Nothing.*

That situation changed by the time world leaders returned to France for the 2015 United Nations Climate Change Conference (COP 21) where faith groups would play an important role in the climate change civil society campaign. By 2015, faith communities would mobilize nearly two million people and work to successfully pressure political leaders to incorporate a 'recommendation to consider loss and damage' into the COP 21 agreement.[30] But this interview was conducted in 2011, and at that time, frustration was mounting.[31]

---

28   Partnership, Faith Community Responses, Policy Responses, Previous Statements.

29   Ibid.

30   Shantha Ready Alonso, "Summary of the COP 21 Climate Agreement," *Climate Justice and Faith*, no. 1 (2016).

31   Randolph Haluza-DeLay, "Religion and Climate Change: Varieties and Viewpoints and Practices," *WIRES Climate Change* 5, no. March/April (2014); Michael Jacobs, "High Pressure for Low Emissions: How Civil Society Created the Paris Agreement," *Juncture* 22, no. 1

During Summit discussions, delegates emphasized the broad shifts in perspective that were still needed to foster political engagement. In a keynote presentation at the 2011 Summit, John Chryssavgis said, "Religious leaders need to enable people to see the world differently. It is for religious leaders to urge the faithful to move from 'what we want' to 'what the world needs,' and communicate that message to our politicians." The attempt to shift the G8 leaders' focus from politics to service was explicitly evident when Rüdiger Noll addressed delegates about the macro economic situation: "Religious leaders offer a long-term perspective to political leaders who have a short-term perspective. But values need to be connected to specific applications," he said. "If we remain on the value level, we can be easily misused by politicians endorsing their behaviour via dialogue. We need to explore with politicians what these values mean on a practical level." Respondents spoke of adopting a "disinterested" attitude toward politics. One of the religious leader members of the ICC said,

> There has been a tendency to see this group as the religious leaders validating everything the G8 does, and not seeing this as an independent body...We are an independent body that wishes to be in dialogue but we are not a subsidiary giving validity...I find myself correcting people all of the time...People will say, "The G8 religious leaders..." I will go, "No, we are not the G8 religious leaders in the way that you mean. We are religious leaders in the G8 countries who have come together to speak to the current meeting of the G8 Summit in particular ways, but we are not a subsidiary in any way. We are a completely independent body that will say whatever it needs to say." That is *really* important.

I asked a respondent from one of the world's poorest regions if there were conditions under which people might oppose the G8 leadership. His response reflected a parliamentary approach to dialogue that includes the voice of the 'loyal opposition':

> I don't believe in the approach of opposing. I believe in the possibility of people expressing and appreciating the divide, condemning the wrong... People need to get involved in politics and say "these mistakes have been done and we have to correct it and behave differently."

(2016); Jack Jenkins and Jeremy Deaton, "250 Faith Leaders Demand Nations Ratify Paris Climate Deal," *ThinkProgress* (2015), https://thinkprogress.org/250-faith-leaders-demand -nations-ratify-paris-climate-deal-c150f6a30ec3#.fo3ozp6zy; Bron Taylor, "Religion to the Rescue (?) in an Age of Climate Disruption" (2015).

In his comments on development, Ji said at the 2011 French F8 Summit:

> People of faith have difficulty articulating in secular contexts our values
> because we don't blow our own trumpets, but the time has come for us
> to articulate so there is a respect for faith. How do you value goodness?
> How do you value love? What is sacrifice? We need to articulate this so we
> can fuse secularity and sacredness for the common good. Rights and re-
> sponsibilities go hand in hand. We have a universal declaration of rights.
> There is no universal declaration of responsibilities. We need one.

In another interview at the 2011 French F8 Summit, one of the delegates was
asked if s/he sees any accountability gaps in global governance. The leader's response reflected an awareness of 'governance without government' dynamics:

> You could probably drive a truck through them. There are gaps, yes. But
> the trouble is, you can't say that the G8 has failed or created gaps be-
> cause there wasn't any understanding of accountability in the first place.
> So, it's not so much a gap as a missing piece of the process...Find ways
> of having the discussion with them saying, "If you are not going to deal
> with these issues, then how can we have them happen?" That is the dis-
> cussion you have. You *don't* say, "Why aren't you doing it?" You put it in
> such a way that they take ownership. You don't say, "Who failed?" You say,
> "Listen, let's agree that we have a problem. I accept your starting point,
> at least for now"...that you see this is not your problem. Then, "let's talk
> together about how we solve the problem."...You put it on the table and
> say, "Let's take mutual ownership of saying there are problems that go
> beyond some things here. What things do we need to put in place to ad-
> dress these problems?"

Also at the 2011 France F8 Summit, Hamilton said, "Politicians rightly push
back." When she speaks with them, she said that they challenge her on climate
change lifestyle issues. Many of the policies leaders are calling for, if they are to
be effective, will involve sacrifice. Are leaders in the churches asking people to
cut back on fossil fuel energy use? "In the real world," said one delegate,

> people have to make very difficult choices. When religious authorities
> come in knowing there are difficult choices to be made, weighing these
> difficult choices...that is what has long-term value. It is taken much more
> seriously than when you say, "We are the moral voices who believe in

goodness and peace." You make it much easier for a politician to take a longer view when you show them how they can articulate outcomes so they are not inconsistent with what they need to produce.

Another 2011 France F8 Summit delegate said,

If you are serious about playing in the real world, you do the things necessary to be able to allow the people who have to function in that world to be able to function in that world. You don't pretend that the world is going to change because you want to be above it...and I don't mean that you compromise or sacrifice your values! It does mean that you start from the recognition that somebody else is living from a different position.

At times, the conversation became frank. One delegate pointed out that when the Universal Declaration of Human Rights was written "here, in Paris, the same country was occupying and humiliating and colonizing a big number of human beings" and "they exempted themselves....I think those who did it know that we know. But this mistake of the past cannot prevent the generation of now to correct those mistakes and not have a double standard." And another delegate said, "It's not about getting close to political leaders, but about being courteous, appropriately supportive and, when necessary, confrontational." Delegates consistently expressed that political leaders have a responsibility to serve the most vulnerable, the most poor, the most marginalized, and the most oppressed. "We gather to speak out of the depths of our religious tradition; to speak out of our truths to challenge the G8 leaders and to recommit ourselves to address the needs of dire poverty," said Hamilton. According to Vendley,

We are here to honor the deepest specificity of our respective faiths. At the same time, and we feel no contradiction, we come together in a spirit of partnership that reaches out to governments and to all other stakeholders linked to service in the spirit of the common good. We recognize that in our particularities of faith we are also citizens of the world, united.

Speakers often used religious imagery full of promise and transformation. In remarks on climate change, Chryssavgis emphasized,

The way we view the world affects how we treat it. We treat it in a godless manner because we view it as godforsaken. Unless we change how we see it, we won't change how we treat it...And if the world is an image that reflects the presence of God, then nothing whatsoever can lack sacredness. If God cannot be worshiped here, then God cannot be seen in heaven, either.

"We must learn to see the world through the eyes of God," he said. "If God saw the world as very good, we too must learn to see the promise of beauty and see the world in its interrelatedness. All things look to God and when God sends forth his breath, all creation happens all over again and the face of the earth is renewed." Metropolitan Emmanuel said to the religious leaders participating in the 2011 F8 Summit,

> The religious perspective and the dialogue that inspires our work is important. We want to relieve human suffering in our world. You are here because you are interested in solutions...How much better for the earth and those who dwell in it if we embrace change in government structures that advance human rights? This will require a new way of seeing things. Let us take measures to preserve our own home, but also our neighbor's.

Cardinal Jean-Pierre Ricard echoed these sentiments in his 2011 F8 Summit address, saying:

> We want to be contributors of peace to all people of all faiths from the spirituality that lives within us. We want to promote the well-being of all people, justice and solidarity between peoples.... We understand that globalization promotes inequalities and creates problems of injustice... We should try to correct the inequities that might cause disquiet.

Marc Stenger spoke at the 2011 F8 Summit about the need for government reform: "Global governance should not just be in the hands of those with political and economic power. It should involve all of us." He called for frank and open dialogue between the G-plus System and the global village through greater geographic representation, civic involvement and interfaith contributions. Andre Karamaga addressed the issue of greater bioregional representation for Africa in global governance, saying "We are tired of having others do things for us, instead of with us. Africa," he said, "should participate in the G8. But more than that, we should be able to ask for Africa's marginalization to stop.... If there is a crisis, let us resolve the crisis." Susanne Tamas (Baha'i delegate from Canada to the 2011 Summit) commented that "the legitimacy of governance depends in large part on the engagement of the voice of people...Systems of global governance must likewise evolve to reflect the fundamental oneness of humanity distinguished by fair representation in collective deliberation and decision-making processes." The positions taken in the 2011 F8 statement that was delivered to the G8 and G20 leaders in 2011, in a manner similar to other communiqués throughout the shadow summit process, reflected democratic principles such as: ensuring "political self-determination"; supplementing rather than undermining the "UN General Assembly and other UN processes"; incorporating the voice of "low income countries"; making the G8/7 and G20 process "more transparent"; and working with civil society to help ensure "substantively enhanced compliance of the G8 with its own commitments."[32] According to Christie, the MDGs served as an ongoing "Rosetta Stone" providing a common language of global concern between secular world leaders and global religious leaders.[33]

Transition Dynamics

Once the target date for the MDGs was in sight, development communities began to ask about what might come next.[34] While some progress had been made by the 2008 mid-point, 2010–2015 became referred to as the MDG 'big push.' The foci on human rights, gender, poor people's adaptation to climate change, equality and social justice increased during the 'big push' despite recognition that several of the targets would not be met by 2015.[35] An 'impacts literature' emerged shifting focus away from norm adoption toward asking how the MDGs actually changed poor people's lives.[36] One of the earlier celebrity moments that served as a harbinger of the shifting dynamics that would accompany the impending 2015 deadline was when Bono spoke at the US National Prayer Breakfast. Bono used the MDG standards as the basis for reframing US development aid history from being one of 'charitable achievement' to that of 'a woefully inadequate legacy.' He spoke about how providing eight million bed nets to protect children from malaria was something to be proud of only until

---

32   F8-France, "Statement of the Bordeaux Religious Leaders Summit."

33   Christie, "In Sundry Places: The Domestic Impact of the F8/F20 International Interfaith Summit Process."

34   Edwin Van Teijlingen et al., "Millennium Development Goals: All Good Things Must Come to an End, So What Next?" *Midwifery* 30, no. 1 (2014).

35   Fukudo-Parr, "Millennium Development Goals: Why They Matter"; Sumner and Lawo, "The MDGs and Beyond: Pro-Poor Policy in a Changing World."

36   R. Manning, "Using Indicators to Encourage Development: Lessons from the MDGs," in *DIIS Report* (Copenhagen: Danish Institute for International Studies, 2009).

one recognized the giant chasm between the scale of the emergency and the scale of the response. "It's not about charity," said Bono,

> it's about justice....[J]ustice is a higher standard. Africa makes a fool of our idea of justice. It makes a farce of our idea of equality. It mocks our pieties. It doubts our concern. It questions our commitment.[37]

And these comments were made *before* the 2008 global financial crisis. The international global economic crisis stimulated an immediate civil society response, with a country countdown to the 2015 MDGs conference that same year.[38] But research increasingly indicated that the MDG shortfalls went beyond time and money to include how the initial shaping of MDG goals had been influenced by a shortage of connections with women and the poor.[39]

International norms have life cycles and, given the increasing instability of the global economy, the ongoing existence of something to replace the MDGs could not be taken-for-granted beyond 2015.[40] While there was talk of replacing the MDGs with SDGs (Sustainable Development Goals), the impending 2015 deadline nevertheless posed a public relations communication challenge. As early as 2006, scholars expressed concern about how the MDG goals were problematic because they created expectations for fulfillment that could potentially undermine the very constituency needed for maintaining sustained engagement.[41] Given the sustained instability of the global economy, MDG scholars D. Hulme and Sakiko Fukudo-Parr emphasized the importance of employing strategies that drew on the MDG norms to influence citizens of rich countries so that they might consider the existence of extreme poverty in an

---

37   Hewson, "Transcript: Bono Remarks at the National Prayer Breakfast."
38   Victor M. Mukonka et al., "Holding a Country Countdown to 2015 Conference on Millennium Development Goals (MDGs)—the Zambian Experience," *BMC Public Health* 14 (2014): 60.
39   Elaine Unterhalter, "Poverty, Education, Gender and the Millennium Development Goals: Reflections on Boundaries and Intersectionality," *Theory and Research in Education* 10, no. 3 (2012); Suzanne Romaine, "Keeping the Promise of the Millennium Development Goals: Why Language Matters," *Applied Linguistics Review* 4, no. 1 (2013).
40   D. Hulme and Sakiko Fukudo-Parr, "International Norm Dynamics and 'The End of Poverty': Understanding the Millennium Development Goals (MDGs)," in *BWPI Working Paper* (Manchester: Brooks World Poverty Institute, 2009).
41   Michael A. Clemens, Charles J. Kenny, and Todd J. Moss, "The Trouble with the MDGs: Confronting Expectations of Aid and Development Success," *World Development* 35, no. 5 (2004).

affluent world to be morally unacceptable.[42] They distinguished 'message entrepreneurs' from 'norm entrepreneurs,' noting that message entrepreneurs are
less motivated by ideational commitment than they are with emphasizing the
organizational imperative to implement norms via actual budget allocations
and the undertaking of practical actions to achieve the norms.[43] But Hulme
and Fukudo-Parr also emphasized that the work of 'norm entrepreneurs' was
equally important for maintaining sustained pressure for political will. MDG
scholars suggested that a more balanced approach that combined both approaches could facilitate treating the goals more as benchmarks than as planning goals, so that the criterion for success could be progressively focused on
the pace of progress rather than on target achievement.[44] Inasmuch as the
first set of MDGs were created against a backdrop of relative political stability
& economic growth, scholars were concerned that the political instability &
flagging international economy of recent years might undermine the political
will necessary for a renewed commitment to MDGs,[45] even as public trust was
declining.[46] Growing protests were contributing to increasing uncertainties.
The arrival of 2015 would be, in social movement terminology, a 'discursive moment' fraught with both crisis and opportunity.[47]

Following the failed political 2009 Copenhagen talks, civil society organizations began to collectively gather into a network called *Beyond 2015* to ensure
that a new set of goals would be adopted. As the network grew, *Beyond 2015* took
advantage of the transition period to engage with the United Nations High-
level Panel on the Millennium Development Goals to help raise the moral and
ethical bar as a new development framework for post-2015 was determined.[48]

---

42   D. Hulme and Sakiko Fukudo-Parr, "International Norm Dynamics And "The End of
      Poverty": Understanding the Millennium Development Goals (MDGs)," in *BWPI Working
      Paper* (Manchester: Brooks World Poverty Institute, 2009).

43   Ibid.

44   Sakiko Fukudo-Parr, J. Greenstein, and D. Stewart, "How Should MDG Success Be Judged:
      Faster Progress or Achieving the Targets?" *World Development* 41, July (2013).

45   United Nations, "The Millennium Development Goals Report 2012," (New York: United
      Nations, 2012).

46   Dan Edelman, "2012 Edelman Trust Barometer Global Results," (www.edelman.com2012).

47   Noram Fairclough, Giuseppina Cortese, and Pratizia Ardizzone, *Discourse and Contem-
      porary Social Change*, Linguistic Insights 54: Studies in Language and Commmunication
      (Bern, Switzerland: Peter Lange, 2007).

48   Hamilton, "Faith in Sustainability: How Faith Communities Have Helped Move the Dis-
      cussion around Sustainability Forward" Hamilton, "Faith in Sustainability: How Faith
      Communities Have Helped Move the Discussion around Sustainability Forward."

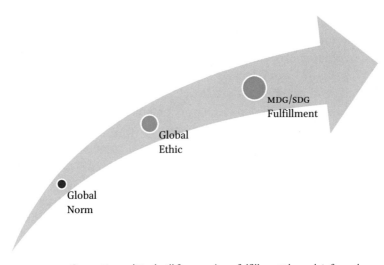

FIGURE 9.1   *Generating political will for MDG/SDG fulfillment through informal dialogue*

F8 leadership participated in this dialogue (see Figure 9.1).[49] Leaders of the 192 UN member states convened their first deliberations concerning the SDGs at the Rio+20 Summit in Rio de Janeiro in 2012. A growing network of UN officials and civil society advocates collaborated to develop the new set of benchmarks via a transparent process to establish new priorities that, unlike the MDGs that came before, would be in solidarity with those actively engaged in the social struggles underway across the world for democracy and basic needs.[50] By 2012, a new set of SDGs was under discussion that would pose goals and challenges for all countries' involvement—"not what the rich should do for the poor, but what all countries together should do for the global wellbeing of this generation and those to come."[51] The *Beyond 2015* network grew from 5 organizations in 3 countries in 2010 to 1,581 organisations from 142 countries by December 2015. The majority of participating civil society organizations were from developing countries: 69% were Southern CSOs and 31% Northern CSOs representing 44 countries in Africa, 38 countries in Europe, 26 countries in Asia, 25 countries in Latin America, 7 countries in the Pacific, and 2 countries in North

---

49   "UN High Panel on the Millennium Development Goals."

50   Patrick Bond, "Global Governance Campaigning and MDGs: From Top-Down to Bottom-up Anti-Poverty Work," *Third World Quarterly* 27, no. 2 (2006).

51   Jeffrey D. Sachs, "From Millennium Development Goals to Sustainable Development Goals," *Lancet* 379 (2012).

America.[52] In the final year, they mobilized issue attention with a 100-day countdown strategy that ran June 17 through September 25, 2015 followed by a media campaign September 24–27. *Beyond 2015* announced the campaign's completion on March 31, 2016 after the UN successfully adopted the new set of SDGs. As with civil society more generally, it is not possible to measure the direct impact *Beyond 2015* had on the UN adoption of the SDGs. What they can say, however, is that their impact was multi-level (global, regional, and national) and that their efforts enriched the post-2015 debate through the sharing of perspectives from people living in poverty and marginalisation, enhanced opportunities for civil society to engage with the UN, shared intelligence on the post-2015 process, and exercised some influence on the final text of the post-2015 agenda.[53]

F20 SDG Dialogue

Within two months of the UN adoption of the 2030 Development Agenda "Transforming our World," the F20 SDG process was identifying how attention to the faith factor might enhance implementation of the newly adopted goals. Durham described how the planning committee, following the 2014 Summit in Brisbane, decided to make sustainable development the central theme of the 2015 meetings in anticipation that the United Nations would likely adopt the new set of goals in the meantime. Sessions were organized to consider how the faith factor plays into each Sustainable Development Goal (SDG). The opening plenary addressed the broad theme of sustainable development, followed by sessions focused on how diverse faith traditions relate to specific sustainability issues such as refugees, peace and sustainable communities, economic development, education, employment, etc.[54] Session summaries and videos of the presentations were made available online at G20Interfaith. org. A few highlights merit mentioning.

Several speakers explicated how faith traditions might enhance SDG fulfillment. For example, faith communities are heavily involved in private sector financing of development initiatives. The giving of alms is built into the faith traditions of many faith groups which translates into hundreds of billions of dollars from the private sector being put toward development efforts.

---

52 Beyond 2015, "Who Was Involved," http://www.beyond2015.org/participating-organisa tions-beyond-2015.

53 "Our Impact," http://www.beyond2015.org/our-impact.

54 Steiner, "G20 Interfaith Summit Summary Report," (2015), 11.

But sustainable development cannot succeed when society fails to the extent that conflict disrupts commerce, so the relationship between religious freedom and fulfillment of the SDGs was frequently explored. Data indicate that 76% of the world's population experiences either government restrictions or social hostilities pertaining to religious freedom. Many speakers logically argued that if SDG fulfillment is hampered by suppression of religious freedom, then the extent of this global problem justifies a specific governance focus on the free exercise of religious freedom or belief. Some of the key points made were:

- There is a value convergence between world religions and the SDGs
- Religious organizations make significant and valuable contributions to elements of the SDGs and economies in many social contexts, including China
- Development of explicit faith-based rationales for commitment to SDG fulfillment would make these contributions more intentional and likely increase SDG fulfillment
- Protection of religious freedom enhances the contributions of faith-based organizations to SDG fulfillment and fosters respect for differing faiths and beliefs, including people with no particular faith
- Protection of religious freedom multiplies trust among employees whose faith and beliefs are respected, helps reduce corruption by allowing faith-based ethics to be voiced, engenders peace by defusing religious tensions, and encourages broader freedoms
- Protection of religious freedom overcomes any over-regulation that might accompany such things as coercive blasphemy laws
- Multiple models exist for the protection of religious freedom and for how government and religion contribute to SDG fulfillment[55]

Faith leaders were already suggesting that the strategies emphasized for SDG implementation might differ from the strategies that were primarily employed for MDG implementation. Speaking from a developed country perspective, Edmund Newell's 2015 F20 presentation directly addressed a strategic shift. His Church of England congregation had been heavily involved in the civil society *Make Poverty History* campaign from which the F8 Initiative emerged. He spoke about the importance of shifting strategies in keeping with the changing times. Multinational companies wield enormous power that transcend national boundaries; the SDGs provide businesses with a diverse set of opportunities for involvement. SDG Goal 2 calls for a doubling of small scale food productivity. SDG Goal 6 calls for universal access to water and sanitation. SDG

---

55   Ibid.

Goal 7 calls for the balance of energy supply to shift to renewables. SDG Goal 8 calls for the decoupling of economic growth from environmental degradation. SDG Goal 9 calls for sustainable industrialization. SDG Goal 12 calls for a reduction of food waste. The fishing industry is affected by SDG Goal 14. The SDGs consistently emphasize subsidy removal and trade liberalization through the involvement of the World Trade Organization. He spoke about how businesses are encouraged to become familiar with the SDGs, align their priorities with SDG goals, decide on how they might contribute and then assess their ongoing progress. But the SDGs are aspirational and voluntary. Implementation of them may be costly, and the SDGs are not legally binding. One of the problems associated with corporate social responsibility is to ensure that commitments represent more than tokenistic ethical window dressing. Management objectives have to align with ethical objectives, but this affects profits. Moreover, sustainable development requires a long-term commitment to a future vision which requires a shift in mindset away from short-termism.

Edmund Newell spoke about how religions have a role to play in influencing ethical investment. Religious groups can meet with businesses and apply shareholder pressure to get people to reflect on how their faith relates to their working lives. He spoke about projects such as the Faith and Work Forum which encourages voluntary change from within the business world. But he was cautionary about the degree of influence faith-based civic engagement might have in the UK national context. In a recent national survey about church reputation, only 20% of respondents regarded the Church of England as a positive voice in society, and only a small percentage of those indicated that it was because of an ethical voice. Religious organizations should not presume that others will automatically consider them to be ethical role models, he said. Nevertheless, people of faith have much to contribute to the SDGs through joint initiatives, lobbying, education, and direct engagement with business to address questions of 'what is business for?'[56]

At the 2015 F20 Summit, Miyake spoke about how the less anthropocentric SDGs present an opportunity to prioritize environmental protection. He explained how Japanese people have lived continuously for 15,000 years on small islands, amidst a fragile environment affected by earthquakes and typhoons. Kyoto became the capital in the 8th century and the area is still surrounded by greenery. Different cultural teachings affect how people relate to the environment. Japan is 68% covered in green forest despite being a small, well-developed country; compare this to Turkey which is 15% covered, Canada is 33% covered, Russia is 48% covered, and Sweden is 67% covered in green

---

56   "G20 Interfaith Summit Summary Report," (2015), 34–35.

forest. Finland is the only country with a higher green coverage ratio than Japan. He then linked these ratios with cultural heroes from the different civilizations. For example, the first human written text from Mesopotamian Clay tablets tell of a Sumerian King Gilgamesh who affirmed deforestation of Lebanon's cypress trees because he opened the land. The story of Noah's ark also justifies deforestation. He identified a linkage between these first cultural heroes and practices that deforest the land over time. To this day, the Middle East has no forest. By way of contrast, the first cultural hero in Japanese myths is of Susanoh, someone with a bad attitude who was living in a divine kingdom. According to tradition, because Susanoh interfered with other deities' cultivation, he was kicked out from heaven and sent to earth where he found a mountain without trees. He pulled out his hairs to plant trees and that is how so many trees came to Japan. This hero taught a diverse approach where different trees were planted and used for different purposes. The people welcomed this cultural hero to be their holy king. Japanese culture emphasizes the continuous planting of trees with respect for the environment. He concluded with a final example from the Shinto tradition that illustrates a sustainable approach to the environment. The Ise Grand Shrine in Japan is a distinctive shrine to the highest Sun Goddess deity that is rebuilt every 20 years since ancient times. An exact replica is built next to the old shrine. Once the copy is completed, the old shrine is collapsed and a new exact replica is rebuilt on the old site. This has been done for thousands of years and serves as a model for sustainable cultural practices.[57]

Upolu Luma Vaai from Fiji brought an islander developing country perspective to the 2014 F20 Summit. He critically analyzed how religion has historically played a huge role in nurturing an oppressive system in the Pacific. He described what he referred to as the One Truth Ideology that has Christian roots in Greek logic, is entrenched in Western culture and promoted by Western philosophies. When this approach was introduced to the Pacific, it suggested that there is only one solitary God who rules, and it promoted uncomfortable relationships with other religious traditions. This notion suggested that the cultural or religious system that best expresses this solitary ruling God should also be treated as universal. This contributed to the reduction of everything into one and has been a problematic contributor to increased poverty, environmental degradation and violence in island communities. The Pacific is more than 70% Christian, so this universal monarchy of the one God ideology supports a foreign system of life to rule the communities. Such an approach is unsustainable, he said, because it introduces a system that disturbs four basic

---

57   Ibid., 64–65.

Pacific harmonies: harmony with the divine, harmony with self, harmony with others, and harmony with the environment. He spoke about how the limited resources of the islands are continually being extracted by logging, fishing and mining companies of the rich countries. Approaches to climate justice have been very top-down, often benefiting wealthier countries at the expense of the most vulnerable smaller islands in the Pacific. He then began to reconstruct a positive alternative as the Pacific Islander contribution to interfaith dialogue, harmony and sustainable development. He described how some Pacific Islands, such as Vanuatu, have implemented a more relational system of well-being entrenched in their Indigenous religious culture as the most economically secure and sustainable way to address poverty and economic injustice. Relationality is the overarching moral value that encompasses the majority, if not all, Pacific cultures. He further explicated their worldview describing aspects involving empathic connection, mutual respect, and communal interconnectivity with so-called 'others.' He described how, in their worldview, the opposite is not a conflicting opposite. Rather, the opposite is a *relational* opposite. In this sense, with the growing attention of postmodernity and the uncertainty associated with the epistemological centers of the world, he suggested that *minor-narratives be regarded as truth-bearing*. He asked attendees to avoid making the mistake of excluding one in favor of the other as is dominant in the One Truth Ideology. Truth, he said, is not fixed, but is featured by the different contextual conditions. Therefore, *all narratives have significance*. Religious freedom is only genuine, he said, when it acknowledges diverse narratives as truth bearing and respects community protocols and codes of behavior. To the extent that the One Truth Ideology is hegemonic, it hinders religious freedom, human development and creativity by excluding, rejecting, and killing the other in favor of a more universal idea of truth. The Pacific relational approach suggests that both individual and community, both male and female, both Western and Pacific, both Christian and non-Christian should be embraced as a collaborative way forward. Religion has a lot to offer development, he said, but if it is to be sustainable, it must deconstruct a colonial religious system that promotes oneness at the expense of diversity. He then posed a question and challenge to participants in the F20 process: Can the One Truth Ideology that has become the basis of some oppressive economic development systems, be challenged and/or confronted by these summits? How can the minor narratives be given greater attention in this process?[58]

The changing dynamics beginning to appear in the F20 process are in keeping with a broader paradigm shift that several civil society organizations have

---

58   Ibid., 92–93.

identified in association with the new goals. Whereas MDGs were organized around a poverty reduction paradigm, the SDGs have adopted a paradigm of environmental as well as social sustainability.[59] Social sustainability is not as pro-poor in approach, is less anthropocentric and more favorable to environmental priorities than the past approach that was taken with the MDGs.

Non-human Agency

As we look to the future, the role religious actors might play in implementation of the UN Sustainable Development Goals goes far beyond the mere 'value added' component of SDG promotion within their respective organizational networks. Religious actors have long been recognized for their ability to provide moral agency; an Ethics in Action Initiative has been formed recently to form a multi-religious consensus in an attempt to establish enough "moral capacity" to "better orient the global economy toward the common good."[60] This could possibly be 'good' news. But world religions have long been critiqued for being anthropocentrically biased toward the human species, overall, and toward the rich at the expense of the poor.[61] Humans with the fewest resources have the smallest buffer from environmental degradation and their health conditions are one of the first anthropogenic indicators – the proverbial 'canaries in the coal mine' so to speak – that the carrying capacity of a given ecosystem has been breached.[62] In September of 2016, the United Nations 70th General Assembly had more than twenty side events focused on the theme of religion and faith, but as the Senior Culture Advisor at the UN Population Fund and Coordinator of the un Inter-Agency Task Force on Religion and Development, Azza Karam, has so wisely pointed out, "elevating the value of morality, and those who speak in its name, is not the same as ensuring inclusive civic discourse, engagement and equitable access."[63] He points out that increasing the rhetoric that "religion matters" does not automatically result in equitable social

59   Peter S. Hill et al., "How Can Health Remain Central Post-2015 in a Sustainable Development Paradigm," *Globalization and Health* 10, no. 18 (2014).

60   Anthony Annett et al., "A Multi-Religious Consensus on the Ethics of Sustainable Development: Reflections of the Ethics in Action Initiative," (2017).

61   Steiner-Aeschliman. *The Religious Construction of Intimacy for Emotional Renewal: The Parallel Protestant Ethic*; "Transitional Adaptation: A Neoweberian Theory of Ecologically-Based Social Change."

62   Freese, *Environmental Connections*.

63   Azza Karam, "The Role of Religious Actors in Implementing the UN's Sustainable Development Goals," *The Ecumenical Review* 68, no. 4 (2016).

inclusion and sustainable development. He warns that prioritizing a largely patriarchal network of religious leaders to reinforce the role of religious actors as
a 'moral compass' risks "compromising on the universality of human rights."[64]
He points out that moral agency does not automatically translate into equitable service provision for the "less privileged regardless of their race, gender,
ethnicity, religion, and class" and that "the credibility of any faith institution is
significantly enhanced through its social service community outreach."[65]

Human agency is not just the solution; it has long been *part of the problem*.
Until we understand that, and adjust our behavior accordingly, our proposed
solutions are more likely to accelerate our collective self-destruction than
secure our common future.[66] We are living in the Age of the Anthropocene
where accelerated global human impacts are inducing environmental changes in planetary ecology, geography, climate, and pollution that have "agentic"
forces in the biosphere that shape human action.[67] *Unsustainable* social behavior results from human exemptionalist manipulations of the atmosphere
and biosphere where, whether intended or unintended, we anthropogenical-
ly alter sedimentation rates, ocean chemistry, carbon dioxide ratios, climate
change, global distribution of plants and animals, and species extinction.[68] If
we unreflexively respond to nonhuman agency by unthinkingly repeating past
behavior by creating even more intense human agency capable of dominating
the forces of nature, we risk becoming *fools*. At what point do the costs associated with large-scale manipulation of the atmosphere and biosphere through
geo-engineering begin to outweigh the benefits? Scholars have critiqued this
type of neo-Promethean manipulation of nature for "assuming straightforward
human agency" as a new human hubris that perpetuates the destructive effects on economic, social and ecological systems.[69] Scholars warn that human
agency in the Age of the Anthropocene can only achieve sustainable social
organization if it departs from the "normative viewpoint of exclusive human

---

64   Ibid., 374.
65   Ibid., 375.
66   Catton, *Overshoot*.
67   Duerbeck, Schaumann, and Sullivan, "Human and Non-Human Agencies in the
      Anthropocene."
68   Mark Williams et al., "The Anthropocene Biosphere," *The Anthropocene Review* 2, no. 3
      (2015).
69   Deborah Bird Rose et al., "Thinking through the Environment, Unsettling the Humani-
      ties," *Environmental Humanities* 1 (2012); Will Steffen et al., "The Anthropocene: Concep-
      tual and Historical Perspectives" (paper presented at the Philosophical Transactions of
      the Royal Society, 2011).

agency (human exceptionalism)" and conceptualizes human beings 'ecologically' as "co-participants within active biospheric systems."[70]

Human agency must itself become *reflexive* if it is to produce sustainable outcomes. Sustainable development involves more than the science of ecosystem management; there are ethical dimensions to the choices that we make. Scholars writing about the new multi-religious consensus on the ethics of sustainable development explain it this way:

> Our productivity and wealth are astounding. The world economy produces $US 127 trillion of output per year at international prices, for an average output per person of $16,770 that is distributed highly unequally across and within countries. With this average level of output per capita, extreme poverty would have ended long ago if countries had acted boldly and in international partnership. Challenges such as extreme poverty, hunger, lack of access to education, and deaths caused by preventable and treatable disease, are anachronisms. Worse, they are choices. Their persistence reflects what Pope Francis has called the "globalization of indifference."[71]

Humans, as a species, cannot live alone. Sustainability cannot be achieved until we de-center human beings enough to exercise our capacity to make choices in a manner that accepts responsibility for the "geophysical force" we have become in societal-environmental relations. Prioritizing the health of the most vulnerable in development circles is a start, but our common future depends not just upon how well we collaborate with people who are different; humans are also dependent upon other life forms. Sustainable development can only be achieved through a human agency capable of "environmental reciprocity instead of simple linear subject-object relationships."[72]

In the days ahead, religious diplomacy – *cosmopiety* – will become more important than ever. Evidence clearly indicates that religion can play a negative role in development. In 2014, the Pew Research Center indicated that religion was implicated in hostilities in a third of the 198 countries that they observed.[73] The Institute for Economics and Peace have estimated that religious factors

---

70   Duerbeck, Schaumann, and Sullivan, "Human and Non-Human Agencies in the Anthropocene," 119–120.

71   Ibid., 1.

72   Ibid., 121.

73   Pew Research Center, "Religious Hostilities Reach Six Year High," (2014), http://www.pew forum.org/2014/01/14/religious-hostilities-reach-six-year-high/.

play a decisive role in at least 14% of those conflicts.[74] In a world where more than 80% of the global population affiliates with some kind of religion,[75] how will the political-religious nexus be negotiated when environmental conditions deteriorate? Empirical studies have already identified a trend of religious organizations playing an increasing role as providers of essential services in developing and fragile countries. States are already responding to pressures to downsize through increased reliance upon non-state providers for service delivery.[76] Religious organizations are turned to as providers of "safe spaces" during humanitarian emergencies and crises in refugee resettlement, as religious organizations "turn churches into hospitals, mosques into kitchens, and temples into first aid centres."[77] As conditions worsen in the days ahead, and existing evidence about current trajectories suggest that conditions are likely to get worse before they can get any better, do we want the forces within religion and politics to be enemies or collaborative partners? Whether we like it or not, everyone is implicated and we are all in this together.

Conclusion

This chapter has described the evolution of a global ethic among world religions and a global norm among world nations in tandem with the turn of the century. The F8/F7/F20 process links the global ethic and the global norm through dialogue. The MDGS/SDGS have become the focal point in this dialogue for the F8/F7/F20 Initiative, but also for civil society, as the most salient and notable solution to problems of global governance; the MDGS/SDGS best clarify among leaders in global governance what "each person's expectation of what the other expects him to expect to be expected to do." Because the MDGS/SDGS are operationalized and measurable, governance tensions with civil society have been, and will continue to be, significantly shaped by the

---

74   Institute for Economics and Peace, "Five Key Questions Answered on the Link between Peace and Religion: A Global Statistical Analysis on the Empirical Link between Peace and Religion," (Sydney, Australia 2014).

75   Pew Research Center, "The Global Religious Landscape," (2012), http://www.pewforum .org/2012/12/18/global-religious-landscape-exec/.

76   Severine Deneulin and Carole Rakodi, "Religion and the Transformation of Development Studies: Re-Assessing the Relationship between Religion and Development," *World Development* 39, no. 1 (2011).

77   Nitschke and Gabriel, "The International Partnership on Religion and Sustainable Development/PaRD: A Global and Inclusive Partnership to Harness the Positive Impact of Religion in Development and Humanitarian Assistance," 381.

arrival and passage of deadlines. The most recent set of goals were success-fully adopted in September of 2015. The shift from the MDGs to SDGs involves a paradigm shift that will continue to shape civil society relations with trans-national governance institutions in the years ahead. Achieving sustainable development will require a new approach to how we relate to one another in the context of changing environmental conditions. Religious contributions will factor in far more than as value-added window dressing. Will the religious-political nexus be diplomatically channelled in a collaborative direction that builds our common future?

CHAPTER 10

Collaboration for a Responsible Future

In this chapter, three governance dimensions of the F8/F7/F20 Initiative case study are explored. The Initiative is discussed as an illustrative example of *cosmopiety* in international relations. Future considerations of governance challenges suggest that cosmopiety may become increasingly important for what it might contribute to international stability. I explore what the F20 might offer transnational relations in the way of governance, and offer suggestions for further research.

Religious Diplomacy in the Age of the Anthropocene

Historically unprecedented primarily human-induced environmental changes will continue to impose conditions that influence transnational relations in the days ahead.[1] Governance under rapidly changing environmental conditions that, to some extent, result from human activities will involve moral pressure to identify and negotiate more responsible paths of action. One way or another, religious voices will likely be drawn into the discussions, only some of whom will have cultivated the capacity for religious diplomacy.

Three governance dimensions can be identified with how *cosmopiety* might function in transnational relations: *deliberative, directional* and *decisional*. Each of these can be illustrated with reference to the F8/F7/F20 Initiative. The *deliberative* dimension of *cosmopiety* brings a broad array of universities, faith groups, religious leaders, development experts, human rights advocates and government officials together to listen and learn about one another's national constraints, priorities, and goals in ways that lead to ongoing relationships. Such deliberations occur throughout the year in a variety of contexts. Organizations such as RfP, WCRP, WFDD, and PaRD bring together a diverse array of stakeholders for dialogue toward this end. At F8/F7/F20 Initiative summits, participants are asked to exchange best practices, make case studies available, and share products (e.g., Coexist House's educational curriculum *Religious Literacy for Organisations*). At the 2017 Germany F20 Summit, participants could

---

1   Dietz, "Drivers of Human Stress on the Environment in the Twenty-First Century."

obtain an add-on certificate by completing the *Self-reliance and Empowerment Course for Refugees* offered by the Religious Freedom and Business Foundation, Launching Leaders and Interweave Solutions. As the Executive Committee plans for future F20 Summits, the sharing of best practices, products and training is one way of contributing to more effective governance.

The *directional* dimension of *cosmopiety* involves problem identification, agenda setting, and priority defining activities. In the case study of the F8/F7/F20 Initiative, problematic tensions have been identified internally along dimensions such as gender and religion, human rights and religion, and environment and religion. The Initiative's agenda routinely dedicates parallel sessions to these topics and often prioritizes plenary session space for panelists to identify problematic areas that merit further dialogue. Once raised, multiple opportunities exist for further dialogue around the issues in informal settings during coffee breaks and around shared meals, sometimes late into the evening. Most summits are convened in hotel settings where experts, leaders, practitioners and government officials are encouraged to disconnect from busy schedules and engage in the dialogue process for three full days. Participants are encouraged to develop friendships and initiate common projects that bring together diverse parties as a strategy for strengthening social cohesion across dimensions of difference. Participants are asked to identify priority areas for dialogue with the G20. The Summit Executive Committee takes this feedback into consideration when developing policy briefs for G-plus System Sherpas.

The *decisional* dimension of *cosmopiety* involves the practical recommendations that are made to the G-plus System that is being shadowed. In the early years of the Initiative, summits developed collaborative statements on specific subjects. More recently, the Initiative is focusing on ongoing early engagement and development of policy briefs on targeted issues such as famine relief and refugee resettlement. The common ground basis for the decisional dimension of governance are issues pertaining to implementation of the MDGs/SDGs that have been adopted by the international community. Summit Executive Committee members have prioritized briefs that focus on the salient humanitarian crises where concrete recommendations are likely to obtain greatest support.

Cosmopiety, illustrated here by the Initiative, can be understood as a form of cultural capital. Once developed, cultural capital can be drawn upon when the system of nation-states must make agonistic (if not undecidable) decisions during times of legitimation crises, weakening states or even state failures. Europe's current refugee crisis underscores the global interconnectedness of the nation-state system and is an important reminder that it takes little for regional instability to 'go global.'[2] When it does, what networks are in place when diplomacy is needed? Religious diplomacy has been theorized as obtaining greater significance during times of crisis and heightened uncertainty. Conditions of uncertainty and crises are expected to increase given the current trajectories of globalization. The cultural capital of cosmopiety may become more important as devolving states increasingly rely upon the private sector to assist with responding to humanitarian crises.

As we look to the future, predictions of increased cosmopiety breaks with the historic trajectory of secularization. The religious-political nexus contains significant predictive slack between past state practices of religious favoritism and the democratic inclusiveness emphasized with *cosmopiety*. The recent waves of nationalism and protectionism render the promise of *cosmopiety* even more uncertain. Nevertheless, futurist scholars have argued that it is unreasonable to root the validity of any theory in the best explanation of its success for cases, such as this, where predictive slack is understandably large.[3] Some of the best public diplomacy moments have been situations where less probable but objectively possible conditions won out over highly probable bleaker alternatives.[4] State fragility and failure has been characterized as a 'wicked problem' that involves conflicting objectives, characterized by multidimensional and complex factors, the resolution of which have important consequences for people's lives.[5]

The traditional dualistic approach to the religious-political nexus is no longer an effective approach to resolving conflict in transnational relations. According to Derick Brinkerhoff, current dialogue around state failures are hampered by a dualistic "naming and taming" dynamic between labelers and labelled; he says the international community is searching for new approaches that will encourage stronger policy realism and coherence.[6] For example, in a study of episodic violent outbursts that targeted minorities in Turkey, Germany, and Serbia, Murray identified three progressive stages in the ideologies that

---

2   For the past ten years, *Foreign Policy* has published The Fund for Peace's rankings of state fragility. For 2015, see The Fund for Peace, "Fragile States Index 2016," (*Foreign Policy,* 2016), http://foreign policy.com/fragile-states-index-2016-brexit-syria-refugee-europe-anti-migrant-boko-haram/.

3   Paul Dragos Aligica, "Prediction, Explanation and the Epistemology of Future Studies," *Futures* 35, no. 10 (2003).

4   Steiner, "Is Religious Soft Power of Consequence in the World Today?"

5   Derick W. Brinkerhoff, "State Fragility and Failure as Wicked Problems: Beyond Naming and Taming," 35, no. 2 (2014); Horst W.J. Rittel and Melvin W. Webber, "Dilemmas in a General Theory of Planning," *Policy Sciences* 4, no. 2 (1973).

6   Brinkerhoff, "State Fragility and Failure as Wicked Problems: Beyond Naming and Taming."

led, in tandem with other variables, to policies conducive to violence: First, nations understood themselves as victimized and disgraced by anti-national forces. Second, the nation was presented as the exclusive bearer of culture and civilized values. Third, fears were expunged by way of the purification of internal and external threats, either nationally as in the cases of Turkey and Serbia, or racially, as was the case in Germany.[7]

Brinkerhoff has proposed a problem-solving approach that looks beyond naming and taming to incorporate lessons from international development practices. Shared understandings get established among key stakeholders with respect to the aims, benefits, costs and tasks associated with needed reforms. Similarly, Innes and Booher[8] propose collaborative rationality as a strategy for working with wicked problems where diverse, interdependent, and authentic dialogue may be better suited than classic dualism to successfully resolve complex, multidimensional problems. Both approaches help to de-escalate tensions by redirecting attention away from the emotional frustrations associated with dualistic boundary maintenance toward the adoption of constructive problem-solving strategies that are better-suited to boundary crossing 'wicked problems.'

One of the boundaries state and government leaders have begun to cross on occasion is the separation between church and state. When dialogue is expanded to include pluralistic and inclusive representation of religion or belief, it becomes clear that nations are not the exclusive bearers of culture and civilized values. Religions bring an important long term perspective, some having existed for millennia. According to Weberian thought, religions exercise a form of traditional rational authority that is privatized during times of relative political stability, routine politics and even at the beginning of a crisis.[9] However, when long-range structural changes and historical accidents lead to legitimation crisis, religious authority can become publicly relevant and important to the unfolding social process.[10] According to Max Weber, even in secularizing Western Europe, religion serves as an important source of authority during

---

7   Elisabeth Hope Murray, *Disrupting Pathways to Genocide: The Process of Ideological Radicalization, Rethinking Political Violence* (Basingstoke, UK: Palgrave Macmillan, 2015).

8   Judith E. Innes and David E. Booher, "Collaborative Rationality as a Strategy for Working with Wicked Problems," *Landscape and Urban Planning* (2016).

9   Wolfgang Schluchter, *The Rise of Western Rationalism: Max Weber's Developmental History* (Berkeley, CA: University of California Press, 1981).

10   Roth and Schluchter, *Max Weber's Vision of History*.

times of social change, contributing to the negotiation of values when changes are needed.[11]

Cosmopiety exists within a complex religious landscape marked by diverse histories with long lasting legacies. It is uncertain which type of religious authority will be most influential in the days ahead. Depending upon the type of engagement, religious influence can increase social tensions or contribute to the collaborative resolution of social problems.[12] Religion becomes most problematic when hegemonic status is granted to a particular religion by a particular state; the ensuing politicization of religion (via political favoritism) has been shown to exacerbate political violence.[13] Indeed, religious regulation and violence have been shown to be empirically correlated.[14] Although many countries have tended to move away from theocracies toward adoption of the Westphalian model, many European countries and Muslim majority nations continue to have established churches and religion as an explicit part of the political system. Other nations have embraced a form of secularism (e.g., France's laïcité) that is dualistic.[15] Religion is also playing an influential role in the recent wave of anti-globalization and protectionism sweeping across Europe and the United States.[16] International religious landscapes are very complex; human migration patterns and global interdependence magnifies and intensifies how religion influences the complex social interactions.

There may be some identifiable common threads across a broad array of RNGOs engaged in public advocacy, only some of whom the F8/F7/F20 Initiative has been bringing together. Several scholars have observed how religious organizations constitute a distinct type of civil society engagement.[17]

---

11 Roslyn W. Bologh, *Love or Greatness: Max Weber and Masculine Thinking-a Feminist Inquiry* (London, United Kingdom: Unwin Hyman, 1990).

12 Haynes, "Religion and International Relations in the 21st Century: Conflict or Co-Operation?"; *Religion and Development: Conflict or Cooperation?*.

13 J. Cesari, *Muslims in the West after 9/11: Religion, Politics and Law* (London, England: Routledge, 2010); Cesari, "Religion and Politics: What Does God Have to Do with It?"

14 Grim and Finke, *The Price of Freedom Denied: Religious Persecution and Conflict in the Twenty-First Century*.

15 Marshall, *Global Institutions of Religion: Ancient Movers, Modern Shakers*; Haynes, "Religion and International Relations in the 21st Century: Conflict or Co-Operation?"

16 Laura King, "European Far-Right Populist Movements Energized by Britain's Brexit Vote and Trump's Victory," *Los Angeles Times*, January 1 2017; Scott, "ACLU Expecting More Religious Freedom Bills in 2017 Than Ever."

17 Berry, "Religion and Sustainability in Global Civil Society"; Ronnie D. Lipschutz, *Global Civil Society and Global Governance: The Politics of Nature from Place to Planet* (Albany,

What we do know is that governance improves when the religious factor is better understood and taken into account.[18] Given that not all religious groups are interested in, or capable of, engaging in constructive dialogue for governance purposes, identification of dialogue partners where they exist becomes important.

Tikkun Olam

Religious diplomacy is not easy, and it can involve great risk. In 2011, Syriac Orthodox Archbishop Yohanna Ibrahim was a plenary speaker at the F8 2011 Summit in France. When religious leaders were discussing migration, Ibrahim spoke about how migration in his home region of Syria was a matter of life or death more than a matter of becoming a refugee. In hindsight, we now know that Syria was on the brink of what would become a devastating civil war. Ibrahim turned to his colleagues at the 2011 Summit and asked, "How does this F8 Summit and other organizations stop this dangerous phenomenon? How do we tell people that they can stay and be safe? Is there any solution for this big problem or do we just come, speak and talk about what is happening here and there?" As Special Rapporteur for the Bordeaux Summit, I recorded his words. I have returned to them, on more than one occasion, and re-read my record of his full presentation. They haunt me. On April 22, 2013, Syriac Orthodox Archbishop Yohanna Ibrahim and Greek Orthodox Archbishop Boulos Yazigi were kidnapped by gunmen as they were walking along the road from the Turkish border to return to their city of Aleppo. There has yet to be confirmation of life or death since their capture, and as I write, no one has yet to accept responsibility for their abduction.[19]

A realist reading of this case study does not ask questions about the merits of the Initiative that participants are not already asking of themselves. The difference between a somewhat dismissive account and an account that takes the process more seriously is that even during times when evidence suggests

---

New York: State University of New York Press, 1996); Thomas Princen and Matthias Finger, *Environmental NGOs in World Politics: Linking the Local and the Global* (New York, New York: Routledge, 1994); Paul Wapner, *Environmental Activism and World Civic Politics* (Albany, New York: State University of New York Press, 1996).

18   Marshall, "Ancient and Contemporary Wisdom and Practice on Governance as Religious Leaders Engage in International Development"; *Global Institutions of Religion : Ancient Movers, Modern Shakers*; "Religious Freedom in US International Development Assistance and Humanitarian Relief: Ideas, Practice and Issues."

19   Wolfgang Danspeckgruber, *Huffington Post* (2014).

that the international order may be shaped more by *conflict of interests* than *harmony of interests*, the inevitability of nihilistic accounts of 'what is' is still challenged and unmasked to unveil the possibilities of 'what could be' even when the probability of achieving a different outcome might be low. The scholar's temptation is to safely write from the vantage point of highest probability and possibility without giving voice to possible alternative futures, especially those that may be objectively possible but highly unlikely. But to *choose* an interpretive account that only gives voice to hegemony over understanding is to reach for a safer account that does not stand the test of time. Even victors bring only partial truths to a common meeting place because social truths are constituted by the narrative truths of every member within the community.

In the Jewish tradition, there is a term—*Tikkun Olam*—that defines the joyful act as repairing the world. What I learned from studying this case study of *cosmopiety* is that common ground can only be made when we reach deep within ourselves to choose peace when we feel like war, to invest in the common good when politics would overwhelm the agenda, to emotionally commit to forgive when the heat of hatred hungers for retribution, to summon the courage to trust when suspicion is all we can hear, and to discern an opportunity for the light of wisdom when darkened doorways obscure the entrance to a way forward in this world.

As the humanitarian crisis in Syria has deepened, Aleppo Archbishop Jeanbart said that Christians have been "forgotten" by the world.[20] When the Syrian Orthodox Patriarch Mar Ignatius Zakka I passed away on March 21, 2014, an already suffering religious community became leaderless. In a somewhat unorthodox move, Christians in Syria and the wider Middle East unanimously nominated Archbishop Mar Gregorios Yohanna Ibrahim by electronic polls to be "The People's Patriarch." If scholars such as Machiavelli (1469–1527) and Thomas Hobbes (1588–1683) were alive today, they might be tempted to say that Syrian Orthodox Christians have elected a dead man as leader of their church.

But have they? The truth is, no one knows for certain. There is no evidence either way. And given the high uncertainty associated with unfolding affairs in the region, the people chose to vote in accordance with their faith. As I prepared to conclude this account of the F8/F7/F20 Initiative, I once again returned to the words that Ibrahim shared with his religious leader colleagues on May 24, 2011 when his region stood on the brink of war. This is what he had to say:

---

20   Christian Peschken and Archbishop Jeanbart, *Christians Forgotten in Syria, Says Aleppo Archbishop*, podcast audio 2016.

Peace in Aramaic is something that everyone seems to want, but very few people know how to successfully achieve...The Ancient Romans said if you want peace, prepare for war which means that unless one destroys the opposing party, you cannot have any peace. The world has not progressed much from the times when the Romans lived. But it is not possible to prepare peace without having good will towards one another, and this is not possible without acknowledging God, without conscience, without listening to the Voice of God speaking in silence. If this Voice is not listened to, God is not listened to and honored...Peace can never be fulfilled if we do not respect others' understanding. Mere coexistence is not enough.... A just peace means rejecting all forms of racism that treats any group as lesser or inferior. As Rev. Martin Luther King, Jr. emphasized, it is not possible to be in favor of some people and not be in favor of justice for all...If we desire to make a statement to a troubled world, our one God calls us to redesign our understanding of living together and respect diversity in peace. We are called to be peacemakers.

Much of this book has been devoted to explaining how and why religious diplomacy is important in transnational relations at this moment in history. The term *cosmopiety* was put forward as a conceptual tool useful for explaining the distinctive historical emergence of a new type of transnational religious engagement: a cosmopolitan stream of religious actors engaged in global governance. In Chapter 3, we considered the broader context of environmental changes, globalization and transnational governance within which this particular case study of *cosmopiety,* the F8/F7/F20 process, is situated. Scientific data consistently indicates that the environmental and social changes, from floods and severe storms to droughts and wildfires, are having greater effects now than in the 20th century. Religious diplomacy has been addressed in the context of the Age of the Anthropocene. None of the key environmental indicators or trends show signs of significant improvement or reversal despite nearly four decades of intense institutional activity aimed at containing an array of environmental threats. Reports consistently emphasize how taking more from ecosystems and natural processes than can be replenished, jeopardizes our common future.

Changing Times

The year 2015 marked a pivotal, although troubled, year of hope for the global community in terms of restoring degraded landscape, reaching global agreement on sustainability goals, spurring companies to cut emissions, urban leaders taking action to cut emissions, groundwork on the Paris agreement, and China prioritizing green financing for their G20 presidency.[21] The shift from MDGs to SDGs reflected a governance shift in focus from poverty eradication to sustainable development. This shift marked the beginning of taking environmental changes into account.[22] But 2016 saw a wave of nationalism sweep across Europe and the United States that has increased the already high sense of uncertainty associated with the future.

Nearly a year after world leaders endorsed the SDGs, a high-level political forum on sustainable development convened at the UN to help make the SDG promise a reality by bringing policymakers together to dialogue about how to accelerate the transition to a sustainable economy.[23] In a telling statement that "crystalized the difference between SDGs and previous international development goals, Norway Prime Minister Erna Solberg affirmed that the 'SDGs have made us all developing countries,' meaning that all countries have work to do to make their societies more equitable and environmentally responsible."[24] This emphasis upon increased collaborative engagement between all countries comes at a time when the 'trust gap' has moved from an all-time high measuring at a 12 point gap between the informed public and mass population in 2016 to the crisis stage (15 point gap). According to the Edelman Trust Barometer, the trust gap is driven by income inequality and divergent expectations of the future. While trust levels among informed publics are the highest ever in 16 years, trust is below 50 percent for the mass population in over sixty percent of the countries surveyed, having barely moved since the Great Recession. The trust disparity has widened and is now at double digit levels in more than half of the countries surveyed. In 2017, the United States presents the largest divide at nearly 21 points followed by the UK (19 points), and France (18 points).[25]

SDG Implementation Challenges

The 2030 Agenda for Sustainable Development sets out an ambitious plan of action for people, the planet and prosperity, with an overarching objective of leaving no one behind. At its core are 17 Sustainable Development Goals

---

21   Harmon and Steer, "Letter from the Chairman & President."

22   Folke et al., "Reconnecting to the Biosphere."

23   Bouye, "6 Lessons on Sustainable Development from the High-Level Political Forum."

24   Ibid., 2.

25   See www.edelman.com/global-results/, Michael Bush, "2016 Edelman Trust Barometer Finds Global Trust Inequality is Growing," *News Release,* 2016, http://www.edelman.com/news/2016-edelman-trust-barometer-release/.

comprising 169 targets. The Agenda represents a holistic plan of action that shifts the development focus from mainly focusing on the needs of poor countries to one that emphasises the well-being and sustainability in all countries.

Initial research indicates that the interest groups involved in SDG implementation do not want to repeat the mistakes made by the more bureaucratically driven MDG process.[26] The top-down approach of the MDGs contributed to lack of ownership, participation, and partnership among too many high-level policy makers and communities, civil society, the Global South, the private sector and other relevant stakeholders who were pivotal to MDG success.[27] MDGs were criticized for setting unrealistic expectations, lacking governance goals, ignoring the role of human rights, being focused on 'short term quick impact' projects rather than addressing complex social systems, and being identical across countries without taking into consideration varying national contexts.[28] Sustained, multi-stakeholder political mobilization is equally, if not more, important for SDG progress.[29] Inclusivity is already being strongly emphasized by many as a national priority in the year since adopting the SDG agenda. Most reporting countries have held civil society consultations and a few countries have reached out to empower civil society organizations. Finland, for example, has created a national civil society coalition called *Society's Commitment to Sustainable Development* that is composed of hundreds of non-state actors, 60 of whom are businesses, which have endorsed their own targets as contributions to the SDGs.[30] High-level leaders are also emphasizing capacity building

---

26   Hill et al., "How Can Health Remain Central Post-2015 in a Sustainable Development Paradigm"; Claire E. Brolan et al., "Back to the Future: What Would the Post-2015 Global Development Goals Look Like if We Replicated Methods Used to Construct the Millennium Development Goals?" *Globalization and Health* 10, no. 19 (2014).

27   B. Sadasivam, "Wooing the MDG Skeptics," *Development* 48 (2005); L. Gold, "Are the Millennium Development Goals Addressing the Underlying Causes of Injustice? Understanding the Risks of the MDGs," *Trocaire Dev Rep* (2005).

28   Devin K. Joshi, Barry B. Hughes, and Timothy D. Sisk, "Improving Governance for the Post-2015 Sustainable Development Goals: Scenario Forecasting the Next 50 Years," *World Development* 70, June (2015).

29   M. Darrow, "The Millennium Development Goals: Milestones or Millstones? Human Rights Priorities for the Post-2015 Development Agenda," *Human Rights Development Law Journal* 15 (2012); Brolan et al., "Back to the Future: What Would the Post-2015 Global Development Goals Look Like if We Replicated Methods Used to Construct the Millennium Development Goals?"; Hill et al., "How Can Health Remain Central Post-2015 in a Sustainable Development Paradigm."

30   Bouye, "6 Lessons on Sustainable Development from the High-Level Political Forum."

as essential to addressing gaps in knowledge, institutional coordination and data management through financial and technical support, best-practice exchanges and research. Stronger communication between government and civil society will be crucial to advancing this agenda.[31] Collaborative engagement is crucial if organizations and structures are to provide the tools, partnerships and systems needed to deliver on SDG promises, particularly in fragile contexts where risk and crisis rapidly evolve.[32]

SDG implementation faces challenges posed by lack of data on several fronts.[33] The list of indicators for adoption by the Statistical Commission is large and unwieldly. The SDGs have 230 indicators compared to the MDGs which used 60 that were harmonized and measurable. A significant number of developing and fragile nations across Asia and Africa lack sufficient data to be used by development professionals and policymakers for indicator establishment. This is problematic because accurate data is crucial for turning the SDGs into practical tools for problem solving by mobilizing governments, academia, civil society, and business. Indicators are necessary for tracking progress and ensuring accountability. Indicators also serve as a management tool for the transformations needed to achieve the SDGs by 2030. It may take five or more years to develop the full indicator. In the meantime, a preliminary index using national cross-country data already available has been put together to provide some preliminary rough estimates and country rankings.[34] The OECD has also proposed a short-hand SDG Index for OECD countries as a simplified way of tracking SDG achievement and determining priorities for implementation in each country.[35] The Overseas Development Institute has developed an SDG Scorecard operative at the regional level that identifies high-priority areas for SDG implementation, but the scope conditions do not allow the data to be used for national comparisons.[36]

---

31 Ibid.
32 OECD, "The Sustainable Development Goals: An Overview of Relevant OECD Analysis, Tools and Aproaches," (2016), http://www.oecd.org/dac/The%20Sustainable%20Development%20Goals%20An%20overview%20of%20relevant%20OECD%20analysis.pdf.
33 Jeffrey D. Sachs, Guido Schmidt-Traub, and David Durand-Delacre, "Preliminary Sustainable Development Goal (SDG) Index and Dashboard," in *SDSN Working Paper* (2016).
34 Ibid., 2–5.
35 OECD, "The Sustainable Development Goals: An Overview of Relevant OECD Analysis, Tools and Aproaches."
36 Sachs, Schmidt-Traub, and Durand-Delacre, "Preliminary Sustainable Development Goal (SDG) Index and Dashboard."

Governance Forecasts

Looking forward, good governance will continue to remain important for implementation of development goals. The level of corruption and poor governance in the developing world has been estimated to result in the unnecessary deaths of 140,000 children and cost \$1 trillion every year.[37] As indexes become available, issue attention will continue to wax and wane in accordance with civil society pressures to meet target dates and goals. Public expectations will still need to be managed. As early as 2006, scholars expressed concern about how the mere existence of MDG goals created expectations for fulfillment that could potentially undermine the very constituency needed for maintaining sustained engagement with poor countries. Making the SDG goals more realistic does not necessarily change the dynamic associated with the creation of tangible and time bound expectations. The work of 'norm entrepreneurs' will likely continue to be equally important for maintaining sustained pressure for political will as will the work of 'message entrepreneurs' so that SDG goals are treated as benchmarks rather than as planning goals. Of course, the process could all break down, too, as a consequence of angry protests fixated on specific targets.

Most governance forecasts in the literature have been short-term, qualitative or prescriptive.[38] A few exceptions have been related to the future of violent conflicts.[39] Long-range, quantitatively and empirically based governance forecasts that predict the future of transitions away from autocracy and the further movement toward democracy in partial democracies are rare. To address this gap in the literature, Joshi and colleagues pioneered a forecast of the future of domestic governance through the year 2060 for 183 countries utilizing a long-term, dynamic, integrated global futures modeling system. The study by Joshi and colleagues examined governance within the broader context of development, including connections to other systems, both domestic and international (e.g., demographic, economic, education, energy, environment, as well as patterns of relationships among states in regional and global networks

---

37   Global Financial Integrity, "Illicit Financial Flows 2004–2013," (2013), http://www.gfin
      tegrity.org/issue/illicit-financial-flows/; M. Hanf et al., "Corruption Kills: Estimating the
      Global Impact of Corruption on Children Deaths," *Plos One* 6, no. 11 (2011).

38   For example, see J. Kurlantzick, *Democracy in Retreat: The Revolt of the Middle Class and
      the Worldwide Decline of Representative Government* (New Haven: Yale University Press,
      2013).

39   For example, see H. Hegre et al., "Predicting Armed Conflict," *International Studies Quarterly* 57, no. 2 (2013).

that strongly affect governance). Although their Base Case did not take many of the environmental conditions into consideration, even their worst case scenario (which did) suggested that timely and effective interventions to strengthen governance and implement pro-poor development policies would result in much greater advances on the Post-2015 Sustainable Development Goals.[40]

Model forecasts are not predictions, and they are sensitive to specific decision rules that can be invalidated by policy changes,[41] so the findings by Joshi and colleagues should be interpreted with caution. That said, the policy change of SDG adoption was the topic of their governance analysis. To the extent that factors can be said to positively influence SDG implementation, they can be argued to improve governance in the future. Elsewhere, inclusion of civil society organizations, secular and faith-based, have been shown to strengthen G-plus System governance and improve national capabilities for implementing pro-poor development policies.[42] There are too many uncertainties associated with the future to suggest that taking bold steps to implement the SDGs is likely to produce greater peace, more democracy and less corruption in the global community. Even without guarantees, the alternative would be much worse.

What an F20 Might Offer

Religious organizations, particularly in the form of public-private partnerships, are becoming recognized for important roles they are anticipated to play in SDG implementation. A milestone occurred when the German Government partnered with the World Bank to co-host *Religion and Sustainable Development: Building Partnerships to End Extreme Poverty* on July 8–9, 2015 where key development stakeholders were asked to present evidence on the effectiveness of religious development work. This initiated a series of meetings that convened diverse key stakeholders that had not been brought together before to create a safe space for candid consultation, discussion and assessment. Over

---

40   Joshi, Hughes, and Sisk, "Improving Governance for the Post-2015 Sustainable Development Goals: Scenario Forecasting the Next 50 Years."

41   R.E. Lucas, "Econometric Policy Evaluation: A Critique," in *The Phillips Curve and Labour Markets*, ed. K. Brunner and A.H. Meltzer (Amsterdam: North Holland, 1976).

42   Hajnal, *The G7/G8 System: Evolution, Role and Documentation*; "The 2006 St. Petersburg Summit and Civil Society"; "Civil Society and the 2008 G8 Hokkaido Summit"; Hajnal and Guebert, "A Civil Society"; Hajnal, "Civil Society at the 2009 G8 Summit in L'Aquila"; "Head to Head: Summits in Canada in June 2010: The Muskoka G8 Meets the Toronto G20"; "The G20"; Kirton, Guebert, and Bracht, "Climate Change Accountability: The G8's Compliance Record from 1975–2011"; Kirton, "G20 Governance for a Globalized World."

time, outreach to different religious actors became normalized and regularized, which created more opportunities to create, consolidate, and coordinate joint efforts. By September 2016, there were twenty side events focused on the theme of religion and faith when the UN gathered for their 70th General Assembly.[43] The formation of intergovernmental efforts such as the International Partnership on Religion and Sustainable Development (PaRD) in 2016 are promising for their expressed commitments to facilitate implementation of the 2030 SDG Agenda.[44] They were one of two groups to focus on religious perspectives across the G20 agenda that were invited to contribute to the 2017 T20 Engagement Group meetings in Germany.[45]

Public-private partnerships are essential to SDG implementation, according to Irina Zaparina, for three main reasons. Firstly, implementation of the seventeen SDG goals requires infrastructure improvements, particularly in developing countries. But there is an infrastructure gap that renders developing economies incapable of meeting the demand for infrastructure investment. Nation-state budgets require additional funds from private investment. Secondly, public-private partnerships not only burden-share, they risk share; this increases a focus on results. Thirdly, public-private partnerships are a best-practices instrument for providing socially inclusive development. Public-private partnerships bring non-profit organizations, government and business together for the creation of new modern institutions and capacity-building activities in developing countries.[46]

The religious sector has much to offer the G-plus System, which is why the F8/F7/F20 process has been convening shadow summits since 2005. By documenting this history, this case study has illuminated an unseen, informal and unrecognized engagement group as a distinctive example of *cosmopiety* in international relations. Theoretical development has made the case for religious diplomacy as one way of creating moral pressure to generate the political will for responsible globalization. The international community has agreed upon a concrete set of SDGs. What an F20 engagement group might offer the G-plus

---

43   Karam, "The Role of Religious Actors in Implementing the UN's Sustainable Development Goals."

44   Nitschke and Gabriel, "The International Partnership on Religion and Sustainable Development/PaRD: A Global and Inclusive Partnership to Harness the Positive Impact of Religion in Development and Humanitarian Assistance."

45   Katherine Marshall, "Urgent Challenges for the G20: What an F20 Might Offer," *Huffington Post*, June 2 2017.

46   Irina Zapatrina, "Sustainable Development Goals for Developing Economies and Public-Private Partnership," *EPPPL* 1 (2016).

System is the diplomatic skills among religious leaders and the human agency within religious networks to help implement them.

At no other point in human history have nations of the world created a vehicle like the MDGs/SDGs which were a state and government initiated set of goals through the UN System. Adopting the implementation of these goals by the religious communities as a Rosetta Stone by which state and religious communities could engage together for the sake of mending the world is not without impact. Religious summitry has certainly had ancillary benefits such as, in Canada, bringing diverse religious communities together who would not have otherwise been aware that they had so much in common, or, as in Russia, raising the religious profile of the Orthodox Church in relation to state authorities, or internationally by providing a basis for strengthening dialogue skills and developing further conversation as global developments permit. Religious summitry has also made contributions to the globalization of democracy and the democratization of globalization, and the social glue that holds it all together, though this too, cannot be measured. The complete round of F8 shadow summits of the G8 have also demonstrated that the secular liberal conceit that faith is antithetical to reason has been set back and, in this context, faith and political reason have been, if not always comfortable, certainly compatible.

The F8/F7/F20 Initiative has evolved since its 2005 ecumenical origins in comparison to its current form in 2017. Although the process has waxed and waned over time, the F8/F7/F20 Initiative is far stronger in 2017 than when it first began. The process has become multi-faith and participative, emphasizing engagement with civil society, local communities and business. The process has remained consistently and persistently engaged with the G-plus System for over a decade, communicating concerns on a wide variety of issues that affirm human dignity, environmental sustainability, and international security. Over time, the process has shifted from high-level religious leader participation toward engaging academia, lawmakers, and opinion makers and advisers to political leaders.

Transnational governance leaders have come to recognize that broad consultation improves the deliberation and policy making process. Although there is some national variation, by and large, seven engagement groups are acknowledged as circling around the G-plus System.[47] The F20 is not yet one of them. To some extent, it may be because, until recently, the religious leader dialogue approach was more oriented to the historic 'fireside chat' model than the pragmatic and practical governance approach to the concrete problem solving of 'wicked problems.' Religious leaders have focused more on their *deliberative*

---

47   Alexander and Loeschmann, "The Solar System of G20: Engagement Groups."

and *directional* functions than their *decisional* functions. They have primarily sought to influence the priorities and agendas of political leaders, and to redirect the direction of society in a more peaceable and sustainable direction than to offer concrete policy recommendations. This may be changing now that two policy briefs (on famine relief and refugee resettlement) have been successfully incorporated into a T20 document that was delivered to the 2017 G20 Sherpas.[48] By way of comparison, most of the recognized engagement partners submit specific policy briefs that offer the G-plus System practical recommendations on pressing global issues. For example, Oxfam publishes specific policy briefs, such as their 2013 *Cracks in Tax: A Plan of Action. Joint Recommendations to the G20 and OECD for Tackling Base Erosion and Profit Shifting,* that resulted in the collaboration of 34 civil society organizations. InterAction has been publishing policy briefs every year since 2005 that have captured the expressed interest of US government officials. The Heinrich Böll Foundation has a G20 program that regularly issues newsletters, briefs and dossiers that offer recommendations on G20 accountability and transparency, development financing and the G20 Development Action Plan.[49] As Peter Hajnal has observed, civic engagement is most effective when it:

· Acknowledges the G-plus System's agenda and consistently dialogues with their agenda priorities
· Takes into account that the summit reflects but one of many other dimensions in the international system, including the UN, WTO, WHO and other organizations
· Works within the operational structure of the G-plus System and process to ensure dialogue
· Starts the dialogue early in the summit process since the agenda-building process is at least a year-long process[50]

Initiative communiqués have certainly commented on policies over the years. Now that they have successfully developed two policy briefs, will this develop into an ongoing series of briefs with sustained engagement? There have been times when the F8/F7/F20 Initiative spoke directly to the G8's agenda (e.g., 2007, 2014, 2015), and engaged with the G-plus System well in advance (e.g., 2010), but at other points, communiqués have appeared entirely detached from the G-plus System's process (e.g., 2006) and summits were convened on

---

48   Marshall, "Urgent Challenges for the G20: What an F20 Might Offer."
49   Hajnal, "The G20," 94–96.
50   "The 2006 St. Petersburg Summit and Civil Society."

short notice with little advance planning (e.g., 2012). The process continues to evolve and seems to have received more organizational support since it began hosting F20 Summits. Varying religious infrastructures within the G-plus System nations will continue to contribute to the complexities associated with summit organization. Some of ICC faith leaders believe the F8/F7/F20 process should continue at least for as long as the G8/G7 and G20 self-appointed global governance situation continues. Other leaders offer more qualified assessments. A year ago, Marshall described the events to date as having had a "somewhat tentative, exploratory character," but that is "hardly surprising given the vast scope of the challenge." At minimum, she describes the "F20" series as "a space worth following."[51] Less than a year later, she is publicly exploring what an F20 might offer the G20: "Among the groups that contribute to the global dialogue that the G20 inspires, an F20 (faith) or R20 (religion) could help ensure that vital human and ethical issues are always part of discussions."[52]

In this book, I have offered an explanation that takes human induced non-human agency into account to explain the enduring viability of the F8/F7/F20 shadow summit process. One can understand why the interfaith dialogue process would continue during the crisis-free years from 2005 to 2007, but why else would the Initiative continue during the financial crisis (2008–2009) and in some ways become even stronger during the crisis-scarred years from 2014 to 2015? It is too soon to predict if ongoing international crisis and waves of protectionism will reinforce or weaken the influence of the Initiative, or do so in a way that strengthens the social fabric. Little is known about how countries that are not members of the G7 and vulnerable countries that have selectively protected religious freedom and entered the global economy (e.g., Saudi Arabia) will accommodate the Initiative when it is their turn to host the F20 Summits. China was reluctant, but in the end, collaborated with religious leaders to host an informal Summit in 2016.

This book adds to the debate over the merits of the F8/F7/F20 Initiative by offering an analysis of the full performance of the forum, the continuing core of the process as a participant in governance, and the historical significance of the integrated whole from conception to its evolved state where this analysis ends in 2017. The Initiative's advantages and disadvantages have been analyzed in relation to its patterns of performance. Several questions were explored such as: How does the Initiative evolve in relation to hosts where religion is regulated differently into public policy by different states? How does the Initiative handle the inevitable tensions that arise in relation to situations that privilege

51   Marshall, "Shadowing the China G20 Summit: An Interreligious Gathering."
52   "Urgent Challenges for the G20: What an F20 Might Offer."

one or very few religions over others? How does the Initiative process these tensions when religious rights, human rights and women's rights diverge? Why didn't the F8 become an ongoing F7? Why did the F8 shift attention to the G20 right when the G7 began to recognize the importance of the faith factor? Why did the initial great endorsers of high-level political engagement, the Anglicans, shift their attention to broader middle-level influence on socio-economic factors over time? Does the Initiative seek a determinative role in the functioning of the state? A systematic examination of the design, evolution, operation and impact of the process was offered as one compelling account of how the F8/F7/F20 Initiative grew, took a particular evolutionary path and performed through 2017.

A theory of religious governance in the Age of the Anthropocene was developed. Peter Beyer's theory of religion and globalization was extended to incorporate (1) the shaping of religion by the political organization of the G-plus System, and (2) human-induced environmental changes. Evidence from the F8/F7/F20 Initiative was provided to illustrate further institutional differentiation of the religious sector. *Cosmopiety* was offered as an ideal type to identify three dimensions of governance associated with a new type of religious engagement in the public sphere. Reflexive human agency that responds to the non-human agency of human-induced environmental changes was theorized as necessary for successful implementation and reorientation of globalization for achievement of sustainable development. Sustainability involves ethics and values as well as science. Religious diplomacy will be an important resource for the successful negotiation of the religious-political nexus. The majority of the world's population is religious. Religiously motivated persons make better friends than enemies.

Further Research

Further research is needed to complement the pluralistic and rational biases underpinning this analysis of the F8/F7/F20 Initiative. For example, researchers might consider further examination of how emotion and conflict influenced evolution of the F8/F7/F20 Initiative and the dialogue process with the G-plus System. Researchers might want to fully explore how the financial burden associated with the Initiative affects the religious infrastructures of host countries. More research is needed to unravel and explain the different responses the G7 and G20 have to the F8/F7/F20 Initiative. Researchers might consider studying how the ongoing F20 process changes in response to the wave of populism and nationalism in Europe and the United States. Further research is also needed on outcomes associated with the Initiative's *deliberative, directional* and *decisional* dimensions of governance. How has bringing leaders, experts and academicians together to listen and learn about one another's national constraints, priorities and goals impacted their behavior and expanded interfaith networks? How have the agenda items they have submitted into the G-plus System become prioritized, if at all, in transnational relations? How have specific concrete agreements that have been specified in collaborative statements been implemented in participating religious networks? Finally, do the *deliberative, directional* and *decisional* dimensions of governance fluctuate in tandem with moments of increasing crisis and high uncertainty? If so, in what ways? What can be learned by any fluctuations in functional relevance? Is there any relationship between dialogue with religious leaders and the perceived legitimacy of national and government leadership?

We may envision a day when the human community is not dominated by the strongest arbiters of power but by a different order that recognizes the full human community. We may imagine a world where collaboration for the sake of the most vulnerable among us is commonly expected behavior. Until that day comes, it remains in the best interest of the global community to find multiple and diverse ways to maintain moral pressure on governance actors to redirect globalization toward more responsible trajectories.

Theoretical Orientation, Methodology, Documentation & Data

This work is set within a theoretical framework of complex, non-linear, multidimensional, self-organizing systems theory that considers biological and socio-economic theories of evolution as interrelated processes.[1] Biophysical environmental conditions are theorized as primary influencers of social-environmental connections along with cultural meanings, but the relationship is not one of simple causality. This represents a departure from sociological frameworks that treat human symbolic means as primary and material biophysical conditions as "secondary and useful only as raw input around which cultural meanings can be constructed."[2] The ecological constraints are considered severe enough to render some of the current growth trajectories unsustainable, and other trajectories subject to limited adaptability.[3] This work focuses upon maximizing the limited human adaptability that might be possible through reorganization.[4] Set within human ecology theory, I closely examine how ideal interests and material forces are once again shaping and influencing the development of societal-environmental relations at this moment in history.

The theoretical breadth of the approach taken in this manuscript merits particular attention. Few assessments of the interfaith movement are informed by an understanding of international relations that examines the full array of performance dimensions such as domestic political management, deliberation, direction setting, decision-making, the delivery of these decisions, and the development of international global governance as constrained by environmental conditions. Few offer a well-specified theoretical explanation for the emergence, evolution, and performance of the interfaith movement that could serve as a foundation for assessing how the movement might develop in the years ahead. For those who consider interfaith dialogue with the G-plus System to be a necessary development, few have offered systemic

---

1　Freese, "Evolution and Sociogenesis: Parts I & II"; Georgescu-Roegen, *The Entropy Law and the Economic Process*; *Energy and Economic Myths*.

2　Freese, *Environmental Connections*, 21–22.

3　Catton, *Overshoot*.

4　Paul Harrison, "Towards a Post-Malthusian Human Ecology," *Human Ecology Review* 1, no. 2 (1994); Gual and Norgaard, "Bridging Ecological and Social Systems Coevolution: A Review and Proposal"; Richard Norgaard, *Development Betrayed: The End of Progress and a Coevolutionary Revisioning of the Future* (London: Routledge, 1994); Dietz, "Drivers of Human Stress on the Environment in the Twenty-First Century."

theories to clarify how this claim is analytically persuasive. Few have considered the realists' supply of changing relative capacities and capabilities of governance and religious institutions together with the mutual vulnerabilities and interdependencies that affect dynamics in the interconnected globalizing world, and how this concentrates and exacerbates demands on all international institutions that claim to meet people's needs in the context of environmental changes. Above all, while some have noted the causal relevance of crisis in generating the interfaith and G-plus System dialogue process, none of these positions can explain why the F8/F7/F20 Initiative continues amidst other existing alternatives.

Given the rapidity with which international relations are shifting in 2018, it becomes important to say a few words about biases underpinning the book. The work is set in the pluralist tradition of international relations theory (e.g., Robert Keohane, Joseph Nye) that emphasizes the complex interdependence of the international system and the new opportunities presented by the growing network of INGOs. The perspective assumes that states can widen their perception of self-interest through economic cooperation and involvement in international institutions. Unlike Machiavelli (1469–1527) and Thomas Hobbes (1588–1683) who both assumed that the quest and struggle for power is at the core of relations among states, this book accepts that pursuit of a *harmony of interests* is feasible, that human beings can rationally recognize that they have some interests in common, and that cooperation is therefore objectively possible. This imposes obvious limitations on the work. The bias toward rationality underpinning this assumption may inadequately explore how emotional appeals to nationalism and self-interest influence international relations. According to E.H. Carr (1892–1982), the international order is shaped more by *conflict of interests* than *harmony of interests;* to the extent that international order exists, it is based on power rather than morality. According to Carr, morality is constructed by the legal system and is itself a product of power.[5] As such, the political framework within which this book is situated may overestimate the future viability of the F8/F7/F20 Initiative.

Certainly, a realist account of the F8/F7/F20 Initiative would present a very different assessment than what is presented here. At minimum, such an approach would emphasize that any attempt by the F8/F7/F20 Initiative to embed morality in the legal order must pay adequate attention to the reality of power. Indeed, I would counter that such an approach has not gone far enough, and would benefit from greater attention to the constraining reality of environmental conditions and what happens to the political-religious nexus under conditions of weak or failed states.

---

5 W. Julian Korab-Karpowicz, "Political Realism in International Relations," *The Stanford Encyclopedia of Philosophy* (2013), https://plato.stanford.edu/entries/realism-intl-relations/#RooReaTra.

In this book, I assume that there can be progress in international relations and that the future does not need to look like the past. In so doing, I avoid the self-fulfilling prophecy that war and environmental destruction are inevitable. That said, I have tried to heed realist school of thought warnings against progressivism, moralism, legalism or other orientations that might lose touch with how power shapes outcomes.[6] In the end, the most significant contribution the F8/F7/F20 Initiative may play in international relations is as a collective historic effort to sustain hope by religious leaders who consistently and persistently 'speak truth to power' and 'unmask power's claims to truth and morality.' The realist school emphasizes that the practical reality is that nation-states must make prudent—not ethical—political decisions.[7] And yet, had it not been for the interwar idealism's press against nihilist probability to realize what was objectively possible, would we have ever seen humanity unite enough to create the League of Nations in 1920, the Kellogg-Briand Pact of 1928, or the United Nations in 1945?[8]

Methodology

The historical sociological method is used here within the framework of human ecology theory. The historical sociological method was chosen for analysis of the Initiative because it is well suited to providing plausible explanations at critical historical moments. This use of 'historical sociology,' as opposed to simply combining history with sociology, challenges explanations in sociology and other transnational fields of research in a manner reminiscent of how historical sociologists expanded sociology to actively engage with global processes in the 1980's.[9] Neo-Weberian historical sociology tends to be combined with international relations in the United Kingdom and with civilizational analyses in Europe.[10] I expand the method to further incorporate environmental factors. Although scholars such as Christian Reus-Smit will undoubtedly

---

6   Muriel Cozette, "Reclaiming the Critical Dimension of Realism: Hans J. Morgenthau and the Ethics of Scholarship," *Review of International Studies* 34, no. 1 (2008); Hans J. Morgenthau, *Politics among Nations: The Struggle for Power and Peace* (New York, New York: McGraw-Hill, 1948); *Truth and Power* (New York, New York: Praeger, 1970).

7   Cozette, "Reclaiming the Critical Dimension of Realism: Hans J. Morgenthau and the Ethics of Scholarship."

8   Korab-Karpowicz, "Political Realism in International Relations."

9   Stephen Hobden and John M. Hobson, *Historical Sociology of International Relations* (Cambridge, England: Cambridge University Press, 2002).

10   Gurminder K. Bhambra, "Historical Sociology, International Relations and Connected Histories," *Cambridge Review of International Affairs* 23, no. 1 (2010).

deem this approach as too rationalistic and materialistic,[11] the theoretical inclusion of non-human agency draws on post-humanist theories to provide a basis for claims that environmental factors influence the co-evolution of societal-environmental relations.[12]

Indeed, historical sociology has been critiqued for many reasons including, but not limited to, the problem of locating agency,[13] for deficiencies in using a linear convergent model of development,[14] and for being too loose and abstract of an orientation that is defined more by what it denies than what it affirms.[15] The use of 'ideal types' compounds exegetical selectivity on the part of the researcher with contextual selectivity in a manner that prohibits methodological certitude.[16] The unavoidable biases that underpin historical sociological studies have been critiqued for maintaining a Eurocentric bias in the way that *sui generis* endogenous processes are abstracted as integral to the connections.[17]

But the benefits of using the historical sociological method outweigh the risks. Historical sociology is contextual in both time and space, and it allows for close attention to historical context and complexity. The most important way the method's weaknesses can be compensated for is for the researcher to make his or her biases and assumptions explicit, and to consider counterfactual analysis of how history might be otherwise.[18] I have attempted to do both throughout this manuscript. I am explicitly locating non-human agency in ecological changes that variously operate at regional, transnational and biospheric levels of analysis. The historical sociological method

---

11   Christian Reus-Smit, "The Idea of History and History with Ideas," in *Historical Sociology of International Relations*, ed. Stephen Hobden and John M. Hobson (Cambridge, England: Cambridge University Press, 2002).

12   Pearson, "Beyond 'Resistance': Rethinking Nonhuman Agency for a 'More-Than-Human' World."

13   Lynn Hankinson Nelson, "Epistemological Communities," in *Feminist Epistemologies*, ed. Linda Alcoff and Elizabeth Potter (London, England: Routledge, 1993).

14   Barry Buzan and Richard Little, *International Systems in World History* (Oxford, England: Oxford University Press, 2001); "International Systems in World History: Remaking the Study of IR," in *Historical Sociology of International Relations*, ed. Stephen Hobden and John M. Hobson (Cambridge, England: Cambridge University Press, 2002).

15   Edgar Kiser and Michael Hechter, "The Role of General Theory in Comparative-Historical Sociology," *American Journal of Sociology* 97, no. 1.

16   Roth and Schluchter, *Max Weber's Vision of History*, 12.

17   Gurminder K. Bhambra, *Rethinking Modernity: Postcolonialism and the Sociological Imagination* (Basingstoke, England: Palgrave, 2007); Bhambra, "Historical Sociology, International Relations and Connected Histories."

18   Kiser and Hechter, "The Role of General Theory in Comparative-Historical Sociology."

makes theory building possible in the context of discovery.[19] Metaphors such as *cosmopiety* are used throughout the text as a form of historical interpretation in keeping with Rosa and Machlis[20] who consider metaphor usage to be an appropriate tool for bridging between old and new ideas during a time of paradigmatic shift. Ulrich Beck's[21] sociology of religion in risk society is critiqued and extended, in accordance with sociological theory building techniques,[22] to question the normative horizon of world risk society, to break with the automatisms of modernization and globalization, and to rediscover the openness of human action to the future by identifying cosmopolitan alternatives in a manner inclusive of religious resources.

Since the F8/F7/F20 Initiative is a singular historic case in a rapidly changing social context, assessment of the historical significance of the F8/F7/F20 process is more suitable to the standards of scientific investigation associated with future studies. Future studies have disentangled the theory of prediction from the theory of explanation that were too closely tied together under the positivist model.[23] The symmetry between prediction and explanation is a myth that rarely converges in the history of scientific inquiry. There are many explanations lacking predictive power (e.g., for the emergence of a new biological species) that are nevertheless meaningful, and there have been significant predictive approaches that lacked serious explanations (e.g., the arithmetic Babylonian technique for forecasting moon cycles and lunar eclipses).[24] Newton powerfully synthesized the two traditions of explanation and prediction, but using the Newtonian synthesis as a validity criterion inappropriately narrows the field of scientific investigation. Rescher[25] speaks of "predictive slack" rather than "fit" between theoretical explanation and prediction to make the point that the epistemological nature of the relationship between the two remains unclear. When it comes to future studies, successful predictions

> are less dependent on statistical information than on knowledge of behavioral regularities, of the intentions and preferences of the relevant people, of the institutional arrangements, group aspirations, traditions, customs, practices,

19   Charles C. Ragin, *The Comparative Method: Moving Beyond Qualitative and Quantitative Strategies* (Berkeley, CA: University of California Press, 1987).

20   Eugene A. Rosa and Gary E. Machlis, "Energetic Theories of Society: An Evaluative Review," *Sociological Inquiry* 53 (1983).

21   Beck, "A God of One's Own"; "The Two Faces of Religion."

22   Freese and Sell, "Constructing Axiomatic Theories in Sociology."

23   Aligica, "Prediction, Explanation and the Epistemology of Future Studies."

24   Ibid.

25   Nicholas Rescher, "Predicting the Future: An Introduction to the Theory of Forecasting," *Philosophy: The Journal of the Royal Institute of Philosophy* 74, no. 287 (1999).

fashions, of national attitudes and climates of opinion, organizational rules and regulations, and so on.[26]

Attentiveness to behavioral regularities are particularly relevant to the study of dialogue in transnational relations, and given the rapidly changing social contexts, the historical explanation for any given moment in time may significantly differ from the items' relevance for the future (e.g., climate change). The outcome of a single election can have ripple effects throughout the system. Sometimes ecosystem regimes shift,[27] sometimes history is discontinuous,[28] and sometimes history might have been otherwise.[29] If we are to avoid the kind of self-fulfilling prophecies that close the future to important possibilities,[30] then we would do well to recognize the appropriateness of "predictive slack" as a helpful protective against the reifications imposed by historical determinism.[31]

Documentation

As with the G-plus System, documentation of the F8/F7/F20 Initiative is dependent upon external scholarship. The University of Toronto's G7, G8 and G20 research groups have developed a comprehensive archive of analytic work that they make accessible to scholars; The Lowy Institute for International Policy publishes a quarterly *G20 Monitor* that brings together policy contributions from a wide cross-section of society interested in feeding into the G20 process; but, the F8/F7/F20 Initiative has received scant scholarly attention. The F8 statements are hosted by the G7 Information Centre at

---

26   Aligica, "Prediction, Explanation and the Epistemology of Future Studies."

27   Aart DeZeeuw, "Regime Shifts in Resource Management," *Annual Review of Resource Management* 6 (2014): 85–104; Carl Folke, Steve Carpenter, Brian Walker, Marten Scheffer, Thomas Elmqvist, Lance Gunderson, and C.S. Holling, "Regime Shifts, Resilience, and Biodiversity in Ecosystem Management," *Annual Review of Ecology, Evolution, and Systematics* 35 (2004): 557–581.

28   Thomas J. Crowley and Gerald R. North, "Abrupt Climate Change and Extinction Events in Earth History," 1988.

29   Stanley Lieberson, "More on the Uneasy Case for Using Mill-Type Methods in Small-N Comparative Studies," *Social Forces* 72 (1994); "Small N's and Big Conclusions: An Examination of the Resaoning in Comparative Studies Based on a Small Number of Cases," *Social Forces* 70, no. 2 (1991).

30   Robert K. Merton, "The Self-Fulfilling Prophecy," *The Antioch Review* 8, no. 2 (1948).

31   Lieberson, "More on the Uneasy Case for Using Mill-Type Methods in Small-N Comparative Studies"; "Small N's and Big Conclusions: An Examination of the Resaoning in Comparative Studies Based on a Small Number of Cases."

University of Toronto.[32] The F7 statement is hosted as a web petition. Griffith University's Centre for Interfaith & Cultural Dialogue hosted information about the first F20 summit and supported the involvement of the Centre's Director, Adams, to help coordinate ongoing F20 meetings. BYU Law's ICLRS now hosts a website for the F20 Initiative where presentation videos and additional information about upcoming and past F20 events are accessible to scholars and the general public. This book documents and describes the importance of the F8/F7/F20 Initiative in the post-secular world of global environmental change. The book seeks to be the first comprehensive, independent, authoritative, analytical account of the F8/F7/F20 Initiative from its ecumenical origins in 2005, through its evolution with the second F20 Summit in Istanbul in 2015, and the beginning of a new recognition phase in 2016. This is not a sanitized account written from the inside of the F8/F7/F20 Initiative. Instead, the approach draws on concepts and theories from environmental sociology, sociology of religion, international relations and global governance to offer an account of F8/F7/F20 governance and the F8/F7/F20 Initiative itself.

Data

Documentation of the F8/F7/F20 Initiative imposes evidentiary demands that exceed those engaged in advocacy work or assessment tasks. Illustrative data are used as informative evidence to develop, not test, a *cosmopiety* theory of risk society in transnational relations. The theory expands the concept of *cosmopiety* from previous applications that have been limited to peacemaking,[33] to be more broadly applicable to issues related to economic development, international finance and environmental change. *Cosmopiety* is introduced as a useful ideal type that partially represents reality so that the meaningfulness and significance of the F8/F7/F20 Initiative can be assessed.

Primary data was gathered over a five year period between 2010 and 2015. The book has benefited from more than 100 private interviews conducted between 2010 and 2015, and by phone and face-to-face contact in Canada, France, the United States, Turkey, China and Germany. F8 interviews and questionnaires (33% response rate) were conducted on May 23 and 24, 2011, in France. F8 interviews and questionnaires (45% response rate) were conducted on May 17, 2012 in Washington, DC. Qualitative interviews of F8 summit hosts were conducted from October 2012 to January 2013 (75% response rate) from Canada. F20 interviews were conducted on November 16 to 18, 2015 in Istanbul, Turkey.

---

32   See http://www.g8.utoronto.ca/interfaith/.

33   Ralph Pellman, "In Pursuit of World Peace: Modernism, Sacralism and Cosmopiety," *Global Change, Peace and Security* 22, no. 2 (2010).

Secondary data was also gathered over a seven year period covering summits occurring between 2005 through 2017. Evidence also comes from impact science and scholarly works on the interfaith movement and the G-plus System, publications by practitioners, biographies of F8/F7/F20 participants, newspaper and other media accounts.

I served as Special Rapporteur for Canada (2010), France (2011), the United States (2012), Turkey (2015), China (2016) and Germany (2017). When possible, *Summit Reports* produced from this role were circulated to presenters for verification. Serving as Special Rapporteur has provided me access to more information (presentations, questionnaires, and qualitative interviews) on those summits than the summits from 2005 to 2009. Although this created an imbalance of information, the additional material gained from firsthand participant observation of what were mostly closed meetings outweighed the drawbacks associated with information discontinuity. Compiled information on the religious and political representation of summit participants for the 9-year F8 cycle was also circulated to summit organizers and the international continuance committee for verification. I am grateful for the feedback from several diplomats and scholars who offered timely and early analyses to assist my work in explaining and understanding the F8/F7/F20 Initiative. I am grateful to the Canadian Council of Churches for providing me access to their records in 2014 of their summit involvement from 2007–2013. At this early stage of the F8/F7/F20 Initiative, the evidence I have gathered may be sufficient to achieve my purpose of providing the first comprehensive, reliable, detailed, independent scholarly account of the F8/F7/F20 Initiative. I look forward to reading better explanations as others build on this foundation to improve our understanding of F8/F7/F20 involvement in global governance.

Institutional Affiliations Reference List

The institutional affiliations for the positions are for purposes of identification only.

Metropolitan E. Adamakis	Secretary-General of F8 (2011); Metropolitan, Greek Orthodox Metropolis of France
Dr. Brian J. Adams	Secretary-General of F20 (2014–2017); G20 Interfaith Summit Executive Committee; Director, Centre for Interfaith and Cultural Dialogue, Griffith University, Australia
Martin Affolderbach	Executive Officer, Church Office of the Evangelical Church in Germany
Patriarch Alexey II	Secretary-General of F8 (2006); 15th Patriarch of Moscow, Russian Orthodox Church, Russia
Sarosh Arif	Alliance of Civilizations Institute, Fatih Sultan Mehmet Waqf University, Turkey
Hon. Lloyd Axworthy	Retired President and Vice Chancellor, University of Winnipeg; Minister of Foreign Affairs and International Development for Canada 1996–1999, Canada
Rev. Hegumen P. Bulekov	Moscow Patriarchate Representative to the Council of Europe, Department for External Relations, the Russian Orthodox Church, France
Desmond Cahill	Professor, RMIT University in Melbourne, Australia
Rev. Dr. James T. Christie	Secretary-General of F8 (2010); G20 Interfaith Summit Executive Committee; Professor of Whole World Ecumenism and Dialogue Theology and Director of the Ridd Institute for Religion and Policy at the University of Winnipeg, Canada
Rev. Dr. John Chryssavgis	Archdeacon of the Ecumenical Patriarchate, Greek Orthodox Archdiocese of America, United States
Dr. Ram Cnaan	University of Pennsylvania, United States
Prof. Dr. Pieter Coertzen	G20 Interfaith Summit International Organizing Committee; Professor, Faculty of Theology, University of Stellenbosch, South Africa
Honourable Roméo Dallaire	Lieutenant-General, Canadian Senator, Founder, Roméo Dallaire Child Soldiers Initiative, Canada

© KONINKLIJKE BRILL NV, LEIDEN, 2018 | DOI 10.1163/9789004365018_013

Dr. W. Cole Durham, Jr.	Secretary-General of F20 (2014–2017); G20 Interfaith Summit Executive Committee; Founding Director, International Center for Law and Religion Studies, Italy; Susa Young Gates Professor of Law, J. Reuben Clark Law School, Brigham Young University
Dr. Kathy Ehrensperger	Co-Secretary-General of F20 (2017); G20 Interfaith Summit German Organizing Committee, Research Professor from Universität Potsdam, Germany
Sharon Eubank	Director of Humanitarian Services, LDS Charities, United States
Prof. Alessandro Ferrari	G20 Interfaith Summit International Organizing Committee; Director, Center on Religion, Law and Economy in the Mediterranean Area; Associate Professor, Department of Law, Economy, and Cultures, University of Insubria, Italy
Max Finberg	Director of Faith-Based and Neighborhood Partnerships, US Department of Agriculture, United States
Marie-Claire Foblets	G20 Interfaith Summit International Organizing Committee; Director, Max Planck Institute for Social Anthropology, Department of Law and Anthropology, Germany
Mussie Hailu Gebrestadik	Regional Director of United Religions Initiative for Africa; Representative to the UN and African Union, Kenya
Nazila Ghanea	Associate Professor International Human Rights Law, University of Oxford, OSCE Advisory Panel of Experts on Freedom of Religion or Belief, United Kingdom
Dr. Brian Grim	Berkley Center for Religion, Peace & World Affairs, United States
Rev. Dr. Karen Hamilton	G20 Interfaith Summit International Organizing Committee; General Secretary, The Canadian Council of Churches, Canada
Rev. Bud Heckman	Secretary-General of F8 (2012); Executive Director, Religions for Peace USA, United States
Sarah Hildebrandt	Director, Millennium Kids, Canada
Right Rev. Christopher Hill	The Lord Bishop of Guildford and Clerk of the Closet in the Ecclesiastical Household of the Royal Household of the Sovereign of the United Kingdom, United Kingdom
Mark Hill QC	Centre for Law and Religion, Cardiff and University of Pretoria, South Africa

Peter Howard	Senior Director of Emergency Response, Food for the Hungry, United States
Bishop Dr. Wolfgang Huber	Secretary-General of F8 (2007); Former Chairperson, Council of the Evangelical Church in Germany, Germany
Linda Hyökki	Alliance of Civilizations Institute, Fatih Sultan Mehmet Waqf University, Turkey
Mar Gregorios Y. Ibrahim	Syriac-Orthodox Archbishop, Metropolitan of Aleppo, Syria
Bhai Sahib B.M. Singh Ji	Trustee, RfP; Chairman, Guru Nanak Nishkam Sewak Jatha, United Kingdom
Dmitry Kabak	President, Open Viewpoint Foundation; Member, Panel of the OSCE/ODIHR Advisory Council on Freedom of Religion or Belief, Kyrgyzstan
Rev. Dr. Andre Karamaga	General Secretary of the All Africa Conference of Churches, Kenya
Prof. Syed Munir Khasru	Chairman, Institute for Policy, Advocacy, and Governance, Bangladesh
Prof. John Kirton	G20 Interfaith Summit International Organizing Committee; Co-Founder and Director, G8 Research Group; Founder and Co-Director, G20 Research Group, Munk School of Global Affairs, University of Toronto, Canada
Elizabeta Kitanović	G20 Interfaith Summit Executive Committee; Executive Secretary for Human Rights and Communication, Conference of European Churches, Belgium
Lena Larsen	Executive Director, Oslo Coalition on Freedom of Religion or Belief, Norwegian Centre for Human Rights, University of Oslo, Norway
Ricky Lashand	G20 Interfaith Summit Secretariat, Administrative Support Officer, Center for Interfaith and Cultural Dialogue, Griffith University, Australia
Lin Li	Director, Department of Islamic Studies, Institute of World Religions, Chinese Academy of Social Sciences, China
Nicta Lubaale	General Secretary for the Organization of African Independent Churches, Kenya
Dr. Tahir Mahmood	G20 Interfaith Summit International Organizing Committee; Distinguished Jurist Chair; Professor of Eminence and Founder Chairman, Amity University Institute of Advanced Legal Studies, India

Shan Manocha	Senior Advisor on Freedom of Religion and Belief, Human Rights Department, OSCE/ODIHR, Warsaw, Poland
Rabbi Richard Marker	Senior Fellow at New York University's George Heyman Jr. Center for Philanthropy, United States
Dr. Katherine Marshall	G20 Interfaith Summit Executive Committee; Senior Fellow, Berkley Center for Religion, Peace, and World Affairs, Georgetown University; Executive Director, World Faiths Development Dialogue, United States
John McArthur	Senior Fellow, Brookings Institution; CEO, Millennium Promise, former Manager & Deputy Director, UN Millennium Project, United States
Rt. Rev. Yoshinobu Miyake	Secretary-General of F8 (2006); G20 Interfaith Summit International Organizing Committee; Superior General, Konko Church of Izuo, Japan
Paul Morris	Professor, Victoria University of Wellington, New Zealand
Dr. Faizan Mustafa	G20 Interfaith Summit International Organizing Committee; Vice Chancellor of NALSAR University of Law, India
Rev. Edmund Newell	Priest, Church of England, Principle, Cumberland Lodge, United Kingdom
Ulrich Nitschke	Head of the Secretariat for International Partnership on Religion and Sustainable Development (PaRD), Germany
Rev. Nichiko Niwano	Secretary-General of F8 (2006); President of Rissho Kossei-kai International Buddhist Congregation, President, World Conference of Religions for Peace Japan, Japan
Rev. Rüdiger Noll	Director of the Church and Society Commission, Associate General Secretary of the Conference of European Churches, Switzerland
Bishop H.E. Msgr. V. Paglia	Secretary-General of F8 (2009); Bishop of Terni-Narni-Amelia and Chairman, Commission for Ecumenism and Dialogue of the Italian Bishops Conference, Italy
Liu Peifeng	Professor, Law School of Beijing Normal University, China
Carmen Asiaín Pereira	Senator, Member of Parliament; President, Latin American Consortium for Freedom of Religion or Belief, Uruguay

Dr. Peter Petkoff	G20 Interfaith Summit Executive Committee; Director, Law and International Relations Programme, Regent's Park College, Oxford and Brunel Law School, United Kingdom
Rev. Francois Pihaate	General Secretary, Pacific Conference of Churches, Tahiti
Dr. Charles Reed	Secretary-General of F8 (2013); Foreign Policy Advisor at Archbishops' Council of the Church of England, United Kingdom
Father Thomas J. Reese	Jesuit, Senior Fellow at the Woodstock Theology Center at Georgetown University, United States
Cardinal Jean-Pierre Ricard	Archbishop of Bordeaux and Bazas, Roman Catholic Church, France
Dr. Mohammad Sammak	Advisor to the Mufti of Lebanon; Secretary General of the Christian-Muslim Committee for Dialogue; Secretary General of the Islamic Permanent Committee; Secretary General of the Executive Committee of the Christian-Muslim Arab Group, Lebanon
David Saperstein	US Ambassador at Large for International Religious Freedom, United States
Dr. Rev. Patrick Schnabel	Co-Secretary-General of F20 (2017); G20 Interfaith Summit German Organizing Committee, Co-Chair, Evangelische Kirche Berlin-Brandenburg-Schlesische Oberlausitz, Kirchlicher Entwicklungsdienst, Germany
Dr. Recep Şentürk	Secretary-General of F20 (2015); G20 Interfaith Summit International Organizing Committee; Director, Alliance of Civilizations Institute, Fatih Sultan Mehmet University; President, Ibn Haldun University, Turkey
Blythe Shupe	G20 Interfaith Summit Secretariat, Communications Specialist, International Center for Law and Religion Studies, J. Reuben Clark Law School, Brigham Young University, United States
John Siebert	Former Executive Director, Project Ploughshares, Canada
Justice Murray Sinclair	Canadian Senator, Chair of the Indian Residential Schools Truth and Reconciliation Commission, Canada
Bishop Marc C.M. Stenger	Bishop of Troyes, Roman Catholic Church, France
Dr. Katrina Lantos Swett	Chair of the US Commission on International Religious Freedom, United States

Dr. Sayyid M. Syeed	National Director, Interfaith and Community, Islamic Society of North America, United States
Rabbi Elías Szczytnicki	Director, Latin American and Caribbean Religions for Peace Regional Office, Peru
Knox Thames	Special Advisor for Religious Minorities in the Near East and South/Central Asia, US Department of State, United States
Donlu Thayer	G20 Interfaith Summit Secretariat, Senior Editor, Print and Electronic Publications, International Center for Law and Religion Studies, J. Reuben Clark Law School, Brigham Young University, United States
Upolu Luma Vaai	Senior Lecturer and Department Head, Department of Theology and Ethics, Pacific Theological College, Fiji
William F. Vendley	Secretary-General of Religions for Peace International, United States
Marco Ventura	Professor, University of Siena, Italy
Canon Guy Wilkinson	Inter Religious Affair's Advisor to the Archbishop of Canterbury, United Kingdom
Rev. Jim Wallis	Founder and Editor, *Sojourners* magazine, United States
Archbishop R. Williams	Secretary-General of F8 (2005); 104th Archbishop of Canterbury, Church of England, United Kingdom
Fang Wen	Professor, Department of Sociology of Peking University, China
Deborah Wright	G20 Interfaith Summit Secretariat, Coordinator and Executive Assistant, International Center for Law and Religion Studies, J. Reuben Clark Law School, Brigham Young University, United States
Dr. Zhuo Xinping	Secretary-General of F20 (2016); President, Society of Chinese Religious Studies; Director, Institute of World Religions, Chinese, China
Prof. Xiaoyun Zheng	G20 Interfaith Summit International Organizing Committee; Deputy Director, Institute of World Religions, Chinese Academy of Social Sciences, China

References

Abu-Nimer, Mohammed, Cole Durham, Manoj Kurian, Katherine Marshall, Ulrich Nitschke, Awraham Soetendorp, and Arnhild Spence. "Engaging Religious Actors in Addressing the Famine Emergency in South Sudan, Nigeria, Somalia, and Yemen." *T20 Policy Vision* (2017). Published electronically May 10. http://www.g20-insights .org/policy_briefs/engaging-religious-actors-addressing-famine-emergency-south -sudan-nigeria-somalia-yemen/.

Achterhuis, H. *De Erfenis Van De Utopie (The Legacy of Utopia)*. Amsterdam, Netherlands: Ambo, 1998.

Adams, Brian. "History of F20 Summits." Interview by Sherrie Steiner, November 17, 2015.

Adams, Brian. Email, March 15, 2017.

Adams, Tim. "Statement by IIF President and CEO Tim Adams on the U.K. Referendum." (2016). Published electronically June 24. https://www.iif.com/press/ statement-iif-president-and-ceo-tim-adams-uk-referendum.

Affairs, Ministry of Foreign. "Summary of the Hokkaido Toyako Summit." (2008). http:// www.mofa.go.jp/policy/economy/summit/2008/news/summary.html.

Affolderbach, Martin. Email, July 15, 2010.

Aidala, Angela A. "Social Change, Gender Roles, and New Religious Movements." *Sociology of Religion* 46, no. 3 (1985): 287–314.

Aidid, Abdi, Sima Atri, Kwaku Boateng, Kate Bruce Lockhart, Carmen Celestini, Julian Dyer, Niamh Fitzgerald, Susan Hammond, Mahdi Husssein, Sara Lee, Rameez Mahmood, and Laura Correa Ochoa. "Report on Civil Society and the 2010 G8 Muskoka Summit." Toronto, Canada: The G8 Research Group. (2010).

Alexander, Nancy, and Heike Loeschmann. "The Solar System of G20: Engagement Groups." *G20 Fundamentals* 4(2016). Published electronically December 8. https:// www.boell.de/en/2016/12/08/solar-system-g20-engagement-groups.

Aligica, Paul Dragos. "Prediction, Explanation and the Epistemology of Future Studies." *Futures* 35, no. 10 (2003): 1027.

Alliance of Religions and Conservation. "Religious Leaders Remind G8 Summit That the Eco Crisis Is a Crisis of the Heart." *News Release,* Published electronically July 1, 2008 http://www.arcworld.org/news.asp?pageID=242.

Almasy, Steve, Pierre Meilham, and Jim Bittermann. "Paris Massacre: At Least 128 Die in Attacks." *CNN* (2015). Published electronically November 14. http://www.cnn .com/2015/11/13/world/paris-shooting/.

Alonso, Shantha Ready. "Summary of the COP 21 Climate Agreement." *Climate Justice and Faith*, no. 1 (2016).

Alterman, J.B., and K. Von Hippel, eds. *Understanding Islamic Charities*. Washington, DC: Center for Strategic and International Studies, 2007.

Anderson, P. *Passages from Antiquity to Feudalism*. London: New Left Books, 1974.

Annett, Anthony, Marcelo Sanchez Sorondo, Jeffrey D. Sachs, and William Vendley. "A Multi-Religious Consensus on the Ethics of Sustainable Development: Reflections of the Ethics in Action Initiative." (2017). Published electronically May 10.

Araral, Eduardo. "Ostrom, Hardin and the Commons: A Critical Appreciation and a Revisionist View." *Environmental Science and Policy* 36 (2014): 11–23.

Argyris, C., and D. Schön. *Organizational Learning: A Theory of Action Perspective*. Reading, PA: Addison-Wesley, 1978.

Armstrong, Karen. *The Great Transformation*. The Beginning of Our Religious Traditions. Toronto, Canada: Vintage Canada, 2010.

Arnold, Denis G., Kenneth E. Goodpaster, and Gary R. Weaver. "Past Trends and Future Directions in Business Ethics and Corporate Responsibility Scholarship." *Business Ethics Quarterly* 25, no. 4 (2015): v–xv.

Arrow, K.J. "Methodological Individualism and Social Knowledge." *American Economic Review* 84 (1994): 1–9.

Audi, R., and N. Wolterstorff. *Religion in the Public Square: The Place of Religious Convictions in Political Debate*. Lanham, MD: Rowman & Littlefield, 1997.

Augman, Rob. "G8-Summit Protests in Germany: Against Globalisation and Its Non-Emancipatory Responses." *Libcom.org* (2007). https://libcom.org/library/g8-summit-protests-germany-against-globalisation-its-non-emancipatory-responses-rob-augm.

Axworthy, Lloyd. *Navigating a New World*. Toronto, Canada: Vintage Canada, 2003.

Ayres, Jeffrey M. "Framing Collective Action." *Journal of World-Systems Research* 10, no. 1 (2004): 11–34.

Bader, Veit. "Religious Pluralism: Secularism or Priority for Democracy?" *Political Theory* 27 (1999): 597–633.

Bader, Veit. "Sciences, Politics, and Associative Democracy: Democratizing Science and Expertizing Democracy." *Innovation: The European Journal of Social Sciences* 27, no. 4 (2014): 420–441.

Bailey, Kenneth D. "System Entropy Analysis." *Kybernetes* 26, no. 6/7 (1997): 674.

Balanche, Fabrice. "The Worst of the Syrian Refugee Crisis Is Coming for Europe." *Business Insider* (2016). Published electronically February 16.

Banchoff, Thomas, ed. *Religious Pluralism, Globalization, and World Politics*. New York, New York: Oxford University Press, 2008.

Banchoff, Thomas, and Robert Wuthnow, eds. *Religion and the Global Politics of Human Rights*. New York, New York: Oxford University Press, 2011.

Barnett, Jon. "Security and Climate Change." *Global Environmental Change* 13 (2003): 7–17.

Barrett, Gary W., and Eugene P. Odumuch. "The Twenty-First Century: The World at Carrying Capacity." *BioScience* 50, no. 4 (2000): 363.

Baruchel, Hanae, and Steve Dasilva. "Global Civil Society Action at the 2005 G8 Gleneagles Summit." (2005).

Baum, Seth D. "The Far Future Argument for Confronting Catastrophic Threats to Humanity: Practical Significance and Alternatives." *Futures* 72 (2015): 86–96.

Baum, Seth D., and Itsuki C. Handoh. "Analysis: Integrating the Planetary Boundaries and Global Catastrophic Risk Paradigms." *Ecological Economics* 107 (2014): 13–21.

Bauman, Zygmunt. *Globalization: The Human Consequences.* New York: Columbia University Press, 1998.

Bauman, Zygmunt. *Liquid Modernity.* Cambridge: Polity Press, 2000.

Bayne, Nicholas. "The G7 Summit and the Reform of Global Institutions." 30, no. 4 (1995): 494.

Bayne, Nicholas. *Staying Together: The G8 Summit Confronts the 21st Century.* United Kingdom: Ashgate, 2005

Beam, Alex. *American Crucifixion: The Murder of Joseph Smith and the Fate of the Mormon Church.* New York, New York: Public Affairs/Perseus Books Group, 2014.

Beck, Ulrich. "Reply and Critiques." In *Reflexive Modernization: Politics, Tradition and Aesthetics in the Modern Social Order,* edited by Beck, Ulrich, Anthony Giddens and S. Lash, 174–216. Stanford, CA: Stanford University Press, 1994.

Beck, Ulrich. *What Is Globalization?* Malden, MA: Polity Press, 2000.

Beck, Ulrich. "The Cosmopolitan Society and Its Enemies." *Theory, Culture & Society* 19, no. 1–2 (2002): 17–44.

Beck, Ulrich. "Critical Theory of World Risk Society: a Cosmopolitan Vision." *Constellations* 16, no. 1 (2009a): 3–22.

Beck, Ulrich. "World Risk Society and Manufactured Uncertainties." *Iris* 1, no. 2 (2009b): 291–299.

Beck, Ulrich. "A God of One's Own." In *Religion's Capacity for Peace and Potential for Violence.* Thousand Oaks, CA: Sage, 2010.

Beck, Ulrich. "Incalculable Futures: World Risk Society and Its Social and Political Implications." *Ulrich Beck: Pioneer in Cosmopolitan Sociology & Risk Society* (2014a): 78.

Beck, Ulrich. "The Reality of Cosmopolitanism." *Ulrich Beck: Pioneer in Cosmopolitan Sociology & Risk Society* (2014b): 65.

Beck, Ulrich. "The Two Faces of Religion." *Ulrich Beck: Pioneer in Cosmopolitan Sociology & Risk Society* (2014c): 128.

Beck, Ulrich. "We Do Not Live in an Age of Cosmopolitanism but in an Age of Cosmopolitization: The 'Global Other' Is in Our Midst." In *Ulrich Beck: Pioneer in Cosmopolitan Sociology and Risk Society,* edited by Ulrich Beck, 169–187. New York, New York: Springer, 2014d.

Beck, Ulrich, and Elisabeth Beck-Gernsheim. *Individualization: Institutionalized Individualism and Its Social and Political Consequences.* London, England, 2002.

Beck, Ulrich, W. Bonss, and C. Lau. "The Theory of Reflexive Modernization: Problematic, Hypotheses and Research Programme." *Theory, Culture & Society* 20, no. 2 (2003): 1–23.

Beck, Ulrich, and Patrick Camiller. "The Truth of Others: A Cosmopolitan Approach." *Common Knowledge*, no. 3 (2004): 430.

Beck, Ulrich, and Ciaran Cronin. "The European Crisis in the Context of Cosmopolitization." *New Literary History*, no. 4 (2012): 641.

Beck, Ulrich, A. Giddens, and S. Lasch. *Reflexive Modernization: Politics, Tradition and Aesthetics in the Modern Social Order.* Stanford, CA: Stanford University Press, 1994.

Beck, Ulrich, and Edgar Grande. "Varieties of Second Modernity: The Cosmopolitan Turn in Social and Political Theory and Research." *British Journal of Sociology* 61, no. 3 (2010): 409–443.

Beck, Ulrich, and Natan Sznaider. "A Literature on Cosmopolitanism: An Overview." *British Journal of Sociology* 57, no. 1 (2006): 153–164.

Bekke, H., W. Kickert, and J. Kooiman. "Public Management and Governance." In *Public Policy and Administrative Sciences in the Netherlands*, edited by W. Kickert and F.A. van Vught, 201–218. London: Harvester-Wheatsheaf, 1995.

Bell, Daniel. *The Cultural Contradictions of Capitalism.* New York, New York: Basic Books, 1996.

Belshaw, Deryke, Robert Calderisi, and Chris Sugden. *Faith in Development: Partnership between the World Bank and the Churches of Africa.* Oxford, UK: Regnum Books, 2001.

Benhabib, Seyla. "Beyond Interventionism and Indifference: Culture, Deliberation and Pluralism." *Philosophy and Social Criticism* 31 (2005): 753–771.

Bennett, W. Lance, Chris Wells, and Deen Freelon. "Communicating Civic Engagement: Contrasting Models of Citizenship in the Youth Web Sphere." *Journal of Communication* 61, no. 5 (2011): 835–856.

Benson, Iain T. "That False Struggle between Believers and Non-Believers." *Oasis* 12, Dec. (2010).

Benton, Raymond Jr. "Business, Ethics, and the Environment: Imagining a Sustainable Future." *Business Ethics Quarterly* 18, no. 4 (2008): 567–581.

Berger, Julia. "Religious Nongovernmental Organisations." *Voluntas: International Journal of Voluntary and Nonprofit Organisations* 14, no. 1 (2003).

Berger, Peter L. *The Desecularization of the World: Resurgent Religion and World Politics.* Grand Rapids, MI: Eerdmans, 1999.

van den Bergh, Jeroen C.J.M. *Evolutionary Economics and Environmental Policy: Survival of the Greenest.* Cheltenham, UK: Edward Elgar Publishing, 2007.

Bernardini, Paola. "Dialogue between the Catholic Church and the Modern World." *Contending Modernities*, March 6, 2014. Published electronically at https://blogs

.nd.edu/contendingmodernities/2014/03/06/dialogue-between-the-catholic
-church-and-the-modern-world/.

Bernstein, Richard J. "Rethinking Responsibility." *Social Research* 61, no. 4 (1994): 833.

Berry, Evan. "Religion and Sustainability in Global Civil Society." *Worldviews: Global Religions, Culture & Ecology* 18, no. 3 (2014): 269–288.

Beyer, Peter. *Religion in the Context of Globalization.* New York: Routledge, 2013.

Beyond 2015. "Who Was Involved." http://www.beyond2015.org/participating-organisations-beyond-2015.

Beyond "Our Impact." http://www.beyond2015.org/our-impact.

Bhagwati, Jagdish N. *In Defense of Globalization.* New York: Oxford University Press, 2004.

Bhambra, Gurminder K. *Rethinking Modernity: Postcolonialism and the Sociological Imagination.* Basingstoke, England: Palgrave, 2007.

Bhambra, Gurminder K. "Historical Sociology, International Relations and Connected Histories." *Cambridge Review of International Affairs* 23, no. 1 (2010): 127–143.

Bhargava, Rajeev. *Secularism and Its Critics.* Oxford, England: Oxford University Press, 2005.

Biermann, Frank. "Planetary Boundaries and Earth System Governance: Exploring the Links." *Ecological Economics* 81 (2012): 4–9.

Black, Laura W. "Blog, Chat, Edit, Text, or Tweet? Using Online Tools to Advance Adult Civic Engagement." *New Directions for Adult and Continuing Education*, no. 135 (2012): 71–79.

Blair, Tony. "Protecting Religious Freedom Should Be a Priority for All Democracies." *The Review of Faith and International Affairs* 10, no. 3 (2012): 5–10.

Blampied, Catherine, Sara Harcourt, Isabelle de Lichtervelde, and Eloise Todd. " The Data Report 2015: Putting the Poorest First." *One,* 2015. https://www.one.org/us/policy/data-report-2015/.

Bloch, Jon P. "A Whisper toward Peace: A Theoretical Analysis of the Council for a Parliament of the World Religions." *Journal for the Scientific Study of Religion* 47, no. 4 (2008): 612–627.

Blumenberg, H. *Saekularisierung und Selbstbehauptung.* Frankfurt, Germany: Suhrkamp, 1974.

Bologh, Roslyn W. *Love or Greatness: Max Weber and Masculine Thinking-a Feminist Inquiry.* London, United Kingdom: Unwin Hyman, 1990.

Bond, Patrick. "Global Governance Campaigning and Mdgs: From Top-Down to Bottom-up Anti-Poverty Work." *Third World Quarterly* 27, no. 2 (2006): 339–354.

Bourguignon, F., A. Bénassy-Quéré, S. Dercon, A. Estache, W. Gunning, R. Kanbur, S. Klasen, S. Maxwell, J. Platteau, and A. Spadaro. "Millennium Development Goals at Midpoint: Where Do We Stand and Where Do We Need to Go?" *European Report on Development*, 2008.

Bouye, Mathilde. "6 Lessons on Sustainable Development from the High-Level Political Forum." (2016). Published electronically August 2. http://www.wri.org/print/444310.

Bradford, Becky. "Is Populism a Threat to Europe's Economies?" *BBC News*, May 26 2016.

Bratsis, Peter. "Legitimation Crisis and the Greek Explosion." 190–196, 2010.

Bratton, Kathleen A. "The Effect of Legislative Diversity on Agenda Setting: Evidence from Six State Legislatures." *American Politics Research* 30, no. 2: 115–142.

Brauch, Hans Günter. "Conceptualising the Environmental Dimension of Human Security in the Un." *International Social Science Journal* 59, no. 193 (2008): 19.

Brenner, R. "Agrarian Class Structure and Economic Development in Pre-Industrial Europe." *Past and Present* 70 (1976): 30–75.

Brett, EA. *Reconstructing Development Theory: International Inequality, Institutional Reform and Social Emancipation.* Basingstoke: Palgrave MacMillan, 2009.

Breyer, Christian, Sirkka Heinonen, and Juho Ruotsalainen. "New Consciousness: A Societal and Energetic Vision for Rebalancing Humankind within the Limits of Planet Earth." *Technological Forecasting & Social Change* (2016).

Brinkerhoff, Derick W. "State Fragility and Failure as Wicked Problems: Beyond Naming and Taming." 35, no. 2 (2014): 333–344.

Brodeur, Patrice. "From the Margins to the Centers of Power: The Increasing Relevance of the Global Interfaith Movement." *Cross Currents* 55, no. 1 (2005): 42–53.

Brolan, Claire E., Scott Lee, David Kim, and Peter S. Hill. "Back to the Future: What Would the Post-2015 Global Development Goals Look Like if We Replicated Methods Used to Construct the Millennium Development Goals?." *Globalization and Health* 10, no. 19 (2014): 1–8.

Brown, Charles S. "Anthropocentrism and Ecocentrism: The Quest for a New Worldview." *Midwest Quarterly* 36 (1995): 191–202.

Brown, Wendy. *Regulating Aversion: Tolerance in the Age of Identity and Empire.* Princeton, NJ: Princeton University Press, 2006.

Bruce, Steve. *Secularization: In Defence of an Unfashionable Theory.* Oxford, UK: Oxford University Press, 2011.

Bruce-Lockhart, Kate, Sima Atri, Mahdi Hussein, Yasmin Alabed, Carmen Celestini, Salvator Cusimano, Niamh Fitzgerald, Lindsay Hart, Alexandra Robertson, Estefania Rueda, Robyn Waler, Sarah Danuro Wang, and Mikayla Wicks. "Report on Civil Society and the 2011 G8 Deauville Summit." (2011) Toronto Canada:, The G8 Research Group.

Brundtland, Gro Harlem. "Report of the World Commission on Environment and Development: Our Common Future (Brundtland Report)." Oslo, Norway: United Nations, 1987.

Brunkhorst, Hauke. "The Legitimation Crisis of the European Union." *Constellations: An International Journal of Critical and Democratic Theory* 13, no. 2 (2006): 165–180.

Buchanan, A., and R. Keohane. "The Legitimacy of Global Governance Institutions." *Ethics and International Affairs* 20 (2006): 405–437.

Buchanan, A., and R. Keohane. "The Legitimacy of Global Governance." In *Human Rights, Legitimacy, and the Use of Force*, edited by A. Buchanan, 105–133. Oxford, UK: Oxford University Press, 2010.

Burns, James MacGregor. *Leadership*. New York: Harper and Row, 1978.

Burrow, Sharan, Mike Callaghan, Tim Costello, Robert Milliner, Holly Ransom, and Heather Smith. "G20 2014: Perspectives from Business, Civil Society, Labour, Think Tanks and Youth." *G20 Monitor* 9, March (2014).

Bush, Michael. "2016 Edelman Trust Barometer Finds Global Trust Inequality is Growing." *News Release*, 2016, http://www.edelman.com/news/2016-edelman-trust -barometer-release/.

Butler, Judith, Jürgen Habermas, Charles Taylor, and Cornel West. *The Power of Religion in the Public Sphere*. New York, NY: Columbia University Press, 2011.

Buzan, Barry, and Richard Little. *International Systems in World History*. Oxford, England: Oxford University Press, 2001.

Buzan, Barry, and Richard Little. "International Systems in World History: Remaking the Study of IR." In *Historical Sociology of International Relations*, edited by Stephen Hobden and John M. Hobson, 200–220. Cambridge, England: Cambridge University Press, 2002.

Bwalya, Kelvin Joseph, and Stephen Mutula. *Digital Solutions for Contemporary Democracy and Government*. Hershey, PA: ICI Global, 2015.

Cahill, Desmond. "The Role of Religious Leaders in the Protection of Vulnerable Groups in the Context of 21st Century Asia." In *Dialogue among Civilizations and Human Destiny Community CASS Forum*. Beijing, China, 2016.

Caldecott, B., and J. McDaniels. "Stranded Generation Assets: Implications for European Capacity Mechanisms, Energy Markets and Climate Policy." (2014).

Callaghan, Mike, Colin Bradford, Barry Carin, David Skilling, and Mark Thirlwell. "Challenges Facing the G20 in 2013." *G20 Monitor* 1, Dec. (2012).

Calo, Zachary R. "Higher Law Secularism: Religious Symbols, Contested Secularisms, and the Limits of the Establishment Clause." *Chicago-Kent Law Review* 87, no. 3 (2012): 811–831.

Calo, Zachary R. "Law in the Secular Age." *European Political Science* 13, no. 3 (2014): 306.

Campbell, C. "The Romantic Ethic and the Spirit of Modern Consumerism." New York: Basil Blackwell, 1987.

Campbell, Katie. "G8 Accountability Report a Big Step Forward for Transparency, but Underscores Unfinished Agenda on Global Hunger." *ActionAid* (2012). Published electronically May 22. https://www.interaction.org/document/g8-accountability -report-big-step-forward-transparency-underscores-unfinished-agenda-global.

Campbell, Joel R., Leena Thacker Kumar, and Steve Slagle. "Bargaining Sovereignty: State Power and Networked Governance in a Globalizing World." *International Social Science Review* 85, no. 3/4 (2010): 107.

Canada, G8. "Muskoka Accountability Report." (2010). http://www.g8.utoronto.ca/summit/2010muskoka/accountability/.

Canadian Council of Churches. "2010 Religious Leaders Summit High Level Financial Budget." 2009.

Canadian Interfaith Conversation. "Charter Vision." http://www.councilofchurches.ca/wp-content/uploads/2013/11/The-Canadian-Interfaith-Conversation-January-2013-Final.pdf.

Canadian Interfaith Conversation. "Doha International Award." (2013). http://www.interfaithconversation.ca/documents-and-responses.

Carrette, Jeremy, and Richard King. *Selling Spirituality: The Silent Takeover of Religion.* New York: Routledge, 2005.

Carrette, Jeremy, and Hugh Miall, eds. *Religious NGOs and the United Nations in New York and Geneva.* Canterbury, United Kingdom: University of Kent, 2013.

Cartlidge, Edwin. "Updated: Appeals Court Overturns Manslaughter Convictions of Six." *Sciencemag.org* (2014). Published electronically Nov. 10. http://www.sciencemag.org/news/2014/11/updated-appeals-court-overturns-manslaughter-convictions-six-earthquake-scientists.

Casanova, J. *Public Religions in the Modern World.* Chicago, IL: Chicago University Press, 1994.

Castells, M. *The Power of Identity.* Cambridge, MA: Blackwell, 1997.

Castilla, Juan Carlos. "Tragedia De Los Recursos De Uso Comun Y Etica Ambiental Individual Responsible Frente Al Calentamiento Global." *Tragedy of the Common Pool Resources and Environmental Ethics Individually Liable to Global Warming* 21, no. 1 (2015): 65–71.

Catton, William R. *Overshoot.* Urbana, Illinois: University of Illinois Press, 1980.

Cesari, J. *Muslims in the West after 9/11: Religion, Politics and Law.* London, England: Routledge, 2010.

Cesari, Jocelyne. "Religion and Politics: What Does God Have to Do with It?" *Religions* 6, no. 4 (2015): 1330.

Chang, Pauline J. "Ecumenical Forum: Poverty is the New Slavery and Silent Tsunami." (2005). *Christian Post.* Published electronically June 30. http://www.christianpost.com/news/ecumenical-forum-poverty-is-the-new-slavery-and-silent-tsunami-3703/.

Chang, K.S., and M.Y. Song. "The Stranded Individualizer under Compressed Modernity: South Korean Women in Individualization without Individualism." *British Journal of Sociology* 61, no. 3 (2010): 540–565.

Chesnokova, Irina. "The Addressee Types of the Internet Open Letters." *Procedia—Social and Behavioral Sciences* 206 (2015): 14–17.

Christie, James. "How Well Does the G8 Deliver: Compliance with G8 Commitments." Tokyo, Japan, 2008.

Christie, James. "In Sundry Places: The Domestic Impact of the F8/F20 International Interfaith Summit Process." In *Dialogue among Civilizations and Human Destiny Community CASS Forum.* Beijing, China, 2016.

Christie, James. Email, June 21, 2016.

Christie, James. Email, July 20, 2016.

Christie, James. Email, May 27, 2016.

Christie, James, and Karen Hamilton, Email exchange, August 2009.

CIGI. "UNU Conference: Expansion, Outreach or Status Quo?" Published electronically July 1, 2008.

Clarke, G. "Faith Matters." *Journal of International Development* 18, no. 6 (2006): 836.

Clarke, G., and M. Jennings. *Development, Civil Society, and Faith-Based Organizations.* London, UK: Palgrave Macmillan, 2008.

Clemens, Michael A., Charles J. Kenny, and Todd J. Moss. "The Trouble with the MDGs: Confronting Expectations of Aid and Development Success." *World Development* 35, no. 5 (2004): 735–751.

Clozel, Lalita. "U.S. Banking Regulators Concerned About Brexit: Report." *American Banker* 181, no. 76 (2016): 1.

Cohen, Raymond. "Putting Diplomatic Studies on the Map." *Diplomatic Studies Programme Newsletter*, 1998.

Cohen, Tamara. "G8 Becomes the G7 as Leaders Kick Russia Out: It's Not a Big Problem, Says Putin's Foreign Minister." *Daily Mail* (2014). Published electronically March 24. http://www.dailymail.co.uk/news/article-2588490/G8-G7-leaders-kick-Russia-Its-not-big-problem-says-Putins-foreign-minister.html.

Connolly, William E. *Why I Am Not a Secularist.* Minneapolis, MN: University of Minnesota Press, 2007.

Considine, M. "The End of the Line? Accountable Governance in the Age of Networks, Partnerships, and Joined-up Services." *Governance* 15 (2002): 21–40.

Costanza, Robert. "Ecosystem Health and Ecological Engineering."*Ecological Engineering* 45 (2012): 24–29.

Cozette, Muriel. "Reclaiming the Critical Dimension of Realism: Hans J. Morgenthau and the Ethics of Scholarship." *Review of International Studies* 34, no. 1 (2008): 5–27.

Cramer, C. "Homo Economicus Goes to War: Methodological Individualism, Rational Choice and the Political Economy of War." *World Development* 30 (2002): 1845–1864.

Crow, Deserai, and Maxwell Boykoff. *Culture, Politics and Climate Change: How Information Shapes Our Common Future.* New York, New York: Routledge/Earthscan, 2014.

Crowley, Thomas J., and Gerald R. North. "Abrupt Climate Change and Extinction Events in Earth History." 1988, 996.

Dadush, Uri, and William Shaw. *Juggernaut: How Emerging Markets Are Reshaping Globalization.* Washington D.C.: Carnegie Endowment for International Peace.

Dafoe, Joanna, and Miranda Lin. "The Choreography of Resistance: Civil Society Action at the 2007 G8 Summit." (2007). http://www.g8.utoronto.ca/evaluations/csed/index.html.

Daly, Herman E. *Steady-State Economics.* San Francisco: W.H. Freeman, 1977.

Damphouse, Julia. "Storming the Stage: An Interview with Emily Laquer." (2017). Published electronically June 16. https://jacobinmag.com/2017/06/g20-summit-protests-eu-globalization-neoliberalism.

Danan, Liora. "A Public Diplomacy Approach to International Religious Freedom." *The Review of Faith and International Affairs* 10, no. 3 (2012): 59–66.

Danspeckgruber, Wolfgang. "A Plea to Free Archbishop Mar Gregorios Yohanna Ibrahim and Archbishop Boulos Yazigi Who Were Kidnapped One Year Ago Today." Huffington Post (2014). Published electronically April 21 http://www.huffingtonpost.com/wolfgang-danspeckgruber/archbishop-mar-gregorios-yohanna-ibrahim-and-archbishop-boulos-yazigi-_b_5186945.html.

Darrow, M. "The Millennium Development Goals: Milestones or Millstones? Human Rights Priorities for the Post-2015 Development Agenda." *Human Rights Development Law Journal* 15 (2012): 55–127.

Davids, Nuraan. "Muslim Women and the Politics of Religious Identity in a (Post) Secular Society." *Studies in Philosophy & Education* 33, no. 3 (2014): 303–313.

Day, Neil. Letter, August 6, 2008.

Deneulin, Severine, and Carole Rakodi. "Religion and the Transformation of Development Studies: Re-Assessing the Relationship between Religion and Development." *World Development* 39, no. 1 (2011): 45–54.

Dennis, Della. "Idealism to Realism: Applying Ecological Science to Society's Environmental Problems: The Sustainable Biosphere Initiative Project Office Creates Implementation Plan." 1992, 219.

DesJardins, Joseph. "Is It Time to Jump Off the Sustainability Bandwagon?" *Business Ethics Quarterly* 26, no. 1 (2016): 117–135.

Development, World Commission on Environment and. *Our Common Future.* Oxford Paperbacks. New York: Oxford University Press., 1987.

Dewey, Joseph. "Our Common Future." Salem Press, 2015.

DeZeeuw, Aart. "Regime Shifts in Resource Management." *Annual Review of Resource Management* 6 (2014):85–104;

Diamond, Jared. *Collapse: How Societies Choose to Fail or Succeed.* Viking, 2004.

Diamond, Miriam L., Cynthia A. de Wit, Sverker Molander, Martin Scheringer, Thomas Backhaus, Rainer Lohmann, Rickard Arvidsson, et al. "Review: Exploring the

Planetary Boundary for Chemical Pollution." *Environment International* 78 (2015): 8–15.

Dickinson, G. Lowes, and Susan Sered. "Prologue: Negotiating Women's Roles and Power in the Practice of World Religions in Contemporary Asia." *Religion* 37, no. 2 (2007): 111–116.

Diehl, Amy B., and Leanne M. Dzubinski. "Making the Invisible Visible: A Cross-Sector Analysis of Gender-Based Leadership Barriers." *Human Resource Development Quarterly* 27, no. 2 (2016): 181–206.

Dietz, Thomas, "Drivers of Human Stress on the Environment in the Twenty-First Century," *Annual Review of Environment and Resources,* 42 (2017):189–213.

Djupe, Paul A. "The Effects of Descriptive Associational Leadership on Civic Engagement: The Case of Clergy and Gender in Protestant Denominations." *Journal for the Scientific Study of Religion* 53, no. 3 (2014): 497.

Dobb, M. *Studies in the Development of Capitalism.* London: Routledge and Kegan Pauul, 1963. 1947.

Donati, Pierpaolo. "Social Capital and Associative Democracy: A Relational Perspective." *Journal for the Theory of Social Behaviour* 44, no. 1 (2014): 24–45.

Dondelinger, Joseph M. "Cultural Contradictions of Soft Power and Islam." *Journal of Interdisciplinary Studies* 20 (2008): 37.

Doyle, W. *Origins of the French Revolution.* New York: Oxford University Press, 1980.

Druskat, Vannessa Urch. "Gender and Leadership Style: Transformational and Transactional Leadership in the Roman Catholic Church." *Leadership Quarterly* 5, no. 2 (1994): 99–119.

Duerbeck, Gabriele, Caroline Schaumann, and Heather Sullivan. "Human and Non-Human Agencies in the Anthropocene." *Ecozon@2015*, no. 1 (2015): 118–136.

Durham, Cole. Email, March 15, 2017.

Easterly, W. "How the Millennium Development Goals are Unfair to Africa." *World Development* 37, no. 1 (2009): 26–30.

Eberle, C.J. *Religious Conviction in Liberal Politics.* Cambridge, MA: Cambridge University Press, 2002.

Eck, Diana. *Encountering God: A Spiritual Journey from Bozeman to Banaras.* Boston: Beacon Press, 2003.

Eck, Diana. "What Is Pluralism?" (2006). Published electronically http://pluralism.org/what-is-pluralism/.

Edelman, Dan. "2012 Edelman Trust Barometer Global Results." Published electronically https://www.edelman.com, 2012.

Edge, Peter. "Law, State and Religion in the New Europe: Debates and Dilemmas." *Journal of Church and State* 55, no. 3 (2013): 1–2.

Ehrenfeld, David. "Globalisation: Effects on Biodiversity, Environment and Society." *Conservation & Society* 1, no. 1 (2003): 99.

Ehrlich, P.R., and A.H. Ehrlich. "Can a Collapse of Global Civilization Be Avoided?" *Proceedings of the Royal Society B: Biological Sciences* 280, no. 1754 (2013): 1–9.

Ellis, Luci, Andy Haldane, and Fariborz Moshirian. "Systemic Risk, Governance and Global Financial Stability." *Journal of Banking and Finance* 45 (2014): 175–181.

Emmeche, Claus. "Bioinvasion, Globalization, and the Contingency of Cultural and Biological Diversity: Some Ecosemiotic Observations." *Sign Systems Studies* 29, no. 1 (2001): 237.

Ethiraj, Sendil K., and Daniel Levinthal. "Bounded Rationality and the Search for Organizational Architecture: An Evolutionary Perspective on the Design of Organizations and Their Evolvability." *Administrative Science Quarterly* 49, no. 3 (2004): 404–437.

Evans, Malcolm. "Introductory Overview." In Article 18: An Orphaned Right, edited by Evans, Malcolm and Kay Carter Washington, D.C.: All Party Parliamentary Group on International Religious Freedom or Belief, 2013. Published electronically https://freedomdeclared.org/media/Article-18-An-Orphaned-Right.pdf.

F7-Germany. "Interreligious Youth Forum on Sustainable Development." (2015). Published electronically https://www.change.org/p/g7-political-leadership-world-religious-leaders-socially-and-politically-engaged-youth-implement-universal-sustainable-development-goals?recruiter=258670861&utm_source=share_petition&utm_medium=email&utm_campaign=share_email_responsive.

F8-Canada. "A Time for Inspired Leadership and Action." (2010). Published electronically http://www.g8.utoronto.ca/interfaith/.

F8-France. "Statement of the Bordeaux Religious Leaders Summit." (2011). Published electronically http://www.g8.utoronto.ca/interfaith/.

F8-Germany. "Just Participation: A Call from Cologne." (2007). Published electronically http://www.g8.utoronto.ca/interfaith/.

F8-Italy. "Iv Summit of Religious Leaders on the Occasion of the G8." (2009). Published electronically http://www.g8.utoronto.ca/interfaith/.

F8-Japan/Kyoto-Osaka. "A Proposal from People of Religion." (2008). Published electronically http://www.g8.utoronto.ca/interfaith/.

F8-Japan/Sapporo. "Call from Sapporo-World Religious Leaders Summit for Peace." (2008). Published electronically http://www.g8.utoronto.ca/interfaith/.

F8-Russia. "World Summit of Religious Leaders." (2006). Published electronically http://www.g8.utoronto.ca/interfaith/.

F8-United Kingdom. "Action on Poverty Needed Now." (2005). Published electronically http://www.g8.utoronto.ca/interfaith/.

F8-United Kingdom. "UK Can Lead G8 in Striking at Causes of Poverty, Say Religious Leaders." (2013). Published electronically http://www.archbishopofcanterbury.org/articles.php/5045/archbishop-joins-call-on-g8-to-strike-at-causes-of-poverty.

F8-United States. "Religious Leaders' Statement for the G8 and G20 Summits." (2012). Published electronically http://www.g8.utoronto.ca/interfaith/.

F20-Australia. "Statement from the G20 Interfaith Summit 2014." (2014). Published electronically November 18. http://www.g20interfaith.org/sites/default/files/2014-interfaith-summit/Consensus-Statement.pdf.

F20-China. "Conference Statement: G20 Interfaith Summit Pacific Regional Preconference." (2016).

Fairclough, Noram, Giuseppina Cortese, and Pratizia Ardizzone. *Discourse and Contemporary Social Change.* Linguistic Insights 54: Studies in Language and Communication. Bern, Switzerland: Peter Lange, 2007.

Faist, Thomas. "The Crucial Meso-Level." In *Selected Studies in International Migration and Immigrant Incorporation*, edited by Martinello, Marco and Jan Rath, 59–90. Amsterdam: Amsterdam University Press, 2009.

Falk, Richard. *Religion and Humane Global Governance.* New York, New York: Palgrave, 2001.

Fang, K., R. Heijungs, and G.R. De Snoo. "Understanding the Complementary Linkages between Environmental Footprints and Planetary Boundaries in a Footprint-Boundary Environmental Sustainability Assessment Framework." *Ecological Economics* 114 (2015): 218–226.

Farrugia, D. "Addressing the Problem of Reflexivity in Theories of Reflexive Modernisation: Subjectivity and Structural Contradiction." *Journal of Sociology* 51, no. 4 (2015): 872–886.

Feindt, P.H. "Reflexive Governance and Multilevel Decision Making in Agricultural Policy: Conceptual Reflections and Empirical Evidence." In *Reflexive Governance for Global Public Goods*, edited by Bronsseau, E., T. Dedeurwaerdere and B. Siebenhuener, 159–178. Cambridge, MA: The MIT Press, 2012.

Fernández-Llamazares, Álvaro, Isabel Díaz-Reviriego, Ana C. Luz, Mar Cabeza, Aili Pyhälä, and Victoria Reyes-García. "Rapid Ecosystem Change Challenges the Adaptive Capacity of Local Environmental Knowledge." *Global Environmental Change Part A: Human & Policy Dimensions* 31 (2015): 272–284.

Findlay, Allan M. "Migrant Destinations in an Era of Environmental Change." *Global Environmental Change Part A: Human & Policy Dimensions* 21 (2011): S50–S58.

Finke, Roger. "Religious Deregulation: Origins and Consequences." *Journal of Church and State* 32, no. 3 (1990): 609–626.

Flores, J.C. "A Phase-Transition Model for the Rise and Collapse of Ancient Civilizations: A Pre-Ceramic Andean Case Study." *Physica A: Statistical Mechanics and its Applications* 440 (2015): 155–160.

Foley, Jonathan. "Boundaries for a Healthy Planet." *Scientific American* 302, no. 4 (2010): 54–57.

Folke, Carl, Steve Carpenter, Brian Walker, Marten Scheffer, Thomas Elmqvist, Lance
   Gunderson, and C.S. Holling. "Regime Shifts, Resilience, and Biodiversity in Ecosystem Management." *Annual Review of Ecology, Evolution, and Systematics* 35 (2004):
   557–581.

Folke, Carl, Åsa Jansson, Johan Rockström, Per Olsson, Stephen Carpenter, F. III,
   Anne-Sophie Stuart Chapin, Gretchen Daily, Kjell Danell, Jonas Ebbesson, Thomas
   Elmqvist, Victor Galaz, Fredrik Moberg, Måns Nilsson, Henrik Österblom, Elinor
   Ostrom, Åsa Persson, Garry Peterson, Stephen Polasky, Will Steffen, Brian Walker,
   and Westley, Frances Crépin. "Reconnecting to the Biosphere." AMBIO: A Journal of
   the Human *Environment* 40, no. 7 (2011): 719–738.

Foucault, Michael. "Governmentality." *Ideology and Consciousness* 6 (1979): 5–21.

Fowler, Charles W. "Maximizing Biodiversity, Information and Sustainability." *Biodiversity & Conservation* 17, no. 4 (2008): 841.

Fox, Jonathan. "Integrating Religion into International Relations Theory." In *Routledge
   Handbook of Religion and Politics*, edited by Jeffrey Haynes, 273–292. New York, New
   York: Routledge, 2009.

Fox, Jonathan. "Religion and State Failure: An Examination of the Extent and Magnitude of Religious Conflict from 1950 to 1996." *International Political Science Review/
   Revue Internationale de Science Politique* 25, no. 1 (2010): 55–76.

Fox, Jonathan, and Shmuel Sandler. *Bringing Religion into International Relations.* Culture and Religion in International Relations. 1st ed, New York: Palgrave Macmillan,
   2004.

Freese, Lee. *Environmental Connections.* Greenwich, Connecticut: JAI Press, 1997a.

Freese, Lee. *Evolutionary Connections.* Greenwich, Connecticut: JAI Press, 1997b.

Freese, Lee. "Evolution and Sociogenesis: Parts I & II." In *Advances in Group Processes*,
   edited by Lawler, E.J. and B. Markovsky, 53–118. Greenwich, CT: JAI Press, 1988.

Freese, Lee, and Jane Sell. "Constructing Axiomatic Theories in Sociology." In *Theoretical Methods in Sociology: Seven Essays*, edited by Freese Lee, 3329–3330. Pittsburgh,
   PA: University of Pittsburgh Press, 1980.

Friedman, Uri. "Russia's Slow-Motion Invasion of Ukraine." *The Atlantic*, August 29,
   2014.

Fukudo-Parr, Sakiko. "Millennium Development Goals: Why They Matter." *Global
   Governance* 10 (2004): 395–402.

Fukudo-Parr, Sakiko, J. Greenstein, and D. Stewart. "How Should MDG Success Be
   Judged: Faster Progress or Achieving the Targets?" *World Development* 41, July (2013):
   19–30.

Fuller, Sylvia, and John Levi Martin. "Women's Status in Eastern NRMs." *Review of Religious Research* 44, no. 4 (2003): 354–369.

G8. "G8 Accountability Tool." Published electronically http://78.41.128.109/images//
   Holding_G8_Accountability_to_Account.pdf.

G20-China. "Equal Participation, Innovative Development: 2016 W20 Meeting Highlights 'She Power' to the World." (2016). Published electronically June 28. http://www.g20.org/English/G20Priorities/Engagement/201606/t20160628_2345.html.

Gallego-Álvarez, Isabel, Mª Galindo-Villardón, and Miguel Rodríguez-Rosa. "Analysis of the Sustainable Society Index Worldwide: A Study from the Biplot Perspective." *Social Indicators Research* 120, no. 1 (2015): 29.

Gasagara, Elie. "Accountability." *World Vision International Accountability Report 2014* (2014). Published electronically http://www.wvi.org/accountability/publication/2014-accountability-report.

Gaziulusoy, A.I., C.A. Boyle, and R. McDowall. "A Conceptual Systemic Framework Proposal for Sustainable Technology Development: Incorporating Future Studies within a Co-Evolutionary Approach." *Civil Engineering & Environmental Systems* 25, no. 4 (2008): 301–311.

Georgescu-Roegen, Nicholas. *The Entropy Law and the Economic Process.* Cambridge, MA: Harvard University Press, 1971.

Georgescu-Roegen, Nicholas. *Energy and Economic Myths.* New York, New York: Pergamon, 1976.

Gerring, John. "Global Justice as an Empirical Question." *PS: Political Science & Politics* 40, no. 1 (2007): 67–77.

Giddens, Anthony. *Runaway World: How Globalization is Reshaping Our Lives.* New York: Routledge, 2003.

Glenn, John. "Global Governance and the Democratic Deficit: Stifling the Voice of the South." 2008, 217.

Global Financial Integrity. "Illicit Financial Flows 2004–2013." (2013). Published electronically http://www.gfintegrity.org/issue/illicit-financial-flows/.

Gold, Jennifer. "Religious Leaders in Peace Call to G8 Leaders." *Christian Today* (2008). Published electronically July 5.

Gold, L. "Are the Millennium Development Goals Addressing the Underlying Causes of Injustice? Understanding the Risks of the MDGs." *Trocaire Development Report* (2005): 23–41.

Gorski, Philip S., and Gülay Türkmen-Dervişoğlu. "Religion, Nationalism, and Violence: An Integrated Approach." *Annual Reviews* 39 (2013): 193–210.

Grant, Kelly. "Paul Martin." *Globe and Mail*, May 31, 2010.

Grant, R.W., and R. Keohane. "Accountability and Abuses of Power in World Politics." *American Political Science Review* 99 (2005): 29–43.

Gray, J. *Black Mass: Apocalyptic Religion and the Death of Utopia.* New York, New York: Farrar, Straux, Giroux, 2007.

Greenawalt, K. *Private Consciences and Public Reasons.* New York, New York: Oxford University Press, 1995.

Grier, Peter. "The Year of Disruption." *The Christian Science Monitor*, December 24, 2016.

Grim, Brian, and Roger Finke. *The Price of Freedom Denied: Religious Persecution and Conflict in the Twenty-First Century.* Cambridge, MA: Cambridge University Press, 2010.

Grim, Brian J., and Jo-Anne Lyon. "G20 Interfaith Summit, Paris Terror and How Religious Freedom Benefits Women." (2015).

Gruending, Dennis. "Justice Tour 2015: Churches Focus on Climate Change and Ending Poverty." (2015). Published electronically May 10. http://rabble.ca/print/blogs/bloggers/dennis-gruending/2015/05/justice-tour-2015-churches-focuses-on-climate-change-and-end.

Grugel, Jean, and Nicola Piper. *Critical Perspectives on Global Governance: Rights and Regulations in Governing Regimes.* New York, New York: Routledge, 2007.

Gual, Miguel A., and Richard B. Norgaard. "Bridging Ecological and Social Systems Coevolution: A Review and Proposal." *Ecological Economics* 69 (2010): 707–717.

Guinane, K. "Muslim Charities and the War on Terror." (2006). Published electronically http://foreffectivegov.org/files/pdfs/muslim_charities.pdf.

Gumrukcu, Selin Bengi. "The Rise of a Social Movement: The Emergence of Anti-Globalization Movements in Turkey." *Turkish Studies* 11, no. 2 (2010): 163–180.

Gupta, A. "Transparency under Scrutiny: Information Disclosure in Global Environmental Governance." *Global Environmental Politics* 8 (2008): 1–7.

Gutterman, David S., and Andrew R. Murphy. *Political Religion and Religious Politics: Navigating Identities in the United States.* Routledge Series on Identity Politics. New York, New York: Routledge, 2016.

Gyapong, Deborah. "Canadian Bishops Pull out of Interfaith Group." *Catholic Register* (2012). Published electronically March 15. http://www.catholicregister.org/item/14064-canadian-bishops-pull-out-of-interfaith-group.

Habermas, Jürgen. *Legitimation Crisis.* Translated by McCarthy, Thomas. Beacon Press, 1975.

Habermas, Jürgen. *Future of Human Nature.* London, UK: Polity Press, 2003.

Habermas, Jürgen. "Religion in the Public Sphere." *European Journal of Philosophy* 14, no. 1 (2006): 1–25.

Habermas, Jürgen, Joseph Ratzinger, and Florian Schuller. *The Dialectics of Secularization: On Reason and Religion.* Freiberg, Germany: Herder Verlag, 2005.

Habib, M. "Globalization and Literature." *Language in India* 15, no. 9 (2015): 14–21.

Hajnal, Peter. *The G7/G8 System: Evolution, Role and Documentation.* Brookfield, Vermont: Ashgate Publishing Company, 1999.

Hajnal, Peter. "The 2006 St. Petersburg Summit and Civil Society." (2006). Published electronically http://www.g8.utoronto.ca/scholar/hajnal_061202.html.

Hajnal, Peter. "Civil Society and the 2008 G8 Hokkaido Summit." (2008). Published electronically http://www.g8.utoronto.ca/evaluations/2008hokkaido/2008-hajnal.html.

Hajnal, Peter. "Civil Society at the 2009 G8 Summit in L'Aquila." (2009). Published electronically November 10. http://www.g8.utoronto.ca/evaluations/2009laquila/2009 -hajnal.html.

Hajnal, Peter. "Head to Head: Summits in Canada in June 2010: The Muskoka G8 Meets the Toronto G20." *Academic Council on the United Nations System* 83, Summer (2010a).

Hajnal, Peter. "The World Religions Summit 2010—Interfaith Leaders in the G8 Nations: Notes of an Observer." (2010b). Published electronically http://www.g8.utoronto.ca/ evaluations/2010muskoka/hajnal-faith.html.

Hajnal, Peter. "The G20." In *Evolution, Interrelationships, Documentation*, 311. Burlington, VT: Ashgate, 2014.

Hajnal, Peter I., and Jenilee M. Guebert. "A Civil Society." In *G8 the Italian Summit 2009: From La Maddalena to L'Aquila*, edited by John Kirton, 186–187. Toronto, Canada: Newsdesk Communications Ltd., 2009.

Halafoff, Anna. "Netpeace and the Cosmopolitan Condition: Multifaith Movements and the Politics of Understanding." *Political Theology* 11, no. 5 (2010): 717–737.

Halafoff, Anna. "The Multifaith Movement." In *Global Risks and Cosmopolitan Solutions*, 181. New York: Springer, 2013.

Haluza-DeLay, Randolph. "Religion and Climate Change: Varieties and Viewpoints and Practices." *WIRES Climate Change* 5, March/April (2014): 261–279.

Hamilton, Karen. "A Few Comments from Karen's Participation in the G8 Religious Leaders' Conference June 5–7, 2007—Koln, Germany." Toronto, Canada: Canadian Council of Churches, 2007.

Hamilton, Karen. "For Just Such a Time as This: Reflections on the Statement 'Translating Shared Concerns into Action.'" Sapporo, Japan, 2008.

Hamilton, Karen. "Inspired Leadership: Civil Society's Contribution to G8 and G20 Summitry." In *G8/G20 the 2010 Canadian Summits: Recovery and New Beginnings*, edited by Kirton, John and Madeline Koch, 308. Toronto, Canada: Newsdesk Media, 2010.

Hamilton, Karen. "UN High Panel on the Millennium Development Goals," *Canadian Council of Churches* (2012a). Published electronically December 6 https://www .councilofchurches.ca/whats-new/un-high-panel-on-the-millennium-development -goals/.

Hamilton, Karen. "Research on the World Summit(s) of Religious Leaders: Karen Hamilton." Interview by Sherrie Steiner (October 2012b).

Hamilton, Karen. "The Open Spiral: The Ongoing Commitments of Faith Leaders." In *G8 the Camp David Summit: The Road to Recovery*, edited by Kirton, John and Madeline Koch, 220–221. Toronto, Canada: Newsdesk Media Group, 2012c.

Hamilton, Karen. "After 13 Years, the Millennium Development Goals Are Still Pertinent." In *G8 the UK Summit Lough Erne: Helping Global Trade to Take Off*, edited by

Kirton, John, Madeline Koch and Nicholas Bayne, 234–235. London, UK: Newsdesk Media, 2013a.

Hamilton, Karen. "Faith in Sustainability: How Faith Communities Have Helped Move the Discussion around Sustainability Forward." *Open Canada.Org* (2013b). Published electronically February 4.

Hamilton, Karen. Email, June 6, 2013.

Hamilton, Karen. "Keeping the Faith: Still Focused on Goals." In *G7 the Brussels Summit: Strengthening the Global Network*, edited by Kirton, John and Madeline Koch, 112–113. London, UK: Newsdesk Media, 2014.

Hamilton, Karen. "The Global Agenda from an Interfaith Perspective." In *G7 Germany: The Schloss Elmau Summit*, edited by Kirton, John and Madeline Koch, 134–135. London, UK: Newsdesk Media, 2015.

Hamilton, Karen. "To Boldly Go: Innovations Originating through the F8 Canadian Interfaith Leaders Summit Which Strengthen Human Destiny and Community." Unpublished paper, 2016.

Hamilton, Karen. *Logo*. Email, 2016.

Hamilton, Karen. Email, June 15, 2017.

Hamilton, Karen, and Brian Adams. "Inspiring Leadership and Action for Development." G20 Turkey: The Antalya Summit, edited by Kirton, John and Madeline Koch, 194–195. London, UK: Newsdesk Media, 2015.

Hanf, M., A. Van-Melle, F. Fraisse, A. Roger, B. Carme, and M. Nacher. "Corruption Kills: Estimating the Global Impact of Corruption on Children Deaths." *Plos One* 6, no. 11 (2011): e26990.

Harmon, James A., and Andrew Steer. "Letter from the Chairman & President." *Pivotal Year: WRI 2015 Annual Report* (2016). Published electronically http://www.wri.org/annualreport/2015/welcome/letter-from-the-chairman-president/.

Harrison, Paul. "Towards a Post-Malthusian Human Ecology." *Human Ecology Review* 1, no. 2 (1994): 265–276.

Hassan, Abul. "Islamic Ethical Responsibilities for Business and Sustainable Development." *Humanomics* 32, no. 1 (2016): 80.

Häyhä, Tiina, Paul L. Lucas, Detlef P. van Vuuren, Sarah E. Cornell, and Holger Hoff. "From Planetary Boundaries to National Fair Shares of the Global Safe Operating Space—How Can the Scales Be Bridged?." *Global Environmental Change* (2016).

Haynes, Jeffrey. *Religion in Third World Politics*. Buckingham, England: Open University Press, 1993.

Haynes, Jeffrey. *Religion in Global Politics*. London, England: Longman, 1998.

Haynes, Jeffrey. "Transnational Religious Actors and International Politics." *Third World Quarterly* 22, no. 2 (2001): 143–158.

Haynes, Jeffrey. "Religion and International Relations in the 21st Century: Conflict or Co-Operation?" *Third World Quarterly* 27, no. 3 (2006): 535.

Haynes, Jeffrey. *Religion and Development: Conflict or Cooperation?* Basingstoke, England: Palgrave Macmillan, 2007.

Haynes, Jeffrey. "Religion and Foreign Policy Making in the USA, India and Iran: Towards a Research Agenda." *Third World Quarterly* 29, no. 1 (2008): 143–165.

Haynes, Jeffrey. "Religion and Foreign Policy." In *Routledge Handbook of Religion and Politics*, edited by Haynes, Jeffrey, 293–307. New York, New York: Routledge, 2009a.

Haynes, Jeffrey. "Transnational Religious Actors and International Order." *Perspectives: Central European Review of International Affairs* 17, no. 2 (2009b): 43–69.

Haynes, Jeffrey. *Religious Transnational Actors and Soft Power.* Surrey, England: Ashgate Publishers, 2012.

Hayward, Susan, and Katherine Marshall. *Women, Religion and Peacebuilding.* Washington, D.C.: United States Institute of Peace Press, 2015.

Hedley, R. Alan. *Running out of Control: Dilemmas of Globalization.* Bloomfield, CN: Kumarian Press, 2002.

Heferen, T. "Finding Faith in Development." *Anthropological Quarterly* 80, no. 3 (2007): 888.

Hefner, Robert. *Civil Islam: Muslims and Democratization in Indonesia.* Princeton, NJ: Princeton University Press, 2000.

Hegre, H., J. Karlesen, H. Nygard, H. Strand, and H. Urdal. "Predicting Armed Conflict." *International Studies Quarterly* 57, no. 2 (2013): 250–270.

Heise, Arne. "Governance without Government." *International Journal of Political Economy* 41, no. 2 (2012): 42–60.

Hew Wai, Weng. "Beyond 'Chinese Diaspora' and 'Islamic Ummah': Various Transnational Connections and Local Negotiations of Chinese Muslim Identities in Indonesia." *SOJOURN: Journal of Social Issues in Southeast Asia* 29, no. 3 (2014): 627–656.

Hewson, Paul David. "Transcript: Bono Remarks at the National Prayer Breakfast." *USA Today*, February 2 2006.

Hill, Peter s., Kent Buse, Claire E. Brolan, and Gorik Ooms. "How Can Health Remain Central Post-2015 in a Sustainable Development Paradigm." *Globalization and Health* 10, no. 18 (2014): 1–5.

Hilton, R. *Bond Men Made Free, Medieval Peasant Movement and the English Rising of 1381.* London: New Left Books, 1973.

Hines, Shawnda. "Faith Leaders to Press for Action During G-20 Summit in Pittsburgh." *Agriculture Week*, October 8 2009.

Hinze, Bradford. *Practices of Dialogue in the Roman Catholic Church.* New York, New York: The Continuum Publishing Group, 2006.

Hipple, Andreas. "The Center for Interfaith Action and the Mdgs: Leveraging Congregational Infrastructures for Maximum Impact on Disease and Poverty." *Cross Currents* 60, no. 3 (2010): 368–382.

Historian, Office of the. "United States Relations with Russia: After the Cold War." (2001–2009). http://2001-2009.state.gov/r/pa/ho/pubs/fs/85962.htm.

Hobden, Stephen, and John M. Hobson. *Historical Sociology of International Relations.* Cambridge, England: Cambridge University Press, 2002.

Holden, Erling, Kristin Linnerud, and David Banister. "Sustainable Development: Our Common Future Revisited." *Global Environmental Change* 26 (2014): 130–139.

Hollis, Aidan, and Peter Maybarduk. "Antibiotic Resistance Is a Tragedy of the Commons That Necessitates Global Cooperation." *The Journal Of Law, Medicine & Ethics: A Journal Of The American Society Of Law, Medicine & Ethics* 43, Suppl. 3 (2015): 33–37.

Holman, Otto. "Trans-National Governance without Supra-National Government: The Case of the European Employment Strategy." *Perspectives on European Politics & Society* 7, no. 1 (2006): 91–107.

Holton, R.J. *The Transition from Feudalism to Capitalism.* London: MacMillan, 1985.

Hou, Zhenbo, and Dirk Willem te Velde. "The Accountability of the G20's Development Agenda: Perspectives and Suggestions from Developing Countries of the Commonwealth and Francophonie." In *Commonwealth-Francophonie-G20 Development Working Group Meeting.* Washington, D.C., 2013.

Hu, Anning. "Gifts of Money and Gifts of Time: Folk Religion and Civic Involvement in a Chinese Society." *Review of Religious Research* 56, no. 2 (2014): 313.

Hulme, D., and Sakiko Fukudo-Parr. "International Norm Dynamics And 'The End of Poverty': Understanding the Millennium Development Goals (MDGs)." In *BWPI Working Paper.* Manchester: Brooks World Poverty Institute, 2009.

Hunter, James Davison, and Kimon Howland Sargeant. "Religion, Women and the Transformation of Public Culture." *Social Research* 60 (1993): 545–570.

Huntington, Samuel P. *The Clash of Civilizations and the Remaking of the World Order.* London: Simon & Schuster, 2003.

Hurd, Elizabeth S. *The Politics of Secularism in International Relations.* Princeton Studies in International History and Politics. Edited by Christiensen, Thomas, G. John Ikenberry and Marc Trachtenberg. Princeton, New Jersey: Princeton University Press, 2007.

Inglis, David, and Roland Robertson. "The Ecumenical Analytic: 'Globalization,' Reflexivity and the Revolution in Greek Historiography." *European Journal of Social Theory* 8, no. 2 (2005): 99–122.

Innes, Judith E., and David E. Booher. "Collaborative Rationality as a Strategy for Working with Wicked Problems." *Landscape and Urban Planning* (2016).

Interaction Council. "In Search of Global Ethical Standards." (1996). Published electronically March 22–24. http://interactioncouncil.org/in-search-of-global-ethical-standards.

Interreligious Youth Forum. "Canceled:Interreligious Youth Forum." Published electronically http://www.iyf2015.de/.

International Norm Dynamics and 'The End of Poverty': Understanding the Millennium Development Goals (MDGS)."International Norm Dynamics and 'The End of Poverty': Understanding the Millennium Development Goals (MDGS)." In *BWPI Working Paper*. Manchester: Brooks World Poverty Institute, 2009.

Iriye, Akira. *Global Interdependence: The World after 1945*. Cambridge, MA: Harvard University Press, 2014.

Jacobs, Michael. "High Pressure for Low Emissions: How Civil Society Created the Paris Agreement." *Juncture* 22, no. 1 (2016).

Jacques, Peter J. "A General Theory of Climate Denial." *Global Environmental Politics* 12, no. 2 (2012): 9–17.

James, Rick. *What Is Distinctive About FBOS? How European Fbos Define and Operationalise Their Faith*. INTRAC, 2009.

James, Thomas E., and Paul D. Jorgensen. "Policy Knowledge, Policy Formation, and Change: Revisiting a Foundational Question." *Policy Studies Journal* 37, no. 1 (2009): 141–162.

Jamrozik, A. *Social Policy in the Post-Welfare State: Australian Society in the 21st Century*. Frenchs Forest, NSW: Longman, 2005.

Jaramillo, Cesar. *Transparency and Accountability: NPT Reporting 2002–2012*. Waterloo, Ontario: Project Ploughshares, 2012.

Jenkins, Jack, and Jeremy Deaton. "250 Faith Leaders Demand Nations Ratify Paris Climate Deal." *ThinkProgress* (2015). Published electronically April 18. https://thinkprogress.org/250-faith-leaders-demand-nations-ratify-paris-climate-deal-c150f6a30ec3/.

Jermier, John M. "Complex Systems Threaten to Bring us Down." *Organization & Environment* 17, no. 1 (2004): 5.

Jessop, Bob. "Hollowing out the 'Nation-State' and Multilevel Governance." In *A Handbook of Comparative Social Policy*, 11–25. Cheltenham: Edward Elgar Publishing, 2004.

Jianguo, Liu, Hull Vanessa, Luo Junyan, Yang Wu, Liu Wei, Viña Andrés, Vogt Christine, et al. "Multiple Telecouplings and Their Complex Interrelationships." *Ecology & Society* 20, no. 3 (2015): 746–762.

Johnston, Douglas, ed. *Faith-Based Diplomacy: Trumping Real Politik*. New York, NY: Oxford University Press, 2003.

Johnston, Douglas, and Cynthia Sampson, eds. *Religion, the Missing Dimension of Statecraft*. New York, New York: Oxford University Press, 1994.

Jonas, Hans. *The Imperative of Responsibility: In Search of an Ethics for the Technological Age*. Chicago: University of Chicago Press, 1984.

Jones, Sam, and Carla Kweifio-Okai. "World Leaders Agree Sustainable Development Goals—as It Happened." *The Guardian* (2015). Published electronically September 25. https://www.theguardian.com/global-development/live/2015/sep/

25/un-sustainable-development-summit-2015-goals-sdgs-united-nations-general
-assembly-70th-session-new-york-live.

Jones, Ben, and Marie Juul Petersen. "Instrumental, Narrow, Normative? Reviewing Recent Work on Religion and Development." *Third World Quarterly* 32, no. 7 (2011): 1291.

Jones, Bruce, Carlos Pascual, and Stephen John Stedman. *Power and Responsibility: Building International Order in an Era of Transnational Threats.* Washington, D.C.: Brookings Institution, 2009.

Joppke, Christian, and Eve Morawska. *Toward Assimilation and Citizenship: Immigrants in Liberal Nation States.* Palgrave MacMillan: New York, NY, 2003.

Joshi, Devin K., Barry B. Hughes, and Timothy D. Sisk. "Improving Governance for the Post-2015 Sustainable Development Goals: Scenario Forecasting the Next 50 Years." *World Development* 70, June (2015): 286–302.

Juergensmeyer, M. *The New Cold War?* Berkeley: University of California, 1993.

Kahiluoto, Helena, Miia Kuisma, Anna Kuokkanen, Mirja Mikkilä, and Lassi Linnanen. "Taking Planetary Nutrient Boundaries Seriously: Can We Feed the People?." *Global Food Security* 3 (2014): 16–21.

Kairos. "Churches' Response to Call to Action #48." http://www.kairoscanada.org/what-we-do/indigenous-rights/churches-response-call-action-48.

Kaldor, Mary. "New & Old Wars: Organized Violence in an Global Era." Cambridge: Polity, 1999.

Karam, Azza. "The Role of Religious Actors in Implementing the UN's Sustainable Development Goals." *The Ecumenical Review* 68, no. 4 (2016): 365–377.

Keachie, Hilary. Email, April 1, 2015.

Kealing, Jonathan. "This Weekend's Terrorist Attacks Are Just a Handful among Hundreds. Most of Them You Don't Hear About." *Public Radio International* (2016). Published electronically March 22. http://www.pri.org/stories/2016-03-22/paris-there-have-been-hundreds-terrorist-attacks-many-have-gone-unnoticed.

Keller, Anna. "World Religious Leaders Urge G8 and G20 Governments to Invest in Peace." (2011). Published electronically May 24. http://www.cimer.org.au/documents/WorldReligiousLeadersUrgeGovernments.pdf.

Kelly, Jon. "In Numbers: Has Britain Really Become More Racist?" *BBC News Magazine*, August 10 2016.

Kennett, Patricia. *Governance, Globalization and Public Policy.* Cheltenham, UK: Edward Elgar Publishing, 2008.

Kenney, Jason. August 6 2010.

Keohane, R.O. "Global Governance and Democratic Accountability." In *Taming Globalization: Frontiers of Governance*, edited by Held, D. and M. Koenig-Archibugi, 130–159. Cambridge, UK: Polity Press, 2003.

Kepel, Gilles. *The Revenge of God: The Resurgence of Islam, Christianity, and Judaism in the Modern World.* Cambridge, UK: Polity Press, 1994.

Kern, Soeren. "Germany's Muslim Demographic Revolution." (2015). Published electronically August 31. http://www.gatestoneinstitute.org/6423/germany-muslim -demographic.

Khan, Muhammad Tariq, Asad Afzal Humayun, Muhammad Sajjad, and Naseer Ahmed Khan. "Languages in Danger of Death—and Their Relation with Globalization, Business and Economy." *International Journal of Information, Business & Management* 7, no. 2 (2015): 239.

Kharade, Jyoti. "G2c E-Governance Project Implementation at Local Level in a Pune Division Context." *BVIMSR Journal of Management Research* 8, no. 1 (2016): 19.

Kim, Chon-Kyun. "Anti-Corruption Initiatives and E-Government: A Cross-National Study." *Public Organization Review* 14, no. 3 (2014): 385.

King, Laura. "European Far-Right Populist Movements Energized by Britain's Brexit Vote and Trump's Victory." *Los Angeles Times*, January 1 2017.

Kingsbury, B., and R.B. Stewart. "Legitimacy and Accountability in Global Regulatory Governance: The Emerging Global Administrative Law and the Design and Operation of Administrative Tribunals of International Organizations." In *International Administrative Tribunals in a Changing World*, edited by S. Flogaitis, 1–20. Esperia, Italy, 2008.

Kirton, John. "What Is the G20?" *G20 Information Centre* (1999). http://www.g20 .utoronto.ca/g20whatisit.html.

Kirton, John. "Hokkaido Analysis: Assessment of the 2008 G8's Climate Change Performance." (2008). http://www.g8.utoronto.ca/evaluations/2008hokkaido/2008 -kirton-climate.html.

Kirton, John. "Leveling the Playing Field." In *G8 the UK Summit Lough Erne: Helping Global Trade to Take Off*, edited by Kirton, John, Madeline Koch and Nicholas Bayne, 36–37. London, UK: Newsdesk Media, 2013a.

Kirton, John. "G20 Governance for a Globalized World." Burlington, VT: Ashgate, 2013b.

Kirton, John J., and Ella Kokotsis. *The Global Governance of Climate Change : G7, G20, and Un Leadership.* Global Environmental Governance. Surrey, England: Routledge, 2015.

Kirton, John, Jenilee Guebert, and Caroline Bracht. "Climate Change Accountability: The G8's Compliance Record from 1975–2011." (2011). Published electronically December 2. www.g8.utoronto.ca/evaluations/climate-acc-111205.pdf.

Kirton, John, Jenilee Guebert, and Shamir Tanna. "G8 and G20 Summit Costs." (2010). Published electronically July 5. http://www.g8.utoronto.ca/evaluations/factsheet/ factsheet_costs.pdf.

Kiser, Edgar, and Michael Hechter. "The Role of General Theory in Comparative-Historical Sociology." *American Journal of Sociology* 97, no. 1: 1–30.

Kitanović, Elizabeta. "The Impact of the G20 Interfaith Summit on the G20." In *Dialogue among Civilizations and Human Destiny Community CASS Forum.* Beijing, China, 2016.

Kokotsis, Ella. "The Muskoka Accountability Report: Assessing the Written Record." *International Organisations Research Journal* 5, no. 5 (2010): 21–24.

Kollar, Nathan R. "The Interfaith Movement in a Liminal Age: The Institutionalization of a Movement." *Journal of Ecumenical Studies* 51, no. 1 (2016): 7.

Koppell, J. "Pathologies of Accountability: Icann and the Challenge of 'Multiple Accountabilities Disorder.'" *Administration Review* 65 (2005): 94–108.

Korab-Karpowicz, W. Julian. "Political Realism in International Relations." The Stanford Encyclopedia of Philosophy (2013). Published electronically April 2. https://plato.stanford.edu/entries/realism-intl-relations/#RooReaTra.

Kovel, Joel. The Enemy of Nature : The End of Capitalism or the End of the World? Vol. 2nd ed., London: Zed Books Ltd., 2007. Book.

Kumar, Neha, and Agnes R. Quisumbing. "Gendered Impacts of the 2007–2008 Food Price Crisis: Evidence Using Panel Data from Rural Ethiopia." *Food Policy* 38, February (2013): 11–22.

Küng, Hans. *Global Responsibility.* New York, New York: Crossroad, 1991.

Küng, Hans. *Yes to a Global Ethic.* UK: UCS Press, 1996.

Küng, Hans. "A Global Ethic for Global Politics and Economics." Oxford, UK: Oxford University Press, 1997.

Küng, Hans. "A Global Ethic: Development and Goals." *Interreligious Insight* (2003). Published electronically January. https://www.scribd.com/document/89957758/33285835-Hans-Kung-a-Global-Ethic-Development-and-Goals.

Kunnie, Julian. *The Cost of Globalization: Dangers to the Earth and Its People.* Jefferson, North Carolina: McFarland & Company, 2015.

Kurlantzick, J. *Democracy in Retreat: The Revolt of the Middle Class and the Worldwide Decline of Representative Government.* New Haven: Yale University Press, 2013.

Lane, Jan-Erik. *Globalization: The Juggernaut of the 21st Century.* New York, New York: Ashgate Publishing, 2008.

Langan, Mark. "A Moral Economy Approach to Africa-EU Ties: The Case of the European Investment Bank." *Review of International Studies* 40 (2014): 465–485.

Langhelle, Oluf. "Sustainable Development: Exploring the Ethics of 'Our Common Future'." *International Political Science Review* 20, no. 2 (1999): 129–149.

Larionova, Marina, and John Kirton. *The G8-G20 Relationship in Global Governance.* Burlington, VT: Ashgate, 2016.

Ledewitz, Bruce. *Church, State, and the Crisis in American Secularism.* Bloomington, Indiana: Indiana University Press, 2011.

Leichtman, Mara A. "Shi'i Islamic Cosmopolitanism and the Transformation of Religious Authority in Senegal." *Contemporary Islam* 8, no. 3 (2014): 261–283.

LePoire, David. "Interpreting 'Big History' as Complex Adaptive System Dynamics with Nested Logistic Transitions in Energy Flow and Organization." *Emergence: Complexity & Organization* 17, no. 1 (2015): 1–16.

Letsch, Constanza, and Nadia Khomami. "Turkey Terror Attack: Mourning after Scores Killed in Ankara Blasts." *The Guardian* (2015). Published electronically October 11. https://www.theguardian.com/world/2015/oct/10/turkey-suicide-bomb -killed-in-ankara.

Lhotta, R., F. Nullmeier, A. Hurrelmann, Z. Krellalaluhova, and S. Schneider. "The Democratic Nation State: Erosion, or Transformation, of Legitimacy: Is There a Legitimation Crisis of the Nation-State?"*European Review* 13, no. 1 (2005): 119–137.

Lieberson, Stanley. "Small N's and Big Conclusions: An Examination of the Resaoning in Comparative Studies Based on a Small Number of Cases." *Social Forces* 70, no. 2 (1991): 307.

Lieberson, Stanley. "More on the Uneasy Case for Using Mill-Type Methods in Small-N Comparative Studies." *Social Forces* 72 (1994): 1225–1337.

Linders, Dennis, Calvin Zhou-Peng Liao, and Cheng-Ming Wang. "Proactive E-Governance: Flipping the Service Delivery Model from Pull to Push in Taiwan." *Government Information Quarterly* 8, no. 4 (2015).

Linnenluecke, Martina K., and Andrew Griffiths. "Firms and Sustainability: Mapping the Intellectual Origins and Structure of the Corporate Sustainability Field." *Global Environmental Change* 23, February (2013): 382–391.

Linnenluecke, Martina K., Jac Birt, John Lyon, and Baljit K. Sidhu. "Planetary Boundaries: Implications for Asset Impairment." *Accounting & Finance* 55, no. 4 (2015a): 911–929.

Linnenluecke, Martina K., Cristyn Meath, Saphira Rekker, Baljit K. Sidhu, and Tom Smith. "Divestment from Fossil Fuel Companies: Confluence between Policy and Strategic Viewpoints." *Australian Journal of Management* 40, no. 3 (2015b): 478.

Lipschutz, Ronnie D. *Global Civil Society and Global Governance: The Politics of Nature from Place to Planet.* Albany, New York: State University of New York Press, 1996.

Lipset, S.M. "Some Social Requisites of Democracy: Economic Development and Political Legitimacy." *Political Science Review* 53 (1959): 69–105.

Lohr, Christy. "Building the Interfaith Youth Movement: Beyond Dialogue to Action." *Reviews in Religion & Theology* 14, no. 4 (2007): 531–534.

Long, Imogen. "Writing Gaullist Feminism: Francoise Parturier's Open Letters 1968–1974." *Modern & Contemporary France* 19, no. 3 (2011): 313–327.

Lord, Janet E., David Suozzi, and Allyn L. Taylor. "Lessons from the Experience of U.N. Convention on the Rights of Persons with Disabilities: Addressing the Democratic

Deficit in Global Health Governance." *Journal of Law, Medicine & Ethics* 38, no. 3 (2010): 564–579.

Lozang Trinlae, Bhikshuni. "Prospects for a Buddhist Practical Theology." *International Journal of Practical Theology* 18, no. 1 (2014): 7–22.

Lubchenco, Jane, Annette M. Olson, Linda B. Brubaker, Stephen R. Carpenter, Marjorie M. Holland, Stephen P. Hubbell, Simon A. Levin, James A. MacMahon, Pamela A. Matson, Jerry M. Melillo, Harold A. Mooney, Charles H. Peterson, H. Ronald Pulliam, Leslie A. Real, Philip J. Regal, and Paul G. Risser. "The Sustainable Biosphere Initiative: An Ecological Research Agenda: A Report from the Ecological Society of America." *Ecology* 72, no. 2 (1991): 371–412.

Lucas, R.E. "Econometric Policy Evaluation: A Critique." In *The Phillips Curve and Labour Markets*, edited by Brunner, K. and A.H. Meltzer, 104–130. Amsterdam: North Holland, 1976.

Lummis, Adair, and Paula Nesbitt. "Women Clergy Research and the Sociology of Religion." *Sociology of Religion* 61, no. 4 (2000): 443–454.

Mackenzie, C. "Autonomy: Individualistic or Social Rational?" In *Risk, Welfare and Work*, edited by Marston, G., J. Moss and J. Quiggin. Melbourne, Australia: Melbourne University Press, 2010.

MacKinnon, Rebecca. "Flatter World and Thicker Walls? Blogs, Censorship and Civic Discourse in China." *Public Choice* 134 (2008): 31–46.

Make Poverty History. "Policy Impact." http://www.makepovertyhistory.com.au/mdg-highlights-and-achievements/.

Manning, R. "Using Indicators to Encourage Development: Lessons from the MDGs." In *DIIS Report*. Copenhagen: Danish Institute for International Studies, 2009.

Marshall, Brent, and Warren Goldstein. "Managing the Environmental Legitimation Crisis." *Organization & Environment* 19, no. 2 (2006): 214–232.

Marshall, Katherine. "A Religious G8." *The Washington Post* (2008a). Published electronically July 4. onfaith.washingtonpost.com/onfaith/Georgetown/2008/07/a_religious_g8.html.

Marshall, Katherine. "Ancient and Contemporary Wisdom and Practice on Governance as Religious Leaders Engage in International Development." *Journal of Global Ethics* 4, no. 3 (2008b): 217.

Marshall, Katherine. "Development, Religion, and Women's Roles in Contemporary Societies." *Review of Faith & International Affairs* 8, no. 4 (2010): 35.

Marshall, Katherine. *Global Institutions of Religion: Ancient Movers, Modern Shakers.* New York, New York: Routledge, 2013a.

Marshall, Katherine. "Religious Freedom in US International Development Assistance and Humanitarian Relief: Ideas, Practice and Issues." *Review of Faith & International Affairs* 11, no. 1 (2013b): 38.

Marshall, Katherine. "Shadowing the China G20 Summit: An Interreligious Gathering." *Huntington Post*, September 5 2016.

Marshall, Katherine. "Urgent Challenges for the G20: What an F20 Might Offer." *Huffington Post*, June 2 2017.

Martin, Paul. "The G20: From Global Crisis Responder to Global Steering Committee." In *The Oxford Handbook of Modern Diplomacy*, edited by Cooper, A.F. and Jorge Heine, and Ramesh Thakur, 729–744. Oxford, UK: Oxford University Press, 2013.

Martin, John Levi, Tod Van Gunten, and Benjamin D. Zablocki. "Charisma, Status, and Gender in Groups with and without Gurus." *Journal for the Scientific Study of Religion* 51, no. 1 (2012): 20–41.

Masson, Paul R., and John C. Pattison. "Financial Regulatory Reform: Using Models of Cooperation to Evaluate Current Prospects for International Agreement." *The Journal of Economic Asymmetries* 6, no. 3 (2009): 119–136.

Mauss, Armand L. "Beyond the Illusion of Social Problems Theory." In *Perspectives on Social Problems*, edited by Henshel, R.L. and A.M. Henshel, 19–39: JAI Press, 1989.

Mayntz, R. "Modernization and the Logic of Interorganisational Networks." In *Societal Change between Market and Organisation*, edited by Child, J., M. Crozier and R. Mayntz, 3–18. Aldershot, UK: Avebury, 1993.

Mayntz, R. "Common Goods and Governance." In *Common Goods: Reinventing European and International Governance*, 15–27. Lanham, MD: Rowman & Littlefield, 2002.

McArthur, John W. "To Boldly Go." In *World Religions Summit 2010*. Winnipeg, Canada, 2010.

McAuliffe, Cameron. "A Home Far Away? Religious Identity and Trans National Relations in the Iranian Diaspora." *Global Networks* 7, no. 3 (2007): 307–327.

McCann, Jack, and Matthew Sweet. "The Perceptions of Ethical and Sustainable Leadership." *Journal of Business Ethics* 121, no. 3 (2014): 373–383.

McDonald, Henry. "Treasury to Foot Most of 50 Million Pound G8 Summit Security Bill." (2013). Published electronically June 3. https://www.theguardian.com/world/2013/jun/03/treasury-g8-summit-security-bill.

McGuire, Meredith. *Religion: The Social Context*. 5th ed. Long Grove, Illinois: Waveland Press, 2002.

McGuire, Patrick. "Brisbane, Australia's 2014 G20 Security Costs Were $500M Less Than Toronto's." (2014). Published electronically November 18. http://www.vice.com/en_ca/read/brisbane-australias-2014-g20-security-costs-were-six-times-lower-than-torontos-647.

McKinney, Laura A. "Foreign Direct Investment, Development, and Overshoot." *Social Science Research* 47 (2014): 121–133.

Meijer, Albert. "E-Governance Innovation: Barriers and Strategies." *Government Information Quarterly* 32, April (2015): 198–206.

Merdjanova, Ina. "Overhauling Interreligious Dialogue for Peacebuilding." *Occasional Papers on Religion in Eastern Europe* 36, no. 1 (2016): 26–33.

Merlini, Cesare. "The G-7 and the Need for Reform." *The International Spectator* 29, no. 2 (1994): 5.

Merton, Robert K. "The Self-Fulfilling Prophecy." *The Antioch Review* 8, no. 2 (1948): 193–210.

Messner, Dirk, and Dennis Snower. "20 Solution Proposals for the G20 from the T20 Engagement Group." Bonn, Germany, 2017.

Meyerson, Frederick A.B. "Population, Development and Global Warming: Averting the Tragedy of the Climate Commons." 1998, 443.

Miewald, Robert D. "The Greatly Exaggerated Death of Bureaucracy." *California Management Review* 13, no. 2 (1970): 65–69.

Ministers, G7 Foreign. *Joint Communiqué.* (2016). Published electronically http://www.mofa.go.jp/mofaj/files/000147440.pdf.

Ministers, G7 Foreign. *Joint Communiqué.* (2017). Published electronically http://www.esteri.it/mae/resource/doc/2017/04/g7_-_joint_communiqu_final.pdf.

Mitchell, George E., and Hans Peter Schmitz. "Principled Instrumentalism: A Theory of Transnational NGO Behaviour." *Review of International Studies* 40 (2014): 487–504.

Miyake, Yoshinobu. "2008 G8 Religious Leaders Summit: Memorandum of Intent." (2008a).

Miyake, Yoshinobu. "Purpose." (2008b). Published electronically http://www.relnet.co.jp/g8/english/purpose1.htm.

Miyake, Yoshinobu. Email, June 14, 2014.

Miyamoto, Keishi, and William Vendley. "Welcome: World Religious Leaders Summit for Peace—On the Occasion of the G8 Hokkaido Toyako Summit." Sapporo, Japan, 2008.

Monheim, Kai. *How Effective Negotiation Management Promotes Multilateral Cooperation: The Power of Process in Climate, Trade, and Biosafety Negotiations.* Routledge Research in Global Environmental Governance. London: Routledge, 2015.

Monitor, African. "The Time to Act Is Now! African Monitor's Response to the G8 Summit 2008." *African Monitor,* 2008.

Morgenthau, Hans J. *Politics among Nations: The Struggle for Power and Peace.* New York, New York: McGraw-Hill, 1948.

Morgenthau, Hans J. *Truth and Power.* New York, New York: Praeger, 1970.

Morris, Paul. "What Is the Role of Religion in Civilizational Dialogue?" In *Dialogue among Civilizations and Human Destiny Community CASS Forum.* Beijing, China, 2016.

Morris, Paul. *Cosmopiety.* New Zealand: Palgrave, 2017.

Morrow, Adrian. "Toronto Police Were Overwhelmed at G20, Review Reveals." *The Globe and Mail* (2011). Published electronically June 23. http://www.theglobeandmail.com/news/toronto/toronto-police-were-overwhelmed-at-g20-review-reveals/article2073215/.

Mosley, Stephen. *The Environment in World History. Themes in World History.* 1st ed, Milton Park: Routledge, 2010.

Moss, Richard H., and Meredith A. Lane. "Decision-Making, Transitions, and Resilient Futures: The Newly Established National Research Council Board on Environmental

Change and Society Explores Insights and Research Frontiers for Understanding Coupled Human-Environment Systems." *Issues in Science and Technology*, no. 4 (2012): 31.

Movius, Lauren. "The Influence of Global Civil Society on Internet Governance Negotiations." *Florida Communication Journal* 43, no. 2 (2015): 1–14.

Mufwene, Salikoko S. "Language Birth and Death." *Annual Review of Anthropology* 33, no. 1 (2004): 201–222.

Mujaddid, Ghulam. "Second Tragedy of Global Commons: Strategic Competition and Conflict over Humanity's Common Assets." *Strategic Studies* 32, no. 4/1 (2013): 85.

Mukonka, Victor M., Sarai Malumo, Penelope Kalesha, Mary Nambao, Rodgers Mwale, Kasonde Mwinga, Mary Katepa-Bwalya, Olusegan Babaniyi, Elizabeth Mason, Caroline Phiri and Pauline K. Wamulume. "Holding a Country Countdown to 2015 Conference on Millennium Development Goals (MDGs)—the Zambian Experience." *BMC Public Health* 14 (2014): 60.

Murphy, J. "Welfare Regimes and Risky Speculations." In *Risk, Welfare and Work*, edited by Marston, G., J. Moss and J. Quiggin, 24–47. Melbourne, Australia: Melbourne University Press, 2010.

Murphy, Karen. *State Security Regimes and the Right to Freedom of Religion and Belief: Changes in Europe Since 2001.* Hoboken: Taylor and Francis 2013.

Murray, Elisabeth Hope. *Disrupting Pathways to Genocide: The Process of Ideological Radicalization. Rethinking Political Violence.* Basingstoke, UK: Palgrave Macmillan, 2015.

Nadon, Christopher. *Absolutism and the Separation of Church and State in Locke's Letter Concerning Toleration.* Cambridge, MA: Gale, 2007.

NATO. "Relations with Russia." (2016). Published electronically May 18. http://www .nato.int/cps/en/natolive/topics_50090.htm.

Naylor, Tristen. "Civil Society Inclusion at Los Cabos 2012." (2012). Published electronically June 26. http://www.g20.utoronto.ca/analysis/120626-naylor.html.

Nelson, Lynn Hankinson. "Epistemological Communities." In *Feminist Epistemologies*, edited by Alcoff, Linda and Elizabeth Potter, 121–160. London, England: Routledge, 1993.

Newell, Peter. "Civil Society, Corporate Accountability and the Politics of Climate Change." *Global Environmental Politics* 8 (2008): 122–153.

Newell, Peter. *Globalization and the Environment: Capitalism, Ecology and Power.* Cambridge, UK: Polity Press, 2012.

Nilsson, Måns, and Åsa Persson. "Analysis: Reprint of 'Can Earth System Interactions Be Governed? Governance Functions for Linking Climate Change Mitigation with Land Use, Freshwater and Biodiversity Protection'." *Ecological Economics* 81, September (2012): 10–20.

Nitschke, Ulrich, and Bennet Gabriel. "The International Partnership on Religion and Sustainable Development/PaRD: A Global and Inclusive Partnership to Harness the Positive Impact of Religion in Development and Humanitarian Assistance." *Ecumenical Review* 68, no. 4 (2016): 378–386.

Nordland, Rod, Christopher Dickey, Martha Brant, and Barbie Nadeau. "First Blood." *Newsweek* 138, no. 5 (2001): 20.

Norgaard, Kari Marie. *Living in Denial: Climate Change, Emotions and Everyday Life.* MIT Press, 2011.

Norgaard, Richard. *Development Betrayed: The End of Progress and a Coevolutionary Revisioning of the Future.* London: Routledge, 1994.

Norgaard, Richard B., and John A. Dixon. "Pluralistic Project Design." *Policy Sciences* 19, no. 3 (1986): 297.

Norman, Bryony. "Monitoring and Accountability Practices for Remotely Managed Projects Implemented in Volatile Operating Environments." *Tearfund.* (2012). Published online at http://betterevaluation.org/sites/default/files/remote_monitoring _and_accountability_practice__web_2.pdf.

Nowlin, Matthew C. "Theories of the Policy Process: State of the Research and Emerging Trends." *Policy Studies Journal* 39, April (2011): 41–60.

Nye, Joseph S. *Soft Power: The Means to Success in World Politics.* New York, New York: Public Affairs, 2004.

O'Connor, James. *The Second Contradiction of Capitalism.* Santa Cruz, CA: Guilford, 1991.

O'Connor, James. *Is Capitalism Sustainable? Political Economy and the Politics of Ecology.* New York: The Guilford Press, 1994.

O'Hara, Phillip Anthony. "Cultural Contradictions of Global Capitalism." *Journal of Economic Issues* 38, no. 2 (2004): 413–420.

OECD. "The 0.7% ODA/GNI Target: A History." *Development Assistance Committee Journal* 3, no. 4 (2002): 9–11.

OECD. "The Sustainable Development Goals: An Overview of Relevant OECD Analysis, Tools and Aproaches." (2016). Published online at http://www.oecd.org/dac/ The%20Sustainable%20Development%20Goals%20An%20overview%20of% 20relevant%20oecd%20analysis.pdf.

Olson, Laura R., Sue E.S. Crawford, and Melissa M. Deckman. *Women with a Mission: Religion, Gender, and the Politics of Women Clergy.* Tuscaloosa: University of Alabama Press, 2005.

Olzak, Susan. "Does Globalization Breed Ethnic Discontent?." *Journal of Conflict Resolution* 55, no. 1 (2011): 3–32.

Ooms, Gorik, David Stuckler, Sanjay Basu, and Martin McKee. "Financing the Millennium Development Goals for Health and Beyond: Sustaining the 'Big Push'." *Globalization & Health* 6 (2010): 17.

Organization, Islamic Culture and Relations. "German Evangelical Church Leaders Meet Iranian Religious Scholars." (2015). Published electronically March 15.

Organization, World Health. "G8 France 2011 New World New Ideas: Deauville Accountability Report." *G8 Commitments on Health and Food Security: State of Delivery and Results* (2011).http://www.who.int/pmnch/media/membernews/2011/20110518 _accountabilityreport.pdf.

Parasher, Tejas, Amanda Coletta, Ryan Kelpin, Jamie Kim, Subin Kweon, Ceecee Lu, Fabio Ponti, et al. "Media Analysis of the G8 and the 2012 Camp David Summit." (2012). http://www.g8.utoronto.ca/evaluations/csed/.

Parekh, B.C. *Rethinking Multiculturalism: Cultural Diversity and Political Theory.* Cambridge, MA: Harvard University Press, 2000.

Partnership, Interfaith. *Faith Community Responses, Policy Responses, Previous Statements.* 2010.

Peace, Institute for Economics and. "Five Key Questions Answered on the Link between Peace and Religion: A Global Statistical Analysis on the Empirical Link between Peace and Religion." Sydney, Australia, 2014.

Peace, Religions for. "Mena Leaders Address Violent Extremism & Advance Citizenship Ahead of G7 Summit." (2016). http://religionsforpeaceaustralia.org.au/2016/05/17/ mena-leaders-address-violent-extremism-advance-citizenship-ahead-of-g7 -summit/.

Peace, The Fund for. "Fragile States Index 2016." *Foreign Policy,* 2016. http://foreignpolicy .com/fragile-states-index-2016-brexit-syria-refugee-europe-anti-migrant-boko -haram/.

Pearson, Chris. "Beyond 'Resistance': Rethinking Nonhuman Agency for a 'More-Than-Human' World." *European Review of History: Revue Européenne d'Histoire* 22, no. 5 (2015): 709–725.

Pedersen, Kusumita P. "The Interfaith Movement: An Incomplete Assessment." *Journal of Ecumenical Studies* 41, no. 1 (2004): 74.

Pedersen, Kusumita P. "Religious Ethics and the Environment." *Journal of Religious Ethics* 43, no. 3 (2015): 558–585.

Peifeng, Liu. "A Reflection on the Rationality and Paradox of Religion and Charity." In *Dialogue among Civilizations and Human Destiny Community CASS Forum.* Beijing, China, 2016.

Pellman, Ralph. "In Pursuit of World Peace: Modernism, Sacralism and Cosmopiety." *Global Change, Peace and Security* 22, no. 2 (2010): 197–212.

Persson, Linn M., Magnus Breitholtz, Ian T. Cousins, Cynthia A. de Wit, Matthew MacLeod, and Michael S. McLachlan. "Confronting Unknown Planetary Boundary Threats from Chemical Pollution." *Environmental Science & Technology* 47, no. 22 (2013): 12619–12622.

Peschken, Christian, and Archbishop Jeanbart. *Christians Forgotten in Syria, Says Aleppo Archbishop.* Podcast audio 2016.

Peters, B. Guy, and John Pierre. "Governance without Government? Rethinking Public Administration." 1998, 223.

Petersen, Marie Juul. "International Religious NGOs at the United Nations: A Study of a Group of Religious Organizations." *The Journal of Humanitarian Assistance* (2010).

Petito, F., and P. Hatzopoulos. *Religion in International Relations: The Return from Exile.* New York, New York: Palgrave MacMillan, 2003.

Pew Research Center. "Religious Hostilities Reach Six Year High." (2014). Published electronically January 14. http://www.pewforum.org/2014/01/14/religious-hostilities -reach-six-year-high/.

Pew Research Center. "The Global Religious Landscape." (2012). Published electronically http://www.pewforum.org/2012/12/18/global-religious-landscape-exec/.

Pew Research Center. "Trends in Global Restrictions on Religion." (2016). Published electronically June 23. http://www.pewforum.org/2016/06/23/trends-in-global -restrictions-on-religion/.

Polk, W.R. "Legitimation Crisis in Afghanistan." *Nation* 290, no. 15 (2010): 22–24.

Ponting, Clive. "The Burden of the Past." *Global Dialogue* 4, no. 1 (2002): 1.

Ponting, Clive. *A New Green History of the World: The Environment and the Collapse of Great Civilizations.* New York, New York: Penguin Books, 2007.

Benedict xvi. "Caritas in Veritate." *Third Encyclical Letter* (2009). Published electronically 29 June. http://w2.vatican.va/content/benedict-xvi/en/encyclicals/documents/hf _ben-xvi_enc_20090629_caritas-in-veritate.html.

Potrafke, Niklas. "The Evidence on Globalisation." *World Economy* 38, no. 3 (2015): 509–552.

Povoledo, Elisabetta. "Italy Orders Jail Terms for 7 Who Didn't Warn of Deadly Earthquake." *New York Times* (2012).

Povoledo, Elisabetta. "Italian Appeals Court Overturns Guilty Verdicts in Earthquake Trial." (2014). Published electronically Nov. 10.

Princen, Thomas, and Matthias Finger. *Environmental NGOs in World Politics: Linking the Local and the Global.* New York, New York: Routledge, 1994.

Putnam, Robert. *Making Democracy Work: Civic Traditions in Modern Italy.* Princeton, NJ: Princeton University Press, 1994.

Radasanu, Andrea. "Introduction: The Pious Sex?." In *The Pious Sex: Essays on Women and Religion in the History of Political Thought,* edited by Radasanu, Andrea, 7. Lanham, MD: Lexington Books, 2010.

Ragin, Charles C. *The Comparative Method: Moving Beyond Qualitative and Quantitative Strategies.* Berkeley, CA: University of California Press, 1987.

Randeria, S. "Beyond Sociology and Sociocultural Anthropology." *Soziale Welt* 50 (1999): 373–382.

Ravenhill, John. "Resource Insecurity and International Institutions in the Asia-Pacific Region." *Pacific Review* 26, no. 1 (2013): 39–64.

Rawls, John. "The Idea of the Public Reasons Revisited." *University Chicago Law Review* 64 (1997): 765–807.

Rayner, J., and K. McNutt. " Valuing Metaphor: A Constructivist Account of Reflexive Governance in Policy Networks." In *5th Annual Conference on Interpretive Policy Analysis*. Grenoble, France, 2010.

Reed, Charles. "The G8: Our Spiritual and Moral Responsibilities: Does the G8 Matter?" In *World Religious Leaders Summit for Peace on the Occasion of the G8 Hokkaido Toyako Summit*. Sapporo, Japan, 2008.

Reed, Charles. "Project Proposal–2013 G8 Religious Leaders' Initiative." London, UK: International Continuance Committee, 2013.

Reinalda, Bob, and Bertjan Verbeek. *Autonomous Policy Making by International Organizations*. London: Taylor and Francis, 1998.

Relations, Office of Governmental. "G8 Religious Leaders' Summit—Mp Dinners Interim Report." Ottawa, Canada, 2010.

Religions, Parliament of the Worlds. "Declaration toward a Global Ethic." (1993). https://parliamentofreligions.org/pwr_resources/_includes/FCKcontent/File/TowardsAGlobalEthic.pdf.

Rescher, Nicholas. "Predicting the Future: An Introduction to the Theory of Forecasting." *Philosophy: The Journal of the Royal Institute of Philosophy* 74, no. 287 (01/01/ 1999): 122–126.

Reus-Smit, Christian. "The Idea of History and History with Ideas." In *Historical Sociology of International Relations*, edited by Hobden, Stephen and John M. Hobson, 120–140. Cambridge, England: Cambridge University Press, 2002.

Rhodes, R.A.W. "The New Governance: Governing without Government." *Political Studies* 44, no. 4 (1996): 652–667.

Rhodes, R.A.W. *Understanding Governance: Policy Networks, Governance, Reflexivity and Accountability*. Philadelphia, PA: Open University Press, 1997.

Rhodes, R.A.W. "Understanding Governance: Ten Years On." *Organizational Studies* 28 (2007): 1243–1264.

Rider, David, and Susan Delacourt. "Pressure Builds on Ottawa for Compensation." *The Star* (2010). Published electronically June 29. https://www.thestar.com/news/gta/2010/06/29/pressure_builds_on_ottawa_for_compensation.html.

Rip, A. "A Co-Evolutionary Approach to Reflexive Governance—and Its Ironies." In *Reflexive Governance for Sustainable Development*, edited by Voss, J.P., D. Bauknecht and R. Kemp, 82–102. Cheltenham, UK: Edward Elgar Publishing, 2006.

Risse, T. "Transnational Actors and World Politics." In *Handbook of International Relations*, edited by Carlsnaes, W., T. Risse and B. Simmons, 255–274. London, England: Sage, 2002.

Risse, T. "Transnational Governance and Legitimacy." In *Fifth Pan-European Conference on International Relations*. The Hague, Netherlands, 2004.

Rittel, Horst W.J., and Melvin W. Webber. "Dilemmas in a General Theory of Planning." *Policy Sciences* 4, no. 2 (1973): 155–169.

Roberts, S. "Misrepresenting Choice Biographies? A Reply to Woodman." *Journal of Youth Studies* 13, no. 1 (2010): 137–149.

Rockström, Johan. "A Safe Operating Space for Humanity." *Nature* 461, no. 7263 (2009): 472–475.

Rockström, J., W. Steffen, K. Noone, A. Persson, C. Folke, B. Nykvist, S. Sörlin, et al. "Planetary Boundaries: Exploring the Safe Operating Space for Humanity." *Ecology and Society* 14, no. 2 (2009).

Rodríguez Bolívar, Manuel Pedro, Jing Zhang, Gabriel Puron-Cid, and J. Ramon Gil-Garcia. "The Influence of Political Factors in Policymakers' Perceptions on the Implementation of Web 2.0 Technologies for Citizen Participation and Knowledge Sharing in Public Sector Delivery." *Information Polity: The International Journal of Government & Democracy in the Information Age* 20, no. 2/3 (2015): 199–220.

Romaine, Suzanne. "Keeping the Promise of the Millennium Development Goals: Why Language Matters." *Applied Linguistics Review* 4, no. 1 (2013): 1–21.

Rosa, Eugene A., and Gary E. Machlis. "Energetic Theories of Society: An Evaluative Review." *Sociological Inquiry* 53 (1983): 152–178.

Rose, Nikolas, and Peter Miller. "Political Power Beyond the State: Problematics of Government." *The British Journal of Sociology* 43, no. 2 (1992): 173–205.

Rose, Deborah Bird, Thom van Dooren, Matthew Chrulew, Stuart Cooke, Matthew Kearnes, and Emily O'Gorman. "Thinking through the Environment, Unsettling the Humanities." *Environmental Humanities* 1 (2012): 1–5.

Rosenbloom, Jonathan. "Local Governments and Global Commons." *Brigham Young University Law Review* 2014, no. 6 (2015): 1489.

Roth, Guenther, and Wolfgang Schluchter. *Max Weber's Vision of History.* Berkeley, CA: University of California Press, 1979.

Rudolph, Susanne Hoeber, and James Piscatori. *Transnational Religion and Fading States.* Boulder, Colorado: Westview Press, 1997.

Russell, Conrad. *The Crisis of Parliaments.* Oxford: Oxford University Press, 1971.

Ruthrauff, John, and Sue Pleming. "Establishing G8 Accountability: Still a Work in Progress." (2013). Published electronically February. https://www.interaction.org/document/establishing-g8-accountability-still-work-progress.

Sachs, Jeffrey D. "From Millennium Development Goals to Sustainable Development Goals." *Lancet* 379 (2012): 2006–2011.

Sachs, Jeffrey D., and Steve Killelea. "Holding G8 Accountability to Account." Institute for Economics and Peace and the Earth Institute, Columbia University, 2011.

Sachs, Jeffrey D., Guido Schmidt-Traub, and David Durand-Delacre. "Preliminary Sustainable Development Goal (SDG) Index and Dashboard." In *SDSN Working Paper*, 2016.

Sadasivam, B. "Wooing the MDG Skeptics." *Development* 48 (2005): 30–34.

Sahliyeh, E. *Religious Resurgence and Politics in the Contemporary World.* New York: State University of New York Press, 1990.

Sainsbury, Tristram. "G20 Outreach to Society in 2015." *G20 Monitor* 18, October (2015).

Scammell, Rosi. "Britain Sees an Increase in Anti-Muslim Attacks." *Religion News Service* (2016). Published electronically June 30. http://national.deseretnews.com/article/20804/britain-sees-an-increase-in-anti-muslim-attacks.html.

Schelling, T.C. *The Strategy of Conflict.* Cambridge, MA: Harvard University Press, 1960.

Schierup, C.U., A. Ålund, and B. Likić-Brborić. "Migration, Precarization and the Democratic Deficit in Global Governance." *International Migration* 53, no. 3 (2015): 50–63.

Schluchter, Wolfgang. *The Rise of Western Rationalism: Max Weber's Developmental History.* Berkeley, CA: University of California Press, 1981.

Schmidt, Jonathan. June 30 2010.

Schneider, Anselm, and Andreas Scherer. "Corporate Governance in a Risk Society." *Journal of Business Ethics* 126, no. 2 (2015): 309–323.

Scholte, J.A. "Global Governance, Accountability and Civil Society." In *Building Global Democracy? Civil Society and Accountable Global Governance*, edited by Scholte, J.A., 8–41. Cambridge, UK: Cambridge University Press, 2011a.

Scholte, J.A. "Introduction." In *Building Global Democracy? Civil Society and Accountable Global Governance*, edited by Scholte, J.A., 1–7. Cambridge: MA:Cambridge University Press, 2011b.

Schrumm, Andrew. "Muskoka Accountability Report: G8 Rhetoric Versus Reality." *Centre for International Governance Innovation* (2010). https://www.cigionline.org/articles/muskoka-accountability-report-g8-rhetoric-versus-reality.

Schweickart, David. "Is Sustainable Capitalism an Oxymoron?." *Perspectives on Global Development & Technology* 8, no. 2/3 (2009): 559–580.

Scott, Eugene. "ACLU Expecting More Religious Freedom Bills in 2017 Than Ever." *CNNPolitics*, December 16 2016.

Seiple, Chris. "Building Religious Freedom: A Theory of Change." *The Review of Faith and International Affairs* 10, no. 3 (2012): 97–102.

Shabani, O.P. "The Role of Religion in Democratic Politics: Tolerance and the Boundary of Public Reason." *Religious Education* 106 (2011): 332–346.

Shackleton, Michael. "Religious Leaders Call for Global Partnership: Members of the Host Committee." *The Japan Times*, July 3 2008.

Shah, Anup. "G8 Summit 2007." *Global Issues* (2007). http://www.globalissues.org/article/719/g8-summit-2007.

Shah, Timothy Samuel, Monica Duffy Toft, and Alfred Stepan. *Rethinking Religion and World Affairs.* Oxford: Oxford University Press, 2011.

Shapardanov, Christopher. Email, 2007.

Sharp, Paul. "Who Needs Diplomats? The Problem of Diplomatic Representation." *International Journal: Canada's Journal of Global Policy Analysis* 52, no. 4 (1997): 609–634.

Sharp, Paul. "For Diplomacy: Representation and the Study of International Relations." *International Studies Review* 1, no. 1 (1999): 33–57.

Sheoin, Tomás. "Controlling Chemical Hazards: Global Governance, National Regulation?" *Social Justice* 41, no. 1/2 (2015): 101–124.

Shorr, David, and Thomas Wright. "The G20 and Global Governance: An Exchange." *Survival: Global Politics and Strategy* 52, no. 2 (2010): 171–198.

Silva, Carlos Nunes. *Citizen E-Participation in Urban Governance: Crowdsourcing and Collaborative Creativity*. Advances in Electronic Government, Digital Divide, and Regional Development. Hershey, PA: Information Science Reference, 2013.

Simpson, Smith. "Of Diplomats and Their Chroniclers." *Virginia Quarterly Review* 71, no. 4 (1995): 755–758.

Sireau, Nicolas. *Make Poverty History: Political Communication in Action*. New York, New York: Palgrave Macmillan, 2009.

Smart Sustainable Development Model Advisory Board. "Report 2015: Smart Sustsainable Development Model." (2015). http://www.itu.int/en/ITU-D/Initiatives/SSDM/Documents/SmartSustainableDevelopmentModel_Report2015.pdf.

Smith, Graeme. *A Short History of Secularism*. London, UK: I.B. Tauris, 2007.

Smith, Heather. "What Is a Sherpa?" *G20 Watch* (2014).

Smith, Kevin B., and Christopher W. Larimer. *The Public Policy Theory Primer*. Boulder, Colorado: Westview Press, 2009.

Smith-Windsor, Brooke A. "Hard Power, Soft Power Reconsidered." *Canadian Military Journal*, Autumn (2000): 51–56.

Snyder, J. *Religion in International Relations Theory*. New York, New York: Columbia University Press, 2011.

Spash, Clive L., and Iulie Aslaksen. "Research Paper: Re-Establishing an Ecological Discourse in the Policy Debate over How to Value Ecosystems and Biodiversity."*Journal of Environmental Management* 159 (2015): 245–253.

Speicher, Sara. "Tutu, Religious Leaders Call on G8 Leaders to Keep Promises on Aids." news release, May 23, 2007.

Stark, Rodney. "Secularization, R.I.P." *Sociology of Religion* 60, no. 3 (1999): 249.

Stearns, Rich. "2015 Annual Report." (2016). https://www.worldvision.org/wp-content/uploads/2015-annual-report-brochure-F3.pdf.

Steffek, J., and P.M. Ferretti. "Accountability or 'Good Decisions?' The Competing Goals of Civil Society Participation in International Governance." *Global Society* 23 (2009): 37–57.

Steffen, Will, and Mark Stafford Smith. "Planetary Boundaries, Equity and Global Sustainability: Why Wealthy Countries Could Benefit from More Equity." *Current Opinion in Environmental Sustainability* 5 (2013): 403–408.

Steffen, Will, Jacques Grinevald, Paul Josef Crutzen, and John R. McNeill. "The Anthropocene: Conceptual and Historical Perspectives." Paper presented at the Philosophical Transactions of the Royal Society, 2011a.

Steffen, Will, Johan Rockström, and Robert Costanza. "How Defining Planetary Boundaries Can Transform Our Approach to Growth." *Solutions: For a Sustainable & Desirable Future* 2, no. 3 (2011b): 59.

Steinberg, Alan. "Exploring Web 2.0 Political Engagement: Is New Technology Reducing the Biases of Political Participation?" *Electoral Studies* 39 (2015): 102–116.

Steiner, Sherrie. "Religious Soft Power as Accountability Mechanism for Power in World Politics: The Interfaith Leaders' Summit(s)." *Sage Open* (2011): 1–16.

Steiner, Sherrie. "Faith-Based Accountability Mechanism Typology: The 2011 Interfaith Summit as Soft Power in Global Governance." *Sage Open* April-June (2012).

Steiner, Sherrie. "Reflexivity in External Religious Leaders' Summit Communication Sequences (2005–2012) to G8 Political Leaders: The Social (Re)Construction of Cosmopolitan Responsibility by World Religious Leaders." *Sage Open* (2013a).

Steiner, Sherrie. "Reflexive Governance Dynamics Operative within Round One of the World Religious Leaders' Dialogue with the G8 (2005–2013)." *Sage Open* 3, no. 4 (2013b).

Steiner, Sherrie. "G20 Interfaith Summit Summary Report." Paper summarizing the 2015 G20 Interfaith Summit, Istanbul, Turkey, 2015.

Steiner, Sherrie. "Is Religious Soft Power of Consequence in the World Today?." In *Religious Diversity Today*, edited by Goulet, Jen-Guy A., 1–34. Santa Barbara, CA: Praeger, 2016a.

Steiner, Sherrie. "G20 Interfaith Summit Summary Report." Paper summarizing the 2016 G20 Interfaith Summit, Beijing, China, 2016b.

Steiner, Sherrie, and Tanner J. Bean, Tye Christensen, Gesine Kurth, and Jad Lehmann-Abi-Haidar. "G20 Interfaith Summit Summary Report." Paper summarizing the 2017 G20 Interfaith Summit, Potsdam, Germany, 2017.

Steiner-Aeschliman, Sherrie. *The Religious Construction of Intimacy for Emotional Renewal: The Parallel Protestant Ethic.* Edited by Greer, Joanne M. and David O. Moberg Vol. 9, Research in the Social Scientific Study of Religion. Stamford, CN: JAI Press, 1998.

Steiner-Aeschliman, Sherrie. "Transitional Adaptation: A Neoweberian Theory of Ecologically-Based Social Change." edited by Freese, Lee, 157–213: JAP Press, 1999.

Stirling, A. "Precaution, Foresight and Sustainability: Reflection and Reflexivity in the Governance of Science and Technology." In *Reflexive Governance for Sustainable Development*, edited by Voss, J.P., D.Bauknecht and R. Kemp, 225–272. Cheltenham, UK: Edward Elgar, 2006.

Strauss, Andrew L., and William C.G. Burns. *Climate Change Geoengineering: Philosophical Perspectives, Legal Issues, and Governance Frameworks.* Cambridge: Cambridge University Press, 2013.

Stromberg, Joseph. "What Is the Anthropocene and Are We in It?" *Smithsonian Magazine* (2013). Published electronically January. http://www.smithsonianmag.com/science-nature/what-is-the-anthropocene-and-are-we-in-it-164801414/.

Suderman, Brenda. "Economics and the Pulpit." *Winnipeg Free Press*, February 3 2008.

Summit, Indigenous People's. "Nibutani Declaration." (2008). http://www.tebtebba.org/index.php/content/100-nibutani-declaration-of-2008.

Sumner, Andrew, and Thomas Lawo. "The MDGs and Beyond: Pro-Poor Policy in a Changing World." In *EADI Policy Paper*: European Association of Development Research and Training Institute, 2010.

Svensson, Göran, Greg Wood, and Michael Callaghan. "A Corporate Model of Sustainable Business Practices: An Ethical Perspective." *Journal of World Business* 45 (2010): 336–345.

Sweetman, P. "Twenty-First-Century Dis-Ease? Habitual Reflexivity or the Reflexive Habitus." *Sociological Review* 51, no. 4 (2003): 528–549.

Swers, Michele. "Research on Women in Legislatures: What Have We Learned and Where Are We Going?." *Women and Politics* 23, no. 1/2 (2002): 167–185.

Symons, Ali. "Faith Leaders Call for Climate Justice." *Anglican Church of Canada News*, October 28 2011.

Tainter, Joseph A. *The Collapse of Complex Societies.* Cambridge: Cambridge University Press, 1990.

Taylor, Bron. "Religion to the Rescue (?) in an Age of Climate Disruption." 2015.

Taylor, Charles. "Modes of Secularism." In *Secularism and Its Critics*, edited by Bhargava, Rajeev. Oxford, England: Oxford University Press, 2005.

Taylor, Charles. *A Secular Age.* Cambridge, MA: Harvard University Press, 2007.

Taylor, Susan Jean. "The 2008 Food Summit: A Political Response to the Food Price Crisis in Gauteng Province, South Africa." *Development Southern Africa* 30, no. 6 (2013): 760–770.

Taylor, Tiffany. "Re-Examining Cultural Contradictions: Mothering Ideology and the Intersections of Class, Gender, and Race." *Sociology Compass* 5, no. 10 (2011): 898.

Taylor-Gooby, P. *Reframing Social Citizenship.* Oxford, England: Oxford University Press, 2009.

Thomas, Neil. "Global Capitalism, the Anti-Globalization Movement and the Third World." *Capital & Class*, no. 92 (2007): 45–78.

Thomas, S. *The Global Resurgence of Religion and the Transformation of International Relations: The Struggle for the Soul of the Twenty-First Century.* Basingstoke, UK: Palgrave Macmillan, 2005.

Thomas, S.M. "A Globalized God: Religion's Growing Influence in International Politics." [In English]. *Foreign Affairs* 89, no. 6 (11 / 01 / 2010): 93–101.

Thomas, S.M. "Taking Religious and Cultural Pluralism Seriously: The Global Resurgence of Religion and the Transformation of International Society." *Millennium* 29, no. 3 (2000): 815–841.

Threadgold, S., and P. Nilan. "Reflexivity of Contemporary Youth, Risk, and Cultural Capital." *Current Sociology* 57, no. 1 (2009): 47–68.

Tillyris, Demetris. "'Learning How Not to Be Good': Machiavelli and the Standard Dirty Hands Thesis." Ethical Theory & Moral Practice 18, no. 1 (2015): 61–74.

Tisdell, Clem. "Global Warming and the Future of Pacific Island Countries." [In English]. International Journal of Social Economics 35, no. 12: 889–903.

Treas, Judith, and Daisy Carreon. "Diversity and Our Common Future: Race, Ethnicity, and the Older American." Generations 34, no. 3 (2010): 38–44.

Tricarico, Antonio. "Minutes of Consultation Meeting with Italian Prime Minister's G8 Sherpa, Ambassador Massolo." Rome, Italy: CRBM, 2009.

Trommel, W. "Good Governance as Reflexive Governance: Towards Second-Order Evaluations of Public Performance." In *EGPA Conference*. Rotterdam, Netherlands, 2008.

Turam, Berna. "The Politics of Engagement between Islam and the Secular State: Ambivalences of 'Civil Society'." *British Journal of Sociology* 55, no. 2 (2004): 259.

UN. "Deputy Secretary-General Says Achieving Sustainable Development Goals Requires 'Coherent and Holistic' Financial, Non-Financial Implementation Means." 2015.

UNEP. *Global Environmental Outlook 2000.* London, UK: Earthscan, 1999.

UNEP. "UNEP Launches Environment and Trade Hub to Support Countries in Sustainable Development Goals Implementation." *News Release,* 2015.

Union, Information Technology. "ICT Facts and Figures 2016." (2016). http://www.itu.int/en/ITU-D/Statistics/Documents/facts/ICTFactsFigures2016.pdf.

University, United Nations. "Global Development Challenges, Desired G8 Responses: A G8-Developing Country Dialogue for the Hokkaido Summit." Tokyo, Japan, 2008.

United Nations. "The Millennium Development Goals Report 2012." New York: United Nations, 2012.

United Nations Non-Governmental Liaison Office. "Stand against Poverty 16–18 October." (2009). https://www.unngls.org/index.php/un-ngls_news_archives/2009/1912-stand-against-poverty-16-18-october.

Unterhalter, Elaine. "Poverty, Education, Gender and the Millennium Development Goals: Reflections on Boundaries and Intersectionality." *Theory and Research in Education* 10, no. 3 (2012): 253–274.

Van Teijlingene, Edwin, Vanora Hundley, Zoe Matthews, Gwyneth Lewis, Wendy J. Graham, James Campbell, Petra ten Hoope-Bender, Zoe A. Sheppard, and Louise

Hulton. "Millennium Development Goals: All Good Things Must Come to an End, So What Next?"*Midwifery* 30, no. 1 (2014): 1–2.

Vandemoortele, Jan. "The MDG Conundrum: Meeting the Targets without Missing the Point." *Development Policy Review* 27, no. 4 (2009): 355–371.

Velde, Dirk Willem te. "Accountability and Effectiveness of the G20's Role in Promoting Development." In *Workshop on an Accountability Mechanism for G20 Development Commitments*. Bali, Indonesia: Overseas Development Institute, 2012.

Vendley, William F. "The Power of Inter-Religious Cooperation to Transform Conflict." *Cross Currents*, Spring (2005): 90–99.

Vendley, William F. "Vatican City: United Call for Moral Awakening on Climate Change." *Religions for Peace Global Newsletter* (2015). Published electronically May.

Ventura, Marco. "Religion as a Resource in G20 Contributions to an Innovative, Invigorated, Interconnected and Inclusive World Economy." In *Dialogue among Civilizations and Human Destiny Community CASS Forum*. Beijing, China, 2016.

Vitillo, Robert, Awraham Soetendorp, Alberto Quatrucci, Azza Karam, Attalah Fitzgibbon, Ulrich Nitschke, and Katherine Marshall. "G20 Policy Makers Should Support Wider Religious Roles in Refugee Resettlement." T20 Policy Brief (2017). Published electronically May 10. http://www.g20-insights.org/policy_briefs/g20 -policy-makers-support-wider-religious-roles-refugee-resettlement/.

Voas, David, and Mark Chaves. "Is the United States a Counterexample to the Secularization Thesis?"*American Journal of Sociology* 121, no. 5 (2016): 1517–1556.

Voss, J.P., and R. Kemp. "Reflexive Governance for Sustainable Development: Incorporating Feedback in Social Problem Solving." In *6th International Conference of the European Society for Ecological Economics*. Lisbon, Spain, 2005.

Voss, J.P. "Sustainability and Reflexive Governance: Introduction." In *Reflexive Governance for Sustainable Development*, edited by Voss, J.P., D. Bauknecht and R. Kemp, 3–28. Cheltenham, UK: Edward Elgar Publishing, 2006.

Voss, Jan-Peter, Dierk Bauknecht, and Rene Kemp. *Reflexive Governance for Sustainable Development*. Cheltenham, UK: Edward Elgar, 2006.

Voytenko, Yuliya, Kes McCormick, James Evans, and Gabriele Schliwa. "Urban Living Labs for Sustainability and Low Carbon Cities in Europe: Towards a Research Agenda." *Journal of Cleaner Production* 123, June (2016): 45–54.

Waldron, J. "Religious Contribution and Public Deliberation." *San Diego Law Review* 30 (1993): 817–848.

Wallach, L.M. "Accountable Governance in the Era of Globalization: The WTO, NAFTA, and International Harmonization of Standards."*University of Kansas Law Review* 50 (2002): 823.

Walsh, Thomas G. "Religion, Peace and the Postsecular Public Sphere." *International Journal on World Peace* 29, no. 2 (2012): 35–61.

Waltzer, M. *Spheres of Justice*. New York, New York: Basic Books, 1983.

Walzer, Michael. *The Paradox of Liberation: Secular Revolutions and Religious Counter-revolutions.* New Haven, CN: Yale University Press, 2015.

Wang, Guoxing. "Financial Crisis: Its Impacts on International Economic System and Geopolitics." *Global Review* 3 (2009): 24–38.

Wapner, Paul. *Environmental Activism and World Civic Politics.* Albany, New York: State University of New York Press, 1996.

Warner, Koko. "Environmental Change and Migration: Methodological Considerations from Ground-Breaking Global Survey." *Population and Environment* 33, no. 1 (2011): 3–27.

Weber, Max. *Economy and Society.* Vol. 1, Los Angeles, CA: Regents of the University of California, 1978.

Weiss, Richard M. "Weber on Bureaucracy: Management Consultant or Political Theorist?" *Academy of Management Review* 8, no. 2 (1983): 242–248.

Welander, Anna, Carl Hampus Lyttkens, and Therese Nilsson. "Globalization, Democracy, and Child Health in Developing Countries." *Social Science & Medicine* 136–137, July (2015): 52–63.

Wen, Fang. "Cultural Self-Consciousness: Transcending the Escape-Proof Net of Social Categorization." In *Dialogue among Civilizations and Human Destiny Community CASS Forum.* Beijing, China, 2016.

Whiteman, Gail, Brian Walker, and Paolo Perego. "Planetary Boundaries: Ecological Foundations for Corporate Sustainability." *Journal of Management Studies* 50, no. 2 (2013): 307–336.

Widmer, P.S., M.C. Schippers, and M.A. West. "Recent Developments in Reflexivity Research: A Review." *Psychology of Everyday Activity* 2, no. 2 (2009): 1–11.

Wilke, Annette. "Individualisation of Religion." *International Social Science Journal* 64, no. 213–214 (2013): 263–277.

Willaime, Jean-Paul. "Religion in Ultramodernity." In *Theorising Religion: Classical and Contemporary Debates*, edited by Beckford, James A. and John Wallis, 77–89. Aldershot: Ashgate, 2006.

Willetts, P. *The Conscience of the World: The Influence of Non-Governmental Organizations in the UN System.* London, England: Hurst & Co., 1996.

Williams, Mark, Jan Zalasiewicz, P.K. Haff, Christian Schwaegerl, Anthony D. Barnosky, and Erle C. Ellis. "The Anthropocene Biosphere." *The Anthropocene Review* 2, no. 3 (2015): 196–219.

Wilson, B. *Religion in Secular Society.* London, UK: C.A. Watts, 1966.

Wimbledon, Lord Singh. "Introduction." *Article 18: An Orphaned Right* (2013). Published electronically https://freedomdeclared.org/media/Article-18-An-Orphaned-Right .pdf.

Winner, Langdon. *The Whale and the Reactor: A Search for Limits in an Age of High Technology.* Chicago, IL: The University of Chicago Press, 1986.

Winter, Stephen. "Engaging with Globalization: A Matter of Life or Death?"*Political Theology* 3, no. 1 (2001): 47.

Woodman, D. "The Mysterious Case of the Pervasive Choice Biography: Ulrich Beck, Structure/Agency and the Middling State of Theory in the Sociology of Youth." *Journal of Youth Studies* 12, no. 3 (2009): 243–256.

Woodman, D. "Class, Individualization and Tracing Processes of Inequality in a Changing World: A Reply to Steven Roberts." *Journal of Youth Studies* 13, no. 6 (2010): 737–746.

Wuthnow, Robert, and Stephen Offutt. "Transnational Religious Connections."*Sociology of Religion* 69, no. 2 (2008): 209–232.

WWF. *Living Planet Report 2012: Biodiversity, Biocapacity and Better Choices*. Gland, Switzerland: World Wildlife Fund International, 2012. Published electronically http://d2ouvy59p0dg6k.cloudfront.net/downloads/1_lpr_2012_online_full_size _single_pages_final_120516.pdf.

WWF. *Living Planet Report 2014: Species and Spaces, People and Places*. World Wildlife Fund International, 2014. Published electronically https://www.worldwildlife.org/ pages/living-planet-report-2014.

WWF. *Living Blue Planet Report 2015: Species Habitats and Human Well-Being*. Gland, Switzerland: World Wildlife Fund International, 2015. Published electronically http://assets.worldwildlife.org/publications/817/files/original/Living_Blue_Planet _Report_2015_Final_LR.pdf?1442242821&_ga=1.102697736.806690505.1466263849.

Yoshida, Reiji. "Chief Cabinet Secretary Is Much More Than Top Government." *Japan Times* (2015). Published electronically May 18. https://www.japantimes .co.jp/news/2015/05/18/reference/chief-cabinet-secretary-much-top-government -spokesman/.

Yukich, G. "Encounters at the Religious Edge: Variation in Religious Expression across Interfaith Advocacy and Social Movement Settings." *Journal for the Scientific Study of Religion* 53, no. 4 (2014): 791–807.

Yukich, Grace, and Ruth Braunstein. "Encounters at the Religious Edge: Variation in Religious Expression across Interfaith Advocacy and Social Movement Settings." *Journal for the Scientific Study of Religion* 53, no. 4 (2014): 791.

Zablocki, Benjamin D. *Alienation and Charisma: A Study of Contemporary American Communes*. New York: Free Press, 1980.

Zapatrina, Irina. "Sustainable Development Goals for Developing Economies and Public-Private Partnership." *EPPPL* 1 (2016): 39–45.

Zeidan, David. *The Resurgence of Religion*. Netherlands: Brill, 2000.

Zinn, Jens O. "Risk, Social Inclusion and the Life Course—Review of Developments in Policy and Research." *Social Policy & Society* 12, no. 2 (2013): 319.

Zucca, Lorenzo. "A Secular Europe: Law and Religion in the European Constitutional Landscape." Oxford, UK: Oxford University Press, 2012.

Index

Abbott, Jim 173
academia
    financial and organizational support 135,
        159–160, 177–178
    global ethic 250
    Secretaries-General from 99
    See also Brigham Young University;
    Griffith University; University of Toronto
    (Munk School of Global Affairs)
accountability
    broad 189–190
    of civil society 194
    dimensions of 188–189
    of F8/F7/F20 Initiative 188–194
    of INGOS 188, 190, 191, 192, 193t
    MDGs as basis for dialogue 255–256, 258
    of RNGOS 188
    and soft power 189–190
    standards 191, 192, 193t, 194 *See also*
    accountability, G-plus System
accountability, G-plus System
    and accountability of F8/F7/F20
        Initiative 190
    F8/F7/F20 Initiative impact 230–236
    monitoring 20–23, 122n70, 178, 194,
        230–236, 290
    standards 191, 192, 193t, 194
    as summit topic 106, 122, 124, 125, 128,
        169–170, 192
*Accountability Report: G20 Anti-Corruption
    Working Group* 22
acidification, ocean 32n50
ActionAid 21, 230–231
Adamakis, Emmanuel 98t, 120, 123, 260, 303
Adams, Brian J.
    closing statement at Australia 2014 162
    as F20 Executive Committee
    member 157
    F20 origins 77
    on goals 82
    as Secretary-General 98t, 135, 140, 144,
        147, 154, 178, 303
adaptive reorganization 28

Adelaide University 160
advisors, engagement with 170–171, 174–175
aerosol loadings 32n50
Affolderbach, Martin 124, 167, 303
Africa
    African participants 105, 109
    aid package from 2007 G8 108
    proposed Scholarship Foundation 110
    as summit topic 106–107, 110, 115, 124
African Consortium for Law and Religion
    Studies 160
Age of the Anthropocene
    anthropocentrism defined 109n27
    governance challenges 26–28
    G-plus System financial
        deliberations 32–35
    at Japan 2008 109–110
    return of religion to public sphere 8–9,
        24
    role of *cosmopiety* 275–280
    SDGs as focus 270–273
    transition science 28–31 *See also*
    environmental issues
AIDS. *See* HIV/AIDS
Albrecht, Harold 173
Alexey II 76, 98t, 99, 103–104, 303
Algeria, fundamentalism in 62
All Africa Conference of Churches 124
Alliance of Civilizations Institute (Fatih
    Sultan Mehmet Vakif University) 160
Alliance to End Hunger 117
All Party Parliamentary Group on Inter-
    national Religious Freedom or Belief
    (2013) 10
Amity Institute of Advanced Legal
    Studies 160
Amity University 160
Anglican Communion
    analysis of Twitter campaign 131–132
    finances 98
    participation 87, 88, 89, 90t, 124
    UK 2013 planning 129–130
Anishnaabe peoples 162

Ankara bombings (2015)   139, 214
Annan, Kofi   103
Antalya, Turkey G20 Summit (2015)   22, 79,
    97t, 142, 235 *See also* Turkey 2015 F7/
    F20 Summit
Anthropocene. *See* Age of the Anthropocene
anti-globalization movement
    costs of   43–44
    emergence of   37–38
    religion's role in   279 *See also* civil society
Arab Spring   127, 209
archaeological artifacts, destruction
    of   139–140
archives and records
    Canadian Council of Churches   157, 189,
        302
    G8/G7/G20 Research Groups (University
        of Toronto)   21, 300
    G8 Information Centre (University of
        Toronto)   21, 94, 300
    Griffith University   301
    ICC and   157
    ICLRS (Brigham Young University)   301
Argentina
    G20 origins   13
    participation at Germany 2017   149
    planning for Argentina 2018   150
Arif, Sarosh   222, 303
Arinze, Francis   155
Armenian Church   124
arms trade   141
Article 18   10
Article 71   223
assessment of F8/F7/F20 Initiative   208–228
    competing   222–228
    information technology   208–211
    international relations   208, 209, 212–214
    redundancy   223–224
    reinforcement   227–228
    rejection   226–227
    replacement   224–226
    secularization   208, 209, 214–222
    self-assessment by G-plus System
        232–233 *See also* impact of F8/F7/F20
        Initiative
assets, impaired   33
associational democracy   67

Australia
    Brisbane G20 Summit (2014)   97t, 137, 235
    G20 origins   13 *See also* Australia 2014 F20
    Summit
Australia 2014 F20 Summit
    academic support   135, 159
    ancillary events   166
    civil society   234
    engagement with business   178
    engagement with political officials   166,
        173
    F20 origins   77, 135–137
    finances   159–160
    media coverage   136, 182
    overview   134–137
    participants   84, 85, 86t, 135, 237
    SDGs as focus   268–269
    Secretaries-General   98t, 135, 136
    statements, briefs, and communi-
        qués   136–137, 162
    videos online   210
Australian Bahá'í Community   160
Austria, Schloss Elmau G7 Summit
    (2015)   22, 97t
autonomy and transnational governance   40
Axelgard, Frederick   77, 135
Axworthy, Lloyd   120, 164, 303

B20   17, 19, 129, 235
Babie, Paul   136
Bahá'í faith, planning and participation   86t,
        118, 123, 124, 147, 173
Bahá'í Local Spiritual Assemblies   173
Baines, Nicholas   188
Bauman, Zygmunt   36–37
Bayne, Nicholas   14
Beck, Ulrich   59–61, 197, 216, 299
Beijing, China F20 Summit (2016). *See* China
    2016 F20 Summit
Belgium, Brussels G7 Summit (2014)   134, 212
Benedict XVI   103, 115
Berkley Center at Georgetown
    University   126
Berlin, Germany T20 Summit (2017)   55,
        149–150, 290
Berlusconi, Silvio   115–116
Beyer, Peter   1, 7, 10, 221

Beyond 2015   176, 237, 263–265
bias   296–297, 298
biodiversity loss   25, 29, 32n50
biofuels   112
biogeochemical flow changes   32n50
biophysical environmental conditions   295
Birmingham, England G8 Summit (1998)   13
Blair, Tony   11, 58
blinders, problem-solving with   201, 206
Block, Kelly   173
Bono   179, 253, 261–262
Bordeaux, France F8/F20 Summit (2011). *See* France 2011 F8/F20 Summit
borders and reflexivity   72, 197
Braid, Peter   173
Brazil and G20 origins   13
Bread for the World   117
BREXIT   44, 48
Brigham Young University
   archives and records   301
   Australia 2014 support   135, 159
   financial support   160–161
   merger of F8/F7/F20 Initiative   78–79, 138
   Summit Secretariat   157
Brinkerhoff, Derick   277–278
Brisbane, Australia G20 Summit (2014)   97t, 137, 235
broad accountability   189–190
The Brookings Institution   21
Brundtland Report   31
Brunel Law and Religion Research Group   160
Brunel University London   160
Brussels, Belgium G7 Summit (2014)   134, 212
Buchanan, A.   189–190, 191, 192, 194
Buddhist faith, planning and participation   86t, 108, 124
Bulekov, Hegumen P.   124, 303
Bulut, Mehmet   180
Bush, George W.   13
business
   B20   17, 19, 129, 235
   F8/F7/F20 Initiative engagement with   178–181, 187
   legitimacy and risk   32

   SDGs and F8/F7/F20 Initiative
      role   266–267
Business 20   17, 19, 129, 235

C20
   Antalya, Turkey G20 Summit (2015)   142
   Brisbane, Australia G20 Summit (2014)   137, 235
   engagement with Sherpas   172
   origins   17, 117
   recognition of   19–20, 137, 213
   Saint Petersburg, Russia G20 Summit (2013)   235
   shift to by RNGOS   227
Cahill, Desmond   145–146, 303
Call to Action #48   245
Camp David, US G8 Summit (2012)   126, 128, 166 *See also* US 2012 F8 Summit
Canada
   F8 origins   83
   G7/G8/G20 origins   13
   Halifax G7 Summit (1995)   20
   Hunstville G8 Summit (2010)   21–22, 43–44, 121, 122n70, 123, 232
   in list of presidencies   97t
   Toronto G20 Summit (2010)   43–44, 121–123 *See also* Canada 2010 F8/F20 Summit
Canada 2010 F8/F20 Summit
   academic support   177
   accountability   122, 169–170, 192
   ancillary events and pre-conferences   163–165, 182, 232
   domestic impact   243–244
   duration of   152
   emphasis on process   205
   engagement with civil society   175–176, 232
   engagement with political officials   119, 120, 159, 168, 169, 170, 172–173, 174
   finances   119–120, 159
   focus on MDGS   120, 254–256
   logo   93
   media coverage   119, 121, 182–183, 205
   overview   117–123
   participants   84, 85, 86t, 87–90, 119, 120, 186

Canada 2010 F8/F20 Summit (cont.)
    reflexivity   207
    religious rituals   162
    Secretary-General   98t
    statements, briefs, and communi-
        qués   89, 96, 118–119, 153, 172, 255–256
    theme   92
    videos online   210
Canadian Catholic Bishops   244
Canadian Council of Churches
    engagement with civil society   175
    financial and organizational
        support   117–118, 160
    Hamilton's role   237
    Justice Tour (2015)   176
    participation survey and constituency
        claims   90t
    records   157, 189, 302
Canadian Council of Imams   118
Canadian Interfaith Conversation
        244–246 See also Canadian Interfaith
        Partnership
Canadian Interfaith Partnership   117–118,
        176, 178, 243–244 See also Canadian
        Interfaith Conversation
Canadian Yeshiva and Rabbinical
        School   256
Cannes, France G20 Summit (2011)   123, 124,
        125–126 See also France 2011 F8/F20
        Summit
Cannes Action Plan for Growth and Jobs   126
Cao, Nanlai   180–181
capitalism, religion's relation to   218–220
Carey, George L.   54, 155
Caritas in Veritate (encyclical)   115
Carr, E.H.   296
carrying capacity   25, 270
Catholic Church
    on Canada 2010 statement   255–256
    constituency survey   90t
    participation   86t, 90t, 103, 114, 124
    pull out from Canadian Interfaith
        Partnership   244
    support for Italy 2009   114
Catholic Committee Against Hunger and
        Development   165
Catholic Social Services   89
celebrities   234, 253, 261–262

censorship   211
Center for Research and Training in Interfaith
        Relations   160
Center on Religion, Law and Economy
        in the Mediterranean Area (Insubria
        University)   160
Centre for Global Studies at the University of
        Victoria   21
Centre for Interfaith and Cultural
        Dialogue   77, 159, 160 See also Griffith
        University
Centre for International Governance
        Innovation   21, 170
Chamber of Commerce, International
        17–18, 231
Chatham House   21
chemical industry   27
chemical pollution as planetary
        boundary   32n50
child health and welfare
    MDGS   252
    RNGOS involvement   89
    as summit topic   117, 121, 128
China
    Christian transnationalism   180–181
    earthquake (2010)   31
    G20 origins   13
    Hangzhou G20 Summit (2016)   19, 22, 30,
        97t, 235
    Islamic Economic Community   180 See
        also China 2016 F20 Summit
China 2016 F20 Summit
    coordination with other events   82, 144
    organizational support for   160
    overview   142–147
    participants   84, 86t, 144, 237
    Secretaries-General   99t, 144, 154
    theme   79, 93 See also Pacific Regional
        Pre-Conference (Suva, Fiji 2016); South
        Asia Regional Pre-Conference (Trivan-
        drum, India 2016)
Chinese Academy of Social Sciences   82,
        144, 160
Chong, Michael   173
Christie, James T.
    as F20 Executive Committee
        member   157
    F20 origins   77, 135

merging of F8/F7/F20 Initiative 77–78, 138

on need for persistence through cycle 105–106

as Secretary-General 98t, 154, 303

on using MDGs as focus 106, 254

Chryssavgis, John 124, 257, 259–260, 303

Churches of the Reformation in Germany 90t

Church of England 97, 99 *See also* Anglican Communion

Church of Jesus Christ of Latter-day Saints (LDS) 77, 78–79, 138

CIDSE 165

Civil G8 Advisory Council (Russia 2006) 102n9

civil society
accountability of 194

Antalya, Turkey G20 Summit (2015) 142, 235

Australia 2014 234

Beyond 2015 176, 237, 263–265

Brisbane, Australia G20 Summit (2014) 137, 235

Camp David, US G8 Summit (2012) 128

Canada 2010 F8/F20 Summit 175–176, 232

Cannes, France G20 Summit (2011) 125–126

deaths 38

Deauville, France G8 Summit (2011) 125–126

effect on international relations 212, 213, 290

emergence of anti-globalization protests 37–38

engagement with F8/F7/F20 Initiative 83, 175–177, 187, 212, 213, 233–234

external relations as measure of impact 233–234

and forecast for conflicts 287

Gleneagles, Scotland G8 Summit (2005) 100

global financial crisis response 262, 263

Hangzhou, China G20 Summit (2016) 235

Heiligendamm, Germany G8 Summit (2007) 107

Hokkaido-Toyako, Japan G8 Summit (2008) 112

Hunstville, Canada G8 Summit (2010) 121

impact of F8/F7/F20 Initiative 229–236

increase in activities 17, 100n3

Italy 2009 115

L'Aquila, Italy G8 Summit (2009) 38, 115–116

Los Cabos, Mexico G20 (2012) 128–129, 235

Make Poverty History campaign 75–76, 100, 102, 227, 253

MDGs as focus 212, 213, 253–254

monitoring by 230–236, 290

NGOs as distinct type of 279

participants in F8/F7/F20 Initiative 83

Pittsburgh, PA G20 Summit (2009) 117

rejection of 226

Roma Civil G8 115–116

Saint Petersburg, Russia G8 Summit (2006) 102n9

Saint Petersburg, Russia G20 Summit (2013) 133, 235

SDGs engagement 284–285

security costs 43–44, 121, 125

statements, briefs, and communiqués 17

as term 75n1

Toronto, Canada G20 Summit (2010) 121–122

Turkey 2015 234

UK 2005 175

UK 2013 130

Web 2.0 184–185, 209–210, 211

World Social Forum (Brazil, 2005) 100n3

See also C20

Civil Society 20. *See* C20

Çizakça, Murat 180

clash of civilizations thesis 144

class consciousness and paradox of emancipation 219

climate agreements 107

climate change
accountability monitoring 231

at Canada 2010 120, 121

Canadian Interfaith Conversation 245

effects 24–26

at France 2011 256, 259–260

climate change (cont.)
  at Germany 2007   107
  governance challenges   26–28
  G-plus System financial
    deliberations   32–35
  at Italy 2009   115, 117
  at Japan 2008   109, 110, 111
  justice tours   121, 164, 176
  letter from UK G8 Team Assistant   169
  at Pacific Regional Pre-Conference (Suva,
    Fiji 2016)   143
  as planetary boundary   32n50
  transition science   28–31
  at Turkey 2015   140
  United Nations Climate Change Confer-
    ences   245, 256
  Vatican faith-leader consultation on sus-
    tainable development and (2015)   177 See
    also Age of the Anthropocene; environ-
    mental issues
Climate Investment Funds   169
Climate Justice Tour (Canada 2010)   121, 164
Cnaan, Ram   135, 303
Coertzen, Pieter   140, 157, 303
collaborative rationality   278
Cologne, Germany F8 Summit (2007). See
  Germany 2007 F8 Summit
Columbia University   177, 232–233
communiqués. See statements, briefs, and
  communiqués
community fracturing from
  globalization   36–37
complexity, efficacy paradox of   201, 203,
  206, 208
Complex Standard   192, 193t, 194
compliance monitoring. See accountability;
  monitoring of G-plus System
Compliance Reports   22
Complutense University   161
conflicts
  cosmopiety and religious
    conflicts   272–273
  forecast for   286–287
  and globalization   36
  as summit topic   109, 110, 111, 121
  United Religions Initiative and   225
Confucianism and corruption
  reduction   54n45
Consejo Argentino para la Libertad
  Religiosa   160

consocial politics   67
Consorcio Latinaamericano de Libertad
  Religiosa   160, 161
consumption pressures. See Age of the
  Anthropocene
controllability as dimension of
  accountability   189
cooperation and harmony of interests   296
coral reefs   26
Corporate Dream, Global Nightmare
  (2005)   100n3
corporate sustainability   31
corruption
  costs   286
  role of RNGOs in addressing   53–54
  as summit topic   124
cosmopiety
  as cultural capital   276–277
  defined   9
  and development collaboration   247–249
  governance dimensions   275–276,
    289–290, 293
  non-human agency   271–272
  and religious conflicts   272–273
  as replacement for secularization   67–74,
    277–280
  role of   275–280, 288–289
  SDGS   70–71, 276
  soft power   69–74
  as term   70–71, 299
cosmopolitan political theory   69–70, 72–74
  See also cosmopiety
Costello, Tim   137
costs
  criticism of F8/F7/F20 Initiative   204–
    205, 206, 226
  housing and transportation   124, 158,
    159, 206
  security   43–44, 121, 125
Council for a Parliament of the World
  Religions   224n165
Cox, Jo   48
cultural barriers to e-governance   211
cultural capital, cosmopiety as   276–277
cultural events at summits   162, 165

Daish (ISIL)   139–140, 214
Daliwal, Sukh   173
Dallaire, Roméo   120, 303
dance and music at summits   162, 165

data collection for this book 301–302
DATA Report 22–23, 230
Davies, Don 173
Deauville, France G8 Summit (2011) 123, 124, 125–126
Deauville Partnership 126, 127
Debt AIDS Trade Africa 104
debt relief and debt cancellation 75–76, 101, 102, 120
decisional governance and *cosmopiety* 275, 276, 293
deforestation 267–268
Deguchi, Juntoku 155
delegation model 83–86, 152–153, 186, 189
deliberative governance and *cosmopiety* 275–276, 289–290, 293
democracy
  associational democracy 67
  expectations of democratic norms 40–41, 42–43
  paradox of 44–45
demonstrations. *See* civil society
Denmark and MDGs commitments 253
Department of Citizenship and Immigration Canada 159
Department of Foreign Affairs (Italy) 114, 158, 171
Dersaadet Kültür Platformu 160
desecularization. *See* religion's return to public sphere; secularization
Deutscher Evangelischer Kirchentag (Germany, 2007) 82, 105, 163
development
  collaboration with religious organizations 247–249
  cosmopiety collaboration 247–249
  engagement with development organizations 187
  Muslim religious organizations 61–62
  official development assistance (ODA) 253
  rejection of F8/F7/F20 Initiative model 226
  shift in F20 goals 82, 283
  as summit topic 101, 106–107, 115, 124, 125, 136, 140 *See also* MDGs (Millennium Development Goals); SDGs (Sustainable Development Goals); sustainable development
Dewar, Paul 173

dialogue
  as central to F8/F7/F20 Initiative 81–82, 85
  dinners (Canada 2010) 119, 120, 159, 173
  importance of in governance 15–16
  and informality 194–197
  MDGs as starting point for 256–261
  of pluralism 71–72
  shift from global governance to development 82, 283
  summit structure 101
  as summit topic 115, 256–261
differentiation 1, 7, 10, 214–222
digital gap 210–211
Dignity Pre-Conference (Germany 2007) 105, 163
dinners, dialogue (Canada 2010) 119, 120, 159, 173
diplomacy
  indices 21
  and perception of process 20
  relation of G-plus System to 15–16
  religious diplomacy as replacement for secularization 68–69 *See also* cosmopiety
directional governance and *cosmopiety* 275, 276, 290, 293
diverse portfolio typology 203, 208
diversity
  of F8/F7/F20 Initiative participants 3, 82–83, 85–87, 86t
  pluralism as engaging with others 71–72
  as summit topic 109, 110, 136
Doha International Award for Interfaith Dialogue 245
domestic interfaith relations 228, 243–246
domestic violence 242
Dondelinger, Joseph 73
double-loop learning 198–199, 202
droughts 27
Durham, W. Cole, Jr.
  as F20 Executive Committee member 157
  F20 origins and merger of F8/F7/F20 Initiative 77, 78
  as Secretary-General 98t, 135, 136, 144, 147, 154, 178, 304
  as speaker 140
  on sustainable development focus 265
  T20 policy briefs (2017) 55, 148–149

Earth Institute (Columbia University)   177,
    232–233
earthquakes   31, 113–114, 162, 164, 207
Ecclesiastical Insurance   159
Eck, Diana   71–72
Economic and Social Council of the United
    Nations (ECOSOC)   223, 225
The Economic Policy Research Foundation of
    Turkey   160
economics
    commitment to open markets   252
    green economy   34
    limits on growth from environmental
    change   25
    as summit topic   147, 148 See also devel-
    opment; financing; global financial crisis
    (1997–1999)
ECOSOC (Economic and Social Council of the
    United Nations)   223, 225
ecosystem pressures. See Age of the Anthro-
    pocene; environmental issues
Ecumenical Advocacy Alliance   106
Edelman Trust Barometer   283
Edgar, Robert   115, 156
education
    MDGS   252
    Pacific Regional Pre-Conference (Suva, Fiji
    2016)   143
    as summit topic   101, 120, 134
    youth summits and pre-conferences   134,
    141
Education for Innovative Societies in the 21st
    Century   229
Edwards, Len   172
efficacy paradox of complexity   201, 203,
    206, 208
e-governance
    and corruption reduction   54n45
    cultural barriers   211
    defined   184
    development of   94
    UK 2013   84, 87, 130, 131–132, 208, 210, 213
    uses   184
Ehrensperger, Kathy   99t, 147, 304
Eliasson, Jan   34–35
Elmau, Austria G7 Summit (2015)   22, 97t
emancipation, paradox of   219
emotions and link to morality   220

employment, as summit topic   136
engagement groups
    Brisbane, Australia G20 Summit
    (2014)   137, 235
    F8/F7/F20 Initiative as potential engage-
    ment group   287–292
    Los Cabos, Mexico G20 (2012)   128–129
    monitoring of G-plus System   21
    phases of   20, 93
    policy briefs by   21, 55, 148–150, 290
    recognition of   18–20, 234–236
    shadow summits by   236
    Solar System of G20   18, 21
    types   17–18, 234
entrepreneurs, message/norm   263, 286
environmental issues
    carrying capacity   25, 270
    cosmopiety, role of   275–280
    deforestation   267–268
    ethics as human-centered   45–46
    from globalization   26–28, 36, 41–42
    governance challenges   26–28
    G-plus System financial
    deliberations   32–35
    as human-induced   24–26
    MDGS   252
    non-human agency   270–273
    Pope Francis on   138
    return of religion to public sphere   1,
    8–9, 24
    and risk   32, 33, 42
    as summit topic   109–110, 120, 121, 136,
    255–256, 267–269
    transition science   28–31 See also Age
    of the Anthropocene; SDGs (Sustain-
    able Development Goals); sustainable
    development
Environment and Trade Hub   34–35
Episcopal Conference of the Italian Bishops
    of the Catholic Church   114, 158
erosion of strategic capabilities   201–202
ethics
    as anthropocentric   45–46
    difficulty separating church and state in
    decision-making   65
    global ethic   247, 250–251, 264
    as summit topic   104
Ethics in Action Initiative   270

Eubank, Sharon 140, 304
Europe
    Euro zone crisis 124n80
    G7 origins 13
    rise of nationalism 41, 48–49, 283
European Central Bank 48
Euro zone crisis 124n80
Evangelical Lutheran Church of
    America 90t
exclusivism *vs.* pluralism 71–72
excursions and events, summit 163–166
expectations, increased
    democratic norms 40–41, 42–43
    from MDGs and SDGs 286
exploring experiments typology 203, 208
external epistemic actors 191
external relations with F8/F7/F20 Initiative
    168–185
    academia 177–178
    business 178–181, 187
    civil society 83, 175–177, 187, 212, 213,
        233–234
    foreign ministers 171
    government advisors 170–171
    heads of state 168–170
    mayors 174
    media engagement 164, 181–185, 205
    members of Parliament 119, 120, 136–137,
        159, 166, 172–174
    political officials 119, 120, 136–137, 159,
        166, 168–175, 233–234
    Sherpas 171–172
    special advisors 174–175

F7 Initiative
    acknowledgment of F8/F7/F20
    Initiative 94, 143
    last statement 154
    merging of F8/F7/F20 Initiative 77–78
    origins 75–77, 134, 153 *See also* F8/F7/F20
    Initiative
F7 Interfaith Youth Summit (Germany,
    2014) 76–77, 119, 134, 153, 167
F7 Interfaith Youth Summit (Germany,
    2015) 77, 141, 154, 158, 166–167, 213
F8/F7/F20 Initiative
    compared to other interfaith
    groups 81–82

critiques of concept 187–188,
    207, 208
evolution 2–4, 75–79, 289
and general return of religion to public
sphere 5–11
merge 77–79, 138
official recognition of 94, 142–143, 171,
    229–230, 287
origins 12–13, 75–79, 83, 94
phases of development 93–94, 150
potential as an engagement
group 287–292
reflexive analysis of 204–208
scholarship on 292–293, 295–296
structure 79–81
suggestions for 287–292
terms 2–3 *See also* accountability;
assessment of F8/F7/F20 Initiative;
cosmopiety; external relations with F8/
F7/F20 Initiative; impact of F8/F7/F20
Initiative; leadership rotation model;
participants in F8/F7/F20 Initiative; pre-
conferences, F8/F7/F20 Initiative; reform,
internal; summits, F8/F7/F20 Initiative
F8 Initiative
    engagement with business 178
    engagement with civil society 175–176
    engagement with political
    officials 168–170
    housing and transportation
    costs 158–159
    merging of F8/F7/F20 Initiative 77–78
    origins 75–76, 83, 100, 227
    summit organization 152–153
    years in cycle 76 *See also* F8/F7/F20
    Initiative
F20 Executive Committee
    directional governance and
    cosmopiety 276
    members 155, 157, 237
    merger 77–78
    nomenclature 2
    participation in T20 94
    planning for Argentina 2018 150 *See also*
    International Continuance Committee
    (ICC)
F20 Initiative
    business engagement 178–181

F20 Initiative (cont.)
  merging of F8/F7/F20 Initiative   77–78
  origins   75–76, 77, 94, 96, 97, 135–137,
      154–155 *See also* F8/F7/F20 Initiative
@F2oNews   185, 210
failures of states   277–278
Faith and Work Forum   267
faith-based organizations (FBOs)
  compared to F8/F7/F20 Initiative   81–82
  growth of   49–50
  links with development and
  cosmopiety   71 *See also* religious non-
  governmental organizations (RNGOs)
Fakuda, Yasuo   171
famine, T20 policy brief (2017)   55, 148–150,
      290 *See also* food security and food
      supply
farming as summit topic   128
Fast, Ed   173
Fatih Sultan Mehmet Vakif Üniversitesi   160
FBOS. *See* faith-based organizations (FBOS)
Federal Ministry for Economic Cooperation
      and Development   54
Ferrari, Alessandro   157, 304
Fiji. *See* Pacific Regional Pre-Conference
      (Suva, Fiji 2016)
finances, G-plus System   32–35, 43–44,
      121, 125
finances, summit
  criticism of F8/F7/F20 Initiative
      204–205, 206, 226
  effect of global financial crisis on   152,
      205, 213
  effect on host country   292
  government support   97, 103, 158, 205
  housing and transportation costs   124,
      158, 159, 206
  overview   158–161
  resources   78–79, 82, 97–99 *See also*
  under specific Summits
financial crisis, global. *See* global financial
      crisis (1997–1999)
Financial Transaction Tax   123
financing
  green   30
  Islamic   140, 180
  of SDGs   34–35
  as summit topic   115, 116, 124, 140, 180

and transnational governance   40
Financing for Development Action
      Agenda   34
Finberg, Max   127, 304
Finland
  civil society coalition   284
  MDGS commitments   253
First Nations peoples. *See* indigenous peoples
first-order reflexivity   198, 199–200, 202, 204
fish and fishing industry   25–26, 29
Fletcher, Steven   119, 172
Floria, Juan Navarro   136
Foblets, Marie-Claire   140, 157, 304
food security and food supply
  and environmental change   27
  famine policy brief by T20 (2017)   55,
      148–150, 290
  food crisis (2007–2008)   111, 116
  Germany F7 2015 Youth Pre-Conference
  Statement   141
  L'Aquila Food Security Initiative   116, 117
  letter from UK G8 Team Assistant   169
  MDGS   252
  planetary boundaries   30
  as summit topic   111, 127, 136
foreign ministers, engagement with   171
forestation   267–268
Foster, Neil   136
France
  Cannes G20 Summit (2011)   123, 124,
      125–126
  Deauville G8 Summit (2011)   123, 124,
      125–126
  F8 origins   83
  G6 origins   12
  G7/G8/G20 origins   13
  in list of presidencies   97t
  Paris terrorist attacks (2015)   138–139,
      213–214
  trust gap   283 *See also* France 2011 F8/F20
  Summit
France 2011 F8/F20 Summit
  coordination with other events   82, 165
  engagement with political officials   168
  INGO Caravan   165
  MDGS use in dialogue   256–261
  overview   123–126
  participants   83, 85, 86t, 123–124

reflexivity 207
Secretary-General 98t
statements, briefs, and
communiqués 96, 125, 261
survey on process and engagement
90–92, 91t
France G8 Summit (2011). *See* Deauville,
France G8 Summit (2011)
France G20 Summit (2011). *See* Cannes,
France G20 Summit (2011)
Francis (pope) 137–138
freshwater use as planetary boundary 32n50
Friends of the Earth 104
Fukudo-Parr, Sakiko 262–263
future studies 299–300

G6 12 *See also* G-plus System
G7
accountability reports 22
as basis for F8/F7/F20 Initiative 2–4
engagement with civil society 234–236
Hamilton on 2015 agenda 142
origins 13, 134
presidencies 97t
recognition of engagement groups 20
recognition of F8/F7/F20 Initiative 94,
143, 171
RfP engagement 224–225
shadowing by Youth Summit 2–3 *See
also* G-plus System; *specific summits*
G7 Elmau Progress Report on Biodiversity 22
G7 Foreign Ministers Meeting (Hiroshima
2016) 94, 143, 171, 224–225
G7/G8/G20 Information Centre (University of
Toronto) 21, 94, 300–301
G7/G8/G20 Research Groups (University of
Toronto)
compliance monitoring 22, 231–232, 233
Compliance Reports 22
coordination with and observation of
Canada 2010 118
distribution of Germany 2007
statement 107
Hamilton's role 237
Japan 2008 preparation 170
materials 21, 300
regional meetings 178
study of F8/F7/F20 Initiative 177

G8
as basis for F8/F7/F20 Initiative 2–4
compared to G20 113
origins 13, 83
presidencies 97t
Russia's removal from 13, 134, 153, 166,
212
self-assessment 232–233 *See also* G-plus
System; *specific summits*
G8 Alternatives Summit (2005) 100n3
G8/G7
about 231n187, 232
contributions from
Secretaries-General 178
Hamilton's role 129, 133, 142, 167,
207–208, 237
Heckman and Hamilton article on US
2012 129, 207–208
G8/G20 People's Summit (Toronto, 2010) 121
G8 Information Centre. *See* G7/G8/G20 Information Centre (University of Toronto)
*G8 Summit Declaration on
Counter-Terrorism* 229
G8 World Religions Summit. *See* F8/F7/F20
Initiative
G20
as basis for F8/F7/F20 Initiative 2–4
compared to G8 113
first communiqué directed at 96, 153
first meeting 113
membership criteria 85
origins 13
participation in F20 84
presidencies 97t
self-assessment 233
shift to shadowing 96, 97, 154, 186
special advisors, engagement with
174–175 *See also* civil society; engagement groups; G-plus System; *specific
summits*
G20 Business Scorecard 231
G20 Development Action Plan 290
G20 (Girls 20) engagement group 19
G20 Financial Inclusion Experts Group 123
G20 Information Centre. *See* G7/G8/G20
Information Centre (University of
Toronto)
#G20Interfaith 185, 210

G20 Interfaith Executive Committee. *See* F20
    Executive Committee
*G20 Interfaith Summit 2017 Summary
    Report*   150
G20 Interfaith Summit International Organiz-
    ing Committee   150, 237
G20 Interfaith Summits. *See* F8/F7/F20
    Initiative
G20 Monitor   21
Gebrestadik, Mussie Hailu   148, 304
gender
    digital gap   210, 211
    impact on religious transnational
        relations   228, 236–243
    Islamic traditions and gender
        equality   242–243
    MDGS   252
    SDGS   241–242
    as summit topic   241–243
Georgetown University   126, 161
Germany
    cancellation of 2015 youth summit   154,
        158, 166–167, 213
    F8 origins   83
    G7/G8/G20 origins   13, 83
    Hamburg G20 Summit (2017)   97t
    Heiligendamm G8 Summit (2007)   43,
        97t, 107, 108
    in list of presidencies   97t
    Muslim demographic revolution   48,
    60 *See also* Germany 2007 F8 Summit;
        Germany 2017 F20 Summit
Germany 2007 F8 Summit
    coordination with other events   82, 105,
        163
    deliberative governance and
        cosmopiety   275–276
    Dignity Pre-Conference   105, 163
    emphasis on process   205
    engagement with political officials   174
    finances   158
    invitation to host   104
    in list of presidencies   97t
    overview   105–108
    participants   83, 84, 86t, 105
    reflexivity   206
    Secretary-General   98t, 154
    statements, briefs, and
        communiqués   106–107
    theme   93

Germany 2017 F20 Summit
    emphasis on process   205
    formation of S20   17
    overview   147–148
    participants   86t, 147–148, 149, 237
    recognition of engagement groups   19
    Secretaries-General   99, 99t, 147
    statements, briefs, and
        communiqués   148–149
    theme   79
Ghanea, Nazila   174, 242, 304
Giddens, Anthony   37
Girls   20, 19
girls education as summit topic   120
Giuliani, Carlo   38
Gleneagles, Scotland G8 Summit (2005)   100,
        253
Global Call to Action Against Poverty   115,
        253
Global Campaign against Poverty   112
Global Change Research Institute (University
        of Maryland)   29
Global Diplomacy Index   21
Global Energy Security   229
global ethic   247, 250–251, 264
global financial crisis (1997–1999)
    civil society response   262, 263
    effect on international relations   212, 213
    effect on summit finances and
        participation   152, 205, 213
    G-plus evolution   13
    MDGS   262, 263
    as summit topic   115
globalization
    an economic process *vs.* political
        process   1–2
    benefits   36
    environmental issues and costs   26–28,
        36, 41–42
    as liquifying modernity   36–37
    and rise of G-plus System   12
    vulnerabilities from   35–38 *See also* anti-
        globalization movement
global norm   247, 249–254, 264, 286
Global Warming 8 Conference (2005)   100n3
goals. *See* MDGS (Millennium Development
        Goals); SDGS (Sustainable Development
        Goals)
Gold Coast, Australia F20 Summit (2014). *See*
        Australia 2014 F20 Summit

governance
  challenges in Age of the
    Anthropocene 26–28
  dialogue, importance of 15–16
  dimensions and *cosmopiety* 275–276,
    289–290, 293
  forecasts 286–287
  as limited technique 45
  reflexive 198–203
  rise of transnational 39–41, 68–69
  shift in F20 goals 82 *See also*
    e-governance; governance without
    government
governance without government
  accountability role of F8/F7/F20
    Initiative 192
  F8/F7/F20 Initiative structure 80–81
  relationship of G-plus System to
    diplomacy 15–16
  religious diplomacy in 68–69
  shift to 38–41 *See also* governance
G-plus System
  dialogue as tool 15–16
  engagement with civil society as measure
    of impact 234–236
  environmental change and financial
    deliberations 32–35
  evolution 12–15
  and F8/F7/F20 Initiative phases of
    development 93–94, 150
  impact of F8/F7/F20 Initiative 228–236
  informality of 14, 195–196
  monitoring of 20–23, 122n70, 178, 194,
    230–236, 290
  origins 12
  presidencies 97t
  relation to diplomacy 15–16
  rise of shadow summits and protests 17,
    236
  security costs 43–44, 121, 125
  self-assessment 232–233
  statements, briefs, and communiqués 14,
    96, 129, 169, 172
  structure 14
  terms 2 *See also* accountability, G-plus
    System; engagement groups; *specific
    summits*
Greece and Euro zone crisis 124n80
Greek Orthodox Church 123, 124
green economy 34

green financing 30
Greenpeace 104
Griffith University
  archival materials 301
  F20 origins 77
  Summit Secretariat 157
  support from 159, 160, 178
Grim, Brian 135, 140, 178, 179, 241–242, 304
Group of Eight. *See* G8
Group of Seven. *See* G7
Group of Twenty. *See* G20
GSott8 115
"Guidelines of the Organisation for
  Economic Co-operation and Devel-
  opment (OECD) for Multinational
  Enterprises," 107

Habermas, Jürgen 56–57, 65–66, 217
Haiti earthquake (2010) 31
Hajnal, Peter
  on engagement groups 19–20, 93, 234,
    235
  on impact of civil engagement 229, 290
  on informality 14
  on monitoring of G-plus System 233
Halafoff, Anna 72–73
Halifax, Canada G7 Summit (1995) 20
Hamburg, Germany G20 Summit (2017) 97t
  See also Germany 2017 F20 Summit
Hamilton, Karen
  address to UN High Panel on MDGs 176,
    237
  article on US 2012 129, 207–208
  on cancellation of Russia 2014 134
  delivery of Canada 2010 statement 172
  on G7 2015 agenda 142
  G8/G7 role 129, 133, 142, 167, 207–208, 237
  as leader/member 157, 237–238,
    239, 304
  merging of F8/F7/F20 Initiative 77, 138
  on need to stay focused on goals 213
  on political pushback 258–259
  proposal on host selection 194
  on religious rituals within summits 161
  as speaker 124, 125, 140
  on youth summit plans 167
Hammour, Mohamad 179
Hangzhou, China G20 Summit (2016) 19,
    22, 30, 97t, 235 *See also* China 2016 F20
    Summit

Hangzhou Comprehensive Account-
ability Report on G20 Development
Commitments 22
hard power 51 *See also* power; soft power
harmony of interests 281, 296
Harper, Stephen 119
Harvard University, Pluralism Project at 71
heads of state, engagement with 168–170
health
  gap 36
  Germany F7 2015 Youth Pre-Conference
    Statement 141
  HIV/AIDS 106, 125, 252
  malaria 169, 252, 254–255
  MDGS 252
  as summit topic 101, 106, 117, 121,
    125, 127
Heavily Indebted Poor Country Initiative
  (HIPC) 75–76
Heckman, Bud 98t, 127, 129, 207–208, 304
Heiligendamm, Germany G8 Summit
  (2007), 43, 97t, 107, 108 *See also* Ger-
  many 2007 F8 Summit
Heinrich Böll Foundation
  engagement groups 19
  monitoring of G-plus System 21, 290
Heinrich Böll Institute
  engagement groups 18, 19
higher law secularism 67
Higher School of Economics 232
Hildebrandt, Sarah 127, 304
Hill, Christopher 105, 254, 304
Hill, Mark 140, 304
Hindu faith participation and support 86t,
  118, 159
Hindu Federation of Canada 159
HIPC (Heavily Indebted Poor Country
  Initiative) 75–76
Hiroshima, Japan G7 Foreign Ministers
  Meeting (2016) 94, 143, 171, 224–225
historical sociological method 297–299
HIV/AIDS 106, 125, 252
Hobbes, Thomas 296
Hokkaido-Toyako, Japan G8 Summit
  (2008) 110, 111–113 *See also* Japan 2008 F8
  Summit
homelessness 164
hosts
  domestic impact 228, 243–246
  effect on process 92

and engagement groups recognition 18–
  19, 235–236
interviews with 301–302
role 80–81, 82
selecting/inviting process 103–104,
  194–195
housing costs 122, 158, 159
Howard, Peter 140, 305
Huber, Wolfgang 98t, 104, 305
Hulme, D. 262–263
human ecology theory 1, 8–9, 295, 297–299
Human Rights and Religious Freedom Pre-
  Conference (Canada 2010) 163–164
human trafficking 141
hunger. *See* food security and food supply
Hunstville, Canada G8 Summit (2010)
  civil society 121
  criticism of 123
  The Muskoka Accountability Report 21–
    22, 122n70, 232
  security costs 43–44 *See also* Canada
    2010 F8/F20 Summit
Huntington, Samuel 144
Hyer, Bruce 173
Hyökki, Linda 222, 305

IBAQ 159
Ibrahim, Gregorios Yohanna 7n21, 124, 280,
  281–282, 305
ICC. *See* International Continuance Committee (ICC)
ICLRS. *See* International Center for Law
  and Religion Studies (Brigham Young
  University)
idealism 192
Ignatius Zakka I 281
IMF (International Monetary Fund) 13, 38,
  107, 224n165
immigration and migration
  from climate change 27
  minority religions and tensions from 146
  and potential legitimation crisis 44
  remittances 105n16
  and return of religion to public
    sphere 48, 60
  scholarship assumptions 60
  as summit topic 115, 140 *See also* refugees
impact of F8/F7/F20 Initiative 228–246
  domestic interfaith relations 228,
    243–246

gender and religious transnational
relations 228, 236–243
on G-plus System 228–236 *See also*
assessment of F8/F7/F20 Initiative
impaired assets 33
impartiality *vs.* separation of church and
state 65
inclusivism *vs.* pluralism 71–72
India
fundamentalism in 62
G20 origins 13
South Asia Regional Pre-Conference
(Trivandrum, 2016) 79, 84, 85, 143, 160,
163
indigenous peoples
Canada 2010 planning and rituals 118,
162
Canadian Interfaith Conversation 245
Indigenous People's Summit (Sapporo,
Japan 2008) 112
Japan 2008 planning 108
land dispossession 36
participation 86t, 108
*United Nations Declaration of the Rights of
Indigenous Peoples* 245
Indigenous People's Summit (Sapporo, Japan
2008) 112
informality
communications and publicity 81
of G-plus System 14, 195–196
of infrastructure 81
leadership rotation model 80–81,
155–156, 194–195
and reform 194–197
and women's leadership 239
information disclosure. *See* transparency
Information Resource Kits 182
information technology 208–211 *See also*
e-governance; Twitter campaign
(UK 2013)
INGO Caravan (France 2011) 165
INGOs. *See* international non-governmental
organizations (INGOs)
Institute for Economics and Peace 232–233,
272–273
Institute for Policy, Advocacy, and
Governance 160, 161
Institute of World Religions 144, 160
institutional affiliations list 306–308
instrumentalism, principled 215–218

Insubria University 160
InterAction 17, 21, 233, 251, 290
Interfaith Bus Tour (Canada 2010) 165
Interfaith Leaders Summits. *See* F8/F7/F20
Initiative
internal reform. *See* reform, internal
International Anglican Communion. *See*
Anglican Communion
International Center for Law and Religion
Studies (Brigham Young University)
Australia 2014 support 135, 159
financial support 160–161
merger of F8/F7/F20 Initiative 78–79, 138
website on F20 Initiative 301
International Chamber of Commerce 17–18,
231
International Consortium for Law and
Religion Studies (Milan) 161
International Continuance Committee (ICC)
archives 157
Canada 2010 statement 118n55
formalizing use of MDGs 254
founding 76, 115, 156, 194
on future of F8/F7/F20 Initiative 291
on government support for Summits 158
Hamilton's role 237
internal reforms 186
merger into F20 Executive
Committee 155
structure and role 156–157
UK 2013 collaborative statement 132–133,
157
US 2012 communications 126
Vendley's participation 177n5 *See also*
F20 Executive Committee
International Doctrine Council (Salvation
Army) 89
International Ecumenical Peace Convocation
(France, 2014) 82
International Labor Organization 248
International Monetary Fund (IMF) 13, 38,
107, 224n165
International NGO Accountability
Charter 188
international non-governmental
organizations (INGOs)
accountability 188, 190, 191, 192, 193t
compared to RNGOs 86–87
exclusion from Russia 2006 102n9
increase in 83

international non-governmental organizations (INGOS) (cont.)
  INGO Caravan (France 2011)   165
  shift of power and responsibilities
  to   39–41 See also non-governmental
  organizations (NGOS); religious
  non-governmental organizations
  (RNGOS)
International Organisations Research
  Institute   232
International Partnership on Religion and
  Sustainable Development (PaRD)   54–55,
  288
international relations
  and F8/F7/F20 Initiative   208, 209,
    212–214, 290
  international relations theory   296 See
  also external relations with F8/F7/F20
  Initiative
International Religious Liberty
  Association   160, 161
International Telecommunication
  Union   209–210
International Trade Union Confederation   17
internet. See information technology; Twitter
  campaign (UK 2013); Web 2.0
The Interreligious Council of Russia   102,
  103
interviews and data collection for this
  book   301–302
Interweave Solutions   276
Ise Grand Shrine   268
Ise-Shima G7 Summit (2016)   22
Ise-Shima Progress Report: G7 Accountability
  on Development and Development-Related
  Commitments   22
ISIL   139–140, 214
Islam
  constituency claims   90t
  development activities by Muslim
  religious organizations   61–62
  e-governance in Islamic cultures   54n45
  extremism   50, 73, 139–140, 214
  financial institutions and financing   140,
    180
  gender equality and Islamic
  traditions   242–243
  German demographic revolution   48, 60
  Islamophobia   50, 222, 243
  Muslim dress   221–222

  participation   86t, 90t, 124
  soft power and Islamic cultures   51–53,
    221
Islamic Economic Community (China)   180
Israel, fundamentalism in   62
Istanbul F7/F20 Summit (2015). See Turkey
  2015 F7/F20 Summit
Italy
  F8 origins   83
  G6 origins   12
  G7/G8/G20 origins   13
  informality of process   195 See also
  Italy 2009 F8 Summit; L'Aquila, Italy G8
  Summit (2009)
Italy 2009 F8 Summit
  domestic impact   243
  engagement with political officials   168
  finances   158, 171
  media coverage   205
  overview   113–117
  participants   86t, 114
  religious rituals   162
  Secretary-General   98t, 155

Japan
  cancellation of 2016 F7 Summit   167
  F8 origins   83
  G6 origins   12
  G7/G8/G20 origins   13
  Hiroshima G7 Foreign Ministers Meeting
    (2016)   94, 143, 171, 224–225
  Hokkaido-Toyako G8 Summit (2008)   110,
    111–113
  in list of presidencies   97t See also Japan
  2008 F8 Summit; Kyoto-Osaka, Japan F8
  Summit (2008); Sapporo, Japan F8 Summit
  (2008)
Japan 2008 F8 Summit
  confusion over hosting and
  leadership   194–195, 204
  domestic impact   243
  duration of   152
  engagement with political officials   168,
    169, 170–171, 174
  finances   108, 159
  media coverage   181–182
  organizers, additional   155
  overview   108–113
  participants   86t, 108–109
  Poverty Excursion   164

reflexivity   207
religious rituals   162
Secretaries-General   98t, 154, 194–195
statements, briefs, and
communiqués   170, 171
themes   93, 109
women as focus   241 *See also* Kyoto-
Osaka, Japan F8 Summit (2008);
Sapporo, Japan F8 Summit (2008)
Japan Broadcasting Company   181–182
Japanese Association of Religious
Organizations   108, 159
Japanese Buddhist Federation   108
Jeanbart, Jean-Clemént   281
Jewish Federation   89
Jewish participation   86t, 124, 147
Ji, Bhai Mohinder Singh   124, 258, 305
Joint Communiqué and acknowledgment of
F8/F7/F20 Initiative   94, 143, 171
Joint Religious Leadership Coordination for
the Summits (JRLCS)   126
Joshi, Devin K.   286–287
Jubilee   253
justice
as summit topic   134, 144
and sustainability   35
Justice Tour ()   2015176
justice tours, climate change   121, 164, 176

Kabak, Dmitry   175, 305
KAIROS   121, 123, 164
Karam, Azza   270–271
Karamaga, Andre   120, 124, 260, 305
Kato, Katsunobu   136–137
Katz, Sam   174
Kaub, Germany Youth Summit 2014   76–77,
119, 134, 153, 167
Keatchie, Hilary   165, 166
Kemp, R.   201–203
Keohane, Robert   45, 189–190, 191, 192, 194
Kerala and South Asia Regional
Pre-Conference (2016)   160
Khasru, Syed Munir   157, 305
Kirchentag (Germany, 2007)   82, 105, 163
Kirton, John
engagement with civil society   175, 232
on informal structure of G-plus
System   14
leadup to Canada 2010   118
as member   157, 305

Kitanović, Elizabeta   145, 157, 305
KOF indices   41
Kohn, Rachel   141, 182
Konko tradition   87, 98t, 124, 147
Koppel, J.   188–189
Küng, Hans   250, 251
Kyoto Chamber of Commerce and
Industry   159
Kyoto Committee for the 2008 G8 Foreign
Ministers Meeting   159
Kyoto Convention Bureau   159
Kyoto-Osaka, Japan F8 Summit (2008)
engagement with political
officials   170–171
finances   159
in list of presidencies   97t
media coverage   181–182
overview   108–113
participants   108
Poverty Excursion   164
religious rituals   162
statements, briefs, and
communiqués   170
theme   93, 109
women as theme   241 *See also* Japan 2008
F8 Summit; Sapporo, Japan F8 Summit
(2008)

L20 (Labor 20)   17, 19, 21, 235
land
dispossession   36
grabs   141
land-system changes as planetary
boundary   32n50
use and transition science   29
L'Aquila, Italy G8 Summit (2009)
civil society   38, 115–116
criticism of   116–117
earthquake   113–114, 162, 164, 207
in list of presidencies   97t *See also* Italy
2009 F8 Summit
L'Aquila earthquake   113–114, 162, 164, 207
L'Aquila Food Security Initiative   116, 117
Larsen, Lena   242–243, 305
Lashand, Ricky   157, 305
Launching Leaders   276
Lauzon, Guy   173
LDS (Church of Jesus Christ of Latter-day
Saints)   77, 78–79, 138
leadership by women   136, 236–241

leadership rotation model
  advantages and disadvantages   156
  informality   80–81, 155–156, 194–195
  and reflexivity   206
  reforms and critique   186, 194–195, 204,
    206, 226
  roles and responsibilities   152, 155–156
  and survey results   92
  transition to follow G20   154
legitimacy
  of business and risk   32
  legitimation crisis   8–9, 44
  political legitimacy and religious
    discourse   55
Leichtman, Mara   73–74
Li, Lin   180, 305
liability as dimension of
  accountability   188–189
Live 8   253
logos   93
London, UK F8 Summit (2005). *See* UK 2005
  F8 Summit
London, UK F8 Summit (2013). *See* UK 2013 F8
  Summit
The London Forum on G8 (2005)   75–76
loop learning   198–202
Los Cabos, Mexico G20 Summit (2012)
  civil society   128–129, 235
  focus   127
  in list presidencies   97t
  statements, briefs, and
    communiqués   96, 129
Los Cabos Communiqué   129
Lough Erne, Northern Ireland G8 Summit
  (2013)   22 *See also* UK 2013 F8 Summit
Lowy Institute for International Policy   21,
  300
Lubaale, Nicta   148, 305
Lunn, Gary   173
Luxembourg, MDGs commitments   253

Machiavelli, Niccolò   296
Ma'din Academy   159–160, 161
Mahmood, Tahir   140, 157, 305
Make Poverty History campaign   75–76, 100,
  102, 227, 253
Make Promises Happen   253
malaria   169, 252, 254–255

Manitoba Interfaith and Immigration
  Council   165
Manitoba Interfaith Council   165
Manocha, Shan   140, 306
MAP (Mutual Assessment Process)   233
marine protected areas   26
Marker, Richard   124, 306
Marshall, Katherine
  dinner hosting at US 2012   155, 165
  as F20 Executive Committee
    member   157, 237, 306
  on future of F8/F7/F20 Initiative   291
  on impact of F20 series   4
  as leader   237, 238, 239, 306
  on new collaborative
    partnerships   248–249
  as speaker   19, 127, 140, 181, 218, 237
  T20 policy briefs (2017)   55, 148–149
  work on intersection of gender and
    religion   241
Martin, Keith   173
Martinez-Torron, Javier   140
Marxist theory   218–219
maternal health, MDGs   252
Matsunaga, Yukei   155
Max Planck Institute for Social
  Anthropology   160, 161
mayors   174
McArthur, John   120, 254–255, 306
McGuinty, David   173
MDG Monitor   252
MDGs (Millennium Development
  Goals)
  Canada 2010   120, 254–256
  civil society focus   212, 213, 253–254
  as consensus on poverty   249
  decisional governance and
    cosmopiety   276
  as focus   105–106, 228, 252–261, 289
  fundamental values   250
  global financial crisis (1997–1999)   262,
    263
  as global norm   249–254, 264, 286
  Hamilton's address to UN High Panel
    on   176, 237
  list of goals   252
  Millennium Development Kids   119, 127,
    131–132, 164–165

official development assistance
(ODA) 253
  as top-down 284
  transition to SDGs 30, 213, 247, 261–265,
    283 *See also* SDGs (Sustainable Devel-
    opment Goals)
meaning, communication by religion 217
Medeniyetler Ittifaki Enstitüsü 160
media, engagement with 164, 181–185, 205
  See also media coverage
Media Communications Pre-Conference
  (Canada 2010) 164, 182
media coverage
  of Australia 2014 136, 182
  of Canada 2010 119, 121,
    182–183, 205
  and government support 181
  of Italy 2009 205
  of Japan 2008 181–182
  Media Communications Pre-Conference
    (Canada 2010) 164, 182
  and moral accountability of INGOs,
    etc. 190–191
  of protests at Canada 2010 G8 and G20
    summits 121
  and reinforcement of messages 228
  of Russia 2006 205
  of terrorism 139n124
  of Turkey 2015 141, 182
  of US 2012 128
Merlini, Cesare 14
message entrepreneurs 263, 286
metaphor usage 299
methodology 295, 297–300
Mexico
  G20 origins 13
  Los Cabos, Mexico G20 Summit
    (2012) 96, 97t, 127, 128–129, 235
Micah Challenge 253
migration. *See* immigration and migration
Millennium Development Goals (MDGs).
  See MDGs (Millennium Development
  Goals)
Millennium Development Kids 119, 127,
  131–132, 164–165
Ministry of Environment (Japan) 159
Ministry of Islamic Affairs (Saudi
  Arabia) 88, 90t

Mitchell, George E. 214–215
Miyake, Yoshinobu
  as Association Member 157
  and cancellation of Japan 2016 F7
    Summit 167
  merging of F8/F7/F20 Initiative 77,
    138
  as Secretary-General 98t, 106,
    108, 109n26, 154, 155, 194–195,
    306
  as speaker 120, 124, 128, 267–268
  visit to Japanese Parliament 136–137
Miyamoto, Keishi 155
Modern Earth Web Design 159
modernity
  liquification by globalization 36–37
  loop learning 198, 199, 201
  second-order reflexivity 199
monetary system. *See* Euro zone crisis;
  financing
Monheim, Kai 20, 215
monitoring of G-plus System 20–23,
    122n70, 178, 194, 230–236, 290 *See also*
    accountability
Montreal Protocol 34
Moqbel, Redwan 163
morality
  accountability role of F8/F7/F20
    Initiative 192
  accountability role of INGOs 190–191
  as construct of legal system 296
  global norm 250
  and informality of G-plus System
    process 196–197
  link to emotion 220
  and reflexivity 197
  reinforcement assessment 228
  relation to power 296–297
  religion as anthropocentrically
    biased 270
  statements as consensus on 85
Mormon Church. *See* Church of Jesus Christ
  of Latter-day Saints (LDS)
Morris, Paul 70–71, 146–147, 306
Moscow, Russia F8 Summit (2006). *See* Russia
  2006 F8 Summit
MP dinners (Canada 2010) 119, 120, 159, 173
multi-faith dialogue 67

Munk School of Global Affairs (University of
    Toronto)
    G7/G8 Information Centre   21, 94, 300
    monitoring of G-plus System   21 *See also*
    G7/G8/G20 Research Groups (University
    of Toronto); *G8/G7*
music and dance at summits   162, 165
The Muskoka Accountability Report   21–22,
    122n70, 232
Mustafa, Faizan   136, 140, 157, 306
Mutual Assessment Process (MAP)   233

Nakayama, Yashuhide   171
Nalsar Hyderabad   160
National Academy of Legal Studies and
    Research (Hyderabad)   161
National Council of Churches USA   90t, 103,
    237
National Federation of UNESCO Associations
    of Japan   159
nationalism
    effect on F8/F7/F20 Initiative   292
    recent rise of   41, 48–49, 277, 283
    relationship between violence, reli-
    gion and   53–54, 55, 212–214 *See also*
    nation-states
The National Research Council (US)   29
National Research University (Moscow)   232
nation-states
    religious diplomacy in   68–69
    religious minorities and   146
    shift to governance without
    government   38–41
    state failures   277–278
    statism as past   80n15 *See also*
    nationalism
Native Americans. *See* indigenous peoples
neocolonialism, globalization as   37
Netherlands, MDGs commitments   253
networks and governance power   39–41
Newell, Edmund   178, 266–267, 306
New Rules for Global Finance   231
Newtonian synthesis   299–300
NGOs. *See* non-governmental organizations
    (NGOs)
Nibutani Declaration   112
1997–1999 global financial crisis. *See* global
    financial crisis (1997–1999)
Nitschke, Ulrich   55, 147, 148–149, 306

Niwano, Nichiko   98t, 109, 154, 306
NodeXL   130
Noll, Rüdiger   124, 257, 306
non-governmental organizations (NGOS)
    as distinct type of civil society   279
    freedom of activity at Russia 2006
    102n9
    lack of participants at US 2012   226
    late accreditation at Los Cabos, Mexico
    G20 (2012)   129
    RNGOS as   49–50
    women's leadership   239 *See also* inter-
    national non-governmental organizations
    (INGOS); religious non-governmental
    organizations (RNGOS)
non-human agency   270–273
norm entrepreneurs   263, 286
norms
    expectations of democratic   40–41,
    42–43
    global   247, 249–254, 264, 286
    norm entrepreneurs   263, 286
    soft power as denying or repudiating   53
Norway, MDGs commitments   253
Norwegian Centre for Human Rights   161
nuclear disarmament and nonproliferation
    at Canada 2010   120, 121
    at Italy 2009   115, 116
    at Japan 2008   109, 110, 111
    monitoring by civil society   231
Nuclear Non-Proliferation Treaty   231
Nye, J.S., Jr.   51, 221

oceans   25–26, 32n50
OECD (Organization for Economic Coopera-
    tion and Development)
    anti-globalization movement target   38
    guidelines   107
    MDGs targets   253
    SDGs index   285
    Trade Union Advisory Committee   17
Office of Legal Counsel (LDS Church)   78
official development assistance (ODA)   253
Öktem, Emre   139
ONE   22–23, 165, 230, 253
One Truth Ideology   268, 269
Ono, Matsushige   170–171
opening and closing, sequential   202–203,
    206–207

Open Letter
    as technique 183
    UK 2013 96, 157, 183–185, 210
open markets, commitment to 252
Organization for Economic Cooperation and
    Development. *See* OECD (Organization for
    Economic Cooperation and
    Development)
Orman, Cüneyt 174–175, 180
Osaka Promotion Committee for the G8
    Finance Ministry Meeting 159
Oslo Coalition on Freedom of Religion or
    Belief 160, 161
"The Other Russia" (shadow summit
    2006) 102n9
"Our Whole Society" Conferences 245
Overseas Development Institute 285
Oxfam 104, 112, 126, 290
Oxford Journal of Law and Religion 160
Oxford Society of Law and Religion 161
Oxford University 161
ozone depletion 32n50, 34

Pacific Conference of Churches 88, 90t
Pacific Regional Pre-Conference (Suva, Fiji
    2016) 79, 84, 85, 143–144, 154, 160, 163, 178
Pacific Theological College 178
    See also Pacific Regional Pre-Conference
    (Suva, Fiji 2016)
Paglia, Vincenzo 98t, 114, 155, 306
paradox of complexity, efficacy 201, 203,
    206, 208
paradox of democracy 44–45
paradox of emancipation 219
PaRD (International Partnership on Religion
    and Sustainable Development)
    54–55, 288
Paris Agreement 30, 148, 177
Paris terrorist attacks (2015) 138–139,
    213–214
Parliamentary Panels (Australia 2014, Turkey
    2015) 166
Parliamentary Petition (Canada 2010) 119,
    173
Parliaments
    engagement with 119, 120, 136–137, 159,
    166, 172–174
    MP dinners (Canada 2010) 119, 120, 159,
    173

Parliamentary Panels (Australia 2014,
    Turkey 2015) 166
participants in F8/F7/F20 Initiative
    delegation model 83–86, 152–153, 186,
    189
    diversity of organizations 3, 82–83,
    85–87, 86t
    first African 105
    heads of state 168–170
    overview 82–93
    participation model 83, 189
    reform efforts 186, 189
    survey of RNGOs (2010) 87–90, 90t
    survey on process and engagement
    (France 2011) 90–92, 91t
    violence against 7 *See also under specific
    Summits*
participation model 83, 189
Parturier, Françoise 183
peace
    cosmopiety in peacebuilding
    movement 73
    Pacific Regional Pre-Conference (Suva, Fiji
    2016) 144
    as summit topic 124, 125, 255–256
    youth summits 134, 141
Peifeng, Liu 144–145, 306
Pereira, Carmen Asiaín 136, 140, 157, 173, 306
Peschke, Doris 124
Petkoff, Peter 140, 157, 307
Pew Research Center 272
Pihaate, Francois 120, 164, 307
Pittsburgh, PA G20 Summit (2009) 117
planetary boundaries 30, 32–33
pluralism
    vs. exclusivism and inclusivism 71–72
    international relations theory 296
    prejudicial 70
    vs. secularization 66–67
Pluralism Project at Harvard University 71
Podoprigora, Roman 175
policy briefs
    by civil society 17
    decisional governance and
    cosmopiety 276
    by engagement groups 21, 55, 148–150,
    290
    by InterAction 17, 290
    by Oxfam 290

policy briefs (cont.)
    T20 (Berlin 2017)   55, 148–150, 290 *See also* statements, briefs, and communiqués
political officials
    engagement with F8/F7/F20 Initiative   119, 120, 136–137, 159, 166, 168–175, 233–234
    external relations as measure of impact   233–234
    foreign ministers   171
    government advisors   170–171
    heads of state   168–170
    mayors   174
    members of Parliament   119, 120, 136–137, 159, 166, 172–174
    pushback   258–259
    special advisors   174–175
pollution   26, 32n50 *See also* environmental issues
Pontifical Academies of Sciences   177
Pontifical Council for Inter-religious Dialogue   114
population pressures. *See* Age of the Anthropocene
populism   292 *See also* nationalism
portfolio typology, diverse   203, 208
post-secularization. *See* religion's return to public sphere
Potsdam, Germany F20 Summit (2017). *See* Germany 2017 F20 Summit
poverty
    at Australia 2014   136
    at Canada 2010   120, 121, 255–256
    environmental issues and   36
    at Germany 2007   106–107
    at Japan 2008   110, 111, 164
    Justice Tour (Canada 2015)   176
    Make Poverty History campaign   75–76, 100, 102, 227, 253
    RNGOs involvement   89
    at UK 2005   101–102
    at US 2012   128 *See also* MDGs (Millennium Development Goals); SDGs (Sustainable Development Goals)
Poverty Excursion (Japan 2008)   164
power
    globalization and community fracturing   37
    relation to morality   296–297

shift to governance without government   38–41 *See also* soft power
"The Power of Dignity" conference (Germany, 2007)   105, 163
prayers during summits   161, 162
pre-conferences, F8/F7/F20 Initiative
    Dignity Pre-Conference (Germany 2007)   105, 163
    Human Rights and Religious Freedom Pre-Conference (Canada 2010)   163–164
    Media Communications Pre-Conference (Canada 2010)   164, 182
    Pacific Regional Pre-Conference (Suva, Fiji 2016)   79, 84, 85, 143–144, 154, 160, 163, 178
    South Asia Regional Pre-Conference (Trivandrum, India 2016)   79, 84, 85, 143, 154, 160, 163
    Turkey 2015   243
prediction   299–300
press conferences
    Canada 2010   182
    shutdown at Los Cabos, Mexico G20 (2012)   129
    summit structure   101 *See also* media, engagement with; media coverage
principled instrumentalism   215–218
problem-solving with blinders   201, 206
process
    emphasis on in Germany and Canada summits   205
    importance of   215
    monitoring of G-plus System   20
    survey on (France 2011)   90–92, 91t
    as topic at China 2016   144–147
    and women's leadership   239 *See also* informality
Project Ploughshares   231
protectionalism   277, 279 *See also* nationalism
Protestant faiths participation   86t, 124 *See also* Anglican Communion; Church of Jesus Christ of Latter-day Saints (LDS)
protests. *See* civil society
public-private partnerships   288
Putin, Vladimir   84, 103, 168–169

Quebec and public use of religious symbols   246n254
Queensland, State of   135, 159

Queensland Churches Together 160
Queensland Intercultural Society 160
Queensland Jewish Interfaith 160
questionnaires and data collection for this
    book 301–302

Rafferty, John 173
rationality
    bias toward 296
    collaborative 278
    over-rationalization 63
Rawls, John 55, 66
records. *See* archives and records
redundant, F8/F7/F20 Initiative as 223–224
Reed, Charles
    changes to model in UK 2013 130
    critique of F8/F7/F20 Initiative
    concept 187–188, 207, 208
    as participant 83
    as Secretary-General 307
Reese, Thomas J. 127, 307
reflexive governance theory 198–203
reflexivity
    and borders 72, 197
    efficacy paradox of complexity 201, 203,
        206, 208
    engagement 197–208
    first-order 198, 199–200,
        202, 204
    indicators 197
    non-human agency 271–272
    as process 198
    reflexive analysis of F8/F7/F20
    Initiative 204–208
    reflexive governance theory 198–203
    religion as governance 57–58
    second-order 198–200, 204
reform, internal 186–208
    accountability 188–194
    delegation model 186, 189
    informality and 194–197
    reflexive analysis 204–208
    reflexive engagement 197–208
    shift to policy recommendations *vs.*
    engagement 186–187
refugees
    fragility and
    interconnectedness 276–277
    potential legitimation crisis 44

and return of religion to public
    sphere 60
Syrian refugee crisis 44, 48, 60,
    280–282
T20 policy brief (2017) 55, 148–150, 290
See also immigration and migration
Regents College 161
reinforcement assessment 227–228
rejection assessment 226–227
relativism *vs.* pluralism 71
Relief Web 252
religion
    capitalism, relation to 218–220
    challenges to state sovereignty 146–147
    communication of meaning 217
    cosmopiety and religious
    conflicts 272–273
    gender and transnational relations 228,
        236–243
    public discourse as 221–222
    relationship between violence,
    nationalism and 53–54, 55, 212–214
    religious ritual within summits 161–163
    See also religion, freedom of; religion's re-
    turn to public sphere; religious extremism
religion, freedom of
    general emphasis on 215
    and limits on fulfilling SDGs 266
    One Truth Ideology 268, 269
    and soft power 52
    as summit topic 104, 124, 135, 147–148
    violence against religious minorities
        7–8, 10
*Religion and Sustainable Development: Build-
    ing Partnerships to End Extreme Poverty*
    (2015) 287
Religions for Peace (RfP). *See* RfP (Religions
    for Peace)
religion's return to public sphere
    cosmopiety as replacement for
    secularization 67–74, 277–280
    criticism of 59–61
    differentiation and 1, 7, 10, 222
    environmental issues as driver 1, 8–9, 24
    human ecology theory 1, 8–9
    immigration and migration 48, 60
    legitimation crisis 8–9
    Muslim religious organizations and
    development 61–62

religion's return to public sphere (cont.)
  principled instrumentalism   215–218
  religious diplomacy   68–69
  and secularization crisis   62–67, 69
  theories   5–11
  transnational relations   47–56
religious extremism
  as homogenizing   73
  as reflection of failed secular politics   62
  research interest in   50
  soft power and   52–53
  as summit topic   104
Religious Freedom and Business
  Foundation   179, 276
religious heritage protection   140
The Religious Leaders Summit. *See* F8/F7/F20
  Initiative
religious non-governmental organizations
  (RNGOS)
  accountability   188
  compared to F8/F7/F20 Initiative   81–82
  compared to INGOS   86–87
  constituency measurements   87–88
  corruption, role in addressing   53–54
  defined   86
  increase in   49–50
  lack of in Turkey 2015 C20   142
  as majority of F8/F7/F20 Initiative
  participants   3
  marginalization by policy makers   3–4
  participation in engagement groups   19
  participation survey   87–90, 90t
  redundancy of F8/F7/F20
  Initiative   223–224
  shift to C20 from F8/F7/F20
  Initiative   227
  soft power of   50–56
religious resurgence. *See* religion's return to
  public sphere
religious summitry. *See* F8/F7/F20 Initiative
remittances   105n16
replacement assessment   224–226
*Report of the Nuclear Safety and Security
  Group*   229
resource pressures. *See* Age of the
  Anthropocene
responsibility as dimension of
  accountability   189
responsiveness as dimension of
  accountability   189

RfP (Religions for Peace)
  about   86t, 225
  compared to F8/F7/F20 Initiative   81
  F8/F7/F20 Initiative support and
  organization   99, 108, 159, 160, 194
  faith-leader consultation on sustainable
  development and climate change
  (2015)   177
  Joint Religious Leadership Coordination
  for the Summits (JRLCS)   126
  leadership struggles   204
  participation   86t
  as replacement for F8/F7/F20
  Initiative   224–225
  thank you letter (2006)   112
  as transnational   89
Ricard, Jean-Pierre   260, 307
Rip, A.   200–201
risk
  analysis and L'Aquila earthquake   114n40
  environmental change and   32, 33, 42
  increase in human-induced   41
risk society   42
ritual within summits, religious   161–163
RNGOS. *See* religious non-governmental
  organizations (RNGOS)
Roma Civil G8   115–116
Rome, Italy F8 Summit (2009). *See* Italy 2009
  F8 Summit
Royal Academy of Jurisprudence and
  Legislation   160, 161
Russia
  cancellation of Russia 2014 F8
  Summit   134, 166, 212
  defense of summit costs   206
  domestic violence laws   242
  engagement with political
  officials   168–169
  F8 origins   83
  G7 post-summit dialogue   13
  G8/G20 origins   13
  in list of presidencies   97t
  non-attendance at 2012 G8   128, 166
  relationship with West   212–213
  removal from G8   13, 134, 153, 166, 212
  Saint Petersburg, Russia G8 Summit
  (2006)   102n9, 104
  Saint Petersburg, Russia G20 Summit
  (2013)   22, 133, 235
  Ukraine, activity in   13, 166, 212

Russia 2006 F8 Summit
  civil society   102n9, 229
  domestic impact   243
  finances and support   99, 103, 212
  in list of presidencies   97t
  media coverage   205
  overview   102–104
  participants   83, 84, 86t, 103, 104, 168–169, 206
  reflexivity   206
  Secretary-General   98t, 99
  statements, briefs, and communiqués   104
Russia 2014 F8 Summit, cancellation   134, 166, 212
Russian Orthodox Church   88, 90t, 103–104, 124 See also Alexey II

S20   17, 19
Saint Petersburg, Russia G8 Summit (2006)   102n9, 104
Saint Petersburg, Russia G20 Summit (2013)   22, 133, 235
Saint Petersburg Accountability Report on G20 Development Commitments   22
Saint Petersburg Plan of Action on Global Energy Security   229
The Salvation Army   88–89, 90t, 159
Samdech Norodom Sirivudh, Prince   155
Sammak, Mohammad   124, 307
Sangris, Fred   164
Sant' Edigio Community   161
Saperstein, David   140, 307
Sapporo, Japan F8 Summit (2008)
  engagement with political officials   169, 171
  finances   159
  overview   108–113
  participants   108–109
  statement   171
  theme   93, 109 See also Japan 2008 F8 Summit; Kyoto-Osaka, Japan F8 Summit (2008)
Sardinia GSott8 (alternative summit)   115
Saudi Arabia
  G20 origins   13
  Ministry of Islamic Affairs   88, 90t
  participation survey and constituency claims   88
Save The Children   121

Savoie, Denise   173
Schelling points   252–254
Schloss Elmau, Austria G7 Summit (2015)   22, 97t
Schmitz, Hans Peter   214–215
Schnabel, Patrick   99t, 147, 307
Science   20, 17, 19
scorecards
  G20 Business Scorecard   231
  Overseas Development Institute   285
Scotland, Gleneagles G8 Summit (2005)   100, 253
SDGs (Sustainable Development Goals)
  adoption of   137–138, 247, 265
  business engagement   179, 266–267
  cosmopiety   70–71, 276
  development of   264–265
  financing of   34–35
  as focus   228, 265–273, 289
  gender equity   241–242
  as global norm/increased expectations from   264, 286
  Hamilton on   142
  implementation challenges   283–285
  indicators   285
  information technology   210
  Millennium Development Kids   164–165
  non-human agency   270–273
  public-private partnerships   288
  as summit topic   141, 143–144, 147
  transition from MDGs   30, 213, 247, 261–265, 283
  2030 Agenda for Sustainable Development   34, 283–284 See also MDGs (Millennium Development Goals); sustainable development
SDG Scorecard   285
second-order reflexivity   198–200, 204
Secretaries-General
  list   98–99t
  pattern   154
  roles and responsibilities   155 See also under specific Summits
secularization
  cosmopiety as replacement for   67–74, 277–280
  crisis of   62–67, 69
  and F8/F7/F20 Initiative   208, 209, 214–222
  higher law secularism   67

secularization (cont.)
  limits of   6, 50, 59
  pluralism *vs.*   66–67
  secularism as term   63
security
  costs   43–44, 121, 125
  letter from UK G8 Team Assistant   169
Seekers Hub Global   159
Seiple, Robert   52
self-assessment by G-plus System   232–233
*Self-Reliance and Empowerment Course for
  Refugees*   276
Senegal and transformation of religious
  authority   73–74
Şensoy, Needet   180
Şentürk, Recep
  as Association Member   157
  on instrumentalism   218
  as Secretary-General   98t, 140, 154, 307
separation of church and state
  cosmopiety   278
  criticism of religion's return to public
  sphere   59–61
  impartiality *vs.*   65
  as limiting religious public
  engagement   55, 65
  pluralism *vs.*   66–67
  US 2012 finances   126
sequential opening and closing   202–203,
  206–207
Shabani, O.P.   65, 66
shadow summits   17, 236 *See also* F8/F7/F20
  Initiative
Sharia law and gender equity   242–243
Sharp, Paul   15
Sherpas
  defined   171
  engagement with   171–172, 290
  role   19n24, 20
Shinto faith, planning and participation   86t, 108
Shupe, Blythe   157, 307
Siebert, John   120, 307
Sikh faith, planning and participation   86t,
  118
Sinclair, Murray   120, 307
Singh, Indarjit   10
single-loop learning   198, 201
Soboleva, Anita   242

Sochi, Russia G8 Summit cancellation
  (2014)   134, 212
social media. *See* Twitter campaign (UK 2013);
  Web 2.0
social science and transition science   29
social security   141
social sustainability   270
Society of Chinese Religious Studies   144
*Society's Commitment to Sustainable
  Development*   284
soft power
  and accountability   189–190
  as attractive   221
  cosmopiety   69–74
  defined   51
  as denying or repudiating norms   53
  engagement with political officials   168
  and Islamic cultures   51–53, 221
  of RNGOS   50–56
  as term   53 *See also* external relations
  with F8/F7/F20 Initiative; power
Solar System of G20   18, 21
Solberg, Erna   283
South, Jubilee   102
South Africa, G20 origins   13
South Asia Regional Pre-Conference
  (Trivandrum, India 2016)   79, 84, 85, 143,
  154, 160, 163
South Korea, G20 origins   13
sovereignty, religion's challenges to
  state   146–147
special advisors, engagement with   174–175
Special Rapporteur   302
Stand Up against Poverty   253–254
state failures   277–278
statements, briefs, and communiqués
  archives/hosting by G8 Information
  Centre   94
  Australia 2014   136–137, 162
  Canada 2010   89, 96, 118–119, 153, 172,
  255–256
  as consensus on morality   85
  decisional governance and
  cosmopiety   276
  distribution by G8 Research Group   107
  as engagement with political
  officials   169–170
  first directed to G20 (Canada 2010)   94,
  96, 153

France 2011   96, 125, 261
future   290–291
Germany 2007   106–107
Germany 2014 Youth Summit   134, 153
Germany 2015 Youth Summit   141, 154, 167, 213
Germany 2017   148–149
G-plus System   14, 96, 129, 169, 172
hosts' role   81
impact of   229–230
by InterAction   17, 290
Japan 2008   170, 171
last F7   154
Los Cabos, Mexico G20 (2015)   96, 129
online presence   94, 210
overview   96–97
Pacific Regional Pre-Conference (Suva, Fiji 2016)   143–144
reflexive analysis   204–208
Russia 2006   104
by Sherpas   172
in summit structure   101
T20 policy briefs   55, 148–150, 290
UK 2013   96, 130, 132–133, 153, 157, 183–185, 210
from UK G8 Team Assistant   169
US 2012   127
statism. See nation-states
Statistical Commission   285
Steiner, Sherrie   192–194, 193t, 302
Stenger, Marc Camille Michel   124, 260, 307
strategic ozone depletion   32n50, 34
subsidy reform   102
The Summit of World Religious Leaders. See F8/F7/F20 Initiative
summitry, religious. See F8/F7/F20 Initiative
summits, F8/F7/F20 Initiative
   aborted events   166–167
   academic support   135, 159–160, 177–178
   committee support, need for   114–115
   duration of   152, 153, 205
   excursions and events   163–166
   future   291
   list of Secretaries-General   98–99t
   organization   152–155, 228
   overview   96–99
   religious ritual in   161–163
   structure   80–81, 101, 195
   tensions in survey   92–93

themes   92–93 See also finances, summit; G-plus System; leadership rotation model; media coverage; statements, briefs, and communiqués; specific summits
Summit Secretariat   157
Sunc, Naty Atz   164
surveys and data collection for this book   301–302
sustainability
   corporate   31
   first appearance as concept   31
   MDGs   252
   planetary boundaries   30, 32–33
   and risk   32, 33
   social   270
   and social justice   35
   as summit topic   110
sustainable development
   faith-leader consultation on sustainable development and climate change (2015)   177
   as focus   265–269
   indices   31
   as oxymoron   1–2
   planetary boundaries   30, 32–33
   reflexivity and non-human agency   271–272
   role of G-plus System   34–35
   as summit topic   136, 140, 147–148, 265–266
   transition science   28–31
   women and   242–243 See also SDGs (Sustainable Development Goals)
Sustainable Development Goals (SDGs). See SDGs (Sustainable Development Goals)
Suva, Fiji. See Pacific Regional Pre-Conference (Suva, Fiji 2016)
Sweden, MDGs commitments   253
Swett, Katrina Lantos   135, 140, 173–174, 307
Syeed, Sayyid M.   124, 308
syncretism vs. cosmopiety   72
synthesis, Newtonian   299–300
Syrian refugee crisis   44, 48, 60, 280–282
Szczytnicki, Elías   127, 308

T20
   Berlin, Germany T20 Summit (2017)   55, 149–150, 290
   briefs   55, 148–150, 290

T20 (cont.)
  Brisbane, Australia G20 Summit
    (2014)   235
  engagement with religious leaders   55,
    148–150, 288
  F20 Executive Committee
    participation   94
  origins   17
  recognition of   19
  Saint Petersburg, Russia G20 (2013)   235
taking-turns   202–203, 206–207
Tamas, Susanne   260–61
taxes as summit topic   133
Tear Fund   123
technology transfer   252
Telecommunication Development
  Bureau   210
temperatures, rising   25–26
terrorism
  Ankara bombings (2015)   139, 214
  effect on international relations   212,
    213–214
  letter from UK G8 Team Assistant   169
  media coverage   139n124
  Paris terrorist attacks (2015)   138–139,
    213–214
  as summit topic   104, 109, 110,
    111, 115
Thames, Knox   140, 174, 308
Thayer, Donlu   157, 308
theoretical framework   295–297
think tank 20. See T20
think tanks
  engagement with   187
  monitoring of G-plus System   21, 22–23
  See also T20
#1000DaysToGo Twitter Campaign   130, 185,
    210
Tikkun Olam   280–282
tithing   71
tolerance vs. pluralism   71
Tony Blair Faiths Act Fellows   119, 165
Toroitich, Isaiah Kipyegon   164
Toronto, Canada G20 Summit (2010)   43–44,
    121–123. See also Canada 2010 F8/F20
    Summit
trade as summit topic   133
Trade Union Advisory Committee
  (OECD)   17

transition science   28–31
translation services   120, 159, 205
transnational governance
  defined   40
  religious diplomacy in   68–69
  rise of   39–41
transnationalism, Christian Chinese   180–181
transnational relations
  cosmopiety   69–74
  impact on gender in religious transna-
    tional relations   228, 236–243
  religion's return to public sphere   47–56
transparency
  as dimension of accountability   188,
    189–190
  monitoring of G-plus System   21–23, 290
  as summit topic   125, 133
Transparency International   21, 231
transportation costs   124, 158, 159, 206
Trivandrum, India. See South Asia Regional
  Pre-Conference (Trivandrum, India 2016)
Trommel, W.   200, 202
Trost, Brad   173
Trump, Donald   49
trust gap   283
Truth and Reconciliation Commission
  (Canada)   120, 245
Turkey
  Ankara bombings (2015)   139, 214
  Antalya G20 Summit (2015)   22, 79, 97t,
    142, 235
  G20 origins   13 See also Turkey 2015 F7/
    F20 Summit
Turkey 2015 F7/F20 Summit
  ancillary events   165, 166, 243
  civil society   234
  engagement with business   178–181
  engagement with political officials   166,
    173–174
  finances   160
  as first F20 Summit   79, 97
  instrumentalized religion   217–218
  introduction of cosmopiety term   70–71
  media coverage   141, 182
  overview   137–142
  participants   84, 85, 86t, 138, 237
  recognition of engagement groups   19
  religious rituals at   162
  SDGs as focus   265–266

Secretaries-General 98t, 140
special advisors 174–175
theme 93
videos online 210
women's rights 140, 222, 241–243
Turkish Muslims in Germany 90t
turn taking 202–203, 206–207
Tutu, Desmond 105
21st International Law and Religion Symposium 77
Twitter campaign (UK 2013) 84, 87, 130, 131–132, 208, 210 *See also* e-governance; Web 2.0
The 2013 Lough Erne Accountability Report 22
2030 Agenda for Sustainable Development 34, 283–284
2030 Development Agenda 265
2012 Religious Leaders' Statement for the G8 and G20 Summits 127

UK 2005 F8 Summit
civil society 175
coordination with other events 82
criticism of 102
finances 158–159
overview 100–102
participants 83, 85, 86t, 101
Secretary-General 98t
theme 92
UK 2013 F8 Summit
finances 99, 205, 208, 213
as internet-only 99, 153, 205, 210, 213
Open Letter 96, 157, 183–185, 210
overview 129–133
participants 83–84, 86t
Secretary-General 98t
statements, briefs, and communiqués 96, 130, 132–133, 153, 157, 183–185, 210
theme 92
Twitter campaign 84, 87, 130, 131–132, 208, 210
Ukraine, Russian activity in 13, 166, 212
UN. *See* United Nations
UNAOC (United Nations Alliance of Civilizations) 224
UN Association of Kansai 159
UNESCO 159, 160, 225

UNICEF 159, 225, 252
United Arab Emirates Ministry of Culture, Youth and Community Development 135, 159
United Church Women 159
United Kingdom
Birmingham, England G8 Summit (1998) 13
BREXIT 44, 48
F8 origins 83
G6 origins 12
G7/G8/G20 origins 13
Gleneagles, Scotland G8 Summit (2005) 100, 253
in list of presidencies 97t
MDGs commitments 253
trust gap 283 *See also* UK 2005 F8 Summit; UK 2013 F8 Summit
United Nations
Article 18 10
Article 71 223
Climate Change Conferences 245, 256
Economic and Social Council of the United Nations (ECOSOC) 223, 225
Environment Programme 34–35
goals and focus of F8/F7/F20
Initiative 82
High Panel on the Millennium Development Goals 176, 237
International Labor Organization 248
involvement of religious organizations in General Assembly 288
lack of convention on freedom of religion 7
MDG Monitor 252
Security Council Resolutions 111, 174
Special Consultative Status 81
Sustainable Development Solutions Network 177
United Religions Initiative and 225
UN World Summit (2005) and official development assistance (ODA) 253 *See also* UNESCO; UNICEF
United Nations Children's Emergency Fund. *See* UNICEF
United Nations Climate Change Conference (COP 17) [Durban, 2011] 245
United Nations Climate Change Conference (COP 21) [Paris, 2015] 256

United Nations Declaration of the Rights of Indigenous Peoples 245

United Nations Department of Economic and Social Affairs 252

United Nations Development Programme MDG Monitor 252

United Nations Economic and Social Council 81

United Nations Educational, Scientific and Cultural Organization. *See* UNESCO

United Nations Environment Programme 34–35

United Nations Framework Convention on climate change 169

United Nations High Panel on the Millennium Development Goals 176, 237

United Nations Security Council Resolution 1325 174

United Nations Security Council Resolution 1540 111

United Nations Sustainable Development Solutions Network 177

United Nations University 170

United Religions Initiative (URI) 224, 225–226

United States
Camp David, US G8 Summit (2012) 126, 128, 166
F8 origins 83
G6 origins 12
G7/G8/G20 origins 13
in list of presidencies 97t
Pittsburgh, PA G20 Summit (2009) 117
rise of nationalism 41, 49, 283
soft power and freedom of religion 52
trust gap 283
Washington, DC G20 Summit (2006) 113
See also US 2012 F8 Summit

Universal Peace Federation (UPF) 81

Universidad Complutense Departamento de Derecho Eclesiástico del Estado 160

Universitas Studiorum Insubriae 160

University of Maryland 29

University of Oxford 160

University of Toronto (Munk School of Global Affairs)
G7/G8 Information Centre 21, 94, 300
monitoring of G-plus System 21 *See also* G7/G8/G20 Research Groups (University of Toronto); *G8/G7*

University of Victoria 21

University of Winnipeg 120, 175, 177

UN World Summit (2005) 253

UPF (Universal Peace Federation) 81

URI (United Religions Initiative) 224, 225–226

US 2012 F8 Summit
ancillary events 165
article on 129, 207–208
expansion of communication strategy to address G20 94
finances 126, 205
hosting by Marshall 155, 165
lack of NGO participants 226
media coverage 128
overview 126–129
participants 84, 86t, 126–127, 226
reflexivity 207
Secretary-General 98t
statements, briefs, and communiqués 127

US Jewish Council of Public Affairs 90t

US National Prayer Breakfast (2006) 253, 261–262

USSR and G7 post-summit dialogue 13
See also Russia

Vaai, Upolu Luma 268, 269, 308

Vatican faith-leader consultation on sustainable development and climate change (2015) 177

Vendley, William F.
France 2011 124, 125, 259
ICC participation 177n5
Japan 2008 155, 169
as Secretary-General 177, 308
Vatican faith-leader consultation (2015) 177

Ventura, Marco 145, 308

Victoria University of Wellington 160

videos, summit 210

violence
domestic violence 242
against F8/F7/F20 Initiative participants 7, 38
at Gleneagles G8 Summit (2005) 100n3
hate crimes against immigrants 48
relationship between nationalism, religion and 53–54, 55, 212–214
religious minorities 7–8, 10
religious regulation 279

religious violence as summit topic 144
state failures 277–278 *See also* conflicts
Volder, Jan de 124
Voss, J.P. 201–203

W20
Antalya, Turkey G20 Summit (2015) 235,
241
Hangzhou, China G20 Summit
(2016) 235
origins 17, 140
recognition of 19, 241
Wallis, Jim 101, 120, 308
Walzer, Michael 62
Washington, DC F8 Summit (2012). *See* US
2012 F8 Summit
Washington, DC G20 Summit (2006) 113
water
oceans and environmental change
25–26, 32n50
planetary boundaries 32n50
as summit topic 128
WCRP (World Conference on Religion and
Peace) 275
WEA (World Evangelical Alliance) 88, 89, 90t
Web 2.0 184–185, 209–211 *See also* Twitter
campaign (UK 2013)
Weber, Max 63, 278–279
Welby, Justin 130
Wen, Fang 145, 308
West Germany and G6 12
See also Germany
WFDD (World Faiths Development
Dialogue) 54, 161, 224n165
Wilke, Annette 59
Wilkinson, Canon Guy 124, 308
Williams, Rowan 76, 83, 98t, 101, 308
Wilson, Tim 135
Winner, Langdon 45
Winnipeg, Canada F8/F20 Summit (2010). *See*
Canada 2010 F8/F20 Summit
Wolfensohn, James D. 3, 54
women
cultural contradictions 219
digital gap 210, 211
F8/F7/F20 Initiative impact on religious
transnational relations 228, 236–243
and global ethic 251
leadership by 136, 236–241
MDGS 252

Muslim dress 221–222
parallel session in Germany 2017 148
as summit topic 128, 140, 148, 222,
241–243
sustainable development and 242–243
Women 20. *See* W20
Woodworth, Stephen 173
World Bank
as anti-globalization movement
target 38
global financial crisis (1997–1999) 13
opposition to dialogue with religious
leaders 3
proposed forum for African
development 107
*Religion and Sustainable Development:
Building Partnerships to End Extreme
Poverty* (2015) 287
WEDD and 224n165
World Conference on Religion and Peace
(WCRP) 275
World Evangelical Alliance (WEA) 88, 89,
90t
World Faiths Development Dialogue
(WFDD) 54, 161, 224n165
World Federalist Movement 159
World Health Organization 231
World Jewish Congress 103
World Parliament of Religions 224n165,
250
World Social Forum (Brazil, 2005) 100n3
The World Summit of Religious Leaders. *See*
F8/F7/F20 Initiative
World Trade Organization 37–38
World Vision
Canada 2010 159
criticism of Canada 2010 123
criticism of Deauville, France G8 Summit
(2011) 126
World Vision Africa, participation survey and
constituency claims 88, 90t
World Vision International 89
Worldwide Sustainable Society Index 31
World Wildlife Fund (WWF) 25
Wright, Deborah 157, 308

Xinping, Zhuo 99t, 144, 154, 308

Y20 17, 19, 235
Yazigi, Boulos 7n21, 280

Young, Terence 173
Yousafzai, Malala 137
Youth 20, 17, 19, 235
youth organizations and summits
  at Canada 2010 119, 165
  cancellation of 2015 summit 77, 141, 154,
    158, 166–167, 213
  engagement and reform 187
  F7 origins 76–77
  at Germany 2014 119, 134, 167
  relation to F20 Executive Committee 78

shadowing G7 2–3
social media 211
as topic in Germany 2017 148
Youth 20, 17, 19, 235

Zaman, Asad 180
Zaparina, Irina 288
Zheng, Xiaoyun 157, 308
Zimmerman, Augusto 135
Zimmermann, Nigel 136